MW00607528

FOR WHEREVER YOUR JOURNEY TAKES YOU

Ask About Our Extended Cruising Areas to Alaska, Canada, Mexico, the Caribbean and the Bahamas!

A policy from BoatU.S. is the best choice for ensuring your peace of mind on the water – no matter how far the voyage.

- Agreed Value Coverage for your Boat, Engine and Boating Equipment
- 24/7 Dispatch for Towing and Claims Assistance
- Consequential Damage Coverage

- Choice of Medical and Liability Limits
- Flexible Premium Payment Plans
- Plus add-on Value Packages to bundle essential coverages boaters need

Start all your journeys with BoatU.S. onboard. Call or visit us online for a fast quote today.

BoatU.S.®
MARINE INSURANCE PROGRAM

800.283.2883
Mention Priority Code 4820
BoatUS.com/insurance

All policies subject to limits and exclusions.

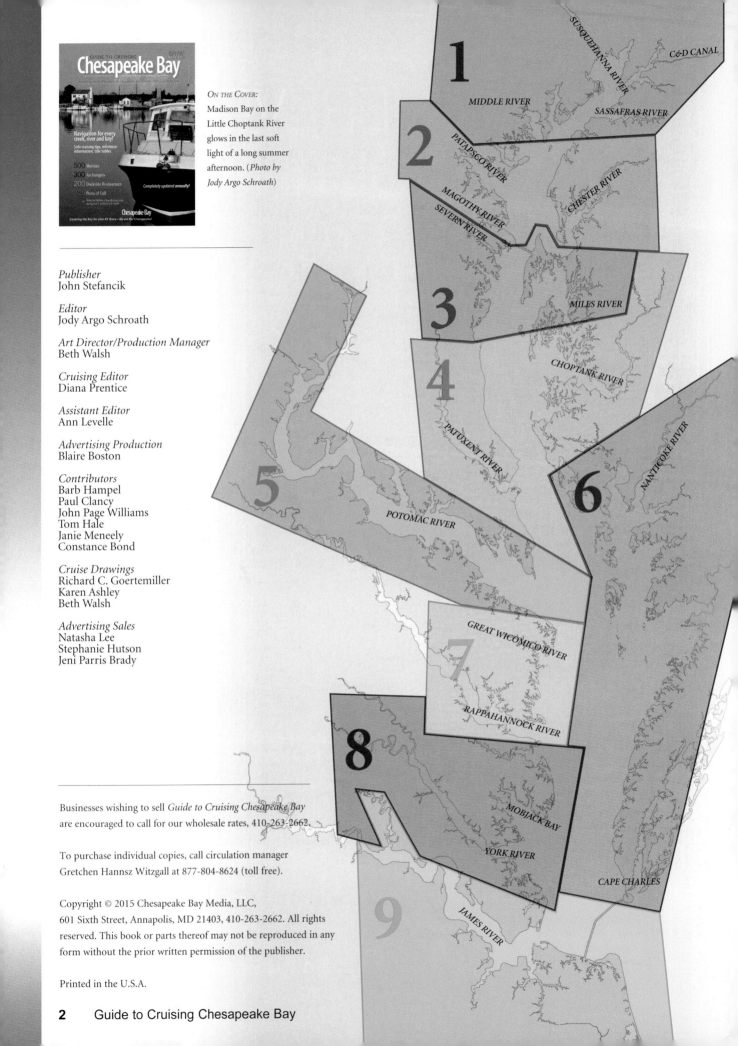

ON THE COVER:
Madison Bay on the Little Choptank River glows in the last soft light of a long summer afternoon. (*Photo by Jody Argo Schroath*)

Publisher
John Stefancik

Editor
Jody Argo Schroath

Art Director/Production Manager
Beth Walsh

Cruising Editor
Diana Prentice

Assistant Editor
Ann Levelle

Advertising Production
Blaire Boston

Contributors
Barb Hampel
Paul Clancy
John Page Williams
Tom Hale
Janie Meneely
Constance Bond

Cruise Drawings
Richard C. Goertemiller
Karen Ashley
Beth Walsh

Advertising Sales
Natasha Lee
Stephanie Hutson
Jeni Parris Brady

Businesses wishing to sell *Guide to Cruising Chesapeake Bay* are encouraged to call for our wholesale rates, 410-263-2662.

To purchase individual copies, call circulation manager Gretchen Hannsz Witzgall at 877-804-8624 (toll free).

Copyright © 2015 Chesapeake Bay Media, LLC, 601 Sixth Street, Annapolis, MD 21403, 410-263-2662. All rights reserved. This book or parts thereof may not be reproduced in any form without the prior written permission of the publisher.

Printed in the U.S.A.

2016 Edition

Guide to Cruising Chesapeake Bay

Welcome to the *Guide to Cruising Chesapeake Bay*

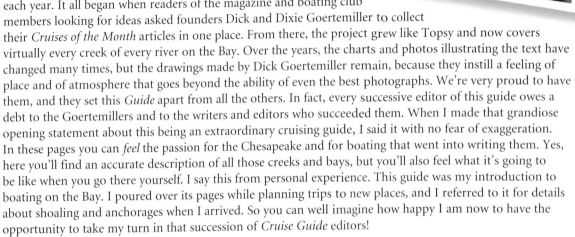

You hold in your hand one of the most extraordinary cruising guides to any body of water anywhere in the world. The Guide to Cruising Chesapeake Bay represents the knowledge and experience of hundreds of Bay cruisers and dozens of *Chesapeake Bay Magazine* editors and writers, accumulated over more than 40 years and updated page-by-page each year. It all began when readers of the magazine and boating club members looking for ideas asked founders Dick and Dixie Goertemiller to collect their *Cruises of the Month* articles in one place. From there, the project grew like Topsy and now covers virtually every creek of every river on the Bay. Over the years, the charts and photos illustrating the text have changed many times, but the drawings made by Dick Goertemiller remain, because they instill a feeling of place and of atmosphere that goes beyond the ability of even the best photographs. We're very proud to have them, and they set this *Guide* apart from all the others. In fact, every successive editor of this guide owes a debt to the Goertemillers and to the writers and editors who succeeded them. When I made that grandiose opening statement about this being an extraordinary cruising guide, I said it with no fear of exaggeration. In these pages you can *feel* the passion for the Chesapeake and for boating that went into writing them. Yes, here you'll find an accurate description of all those creeks and bays, but you'll also feel what it's going to be like when you go there yourself. I say this from personal experience. This guide was my introduction to boating on the Bay. I poured over its pages while planning trips to new places, and I referred to it for details about shoaling and anchorages when I arrived. So you can well imagine how happy I am now to have the opportunity to take my turn in that succession of *Cruise Guide* editors!

Now, with all that said, let's get down to practical matters and look at how the *Guide* is put together, most of which is so obvious that even I can understand it. For example, if you look at the map on page 2, you'll see that the *Guide* divides the Bay into nine sections, top to bottom. Then if you look at the page opposite that map, you'll find each section further broken down into rivers, creeks and ports,

with page numbers for each. When you go to those pages, you'll find the marina information for that area. (Restaurant information, however, remains in the back of the *Guide*, beginning on page 358.) Following the *Table of Contents*, you'll find information about events, crabbing, big ships, shoaling and other stuff that's either important or interesting, including excerpts from the Barrie brothers, early 20th-century yachtsmen.

Here are a few more items of interest. First, you'll note that we've put together a lot of important reference information, with phone numbers and so forth, on a pull-out card. The idea is that you (and I) will tear this out and post it near the helm or the nav station (if you are lucky enough to have one of those). Or you can simply use it as a handy place holder in the *Guide* for your next cruise.

You get the drift. Also we now have 35 Ports of Call, which will give you a more complete picture of some of the Bay's most popular destinations. We recently added four new ones—Rudee Inlet, Kent Narrows, National Harbor and Georgetown on the Sassafras—and we have a few more in mind.

Which raises a point. We try very, very hard to get everything right, but it's a big Bay and sometimes we miss something, or worse, get it wrong. Please let us know any and all changes that you feel should be made, big or small. It's all good. You can call me at the office (410-263-2662), email me at *jody@chesapeakeboating.net* or send me a note (or marked-up pages) at Cruise Guide, 601 Sixth St., Annapolis, MD 21403.

Thanks! Happy cruising! And if you see me out there on *Moment of Zen*, wave like crazy.

— Jody Argo Schroath
Editor

Four Boatyards, Three States, One Company To Help You Cruise

ZMI Herrington Harbour
Herring Bay, MD

ZMI Deltaville Yard
Rappahannock, VA

ZMI Mathews Yard
Mobjack Bay, VA

ZMI Southport Yard
Southport, NC

For more than three decades, Zimmerman Marine has specialized in boat maintenance, repairs, and refits.

BEST OF THE BAY
2015
Chesapeake Bay
Magazine

ZIMMERMAN MARINE

1-804-725-3440 • info@zimmermanmarine.com • www.zimmermanmarine.com

VDH VIRGINIA
DEPARTMENT
OF HEALTH
Protecting You and Your Environment
www.vdh.virginia.gov

KEEP OUR
WATER CLEAN—
USE PUMPOUTS

Raw and partially treated vessel sewage discharged into our waterways poses a potential threat to public health and the environment. Prevent the discharge of sewage into our waters: use pump–outs and dump station facilities.

For a list of marinas with sewage pump–out stations in Virginia please visit the Virginia Department of Health Marina Program web site at:
www.vdh.virginia.gov/EnvironmentalHealth/onsite/marina

To report malfunctioning sewage pump–out stations or for information on grant funded facilities in Virginia:
Please contact **(804) 864–7467 / (804) 864–7468**

Virginia Department of Health
109 Governor Street, Fifth Floor
Richmond, Virginia 23219

Cruising the Chesapeake Bay

They say that if you could unravel the Chesapeake Bay shoreline and lay it out in one long ribbon, it would reach from the Washington Monument (the one in D.C.) all the way to Alaska. Considering the nooks and crannies that make up the edges of the Bay, that's a lot of waterfront. Add to that the natural harbors where towns and fishing villages flourish, and you have even more intriguing places to explore. It would probably take a lifetime to delve into each beckoning cove or wind past every bend in the Bay's rivers, and for someone just beginning the Chesapeake journey, it's hard to imagine covering much territory in one cruising vacation. The truth is, you can't possibly experience all the Bay has to offer in one short season, no matter how hard you try or how fast your boat will get you there. You can, however, choose wisely as to where you think you'd like to go, and, using this guide as a resource, you can know what to expect when you arrive. We certainly don't tell you everything about the Bay, but we do try to give you a heads up on a lot of interesting places to visit and a sneak peak at some of the lovelier spots. And not all of the Bay is easy going—we try to prepare you for the bumpy stretches as well, where an unprepared vessel could run into trouble.

There are plenty of ways to cruise the Bay. Some boaters are just passing through as they transit north and south along the Intracoastal Waterway. For them the Chesapeake repre-sents a relatively sheltered patch of broad water with more than a few interesting places to stop and rest before moving on. Easy in, easy out—that's what they are looking for. Others like to linger longer, following a particular river to its head, or savoring the natural beauty of the Bay itself. Of course the Chesapeake has plenty of homegrown boaters who make week-end forays out and across Bay waters or take extended trips to see what the region has to offer beyond their own riverscape. For anyone who's just beginning a romance with the Bay, here's a thumbnail sketch, from top to bottom.

Upper Bay

The northern reach of the Chesapeake Bay offers wide navigable rivers that lead through rural countryside to some of the most scenic gunkholes around. Here you'll find the C&D Canal, lead-ing to Philadelphia and Delaware Bay. Here you can tuck into freshwater rivers like the Bohemia and the Sassafras to find cozy coves, perfect for jellyfish-free swims. Or you can set your course for the boom and bustle of Baltimore, one of the nation's busi-est ports. The Susquehanna's rocky fall line stops boaters at Port Deposit, Md., but the rest of the northern Bay invites boaters to explore, come ashore and fall in love with Chesapeake Country.

Be aware that commercial shipping regularly heads in and out of the Patapsco River, crossing the Bay to go either north or south. These huge vessels then stay close to the

Eastern Shore and follow the main channel. If you feel inclined to do so too, you may want to do so on the outside. There's plenty of water, and you won't have to be constantly looking over your shoulder. There is also considerable tug-and-tow traffic here, which does not always follow the channels and is hard to spot in a summer haze.

Nighttime cruising in the Upper Bay can be confusing because the shores lie so close together that it's hard to distinguish navigational lights from the lights on land—though this is considerably less of a problem with today's chartplotters. If you do get confused, it's wise to pull in near shore and anchor till you have better visibility.

Middle Bay

With Annapolis and St. Michaels, two of the Bay's favorite ports of call, with rivers and creeks bristling with docks, and with fleets of cruising visitors arriving every season, it's no wonder that the middle swath of the Chesapeake Bay, just below the Bay Bridge, is alive with boats on the move. This is undoubtedly one of the most active stretches for recreational boating on the Bay. But there's plenty of room for everyone, and plenty to do and see, whether you're looking for a quiet creek or a day on the town.

The shipping channels here are active, and commercial vessels often anchor off the mouth of the Severn River as they await clearance into the Port of Baltimore. Ships traveling north hug the Eastern Shore until they are parallel with the Severn River. At that point they make a beeline for the center spans of the Bay Bridge then cross to the Western Shore to follow the Craighill Channel into the Patapsco River.

From spring till late fall, commercial crabbers are hard at work in this part of the Bay, and crab pots seem to be everywhere. Truth is, they won't be inside the channel unless they get blown there by the wind or current. You can avoid them by staying in the channel—just keep an eye out for ships following the same course.

Potomac River

The roughest stretch of water on the Chesapeake Bay lies at the mouth of the Potomac River. The Potomac is a grand freshwater tributary, funneling tons of water and sediment from the Maryland and Virginia highlands in the Bay. You can imagine that it packs a wallop when it hits the more saline water of the Bay proper. Wind and tide can create havoc here, working at cross purposes to the water spilling out of the river's channel. It's often a rock-and-roll ride for boats cutting straight across the Potomac's mouth. To avoid this, boaters moving north and south can head farther east and cut up behind Smith and Tangier islands to ensure a smoother ride.

But then they will miss one of the Bay's finest cruises: the Potomac River. The lower section of the Potomac is rich in

deep-water rivers, like the Coan and Yeocomico on the south shore and Smith Creek and St. Marys River on the north.

Facilities are to be found all the way up the Potomac, as are lovely anchorages and scenes right out of the history books. You'll wind past lovely old resort towns like Colonial Beach, quaint fishing villages like Cobb Island and scores of sheltered gunkholes—all the way to Alexandria, Va, and Washington, D.C.

Lower Bay

The Lower Chesapeake Bay gives boaters plenty of room to move around in. This is a sailor's paradise. At the same time, the wide open mouth of the Bay creates a long fetch from the Atlantic and little protection from a northeast blow. But don't worry. There are always plenty of places to duck in and sit out the blow.

The Eastern Shore of Virginia tends to be shallow, which means that boats drawing much more than 5 feet can run into problems trying to ease into many of the creeks and inlets of the lower shore. Onancock Creek is one of the welcome exceptions, providing deep water inland as far as Onancock, sometimes called the "St. Michaels of the south."

Boaters have much to choose from on the lower Western Shore: the Rappahannock, Piankatank, York and James rivers offer deep open water for most of their length. Traditional boatbuilders still dot these shores, launching state-of-the-art sportfishermen and ocean-ready cruising boats, as well as classic fishing skiffs. You'll also find plenty of full-service boat facilities and a warm welcome from the folks who operate them.

Bay Lighthouses

From Thimble Shoal at the mouth of the Bay to Concord Point at the mouth of the Susquehanna River, lighthouses have long marked the channels leading north and south on the Chesapeake. Once manned by intrepid keepers who kept the lamps burning and the fog horns going for days on end, the lighted towers have nearly all been supplanted by—or converted to—modern automated structures. Many of the lighthouses have been removed from their original positions and reestablished as shoreside attractions. **Thomas Point Lighthouse**, at the mouth of the South River, remains the only screwpile-style lighthouse still in its original location (the Annapolis Maritime Museum offers tours; *www.amaritime. org*). Several other old lighthouses that remain in their original location have been sold to private individuals, who use them as family retreats and vacation houses.

Regardless of their status, the lighthouses remain a fascinating part of Bay history, engaging the imagination of boaters who pass them by or explore them in their new land-based locations. The **Hooper Strait Lighthouse**, for example, now stands on Navy Point, at the entrance to the St. Michaels harbor where it marks the location of the Chesapeake Bay Maritime Museum. The **Seven-Foot Knoll Lighthouse** which once watched the mouth of the Patapsco River, is open for tours in Baltimore's Inner Harbor. These and several of those that remain in place have been decommissioned: the **Concord Point Lighthouse** in Havre de Grace, and the **Cove Point Lighthouse**, north of the

Patuxent River are two that are open to visitors.

One lighthouse is famously haunted. Point Lookout is a long thin peninsula that reaches out from the mouth of the Potomac River. Here Yankee troops established a Confederate prisoner-of-war camp in the waning days of the Civil War. The **Point Lookout Lighthouse** cast its light over scores of cold ragged men who suffered through the cold and wind with little to protect them from the elements. Many died from smallpox and exposure. People familiar with the lighthouse say the soldiers never left completely and that ghostly figures are still visible along the shoreline at night or in the lighthouse itself. The deteriorating keepers' building is not open to the public, except occasionally for special haunted Halloween tours.

Boaters interested in visiting some of the Bay's lighthouses can join in the Maryland Lighthouse Challenge when volunteers from the Chesapeake Chapter of the U.S. Lighthouse Society, in tandem with local governments and lighthouse operators, throw a simultaneous open house and encourage lighthouse buffs to visit as many as they can reach in a single weekend. The event is held every other year, with the next event set for 2017. See *www.cheslights.org* for information, directions and approximate driving times between lighthouses. Shuttle service is provided to a handful of hard-to-reach lights. Participating lighthouses are open extended hours for the Challenge; for safety reasons, not all are open to the public for interior tours. Call or visit their websites for regular hours of operation.

PURE. PURSUIT.

Pursuit delivers innovation and excellence in the perfect sized packages. A combination of finely engineered features designed with a timeless and elegant, yacht-like exterior that withstands the extremes of offshore conditions and in-shore activities with ease.

OS 325
OFFSHORE

Contact Grande Yachts, your Pursuit Factory Authorized Dealer and experience the excitement of Pursuit.

DC 325
DUAL CONSOLE

SC 365i
SPORT COUPE

GRANDE YACHTS
grandeyachts.com

411 Winchester Creek Rd., Grasonville, MD 21638 | Tel (410) 286-1350
301 Pier One Rd., Stevensville, MD 21666 | Tel (410) 643-5800
36624 Dupont Blvd., Selbyville, DE 19975 | Tel (302) 436-2628

 PURSUIT

pursuitboats.com

 YAMAHA

With unmatched inner strength and efficiency, combined with the reliability and precision performance of the Yamaha engines, you'll have an exceptional ride and efficient fuel consumption.

ANNAPOLIS SCHOOL OF SEAMANSHIP

The Mariner's Source for Hands-On Training

USCG Captain's License

- Master to 100 Ton
- OUPV (Six-Pack)
- Upgrade to Master
- License Renewal
- Sailing and Towing Endorsements
- First Aid/CPR

Hands-On Classes

- Diesel Engines
- Outboard Engines
- Electrical Systems
- Navigation
- Safety and Seamanship
- Marine Weather

Onboard Training

- Docking and Maneuvering
- Anchoring
- Coastal Cruising
- Emergencies
- New Boater Training

Call us or visit our website for complete class schedule

www.AnnapolisSchoolofSeamanship.com
(410) 263-8848 • (866) 369-2248

Training Facility at 601 Sixth Street • Annapolis, MD

A Barrie Brothers Cruise

In July of 1897, two brothers, Robert and George Barrie, sailed their boat down from Philadelphia, transited the C&D Canal and emerged into a brand new cruising ground—the Chesapeake Bay. They were enraptured. Robert Barrie wrote:

> "Most sailing people do not realize what magnificent cruising waters we have in that noble bay, the Chesapeake, which might reasonably be called a sea. . . . The scenery is varied, and always picturesque; whether the pleasant sheltered bays of the Eastern Shore, the bold bluffs of the Patuxent, or that of the tropic-like pine-fringed Piankatank. Fish, oysters, and game are all plentiful and cheap. The supply of crabs, indeed, seems to be inexhaustible."

Over the years, the Barries returned again and again, recording their experiences for boating magazines of the day. Along the way, George and Robert Barrie became the first of millions of cruisers to revel in the Bay. What follows is an excerpt of their first cruise. The brothers are determined to get all the way down the Bay . . .

One July evening in 1897 we left the anchorage of the Corinthian Yacht Club, Tinicum Island, Delaware River, about five o'clock, light head air, but with tide got down to Claymont; tide ran awhile longer, but we stopped there on account of a good anchorage. Went very well with the small mainsail, small jib, and balloon staysail.

About three o'clock we got a breeze, and worked down. Got off jib and shot into canal dock under balloon staysail and main, lowering latter as we neared. Locked in at once, paid tolls four and towage three dollars, got provisions,

mailed letters, and got off about four o'clock, but lost time almost at once by going aground in passing a steamer. Aside from the entrances, there is only one lock in the canal, that at St. George's, which is a rise. Just beyond it the canal opens out into quite a lake, where, we were told, there is good shooting in the fall.

Arrived at western lock, Chesapeake City, about eight o'clock, and were lowered about fourteen feet into the Chesapeake, here really Back Creek, where we tied up to a siding for the night. Took on two hundred pounds of ice, some milk, and other trifles. In the evening no mosquitoes, wonderful to relate.

Next morning, by appointment with the tug, we were up at five o'clock, but as some expected schooners were late we did not get away for a couple of hours. The tug, for a dollar and a half, took us down to the Elk River; there we made sail, setting balloon staysail and jib topsail, and ran down the Elk,

SW 1/4 W., to the mouth of the river, passed Turkey Point at ten o'clock, and shortly after had a squall out of the East which caused us to stow the jib topsail. The wind continued easterly, and, notwithstanding there was very little of it, we made fair time, passing Betterton on the south side of the Sassafras River, at a little after eleven o'clock. About noon we were off Still Pond; then, as thunderstorms were about and wind seemed to be dying out, we decided to anchor for the day in the cove at the mouth of Worton's Creek, where we let go in fourteen feet.

We then rigged up the spritsail on the dinghy and beat up to a lonely-looking pier, where we found an old man who knew absolutely nothing. However, at a farmhouse, after a long argument, we induced the people to part with four young chickens, for which they asked only a dollar, and then some peas, beets, and squash. Sailed back to Mona through brisk puffs, and were soon shelling peas, our legs hanging over the counter. The man scalded and picked the chickens. At sundown we had a bully dinner of the above-mentioned purchases: two chickens, fried Maryland style in cracker dust, were delicious. After that we went ashore and bought a few crabs from a lone boy. Then sailed awhile in the gloaming, and at nine o'clock went to bed and slept like tops.

Sunday, wind southeasterly and occasional light rain; sailed out at seven, after breakfast, and were able to stand down the Bay; passed Tolchester Beach at eight as two men-of-war were making colors. One seemed to be a battleship, and the other looked like the dispatch boat Dolphin. They appeared to have on board the Maryland Naval Reserves, as they had an old hulk with them. About this time it began to blow and we were soon boiling along. As we got to Swan Point the squall got harder and the rain heavier; here the wire of the port backstay runner parted at the bend, having been set up too tightly the night before and now made tighter with the rain. We had a regular soak of it down to Sandy Point, then the nearby Eastern Shore smoothed the water some. Here we passed under the stern of the United States schooner Matchless, anchored, apparently on some scientific job. Ran in to Annapolis and anchored at noon among the schooners off the Academy, in about three fathoms.

On Monday we had a light southeasterly wind, which made the beat out of the harbor take nearly two hours. When abreast of Tolly Point buoy we got a fresh breeze with rain from the northeast; running down S 1/2 E or so, we made good time, the wind freshening all the while: when abreast of the mouth of Eastern Bay it came very hard and a good sea on; rapidly getting worse, passing Poplar Island we had all we could stagger under with the small mainsail and small jib.

Knowing we would have to beat up when through the Sharp's Island Channel, we shook her up and put in two reefs; the sea washing us meanwhile. When squared away we rushed for the lighthouse off Sharp's Island, then bore up when we thought we were far enough down to clear the bar running down from Tilghman's Island, at the north mouth of the Choptank. It blew a gale and we thought the mast would carry away. In our carefulness we kept much farther down than necessary, and passed far south of the black buoy.

It was blowing so hard we felt we must find some place to anchor, and as it looked so wicked to westward we knew we must do so soon. Running to the east, in Tripp's Bay, we found it too exposed and went about to try to fetch Black Walnut Cove. Soon a tropical downpour shut out everything: fortunately it beat down the sea, and going about we fetched behind Cook's Point, where we let go in about three fathoms. It was roaring down the Choptank from the northeast, but we lay pretty comfortably behind the point. We stripped and had some hot soup; this was about two o'clock. In an hour the worst was over, having blown a gale for just two hours: we made sail, and although we had plenty of rain, we worked up to the sleepy little village of Oxford and anchored opposite the School House green at about five o'clock. The evening was quiet: and as there were occasional showers we set the awning.

Tuesday, it was blowing and raining from the southeast, and we were unable, as we had expected, to do some refitting. Crabbed in the afternoon.

On Wednesday it was bright and clear in the morning: we soon dried everything; put the dinghy on the beach to dry, and then gave the deck a coat of varnish. After lunch, about two o'clock, Mr. W. O'Sullivan Dimphel came along in his

George Barrie at the helm of Oomo, which he sailed on the Bay in a later cruise; facing page: a yacht heels hard on the wind as it beats down the Bay.

George Barrie and a friend picnic ashore; opposite page: the Barries under sail; Robert Barrie .

launch: we exchanged enthusiastic welcomes, and had a few drinks; he insisted on taking us over to his place on the north shore of the Tred Avon River, at the mouth of Plaindealing Creek. Mrs. Dimphel kindly gave us tea, and D. insisted that we sail over next morning and fill our tanks, the water at Oxford being rank poison, as George had learned. Dimphel showed us plans and models of his yawl Panola, which is the Indian name for cotton seed, and in the early evening took us back in the launch.

Friday was cool and clear, with fair breeze from the southwest. After early breakfast we were away at six o'clock; a dead beat all the way out. Air got very light at Cook's Point, and kept so all the way down the channel behind Sharp's Island; standing in too far towards the long pier where we grounded on a hard sandbar; lowered everything at once and pushed off with the boat boom.

The breeze freshened then, and after a couple of tacks we were able to clear the south end of Sharp's Island, and stand all the way across the bay. The western shore is very fine; bold, with cliffs about a hundred feet high, in between which are green valleys, or gullies, running down to the bay. As the breeze freshened we soon ran due south, close-hauled, down to Cove Point Light. Here it blew very fresh, and the bobble, as the local men call it, was bad, the tide running out the

Patuxent making a short confused sea, and we got pretty well washed. *Mona* pitched very badly, and the jerks were hard on the forestay.

We got a hard dusting heading up to Drum Point Light, where we anchored with some schooners in the cove. The boat that followed us, a heavy working schooner, had only a reefed mainsail and jib; showing how hard it was blowing. We went ashore, and the surf on the beach was so bad that we had to take off our shoes and roll up trousers to make a landing. Hauled the boat up under the cliff; it was too steep to climb, but we found a sort of ladder made of two logs and cross planks. At the top was a great deserted house; found a store, but it was locked up. As we were coming back met a man on a horse, who turned out to be the postmaster of Drum Point Landing; he kindly took our letters and told us where we could get milk: we found it in an old ramshackle house. The pull back to the boat was very tough. Having only had chocolate and bread and jam during the day we were very hungry. After dinner we rigged up preventer forestay of our tow line, and felt easier about the mast.

The steamer came down the river using her searchlight, and, as one passenger was going to Baltimore, she was signaled and made her landing, and so we knew our letters had gone. At half after four we were up and getting under way,

and at five, as we ran out of the cove, the sun rose in a magnificent immense red ball. We passed Cedar Point Light, and the breeze freshened so that at eight o'clock we had made the fifteen miles to Point No Point buoy in three hours. We had light airs after that and did not round Stingray Point and anchor in the bay-like mouth of the Piankatank until four o'clock in the afternoon. Then we put sail on the dinghy and sailed in to a wharf on the north shore, which we learned was called Jackson's Landing, and where we were able to send telegrams via telephone to West Point, forty miles away on the York River. Back for dinner, and in the evening had a strong west wind, which came warm but dry and pine-laden. At sunset the scene was lovely: the bay seemed like a tropical one, with white sand beaches surrounded with tall pines, each with a clump of branches at the top, sixty feet up; exactly like the palms in the East Indies. A glowing red sun and a pale pink and green sky completed the really tropical scene. That night we lounged on deck until after dark, and felt quite as though we had gone foreign: say to the South Sea Islands.

Next morning we found a fresh northwest wind, and were under way at five o'clock, eating breakfast as we rounded Cherry Point. Then we put the dinghy on deck and made very fair time down past the Wolf Trap, and kept going until abreast of New Point Comfort, where the breeze began to die out. Below York Spit it died away altogether, and by eleven o'clock we were in the doldrums. We were delighted with the clearness of the water; could see everything below distinctly, not merely the outline, but each seam in the copper: discovered a small piece was loose near the rudder stock where it chafes. This calm kept up for a couple of hours and then we got a light easterly wind, which worked us down to the

Thimble; there the flood tide caught us and rushed us into Old Point. The entrance to the anchorage is very narrow and good steerage way is necessary; a steamer coming out from the wharf bothered us, but we worked inside the bar, near the Hotel Chamberlin, and anchored among the pilot boats in three fathoms; the chart gives no idea of the amount of space and the depth of water there is in there.

We arrived at four o'clock in the afternoon, and after furling the sails and setting awning, had early dinner; dressed and went ashore, walked through the hotels, all about the fort and over to Hampton, where we saw the old church, built in 1726. Back and read Sunday papers.

On Monday we went over to Norfolk by boat to Willoughby's Spit, and then by trolley through the pines. Saw some immense strawberry beds.

In Norfolk, wandered about, saw fine old residences, then over to Gosport, where we inspected the Navy yard and went aboard the new gunboat *Nashville* and over the *Amphitrite*, and through the boat shops. Back to Norfolk and had lunch, bought a ham; then back on board *Mona*. In the evening it rained, but we were very comfortable under the awning: crabbed and caught a dozen.

The following day, the brothers set off to retrace their route, crawling into Oxford on Wednesday on a dying breeze. Here they deserted the ship, catching a train at one and arriving in Philadephia at five. The hired crewman got a hand to help him and returned the boat to Corinithian Yacht Club a few days later.

If you'd like to read more about the Barrie brothers or to read all of their cruises, which were published in 1909 as Cruises Mainly in the Bay of the Chesapeake, *you'll find them on our website,* ChesapeakeBoating.net.

Captain John Smith's Water Trail

A First for the Bay

Captain John Smith was the quintessential small boat explorer. In his remarkable voyages of the Chesapeake Bay (1607-1609), he and his crews covered 3,000 miles in a 30-foot open shallop, mapping the Bay and its rivers with astonishing accuracy given his relatively simple tools: a compass, a sextant, an hourglass and a notebook. Now his 1,700-mile route has become the nation's first aquatic national historic trail, and the National Oceanic and Atmospheric Administration's series of data-gathering "talking" buoys make that history, as well as real-time water information, available to boaters. The water trail guide for boaters can be accessed at *smithtrail.net*. The smart buoys can be accessed at 877-286-9229 or at *www.buoybay.org*. The Smart Buoys app is available free for smartphones. In addition to a narration of the natural and cultural history for the areas covered, the buoys provide up-to-the-minute data on wave height and direction, wind speed and direction, temperature, nettle probability and environmental data such as dissolved oxygen.

CAPTAIN JOHN SMITH WATER TRAIL
Waterways & Points of Interest

(Map of Chesapeake Bay showing waterways and points of interest, with numbered buoy locations 1–10, and labeled locations including Garrett Island, Havre de Grace, Chesapeake City, Baltimore, Elkridge, Rock Hall, Annapolis, Great Falls, Little Falls, Washington, D.C., Lyons Cr., Choptank R., Bloodsworth Island, Nomini Cr., Cedar Straits, Tangier Island, Onancock, Lancaster Cr., Stingray Pt., Occohannock Cr., Mattaponi R., Pamunkey R., Chickahominy R., York R., Pamunkey R., Cape Charles, Henricus Park, Jamestown, James R., Norfolk, Nansemond R., Elizabeth R., Potomac Cr., Aquia Cr., Rappahannock R., Patuxent R., Severn R., Sassafras R., Susquehanna R., Bush R., Gunpowder R., Patapsco R., Magothy R., Chester R., Eastern Bay, Pocomoke R., Chesapeake Bay)

The Bay's Smart Buoys

1 **Elizabeth River off Norfolk**
   Lat: 36.8455   Long: -76.298

2 **Jamestown**
   Lat: 37.2042   Long: -76.7775

3 **Stingray Point**
   Lat: 37.5674   Long: -76.2572

4 **Potomac River off Point Lookout**
   Lat: 38.0333   Long: -76.3375

5 **Upper Potomac River south of Woodrow Wilson Bridge**
   Lat: 38.7877   Long: -77.0357

6 **Severn River off Annapolis**
   Lat: 38.9631   Long: -76.4475

7 **Patapsco River mouth**
   Lat: 39.1519   Long: -76.3912

8 **Susquehanna River off Havre de Grace**
   Lat: 39.5437   Long: -76.0748

9 **Gooses Reef off the Little Choptank River**
   Lat: 38.5563   Long: -76.4147

10 **First Landing at the mouth of the Bay**
   Lat: 36.9793   Long: -76.0436

NOAA

The Ethanol Project

As the EPA approves increasingly large ethanol levels in gasoline (15 percent for cars and 10 percent for everything else), a number of marinas around the Bay are offering ethanol-free gas in locations where it's not otherwise mandated by the EPA's Clean Air Act. (Go to *ChesapeakeBoating.net* for a list of EPA Clean Air Act counties in Maryland, DC, and Virginia, where the sale of ethanol-free gasoline is not permitted.) We have put together as complete a listing as we can on non-ethanol fuel docks. If you know of a marina that sells ethanol-free gasoline, please email us at *Channel9@ChesapeakeBoating.net*. Meanwhile, here is our current list of marinas that sell non-ethanol gasoline:

MARYLAND

Atlantic Ocean
Sunset Marina, Ocean City (410-213-9600)
Bahia Marina, Ocean City (410-289-7438)
Wicomico Yacht Club, Wicomico River (410-219-5248)

VIRGINIA

York River
Crown Pointe Marina, York River, Hayes (804-642-6177)

Rappahannock River
Norton Yacht Sales, Broad Creek, Rappahannock River, Deltaville (804-776-9211)
Norview Marina, Broad Creek, Rappahannock River, Deltaville (804-776-6463)
Chesapeake Cove Marina, Broad Creek, Deltaville (804-776-6855)
Deltaville Yachting Center, Broad Creek, Rappahannock River, Deltaville (804-776-9898)
Deltaville Marina, Jackson Creek, Piankatank River (804-776-9812)
Yankee Point Sailboat Marina, Myer Creek, Corrotoman River, Lancaster (804-462-7018)
Tides Marinas, Carter Creek, Rappahannock River, Irvington (804-438-5000)

Chesapeake Bay
Chesapeake Boat Basin, Indian Creek, Northern Neck, Kilmarnock (804-435-3110)
Horn Harbor Marina   Port Haywood (804-725-3223)

Great Wicomico River
Ingram Bay Marina, Tripp Creek, Great Wicomico River, Heathsville (804-580-7292)
Buzzards Point Marina, Cockrell Creek, Great Wicomico River, Reedville (804-453-3545)

Little Wicomico River
Smith Point Marina, Little Wicomico River, Reedville (804-458-4077)

Potomac River
White Point Marina, Shannon Branch, Yeocomico River, Kinsale (804-472-2977)
Olverson's Lodge Creek Marina, Yecomico River (804-529-6868)
Cole's Point Plantation, Potomac River, Coles Point (804-472-3955)
Stepp's Harbor View, Mattox Creek, Colonial Beach (804-224-9265)

Virginia Eastern Shore
Deep Creek Marina and Boatyard, Deep Creek, Pocomoke River (757-787-4565)
Wharf at Onancock, Onancock Creek, Onancock (757-787-7911)
Davis Wharf Marina Serives, Occohannock Creek, Occohannock (757-442-9242)
Cape Charles Town Harbor, Cape Charles (757-331-2357)

Ships on the Bay

A major shipping channel runs the length of the Chesapeake Bay and big ships must often keep to a narrow channel. It is up to you to stay clear. The U.S. pilots aboard commercial ships in the Bay monitor VHF channel 13 for ship-to-ship messages. Talk to the pilot; be sure he sees you and knows your intentions. It can take less than 10 minutes for a fast ship to reach you once you spot it in clear weather, and in hazy weather it takes a lot less.

When the ship's engines are put "full astern," there's nothing more the pilot can do. He may lose control of the ship, but reversing will in most cases swing the ship's bow to starboard. If you have a choice, try to escape on his port side. It takes 4 to 6 minutes and 2,000 to 4,000 feet for a ship to stop after its engines are reversed.

Watch out for tugs towing barges, especially at night when they may be poorly lit. They also may not be in the channel. Commercial fishing vessels, though more maneuverable, sometimes haul nets that can be deceptively long.

To see where the ships are, monitor their AIS signal on sites like *www.shipfinder.com* and *www.marinetraffic.com*. Or download the apps on your phone or tablet.
Meanwhile:

- Keep a constant lookout, especially astern.
- Stay out of the way. Avoid traveling in the ship channels, when the visibility is poor. Never anchor in a channel.
- Be visible. At night, make sure your navigation lights are bright and not obscured by sails or flags. If you see a vessel's running lights and don't think you've been seen, begin to get out of the way. Use flashlights, a spotlight or a white flare to indicate your position. Carry a radar reflector as high on the boat as you can.
- Watch the ship's lights—sidelights as well as masthead lights. If you see only one sidelight, or if one is much brighter than the other, you can be fairly sure you are not in the direct path of the ship. If you see both sidelights, you're dead ahead—MOVE OUT FAST.
- Know whistle signals. Five or more short blasts means "Danger!" If the signal is for you, make way fast.
- Use binoculars, especially at night, to help determine ships' lights and direction (7x50 is best for night vision).

Hopelessly Devoted . . .

to sharing everything we now
about the Chesapeake
with our readers!!

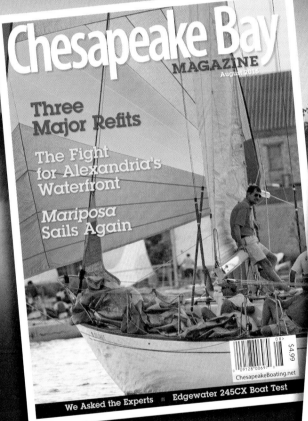

*11 issues per year
for $25.95*

to place your order call
877 804-8624
or visit us online at **ChesapeakeBoating.net**

NO SLIP?
NO PROBLEM.

SNAG-A-SLIP is a FREE online boat slip reservation system that allows boaters to explore marinas by region and search for slip availability based on travel dates, length, beam, draw and power requirements. Boaters can pick their preferred marina after reviewing amenities, location and availability – and then book immediately with ease and confidence!

Snag-A-Slip is based in the Chesapeake Bay and showcases awesome marinas up and down the East Coast. We are expanding daily, so be sure to check our site regularly for new marina additions! You can contact us at hello@snagaslip.com.

www.snagaslip.com

This service is a long-time coming and it makes it so much easier for the boater to find, compare and book slips. We've been extremely satisfied with Snag-A-Slip and their partner marinas. - Todd Anderbery, PA

SNAG-A-SLIP™
EXPLORE. BOOK. BOAT.™

Looking for a Marina? If there is a marina you would like to see on our site, we'd love to hear about it. Drop us a line at hello@snagaslip.com!

The Cruiser's Newest Reference!

2016
Atlantic Coast & ICW
Planning and Facilities Guide

Your A to Z Reference for Making a Successful Trip from Maine through Florida

How to Plan Your Cruise on the Intracoastal Waterway

- ◆ Cruise Guide & App Reviews
- ◆ Finding & Using Government Resources
- ◆ Photos, Charts & Schedules for Bridges Along the Route
- ◆ Latest Facilities Information
- ◆ Putting It All Together for a Fun & Relaxing Cruise

from the publishers of
Chesapeake Bay

Available in Print and on the Web

Wanna Go Crabbing?

CBM staff

Catching a mess of hard crabs is a favorite pastime of Bay boaters. It's as easy as "chicken necking"—tying a piece of raw chicken to a long piece of string, dropping the baited line in the water and waiting for a crab to come along. When you see the string begin to move through the water, you'll know a crab is walking away with the bait. Ever so gently pull on the string, and the bait and crab will rise slowly to the surface. As soon as they are visible, quickly scoop them both into your dip net. Shake the crab into a waiting bushel or bucket, give it a covering of nice cool sea grass, drop the baited line back in the water and wait. The number of baited lines you set is limited only by the size of your dock or your boat and how many chicken necks you can spare. Catching a couple dozen crabs for dinner does not require a license, but be aware of the crabbing regulations in Virginia and Maryland.

Virginia: Unlicensed recreational crabbers may use a hand line, a dip net or two crab pots to catch up to one bushel of hard crabs and two dozen soft crabs (or peelers) daily per boat, or, from a dock of bulkhead, per person. Anything else requires a gear license. For all of the regulations—which change regularly as the states work to preserve the crab popu-

lation on the Bay, see *www.mrc.state.va.us.*

Maryland: Beginning January 1, 2014, all crab pots used off private shoreline property must be registered. The online registration may be done through the DNR Compass System at *compass.dnr.maryland.gov.* Call 410-260-3220 for assistance or visit your local DNR Service Center. From April 1 through December 15, no female crabs may be taken. Unlicensed recreational crabbers may use a hand line, a dip net or two registered crab pots* to catch up to two dozen male hard crabs or one dozen male soft crabs (or peelers) daily, not to exceed four dozen hard crabs or one dozen soft crabs per boat. You must throw the female crabs back (they are marked by a wide, triangular "apron" on their underside). There is no crabbing permitted in Maryland waters on Wednesdays, except with registered crab pots off private docks, hand lines or dip nets. For the latest regulations and size restrictions, see *www.dnr. state.md.us*).

* Maryland prohibits the use of spring-loaded collapsible crab traps. All collapsible traps must be manually operated in order to catch a crab. (This prevents the inadvertent entrapment of other Bay critters, like terrapins.)

Crab Pots & Fish Nets — Watch Out!

Few experiences are more exhilarating than cruising silently through the dark, with only the blinking lights of the markers and the comfort of your chartplotter for company. Few experiences are more certain to bring all that to a halt than snagging a crab pot—or much worse, clipping the stout poles of a pound net. You can believe yourself to be far enough offshore to avoid these twin bugaboos of the recreational boater, but you can never be absolutely certain. And because neither crab pots nor pound nets appear on any chart, only a resolute look-out will assure your safety.

From spring till late fall, commercial crabbers are hard at work on the Bay, harvesting crabs as they migrate north in the warmer months, then back to the mouth of the Bay to winter over. These watermen are most often using traditional white deadrise workboats, which give them a long cockpit for hauling traps and stowing bushels. Their season starts in April and runs through early November, when crabbers have to pull their pots for the winter.

Crab traps are most commonly marked by floats that bear the license number of the owner. They are large wire-mesh cages with a central bait holder and openings for crabs to enter. Running too close to one of the crab floats risks snagging the float line on your propeller, stopping you dead in the water. Should you snag one of these, DO NOT CUT the line until you have retrieved the trap from the Bay bottom. If possible, refasten the line and drop the trap back in the water. If you can't do this for some reason, drop the pot (the trap itself) off at the nearest public wharf or marina, with the crabber's license number attached (if possible). Or hail a nearby commercial crabber if you see one. He (or she) might well be willing to take the pot off your hands.

"Ghost" traps litter the bottom of the Bay and continue to trap crabs and turtles that can't escape. Should you raise one of these long dormant traps, dispose of it properly on dry land just as you would any other kind of debris.

Crabbers also work **trotlines**—especially on the Eastern Shore. These are long baited lines marked on either end with a float (often something as simple as an empty bleach bottle). The lines lie on the bottom between the floats, so it's safe to travel over them if you must. If a crabber is working his line, give it a wide berth; the baited line is rising from the bottom and falling again as the crabber works his way along it.

Pound nets are another mariner's hazard. You will see them in Eastern Bay, at the mouth of the Choptank River, north of Herring Bay and between the Great and Little Wicomico rivers, among many other places. Pound nets can be hard to see in low light or rough weather. Made of cut saplings, they look like a line of fencing material sticking out of the water. They are supposed to be lit on either end, but dead batteries and harsh conditions take their toll on the lighting fixtures. The state of Maryland lists the locations of licensed pound nets at: *www.dnr.state.md.us/fisheries/commercial/poundnetsites.html*. (Virginia does not.)

In Virginia waters, state law requires that **gill nets** must be clearly marked at both ends with a square flag suspended at least two feet above the water. These flags are blaze orange and the poles from which they're suspended must be marked with either reflectors or reflective tape. Drift or anchor gill nets must be marked at one end with a square flag of any color and at the other end with a triangular flag or a floating ball of an identical color. Flags must be suspended three feet above the water and the poles or balls also must be marked with reflective material. Skirt either end of these flag or floating ball configurations, but don't run between them.

Nettles, Rays, Ticks and Snakes!

So there you are, off the boat and enjoying a cooling swim. Suddenly you are surrounded by a ghostly school of **cownose rays**. Yikes! Should you be worried? Oddly enough, the answer is yes and no. Few stings from rays are reported each year—though that original Chesapeake cruiser, John Smith, would have a few things to say on the subject. He was stung by a ray's poisonous tail near the Rappahannock River, but survived the ordeal. Rays can be found on the Bay from May through October, migrating as far north as Kent Island. So if you see rays, give them a wide berth and they'll do the same to you. Besides, there's another kind of critter lurking in the water that can give you a lot more trouble: nettles.

Sea nettles, or jellyfish, can make swimming in portions of the Chesapeake downright unpleasant. Those long silky tentacles carry an acidic toxin that burns human skin. The more tender the skin, the greater the reaction; young children find them terribly painful. An ice cube and a sprinkle of baking soda may help take out the sting; some folks swear by meat tenderizer. Having both on board is not a bad idea. Sea nettles loathe fresh water, so the farther north you go on the Bay, the fewer you'll find. The Chesapeake Bay bridges are the general line of demarcation between nettle-full and nettle-free water, although during unusually dry summers, nettles have reached as far as Worton Creek. Some Bay boaters invest in inflatable portable boat pools to make swimming more pleasant (they serve also to keep kids close to the

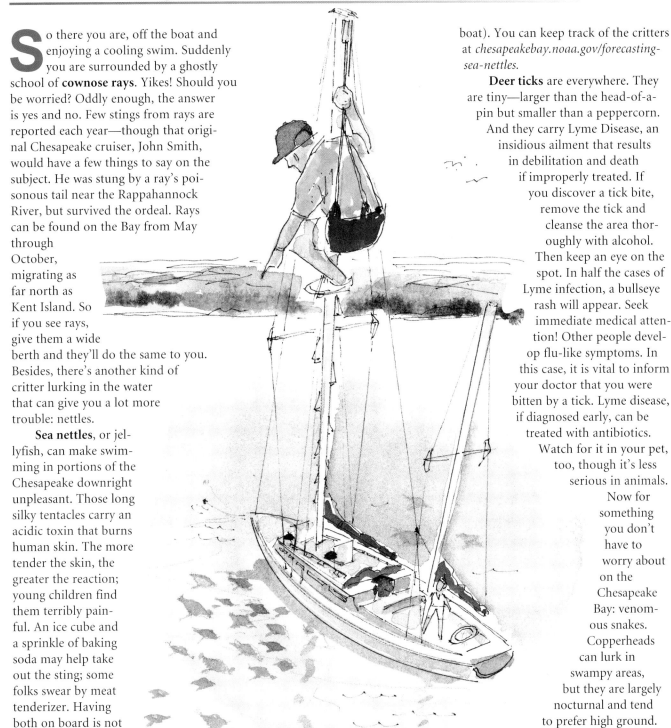

boat). You can keep track of the critters at *chesapeakebay.noaa.gov/forecasting-sea-nettles.*

Deer ticks are everywhere. They are tiny—larger than the head-of-a-pin but smaller than a peppercorn. And they carry Lyme Disease, an insidious ailment that results in debilitation and death if improperly treated. If you discover a tick bite, remove the tick and cleanse the area thoroughly with alcohol. Then keep an eye on the spot. In half the cases of Lyme infection, a bullseye rash will appear. Seek immediate medical attention! Other people develop flu-like symptoms. In this case, it is vital to inform your doctor that you were bitten by a tick. Lyme disease, if diagnosed early, can be treated with antibiotics. Watch for it in your pet, too, though it's less serious in animals.

Now for something you don't have to worry about on the Chesapeake Bay: venomous snakes. Copperheads can lurk in swampy areas, but they are largely nocturnal and tend to prefer high ground. Water moccasins have been reported by people in the southern Bay, but are seldom verified. They are more likely to have encountered a northern water snake, which mimics the coloring of the cottonmouth and copperhead. You will see these in broad daylight, basking along the shore or swimming across deep water—two clues that they are harmless. Nevertheless, leave them alone. If threatened, they will behave defensively.

Chesapeake Weather

Good cruising weather on the Chesapeake Bay usually extends from mid-April until the end of October and often late into November. With a protected steering station, however, or a lot of warm clothes, this can be extended indefinitely. During the spring and fall especially, boaters can expect good winds, warm sunny days and comfortable nights for sleeping, with only an occasional shower and thunderstorm. Summertime can be more unpredictable as days get hotter, nights more humid. Winds tend to drop off during the day in the hottest weather. Sailors should plan on early starts and mid-day layovers. And of course, winter cruising brings its own set of caveats with good winds but wicked storms . . . and ice.

Summer cruisers learn to keep an eye out for the infamous **Chesapeake squalls.** These squalls usually appear during the hottest days and can strike with sudden intensity. You may be cruising along with a moderate breeze and suddenly notice an oppressive, humid heat bearing down on you. The breeze may drop off completely, then clock around to come from a different direction. Often these storms occur in the late afternoon, around three or four o'clock. To the west-northwest the sky may show a distinct coppery glow. Shortly, a line of black clouds will begin to advance toward you. As the clouds draw near, you will see feathery, gray–white clouds and then feel a sudden chill minutes before the wind hits. Short, steep waves will build up, often accompanied by torrential, stinging rain.

What's the best plan? Those with fast boats can run for shelter when they see the storm line coming. Others should button up their boats and power into the wind till the squall blows itself out, usually 15 or 20 minutes (infrequently, up to an hour). Sailors may want to keep a small headsail up to help steady the boat. Powerboats should slow down so that they are off plane. Be aware of the leeward shore and try to get well off before any storm hits. Keep your boat pointed toward the storm and into the waves. While this could be uncomfortable, it is by far safer. Give yourself enough throttle for steerage. Some boaters will work their throttle to better "ride" the waves as they pass under the boat.

Being prepared for heavy weather will give you more confidence as waves and weather start to hammer your boat. Have life jackets close to hand and wear them in any rough conditions. Make sure your bilge pump is working and your scuppers are clear. Know what your options are before you set out, and calculate distance and time between safe havens along your route.

Chesapeake squalls can be frightening, but boats built for Bay cruising are designed to take a beating. Stay aboard your vessel and don't panic. Calling for a rescue can put others in danger and can result in unecessary damage. Bear in mind that your boat is the safest place to be; it will float far longer than you will.

Any veteran cruiser will tell you that stormy weather brings its own rewards: dazzling sunsets and cooler temperatures that promise a good night's sleep.

Dockside Dining

Whether you're looking for a bushel of fresh steamed crabs or something more avant garde, you'll find it on the Chesapeake waterfront, or just a short stroll from it. Many marinas now offer some kind of eatery, from basic bar-and-grills where you can get a beer and a burger to upscale dining where gourmet specialties are the draw. Some marinas offer both. If that's not enough to fill a hungry belly, look beyond the water's edge. Small towns and villages offer a whole slew of dining opportunities these days, from creative bistros to elegantly refurbished historic inns and taverns. Because of the plethora of eateries that lie within a stone's throw of the water, we won't even try to name them all in this guide. With some exceptions, we try instead to indicate where they are, in general, so visiting boaters can walk into town and discover them for themselves. Dining facilities not associated with specific marinas and that offer dockage are listed.

Getting to dinner shouldn't be a problem. If you're anchored out or moored, many harbors now offer water taxi service that will get you ashore without having to launch your dinghy: Chesapeake City, Georgetown (on the Sassafras), Annapolis and St. Michaels are a few. Chesapeake Beach, Rock Hall and Colonial Beach are among those offering fun little trolleys to haul you up the road and back. Even better, plenty of waterside watering holes offer free dockage to patrons. On the weekends, however, competition for these ringside slips can be stiff. Since these are generally available on a first-come-first-served basis, plan accordingly. Call ahead, by marine radio or phone, to see whether the marina/restaurant will take reservations. And if you know you want to go to a particular restaurant, make a reservation days in advance—even in the off season. The same rules apply if the restaurant you're heading for offers free dockage at a cooperating marina. Call the dockmaster to let him or her know of your planned arrival and get a slip assignment.

Here's a great cruising tip: If you're looking for a unique dining experience, check out one of the many church suppers or community fish fries that crop up on the calendar. These are usually fundraisers in support of historic churches or local firehalls—like the annual crabcake, ham and oyster dinner (July) at Trinity Church in St. Mary's City. Then there are the Bay's many popular festivals, such as the Seafood Festival on Tilghman Island or the Urbanna, Va., Oyster Festival. Check out the calendar at *www. ChesapeakeBoating.net* for current listings.

Chesapeake Bay Events

Here is a sampling of events held annually around the Bay. It's far from comprehensive, so be sure to check in with the "Cruiser's Calendar" at *www.ChesapeakeBoating.net* for a complete and up-to-date listing.

April

Bay Bridge Boat Show, Stevensville, Md., *www.usboat.com*

May

Blue Angels Fly-Over, Severn River, Annapolis, *www.usna.edu*

Chestertown Tea Party Festival, *www.chestertownteaparty.org*

Smith Island Day/Crab Skiff Races, Ewell, Md., *www.smithisland.org*

Solomons Maritime Festival, Solomons, Md., *www.calvertmarine museum.org*

June

Alexandria Waterfront Festival, Alexandria, Va., *www.waterfront festival.org*

Antique & Classic Boat Festival, St. Michaels, Md., *www.cbmm.org*

Blackbeard Festival, Hampton, Va., *www.blackbeardpiratefestival.com*

Cobb Island Day Festival, Cobb Island, Md., 301-259-4632

Cock Island Race, Portsmouth, Va., *www.portsmouthboatclub.org*

Eastport-A-Rockin', Annapolis/Eastport, *www.eastportarockin.com*

Harborfest, Norfolk, *www.festevents.org*

St. Mary's Maritime HeritageFestival Historic St. Mary's City, Md., *www.stmaryscity.org*

Seafood Festival, Tilghman, Md., *www.tilghmanmd.com*

July

Cambridge Classic Powerboat Regatta, Cambridge, Md., *www.cpbra.com*

Governor's Cup Log Canoe Races, St. Michaels, Md., *www.blogcanoe.com*

J. Millard Tawes Crab & Clam Bake, Crisfield, Md., *www.crisfieldchamber.com*

Screwpile Lighthouse Challenge Regatta, Solomons, Md., *www.screwpile.net*

Watermen's Heritage Celebration, Yorktown, Va., *www.watermens.org*

Chesapeake Bay Events

August

Governor's Cup Yacht Race, (overnight) Annapolis to St. Mary's City, Md., *www.smcm.edu/govcup*

Mari-Fest, Havre de Grace, Md., *www.hdgmaritimemuseum.org*

Seafood Feast-i-Val, Cambridge, Md., *www.seafoodfeastival.com*

Thunder on the Narrows, Kent Narrows, *www.kentnarrowsracing.com*

September

Antique & Classic Boats Show, Reedville, Va., *www.rfmuseum.org*

Harborfest, Onancock, Va., *www.onancock.org*

Maryland Seafood Festival, Sandy Point, *mdseafoodfestival.com*

National Hard Crab Derby, Crisfield, Md., *www.crisfieldchamber.com*

Rendezvous, Mile Marker Zero, Portsmouth, Va., *www.tyamarina.com*

Skipjack Races & Festival, Deal Island, Md., *skipjack.net/races*

Trawler Fest, Baltimore, *www.passagemaker.com*

October

Fells Point Fun Festival, Baltimore, *www.preservationsociety.com*

Great Chesapeake Bay Schooner Race, Baltimore to Portsmouth, *www.schoonerrace.org*

Mid-Atlantic Small Craft Festival, St. Michaels, Md., *www.cbmm.org*

Patuxent River Appreciation Days, Solomons, Md., *www.calvertmarine museum.org*

St. Mary's County Oyster Festival, Leonardtown, Md., *www.usoysterfest.com*

Tilghman Island Day, Tilghman, Md., *www.tilghmanmd.com*

Turkey Shoot Regatta, Lancaster, Va., *www.turkeyshoot.org*

U.S. Sailboat & U.S. Powerboat Shows, Annapolis, *www.usboat.com*

November

Downrigging Days, Chestertown, Md., *www.sultanaprojects.org*

Urbanna Oyster Festival, Urbanna, Va., *www.urbannaoysterfestival.com*

4th of July Fireworks Displays

(Please call to verify dates and times.)

Annapolis, Spa Creek, 410-263-7958

Baltimore, Inner Harbor, 410-837-4636

Cambridge, Md., Choptank River, 410-228-4020

Cape Charles, Va., Bayfront, 757-331-2304

Chesapeake Beach, Md., Rod 'N Reel Restaurant, 410-257-2230

Chestertown, Md., 410-778-0500

Colonial Beach, Va., 804-224-7181

Crisfield, Md., Somers Cove Marina, 410-968-0925

Deltaville, Va., 804-776-6461

Georgetown, Md., Sassafras River, 410-275-1200

Gloucester Point, Va., York River, 866-847-4887

Friendship, Md., Herrington Harbour South Marina, 301-855-8435

Hampton, Va., Ft. Monroe, 757-788-3151

Havre de Grace, Md., 410-939-4362

Irvington, Va., Tides Inn, 804-438-5000

Kent Narrows, Md., Chesapeake Exploration Center, 410-758-0835

Middle River, Md., Eastern Yacht Club, 410-687-1002

Newport News, Va., James River, 757-926-1400

Norfolk, Town Point Park, 757-441-2345

North East, Md., Town Park, 410-287-5801

Oxford, Md., Tred Avon Yacht Club, 410-226-5269

Portsmouth, Va., North Landing, 757-393-8481

Poquoson, Va., 757-868-3588

Reedville, Va., Cockrell Creek, 804-453-6529

Rock Hall, Md., Harbor, 410-778-0416

St. Michaels, Md., Miles River Yacht Club, 410-745-9511

Smithfield, Va., Pagan River, 757-357-2291

Solomons, Md., Patuxent River, 410-326-1950

Urbanna, Va., Town Marina, 804-758-0464

Washington, D.C., Washington Monument grounds, 202-619-7225

Yorktown, Va., York River, 757-890-3500

Chesapeake Bay Museums

The Chesapeake Bay region is full of museums celebrating the region's maritime, natural and social history. Those listed here are either accessible from the water or are of particular interest to visiting cruisers. Those highlighted have docking facilities on the immediate premises (water depths vary; call ahead). Museums charging admission are noted with a $; those that don't welcome donations. Many of these organizations are small and volunteer-dependent, so they may have restricted hours. Check their websites or call for more information.

Upper Bay Museums

Historic Ships in Baltimore, Inner Harbor, 410-539-1797; *www.historicships.org*. Five historic landmarks, including *USS Constellation, USS Torsk, USCGC Taney*, Lightship *Chesapeake* and the Seven Foot Knoll Lighthouse. $

Baltimore Museum of Industry, Inner Harbor, 410-727-4808; *www.thebmi.org*. Celebrates Baltimore's industrial past, including seafood packing and the maritime trades. $

C&D Canal Museum, Chesapeake City, Md., 410-885-5622; *www.nap.usace. army.mil/sb/c&d.htm*. Weekdays.

Concord Point Lighthouse, Havre de Grace, Md., 410-939-3213. 1827 beacon and light keeper's house. Weekends.

Decoy Museum, Havre de Grace, Md., 410-939-3739; *www.decoymuseum.com*. Decoys, carving demonstrations. $

Fort McHenry National Monument/ Historic Shrine, Baltimore, 410-962-4290; *www.nps.gov/fomc*. Battle site that inspired "The Star-Spangled Banner." $

Geddes Piper House, Chestertown, Md., 410-778-3499; *www.kentcountyhistory. org*. Restored 1784 house. Tue.-Sat. $

Havre de Grace Maritime Museum, Havre de Grace, Md., 410-939-4800; *www.hdg maritimemuseum.org*. Maritime history exhibits, boatbuilders school. $

Maryland Historical Society, Baltimore, 410-685-3750; *www.mdhs.org*. Bay and Port of Baltimore history. Wed.-Sun. $

Mt. Harmon, Earleville, Md., *www.mount harmon.org*. 410-275-8819. Colonial plantation manor house. The museum opened a new dock directly below the plantation house in the spring of 2014. Thu.-Sun. $

National Aquarium in Baltimore, Inner Harbor, 410-576-3800; *www.aqua.org*. Marine and freshwater animals; ocean, coral reef exhibits; Immersion Theater. $

Paw Paw Museum, Port Deposit, Md., 410-378-4480; *www.portdeposit.com/history/ pawpaw*. Local historic artifacts. Second & fourth Sun., first Sat.

Rock Hall Museum, Rock Hall, Md., 410-639-7611; *www.rockhallmd.com/ museum*. Boat models, watermen's gear, re-created decoy workshop. Weekends.

Susquehanna Museum/Lock House, Havre de Grace, Md., 410-939-5780; *www.lockhousemuseum.org*. History of Susquehanna and Tidewater Canal. Weekends.

Tolchester Beach Revisited, Rock Hall, Md., 410-778-5347; *www.rockhallmd. com/tolchester*. History of 19th-century amusement park. Weekends.

Upper Bay Museum, North East, Md., 410-287-2675. Fishing, hunting artifacts. Dinghy and small-boat dock. Wed.-Sun.

Waterman's Museum, Rock Hall, Md., 410-778-6697; *www.havenharbour.com/ hhwatmus.htm*. Open on demand.

Middle Bay Museums

Alexandria Seaport Center, Alexandria, Va., 703-549-7078; *www.alexandriasea port.org*. Boatbuilding workshops Tue. evenings.

Annapolis Maritime Museum, Annapolis, 410-295-0104; *www.annapolismaritime museum.org*. Local maritime heritage, interactive exhibit center; tours to Thomas Point Shoal Lighthouse ($). Dinghy landing. Weekends.

Banneker-Douglass Museum, Annapolis, 410-216-6180; *www.bdmuseum.com*. African American culture and history. Tue.-Sat.

Calvert Marine Museum, Solomons, Md., 410-326-2042; *www.calvertmarine museum.com*. Maritime & estuarine history, paleontology, lighthouse tours, fisheries exhibit. $

Capt. Salem Avery House, Shady Side, Md., 410-867-4486; *www.averyhouse.org*. 1860s waterman's house/museum. Sun.

Chesapeake Bay Maritime Museum, St. Michaels, Md., 410-745-2916; *www. cbmm.org*. Chesapeake maritime history, lighthouse tours, restored workboats and boatbuilding workshops. $

Chesapeake Beach Railway Museum, Chesapeake Beach, Md., 410-257-3892; *www.chesapeake-beach.md.us*. History of local resort and railway that served it.

Colonial Beach Museum, Colonial Beach, Va., 804-224-3379. Local history, casino-era exhibits. Weekends.

Delmarva Discovery Center, Pocomoke City, Md., 410-957-9933; *www.delmar vadiscoverycenter.org*. Heritage of Pocomoke River watershed. Wed.-Sat.

Dorchester County Historical Society, Cambridge, Md., 410-228-7953; *www. dorchesterhistory.org*. Historic house tours (by appointment). Agricultural, carvers museums. Tue.-Sat. $

Gadsby's Tavern Museum, Alexandria, Va., 703-838-4242; *www.gadsbystavern.org*. Restored Colonial tavern and hotel. Daily and Fri. evening lantern tours. $

Historic Annapolis Foundation, Annapolis, 410-267-7619, 800-603-4020; *www. annapolis.org*. Operates William Paca House & Garden, HistoryQuest, tours. $

Historic London Town & Gardens, Edgewater, Md., 410-222-1919; *www.historic londontown.com*. Colonial house, excavation site of early 1700s town. Wed.-Sun. $

Historic St. Mary's City, Md., 240-895-4990, 800-762-1634; *www.stmaryscity. org*. Site of state's first capital; *Maryland Dove* replica ship, living history, archaeological sites. Wed.-Sun. $

Historical Society of Talbot County, Easton, Md., 410-822-0773; *www.hstc.org*. Museum (free) open Mon.-Sat. Tours of three historic homes Tue.-Sat. $

Kinsale Museum, Kinsale, Va., 804-472-3001. Colonial port and steamboat era exhibits. Fri.-Sun.

Mount Vernon, Alexandria, Va., 703-780-2000; *www.mountvernon.org*. George Washington's estate and gardens, interactive exhibit hall. $

Oxford Museum, Oxford, Md., 410-226-0191; *www.oxfordmuseum.org.* Town & maritime artifacts. Mon, Wed., Fri.-Sun.

Piney Point Lighthouse Museum, Piney Point, Md., 301-769-2222; *www.co. saint-marys.md.us/recreate/museums.* "Lighthouse of Presidents" Fri.-Mon. $

Point Lookout Lighthouse/Civil War Museum, Point Lookout, Md., 301-872-5085; *www.pointlookoutlighthouse.com.* History of Civil War POW camp & old Point Lookout Lighthouse.

Richardson Maritime Museum, Cambridge, Md., 410-221-1871; *www.richardsonmuseum.org.* Boatbuilding history, ship's models. Wed., Sat. & Sun. Ruark Boatworks: Model & building workshops Tue. evenings, Mon., Wed. & Fri.; tours Sat.

St. Clements Island Museum, Coltons Point, Md., 301-769-2222, *www.co.saint-marys.md.us/recreate/museums.* Traces journey of first English settlers. $

St. Mary's Square Museum, St. Michaels, Md., 410-745-9561. Town history and memorabilia. Weekends.

Smallwood's Retreat, Pisgah, Md., 301-743-7613; *dnr2.maryland.gov/publiclands/ Pages/southern/smallwood.aspx.* Plantation home. Weekends, Sun. only June 15-Labor Day.

Smith Island Cultural Museum, Ewell, Md., 800-521-9189; *www.smithisland. org.* Island history and cultural life. $

Sotterley Plantation, Hollywood, Md., 301-373-2280; *www.sotterley.org.* Historic plantation and manor house. House tours Tue.-Sun. $

Sturgis One Room School Museum, Pocomoke City, Md., 410-957-1913; *www.pocomokeriver.org..* African American history. Tue.-Sat.

Tangier History Museum, Tangier Island, 757-805-5863; *www.tangierhistorymuseum. org.* Island's unique history & language and it's uncertain future.

J. Millard Tawes Historical Museum, Crisfield, Md., 410-968-2501; *www. crisfieldheritagefoundation.org.* History of lower Bay & its seafood industry. $

Harriet Tubman Museum, Cambridge, Md., 410-228-0401. Harriet Tubman and Underground Railroad. Tue.-Sat.

U.S. Naval Academy Museum, Annapolis, 410-293-2108; *www.usna.edu/Museum.* Historical exhibits, ship's instruments, Robinson naval print collections.

Ward Brothers Workshop, Crisfield, Md., 410-968-2501; *www.crisfieldheritagefoundation.org.* Restored workshop of local decoy artists. Appointment only. $

Ward Museum of Wildfowl Art, Salisbury, Md., 410-742-4988; *www.wardmuseum.org* Comprehensive collection of carvings. $

Lower Bay Museums

Cape Charles Museum, Cape Charles, Va., 757-331-1008. Railroads, boatbuilding.

Casemate Museum at Fort Monroe, Hampton, Va., 757-788-3391; *www.monroe.army.mil.* Old Point Comfort, Ft. Monroe and Civil War history.

Deltaville Maritime Museum, Deltaville, Va., 804-776-7200; *www.deltavilleva.com/ museumpark.* Boatbuilding artifacts and models. Dinghy dock. Call for hours.

Gwynn's Island Museum, Grimstead, Va., 804-725-7949. Island, merchant marine history. Fri.-Sun.

Hampton History Museum, Hampton, Va., 757-727-1610; *www.hampton.gov/history _museum.* Port of Hampton history. $

Hampton Roads Naval Museum/*USS Wisconsin*, Norfolk, 757-322-2987; *www.hrnm.navy.mil.* Lower Bay naval history, World War II battleship tours.

Historic Christ Church/Carter Reception Center, Weems, Va., 804-483-6855; *www.christchurch1735.org.* History of 1735 church & its patron, Robert Carter.

Historic Jamestowne, Va., 757-229-1733; *www.historicjamestowne.org.* James Fort site and archaeological museum. $

Isle of Wight Museum, Smithfield, Va., 757-357-7459. Smithfield Ham exhibits, Civil War artifacts. Tue.-Sun.

Jamestown Settlement, Jamestown, Va., 757-253-4838, 888-593-4682; *www.historyisfun.org.* Living history portrayals, exhibit gallery on America's first permanent English colony. $

Ker Place, Onancock, VA, 757-787-8012; *www.kerplace.org.* Regional history and 19th century plantation life. Tue.-Sat. $

The Mariners' Museum, Newport News, Va., 800-581-7245, 757-596-2222; *www. mariner.org.* Figureheads, half models, scrimshaw, small craft collections, library and archives. *USS Monitor* Center. $

Nauticus, the National Maritime Center, Norfolk, 800-664-1080, 757-664-1000; *www.nauticus.org.* Maritime-themed science center with interactive exhibits. $

Naval Shipyard & Lightship Museums, Portsmouth, Va., (Shipyard Museum 757-393-8591), (Lightship Museum 757-393-8741) *www.portsnavalmuseums.com.* Naval and naval shipyard history, lightship service exhibits. $

Old Coast Guard Station, Virginia Beach, 757-422-1587; *www.oldcoastguardstation. com.* U.S. life-saving service/Coast Guard history, shipwreck exhibit. $

Reedville Fishermen's Museum, Reedville, Va., 804-453-6529; *www.rfmuseum.org.* Menhaden fishing history, boatbuilding workshop, restored workboats. $

Steamboat Era Museum, Irvington, Va., 804-438-6888; *www.steamboateramuseum.org.* Steamboat artifacts. Thu.-Sun.

Virginia Air & Space Center, Hampton, Va., 757-727-0900; *www.vasc.org.* Historic spacecraft & aircraft, interactive aviation gallery, IMAX theater. $

Virginia Aquarium & Marine Science Center, Virginia Beach, 757-385-3474; *www.vmsm.com.* Aquariums, touch tanks, IMAX 3D theater. $

Watermen's Museum, Yorktown, Va., 757-887-2641; *www.watermens.org.* Virginia watermen's history. Tue.-Sun. $

Yorktown Victory Center, 757-253-4838, 888-593-4682; *www.historyisfun.org.* Living history museum depicting life of Revolutionary War soldiers. $

Navigator's Reference

Bay Charts

The use of old or outdated charts is never a good idea, especially on the Chesapeake Bay where erosion and silting make swift changes to even freshly dredged channels. Thanks to the internet, access to downloadable charts and chart corrections is available now in a timely fashion. Look for NOAA chart updates at *www.nauticalcharts.noaa.gov*. This site is also your source for links to downloadable recent and historic Coast Pilot books (PDF format).

Maptech sells officially certified NOAA digital navigation charts and companion CDs with navigation software for your PC. For more information, visit their website, *www.maptech.com*. The company also sells ChartKits, with reproductions of government charts for many areas, including the Chesapeake and Delaware bays.

NOAA Charts-On-Demand paper charts are distributed by OceanGrafix, *www.OceanGrafix.com*. They and the NOAA digital navigation charts offered by Maptech are available for sale the day after NOAA releases a new edition.

Accessing Tidal Lands

Exploring in your dinghy, you spot a sandy beach on an isolated spit of land—an ideal spot to pull ashore. But how far from the waterline can you wander without trespassing on what could be private land? In Maryland, case law has determined that submerged public trust lands extend to the *mean highwater* mark on shore, which gives boaters a degree of flexibility for landing dinghies or walking pets (you will still be expected to collect any droppings). Virginia law, however, establishes the *mean low water* mark as the boundary of submerged public trust lands in tidal areas.

Accident Reports

Accidents resulting in death or significant injury, or major damage to or loss of the boat, must be reported to the appropriate agency.

Maryland: Natural Resources Police, 580 Taylor Ave., Annapolis, MD 21401; 410-260-8888 (emergencies); *www.dnr.maryland.gov/nrp*.

Virginia: Law Enforcement Division, Dept. of Game and Inland Fisheries, P.O. Box 11104, Richmond, VA 23230; 804-367-1258 (emergencies); *www.dgif.virginia.gov/boating/accident.asp*.

District of Columbia: Metropolitan Police Department Harbor Patrol, 550 Water St., SW, Washington, D.C. 20024; 202-727-4582; *www.mpdc.dc.gov* (click on "Specialized Units").

Bay Bridge

The twin spans of the Bay Bridge, which link Sandy Point on the west and Kent Island on the east, have vertical clearances of 186 feet at their apex. Closer to the shorelines, clearances are considerably lower: 19 feet between piers 11 and 12 on the eastbound span and 30 feet at the eastern end of the westbound span.

Boating Laws

Virginia: Recently passed legislation requires all personal watercraft (PWC) operators 35 or younger to have passed a boating safety course; no one under age 14 may operate a PWC under any circumstances. By 2016, those operating motorboats (10 hp and above) will require boating safety certification.

Maryland: Anyone born after July 1, 1972 must have passed a boating safety course. Regardless of certification, operators of any PWC must be at least 16. All children under the age of 13 must wear a life jacket while on deck underway in Maryland waters in a recreational vessel under 21 feet.

Boating Safety Classes: For boating courses and courtesy marine examinations in your region, visit these websites: U.S. Coast Guard Auxiliary, *www.cgaux.org*, U.S. Coast Guard Office of Boating Safety, *www.uscgboating.org*, or *www.boatcourse.com*.

Use of Cell Phones vs. VHF: As useful as cellphones are, they *cannot* take the place of the VHF, which is intended for vessels of all sizes (even the littlest day fishing boat) and whose primary purpose is safety. Keep the VHF turned on and tuned to Channel 16. The VHF informs and protects boaters in a wide variety of situations, and could mean the difference between life and death in the event of a boating emergency or mayday.

Homeland Security

With bases in Norfolk, Solomons and Annapolis, the Bay is teeming with military ships. Boaters must not approach within 100 yards of any U.S. Naval vessel and must slow to a minimum speed if you are within 500 yards. If for any reason you are unable to comply with this regulation, contact the ship or its Coast Guard escort on VHF-FM channel 16.

Should you observe irregular behavior or suspect unauthorized activity call the Coast Guard's America's Waterway Watch at 877-249-2824 and provide as much detail as you can.

Tidal Differences

	High Water hr. min.	Low Water hr. min.		High Water hr. min.	Low Water hr. min.
Corrections: Hampton Roads tide tables:			Worton Creek entrance, Md.	+1 11	+1 13
Kiptopeke Beach, Va.	-0 39	-0 30	Sassafras River, Betterton, Md.	+2 31	+2 18
Cape Charles Harbor, Va.	-0 11	+0 01	Elk River, Old Town Point Wharf, Md.	+3 17	+3 00
Pungoteague Creek, Va.	+2 26	+2 42	Northeast River, Charlestown, Md.	+3 42	+3 58
Onancock, Va., Onancock Creek	+2 56	+3 14	Havre de Grace, Md., Susquehanna River	+3 11	+3 30
Tangier Sound Light, Va.	+2 55	+2 53	Pooles Island, Md.	+0 55	+0 49
Pocomoke River, Shelltown, Md.	+3 33	+4 11	Back River, Rocky Point, Md.	+0 46	+0 38
Pocomoke River, Pocomoke City, Md.	+5 50	+6 10	Sevenfoot Knoll Light, Md.	-0 06	-0 10
Crisfield, Md., Little Annemessex River	+3 51	+4 00	Patapsco River, Fells Point, Md.	+0 09	+0 16
Smith Island, Ewell, Md.	+4 00	+4 26	Baltimore Harbor, Middle Branch, Md.	+0 26	+0 28
Chance, Md.	+4 41	+4 53	Magothy River, Mountain Point, Md.	-0 14	-0 09
Wicomico River, Whitehaven, Md.	+5 28	+5 42	Sandy Point, Md.	-1 21	-1 25
Nanticoke River, Roaring Point, Md.	+5 01	+5 30	Annapolis, Md., Severn River	-1 38	-1 49
Nanticoke River, Vienna, Md.	+7 42	+7 45	Thomas Point Shoal Light, Md.	-2 04	-2 16
Smith Point Light, Va.	+3 30	+3 30	Rhode River, County Wharf, Md.	-2 04	-2 14
Little Wicomico River, Sunnybank, Va.	+5 42	+5 40	Galesville, Md., West River	-1 48	-1 38
Great Wicomico River Light, Va.	+2 59	+3 06	Rose Haven, Md.	-2 47	-2 49
Dividing Creek, Va.	+2 38	+2 36	Chesapeake Beach, Md.	-2 52	-3 04
Windmill Point Light, Va.	+1 48	+2 06	Long Beach, Md.	-4 10	-4 12
Stingray Point Light, Va.	+1 05	+1 27	Cove Point, Md.	-4 05	-4 27
Rappahannock River, Windmill Point, Va.	+1 56	+2 13	Solomons Island, Md., Patuxent River	-4 45	-4 52
Rappahannock River, Orchard Point, Va.	+2 29	+2 46	Broomes Island, Md., Patuxent River	-4 29	-4 21
Urbanna, Va., Rappahannock River	+2 45	+3 04	Point No Point, Md.	-5 27	-5 39
Tappahannock, Va. Rappahannock River	+4 35	+5 13	Point Lookout, Md.	-5 26	-5 36
Piankatank River, Jackson Creek, Va.	+1 31	+1 59			
Wolf Trap Light, Va.	-0 07	+0 27			
Mobjack Bay, New Point Comfort, Va.	-0 07	+0 01	**Corrections: Washington tide tables (Potomac River):**		
Mobjack Bay, Mobjack, Va., East River	-0 22	-0 03	Lewisetta, Va., Coan River	-6 22	-7 19
Perrin River, Va., York River	+0 13	+0 03	Kinsale, Va., Yeocomico River	-6 04	-6 47
Yorktown, Va., York River	+0 11	+0 06	St. Mary's City, Md., St. Mary's River	-6 21	-7 02
West Point, Va., York River	+2 07	+2 33	Piney Point, Md.	-6 12	-7 10
Poquoson River, York Point, Va.	-0 07	+0 01	Ragged Point, Coles Neck, Va.	-5 53	-6 57
Back River, Messick Point, Va.	-0 26	-0 05	Leonardtown, Breton Bay, Md.	-5 50	-6 33
Norfolk, Va., Elizabeth River	+0 18	+0 15	Mount Holly, Nomini Creek, Va.	-5 09	-5 48
Nansemond River, Pig Point, Va.	+0 37	+0 35	Colton's Point, Md.	-5 31	-6 38
Smithfield, Va., Pagan River, James River	+1 29	+1 23	Wicomico Riv., Cobb Pt. Bar Light, Md.	-5 41	-6 22
James River, Jamestown Island, Va.	+2 58	+3 31	Colonial Beach, Va.	-5 27	-6 12
Chickahominy River, Ferry Point, Va.	+3 56	+4 21	Dahlgren, Upper Machodoc Creek, Va.	-5 00	-5 45
Jordan Point, James River, Va.	+6 11	+6 34	Port Tobacco River, Goose Bay, Md.	-4 20	-5 01
Little Creek, Va.	-0 48	-0 50	Aquia Creek, Va.	-1 46	-2 26
Lynnhaven Inlet, Va.	-0 09	+0 06	Mattawoman Creek, Deep Point, Md.	-1 12	-1 38
Cape Henry, Va.	-0 48	-1 10	Occoquan Bay, High Point, Va.	-1 02	-1 28
			Mount Vernon, Va.	-0 17	-0 42
			Alexandria, Va.	+0 08	-0 17
Corrections: Baltimore tide tables:					
Hooper Island Light, Md.	-5 03	-5 13			
Little Choptank River, Taylors Isl., Md.	-3 05	-3 15			
Sharps Island Light, Md.	-3 47	-3 50			
Choptank River Light, Md.	-3 13	-3 08			
Cambridge, Md., Choptank River,	-2 44	-2 41			
Oxford, Md., Tred Avon River	-3 01	-2 50			
Dogwood Harbor, Md.	-3 04	-2 53			
St. Michaels, Md., Miles River	-2 14	-1 58			
Wye East River, Wye Landing, Md.	-2 01	-1 41			
Kent Island Narrows, Md.	-1 40	-1 28			
Bloody Point Bar Light, Md.	-2 42	-2 44			
Chester River, Love Point, Md.	-0 20	-0 36			
Queenstown, Md., Chester River	-0 04	-0 14			
Chestertown, Md., Chester River	+0 47	+0 34			
Swan Creek, Deep Landing, Md.	-0 08	-0 09			

Hampton Roads, VA, 2016

Times and Heights of High and Low Waters

MAY

Day	Time (h m)	Height (ft)	Time (h m)	Height (ft)	Time (h m)	Height (ft)	Time (h m)	Height (ft)
1 Su	04:35 AM	2.5	10:57 AM	0.2	05:04 PM	2.5	11:25 PM	0.2
2 M	05:39 AM	2.6	11:55 AM	0.1	06:07 PM	2.7		
3 Tu	12:30 AM	0.1	06:40 AM	2.7	12:51 PM	-0.1	07:06 PM	3.0
4 W	01:31 AM	-0.1	07:38 AM	2.8	01:45 PM	-0.2	08:03 PM	3.2
5 Th	02:29 AM	-0.3	08:34 AM	2.8	02:38 PM	-0.3	08:57 PM	3.3
6 F ●	03:23 AM	-0.4	09:27 AM	2.9	03:29 PM	-0.4	09:50 PM	3.4
7 Sa	04:16 AM	-0.4	10:19 AM	2.9	04:21 PM	-0.4	10:42 PM	3.4
8 Su	05:09 AM	-0.4	11:11 AM	2.8	05:12 PM	-0.4	11:34 PM	3.3
9 M	06:01 AM	-0.3	12:03 PM	2.7	06:05 PM	-0.2		
10 Tu	12:27 AM	3.2	06:54 AM	-0.2	12:56 PM	2.6	06:59 PM	-0.1
11 W	01:21 AM	3.0	07:48 AM	0.0	01:52 PM	2.5	07:55 PM	0.1
12 Th	02:17 AM	2.8	08:42 AM	0.1	02:49 PM	2.4	08:55 PM	0.2
13 F ◐	03:16 AM	2.6	09:38 AM	0.2	03:49 PM	2.4	09:56 PM	0.3
14 Sa	04:15 AM	2.4	10:33 AM	0.3	04:48 PM	2.4	10:58 PM	0.4
15 Su	05:13 AM	2.3	11:25 AM	0.3	05:43 PM	2.4	11:56 PM	0.4
16 M	06:08 AM	2.3	12:15 PM	0.3	06:34 PM	2.5		
17 Tu	12:50 AM	0.3	06:57 AM	2.3	01:00 PM	0.3	07:21 PM	2.6
18 W	01:38 AM	0.3	07:42 AM	2.3	01:43 PM	0.2	08:04 PM	2.7
19 Th	02:22 AM	0.2	08:24 AM	2.3	02:24 PM	0.2	08:44 PM	2.7
20 F	03:04 AM	0.1	09:04 AM	2.3	03:03 PM	0.1	09:23 PM	2.8
21 Sa ○	03:44 AM	0.1	09:42 AM	2.3	03:42 PM	0.1	10:00 PM	2.8
22 Su	04:23 AM	0.1	10:19 AM	2.3	04:19 PM	0.1	10:37 PM	2.8
23 M	05:02 AM	0.1	10:57 AM	2.3	04:57 PM	0.2	11:14 PM	2.8
24 Tu	05:41 AM	0.1	11:34 AM	2.3	05:36 PM	0.2	11:53 PM	2.8
25 W	06:21 AM	0.1	12:14 PM	2.3	06:17 PM	0.2		
26 Th	12:34 AM	2.7	07:03 AM	0.1	12:58 PM	2.3	07:04 PM	0.3
27 F	01:20 AM	2.7	07:48 AM	0.1	01:47 PM	2.4	07:56 PM	0.3
28 Sa	02:10 AM	2.6	08:37 AM	0.1	02:41 PM	2.4	08:55 PM	0.3
29 Su ◑	03:07 AM	2.5	09:31 AM	0.1	03:40 PM	2.5	09:59 PM	0.2
30 M	04:08 AM	2.5	10:27 AM	0.0	04:42 PM	2.7	11:06 PM	0.2
31 Tu	05:11 AM	2.5	11:24 AM	-0.1	05:44 PM	2.8		

JUNE

Day	Time (h m)	Height (ft)	Time (h m)	Height (ft)	Time (h m)	Height (ft)	Time (h m)	Height (ft)
1 W	12:11 AM	0.0	06:14 AM	2.5	12:22 PM	-0.2	06:44 PM	3.0
2 Th	01:13 AM	-0.1	07:14 AM	2.6	01:18 PM	-0.3	07:42 PM	3.2
3 F	02:11 AM	-0.2	08:12 AM	2.6	02:14 PM	-0.3	08:38 PM	3.3
4 Sa	03:07 AM	-0.3	09:07 AM	2.7	03:08 PM	-0.4	09:32 PM	3.3
5 Su ●	04:00 AM	-0.4	10:00 AM	2.7	04:00 PM	-0.4	10:25 PM	3.3
6 M	04:52 AM	-0.3	10:52 AM	2.7	04:53 PM	-0.3	11:16 PM	3.2
7 Tu	05:42 AM	-0.3	11:44 AM	2.6	05:45 PM	-0.2		
8 W	12:07 AM	3.0	06:32 AM	-0.2	12:35 PM	2.6	06:37 PM	-0.1
9 Th	12:57 AM	2.9	07:21 AM	-0.1	01:27 PM	2.5	07:31 PM	0.1
10 F	01:48 AM	2.7	08:10 AM	0.1	02:20 PM	2.4	08:26 PM	0.2
11 Sa	02:39 AM	2.5	08:59 AM	0.2	03:13 PM	2.4	09:22 PM	0.3
12 Su ◐	03:32 AM	2.3	09:49 AM	0.2	04:07 PM	2.4	10:20 PM	0.4
13 M	04:26 AM	2.2	10:38 AM	0.3	05:01 PM	2.4	11:17 PM	0.4
14 Tu	05:19 AM	2.1	11:27 AM	0.3	05:53 PM	2.5		
15 W	12:12 AM	0.4	06:11 AM	2.1	12:15 PM	0.3	06:42 PM	2.5
16 Th	01:03 AM	0.3	07:00 AM	2.1	01:01 PM	0.2	07:28 PM	2.6
17 F	01:50 AM	0.3	07:46 AM	2.2	01:46 PM	0.2	08:11 PM	2.7
18 Sa	02:35 AM	0.2	08:30 AM	2.2	02:30 PM	0.2	08:53 PM	2.7
19 Su	03:17 AM	0.1	09:12 AM	2.2	03:12 PM	0.1	09:34 PM	2.8
20 M ○	03:58 AM	0.1	09:53 AM	2.3	03:53 PM	0.1	10:13 PM	2.8
21 Tu	04:38 AM	0.0	10:33 AM	2.3	04:34 PM	0.1	10:53 PM	2.8
22 W	05:18 AM	0.0	11:14 AM	2.4	05:16 PM	0.1	11:34 PM	2.8
23 Th	05:59 AM	0.0	11:56 AM	2.4	06:01 PM	0.1		
24 F	12:17 AM	2.8	06:41 AM	0.0	12:41 PM	2.5	06:49 PM	0.1
25 Sa	01:02 AM	2.7	07:26 AM	0.0	01:30 PM	2.5	07:42 PM	0.1
26 Su	01:52 AM	2.6	08:14 AM	-0.1	02:23 PM	2.6	08:41 PM	0.2
27 M ◑	02:47 AM	2.5	09:06 AM	-0.1	03:21 PM	2.7	09:44 PM	0.2
28 Tu	03:46 AM	2.5	10:01 AM	-0.1	04:22 PM	2.8	10:50 PM	0.1
29 W	04:49 AM	2.4	10:59 AM	-0.1	05:25 PM	2.9	11:55 PM	0.1
30 Th	05:53 AM	2.4	11:59 AM	-0.2	06:27 PM	3.0		

JULY

Day	Time (h m)	Height (ft)	Time (h m)	Height (ft)	Time (h m)	Height (ft)	Time (h m)	Height (ft)
1 F	12:58 AM	0.0	06:55 AM	2.4	12:58 PM	-0.2	07:27 PM	3.1
2 Sa	01:56 AM	-0.1	07:54 AM	2.5	01:55 PM	-0.3	08:23 PM	3.2
3 Su	02:52 AM	-0.2	08:50 AM	2.6	02:50 PM	-0.3	09:17 PM	3.2
4 M ●	03:43 AM	-0.2	09:43 AM	2.6	03:43 PM	-0.3	10:08 PM	3.2
5 Tu	04:33 AM	-0.2	10:33 AM	2.6	04:34 PM	-0.2	10:57 PM	3.1
6 W	05:20 AM	-0.2	11:22 AM	2.6	05:24 PM	-0.1	11:44 PM	2.9
7 Th	06:05 AM	-0.1	12:10 PM	2.6	06:13 PM	0.0		
8 F	12:29 AM	2.8	06:49 AM	0.0	12:57 PM	2.6	07:02 PM	0.1
9 Sa	01:14 AM	2.6	07:33 AM	0.1	01:44 PM	2.5	07:52 PM	0.3
10 Su	01:59 AM	2.4	08:16 AM	0.2	02:32 PM	2.4	08:43 PM	0.4
11 M	02:45 AM	2.3	09:01 AM	0.3	03:21 PM	2.4	09:37 PM	0.5
12 Tu ◐	03:34 AM	2.1	09:48 AM	0.3	04:13 PM	2.4	10:33 PM	0.5
13 W	04:27 AM	2.1	10:38 AM	0.4	05:06 PM	2.4	11:29 PM	0.5
14 Th	05:21 AM	2.0	11:29 AM	0.4	05:59 PM	2.5		
15 F	12:23 AM	0.5	06:15 AM	2.1	12:20 PM	0.3	06:50 PM	2.6
16 Sa	01:14 AM	0.4	07:06 AM	2.1	01:09 PM	0.3	07:38 PM	2.7
17 Su	02:02 AM	0.3	07:55 AM	2.2	01:57 PM	0.2	08:23 PM	2.8
18 M	02:47 AM	0.2	08:41 AM	2.3	02:43 PM	0.1	09:06 PM	2.9
19 Tu ○	03:30 AM	0.1	09:25 AM	2.4	03:28 PM	0.1	09:49 PM	2.9
20 W	04:11 AM	0.0	10:08 AM	2.5	04:13 PM	0.0	10:31 PM	3.0
21 Th	04:53 AM	-0.1	10:51 AM	2.6	04:58 PM	0.0	11:14 PM	3.0
22 F	05:34 AM	-0.1	11:36 AM	2.7	05:45 PM	0.0	11:58 PM	2.9
23 Sa	06:17 AM	-0.1	12:23 PM	2.8	06:36 PM	0.0		
24 Su	12:45 AM	2.8	07:03 AM	-0.1	01:12 PM	2.8	07:29 PM	0.1
25 M	01:35 AM	2.7	07:51 AM	-0.1	02:06 PM	2.8	08:28 PM	0.1
26 Tu ◑	02:30 AM	2.6	08:43 AM	-0.1	03:04 PM	2.9	09:30 PM	0.2
27 W	03:29 AM	2.5	09:40 AM	0.0	04:06 PM	2.9	10:36 PM	0.2
28 Th	04:33 AM	2.4	10:40 AM	0.0	05:11 PM	2.9	11:42 PM	0.2
29 F	05:38 AM	2.4	11:42 AM	0.0	06:15 PM	3.0		
30 Sa	12:44 AM	0.1	06:41 AM	2.4	12:43 PM	0.0	07:15 PM	3.1
31 Su	01:42 AM	0.1	07:40 AM	2.5	01:41 PM	-0.1	08:11 PM	3.1

AUGUST

Day	Time (h m)	Height (ft)	Time (h m)	Height (ft)	Time (h m)	Height (ft)	Time (h m)	Height (ft)
1 M	02:35 AM	0.0	08:35 AM	2.6	02:36 PM	-0.1	09:03 PM	3.1
2 Tu ●	03:24 AM	-0.1	09:26 AM	2.7	03:28 PM	-0.1	09:50 PM	3.1
3 W	04:10 AM	-0.1	10:13 AM	2.7	04:16 PM	-0.1	10:35 PM	3.0
4 Th	04:53 AM	-0.1	10:58 AM	2.8	05:02 PM	0.0	11:17 PM	2.9
5 F	05:34 AM	0.0	11:40 AM	2.7	05:47 PM	0.1	11:58 PM	2.8
6 Sa	06:13 AM	0.1	12:22 PM	2.7	06:31 PM	0.2		
7 Su	12:38 AM	2.6	06:52 AM	0.2	01:04 PM	2.6	07:16 PM	0.4
8 M	01:17 AM	2.5	07:32 AM	0.3	01:47 PM	2.6	08:03 PM	0.5
9 Tu	01:59 AM	2.3	08:14 AM	0.4	02:33 PM	2.5	08:53 PM	0.6
10 W ◐	02:45 AM	2.2	08:59 AM	0.5	03:23 PM	2.5	09:47 PM	0.7
11 Th	03:36 AM	2.1	09:49 AM	0.5	04:18 PM	2.5	10:44 PM	0.7
12 F	04:32 AM	2.1	10:43 AM	0.5	05:14 PM	2.5	11:41 PM	0.6
13 Sa	05:30 AM	2.1	11:39 AM	0.5	06:10 PM	2.6		
14 Su	12:36 AM	0.5	06:27 AM	2.2	12:33 PM	0.4	07:02 PM	2.7
15 M	01:26 AM	0.4	07:20 AM	2.3	01:26 PM	0.3	07:51 PM	2.9
16 Tu	02:13 AM	0.3	08:09 AM	2.5	02:16 PM	0.2	08:37 PM	3.0
17 W	02:57 AM	0.1	08:56 AM	2.7	03:04 PM	0.1	09:22 PM	3.1
18 Th ○	03:40 AM	0.0	09:42 AM	2.8	03:52 PM	0.0	10:07 PM	3.1
19 F	04:23 AM	-0.1	10:27 AM	3.0	04:40 PM	0.0	10:52 PM	3.1
20 Sa	05:07 AM	-0.2	11:14 AM	3.1	05:29 PM	0.0	11:38 PM	3.1
21 Su	05:51 AM	-0.2	12:02 PM	3.1	06:21 PM	0.0		
22 M	12:26 AM	3.0	06:38 AM	-0.1	12:53 PM	3.1	07:16 PM	0.1
23 Tu	01:18 AM	2.8	07:28 AM	-0.1	01:48 PM	3.1	08:14 PM	0.2
24 W	02:14 AM	2.7	08:23 AM	0.0	02:48 PM	3.1	09:17 PM	0.3
25 Th ◑	03:15 AM	2.6	09:22 AM	0.1	03:52 PM	3.0	10:23 PM	0.3
26 F	04:20 AM	2.5	10:26 AM	0.2	04:59 PM	3.0	11:29 PM	0.3
27 Sa	05:27 AM	2.5	11:31 AM	0.2	06:04 PM	3.0		
28 Su	12:30 AM	0.3	06:31 AM	2.6	12:33 PM	0.2	07:04 PM	3.0
29 M	01:26 AM	0.2	07:28 AM	2.6	01:31 PM	0.1	07:58 PM	3.1
30 Tu	02:16 AM	0.2	08:20 AM	2.8	02:23 PM	0.1	08:46 PM	3.1
31 W	03:02 AM	0.1	09:07 AM	2.8	03:12 PM	0.1	09:30 PM	3.0

SEPTEMBER

Day	Time (h m)	Height (ft)	Time (h m)	Height (ft)	Time (h m)	Height (ft)	Time (h m)	Height (ft)
1 Th ●	03:43 AM	0.1	09:50 AM	2.9	03:57 PM	0.1	10:10 PM	3.0
2 F	04:22 AM	0.1	10:30 AM	2.9	04:39 PM	0.2	10:49 PM	2.9
3 Sa	04:59 AM	0.2	11:09 AM	2.9	05:20 PM	0.2	11:26 PM	2.8
4 Su	05:36 AM	0.2	11:47 AM	2.9	06:01 PM	0.3		
5 M	12:02 AM	2.7	06:12 AM	0.3	12:25 PM	2.8	06:42 PM	0.5
6 Tu	12:39 AM	2.5	06:49 AM	0.4	01:05 PM	2.7	07:25 PM	0.6
7 W	01:18 AM	2.4	07:29 AM	0.5	01:48 PM	2.7	08:12 PM	0.7
8 Th	02:01 AM	2.3	08:13 AM	0.6	02:36 PM	2.6	09:04 PM	0.8
9 F ◐	02:51 AM	2.2	09:03 AM	0.7	03:30 PM	2.6	10:00 PM	0.8
10 Sa	03:47 AM	2.2	10:00 AM	0.7	04:29 PM	2.6	10:59 PM	0.7
11 Su	04:49 AM	2.2	11:00 AM	0.6	05:28 PM	2.7	11:55 PM	0.6
12 M	05:49 AM	2.4	11:59 AM	0.5	06:24 PM	2.8		
13 Tu	12:48 AM	0.5	06:45 AM	2.5	12:56 PM	0.4	07:17 PM	2.9
14 W	01:36 AM	0.3	07:38 AM	2.7	01:50 PM	0.2	08:07 PM	3.1
15 Th	02:23 AM	0.1	08:27 AM	3.0	02:41 PM	0.1	08:54 PM	3.2
16 F ○	03:08 AM	0.0	09:15 AM	3.2	03:31 PM	0.0	09:42 PM	3.2
17 Sa	03:53 AM	-0.1	10:03 AM	3.3	04:22 PM	-0.1	10:29 PM	3.2
18 Su	04:38 AM	-0.2	10:51 AM	3.4	05:13 PM	-0.1	11:17 PM	3.1
19 M	05:25 AM	-0.2	11:42 AM	3.4	06:05 PM	0.0		
20 Tu	12:08 AM	3.0	06:15 AM	-0.1	12:34 PM	3.4	07:01 PM	0.1
21 W	01:01 AM	2.9	07:07 AM	0.0	01:30 PM	3.3	07:59 PM	0.2
22 Th	01:59 AM	2.7	08:04 AM	0.1	02:31 PM	3.1	09:02 PM	0.3
23 F ◑	03:01 AM	2.6	09:07 AM	0.3	03:37 PM	3.0	10:08 PM	0.4
24 Sa	04:09 AM	2.6	10:13 AM	0.4	04:45 PM	3.0	11:12 PM	0.4
25 Su	05:16 AM	2.6	11:19 AM	0.4	05:50 PM	2.9		
26 M	12:12 AM	0.4	06:18 AM	2.6	12:22 PM	0.4	06:48 PM	2.9
27 Tu	01:05 AM	0.3	07:13 AM	2.7	01:18 PM	0.3	07:39 PM	2.9
28 W	01:52 AM	0.3	08:01 AM	2.9	02:08 PM	0.3	08:25 PM	2.9
29 Th	02:34 AM	0.2	08:45 AM	2.9	02:54 PM	0.2	09:06 PM	2.9
30 F	03:13 AM	0.2	09:25 AM	3.0	03:36 PM	0.2	09:44 PM	2.9

OCTOBER

Day	Time (h m)	Height (ft)	Time (h m)	Height (ft)	Time (h m)	Height (ft)	Time (h m)	Height (ft)
1 Sa ●	03:50 AM	0.2	10:02 AM	3.0	04:15 PM	0.2	10:20 PM	2.8
2 Su	04:25 AM	0.2	10:39 AM	3.0	04:54 PM	0.3	10:54 PM	2.7
3 M	05:00 AM	0.3	11:15 AM	3.0	05:33 PM	0.4	11:29 PM	2.6
4 Tu	05:35 AM	0.4	11:51 AM	2.9	06:12 PM	0.5		
5 W	12:05 AM	2.5	06:12 AM	0.4	12:28 PM	2.8	06:52 PM	0.6
6 Th	12:43 AM	2.4	06:50 AM	0.5	01:09 PM	2.7	07:37 PM	0.6
7 F	01:25 AM	2.3	07:33 AM	0.6	01:55 PM	2.7	08:26 PM	0.7
8 Sa	02:13 AM	2.3	08:23 AM	0.7	02:47 PM	2.6	09:20 PM	0.7
9 Su ◐	03:09 AM	2.3	09:20 AM	0.7	03:45 PM	2.6	10:17 PM	0.7
10 M	04:11 AM	2.3	10:24 AM	0.7	04:47 PM	2.7	11:14 PM	0.6
11 Tu	05:14 AM	2.5	11:28 AM	0.5	05:47 PM	2.7		
12 W	12:08 AM	0.4	06:13 AM	2.7	12:28 PM	0.4	06:43 PM	2.9
13 Th	01:00 AM	0.2	07:08 AM	2.9	01:25 PM	0.2	07:36 PM	3.0
14 F	01:49 AM	0.0	08:00 AM	3.1	02:19 PM	0.0	08:27 PM	3.1
15 Sa	02:36 AM	-0.1	08:50 AM	3.4	03:12 PM	-0.1	09:17 PM	3.1
16 Su ○	03:24 AM	-0.3	09:40 AM	3.5	04:04 PM	-0.2	10:07 PM	3.1
17 M	04:12 AM	-0.3	10:31 AM	3.6	04:56 PM	-0.2	10:57 PM	3.0
18 Tu	05:02 AM	-0.3	11:22 AM	3.5	05:49 PM	-0.1	11:49 PM	2.9
19 W	05:53 AM	-0.2	12:16 PM	3.4	06:44 PM	0.0		
20 Th	12:44 AM	2.8	06:48 AM	0.0	01:13 PM	3.3	07:42 PM	0.1
21 F	01:42 AM	2.7	07:46 AM	0.1	02:13 PM	3.1	08:43 PM	0.2
22 Sa ◑	02:45 AM	2.6	08:50 AM	0.3	03:18 PM	2.9	09:46 PM	0.3
23 Su	03:52 AM	2.5	09:56 AM	0.4	04:24 PM	2.8	10:47 PM	0.4
24 M	04:57 AM	2.5	11:03 AM	0.4	05:27 PM	2.7	11:45 PM	0.3
25 Tu	05:58 AM	2.6	12:04 PM	0.4	06:23 PM	2.7		
26 W	12:36 AM	0.3	06:51 AM	2.7	12:59 PM	0.3	07:13 PM	2.7
27 Th	01:21 AM	0.2	07:38 AM	2.8	01:48 PM	0.3	07:58 PM	2.7
28 F	02:03 AM	0.2	08:20 AM	2.9	02:32 PM	0.2	08:38 PM	2.6
29 Sa	02:41 AM	0.2	08:59 AM	2.9	03:13 PM	0.2	09:15 PM	2.6
30 Su ●	03:18 AM	0.1	09:36 AM	3.0	03:52 PM	0.2	09:51 PM	2.6
31 M	03:54 AM	0.2	10:11 AM	3.0	04:30 PM	0.2	10:26 PM	2.5

LUNAR DATA
- ● -New Moon
- ◐ -First Quarter
- ○ -Full Moon
- ◑ -Last Quarter

Time meridian 75° W. 0000 is midnight. 1200 is noon. Heights are referred to mean lower low water which is the chart datum of soundings. For tidal differences see page 29.

All times given are Eastern Standard Time; add one hour for Daylight Savings Time. To find actual depths of water at a given time, add the height of the tide to the charted depth. If the height of the tide is negative (has a minus sign before the tabular height), it should be subtracted from the charted depth.

Washington, DC, 2016

Times and Heights of High and Low Waters

MAY

Day	Time (h m)	Height (ft)
1 Su	03:26 AM 10:19 AM 03:43 PM 10:56 PM	3.0 0.5 3.1 0.4
2 M	04:27 AM 11:32 AM 04:50 PM 11:57 PM	3.2 0.4 3.1 0.3
3 Tu	05:25 AM 12:40 PM 05:53 PM	3.3 0.3 3.2
4 W	12:55 AM 06:21 AM 01:42 PM 06:52 PM	0.2 3.5 0.2 3.2
5 Th	01:51 AM 07:14 AM 02:40 PM 07:47 PM	0.2 3.7 0.0 3.3
6 F ●	02:44 AM 08:06 AM 03:35 PM 08:41 PM	0.1 3.8 -0.1 3.3
7 Sa	03:37 AM 08:56 AM 04:28 PM 09:34 PM	0.1 3.8 -0.1 3.3
8 Su	04:29 AM 09:47 AM 05:21 PM 10:27 PM	0.1 3.8 -0.1 3.2
9 M	05:22 AM 10:38 AM 06:12 PM 11:20 PM	0.1 3.7 -0.1 3.2
10 Tu	06:15 AM 11:31 AM 07:04 PM	0.2 3.6 0.0
11 W	12:16 AM 07:09 AM 12:27 PM 07:56 PM	3.1 0.3 3.4 0.1
12 Th	01:13 AM 08:05 AM 01:26 PM 08:48 PM	3.1 0.4 3.2 0.2
13 F ◐	02:12 AM 09:02 AM 02:28 PM 09:40 PM	3.0 0.4 3.1 0.3
14 Sa	03:10 AM 10:01 AM 03:30 PM 10:32 PM	3.0 0.5 3.0 0.4
15 Su	04:08 AM 10:59 AM 04:29 PM 11:23 PM	3.1 0.5 2.9 0.4
16 M	05:02 AM 11:55 AM 05:25 PM	3.1 0.5 2.9
17 Tu	12:12 AM 05:52 AM 12:49 PM 06:16 PM	0.4 3.2 0.4 2.9
18 W	12:58 AM 06:39 AM 01:39 PM 07:04 PM	0.4 3.2 0.4 2.9
19 Th	01:42 AM 07:22 AM 02:26 PM 07:49 PM	0.4 3.3 0.3 2.9
20 F	02:23 AM 08:01 AM 03:11 PM 08:31 PM	0.4 3.3 0.3 2.9
21 Sa ○	03:02 AM 08:38 AM 03:53 PM 09:11 PM	0.4 3.3 0.3 2.9
22 Su	03:40 AM 09:11 AM 04:33 PM 09:48 PM	0.4 3.3 0.3 2.9
23 M	04:17 AM 09:42 AM 05:12 PM 10:23 PM	0.5 3.3 0.3 2.9
24 Tu	04:54 AM 10:14 AM 05:49 PM 10:58 PM	0.5 3.3 0.3 2.9
25 W	05:34 AM 10:51 AM 06:27 PM 11:35 PM	0.5 3.3 0.3 2.9
26 Th	06:17 AM 11:34 AM 07:07 PM	0.5 3.3 0.3
27 F	12:18 AM 07:05 AM 12:22 PM 07:50 PM	3.0 0.5 3.3 0.3
28 Sa	01:06 AM 07:59 AM 01:16 PM 08:37 PM	3.0 0.5 3.2 0.3
29 Su ◑	02:01 AM 09:00 AM 02:16 PM 09:29 PM	3.1 0.5 3.1 0.3
30 M	03:00 AM 10:07 AM 03:21 PM 10:26 PM	3.2 0.5 3.1 0.3
31 Tu	04:00 AM 11:17 AM 04:28 PM 11:25 PM	3.3 0.4 3.1 0.2

JUNE

Day	Time (h m)	Height (ft)
1 W	05:00 AM 12:23 PM 05:31 PM	3.4 0.3 3.1
2 Th	12:25 AM 05:57 AM 01:24 PM 06:31 PM	0.2 3.6 0.1 3.1
3 F	01:24 AM 06:52 AM 02:22 PM 07:28 PM	0.1 3.7 0.0 3.1
4 Sa	02:21 AM 07:45 AM 03:17 PM 08:23 PM	0.1 3.7 -0.1 3.2
5 Su ●	03:16 AM 08:37 AM 04:10 PM 09:16 PM	0.1 3.8 -0.1 3.2
6 M	04:10 AM 09:28 AM 05:01 PM 10:08 PM	0.1 3.7 -0.1 3.2
7 Tu	05:02 AM 10:19 AM 05:51 PM 11:00 PM	0.1 3.6 -0.1 3.1
8 W	05:55 AM 11:11 AM 06:40 PM 11:53 PM	0.2 3.5 0.0 3.1
9 Th	06:47 AM 12:04 PM 07:28 PM	0.3 3.3 0.1
10 F	12:46 AM 07:40 AM 01:00 PM 08:15 PM	3.1 0.4 3.1 0.2
11 Sa	01:41 AM 08:34 AM 01:57 PM 09:03 PM	3.0 0.4 3.0 0.3
12 Su ◐	02:37 AM 09:29 AM 02:56 PM 09:50 PM	3.0 0.5 2.9 0.4
13 M	03:32 AM 10:25 AM 03:53 PM 10:37 PM	3.0 0.5 2.8 0.4
14 Tu	04:25 AM 11:21 AM 04:49 PM 11:24 PM	3.1 0.5 2.8 0.4
15 W	05:16 AM 12:15 PM 05:42 PM	3.1 0.5 2.7
16 Th	12:11 AM 06:03 AM 01:07 PM 06:31 PM	0.4 3.1 0.4 2.7
17 F	12:58 AM 06:47 AM 01:55 PM 07:18 PM	0.4 3.2 0.4 2.8
18 Sa	01:43 AM 07:28 AM 02:41 PM 08:02 PM	0.4 3.2 0.3 2.8
19 Su	02:28 AM 08:06 AM 03:25 PM 08:42 PM	0.4 3.2 0.3 2.8
20 M ○	03:11 AM 08:41 AM 04:07 PM 09:20 PM	0.4 3.3 0.2 2.8
21 Tu	03:54 AM 09:16 AM 04:47 PM 09:57 PM	0.4 3.3 0.2 2.9
22 W	04:37 AM 09:52 AM 05:27 PM 10:33 PM	0.4 3.3 0.2 2.9
23 Th	05:21 AM 10:32 AM 06:07 PM 11:12 PM	0.4 3.3 0.2 3.0
24 F	06:07 AM 11:16 AM 06:47 PM 11:56 PM	0.4 3.3 0.2 3.0
25 Sa	06:56 AM 12:05 PM 07:30 PM	0.4 3.3 0.2
26 Su	12:44 AM 07:51 AM 12:59 PM 08:16 PM	3.1 0.4 3.2 0.2
27 M ◑	01:38 AM 08:51 AM 01:58 PM 09:06 PM	3.2 0.4 3.1 0.2
28 Tu	02:36 AM 09:57 AM 03:03 PM 10:02 PM	3.3 0.4 3.0 0.2
29 W	03:37 AM 11:03 AM 04:09 PM 11:01 PM	3.4 0.3 3.0 0.2
30 Th	04:38 AM 12:07 PM 05:14 PM	3.4 0.2 3.0

JULY

Day	Time (h m)	Height (ft)
1 F	12:03 AM 05:37 AM 01:08 PM 06:14 PM	0.2 3.5 0.1 3.0
2 Sa	01:05 AM 06:34 AM 02:05 PM 07:12 PM	0.1 3.6 0.0 3.0
3 Su	02:03 AM 07:29 AM 02:59 PM 08:06 PM	0.1 3.6 -0.1 3.1
4 M ●	02:59 AM 08:21 AM 03:51 PM 08:58 PM	0.1 3.6 -0.1 3.1
5 Tu	03:53 AM 09:12 AM 04:40 PM 09:48 PM	0.1 3.6 -0.1 3.1
6 W	04:44 AM 10:02 AM 05:26 PM 10:37 PM	0.1 3.5 -0.1 3.1
7 Th	05:34 AM 10:51 AM 06:12 PM 11:26 PM	0.2 3.4 0.0 3.1
8 F	06:23 AM 11:40 AM 06:55 PM	0.3 3.2 0.1
9 Sa	12:15 AM 07:12 AM 12:30 PM 07:37 PM	3.1 0.4 3.1 0.2
10 Su	01:05 AM 08:01 AM 01:22 PM 08:18 PM	3.0 0.5 2.9 0.3
11 M	01:55 AM 08:53 AM 02:16 PM 08:59 PM	3.0 0.5 2.8 0.4
12 Tu ◐	02:47 AM 09:46 AM 03:12 PM 09:42 PM	3.0 0.6 2.7 0.4
13 W	03:40 AM 10:41 AM 04:08 PM 10:28 PM	3.0 0.6 2.6 0.5
14 Th	04:32 AM 11:36 AM 05:03 PM 11:19 PM	3.0 0.6 2.6 0.5
15 F	05:22 AM 12:30 PM 05:55 PM	3.0 0.5 2.6
16 Sa	12:12 AM 06:09 AM 01:21 PM 06:44 PM	0.5 3.1 0.5 2.7
17 Su	01:05 AM 06:53 AM 02:09 PM 07:29 PM	0.4 3.1 0.4 2.7
18 M	01:56 AM 07:34 AM 02:55 PM 08:11 PM	0.4 3.2 0.3 2.8
19 Tu ○	02:45 AM 08:14 AM 03:38 PM 08:51 PM	0.4 3.3 0.2 2.9
20 W	03:33 AM 08:53 AM 04:21 PM 09:29 PM	0.3 3.3 0.1 3.0
21 Th	04:20 AM 09:33 AM 05:02 PM 10:08 PM	0.3 3.3 0.1 3.0
22 F	05:07 AM 10:16 AM 05:42 PM 10:49 PM	0.3 3.4 0.1 3.1
23 Sa	05:55 AM 11:01 AM 06:24 PM 11:33 PM	0.3 3.3 0.1 3.2
24 Su	06:46 AM 11:50 AM 07:07 PM	0.3 3.3 0.1
25 M	12:22 AM 07:42 AM 12:43 PM 07:54 PM	3.3 0.3 3.2 0.1
26 Tu ◑	01:15 AM 08:41 AM 01:43 PM 08:45 PM	3.3 0.3 3.1 0.1
27 W	02:14 AM 09:44 AM 02:47 PM 09:43 PM	3.4 0.3 3.0 0.2
28 Th	03:16 AM 10:49 AM 03:54 PM 10:45 PM	3.4 0.3 2.9 0.2
29 F	04:20 AM 11:51 AM 04:59 PM 11:49 PM	3.4 0.2 2.9 0.2
30 Sa	05:22 AM 12:51 PM 06:00 PM	3.4 0.1 3.0
31 Su	12:51 AM 06:21 AM 01:47 PM 06:57 PM	0.2 3.5 0.1 3.0

AUGUST

Day	Time (h m)	Height (ft)
1 M	01:49 AM 07:16 AM 02:40 PM 07:50 PM	0.1 3.5 0.0 3.1
2 Tu ●	02:44 AM 08:08 AM 03:29 PM 08:40 PM	0.1 3.5 0.0 3.2
3 W	03:36 AM 08:57 AM 04:15 PM 09:28 PM	0.1 3.5 0.0 3.2
4 Th	04:25 AM 09:44 AM 04:59 PM 10:13 PM	0.1 3.4 0.0 3.2
5 F	05:12 AM 10:29 AM 05:40 PM 10:57 PM	0.2 3.3 0.1 3.2
6 Sa	05:57 AM 11:14 AM 06:18 PM 11:41 PM	0.3 3.2 0.2 3.1
7 Su	06:41 AM 11:58 AM 06:53 PM	0.4 3.1 0.3
8 M	12:24 AM 07:26 AM 12:44 PM 07:26 PM	3.1 0.5 2.9 0.4
9 Tu	01:08 AM 08:12 AM 01:32 PM 08:00 PM	3.1 0.6 2.8 0.4
10 W ◐	01:54 AM 09:01 AM 02:25 PM 08:40 PM	3.0 0.7 2.7 0.5
11 Th	02:44 AM 09:55 AM 03:21 PM 09:29 PM	3.0 0.7 2.6 0.5
12 F	03:37 AM 10:52 AM 04:19 PM 10:25 PM	3.0 0.7 2.6 0.6
13 Sa	04:32 AM 11:49 AM 05:15 PM 11:27 PM	3.0 0.7 2.6 0.6
14 Su	05:26 AM 12:43 PM 06:06 PM	3.0 0.6 2.7
15 M	12:29 AM 06:16 AM 01:34 PM 06:54 PM	0.5 3.1 0.4 2.8
16 Tu	01:27 AM 07:03 AM 02:22 PM 07:38 PM	0.4 3.2 0.3 2.9
17 W	02:21 AM 07:47 AM 03:07 PM 08:20 PM	0.4 3.3 0.2 3.0
18 Th ○	03:12 AM 08:31 AM 03:50 PM 09:01 PM	0.3 3.4 0.1 3.2
19 F	04:02 AM 09:14 AM 04:33 PM 09:42 PM	0.2 3.4 0.1 3.3
20 Sa	04:51 AM 09:59 AM 05:15 PM 10:25 PM	0.2 3.4 0.0 3.4
21 Su	05:41 AM 10:45 AM 05:58 PM 11:11 PM	0.2 3.4 0.0 3.5
22 M	06:34 AM 11:35 AM 06:44 PM	0.2 3.3 0.1
23 Tu	12:00 AM 07:29 AM 12:29 PM 07:33 PM	3.5 0.3 3.2 0.1
24 W	12:54 AM 08:28 AM 01:28 PM 08:28 PM	3.5 0.3 3.1 0.2
25 Th ◑	01:53 AM 09:30 AM 02:34 PM 09:28 PM	3.4 0.3 3.0 0.3
26 F	02:58 AM 10:32 AM 03:41 PM 10:32 PM	3.4 0.3 2.9 0.3
27 Sa	04:05 AM 11:34 AM 04:46 PM 11:37 PM	3.3 0.3 2.9 0.3
28 Su	05:09 AM 12:32 PM 05:47 PM	3.3 0.2 3.0
29 M	12:38 AM 06:09 AM 01:27 PM 06:42 PM	0.2 3.4 0.1 3.1
30 Tu	01:35 AM 07:03 AM 02:18 PM 07:34 PM	0.2 3.4 0.1 3.2
31 W	02:29 AM 07:54 AM 03:05 PM 08:21 PM	0.1 3.4 0.1 3.2

SEPTEMBER

Day	Time (h m)	Height (ft)
1 Th ●	03:18 AM 08:41 AM 03:48 PM 09:06 PM	0.1 3.4 0.1 3.3
2 F	04:05 AM 09:25 AM 04:29 PM 09:48 PM	0.2 3.4 0.1 3.3
3 Sa	04:49 AM 10:07 AM 05:06 PM 10:28 PM	0.2 3.3 0.2 3.3
4 Su	05:31 AM 10:47 AM 05:39 PM 11:05 PM	0.3 3.2 0.3 3.2
5 M	06:11 AM 11:27 AM 06:08 PM 11:42 PM	0.4 3.1 0.4 3.2
6 Tu	06:50 AM 12:07 PM 06:36 PM	0.5 2.9 0.4
7 W	12:18 AM 07:30 AM 12:49 PM 07:09 PM	3.1 0.6 2.8 0.5
8 Th	12:57 AM 08:14 AM 01:35 PM 07:52 PM	3.1 0.7 2.7 0.5
9 F ◐	01:42 AM 09:05 AM 02:29 PM 08:42 PM	3.0 0.8 2.7 0.6
10 Sa	02:35 AM 10:03 AM 03:29 PM 09:41 PM	3.0 0.8 2.6 0.6
11 Su	03:36 AM 11:03 AM 04:29 PM 10:48 PM	3.0 0.7 2.7 0.6
12 M	04:38 AM 12:01 PM 05:25 PM 11:56 PM	3.0 0.6 2.8 0.5
13 Tu	05:37 AM 12:55 PM 06:16 PM	3.1 0.5 2.9
14 W	12:59 AM 06:30 AM 01:45 PM 07:03 PM	0.4 3.2 0.3 3.1
15 Th	01:57 AM 07:20 AM 02:33 PM 07:48 PM	0.3 3.3 0.2 3.2
16 F ○	02:51 AM 08:07 AM 03:18 PM 08:32 PM	0.2 3.4 0.1 3.4
17 Sa	03:43 AM 08:54 AM 04:03 PM 09:16 PM	0.1 3.4 0.0 3.5
18 Su	04:34 AM 09:41 AM 04:47 PM 10:02 PM	0.1 3.4 0.0 3.6
19 M	05:26 AM 10:29 AM 05:33 PM 10:49 PM	0.1 3.4 0.0 3.7
20 Tu	06:19 AM 11:20 AM 06:22 PM 11:39 PM	0.1 3.3 0.1 3.6
21 W	07:14 AM 12:14 PM 07:14 PM	0.2 3.2 0.1
22 Th	12:34 AM 08:12 AM 01:14 PM 08:12 PM	3.5 0.2 3.0 0.2
23 F ◑	01:34 AM 09:12 AM 02:19 PM 09:14 PM	3.4 0.3 2.9 0.3
24 Sa	02:41 AM 10:12 AM 03:26 PM 10:18 PM	3.3 0.3 2.9 0.3
25 Su	03:50 AM 11:12 AM 04:31 PM 11:22 PM	3.2 0.3 2.9 0.3
26 M	04:55 AM 12:09 PM 05:30 PM	3.2 0.2 3.0
27 Tu	12:22 AM 05:54 AM 01:02 PM 06:25 PM	0.2 3.2 0.2 3.1
28 W	01:18 AM 06:47 AM 01:51 PM 07:14 PM	0.2 3.3 0.1 3.2
29 Th	02:10 AM 07:36 AM 02:36 PM 08:00 PM	0.1 3.3 0.1 3.3
30 F	02:58 AM 08:21 AM 03:18 PM 08:42 PM	0.1 3.3 0.1 3.3

OCTOBER

Day	Time (h m)	Height (ft)
1 Sa ●	03:43 AM 09:03 AM 03:56 PM 09:21 PM	0.1 3.2 0.2 3.3
2 Su	04:26 AM 09:43 AM 04:31 PM 09:58 PM	0.2 3.1 0.2 3.3
3 M	05:05 AM 10:21 AM 05:01 PM 10:32 PM	0.3 3.1 0.3 3.3
4 Tu	05:43 AM 10:58 AM 05:28 PM 11:03 PM	0.4 3.0 0.3 3.2
5 W	06:19 AM 11:34 AM 05:57 PM 11:35 PM	0.5 2.9 0.4 3.2
6 Th	06:55 AM 12:11 PM 06:33 PM	0.6 2.8 0.4
7 F	12:12 AM 07:34 AM 12:52 PM 07:17 PM	3.1 0.6 2.7 0.5
8 Sa	12:55 AM 08:20 AM 01:40 PM 08:09 PM	3.1 0.6 2.7 0.5
9 Su ◐	01:47 AM 09:16 AM 02:38 PM 09:08 PM	3.0 0.6 2.7 0.6
10 M	02:47 AM 10:17 AM 03:40 PM 10:15 PM	3.0 0.6 2.7 0.5
11 Tu	03:54 AM 11:17 AM 04:41 PM 11:26 PM	3.0 0.5 2.8 0.5
12 W	04:59 AM 12:14 PM 05:37 PM	3.0 0.4 3.0
13 Th	12:33 AM 05:58 AM 01:07 PM 06:28 PM	0.4 3.1 0.2 3.1
14 F	01:34 AM 06:52 AM 01:57 PM 07:17 PM	0.2 3.2 0.1 3.3
15 Sa	02:30 AM 07:43 AM 02:45 PM 08:05 PM	0.1 3.3 0.0 3.5
16 Su ○	03:24 AM 08:32 AM 03:33 PM 08:52 PM	0.0 3.3 -0.1 3.6
17 M	04:17 AM 09:22 AM 04:21 PM 09:39 PM	-0.1 3.3 -0.1 3.7
18 Tu	05:09 AM 10:12 AM 05:11 PM 10:28 PM	-0.1 3.3 -0.1 3.6
19 W	06:02 AM 11:04 AM 06:02 PM 11:20 PM	-0.1 3.2 0.0 3.5
20 Th	06:57 AM 11:59 AM 06:57 PM	0.0 3.0 0.0
21 F	12:16 AM 07:53 AM 12:58 PM 07:56 PM	3.4 0.1 2.9 0.1
22 Sa ◑	01:17 AM 08:50 AM 02:02 PM 08:57 PM	3.2 0.1 2.9 0.2
23 Su	02:23 AM 09:48 AM 03:07 PM 10:00 PM	3.1 0.2 2.8 0.2
24 M	03:31 AM 10:45 AM 04:10 PM 11:02 PM	3.0 0.2 2.9 0.2
25 Tu	04:35 AM 11:40 AM 05:08 PM	3.0 0.1 2.9
26 W	12:01 AM 05:33 AM 12:32 PM 06:02 PM	0.2 3.0 0.1 3.0
27 Th	12:56 AM 06:25 AM 01:20 PM 06:51 PM	0.1 3.0 0.1 3.1
28 F	01:47 AM 07:13 AM 02:04 PM 07:35 PM	0.1 3.0 0.1 3.1
29 Sa	02:35 AM 07:58 AM 02:45 PM 08:16 PM	0.1 3.0 0.1 3.2
30 Su ●	03:20 AM 08:40 AM 03:23 PM 08:54 PM	0.1 2.9 0.1 3.2
31 M	04:02 AM 09:19 AM 03:58 PM 09:29 PM	0.1 2.9 0.1 3.1

LUNAR DATA

- ● -New Moon
- ◐ -First Quarter
- ○ -Full Moon
- ◑ -Last Quarter

Time meridian 75° W. 0000 is midnight. 1200 is noon. Heights are referred to mean lower low water which is the chart datum of soundings. For tidal differences see page 29.

All times given are Eastern Standard Time; add one hour for Daylight Savings Time. To find actual depths of water at a given time, add the height of the tide to the charted depth. If the height of the tide is negative (has a minus sign before the tabular height), it should be subtracted from the charted depth.

Baltimore, MD, 2016

Times and Heights of High and Low Waters

MAY

Day	Time (h m)	Height (ft)
1 Su	02:12 AM 08:30 AM 02:25 PM 09:20 PM	1.3 0.4 1.5 0.4
2 M	03:09 AM 09:43 AM 03:26 PM 10:07 PM	1.5 0.4 1.5 0.3
3 Tu	04:05 AM 10:53 AM 04:25 PM 10:53 PM	1.6 0.3 1.4 0.3
4 W	05:01 AM 11:57 AM 05:22 PM 11:38 PM	1.8 0.3 1.4 0.2
5 Th	05:54 AM 12:58 PM 06:16 PM	1.9 0.2 1.4
6 F ●	12:24 AM 06:47 AM 01:56 PM 07:09 PM	0.2 2.0 0.2 1.3
7 Sa	01:10 AM 07:39 AM 02:52 PM 08:02 PM	0.1 2.1 0.2 1.3
8 Su	01:58 AM 08:30 AM 03:47 PM 08:56 PM	0.1 2.1 0.2 1.3
9 M	02:49 AM 09:22 AM 04:42 PM 09:50 PM	0.2 2.0 0.2 1.3
10 Tu	03:43 AM 10:14 AM 05:35 PM 10:46 PM	0.2 1.9 0.3 1.3
11 W	04:42 AM 11:09 AM 06:29 PM 11:44 PM	0.3 1.8 0.3 1.3
12 Th	05:47 AM 12:05 PM 07:21 PM	0.4 1.7 0.4
13 F ◐	12:44 AM 06:58 AM 01:04 PM 08:12 PM	1.3 0.5 1.5 0.4
14 Sa	01:44 AM 08:11 AM 02:02 PM 08:59 PM	1.4 0.5 1.4 0.4
15 Su	02:44 AM 09:22 AM 02:59 PM 09:42 PM	1.5 0.5 1.4 0.4
16 M	03:41 AM 10:26 AM 03:52 PM 10:21 PM	1.5 0.5 1.3 0.4
17 Tu	04:33 AM 11:23 AM 04:41 PM 10:56 PM	1.6 0.5 1.3 0.4
18 W	05:20 AM 12:15 PM 05:26 PM 11:29 PM	1.7 0.5 1.2 0.4
19 Th	06:02 AM 01:02 PM 06:08 PM	1.7 0.5 1.2
20 F	12:01 AM 06:41 AM 01:46 PM 06:50 PM	0.4 1.8 0.5 1.2
21 Sa ○	12:35 AM 07:16 AM 02:27 PM 07:31 PM	0.4 1.8 0.5 1.2
22 Su	01:09 AM 07:50 AM 03:06 PM 08:12 PM	0.4 1.8 0.4 1.2
23 M	01:45 AM 08:23 AM 03:45 PM 08:54 PM	0.4 1.8 0.4 1.2
24 Tu	02:24 AM 08:59 AM 04:23 PM 09:37 PM	0.4 1.8 0.4 1.2
25 W	03:06 AM 09:38 AM 05:02 PM 10:22 PM	0.5 1.8 0.4 1.2
26 Th	03:53 AM 10:20 AM 05:43 PM 11:09 PM	0.5 1.8 0.4 1.3
27 F	04:47 AM 11:08 AM 06:25 PM	0.5 1.7 0.4
28 Sa	12:00 AM 05:50 AM 12:00 PM 07:09 PM	1.3 0.6 1.7 0.4
29 Su ◑	12:55 AM 07:02 AM 12:55 PM 07:54 PM	1.4 0.6 1.6 0.4
30 M	01:52 AM 08:19 AM 01:53 PM 08:40 PM	1.5 0.6 1.5 0.3
31 Tu	02:50 AM 09:36 AM 02:53 PM 09:26 PM	1.7 0.6 1.4 0.3

JUNE

Day	Time (h m)	Height (ft)
1 W	03:47 AM 10:48 AM 03:53 PM 10:14 PM	1.8 0.5 1.4 0.2
2 Th	04:44 AM 11:53 AM 04:52 PM 11:02 PM	2.0 0.4 1.3 0.2
3 F	05:38 AM 12:54 PM 05:50 PM 11:51 PM	2.1 0.4 1.3 0.2
4 Sa	06:31 AM 01:51 PM 06:46 PM	2.1 0.3 1.3
5 Su ●	12:41 AM 07:23 AM 02:44 PM 07:41 PM	0.2 2.2 0.3 1.3
6 M	01:33 AM 08:14 AM 03:35 PM 08:36 PM	0.2 2.1 0.3 1.3
7 Tu	02:27 AM 09:04 AM 04:24 PM 09:31 PM	0.3 2.1 0.3 1.3
8 W	03:22 AM 09:54 AM 05:11 PM 10:25 PM	0.3 1.9 0.4 1.4
9 Th	04:21 AM 10:43 AM 05:58 PM 11:21 PM	0.4 1.8 0.4 1.4
10 F	05:24 AM 11:34 AM 06:42 PM	0.5 1.7 0.4
11 Sa	12:18 AM 06:31 AM 12:24 PM 07:25 PM	1.4 0.6 1.6 0.4
12 Su ◐	01:16 AM 07:41 AM 01:15 PM 08:05 PM	1.5 0.7 1.5 0.4
13 M	02:14 AM 08:52 AM 02:06 PM 08:44 PM	1.5 0.7 1.4 0.4
14 Tu	03:10 AM 09:59 AM 02:57 PM 09:22 PM	1.6 0.7 1.3 0.4
15 W	04:03 AM 11:00 AM 03:47 PM 09:59 PM	1.7 0.7 1.2 0.4
16 Th	04:51 AM 11:54 AM 04:37 PM 10:37 PM	1.8 0.6 1.2 0.4
17 F	05:33 AM 12:43 PM 05:26 PM 11:16 PM	1.8 0.6 1.2 0.4
18 Sa	06:12 AM 01:27 PM 06:14 PM 11:56 PM	1.9 0.6 1.1 0.4
19 Su	06:48 AM 02:07 PM 07:00 PM	1.9 0.5 1.2
20 M ○	12:36 AM 07:23 AM 02:46 PM 07:45 PM	0.4 1.9 0.5 1.2
21 Tu	01:19 AM 07:59 AM 03:23 PM 08:29 PM	0.4 1.9 0.4 1.2
22 W	02:02 AM 08:37 AM 04:00 PM 09:13 PM	0.4 1.9 0.4 1.3
23 Th	02:49 AM 09:17 AM 04:37 PM 09:59 PM	0.5 1.9 0.4 1.3
24 F	03:40 AM 10:01 AM 05:15 PM 10:48 PM	0.5 1.9 0.4 1.4
25 Sa	04:37 AM 10:48 AM 05:54 PM 11:39 PM	0.6 1.8 0.3 1.5
26 Su	05:43 AM 11:37 AM 06:35 PM	0.6 1.7 0.3
27 M ◑	12:35 AM 06:56 AM 12:31 PM 07:18 PM	1.6 0.6 1.6 0.3
28 Tu	01:33 AM 08:15 AM 01:27 PM 08:04 PM	1.7 0.7 1.5 0.3
29 W	02:32 AM 09:32 AM 02:26 PM 08:53 PM	1.8 0.6 1.4 0.2
30 Th	03:31 AM 10:44 AM 03:27 PM 09:44 PM	1.9 0.6 1.3 0.2

JULY

Day	Time (h m)	Height (ft)
1 F	04:29 AM 11:49 AM 04:29 PM 10:36 PM	2.0 0.5 1.3 0.2
2 Sa	05:25 AM 12:47 PM 05:29 PM 11:30 PM	2.1 0.5 1.2 0.2
3 Su	06:18 AM 01:40 PM 06:28 PM	2.1 0.4 1.3
4 M ●	12:25 AM 07:10 AM 02:29 PM 07:23 PM	0.2 2.1 0.4 1.3
5 Tu	01:19 AM 07:59 AM 03:15 PM 08:17 PM	0.3 2.1 0.4 1.3
6 W	02:13 AM 08:46 AM 03:58 PM 09:09 PM	0.3 2.0 0.4 1.4
7 Th	03:07 AM 09:31 AM 04:39 PM 10:01 PM	0.4 1.9 0.4 1.4
8 F	04:01 AM 10:16 AM 05:18 PM 10:53 PM	0.5 1.8 0.4 1.5
9 Sa	04:58 AM 10:59 AM 05:54 PM 11:46 PM	0.6 1.7 0.4 1.5
10 Su	05:59 AM 11:42 AM 06:30 PM	0.7 1.6 0.4
11 M	12:40 AM 07:05 AM 12:27 PM 07:05 PM	1.5 0.8 1.4 0.4
12 Tu ◐	01:35 AM 08:15 AM 01:13 PM 07:43 PM	1.6 0.8 1.3 0.4
13 W	02:30 AM 09:25 AM 02:03 PM 08:23 PM	1.7 0.8 1.3 0.4
14 Th	03:23 AM 10:29 AM 02:57 PM 09:06 PM	1.7 0.8 1.2 0.4
15 F	04:12 AM 11:25 AM 03:53 PM 09:51 PM	1.8 0.7 1.2 0.4
16 Sa	04:57 AM 12:14 PM 04:48 PM 10:38 PM	1.8 0.7 1.1 0.4
17 Su	05:38 AM 12:58 PM 05:40 PM 11:25 PM	1.9 0.6 1.2 0.4
18 M	06:17 AM 01:37 PM 06:30 PM	1.9 0.5 1.2
19 Tu ○	12:13 AM 06:56 AM 02:15 PM 07:17 PM	0.4 1.9 0.5 1.2
20 W	01:00 AM 07:35 AM 02:51 PM 08:02 PM	0.4 1.9 0.4 1.3
21 Th	01:49 AM 08:15 AM 03:27 PM 08:48 PM	0.4 1.9 0.4 1.4
22 F	02:40 AM 08:58 AM 04:03 PM 09:35 PM	0.5 1.9 0.4 1.5
23 Sa	03:35 AM 09:42 AM 04:40 PM 10:25 PM	0.5 1.9 0.3 1.6
24 Su	04:34 AM 10:28 AM 05:19 PM 11:18 PM	0.6 1.8 0.3 1.7
25 M	05:41 AM 11:17 AM 06:00 PM	0.6 1.7 0.3
26 Tu ◑	12:14 AM 06:55 AM 12:09 PM 06:45 PM	1.8 0.7 1.5 0.3
27 W	01:13 AM 08:13 AM 01:06 PM 07:34 PM	1.9 0.7 1.4 0.2
28 Th	02:14 AM 09:29 AM 02:07 PM 08:27 PM	1.9 0.7 1.3 0.2
29 F	03:16 AM 10:37 AM 03:10 PM 09:24 PM	2.0 0.6 1.3 0.2
30 Sa	04:16 AM 11:38 AM 04:14 PM 10:23 PM	2.0 0.6 1.3 0.3
31 Su	05:14 AM 12:33 PM 05:16 PM 11:22 PM	2.1 0.5 1.3 0.3

AUGUST

Day	Time (h m)	Height (ft)
1 M	06:07 AM 01:21 PM 06:13 PM	2.1 0.5 1.3
2 Tu ●	12:18 AM 06:56 AM 02:06 PM 07:07 PM	0.3 2.0 0.5 1.4
3 W	01:12 AM 07:42 AM 02:47 PM 07:58 PM	0.3 2.0 0.4 1.4
4 Th	02:04 AM 08:25 AM 03:24 PM 08:46 PM	0.4 1.9 0.5 1.5
5 F	02:53 AM 09:06 AM 03:58 PM 09:34 PM	0.5 1.8 0.5 1.5
6 Sa	03:43 AM 09:44 AM 04:30 PM 10:21 PM	0.6 1.7 0.5 1.6
7 Su	04:34 AM 10:23 AM 05:00 PM 11:09 PM	0.7 1.6 0.4 1.6
8 M	05:28 AM 11:02 AM 05:31 PM 11:59 PM	0.7 1.5 0.4 1.6
9 Tu	06:29 AM 11:43 AM 06:06 PM	0.8 1.4 0.4
10 W ◐	12:49 AM 07:36 AM 12:28 PM 06:45 PM	1.7 0.9 1.4 0.4
11 Th	01:41 AM 08:45 AM 01:18 PM 07:29 PM	1.7 0.9 1.3 0.4
12 F	02:33 AM 09:50 AM 02:15 PM 08:19 PM	1.7 0.8 1.2 0.5
13 Sa	03:24 AM 10:46 AM 03:14 PM 09:12 PM	1.8 0.8 1.2 0.5
14 Su	04:13 AM 11:35 AM 04:13 PM 10:07 PM	1.8 0.7 1.2 0.5
15 M	04:59 AM 12:18 PM 05:08 PM 11:01 PM	1.9 0.6 1.3 0.5
16 Tu	05:43 AM 12:58 PM 05:59 PM 11:55 PM	1.9 0.6 1.3 0.5
17 W	06:26 AM 01:35 PM 06:48 PM	1.9 0.5 1.4
18 Th ○	12:48 AM 07:09 AM 02:11 PM 07:35 PM	0.5 1.9 0.5 1.5
19 F	01:40 AM 07:52 AM 02:47 PM 08:22 PM	0.5 1.9 0.4 1.6
20 Sa	02:35 AM 08:36 AM 03:23 PM 09:11 PM	0.5 1.9 0.4 1.7
21 Su	03:32 AM 09:21 AM 04:01 PM 10:02 PM	0.5 1.8 0.3 1.8
22 M	04:34 AM 10:08 AM 04:41 PM 10:56 PM	0.6 1.7 0.3 1.9
23 Tu	05:42 AM 10:57 AM 05:25 PM 11:53 PM	0.6 1.6 0.3 1.9
24 W	06:54 AM 11:51 AM 06:14 PM	0.7 1.5 0.3
25 Th ◑	12:53 AM 08:08 AM 12:50 PM 07:09 PM	2.0 0.7 1.4 0.3
26 F	01:56 AM 09:19 AM 01:54 PM 08:10 PM	2.0 0.7 1.3 0.3
27 Sa	03:01 AM 10:23 AM 03:00 PM 09:15 PM	2.0 0.6 1.3 0.4
28 Su	04:03 AM 11:20 AM 04:05 PM 10:20 PM	2.0 0.6 1.3 0.4
29 M	05:01 AM 12:10 PM 05:05 PM 11:20 PM	2.0 0.6 1.4 0.4
30 Tu	05:53 AM 12:55 PM 06:01 PM	2.0 0.5 1.5
31 W	12:16 AM 06:40 AM 01:35 PM 06:51 PM	0.4 1.9 0.5 1.5

SEPTEMBER

Day	Time (h m)	Height (ft)
1 Th ●	01:08 AM 07:21 AM 02:11 PM 07:38 PM	0.4 1.9 0.5 1.6
2 F	01:56 AM 08:00 AM 02:43 PM 08:23 PM	0.5 1.8 0.5 1.6
3 Sa	02:42 AM 08:36 AM 03:11 PM 09:06 PM	0.6 1.7 0.5 1.7
4 Su	03:28 AM 09:11 AM 03:38 PM 09:49 PM	0.6 1.7 0.5 1.7
5 M	04:14 AM 09:47 AM 04:06 PM 10:32 PM	0.7 1.6 0.4 1.7
6 Tu	05:04 AM 10:25 AM 04:37 PM 11:15 PM	0.8 1.5 0.4 1.7
7 W	06:00 AM 11:05 AM 05:13 PM	0.8 1.4 0.4
8 Th	12:01 AM 07:00 AM 11:51 AM 05:55 PM	1.7 0.9 1.3 0.5
9 F ◐	12:48 AM 08:04 AM 12:43 PM 06:43 PM	1.7 0.9 1.3 0.5
10 Sa	01:39 AM 09:05 AM 01:41 PM 07:38 PM	1.7 0.8 1.2 0.5
11 Su	02:32 AM 10:00 AM 02:42 PM 08:38 PM	1.8 0.8 1.2 0.5
12 M	03:26 AM 10:49 AM 03:41 PM 09:41 PM	1.8 0.7 1.3 0.5
13 Tu	04:17 AM 11:32 AM 04:38 PM 10:42 PM	1.8 0.6 1.4 0.5
14 W	05:07 AM 12:11 PM 05:30 PM 11:41 PM	1.8 0.6 1.5 0.5
15 Th	05:54 AM 12:49 PM 06:20 PM	1.9 0.5 1.6
16 F ○	12:38 AM 06:40 AM 01:26 PM 07:09 PM	0.5 1.9 0.4 1.7
17 Sa	01:34 AM 07:25 AM 02:03 PM 07:58 PM	0.5 1.8 0.3 1.8
18 Su	02:31 AM 08:11 AM 02:42 PM 08:49 PM	0.5 1.8 0.3 1.9
19 M	03:31 AM 08:58 AM 03:22 PM 09:41 PM	0.5 1.7 0.2 2.0
20 Tu	04:33 AM 09:47 AM 04:06 PM 10:35 PM	0.5 1.6 0.2 2.0
21 W	05:39 AM 10:40 AM 04:54 PM 11:32 PM	0.6 1.5 0.2 2.0
22 Th	06:47 AM 11:37 AM 05:49 PM	0.6 1.4 0.3
23 F ◑	12:33 AM 07:56 AM 12:38 PM 06:51 PM	2.0 0.6 1.3 0.3
24 Sa	01:37 AM 09:01 AM 01:44 PM 08:00 PM	1.9 0.6 1.3 0.4
25 Su	02:42 AM 10:00 AM 02:51 PM 09:10 PM	1.9 0.6 1.3 0.4
26 M	03:45 AM 10:53 AM 03:56 PM 10:17 PM	1.8 0.5 1.4 0.4
27 Tu	04:42 AM 11:40 AM 04:55 PM 11:18 PM	1.8 0.5 1.5 0.4
28 W	05:31 AM 12:21 PM 05:48 PM	1.8 0.5 1.5
29 Th	12:13 AM 06:14 AM 12:58 PM 06:35 PM	0.5 1.7 0.5 1.6
30 F	01:02 AM 06:53 AM 01:29 PM 07:20 PM	0.5 1.7 0.4 1.7

OCTOBER

Day	Time (h m)	Height (ft)
1 Sa ●	01:49 AM 07:29 AM 01:57 PM 08:01 PM	0.5 1.6 0.4 1.7
2 Su	02:33 AM 08:04 AM 02:23 PM 08:40 PM	0.6 1.5 0.4 1.7
3 M	03:17 AM 08:39 AM 02:49 PM 09:18 PM	0.6 1.5 0.4 1.7
4 Tu	04:01 AM 09:15 AM 03:18 PM 09:56 PM	0.7 1.4 0.4 1.8
5 W	04:47 AM 09:53 AM 03:51 PM 10:35 PM	0.7 1.3 0.4 1.7
6 Th	05:36 AM 10:35 AM 04:29 PM 11:16 PM	0.7 1.3 0.4 1.7
7 F	06:29 AM 11:22 AM 05:13 PM	0.7 1.2 0.4
8 Sa	12:01 AM 07:25 AM 12:15 PM 06:04 PM	1.7 0.7 1.2 0.5
9 Su ◐	12:51 AM 08:20 AM 01:12 PM 07:03 PM	1.7 0.7 1.2 0.5
10 M	01:45 AM 09:12 AM 02:12 PM 08:09 PM	1.7 0.6 1.2 0.5
11 Tu	02:41 AM 09:59 AM 03:12 PM 09:18 PM	1.7 0.6 1.3 0.5
12 W	03:36 AM 10:42 AM 04:09 PM 10:25 PM	1.7 0.5 1.4 0.5
13 Th	04:29 AM 11:23 AM 05:03 PM 11:29 PM	1.7 0.4 1.5 0.4
14 F	05:20 AM 12:02 PM 05:55 PM	1.7 0.3 1.7
15 Sa	12:30 AM 06:09 AM 12:42 PM 06:46 PM	0.4 1.6 0.2 1.8
16 Su ○	01:29 AM 06:57 AM 01:22 PM 07:37 PM	0.4 1.6 0.1 1.9
17 M	02:28 AM 07:46 AM 02:03 PM 08:28 PM	0.4 1.5 0.1 2.0
18 Tu	03:28 AM 08:36 AM 02:48 PM 09:21 PM	0.4 1.4 0.1 2.0
19 W	04:28 AM 09:28 AM 03:36 PM 10:15 PM	0.4 1.4 0.1 2.0
20 Th	05:30 AM 10:23 AM 04:29 PM 11:12 PM	0.4 1.3 0.1 1.9
21 F	06:33 AM 11:22 AM 05:29 PM	0.4 1.2 0.2
22 Sa ◑	12:11 AM 07:35 AM 12:25 PM 06:36 PM	1.9 0.4 1.2 0.3
23 Su	01:14 AM 08:34 AM 01:32 PM 07:49 PM	1.8 0.4 1.2 0.3
24 M	02:17 AM 09:29 AM 02:38 PM 09:01 PM	1.7 0.4 1.3 0.4
25 Tu	03:17 AM 10:18 AM 03:42 PM 10:09 PM	1.6 0.4 1.3 0.4
26 W	04:10 AM 11:02 AM 04:40 PM 11:09 PM	1.5 0.3 1.4 0.4
27 Th	04:58 AM 11:41 AM 05:32 PM	1.5 0.3 1.5
28 F	12:04 AM 05:40 AM 12:14 PM 06:18 PM	0.4 1.4 0.3 1.5
29 Sa	12:54 AM 06:19 AM 12:44 PM 07:00 PM	0.4 1.4 0.2 1.6
30 Su ●	01:40 AM 06:56 AM 01:11 PM 07:39 PM	0.4 1.3 0.2 1.6
31 M	02:24 AM 07:32 AM 01:39 PM 08:15 PM	0.5 1.2 0.2 1.6

LUNAR DATA
- ● -New Moon
- ◐ -First Quarter
- ○ -Full Moon
- ◑ -Last Quarter

Time meridian 75° W. 0000 is midnight. 1200 is noon. Heights are referred to mean lower low water which is the chart datum of soundings. For tidal differences see page 29.

All times given are Eastern Standard Time; add one hour for Daylight Savings Time. To find actual depths of water at a given time, add the height of the tide to the charted depth. If the height of the tide is negative (has a minus sign before the tabular height), it should be subtracted from the charted depth.

C&D Canal to Back River

The Elk, Bohemia, Northeast, Susquehanna,
Sassafras, Gunpowder, Bush and Middle Rivers
Still Pond and Worton and Fairlee Creeks

Though many tributaries feed the Chesapeake, it is the freshwater Susquehanna River, pouring through Conowingo Dam above Port Deposit, Md., that contributes the greatest volume. That mighty river spills out onto the shallow Susquehanna Flats, mingles with the Northeast River at the western rim of Elk Neck, then joins the Elk River (which feeds into the C&D Canal) to create the narrow beginnings of Chesapeake Bay. Where the rivers join at the head of the Bay, Turkey Point Light shines like a small diamond atop the cliffs at Elk Neck State Park.

In contrast to the lowlands of most of the Eastern Shore, the upper Bay's eastern creeks and rivers are carved into tree-topped bluffs, while much of the western shore is a vast phragmites-fringed salt marsh. The bulk of this western territory, including Pooles Island, belongs to Aberdeen Proving Ground and is used for munitions testing. Aberdeen is delineated on navigational charts as a huge restricted area running from Spesutie Island along the lower lip of Susquehanna Flats south to about mid-Dundee Creek. (The *U.S. Coast Pilot*

details prohibitions and conditions for public use.) Seneca Creek and Middle River to the southwest are outside the restricted area. Surprisingly, the proving ground, home to the Susquehanna National Wildlife Refuge, offers some good wildlife habitat. There are several bald eagle nests, and it's a favorite destination for deer. Boaters can occasionally see bucks swimming between the Eastern Shore and Aberdeen, antlers and rump floating high above the waves as they plow along. Canada Geese fly overhead, and great blue herons glide along both shores.

Because there is so much fresh water in the upper Bay, there are virtually no sea nettles. Fishing is good. Anglers flock to the Susquehanna Flats in early spring for catch-and-release fishing for rockfish. Protected anchorages dot rivers and creeks from Port Deposit on the Susquehanna and Chesapeake City on the C&D Canal through Middle River, though the mouths of the eastern creeks are a bit exposed during western storms. The sunsets, splashed rose and gold against the bronze-colored bluffs, are spectacular.

Section 1

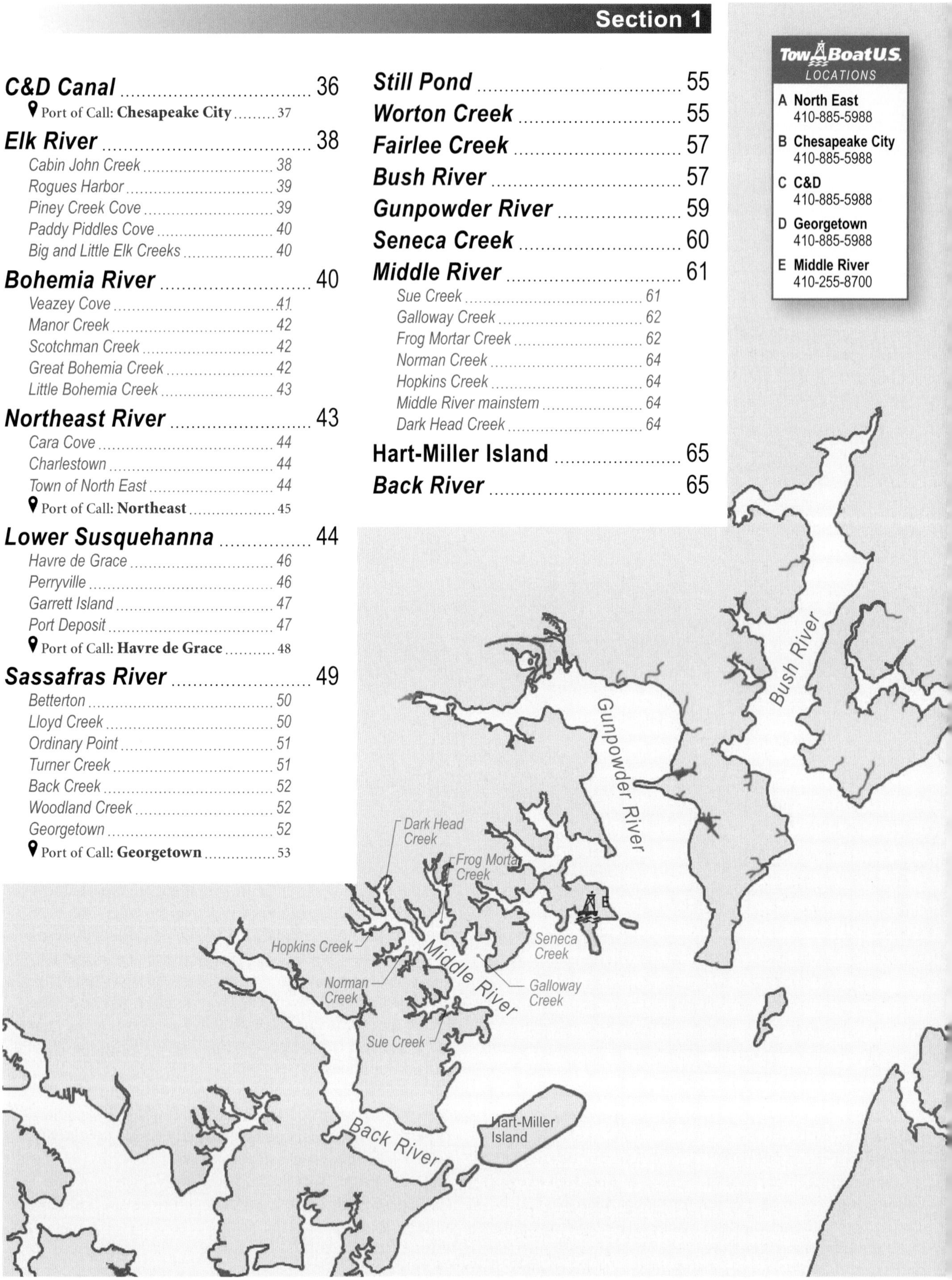

Tow BoatU.S.
LOCATIONS
A North East 410-885-5988
B Chesapeake City 410-885-5988
C C&D 410-885-5988
D Georgetown 410-885-5988
E Middle River 410-255-8700
Bush River
Gunpowder River
Dark Head Creek
Frog Morta
Creek
E
Hopkins Creek
Middle River
Seneca Creek
Norman Creek
Galloway Creek
Sue Creek
Back River
art-Miller
Island

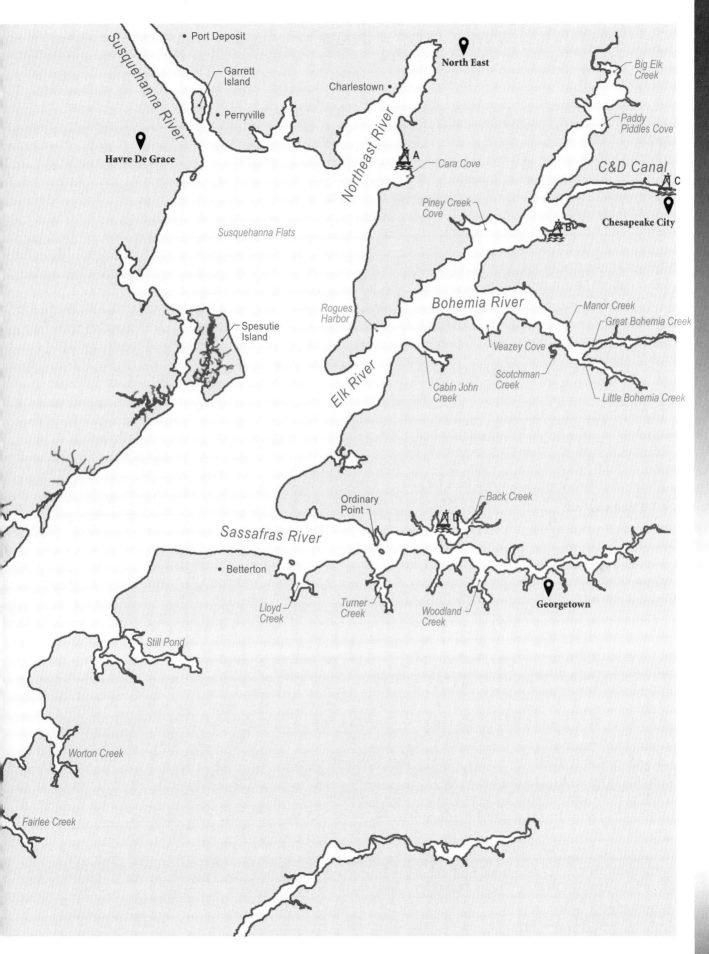

- Port Deposit

Susquehanna River

- Garrett Island

Charlestown •

North East

Big Elk Creek

- Perryville

Havre De Grace

Northeast River

A

Cara Cove

Paddy Piddles Cove

C&D Canal

C

Piney Creek Cove

B

Chesapeake City

Susquehanna Flats

Bohemia River

Manor Creek

Great Bohemia Creek

Rogues Harbor

Veazey Cove

Spesutie Island

Scotchman Creek

Little Bohemia Creek

Elk River

Cabin John Creek

Ordinary Point

Back Creek

Sassafras River

Georgetown

• Betterton

Lloyd Creek

Turner Creek

Woodland Creek

Still Pond

Worton Creek

Fairlee Creek

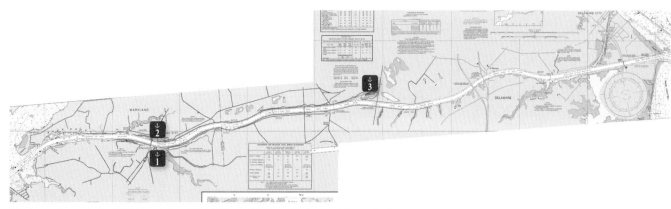

Western entrance to the C&D Canal; from NOAA Chart 12277—not to be used for navigation.

C&D Canal

As you slip between the protective jetties marking its unpretentious entrance from the Delaware River or enter Back Creek from the Elk River, there is little to indicate the magnitude of effort which was and is the **Chesapeake and Delaware Canal**. The C&D Canal opened for business in 1829. At that time it had a waterline width of 66 feet, a bottom width of 36 feet and a depth of 10 feet. The present channel was deepened to 35 feet under a long-term improvement program.

The canal—a vital link on the Intracoastal Waterway connecting the Chesapeake and Delaware bays—is government-owned (supervised by the Army Corps of Engineers) and toll-free. Of the five bridges crossing the canal, four are fixed with a minimum clearance of 135 feet. The remaining bridge, the railroad lift bridge at Summit North, has a vertical clearance of 133 feet when raised, 45 feet when down. The span is kept up and lowered only for train crossings or for maintenance. Closings are announced on channel 13, the working channel for commercial activity on the canal.

Be careful of freighters and tugs towing barges. They can be remarkably quiet, so check astern frequently. Above all, be mindful of the current, which throughout the canal changes direction during high and low tide, which averages 2 to 3 knots. The flow is eastward during the interval from low to high tide there; westward from high to low tide. (Check the Reedy Point tide table for tidal information.)

The channel is marked with buoys and lights from each entrance, and the system reverses itself at **Chesapeake City**, the only town on the canal. Between the Delaware entrance and Chesapeake City, a distance of approximately 12 miles, even numbers and flashing red lights are on the north side and odd numbers and flashing green lights are on the south side. As you enter from the Elk River, even numbers and flashing red lights are on the south side and odd numbers and flashing white or green lights are on the north side.

Traffic control lights directed at boaters are located at Old Town Point Wharf (Maryland) and Reedy Point (Delaware). A green light indicates the canal is open to traffic; a red light indicates that it is closed (as is the case during dense fog, for example). It's wise to stay out of the middle in case you run into an emergency—a stalled engine, perhaps. A large ship looming around the next bend can neither stop nor maneuver around an incapacitated craft.

Just below the railroad bridge on the north side of the canal Summit North Marina offers fuel and slips for transients. Transiting the canal under sail between Reedy Point and Welch Point is prohibited. Vessels proceeding with the current have the right-of-way. However, small pleasure craft relinquish that right to deeper-draft vessels with limited maneuverability. At

continued on page 34

● On Premises
➤ Nearby

C&D Canal	MLW	Overnight Slips	Gas	Diesel	Propane	Electric	Showers	Laundry	Restaurant	Lodging	Pool	Pump-out	Ice	Marine Supplies	Groceries	Bait	Boat Repair	Haul-out Services	Launch Ramp	Wi-Fi	Other
Chesapeake Inn & Marina C&D Canal 410-885-2040; www.chesapeakeinn.com	6'	●	➤	➤			●	●		●	➤		●	●					➤		
Schaefer's Canal House C&D Canal 410-885-7200; www.schaeferscanalhouse.com	15'	●	●	●			●			●							●				Bulkhead docking, restaurant, ships store
Summit North Marina C&D Canal 302-836-1800; www.summitnorthmarina.com	10'	●	●	●		●	●	●	●	●	➤	●	●	●	●	●	●	➤	●	●	➤	●	State park, floating docks, full-service yard

Port of Call

Chesapeake City

Visit this historic port town divided by the Chesapeake & Delaware Canal, and on any given day you may witness a parade of vessels gliding by: freighters flying flags of exotic ports, tugs pulling heavily laden barges, military ships en route to their assignments and pleasure craft of every size and design. Residences cluster north of the waterway, while to the south the town center embraces visitors with hospitality, warmth and sophistication.

Chesapeake City history revolves around the Chesapeake & Delaware Canal, whose story unfolds through photographs, artifacts and models in the stone buildings that now comprise the C&D Canal Museum. The main exhibit room served as the original pump house in the days when the canal still had locks. In a wing abutting the room, visitors get an awe-inspiring look at the nation's oldest and largest steam engines, still on their original foundations, and the mammoth waterwheel that they powered, which could lift 1.2 million gallons of water per hour into the lock.

For more local lore, pay a small fee and take a guided walking tour (five-person minimum, call 410-885-2415 for information) featuring a number of historic landmarks. Sinking Springs Herb Farm, a 130-acre farm at the edge of North Chesapeake City, conducts garden tours, some that include a luncheon featuring herb dishes (call 410-398-5566 for reservations and transportation information). Canal and upper Bay history come alive on narrated cruises aboard the a deadrise berthed at the town dock (reservations required, call 410-885-5088). Take a ride around town courtesy of the city's free bicycles (sign up at Canal Lock Antiques, 105 Bohemia Ave.). Or make an appointment to tour the Hersch Mini Museum, showcasing household items from the late 1800s (call 410-885-5889).

Chesapeake City is eminently walkable. Nearly a dozen antiques shops and art galleries share the spotlight with one-of-a-kind ventures tucked into the compact business district, along with a variety of restaurants and B&Bs (*www.bedandbreakfast.com*). The restored Bayard House offers Eastern Shore cuisine and canal views as well as pub fare in its Hole in the Wall Tavern. The more casual Bohemia Cafe, which offers fresh baked goods and take-out, is the only place in town that opens for breakfast. Waterfront dining is available at the Chesapeake Inn Restaurant and Marina. The Canal Creamery scoops up ice cream. Across the canal, the Giordano family has renovated and reopened the old Schafer Canal House with new docks, a restaurant overlooking the canal and an outdoor dining patio and bar.

Chesapeake City is a fairly low key place, where activities tend to revolve around the arts and local heritage. On Sunday evenings in July and August, the Summer Music in the Park concert series takes place in Pell Gardens (bring a blanket or lawn chair). An annual Ghost Walk takes place at the end of October (call 410-885-2415). For a number of years, the city's big event was Canal Days, when all heck would break loose along the waterfront on the last Saturday in June. But that event has been suspended, at least for the time being, due primarily to safety concerns with such a large group of boats and people concentrated in a small area.

Boaters should be stocked up before they transit the C&D Canal, but if they do run short of basics, they may be able to hitch a ride to a convenience mart just south of town along Route 213.

Information: Chesapeake City Civic Association, 410-885-2415.

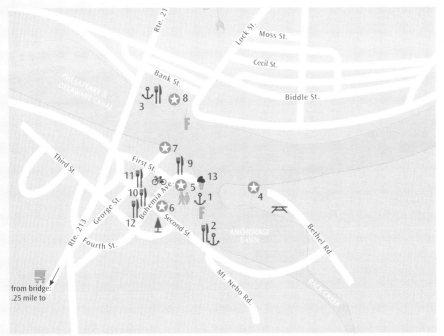

Chesapeake City

⚓ **Marinas/Dockage**
1 Town Dock
2 Chesapeake Inn Restaurant & Marina
3 Schaefer's Canal House

⚙ **Points of Interest**
4 C & D Canal Museum
5 Franklin Hall-Pell Gardens
6 Town Hall
7 George Street Overlook (observation deck)
8 Pilots' Association

🍴 **Dining**
2 Chesapeake Inn Restaurant & Marina
3 Schaefer's Canal House
9 Bayard House Restaurant
10 The Tap Room
11 Bohemia Cafe and Bakery
12 Southside's Bar and Grill

🍦 **Ice Cream**
13 Canal Creamery

🛒 **Groceries**   🪑 **Picnic Area**
🌳 **Park**   F **Pedestrian**
🚻 **Public Restrooms**   **Ferry**
🚲 **Bicycles**   **Landings**

C&D Canal continued from page 32

night, the entire canal is illuminated with amber lights located about 140 feet from the edge of the channel.

Pilots embark and disembark from ships on the north shore at Chesapeake City. Keep clear of their launches. In an emergency, the dispatcher monitors channel 16. Marinas on the canal also monitor 16 and use 9 as their working channel. Harbour North Marina, located in the Elk River near the western entrance to the canal, offers on-water boater assistance (for fuel, engine problems, etc.) in the C&D and Elk River areas, The service is available seven days a week. Call on VHF or 410-885-5656.

In addition to being a point where ships transiting the Bay transfer pilots, Chesapeake City serves thousands of recreational boaters every year. The small scale of the town, with its shops and inns and casual and fine dining, makes it a charming place to explore on foot. The access point is along the canal's southern side through **Back Creek Basin** which carries depths of 10-12 feet on average, though the entrance is subject to periodic shoaling. To starboard, just beyond the entrance, is a floating public dock where boaters may stay for free for up to 24 hours. The dockmaster monitors VHF channel 13, or can be reached by phone at 443-350-2442. Continuing to port, you'll find limited dockage at Chesapeake Inn (mostly for shallower drafts) and some anchoring space with good holding. On the other side of the canal, at Chesapeake City North, you'll find plenty of docking, fuel, a restaurant and a great view of the canal at the newly refurbished Schaefer's Canal House, which sits directly on the canal between the pilot's station and the highway bridge. When docking anywhere here, be mindful of the strong current, and, when anchoring, allow enough room to swing.

The C&D CANAL MUSEUM occupies the original pump house and engine house of the old canal. Easily accessible, it is a short walk from any part of the waterfront. Visitors can follow a sidewalk that leads around the anchorage basin or the path from the dock on the basin's northeastern corner where small boats may tie up temporarily. (The dock lies to the east of a public boat launch.) The museum offers an in-depth look at the history of the canal and includes displays of much of the early machinery used to operate the locks.

Between mid-April and mid-October, the tour boat *Miss Clare* provides ferry service between the south and north shores of the busy canal. Pedestrians not only can get a ride aboard Captain Ralph Hazel's workboat-style vessel, but are also likely to pick up some local lore from the lifelong city resident at the helm. Boaters can catch the ferry at the town dock at the mouth of Back Creek basin on the south shore, or at a dock that lies at the foot of Lock Street on the north shore. (The ferry schedule is posted at the town dock or is available by calling 410-885-5088.) Chesapeake Inn & Marina offers a launch service for patrons in anchored boats. To arrange for a pick up, hail them on VHF channel 16 or call the inn at 410-885-2040.

Elk River

The **Elk River** is a glistening, silvery ribbon of water that separates the hills to the west from the gently rolling countryside to the east. The view here is nothing short of spectacular. The beginning of the river serves as an entrance to the C&D Canal. In this area ships can come down on you quickly, so be ready to get out of the way. The river is rather narrow at this point, and as you might expect the current can be strong.

Cabin John Creek

From Turkey Point, it is about two miles to the mouth of ❶ **Cabin John Creek** to starboard. There is a good beach on the creek's south side. Many boaters, reluctant to expose

● *On Premises*
➤ *Nearby*

	MLW	Overnight Slips	Gas	Diesel	Propane	Electric	Showers	Laundry	Restaurant	Lodging	Pool	Pump-out	Ice	Groceries	Marine Supplies	Boat Repair	Bait	Haul-out Services	Launch Ramp	Wi-Fi	Other
Elk River																					
The Cove Marina Elk River 410-620-5505; www.thecovemarina.com	4'	●	➤	➤	➤	●	●	●	●	➤	➤		●	●	●	●	➤	●	●	●	●	Park area with gas grills, pet area, bike paths
Harbour North Marina Elk R./C&D Canal 410-885-5656; www.sunsetcafemd.com	3'	●	●	●	➤	●	●	●		●			●	●	●	➤	●	➤	●	●	➤	●	Waterfront bar & restaurant with sunset views
Locust Point Marina Elk R./Locust Point 410-392-4994; www.locustpointmarina.com	3'	●	➤	➤	●	●	●		➤	➤	●	●	●	●	➤	●	➤	●	●	●	●	Wi-Fi, MD Clean Marina, Marine services
Taylor's Marina Elk River 410-392-3588; www.liquidfun.com	4'	●	➤	➤		●	●			➤		●	●		●		●		●	●	●	●	Wi-Fi, MD Clean Marina
Triton Marina Elk R./Plum Pt. 410-620-3060; www.tritonmarina.com	5'	●	●			●	●	➤	●	➤		●	●	➤	●	➤	●	➤	●	●		Full service, high/dry boatel, floating slips, boat sales

themselves to the wider Elk and Bohemia rivers, "duck in" to Cabin John Creek for the night. They don't do much farther than half a mile, however, because after that the depth drops from about 5 feet to 2. On summer weekends, Cabin John can be congested with small pleasure boats, but most of these are local and return home at dusk.

Rogues Harbor

Across from Cabin John Creek you will find a boating facility at ❷ **Rogues Harbor** in ELK NECK STATE PARK. The depths in Rogues Harbor range from 3 to 5 feet. Although the charts show 3 feet near the southwest shore, it's best not to venture too close to shore at any point. Visitors to this cove report that boats here generally anchor well out from the sandy beach.

High on one of the bluffs surrounding the cove you can see campers in Elk Neck State Park (410-287-5333). In addition to wooded sites for tents and RVs, there are rustic cabins (built in the late 1930s by the Civilian Conservation Corps) that may be rented from April through October. This lovely park also offers four launching ramps, boat and motor rentals, a pier and concession building with gas, tackle, bait and other supplies. An extensive, protected beach lines the Northeast River side of the neck. Motorists can reach the park by taking Route 272 from the town of North East. Rogues Harbor is located approximately 10 miles south of North East.

Rogues Harbor provides fair protection in blows from the north and northwest. However, the harbor is vulnerable to winds from the south, southwest and east. It is a beautiful daytime anchorage, but its proximity to the heavily traveled shipping lanes on the Elk River make it unsuitable for an overnight stay.

Piney Creek Cove

Continuing up the Elk, across from Old Town Point Wharf to starboard, ❸ **Piney Creek Cove** lies to port. The mouth of Piney Creek Cove, from Oldfield Point to Hylands Point, is a little more than a mile wide, narrowing slightly. Depths of 4 to 6 feet continue toward the northeastern shoreline but diminish considerably along the northwestern

and southern shores.

Once you enter the cove, you'll find good shelter from the north and west. This is a good place to pause and enjoy the beauty of the high headlands of Elk Neck and the gently rolling countryside across the way. You can swim in nettle-free water, safely out of the busy channel.

The next creek to starboard is **Herring Creek**, just beyond Courthouse Point, where there's a marina offering slips and services to shallow-draft boats.

Beyond Back Creek, the point where the C&D Canal branches off from the Elk River, shoaling has been a problem for boaters traveling farther up the river. In response, the state and county dredged a 50-foot wide channel from Welch Point (labeled Welsh Point on some charts) to just above Locust Point. Depths near Locust Point (the site of the northernmost marina on the river) are now reported to range from 5 feet at low tide to 8 feet at high tide.

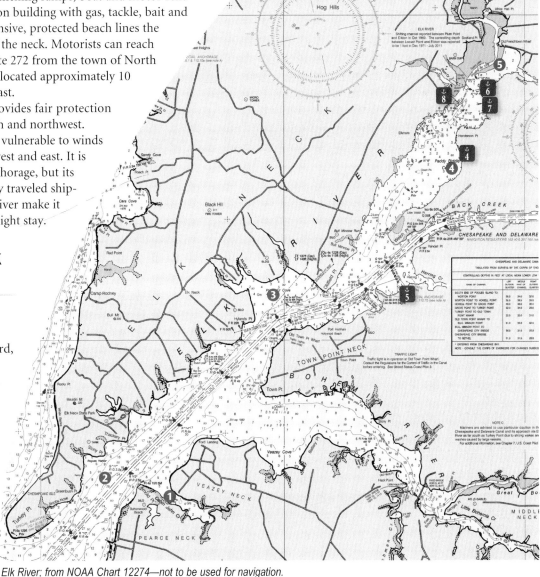

Elk River; from NOAA Chart 12274—not to be used for navigation.

Paddy Piddles Cove

A couple of miles upstream from Welch Point is a delightful anchorage (to starboard) called ❹ **"Paddy Piddles Cove,"** noted on some charts as "Paddy Biddle Cove" and on others as "Paddy Bibble Cove." You will find marinas on either side of the river a little more than a mile farther upstream, offering berths, electricity, hull and motor repairs, haul-out facilities, hardware, groceries, and toilet and shower facilities. A restaurant, Triton Bar and Grill, is located at Triton Marina.

Big and Little Elk Creeks

The channel is marked to the junction of ❺ **Big** and **Little Elk creeks**. If depths are a concern anchor at Paddy Piddles Cove and use a dinghy to explore farther. There is a 2 $1/3$-foot tidal range and a current velocity of just over half a knot in this area.

It's said that Captain John Smith named the Elk River because he saw a resemblance to the horns of an elk in the big and little creeks that join to form the river at Elk Landing.

At one time, the Elk River was quite deep because Frenchtown was a major embarkation point for ports along the Chesapeake Bay. Continental Army soldiers, on their way to their ultimate victory at Yorktown, embarked here. Frenchtown was burned by Admiral Cockburn of the British Navy in 1813 and never rebuilt.

Just 1 Mile
from the ICW
Look for our lighthouse
at the entrance

Close to Home—
Close to the Bay

Full service marina with covered and open slips available now.

- Gas, diesel, pumpout
- Pool • Nettle-free beach
- 50 channel cable TV • Ship's store
- Slipholder fuel discounts
- New 50T lift • Full service and parts
- Mechanics on duty 6 days
- A/C heads & laundry • Picnic peninsula
- Water taxi service to moorings

Why rent a slip when you can buy?

Contact us about slip ownership opportunities

410-885-2706

BOHEMIA BAY YACHT HARBOUR

1026 Town Point Road • Chesapeake City, MD 21915
www.bbyh.com • e-mail: ken@bbyh.com

About a mile upstream from Elk Landing (along narrow, crooked channels with numerous snags and unmarked shoals suitable for only the most intrepid kayakers) is the town of **Elkton**, which was founded early in the 18th century. At that time Elkton was quite a crossroads as it caught the traffic moving between the Bay and Philadelphia.

The county seat of Cecil County was moved from Charlestown to Head of Elk in 1786, and the town began to grow. Elkton managed to escape the fate of Frenchtown in the War of 1812 when the guns of Fort Defiance, about a mile down the river, drove the British away.

Originally, the river at Elkton was deep enough for ships to unload their wares behind the buildings on Main Street and later steamboats docked at the town wharf. Big Elk Creek silted in, however, and the last steamboat left Elkton in 1917.

Years later, Elkton briefly thrived from another "industry." This became the place to go for quick marriages, because, unlike its neighboring states, Maryland required no waiting period for people wishing to marry, and Elkton was the closest town across the state line from the north. Marriages became big business, and wedding chapels lined Main Street. When Maryland established a 48-hour waiting period in 1938, business quickly dropped off.

Bohemia River

Along the Elk River, whether southbound from the C&D or plying up from Turkey Point toward flashing red "14" at the mouth of the **Bohemia River**, you're in one of the most beautiful stretches in all of Bay country. The Bohemia's steep, majestic southern shoreline provides a sharp contrast to those flatter horizons farther down the Bay, and its banks, thick with trees, conceal much of the modern encroachment. This is rural countryside, and while its north shore is less dramatic, the overall effect is perhaps more reminiscent of the Hudson River than a Chesapeake tributary.

Despite charted depths of 7 to 8 feet, this lovely river's broad, inviting mouth is fraught with both charted and uncharted shoals, especially along its northern entrance near Town Point, where all vessels should exercise care. Boats drawing up to 4 $1/2$ feet will probably find no issues, but those with deeper drafts intent on cruising beyond its entrance will want to pay close attention to the tides. The tidal range can be two or more feet, but along with predicted water levels wise skippers will also be mindful of the influence wind direction may have on the rise and fall of tidal waters in this region.

A convenient anchorage for those cruising the Intracoastal Waterway's well-traveled route is just inside the Bohemia's southern shore near Ford Landing. Less than a mile east of "14" in the Elk River, its charted depths of 7 to 9 feet make it an ideal stopover in calm weather or southerly winds. With high banks, fine sandy bottom and gradually sloping beach, it's also attractive. The only drawback could be an occasional wash from a tug or freighter chugging along the ships channel, but distance usually minimizes the swells.

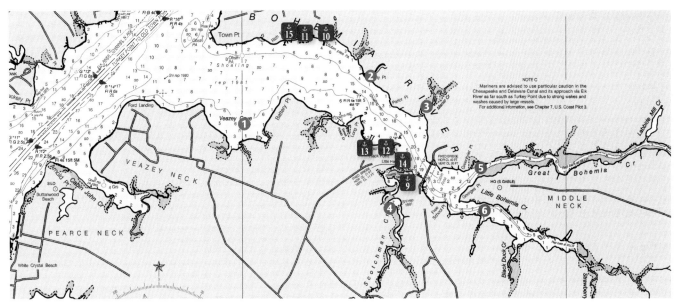

Bohemia River; from NOAA Chart 12274—not to be used for navigation.

Veazey Cove

Another anchorage lies a little beyond Ford Landing in ❶ **Veazey Cove**, a broad curve along the Bohemia's southern shoreline. This is a popular spot for local boaters who find its shallow, nettle-free water ideal for swimming. Boats that would have trouble in the 3- to 6-foot depths closer to shore might choose to sound their way in carefully. Drop the hook in about 7 feet approximately halfway inside the cove.

While the cove doesn't allow a direct sunset view, it does offer good protection from everything but northerly winds.

Summer weekends usually fill it with all manner of powerboats, houseboats and centerboard sailboats anchored in the shallows, sterns close to the beach for swimming and social wading. Although a good many boats may remain in the cove overnight, their numbers dwindle at dusk.

To explore farther east in the expansive lower Bohemia, proceed carefully, favoring the center while anticipating the aforementioned shoaly areas. About two miles upstream, the river squeezes closer to its banks where red flashing "2" marks shallows along the southern shore. Don't venture too far left of this mark, however, since it's even shallower near ❷ Stony

● On Premises
➤ Nearby

Bohemia River	MLW	Overnight Slips	Gas	Diesel	Propane	Electric	Showers	Laundry	Restaurant	Lodging	Pool	Pump-out	Ice	Groceries	Marine Supplies	Bait	Boat Repair	Haul-out Services	Launch Ramp	Wi-Fi	Other
Bohemia Anchorage Bohemia R. 410-275-8148	6'-8'	●	➤	➤		●	●	➤	➤	➤		●	●	➤	➤	➤	●	●	●		Covered, yr-round lifts, wood repairs
Bohemia Bay Yacht Harbour Bohemia R. 410-885-2601; www.bbyh.com	5'	●	●	●		●	●	●			●	●	●		●			●	●		●	Full service yard; 50-ton lift, marine accessories, Wi-Fi
Bohemia Vista Marina Bohemia R. 410-885-2056; www.bohemiavistamarina.com	5'	●	➤	➤		●	●	●	➤	➤		●	●	●	➤	➤	●	●	●	●	●	New floating piers, full-service dept. 35-ton lift
Hack's Point Bohemia R. 410-275-9151; www.hackspointmarina.com	6'	●	➤	➤	➤	●	●	●	➤	➤		●	●	➤	➤	➤	●	●	●	●	●	Floating docks, full-service dept. public ramp
Long Point Marina Bohemia R. 410-275-8181	3'		●			●	●	●				●	●	➤	●			●	●	➤		MD Clean Marina, full working boatyard
Richmond's Marina Bohemia R./Scotchman's Cr. 410-275-2061	7'	●	➤	➤	➤	●	●	●	➤	➤		●	●	➤	➤	➤	●	●	●	●		Floating docks, lifts, full-service, bath house, heat, A/C
Two Rivers Yacht Basin Bohemia R. 410-885-2257	4'	●	●			●	●	●				➤	●		●			●	●		➤	

Bohemia River continued

Point to the north. Here the river's natural channel deepens considerably as it turns southeasterly toward the fixed bridge at Route 213 (vertical clearance 30 feet), a little more than a mile beyond "2". Past the bridge is the confluence of the two tributaries forming the Bohemia.

The river's most popular anchorage is south of Stony Point, off the channel and north of flashing fixed aid to navigation "2". White DNR buoys mark the 6-knot speed limit in this area and with the Bohemia's entire length stretching to the west, boaters enjoy watching the sun disappear beyond Elk Neck and the river's own spectacular display of vivid tones.

Manor Creek

Just off ❸ **Manor Creek**, cruisers have reported depths of 4 and 5 feet about 30 feet from the mouth and with good holding in the sandy mud bottom. Indigenous wildlife seem to like it here and birds swoop and dive around the creek's shallow entrance.

East of Manor Creek, a 1920s Georgian-style brick mansion with multiple chimneys stands on land formerly owned by one of the most important figures in early Maryland and Eastern Shore history, Augustine Herman. A native of Bohemia (now part of the Czech Republic), Herman was dispatched from his adopted home in New Amsterdam (New York City) to Maryland in 1659 to settle a boundary dispute. Soon afterward, he proposed to Lord Baltimore that he map the state and the Chesapeake Bay in return for a grant of land between the Elk River and the river he would rename for his homeland (the waterway was then known as the Oppoquermine). Herman spent 10 years working on his map of the Chesapeake. He did a remarkable job, creating the first truly accurate map of the entire Bay area. Mariners relied on it for years to come. The map was beautifully engraved in London by the renowned William Fairthorne. The current stately home was constructed by a descendant of Herman's after the original Bohemia Manor was destroyed.

In addition to beauty, the Bohemia River offers a fistful of marinas that provide a full range of services. Several of these are clustered together on the north shore about a mile upriver from Town Point at the mouth. Others are along the southern side near Long Point, Hacks Point and the Maryland Route 213 bridge. Note that the entrance channels to a couple of the marinas can be shallow, but at least two, Bohemia Vista Yacht Basin and Hack's Point Marina on opposite sides of the river, have recently dredged their channels.

Scotchman Creek

Stores and restaurants are not always close, but a few eateries offer dockside delivery service. Facilities along the southern shore are accessible to Hacks Point General Store, which is known for its convenience sundries, good coffee, a thick stack of horse magazines for browsing, and great sandwiches. Within easy walking distance to the store is Richmond's Marina in ❹ **Scotchman Creek**, located just beyond Glebe

Road's fixed bridge near the mouth of the creek (vertical clearance 11 feet). If height and draft keep you from entering this narrow tributary, consider taking the dinghy to explore its wooded miles of quietude.

Great Bohemia Creek

Boats of shallower draft and of low enough profile to navigate under the Route 213 Bridge are in for a treat in ❺ **Great Bohemia Creek**. Depending on the tide and size of your boat, the unmarked channel (pay attention to chart and depthfinder) could lead you lazily through rolling horse country. The famous thoroughbred farms here have had owners ranging from the colorful (the late Allaire duPont) to the celebrity (composer Burt Bacharach) and among the many equine past champions that once called these pastures home are Kelso and Northern Dancer. Some of the coun-

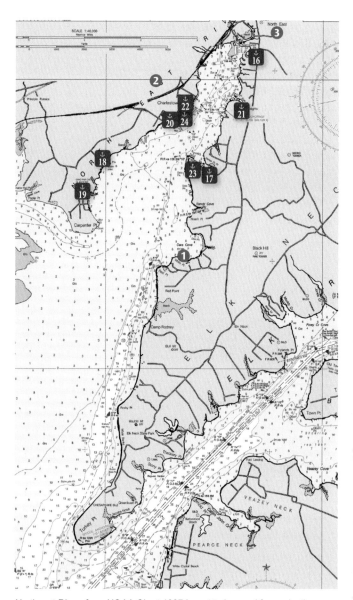

Northeast River; from NOAA Chart 12274—not to be used for navigation.

try's leading breeders still populate the nearby paddocks. A local travel agency (Hill Travel, 800-874-4558) offers outsiders the rare opportunity to visit these farms.

Little Bohemia Creek

To the south of Great Bohemia Creek, **❻ Little Bohemia Creek** is navigable for about a mile above the bridge. Wider and deeper with high banks, the channel carries about 7 feet close to the southern shore around Free School Point, about a half-mile beyond the bridge. Deeper water then hugs the northern banks for a while before the channel ends in shallows. Though sheltered, in mid-season you may share the area with water-skiers.

Just above the headwaters of the Bohemia River is "Old Bohemia," St. Francis Xavier Jesuit Mission. Established in 1704, it served the Catholic population of the entire Delmarva Peninsula and southeastern Pennsylvania (and was the haven to which James Michener's character Rosalind brought her two sons in his novel *Chesapeake*). Bohemia Academy was founded in 1745, at a time when Catholic schools were illegal, and was the Jesuits' immediate predecessor to Georgetown University in Washington, D.C.

The chart shows 8 feet of water behind Free School Point, and the bottom is hard sand. After Free School Point the channel veers to the north shore, with depths ranging from 5 to 15 feet for about a mile. This is verdant land, worth a visit.

Northeast River

Turkey Point can be one of the roughest spots in the upper Bay because this is where the Elk, Sassafras and Susquehanna rivers all join forces, setting up a battle of wills between the incoming or outgoing tidal flow of the various rivers as they meet the Bay. Throw in contrary winds bending around each of the points of land, and you can find yourself in a right good stew. Once you have safely rounded Turkey Point, however, take time to admire the scenery. The deepwater shoreline to starboard is one of Elk Neck State Park's beaches. At one time, the area was inhabited by tribes of Iroquois Indians—primarily the powerful Susquehannocks—and thousands of Indian artifacts have been found along the banks of the Elk and Northeast rivers. This further enhances the already popular pastime of beachcombing for driftwood along these shores.

In 1936, Dr. William L. Abbott willed 368 acres of his estate, including his home, to the state of Maryland to be used for recreation, and thus Elk Neck State Park was established. Over the years, the park has acquired additional land and now consists of nearly 2,200 acres, with topography that varies from sandy beaches and marshlands to heavily wooded bluffs rising more than 100 feet above the Northeast River. There is fishing in both the Elk and Northeast rivers.

The mouth of the **Northeast River** begins not at Turkey Point but at Red Point, five miles upstream. Its marked chan-

● On Premises
➤ Nearby

Northeast River	MLW	Overnight Slips	Gas	Diesel	Propane	Electric	Showers	Laundry	Restaurant	Lodging	Pool	Pump-out	Ice	Groceries	Marine Supplies	Bait	Boat Repair	Haul-out Services	Launch Ramp	Wi-Fi	Other
Anchor Marina North East R. 410-287-8280; www.anchorboat.com	8'	●	●			●		●			●	●		●		●		●	●	●	
Bay Boat Works Northeast R. 410-287-8113; www.bayboatworks.com	4'	●	●	●		●	●					●	●		●		●	●	●		MD Clean Marina, pumpout boat, taxi service
Charlestown Marina Northeast R./Charlestown 410-287-8125; www.charlestownmarina.com	6'	●	●	➤	➤	●	●	●	➤	➤		●	●	➤	●	➤	●	●	➤	●	Full-service, family owned and operated, with ship store
Craft Haven Campground & Marina Northeast R./Charlestown 410-642-2515	3'	●			●	●	●		➤	➤			●						●		
Lee's Marina Northeast R./Charlestown 410-287-5100; www.leesmarina.com	4'	●	➤	➤	➤	●	●	➤	●	➤	➤	●	●	●	●	➤	●	●	➤	●	Transient slips, marine store, service dept.
McDaniel Yacht Basin, Inc Northeast R. 410-287-8121 or 800-320-6231; www.mcdanielyacht.com	6'	●	●	●	➤	●	●	●	➤	➤	●	●	●	➤	●	➤	●	●		●	Canvas shop, repairs, prop shop, storage, boat sales
North East River Marina Northeast R. 410-287-5298; www.northeastrivermarina.com	3.5'	●	➤	➤		●	●		➤	➤		●	●	➤	●	➤	●	●	●	●	Rental boats; Mercruiser, OMC & Volvo parts
Shelter Cove Yacht Basin and Marina Northeast R. 410-287-9400; www.jacksonmarinesales.com	5'	●	●	●	➤	●	●	●	➤	➤	●	●	●	➤	●	●	●	●	➤	●	BoatUS; Hi-Dri storage, full service, parts store, Clean marina
Wellwood Marina and Restaurant Northeast R./Charlestown 410-287-6666; www.wellwoodclub.com	6'	●			●	●	●	●			●	●	➤	●		●		●	●		Live music Fri.–Sun; carry-out wine & beer

Northeast River *continued*

nel hugs the eastern shoreline, passing Hance Point and leading to the communities of Charlestown and North East. Except for a few generous pockets in the northern region, the entire tributary's depths run in the single digits, so deeper draft vessels will be navigating the area cautiously. Be aware of shoaling west of Cara Cove where 5 feet is reported between "7" and "8".

Cara Cove

❶ **Cara Cove**, just past Red Point to starboard, is about a half-mile wide and a half-mile long with depths of 4 to 5 feet and tidal range of nearly 2 feet. For shallower drafts, it offers fair protection from south and east. Most of the cove's shoreline is private property; please don't trespass.

Past the cove, several large marine facilities are located along both shores from Hance Point and beyond. Nearly all have slips, fuel and repairs; only Anchor Marina at North East, however, has dockside depths of more than 6 feet. Two clubs on the eastern side (Hances Point Y.C. and Northeast River Y.C.) offer reciprocity to other members within the Chesapeake Bay Yacht Clubs Association.

You can get a pumpout here from Bay Boat Works, whose traveling pumpout boat serves the area. Available daily from 8 am until 3 pm (April through October) call 410-287-8113 to make arrangements.

Charlestown

❷ **Charlestown**, on the river's western shore, was established in 1742 as a shipping center for the head of Chesapeake Bay. Charlestown and Baltimore had their beginnings about the same time, and the two ports were rivals until the Revolutionary War, when Charlestown lost out to Baltimore's superior facilities and location. The hurricane of 1786 struck another blow. Prior to this storm, ships had to navigate a precarious channel to Havre de Grace by way of Charlestown. The hurricane cut the Locust Point Channel, which made Havre de Grace an easily accessible deepwater port. In a final blow, the Cecil County seat was moved from Charlestown to Elkton in 1780.

Today Charlestown is a quiet summer resort with a number of historic houses, including the Tory House, which is open to the public on the third Sunday of the month May through September and by appointment (410-287-8262). The old wharf where ships once unloaded their cargo is gone, but a stone wharf has been built on its cribbing. Small boats can tie up at the short dock at its tip.

Charlestown has several marinas with transient slips, including the Wellwood and North East River Marina. Charlestown Marina also has fuel. A nearby public park provides an opportunity for picnicking, fishing and general recreation, with restrooms near the public boat ramp. Boaters can dock and dine at the Wellwood and, on the same grounds, the River Shack, where you can get great steamed crabs and other carryout dinners. A deli and limited groceries are accessible from the marina district, as are several inviting antiques shops.

Town of North East

The village of ❸ **North East** lies 1.7 miles beyond Charlestown. Outside of the town there is an anchorage basin with an adjoining public park. The entrance (green "17") has shoaled to 6 feet or less, but the basin is deep, with a gravel bottom. Anchoring here is fine in quiet weather, but less so when the wind rears up from the southwest to northwest quadrants.

Also within the basin you'll find NORTH EAST COMMUNITY PARK. Its slips are available at no charge for day use on a first-come first-served basis. Most points of interest lie a half-mile from the park. There's another anchorage area east of the channel near a home that resembles a screwpile lighthouse. Shallow-draft boats may tie up to the bulkhead along the UPPER BAY MUSEUM on **Northeast Creek** adjacent to the park. There is also a launch ramp (small fee) at nearby Anchor Marina. Also, many of the marinas located south of town offer courtesy transportation into the village.

Lower Susquehanna

The Chesapeake Bay is the drowned river valley of the Susquehanna. To understand the term "drowned river," envision perhaps a million years ago when there was no Bay, only level land through which a river flowed slowly from the northern reaches of what is now New York state some 450 miles to the sea—draining an area on the Atlantic coast second in size only to the St. Lawrence Seaway.

According to geologists, over the course of time, what we now call the Eastern Shore sank beneath the sea not once, but four times. The first time the land emerged above sea level (according to theory), the Susquehanna River, blocked by a great shoal of detritus, was diverted to the south for 150 miles before finding an outlet to the Atlantic. Gradually, the land at the mouth of the river sank again until sea water ran in and flooded it, cutting off all the tributaries from the main river and, in fact, drowning the Susquehanna and creating the Chesapeake Bay.

Coming from the North East River, shallow draft vessels with local knowledge can skim the northern edge of the broad **Susquehanna Flats** to reach the mouth of the Susquehanna and Havre de Grace. The Flats once attracted duck hunters from around the world as millions of migrating water fowl paused to fish its shallow waters. The hunters were so successful that the population has never recovered. But other varieties of wildlife still abound, and the Flats remains a favorite haunt of hunters, fishermen and crabbers.

Most boaters, no matter which direction they are coming from, must take the southern route around the Flats, crossing the Bay just south of Turkey Point to pick up the red and green mid-channel buoy "A" about a mile west. From there, they continue northwest from "A" to green "1". To port, is **Spesutie Island**, which was prominent in the early history of the Bay, but now is part of the Aberdeen Proving Ground, and so off limits to recreational boaters. Buoys mark the

continued on page 46

Port of Call

North East

This small town overflows with antiques shops, gift shops and restaurants, all located in a pleasant, strollable business district. Originally an industrial center that evolved around a flour mill and an iron works, North East remains water-oriented, although its marinas are situated a mile or two south of town— except Anchor Marina, which has transient slips and is located across from the town dock. The closest dockage to the historic town center are the slips located at the town park. These are available for daytime use on a first-come, first-served basis. Transients dining at nearby Nauti Goose Saloon can tie up there overnight, but there are no amenities.

The Upper Bay Museum, housed in a 19th-century fish house adjacent to the town park, preserves the heritage of the region's wildfowl hunters as well as its recreational and commercial fishermen. Its fascinating collection includes decoys, gunning rigs, antique marine engines and mahogany miniatures.

Commercial fishermen are still a backdrop along the Northeast River, which makes a visit to the famous Herb's Tackle and Barber Shop on Main Street essential. If you are eager to sample local seafood, grab a mallet at Woody's, one of the Bay's classic crabhouses, perched on the town's main drag. Visitors can watch weavers handcraft baskets from fine, grain-cut white oak at Day Basket Company, where workers use the same techniques the Day brothers used when they established the company in 1876. (Call 410-287-6100 for times.)

The main body of the town is a pleasant walk north of the town park, and the story of the town itself begins at St. Mary Anne's Episcopal Church, whose current building dates to 1742. Besides serving as a house of worship, the church also operated as a school. During the War of 1812, the building was requisitioned as a military barracks. The surrounding graveyard, one of the oldest in Maryland, contains the graves of Susquehannock Indians from the 1600s. A street map on the town's website (*www.northeastmd.org/about.php*) identifies over a dozen historic buildings visible on a walking tour.

Behind the appealing facades of the business district's mix of refurbished buildings, shopkeepers sell all manner of fun and funky collectibles, gifts, antiques, items for your pet and delicious foodstuffs. The aroma of coffee lures visitors into Beans, Leaves, Etc., which also sells teas, spices, gourmet foods and gifts. The 5&10 Antique Market also features a coffee stand and sells delicious rich chocolates. General groceries are available at several markets in town. Boaters with access to a car can venture to one of several shopping centers along Route 40.

Aside from the Nauti Goose and Woody's, walkers can find an assortment of eateries, includings Woody's Ice Cream Alley and Steak and Main.

North East's calendar is dotted with celebrations of Americana and the Chesapeake Bay: in June, Flag Day (observed with music and a flag-raising ceremony) and the Mid-Atlantic Chevelle Show (the largest gathering of these classic cars on the East Coast); in August, Thunder on the Chesapeake Bay Poker Run, (a two-day event featuring prizes, contests and a banquet); in September, Yesterdays (a street festival highlighted by an auction, crafts, music and food), and in October, the Upper Bay Decoy Show.

Information: North East Chamber of Commerce, 800-CECIL95, *www.northeastchamber.org.*Cecil County Tourism, 800-232-4595, *www.seececil.org*; the Town of North East, 410-287-5801, *www.north eastmd.org*;

North East

⚓ **Marinas/Dockage**
　1 Municipal Docks
　2 Anchor Marina

⊙ **Points of Interest**
　3 Upper Bay Museum
　4 Day Basket Factory
　5 St. Mary Anne's Episcopal Church

❓ **Information (**Town Hall)

🍴 **Dining**
　6 Nauti Goose Saloon (patron dockage)
　7 Woody's Crab House
　8 Black Pearl Surf and Turf Grill
　9 Steak and Main
　10 Pickled Herring Pub

🍴 **Groceries/Carryout**
　11 North East Grocer
　12 Stop and Go

🍦 **Ice Cream**
　13 Woody's Ice Cream Alley

⚓ **Park**

Ⓜ **Marine Supplies**

🏪 **Shopping Center**

📖 **Library**

℞ **Pharmacy**

✉ **Post Office**

🧺 **Laundromat**

🎡 **Playground**

🚻 **Public Restrooms**

Lower Susquehanna *continued from page 40*

restricted area, which is also patrolled.

After red "2", the channel veers to port in the eighth of a mile or so between "2" and green "3". It is imperative you stay between the buoys as the channel threads its way through the Flats. This should be no problem, however, since the channel is approximately 200 feet wide—though sharing the channel with a barge on its way to or from Havre de Grace can make it feel a little tight. After green "9" you'll spot the 38-foot Fishing Battery Light, which was taken off the Coast Guard Light List in 2010. The facility is falling sadly into decay, but its little island remains a popular spot for overnight anchoring and swimming. The distance from green "3" to red "18" off Havre de Grace is about 4.3 miles.

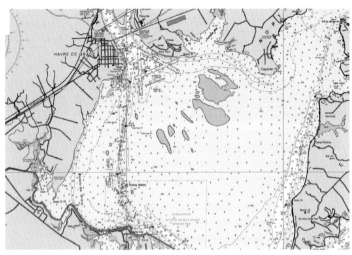

Susquehanna Flats; from NOAA Chart 12274—not to be used for navigation.

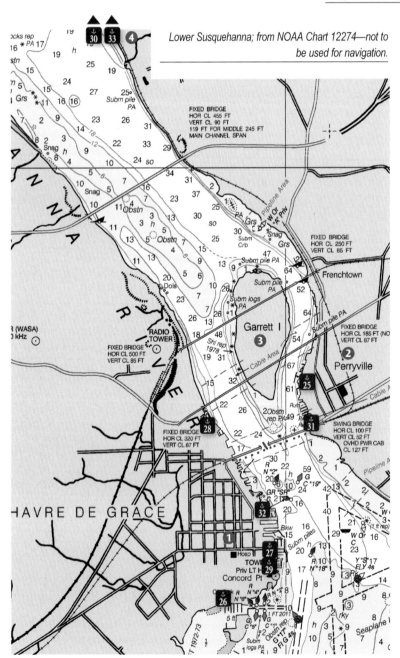

Lower Susquehanna; from NOAA Chart 12274—not to be used for navigation.

Havre de Grace

There are several marinas offering a full range of services at ❶ **Havre de Grace.** (The town was named by General Lafayette, and means "Harbor of Mercy" or "Pleasing Harbor" or "Harbor of Thanks"—you get the idea). Tidewater's ships store is located on the water at the marina, and West Marine, near Lewis Lane on Route 40, is a little more than a mile on foot from the City Yacht Basin. Boaters can find transient slips and a launch ramp ($10) at Havre de Grace City Yacht Basin, the municipal marina at Tydings Park. Heed the speed limit buoys that begin at the basin. Mean tidal range in this area is just under 2 feet, but you find plenty of depth.

Anchorages may be found on the west side of the channel, just beyond Tidewater Marina; just before the railroad bridge; and between the channel and city transient docks at Concord Point in about 6 to 8 feet of water—though wakes and a long southerly and easterly fetch can be an issue here. The water in front of Tidewater Marina is pretty much occupied by mooring balls. If you see a vacant one, call Tidewater on VHF to see if it's available. Wakes and noise from passing trains can sometimes be a bother here, but it's one more way to experience this lovely town. However you choose to visit, you'll find lots to see and do, including museums, parks, restaurants and a first-rate ice cream parlor.

Perryville

At the entrance to the Susquehanna River, you may be stymied by the first of four bridges that cross the navigable section of the river. This Amtrak bridge, used by high-speed Acela trains, has an official closed height of 52 feet at high tide, but often has less because of the rivers volatile levels. So study the tide boards carefully. This is a swing bridge, however, and will open with 24 hours notice. (Call 267-228-0540.)

Beyond the first bridge and across the river from Havre de Grace, ❷ **Perryville's** marinas offer guests most marine services. Owen's Marina and Perryville Yacht Club (formerly Riverwalk Marina) both provide access to town. In 2012, Perryville opened its Rodgers Tavern Dock and Floating Pier. The new facility has room for 12 transient boats, electric hook-ups and an 86-foot T-head for larger boats. Nearby is a community boat ramp. Historic Rodgers Tavern hosted many famous figures from America's Revolutionary past, including George Washington, who was a frequent guest. Call Perryville Town Hall at 410-642-6066 or visit *www.perryvillemd.org.*

Perryville is the only place in the area with train service within walking distance of the marinas. MARC rail service is offered from Perryville to Baltimore and Washington, D.C. For information and schedules, visit *www.mtamaryland.com.*

The railroad and Perryville have a long history. During the late 1800s, Perryville became a major rail center, serving as a central point for the Wilmington to Baltimore line. During the winter of 1853, tracks were laid across the ice on the Susquehanna River and used through the entire winter.

Garrett Island

❸ **Garrett Island** divides the river channel at this point. The heavily wooded island was once envisioned as a picturesque area for the campus of the first university in the Northern Hemisphere. Unfortunately, that early visionary, Edward Palmer, died in 1625, only three years after he acquired the island. For a short time, the island was known as Watson's Island, then Garrett's Island in honor of the railroad president who administered the Baltimore & Ohio Railroad during the Civil War. Now it's administered by the U.S. Fish & Wildlife Service as part of the wide-ranging BLACKWATER NATIONAL WILDLIFE REFUGE. If you choose the west channel around Garrett Island, pay particular attention to your depthfinder, since running aground on the rocks here could mean more than a bent shaft or damaged keel.

Port Deposit

The east channel around the island carries more than 50 feet of water. In fact, cruisers will find at least 14 feet of water in the channel all the way to ❹ **Port Deposit**, about 4 miles from flasher "A" at the mouth of the Susquehanna. There is at least 85 feet of vertical clearance under the three fixed bridges that cross the river between Perryville

continued on page 49

● On Premises
➤ Nearby

	MLW	Overnight Slips	Gas	Diesel	Propane	Electric	Showers	Laundry	Restaurant	Lodging	Pool	Pump-out	Ice	Groceries	Marine Supplies	Bait	Boat Repair	Haul-out Services	Launch Ramp	Wi-Fi	Other
Susquehanna River																					
Covenant Marine Susquehanna R./Perryville 410-642-6359; www.covenantmarine.com	10'+	●				●	●	➤	➤	➤	➤	●	●	➤	●	➤	●	●	●	●	
Havre De Grace City Yacht Basin Susquehanna R./Havre de Grace 410-939-0015; www.havredegracemd.com	6'	●	●	●	➤	●	●	➤	➤	➤		●	●	➤	➤	●	➤	➤		●	New piers, Promenade Grille, pump-out
Havre de Grace Marine Center, Log Pond Susquehanna R./Havre de Grace 410-939-2221; www.hdgmarinecenter.com	6'	●	➤	➤	➤	●	●	●	➤	➤		●	●	➤	➤		➤	➤	➤		Full brokerage; floating dock for transients
Havre de Grace Marine Center, Water Street Susquehanna R./Havre de Grace 410-939-2161 ; www.hdgmarinecenter.com	6'	●	➤	➤	➤	●	●	➤	➤	➤		➤	➤	●			●	●	➤		Full brokerage; floating docks
Penn's Beach Marina at Heron Harbor Susquehanna R./Havre de Grace 410-939-4444; www.pennsbeachmarina.com	5'-8'	●	➤	➤	➤	●	●		➤		●	●	●	➤	➤	➤	➤	➤	➤		Floating dock, up to 100 amp electric service
Port Deposit Marina Park Susquehanna R./Port Deposit 410-378-2121; www.portdeposit.org/visitor-s-center	8'		➤					➤	➤							➤			●		300 feet of free floating docks for transients
Rodgers Tavern Dock and Pier Susquehanna R./Perryville 410-642-6066; www.perryvillemd.org	7'	●			●			➤	➤	➤	➤		➤		➤				●		12 slips, 86-ft. T-head
Tidewater Marina Susquehanna R./Havre de Grace 410-939-0950 or 800-960-TIDE; www.TidewaterMarina.com	8'	●	●	●	➤	●	●	●	➤	●		●	●	➤	●	➤	●	●	●	●	Marine store; free shuttle, Wi-Fi, moorings
Tome's Landing Marina Susquehanna R./Port Deposit 410-378-3343; www.tomeslandingmarina.com	8'	●				●		➤	➤			●	●			●	➤	●	●	➤	Enclosed boatel; boat sales, factory auth. repairs

Port of Call
Havre de Grace

Havre de Grace's broad avenues and quiet streets exude old-fashioned charm, the kind inspired by grand Victorian homes with sweeping porches and shops fronting beautifully preserved buildings. Quality museums, art galleries, specialty shops and restaurants whose cuisines range from sophisticated to down-home make any cruise here worth the trip. But be prepared to walk. The town stretches along the shoreline at the mouth of the Susquehanna River, so it is long and narrow, with attractions at both ends.

Museums and parks are an integral part of the city. Northern-most is the Susquehanna Museum of Havre de Grace, housed in a restored locktender's house along the old Susquehanna & Tidewater Canal. Only vestiges of the canal remain, but its story is recounted at the museum through special events and in guided tours. Prominent on the town's southern perimeter is Concord Point Lighthouse (1827), the John O'Neill House (the restored home of the lighthouse keeper, across the street from the lighthouse) and the Havre de Grace Maritime Museum, where photographs, artifacts and wooden boat projects help preserve the region's past. Nearby, the Havre de Grace Decoy Museum's extensive collections and imaginative displays celebrate the traditional art of decoy carving.

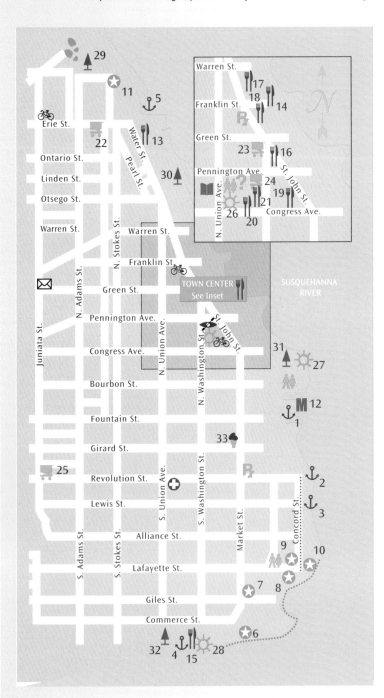

Havre de Grace

⚓ **Marinas/Dockage**
1 Tidewater Marina
2 Log Pond Marina
3 Penns Beach at Heron Harbor
4 Havre de Grace Yacht Basin
5 Havre de Grace Marina

⚙ **Points of Interest**
6 Boardwalk Promenade
7 Havre de Grace Decoy Museum
8 Havre de Grace Maritime Museum
9 John O'Neill House
10 Concord Point Lighthouse
11 Susquehanna Museum/Canal Lock House

Ⓜ **Marine Supplies**
12 Tidewater Marina

🍴 **Dining**
13 Price's Seafood
14 Tidewater Grille (dockage for patrons)
15 Promenade Grill
16 Laurrapin Grill
17 Ritz Gourmet Cafe
18 MacGregor's Restaurant
19 Lacucina Italian Restaurant
20 Java by the Bay
21 Vineyard Wine Bar

🛒 **Groceries**
22 Sam's Deli
23 Goll's Bakery
24 Farmer's Market (Sat. mornings, seasonal)
25 Royal Farm Store

☼ **Recreation/Entertainment**
26 Opera House Theater/Tidewater Players
27 *Lantern Queen* riverboat
28 Skipjack *Martha Lewis*

▲ **Parks**
29 North Park
30 Jean S. Roberts Memorial Park
31 Hutchins Memorial Park & Fishing Pier
32 Tydings Park

🍦 **Ice Cream**
33 Bomboy's Ice Cream and Candy

🚲 **Bicycles**
■ **Library**
⊙ **Hospital**
···· **Boardwalk Promenade**
···· **Sidewalk Promenade**
🐾 **Loop Trail starts** (dog-friendly)
? **Information/Visitor Center**
✉ **Post Office**
℞ **Pharmacy**
🚻 **Public Restrooms**
🛶 **Kayak Rentals**

Not far from the museums, a wooden promenade provides expansive views of the Susquehanna and glimpses of wildlife. At the promenade's southern end sits Tydings Park, an oasis that includes a launch ramp, pavilion, snack bar, picnic grounds (with grills) and a colorful playground.

The Visitor Center on Pennington Ave. offers guide maps to help you explore the historic district's many sights and easily locate restaurants and shops. Activities abound. Enjoy a cruise aboard the skipjack *Martha Lewis* or the *Lantern Queen*, a replica Mississippi riverboat (public dinner cruises); attend a production by the Tidewater Players; parasail above the city; arrange for a taxi (410-939-0900) to one of five nearby public golf courses, including Bulle Rock, home of the LPGA championship; go for a kayak tour of the Susquehanna Flats offered by Chesapeake Cycle & Sport (410-939-TREK) or have them deliver a rental bike to your boat; Biller's Bikes (443-502-2377) makes bike deliveries as well.

Establishments of all kinds line the architecturally diverse business district, including several grand Victorians that now serve as B&Bs (*www.bedandbreakfast.com*). Look for the Saturday morning farmers' market (May-October). For sweets, try Goll's Bakery.

The variety of dining in Havre de Grace is as wide as the mansion-lined streets in the city's historic neighborhoods. Whether you're sitting down to a traditional crab feast at Price's Seafood or grabbing a savory snack in one of the neighborhood bars, you're sure to find your surroundings as pleasing as your meal. The Tidewater Grille is the only downtown restaurant with dockage for diners, but an assortment of dining options are within easy walking distance of any marina. For a special treat, stop by Bomboy's on Market St., where you will find both wonderful hand-made candy and ice cream.

Beginning in May, local businesses stay open until 8 p.m. on the first Friday of the month, and downtown bustles with activities and music. The beat continues at the Friday Concert in the Park series held during July and August in Tydings Park, or tune in to acoustic performers at the Maritime Museum on Monday nights in July.

Many events on Havre de Grace's busy calendar reflect the arts and the city's heritage. Among the calendar's highlights are the citywide Decoy and Wildlife Art Festival in May; an old-fashioned Fourth of July celebration (parade, carnival and fireworks); in August, the city's Seafood Festival and the Maritime Museum's Mari-Fest (living history displays, boat building, music and the nearly-famous Crab Soup Cook-off); and in September, the Decoy Museum's Duck Fair (artists, carvers, and retriever dog demonstrations).

Information: Havre de Grace Office of Tourism & Visitor Center, 800-851-7756 or 410-939-2100, *www.hdgtourism.com*; Harford County Office of Tourism, 888-544-4695, *www.harfordmd.com*.

Port Deposit continued from page 47

continued from page 47

and Port Deposit.

Port Deposit was once a leading supplier of granite, evidence of which can be seen in the cliffs rising above the river and in the town's lovely terraced gardens. At the southern end of town, Marina Park features a public launch ramp (fee charged) and 300 feet of first-come, first-served free dock space for visiting boats along a floating dock. (There is no electric hook-up.) Anglers can buy bait and tackle at a shop across the street. No amenities are available at the town facility, but busy nextdoor Tome's Landing Marina, a boatel and repair facility, offers gas and marine supplies, though no transient slips. Nearby Lee's Landing Restaurant provides docking for patrons.

Port Deposit is about as far as you can cruise on the Susquehanna, and a glance upstream will reveal the reason—rocks. Captain John Smith, who explored the river in 1608, named this portion of it "Smith's Fayles."

The Susquehanna alone is responsible for half of the Bay's supply of fresh water. But in times of heavy rains, the Susquehanna sends a tremendous burden of silt, sewage and debris into the Bay. The water level at Port Deposit rises too when the upriver Conowingo Dam opens its floodgates, so the town has a muli-level warning system for its residents.

Sassafras River

The **Sassafras River** is one of the most beautiful rivers on the Eastern Shore. Because of its east-west alignment, sunrises and sunsets are spectacular as light pours into its basins. Gently rolling emerald hills, with an occasional splash of golden wheat, blend with steep wooded banks rising to heights of 80 feet above the winding river. Around each bend awaits a new and exciting panorama, from historic homes to the marinas of Georgetown.

The Sassafras's grass-fringed creeks and rolling fields have land titles that go back to the original grants from Charles II and Lord Baltimore. (Kent County, on the river's south shore, has some of the richest farmland in the nation.) Here you can enjoy the grouchy, deep-throated conversations of blue herons and bullfrogs, the thickets of shadbush and dogwood, and the occasional glimpse of coyotes, bald eagles, fox and white-tail deer.

Unlike many of the tantalizing but shoal tributaries on the Eastern Shore, the deep-water Sassafras can accommodate boats with drafts up to 13 feet. Though brackish at the mouth, the water soon freshens, which means no sea nettles and excellent swimming. The fishing is good, too, including good-sized rockfish. Bass tournaments are a local fixture.

Visit the Sassafras on a weekday, if at all possible. If you

Sassafras River; from NOAA Chart 12274—not to be used for navigation.

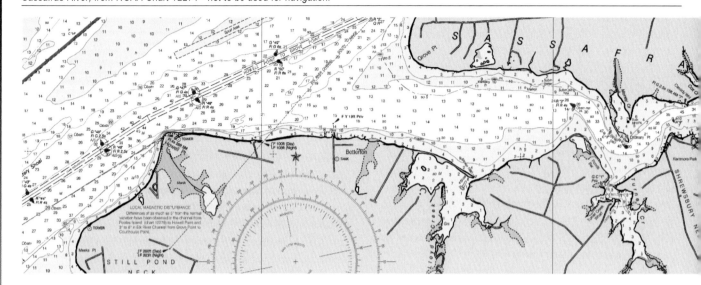

Sassafras River *continued*

arrive on a weekend, chances are you will encounter a "wall" of boats coming at you. Negotiating the wakes can sometimes be more trouble than negotiating a summer Bay squall. (There are speed buoys between Ordinary Point and Knight Island to reduce wake.) But no matter when you go, the Sassafras River is definitely worth the effort.

The mouth of the Sassafras from Grove Point to Howell Point opens wide (over 3 miles) and deep with water navigable all the way across. Five miles from its mouth, the river squeezes down to a half-mile wide at a flashing red "2", which marks a long shoal at a sharp southerly bend. This buoy and the next three (a green "3" and "5" and a red "6") are in fairly deep water, but give the navigational aids upriver a wide berth, since they rest directly on the shoals they mark.

Betterton

About two miles from Howell Point, ❶ **Betterton** appears on the south shore of the Sassafras. Most of the riverbanks are hilly bluffs, but Betterton is located in a break in the bluffs that opens into a valley with about a half-mile of sandy beach.

For the first half of the 20th century, Betterton on the Bay was the Chesapeake's foremost beach resort, boasting a boardwalk, a dance pavilion and numerous hotels and cottages filled with vacationers who arrived by steamboat. Like other Bay resorts tied to the steamboat era, Betterton thrived as long as the steamboats did. With the opening of the Bay Bridge in 1952, automobiles began to carry families to more distant resorts and Betterton slid into decline. Still, Betterton today is perfect for cruisers seeking a swimming beach where sea nettles are almost unheard of. Although the old hotels are gone, the town boasts a 500-foot boardwalk, a bathhouse, a shady picnic grove, benches and a hilltop pavilion.

A county-operated fishing and docking pier features 12 feet of water at its end, slips for 11 transient boats, a fishing

jetty with a surfaced walkway and a boat ramp at the east end of the beach. To top it all off, the beach has a gradual drop-off, the sand is plentiful and waves are non-existent, except for occasional ship wakes.

Boaters are welcome to use the dock and slips on a first-come, first-served basis. (Call the Kent County Office of Public Works at 410-778-7439.) You are allowed to dock for one night only, but there is no fee for the slips. (The dock is relatively exposed, so check weather conditions before deciding to tie up for the night.) Powerboats may not land on the main swimming beach, but should be able to get close to shore west of the beach (watch for the marked rocky shoal). Many boaters simply anchor and swim or dinghy ashore.

Condominiums have been built where hotels once stood overlooking the east end of the beach. Still, most of the town consists of big, rambling homes that once housed the many summer visitors who arrived by steamboat. (For information on Betterton, visit *www.kentcounty.com*.)

As an anchorage, Betterton is wide open to northerlies and westerlies, but it does lie in the lee of the Bay's predominant summer southerlies. Other more protected anchorages are to be found nearby if unsettled weather threatens.

Lloyd Creek

❷ **Lloyd Creek** has become one of the most popular spots on the Sassafras for local boaters to swim and picnic on a hot summer afternoon. But unless you have local knowledge or a shallow-draft boat, you might want to use your dinghy for exploration. Inside its leafy confines, you'll discover a slice of the world that seems far removed from the humdrum of every day life. Just be mindful of the strong current at the entrance.

Lloyd Creek is difficult to find because a long spit of land runs for almost a mile across its mouth, leaving only a narrow opening at its east end. Don't mistake this entrance for the one at Ponds Bar, another spit of land approximately a half-

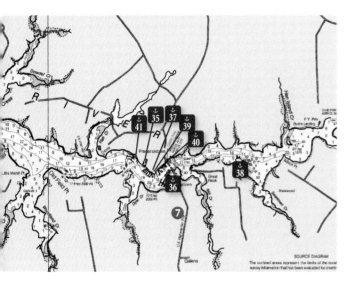

Ordinary Point

Before the rip-rapping of its shoreline sent visitors elsewhere, the sandy beach along ❸ **Ordinary Point** was probably the most popular anchorage on the Sassafras. Ordinary Point was named for the tavern, or "ordinary," that operated there a couple of centuries ago in conjunction with a ferry. A solitary pair of stone steps remains on the beach, perhaps a remnant of the tavern or a later structure. The spot has also been known as Ornery Point, either because sailors had so much trouble weathering the point in a head wind, or—as some maintain—that's how the locals pronounced Ordinary.

Names notwithstanding, just inside the point at the mouth of **Money Creek** you will see the sandy beach. In years past, you'd find two to three dozen boats anchored here on a weekend, but recent erosion-control measures have effectively cut off access to the beach, sending boaters instead to Lloyd Creek. Despite that, the point's protected east side offers a good anchorage, with depths of 5 and 6 feet and a nice sandy bottom. Depending on how far into the creek you go (it shoals rapidly from 4 feet to 1), the point provides a degree of protection from upstream wakes.

Turner Creek

Directly across from Ordinary Point you'll find ❹ **Turner Creek**, one of the northern Bay's loveliest anchorages. The creek has a deep but narrow entrance. The channel is well-marked, so simply keep to the path. There is a small privately maintained green marker C "1" to starboard just inside the creek's entrance. Keep slightly to starboard of the center of the creek to avoid the sand spit to port, since a good portion of it is covered at high

mile before the next creek on the south shore, Turner Creek.

Lloyd Creek's constricted entrance and tricky current can be daunting to first-time explorers, but just stay close to the high bank on the port side. While charts indicate 8 feet of water, some cruisers have reported more. Immediately upon entering the creek turn to starboard to avoid shoaling directly ahead. Without making this turn, the unwary can suddenly find themselves at depths of 18 inches or less.

The "best" depths, 2 to 4 feet, can be found along the spit separating Lloyd Creek from the Sassafras, but even inching your way cautiously toward the tiny wooded island near the west bank can result in a grounding, whether you're in a dinghy or a deadrise.

● *On Premises*
➤ *Nearby*

		MLW	Overnight Slips	Gas	Diesel	Propane	Electric	Showers	Laundry	Restaurant	Lodging	Pool	Pump-out	Ice	Groceries	Marine Supplies	Bait	Boat Repair	Haul-out Services	Launch Ramp	Wi-Fi	Other
Sassafras River																						
5	**Duffy Creek Marina** Sassafras R. 410-275-2141; www.duffycreekmarina.com	6'	●	●	●		●	●	●	➤	➤	●	●	●	➤	●	➤	●	●	●	●	Secluded wake-free basin, beach, picnic areas
6	**Georgetown Yacht Basin** Sassafras R./Georgetown 410-648-5112; www.gybinc.com	13'	●	●	●	●	●	●	●	●	●	●	●	●	●	●	➤	●	●	●	●	moorings, 110-ton lift, full service, Kitty Knight House, beach, kayaks
7	**Granary Marina** Sassafras R./Georgetown Harbor 410-648-5112; www.gybinc.com	12'	●	➤	➤	➤	●	●	●	➤	➤	●	●	●	➤	➤	➤	➤	➤	●	Slips to 140ft; 240v, 100amp. Sassafras Grill, Granary restaurants
8	**Gregg Neck Boat Yard** Sassafras R./Swantown Crk 410-648-5360 or 410-648-5173	10'	●			➤	●	●	➤	➤	➤		●	●		●		●	●	●	●	Used boats, pile driving, crane, dock maintenance
9	**Sailing Associates** Sassafras R./Georgetown Harbor 410-275-8171 or 275-8172; www.sailingassociates.com	12'	●	➤	➤		●	●	➤	➤	➤	●	●	●	●	➤	●	●	➤	●	Deep slips; moorings, beach, picnic area, full service, pet friendly
0	**Sassafras Harbor Marina** Sassafras R./Georgetown 410-275-1144; www.sassafrasharbormarina.com	12'	●	➤	➤	●	●	●	●	●	●	●	●	●	●	●	●	●	➤	●	Covered slips, floating docks, activities ctr, 70-ton lift, Wi-Fi
1	**Skipjack Cove Yachting Resort** Sassafras R./Georgetown 410-275-2122 or 1-800-BOATSLIP; www.skipjackcove.com	12'+	●	●	●	➤	●	●	●	●	●	●	●	●	●	●	●	➤	●	➤	●	Pool, tennis, Wi-Fi, lounge, exercise room

Turner Creek *continued*

tide. Then stay along the beach to the right (10 feet of water carries to the marsh line) and continue to follow the private markers. Inside you'll see a small bay and, ahead, an old granary set on a county pier. There is also a public launch ramp at TURNER'S CREEK PARK. (A county permit is required to use the ramp. Call the Office of Public Works at 410-778-7439.) You may tie up overnight at the pier (no electricity) or temporarily along the bulkhead in an area reserved for recreational use. (Workboats also occupy the bulkhead.) Depths at the pier and bulkheads are 10 to 15 feet. The "No Docking" sign prohibits overnight dockage at the bulkheads only.

A good place to anchor is off the bulkheaded area, although depths are less. Several boats of moderate size can fit comfortably in here. Shallower-draft boats can move farther upstream where the water is about 4 feet deep. The anchorage affords excellent protection, and the scenery is at its upper Eastern Shore best.

The 143-acre Turner's Creek Park (410-778-1948) features a large pavilion on the hillside overlooking the anchorage. It's suitable for cruise gatherings or private picnics. You can tie up to use the heads, hike on the trails, fish off the pier or visit the KENT COUNTY FARM MUSEUM (*www.kentcounty.com/farmmuseum*). The restrooms, which are locked in the evening, are located on the ground level of Lathim House (c. 1700), perched high on the hill. There is sometimes a maintained port-a-potty on site.

Back Creek

You'll find another fine Sassafras anchorage across the river, behind **Knight Island** on ❺ **Back Creek**. The distance from Ordinary Point to the entrance of Back Creek is about 1¹⁄₂ miles. After passing red "6", you should see the tip of Knight Island—in fact a wooded peninsula rather than an island—

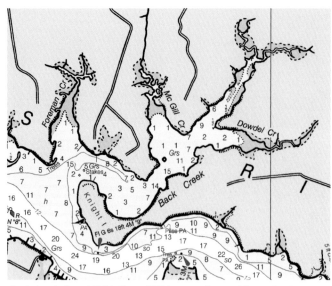

Back Creek; from NOAA Chart 12274—not to be used for navigation.

dead ahead. Between red "6" and red "8", the channel veers to starboard. Between these two buoys, begin easing to port and head to the entrance of Back Creek, careful to give Knight Island a wide berth by favoring the river's north bank until you have cleared the creek's entrance.

On the north shore, you'll find 5 to 10 feet of water. It's possible to anchor just inside the point of the island, but to play it safe head farther in. The anchorage in **Foreman Creek**, west of Back Creek, is a pretty spot, but the bottom appears to be soft mud, and in a strong westerly wind the anchor may drag.

On the bluffs just above the Back Creek anchorage you'll see MOUNT HARMON PLANTATION, whose 1730 brick manor house is open for tours (call 410-275-8819 for hours). Harmon recently opened a small landing in front of the plantation home, suitable for dinghies and small shallow-draft boats.

Woodland Creek

Three miles from Ordinary Point, between buoys red "10" and red "12" to starboard, lies ❻ **Woodland Creek**. Those new to cruising the Sassafras might miss this shallow but delightful anchorage and continue upriver instead. The majority of boats anchor in about 7 feet opposite Old Field Point on the creek's east shore. Farther into the creek you'll find **Daffodil Island** with 4 feet of water near its northeast shore. For deeper drafts. a good anchorage lies across the river, north and east of red "10". A three-quarter-mile stretch of uninhabited shoreline offers deep water up to a sandy beach. Tall, wooded cliffs give protection from all but southerly winds.

Georgetown

❼ **Georgetown**, on the south bank of the Sassafras in Kent County, and **Fredericktown**, on the north bank in Cecil County, are believed to be named for King George II and his son Frederick, the Prince of Wales. The area encompassed

continued on page 54

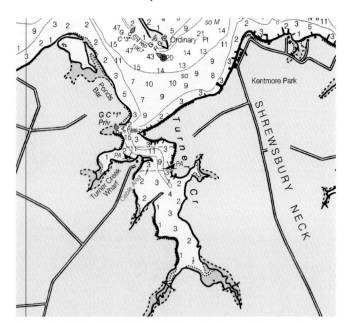

Turner Creek; from NOAA Chart 12274—not to be used for navigation.

Port of Call

Georgetown

Where else could you spend the day cruising up one of the Chesapeake's most beautiful and unspoiled river's before slipping into one of several first-class marinas or securing to a mooring ball in one of the Bay's great natural harbors, and then enjoy an evening ashore, dine on homestyle food in a historic house or a gourmet meal in an unasuming little restaurant at the edge of the water—all the while being treated to one of the finest sunsets around? Georgetown on the Sassafras River, of course! Here you'll find no traffic, no hustle and bustle, but instead a bushel-full of cruising amenities and the good company of hundreds of boats of every size and description.Yes, that's Georgetown, Md., or more accurately, the twin un-cities of Georgetown and Fredericktown, known to boaters simply as Georgetown. In fact, the two lie about nine miles upriver, Georgetown on the south side and Fredericktown across the bascule bridge on the north side.

Although both communities were established before the Revolutionary War as shipping ports for tobacco and then grains, both were effectively razed by the British during the War of 1812 and were never rebuilt. Instead, in the centuries that followed, the twin settlements slowly shifted from a commercial shipping site to a favorite anchorage for the emerging legion of yachtsmen. And so it remains today, with four busy marinas, a large mooring field, several fine restaurants, a couple of well-stocked ship's stores, repair facilities second to none, an ice cream shop, a nice little beach, a good-sized gift shop and an open invitation to kick back and relax.

But don't be mislead. Although Georgetown has a lot to offer the boater, it doesn't have any kind of downtown shopping district or neigh-borhoods of interesting old homes. No, the British took care of all that when they burned the shops and houses . . . except, famously for the house of the redoubtable Kitty Knight. According to legend, she pleaded with the British to spare her home, which they did, as well as the one next to it. Now the two buildings are connected and welcome hundreds of visitors every month as one of the Chesapeake's most famous eating establishments, the Kitty Knight House. The sunset from the porch is a legend in itself. Slightly upstream, Norm's Kitchen, part of the Sassafras Habor Marina complex, offers comfort food reinvented; just upstream from that the Granary & Sassafras Grill offers inventive dishes as well. And finally, the resort-style Skipjack Harbor Marina serves great crab cakes and more at Signals.

For groceries, pharmacy, liquor store and plenty of antiques shops, borrow a marina bicycle or take a hike into charming Galena, just over a mile south on Rte. 213. On the way, you can stop to fortify yourself at local favorite Twinnies restaurant.

Information: www.kentcounty.com and the marina websites

Georgetown

⚓ **Marinas/Dockage**
  1 Skipjack Cove Yachting Resort
  2 Sassafras Harbor Marina
  3 Georgetown Yacht Basin
  4 Duffy Creek Marina
  5 Granary Marina
  6 Sailing Association

⊕ **Points of Interest**
  7 Kitty Knight House

🍴 **Dining**
  1 Signals Restaurant
  2 Norm's Kitchen at Sassafras Harbor Cafe
  7 Kitty Knight House
  5 Granary Restaurant & Sassafras Grill

🍦 **Ice Cream**
  3 HarborView Ice Cream

🛏 **Lodging**
  7 Kitty Knight House Inn

Sassafras Harbor Marina

1George St., PO Box 68, Georgetown, MD * 410-275-1144

Travel up the Sassafras River into
Georgetown Harbor, we are on the
north shore just before the bridge.
TRANSIENTS WELCOME!

Full Service Marina

Open & Covered Slips * Service Department
70 Ton Travel Lift * Private A/C Bath Houses
Pool * Banquet Hall * Restaurant * Yacht Sales

Harbor Marine Store & Heron's Nest Gift Shop
~ Open year round ~
Parts, Electronics, Apparel and much more!

e-mail: shmarina@baybroadband.net
www.sassafrasharbormarina.com

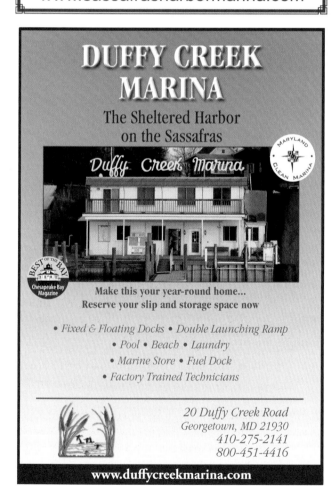

DUFFY CREEK MARINA

The Sheltered Harbor
on the Sassafras

Make this your year-round home...
Reserve your slip and storage space now

• *Fixed & Floating Docks* • *Double Launching Ramp*
• *Pool* • *Beach* • *Laundry*
• *Marine Store* • *Fuel Dock*
• *Factory Trained Technicians*

20 Duffy Creek Road
Georgetown, MD 21930
410-275-2141
800-451-4416

www.duffycreekmarina.com

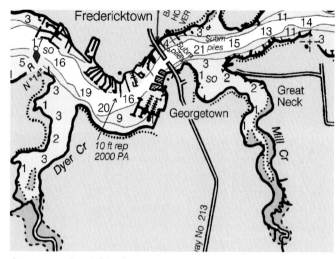

Georgetown; from NOAA Chart 12274—not to be used for navigation.

Georgetown *continued from page 52*

by the two villages, which are linked by the Route 213 draw-bridge, is commonly referred to as Georgetown.

All of the river's marinas (except one above the bridge) are handily clustered here, providing boaters with just about everything, including chartering. Georgetown Yacht Basin, Sassafras Harbor Marina and Skipjack Cove Yachting Resort all have on-site restaurants. Duffy Creek Marina has a boat ramp (call 410-275-2141 to reserve parking). Sailing Associates offers moorings and slips. And the Granary Marina offers some of the best sunsets around. The tidal range is 2 feet.

Georgetown Yacht Basin offers visiting cruisers a number of services, among them moorings for short- or long-term rental, loaner bicycles, a rental van and a new water taxi service that serves the harbor (hail them on VHF channel 71). Georgetown harbor's Fourth of July boat parade and fireworks are a perennial favorite.

Perhaps Georgetown's most famous resident was Miss Kitty Knight, who reportedly convinced British soldiers to spare her house when they burned the town in the War of 1812. Her home now serves as a restaurant and inn. Nearby is the Harbor View Ice Cream shop.

Georgetown Yacht Basin sells basic food items in its small marina store, while Sassafras Harbor Marina has a good-sized ship's store, as well as a gift shop and a restaurant. An organic farm offers vegetables in season on Fridays and Saturdays. Additionally, Sassy River Market (formerly Otwell's) is less than 2 miles away (410-648-5111).

The Route 213 bascule bridge (closed clearance 4 feet MHW) opens on request except during rush hours during boating season. Off season, it opens on request except at night, when it needs 6-hour notice. Although a short run, the river above the bridge is delightful. The channel is deep (10 to 12 feet) in the middle of the river. Chartbooks generally end less than a mile above the bridge, but cruisers will find at least 9 feet of water to Gregg Neck Boat Yard, one of the last classic boatyards on the northern Bay. By dinghy, you can explore all the way to U.S. Route 301.

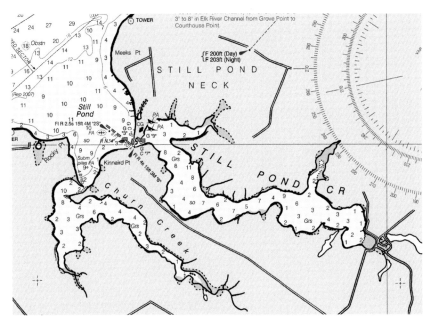

Still Pond; from NOAA Chart 12274—not to be used for navigation.

Still Pond

Although exposed to thunderstorms from the west, **Still Pond**'s wide basin provides one of the best anchorages around on a sultry summer weekend. This broad indentation on the Eastern Shore is located a couple miles south of the Sassafras River, a couple miles north of Worton Creek, and about five miles northeast of Pooles Island. With its easy access off the Bay, mostly jellyfish-free waters and a ring of high bluffs to protect boaters from easterly and southerly winds, Still Pond is a perennial favorite of cruisers.

The best side of the Still Pond anchorage is the southwest shore, where deep water reaches almost to its sandy beach. Any summer weekend will find boats lined along this entire stretch. Swimming, fishing, crabbing and shelling are popular pastimes for the gunkholers who take full advantage of Still Pond's 9- to 11-foot depths. Water-skiers, personal watercraft and children on rafts weave among the many anchored boats.

Churn Creek branches off the southern shore of the Still Pond basin. Some cruisers like to dinghy over to the entrance of this creek and, on inner tubes and floats, gently ride its swift current through the narrow cut. Others with inflatable and fiberglass kayaks stowed on deck enjoy the large pond they find after struggling over the sandbars at the entrance, and families love the sandy beach along Churn Creek's south shore. Just be careful your outboard doesn't "churn" up the sand getting in.

To escape threatening weather or the party scene in the main anchorage, skippers of shallow draft vessels often head for nearby **Still Pond Creek**. The creek is surrounded by high bluffs, which create a scenic, protected anchorage, though it could be an uncomfortable spot on hot muggy summer days

if a breeze can't find its way in.

To reach Still Pond Creek, head east down the center of the basin, toward the indentation in the cliffs. As you approach the basin's eastern shore, the long sand spit extending into Still Pond Creek's narrow entrance becomes clear. A series of buoys marks the channel in, which generally carries 4 to 7 feet. Some boaters report a "hump" lying midway between the marks at the creek's entrance, with as little as 2 feet at low tide.

The space between the sandbar to port and the beach to starboard is very narrow. Recent advice from cruisers suggests that you stay close to "G9" then head to starboard to stay close to the piers, where the deepest water lies. Markers are moved about, and some shoals are no longer marked at all, so watch what you see in the water rather than relying exclusively on your chartplotter or charts.

Farther upstream the creek broadens considerably. Many boaters drop anchor here in 5 to 8 feet of water. You may find enough water to carry you more than a mile down the three-mile-long creek. There's little traffic, and many boats just hunker down right in the center of the creek—making sure to show an anchor light, of course.

Still Pond Creek's serenity is inviting. Except for a few farms, the creek's heavily wooded shore appears unspoiled. Not far inside the southern entrance, boaters might glimpse a brick Georgian mansion, Brayton, just visible through the trees in summer.

Worton Creek

Located right off the Bay, **Worton Creek** lies just south of Still Pond and roughly east of Pooles Island. The narrow width of the Bay here requires boaters to keep a lookout for commercial traffic. Remember, ships and tug-and-barge units move along at a spritely clip on this stretch of the shipping channel. Boaters must stay clear.

If you're heading for Worton Creek from the north or south, you can follow the line of buoys running along the Eastern Shore, staying just east of the main shipping lanes in plenty of water. But keep a sharp watch, for some of the shallower-draft commercial vessels also run outside the channel.

The broad approach to Worton Creek lies well outside of the shipping channel's range. Protected from the north and east by a long cliff that runs from Worton Point to the bottleneck of the creek's entrance, the area along this approach is a favorite anchorage with good holding for both powercraft and sailboats. (Watch for ospreys and eagles soaring above the cliff.) With its open west side, Worton usually affords a breeze at night and freedom from bugs. The water is deep, 9 feet tapering to 6 feet within 400 feet of the shore. Only a strong westerly will give

Worton Creek continued

you problems, as the forested creek offers adequate protection from northerly and easterly winds.

When the gentle curve of the land to the north is bright with the setting sun, the sandy beach will invite you for a stroll. At various points along the way you'll find sections of timbers, some bolted together, suggesting a shipwreck many years ago. A most delightful feature is the Bay bottom itself. Standing neck deep, you'll find yourself walking on sand, not slimy mud.

To enter the creek proper, head toward red "2". Dead ahead you can see Green Point Landing Marina. Continue to green "3" and "5." You'll find 9 feet of water in this part of the channel, gradually decreasing as you wind your way in. Keep close to the buoys, but don't cut straight between them; a small annoying shoal juts out from the northeast shore between these marks. Once past the navigational aids, stay well to the south side of Worton to avoid a very shoal dredge spoil section in the center. At "5", the channel seems to pass right over a shoal area, but you won't find it registering on your depthsounder and locals say it doesn't exist.

As you round the long sand spit to starboard, you'll see a small fleet of boats on moorings. (The spit is private property and is posted.) There are lovely anchorages in the two coves here. Surrounded by trees, they offer protection to boats riding out a storm. Before proceeding, you might want to anchor and enjoy a refreshing, nettle-free swim. Only on rare occasions, such as an extended drought, does a sea nettle ever find its way this far north.

The next marina (also to port) is the Wharf at Handy's Point. About a half mile farther up the creek is Worton Creek Marina, which has been catering to boaters since 1949. Worton Creek and Green Point Landing marinas have fuel and marine supplies. All three have ice, restrooms and showers.

Buck Neck Landing, a public dock used by local watermen, is adjacent to Worton Creek Marina. The Harbor House Restaurant, perched on a wooded bluff overlooking Worton Creek Marina, is open for dinner year round, but closed on Mondays. Boaters can dinghy in to the landing and walk up.

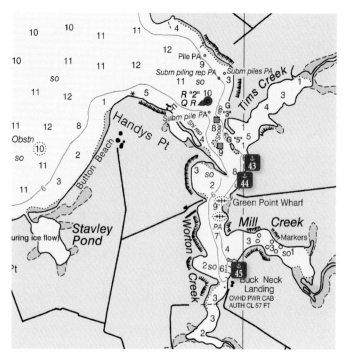

Worton Creek; from NOAA Chart 12278—not to be used for navigation.

Reservations are recommended (410-778-0669). The restaurant has operated for over fifty years, and its reputation for fine fare is undiminshed.

Worton Creek carries 6 to 9 feet to the Wharf at Handy's Point. But where charts show 7 feet near Mill Creek, cruisers report only 5 to 6 feet at low tide to Worton Creek Marina. If you'd rather drop the hook, anchoring space is available opposite the marinas on the western side of the creek. You can row ashore to the marina's floating dinghy dock and make use of its facilities for a small fee.

Tims Creek on the north shore offers an enticing anchorage for small boats. You'll find powerboats anchored stern to the beach here. To enter, start cutting in about halfway between green "5" and a small private green marker, and stay close to the east bank for approximately 50 yards. Then

● On Premises
➤ Nearby

Worton & Fairlee Creeks

	MLW	Overnight Slips	Gas	Diesel	Propane	Electric	Showers	Laundry	Restaurant	Lodging	Pool	Pump-out	Ice	Groceries	Marine Supplies	Bait	Boat Repair	Haul-out Services	Launch Ramp	Wi-Fi	Other
Great Oak Landing ⚓42 Fairlee Cr.; 410-778-5007 or 800-LANDING; www.mearsgreatoaklanding.com	8'	●	●	●		●	●	●	●	●	●	●	●	●	●		●	●	●	●	Tennis, hot tub, basketball, volleyball, pool
Green Point Landing ⚓43 Worton Cr. 443-480-2507	10'	●	●	●		●	●					●	●		●		●	●	➤	●	Full-service marina, slips and moorings, Wi-Fi
Wharf at Handy's Point ⚓44 Worton Cr. 410-778-4363; www.thewharfathandyspoint.com	9'	●	➤	➤	➤	●	●		●	➤	➤	➤	●	●	➤	●		●		●	full-service yard 35-ton lift
Worton Creek Marina ⚓45 Worton Cr. 410-778-3282; www.wortoncreek.com	6'	●	●	●	●	●	●	●	●			●	●	●	●		●			●	60' slips, picnic area, 25- and 70-ton lift, pool, restaurant

make your turn to port and cross the creek until you are behind the sandbar.

This area of Kent County, bounded on the north by the Sassafras and on the south by the Chester River, has a rich, water-influenced history. In 1695, Georgetown and Chestertown were both designated official Ports of Entry (complete with customs houses and crown agents). The shoreline in between these towns, including Worton Creek, was thick with smugglers and contraband. It is easy to see how attractive this area's secluded creeks and inlets were to shippers who wanted to avoid paying duty on goods arriving from abroad. Although housing developments have sprouted up here and there along the shoreline, there are still empty stretches remaining with only an occasional home or colonial foundation visible.

These shores also saw the landing of British soldiers during the War of 1812. The Battle of Caulk's Field resulted from an unexpected clash between Kent County militia and British regulars. The British frigate *Menelaus* had dropped a regiment onto the beach at Tolchester on the Bay, intent upon raiding and burning a nearby farm. But the invaders were spotted by a couple of locals who quickly delivered the news to the local militia, led by Philip Reed. The bloody battle that followed left the British commander, Peter Parker, mortally wounded and the Brits in full retreat. Local legend has it that the fallen Parker, was "embalmed" in a keg of rum and returned to his homeland.

Fairlee Creek

Approaching **Fairlee Creek** from the north, the most direct route is to stay at the eastern edge of the shipping channel. At Howell Point the channel comes in very close to shore (three-tenths of a mile off) and from this point it begins to veer to starboard. You'll find enough water to stay to port of the markers, being careful, of course, to give Worton Point a wide berth and to avoid the many crab pots located there.

You can continue southerly well outside the ship channel, as long as your crew keeps a lookout for the crab pots, until you arrive at red "2F" marking the narrow entrance into Fairlee Creek. At Fairlee, it is imperative that you follow the markers and believe them! You not only have to deal with a strong current, but also precious few navigation aids to guide the way through the 75-foot-wide entrance. However, you should find depths of about 8-foot in the channel's center.

In effect, from red "2F" you head right for the beach, then turn and run parallel to it until you get to the narrow bottleneck entrance of the creek itself. Entering Fairlee Creek is always an experience, particularly on a busy weekend. When the tide is rushing in with you, the sharp turn to starboard around a spit of land can be tricky to negotiate. The small boats crisscrossing the channel don't do much to help the situation, either. Once past the spit, you'll find plenty of water, as evidenced by the size of the boats in the creek. A popular spot for cruisers making the Intracoastal run, Fairlee Creek can be a busy place.

There is a good anchorage behind the sand spit. Fairlee

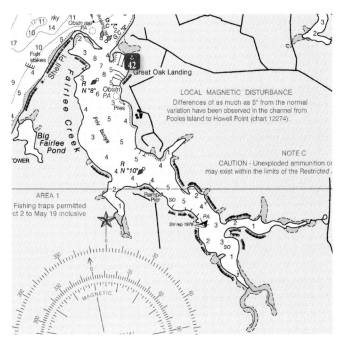

Fairlee Creek; from NOAA Chart 12278—not to be used for navigation.

Creek itself is a good anchorage, although too broad for protection in the blustery off-season. But on hot summer nights when the open water encourages a cooling breeze, it's just the ticket.

Inside the creek, Mears Great Oak Landing lies to port. It offers slips for transients, gas and diesel fuel, and a pumpout station. The country club-like complex provides a wide range of amenities, including restaurants and bars, lodging, a pool, golf and tennis. Don't be surprised if you see several palm trees along the shoreline as well.

The area inside the creek mouth, near the marina, is bustling—no place to stop on a weekend if you're looking for peace and quiet. For more seclusion, motor past the ever-present group of anchored yachts near the mouth. Upstream you'll find a fairly pristine, wooded environment in which to set the hook. The creek holds 5 feet of water, then 4, nearly to its head. For some reason, very few cruisers seem to venture much past the marina. However, they will find excellent holding conditions in the upper portion of the creek in soft to firm mud.

Leaving Fairlee Creek for points south, deep water lies east of Tolchester Channel and close to shore. But be on the lookout for fish traps, especially about a mile south of Fairlee Creek, where the northbound channel turns west, and again outside the channel as you head toward Swan Point Bar.

Bush River

Many cruisers avoid this section of the Western Shore because of its association with ABERDEEN PROVING GROUND (APG). They're missing a special treat. The **Bush River**—or Captain John Smith's "Willowbyes Flu"—is a scenic waterway. But restrictions *do* exist because of ordnance testing at Aberdeen

Bush River *continued*

Proving Grounds. A navigational restriction exists as well, namely, the squat 12-foot vertical clearance at the Amtrak railroad bridge about 7 miles upstream. Those who pass through during the rigid schedule of bridge openings, or those who have smaller or trailerable craft (there are several surfaced ramps above the bridge), are in for a pleasant surprise.

Bush River's entrance is marked by red nun "2", less than 2 miles east of the main shipping channel's "39" and "40", which are located south of the entrance to Still Pond. From nun "2" to green "3" the distance is 1¹/₂ miles. To starboard you pass Bush River Neck, site of one of the most important early settlements in the area—perhaps because of the richness of the soil, and perhaps because it could easily be defended against Indians. Baltimore Town on the Bush predates the present city of Baltimore by more than half a century, yet by 1773, Baltimore on the Bush was known only by tradition. Another town lost to history is Harford Town on Bush, where on March 22, 1774, the first term of court was held. Also at Harford Town on Bush, the French troops of Count de Rochambeau camped on their way north from the victory at Yorktown.

Aberdeen Proving Ground, which extends to both sides of the river, was established in 1917 after the original Ordnance Proving Ground at Sandy Hook, N.J., became inadequate. The establishment of Aberdeen, however, heralded the demise of one of the oldest and most historic playgrounds in the nation. From colonial times, the Susquehanna River Flats and the Bush and Gunpowder River Necks had been famous for duck and goose hunting and fishing. Many elaborate clubhouses were built to accommodate sportsmen, including Congressmen and other prominent individuals.

Now Aberdeen is the hub of all ordnance activities for the U.S. Army in research, development and testing of arms, ammunition, tanks and combat vehicles. APG restricts boating operations in portions of the Bush and Gunpowder rivers, but tries to keep to a regular munitions testing
schedule in order to enable boaters to enter restricted waters most of the time, when the ranges are quiet or when the testing is elsewhere. The best procedure is either to radio one of the patrol boats in the area when you arrive and request passage or call the Range Operations office (410-278-3971 or 410-278-2256) before making the trip. The assured quiet times are limited: Monday through Thursday, 5 p.m. to 7:30 a.m.; weekends, 5 p.m. Friday to 7:30 a.m. Monday; federal (not state) holidays, and from 5 p.m. the day preceding the holiday to 7:30 a.m. the day after the holiday. That said, both the Bush and Gunpowder are generally open for passage through. Once in a while, however, even quiet hours may give way to the demands of the testing schedule. (For more information, visit the center's website at *www.atc.army.mil*).

Once you do get inside, there are some more restrictions. Authorized uses of the restricted area include navigation to traverse waters, fishing, anchoring and water-skiing (no closer than 200 meters, or 220 yards, from the shoreline). However, going ashore in the restricted area is *strictly forbidden* and carries a heavy fine. Swimming, scuba diving and other out-of-boat activities other than water-skiing are also prohibited. The Bush and Gunpowder rivers' tributaries and creeks within APG waters (except Lauderick Creek on the Bush) are closed to the public at all times, and anchoring is prohibited in a few areas due to safety concerns. Fishing is prohibited on the eastern side of the Bush between Pond Point and Chelsea Chimney. (*See map on this page.*)

But despite all the restrictions, you'll find the Bush worth the trip . . . really. On the western shore of the Bush, there are anchorages at ❶ **Doves Cove** and ❷ **Lauderick Creek** below the railroad bridge. The minimum channel depth up to the bridge is 7 feet. The bridge is a bascule span with a horizontal clearance of 35 feet and a vertical clearance of 11.5 to 12 feet.

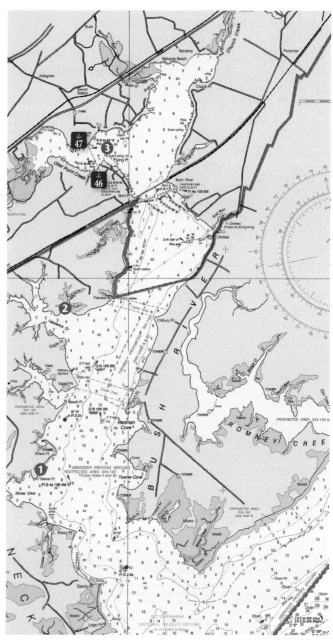

Bush River; from NOAA Chart 12274—not to be used for navigation.

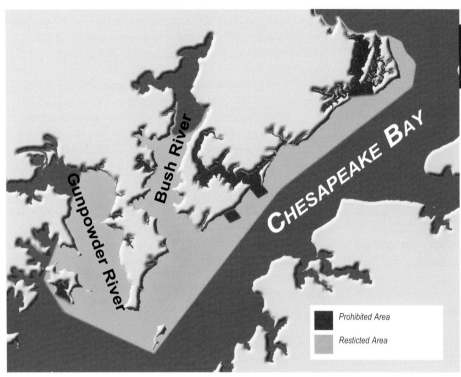

Restricted areas along the Gunpower and Bush rivers, as well as the Bay shoreline south of the Susquehanna Flats.

Gunpowder River

Like Bush, much of the **Gunpowder River** is bounded by Aberdeen Proving Ground. Some of the river's accessible shoreline, however, belongs to GUNPOWDER FALLS STATE PARK which, at 18,000 acres, is Maryland's largest. A favorite with anglers, it's a small-boat tributary, carrying at least 5-foot depths to the fixed railroad bridge (11 to 12 feet MHW vertical clearance) below Joppatowne. Gunpowder has two marinas, one up- and one downstream.

The river's name was likely inspired by the mineral saltpeter found along its shores in the 17th century and used for making gunpowder. Saltpeter Creek is a Gunpowder tributary. Another of the Gunpowder's natural resources, iron ore, became the foundation of a thriving industry here. From the mid-18th century into the 19th century, iron mines operated along the river, extracting ore that was then shipped to local furnaces.

On the Gunpowder, you'll likely encounter fishing skiffs and water-skiers—both permissable activities. The Proving Ground does have regulations governing restricted areas near the shoreline. Water-skiers, for example, cannot touch any dry or subaqueous land or come closer than 200 meters of any shoreline. Swimming and scuba diving are prohibited.

Each year a fixed schedule of limited openings is set for the entire boating season. (To see the schedule, visit the Bush River Yacht Club site, *www.bushriveryachtclub.org.*)

Beyond the bridge the Bush gives the appearance of a large lake, mirroring the gently rolling hills that dip into the tranquil depths. To port a half mile above the railroad bridge, ❸ **Otter Point Creek** carries depths of 3 feet for one mile above its entrance. Otter Point Creek Marina and Flying Point Marina provide surfaced ramps, repairs, slips and other marine services.

● *On Premises*
➤ *Nearby*

	MLW	Overnight Slips	Gas	Diesel	Propane	Electric	Showers	Laundry	Restaurant	Lodging	Pool	Pump-out	Ice	Groceries	Marine Supplies	Bait	Boat Repair	Haul-out Services	Launch Ramp	Wi-Fi	Other
Bush River																					
Flying Point Marina Bush R. 410-676-7311; www.flyingpointmarina.com	3'	●	●			●	●					●	●	●	●	●	●		●		Full boat service, canvas shop, parts, deli
Otter Creek Marina Bush R./Otter Point Cr. 410-688-3422; www.ottercreekmarina.com	5'	●	●			●	●						●	●		●	●	●	●		Full-service marina
Gunpowder River																					
Dundee Creek Marina Gunpowder R./Dundee Cr.; 410-335-9390; www.dnr.state. md.us/publiclands/central/gunpowderdundee.asp	4'		●			●						●	●		●	●			●		Snacks, motor & row-boat rentals, picnic area
Gunpowder Cove Marina/Marinemax Gunpowder R./Taylor's Cr. 410-679-5454; www.marinemax.com	5'	●	●			●	●	➤		➤	●	●	➤	●			●	●	➤		wet and dry storage

Gunpowder River *continued*

The Gunpowder's mouth is tucked between Hart-Miller Island to the southwest and Pooles Island to the southeast. While Hart-Miller is a mecca for pleasure craft, the uninhabited Pooles Island—originally called Powells Island after a member of Captain Smith's party—lies within the Proving Ground's off-limits area. Going ashore here is prohibited. The danger is unexploded ammunition and chemical weapons that lie under water or buried in sediments.

Exploring this picturesque and largely uninhabited river begins at lighted red "2G" at the mouth of the Gunpowder. From here continue northward for nearly a mile to red "4", then swing northeast to red "6". Be mindful to stay where it's known to be safe, particularly west of **Spry Island Shoal** and the shallows around **Rickett Point** on Gunpowder Neck. Numerous charted submerged logs, wrecks, snags and shoals lurk outside the channel to either side.

Once you've reached green "7", the wide Gunpowder surrounds you with about 6- to 9-foot depths. To port, west of green "9", two shallow tributaries enter: ❶ **Saltpeter Creek**, the southerly branch, and ❷ **Dundee Creek** to the north. The charts may show some areas of 6 and 7 feet as you enter, but depths generally run 3 to 5 feet and less, so proceed with caution.

The slips at Dundee Creek Marina in Gunpowder Falls State Park are reserved for long-term lease, but the facility offers pumpouts and gas for the boating public as well as snacks and marine and fishing supplies. Launch ramps provide anglers and nature lovers with access to the marshy waters of Dundee Creek as well as the Gunpowder itself.

Farther north along the Gunpowder, green "11" sits opposite Maxwell Point. In this area on the western shore is ❸ **Hammerman Day Use Area**, a segment of Gunpowder Falls State Park. This popular recreational site has trails, food concessions, picnic facilities, a playground and an extensive guarded beach for swimming. In addition, a separate beach is designated for water sports. If you don't have your own equipment, Ultimate Watersports has a concession where you can rent it. Pets are prohibited in the Hammerman area.

About six nautical miles from the mouth of the Gunpowder, and below the fixed railroad bridge, a line of buoys leads to the dredged channel (5 feet) to Taylors Creek and Joppatowne. Once inside **Taylors Creek**, you'll pass Mariner Point Park to starboard, a county facility featuring four boat ramps, three fishing piers, picnic pavilions and a small visitors center. Boaters can dinghy into shore here, but there are no tie-up facilities.

It's interesting that Old Joppa Town once rivaled Baltimore as a shipping port and even served as Baltimore County's seat from 1712–1768. Today's ❹ **Joppatowne**, a suburban community, is now part of Harford County and welcomes waterborne visitors at MarineMax Gunpowder Cove Marina. The facility has 290 wet slips and 400 high and dry, as well as accommodations for transients, gas, marine supplies and repairs. Stores and restaurants are nearby.

Beyond the railroad bridge, the ❺ **Bird River**, popular with kayakers, has depths of 2 to 3 feet and much less. The Gunpowder itself forms at Days Cove, where the Great Gunpowder Falls merges with Little Gunpowder Falls. The river is tamer than it once was, before dams built upstream stemmed much of its fury.

Seneca Creek

Seneca Creek opens directly on the Bay between the mouths of the Gunpowder and Middle rivers. Approaching Middle River, pick up Pooles Island Light nearly a mile south of Pooles Island. Set a course for flashing red "2G", which is just over 3 miles to the northwest. Continuing northwest be mindful of shoals and submerged piles south of Carroll Island's Lower Island Point. Proceed toward the 15-foot red flasher "2S", about a mile or so beyond "2G". The red and white stacks of the BG&E power plant make good landmarks for spotting Seneca Creek's marked channel which carries 5–8 feet for about 2 miles.

Gunpowder River, from NOAA Chart 12274—not to be used for navigation.

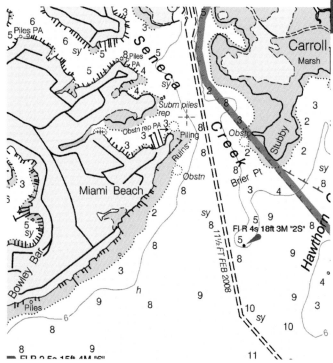

Seneca Creek; from NOAA Chart 12278—not to be used for navigation.

Middle River

While neither a rural retreat nor an urban center, **Middle River** is nevertheless a very popular homeport for legions of boaters and a convenient cruising stopover between the C&D Canal and Annapolis. It's easy to enter, free of hazards and bursting with marinas.

Historic Glenn L. Martin State Airport between Frog Mortor and Dark Head creeks, creates a kind of center point for the river's history and remains one of visiting cruisers' favorite diversions, although the only craft larger than private planes using the airport today are those of the Air National Guard. Once, however, the river thundered with the sound of sea planes, jets and cargo carriers taking off and landing from the world-famous aircraft manufacturer. Now the GLENN L. MARTIN MARYLAND AVIATION MUSEUM, located in Hangar 5, traces state aviation history as far back as 1784, when the nation's first balloon ascension took place in Baltimore. (Call 410-682-6122 for current hours.)

A 6-knot speed limit is enforced on Middle River at times of peak boat traffic. This is a residential area and the once-small cottages owned by Baltimoreans have been steadily upgraded. The river can get pretty active, with substantial traffic from small powerboats on summer weekends, but things should be fairly calm most nights.

Entering the channel, pick up green "3" about $1^1/_4$ mile north of Hart-Miller Island and note the green lighted fixed mark "5" marking Booby Point to port as you enter the river. Red "6" is located at the beginning of the channel near Bowley Bar. For most boaters, the channel is superfluous as good depths obtain throughout most of the river.

Sue Creek

❶ **Sue Creek**, on the south shore, is easiest to enter on a course from red "6" to green "1" next to Sue Island Yacht Basin to avoid shoals on both sides. Pass near green "1" at the entrance and stay close to the piers of the historic Baltimore Yacht Club to avoid the shallow area on the right. Long-legged sailboats can anchor near the club, while others can head upstream to attractive surroundings in 5 feet.

Many boats anchor in the cove in front of the power plant, one of the relatively few places to anchor in Seneca Creek. The creek is lined with residential properties and docks. Cruisers will find three marinas located on Seneca Creek: Beacon Light, which offers gas, some repair services but no transient slips; Goose Harbor, which also offers gas and repairs but no transient slips; and Porter's Seneca Marina, a 100-slip facility that accepts transients and offers gas, repair services, marine supplies and other amenities.

Despite the many residences along its shores, Seneca Creek remains a quieter tributary of the Middle River area than some of its neighbors. After a meal or a night of dancing ashore at one of Middle River's popular restaurants, you might want to move over to Seneca Creek for an overnight slip or anchorage. It is a beautiful refuge, located close to the Bay and with plenty of the options Bay boaters love.

● *On Premises*
➤ *Nearby*

Middle River/Seneca Creek	MLW	Overnight Slips	Gas	Diesel	Propane	Electric	Showers	Laundry	Restaurant	Lodging	Pool	Pump-out	Ice	Groceries	Marine Supplies	Boat Repair	Bait	Haul-out Services	Launch Ramp	Wi-Fi	Other
All Star Marine Middle R. 410-574-8281; *www.allstarmarineonline.com*	5'						●			●						●	●		●		Boatel, full-service marina, new & used sales
Baltimore Boating Center Middle R./Sue Cr. 410-687-2000; *www.baltimoreboatingcenter.com*	5.5'	●	➤	➤		●	●	●	➤	➤		●	●	➤	●	●	●	●	●	●	Hi/Dry; new/used boat sales, engine parts/svc, paddleboard rental
Beacon Light Marina Middle R./Seneca Cr. 410-335-6200; *www.beaconlightmarina.com*	4'		●			●	●	➤	➤	➤		●	●	➤	●	➤	●	●	●		New bulkheads, catwalks and electric. Wi-Fi

Galloway Creek

② **Galloway Creek** on the north shore boasts a large marina at its mouth (and the mouth of Middle River). Bowleys Quarters offers slips, fuel and repairs. The creek itself might be a bit open for anchoring, except on still summer nights, but depths are 5 to 6 feet over a large area. Enter close to Bowleys on the right-hand side to avoid the long shoal off Log Point.

Frog Mortar Creek

Farther upriver to starboard, ③ **Frog Mortar Creek** is well worth a visit. (A family named Throckmorton once owned land here; Frog Mortar is said to be a local corruption of their name.) It's an uncomplicated, stay-in-the-middle sort of creek with several attractive places to anchor. Try the spot near red "4", where the airport side of the creek is nicely wooded. *Please take note:* Small craft with mast heights over 37 feet from the waterline create an obstruction to aircraft using the airport's Runway 33 (just below red "2"). When visibility is less than one statute mile, operators of such vessels transiting the area should call the control tower (410-238-1008) to alert approaching aircraft.

In addition to restaurants, there are several marinas—Long Beach Marina, Maryland Marina, Tradewinds Marina and Parkside Marina—offering fuel, slips, repairs, groceries and other amenities. One marina, Chesapeake Yachting Center, also has a shopping center next door with stores selling groceries, hardware and liquor, a bank, several eateries and a Wal-Mart.

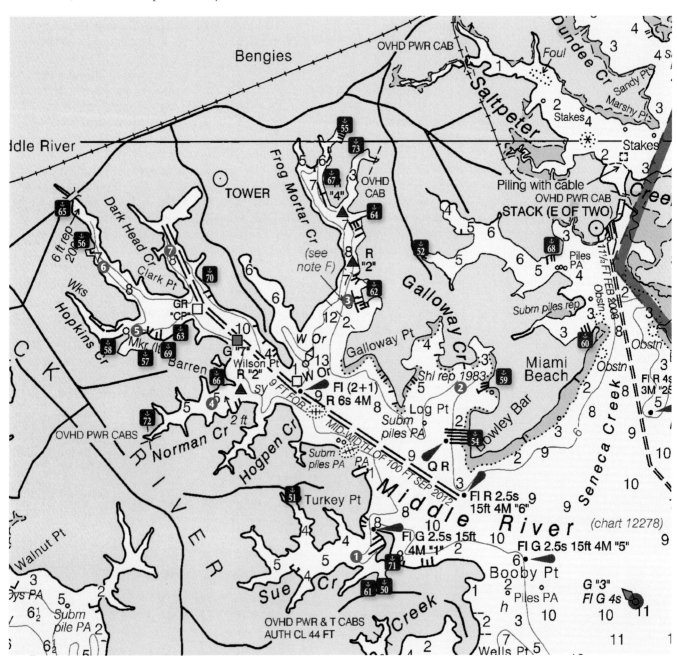

Middle River; from NOAA Chart 12273—not to be used for navigation.

● On Premises
➤ Nearby

Middle River/Seneca Creek continued

	MLW	Overnight Slips	Gas	Diesel	Propane	Electric	Showers	Laundry	Restaurant	Lodging	Pool	Pump-out	Ice	Groceries	Marine Supplies	Bait	Boat Repair	Haul-out Services	Launch Ramp	Wi-Fi	Other
Bowley's Marina Mouth of Middle R. 410-335-3553; www.bowleysmarina.com	8'	●	●	●		●	●		●			●	●	●		●		●	●	●	Volleyball, bar/lounge, grills, haul outs, mechanic
Chesapeake Yachting Center Middle R./Frog Mortar Cr. 410-335-4900; www.chesapeakeyachting.com	6'	●	●	●	➤	●	●	●	➤	➤	●	●	●	➤	●	➤	●	●	➤	●	Connects to shopping center
Cutter Marine Yacht Basin Head of Middle R. 410-391-7245; www.cuttermarina.com	6'	●	➤	➤		●	●		➤	➤	●	●	●		●		●	●	●	●	Floating piers, hurricane hole, 25-ton lift
Deckelman's Boat Yard Middle R./Hopkins Cr. 410-391-6482	8'		➤	●		●	➤	➤	➤	➤		➤	➤	➤	●	●	●		➤		Full-service yard, 40-ton lift, towing & salvage
Essex Marina & Boat Sales Middle R./Hopkins Cr. 410-686-3435; www.essexboatsales.com	7'	●	➤	➤	➤	●		➤	➤	➤		●	●		●	●	●		➤	●	Full-service marina & yard, brokerage, store
Galloway Creek Marina Middle R./Galloway Cr. 410-335-3575	5'					●	●					●					●	●			Deep water slips, haul out, marine service
Goose Harbor Marina Middle R./Seneca Cr. 410-335-7474; www.gooseharbor.com	6'		●			●	●	●			●	●	●								Boat rentals, sales, beach, clubhouse
Holly Neck Marina Middle R./Sue Cr. 410-574-3988	4'		➤	➤		●	●		➤			➤	●			●					
Long Beach Marina Middle R./Frog Mortar Cr. 410-335-8602; www.longbeachmarinaonline.com	8'	●	●	●	➤	●	●	➤	➤	●	●	●	➤	●	●	●	●		●		Boat ramp, picnic pavilion, friendly staff
Markley's Marina Middle R./Hopkins Cr. 410-687-5575	6'		➤	➤		●	●	●	➤			➤	➤	➤	➤		●	●			
Maryland Marina Middle R./Frog Mortar Cr. 410-335-8722; www.marylandmarina.net	7'	●	➤	➤	➤	●	●			●	●	●		●		●	●		●	●	Service, Wi-Fi, Sunset Cove Cafe, live web cam
Middle River Landing Marina Middle R. 410-686-0771; www.middleriverlandingmarina.com	6'	●				●	●		➤	➤		●	➤	➤	●			●			Well protected harbor, 100 slips
Norman Creek Marina Middle R./Norman Cr. 410-686-9343; www.normancreekmarina.com	7'	●	●	●	➤	●	●	➤	➤			●	●		●		➤	➤	➤		Fuel, snacks, slips, Md Clean marina
Parkside Marina Middle R./Frog Mortar Cr. 410-344-1187; www.parksideboating.com	6'	●	➤			●	●					●	●				➤	➤	➤	●	Floating piers, A/C bathrooms; picnic area
Porter's Seneca Marina Middle R./Seneca Cr. 410-335-6563; www.porterssenecamarina.com	8'	●	●	➤		●	●	➤		●	●	●		●		●	●		●	●	Sheltered; floating piers w/ mounted electric, floating gas dock
River Watch Restaurant & Marina Middle R./Hopkins Cr. 410-687-1422; www.riverwatchrestaurant.com	21'	●	➤	➤	➤	●	●	➤	●	➤		●	➤	➤	➤	➤	➤		●		Live music Thurs.–Sun.; deck parties, covered dining
Stansbury Yacht Basin Middle R./Dark Head Cr. 410-686-3909; www.stansburyyachtbasin.com	10'	●	●	➤	➤	●	●		➤			●	●	●	●	➤	●	●	●	●	Floating docks
Sue Island Marina Middle R./Sue Cr. 410-574-7373	4'		➤	➤	➤	●	●	➤	➤	➤		●		➤			●	●			Marine towing; dock bar & crab deck w/light fare
Sunset Harbor Marina Middle R./Norman Cr. 410-687-7290 or 877-420-9575; www.sunsetharbor.com	4'	●	➤			●	●		➤			●	●		●		●	●		●	Picnic area, grills; indoor rack storage to 38'
Tradewinds Marina Middle R./Armstrong Cr. 410-335-7000; www.tradewindsmarina.com	6'	●	●	➤	➤	●	●	➤	➤			●	●	●		●	➤	●	●		●	Floating piers, lift slips

10 Minutes to the Bay...
Middle River, MD

BOWLEYS MARINA

Sales, Lease and Management by
Coastal Properties Management, Inc.

PURCHASE or LEASE!

FAMILY ORIENTED MARINA
- New Playground • Picnic Areas/Gazebos
- Clean Restrooms/Laundry • Gated Facility • Pool/Clubhouse

FULL SERVICE MARINA
- Boat Ramp/Pump Out Facility • Mechanic On-site
- 10-Ton Fork Lift/30-Ton Travel Lift

Deep Draft and No Height Restrictions

410.335.3553 | BowleysMarina.com

New: Generation 3 Pier

MARYLAND MARINA
UNIQUE AMONG MARINAS

On Scenic Frog Mortar Creek

★ SERVING THE BOATING COMMUNITY FOR 70 YEARS ★

- **NEW PIER FEATURES**
  Premier Ipe wood w/longer,
  wider finger piers, slip-side
  holding tank pump out. 30'+
  slips have dedicated T30A or
  S50A electric
  New piping extends water
  service March to December

- **YACHT CARE**
  Hull & deck refinishing
  Insurance & restoration work
  Sailboat Rigging

- **MARINA SERVICES**
  360 Slips
  Ground level rack service
  200 trailer boat spaces
  Dual concrete ramp
  Winter Storage

- **MARINE STORE**
  Do-it-yourself store
  Discount Marine Hardware
  Sailboat hardware

- **EXTRA FEATURES**
  Live Web Cam
  Free WiFi
  Air Conditioned Bath
  House and Showers
  Sunset Cove Café
  Park Pavillion and Playground
  Free Pump-out Station

MEMBER MTAM
Marine Trades
Association of Maryland

410.335.8722 ✕ Interlux

3501 Red Rose Farm Rd. Middle River, MD 21220
www.MarylandMarina.net • info@MarylandMarina.net
7 miles from The Avenue at White Marsh

Norman Creek

❹ **Norman Creek** is attractive and offers the services of two marinas—Norman Creek Marina and Sunset Harbor Marina. It's narrow and a bit shallow (5 feet) for many cruising boats, however.

Hopkins Creek

❺ **Hopkins Creek** has marinas (Bay Boat Supplies and Marina; Essex Marina; Riverwatch Marina), a famous boat-yard (Deckelman's), restaurants and a pretty place to anchor in 7 feet near the north shore. The east and west branches of the creek are separated by a sharp point of land at the end of which is a privately maintained mini-lighthouse with a flashing amber light. Although this light can be helpful for night passages, it is not an official navigational aid.

Middle River mainstem

Leave Clark Point to starboard to enter ❻ **the headwaters of Middle River**, where there's a very attractive anchorage in 8 feet, surrounded by woods. You'll find good storm protection here, but it might be a bit too sheltered and buggy for a hot summer night. Here you'll find transient slips at Cutler Marina Yacht Basin and Riley Marina.

Dark Head Creek

❼ **Dark Head Creek** leads to a basin next to an industrial complex that has grown up at Martin aircraft company's old factory. You'll find a full-service marina (Stansbury Yacht Basin) and a restaurant on Dark Head Creek. WILSON POINT PARK, completed in 2007, provides a double boat ramp with 4-foot depths, two fishing piers, picnic areas, a board-walk, walking paths and an athletic field for boaters who can access the facility. The aviation museum is a short walk from here.

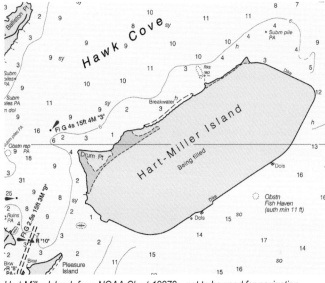

Hart-Miller Island; from NOAA Chart 12278—not to be used for navigation.

Hart-Miller Island

Hart-Miller Island draws hundreds of boaters every summer with its accommodating anchorage, public beach and campsites. Its waters are protected and relatively fresh so swimmers can enjoy themselves without fear of sea nettles.

Located at a large cove off the mouths of Back and Middle rivers, it is one of the few islands in the Chesapeake that is growing—not diminishing—in size. The state of Maryland and the federal government have created this recreational outpost from two separate entities that were shrinking in acreage.

The half-mile section between Miller Island and its southern neighbor, Hart Island, was developed into a sandy beach when a 1,200-acre impoundment area was constructed. Surrounded by a dike on the eastern (Bay) side of the island, the impoundment served as a dumping ground for spoils dredged from Baltimore Harbor and its shipping channels. The ambitious project began in 1981 and accepted dredge spoils till 2009, surpassing expectations. (The impoundment area is off-limits to the public.)

A century ago, a bridge connected Miller Island to the mainland, allowing for the development of Miller Island Ducking Club. Neither the bridge nor the club remains.

If you approach Hart-Miller from the south, a distinctive 105-foot light tower (it has a red top with a white bottom) located at the end of the Craighill Channel Range will help you locate the narrow entrance channel that separates the mainland from wooded Pleasure Island (just south of Hart-Miller). Leave the tower to starboard as you go through the well-marked channel leading to the anchorage in **Hawk Cove**.

The charts report a depth of 5 feet in this channel. Dredging in 2010 has taken care of much of the reported shoaling, but keep an eye out and use caution. This summer's storms already may have made their own alterations.

The anchorage may have upwards of 1,000 boats on any given holiday weekend, and summer weekends are always packed. You'll hear the sounds of music and families at play, and catch the aroma from beach cookouts. The considerable number of boaters who relax and play here have attracted private concessionaires who sell snacks and sodas from barges anchored amid the gathering multitude.

The smaller part of the island that has been set aside as a state park is open from May through September. Here boaters anchor out and dinghy in. Those with a shallow draft, drop their hooks near the beach and simply wade to shore. South of the 3,000-foot-long beach, a primitive camping area shaded by tall trees is available on a first-come, first-served basis. Establish your campsite, and a park ranger will find you later and collect the $6 fee. Pets are now permitted.

A zig-zagging wooden deck and walkway encourage explorations ashore; an observation tower offers a panoramic view of the Bay. There are public restrooms but no trash containers, so campers and picnickers must pack out their trash. Glass containers are prohibited.

The Maryland Department of Natural Resources keeps a close watch on the island, but does not maintain a manned station there. In an emergency, or for assistance, contact rangers on the water and the Coast Guard on channel 16. Otherwise, call 410-592-2897 to reach park personnel.

Boaters staying overnight should be aware of wind conditions. With breezes out of the north or west, the island offers no protection. If the breeze is out of the east or south, the air will be calm enough to give the numerous resident mosquitoes a feast—you. Have the insect repellent handy.

Back River

Experienced cruisers know the Bay is full of surprises, but few are prepared for the pleasant surprise of **Back River**. In many people's minds, Back River has no obvious entrance to the Bay, being nestled quietly between Middle River and the Patapsco River, west of Hart-Miller Island.

Back River is surprisingly wide (almost a mile in places) and relatively short, just over 6 miles to a fixed bridge (vertical clearance 16 feet). ROCKY POINT PARK is located on the north shore at the river's entrance, and the shore is lined with homes.

To starboard, just inside Cedar Point off the state park, you may see other boats anchored. The charts show depths

Your Boat Could Go From This To This...

BEFORE

Custom fiberglass fabrication and alterations Structural/cosmetic gel coat, blister repair, hardtops, Awlgrip Certified technicians

AFTER

CALL TODAY FOR A FREE ESTIMATE!

www.PortersSenecaMarina.com

PORTER'S SENECA MARINA
918 Seneca Park Rd.
Middle River, MD 21220
410-335-6563

Interlux. yachtpaint.com   MERCURY MerCruiser   ABYC. Setting Standards for Safer Boating

Hart Miller Island *continued*

of 4 to 6 feet here, and it appears this would be a good anchorage in almost anything except a southerly blow.

In **Greenhill Cove** below Todd Point, just past fixed daymark "7", the chart indicates only 2 feet at the extreme end of the cove, but there are many large boats tied at the residences there. The cove is surrounded by houses on three sides, with a marsh on the fourth. The cove is more protected than the one behind Cedar Point, but noise from an adjacent highway (Interstate 695) can make spending the night here a little uncomfortable.

The river's soft curves make a cruise upriver interesting. As you proceed up Back River, the shoreline becomes a panorama of change—grassy marshes, tiny bluffs, little suburban areas and a generous scattering of marine facilities, particularly on the river's northeastern shore near Essex, Md.

Heading upriver under power, you may see a huge flock of seagulls following along. This might be mystifying, until you observe that your engine props are actually churning up tiny fish for a seagull feast. Locals explain that the river tends to be silty. Its loose bottom often misleads boaters into thinking they are disturbing the bottom mud when they are only agitating the particle-filled water.

Another park occupies about 10 acres on the northeastern shore at Cox Point. Its narrow finger of land holds a launch ramp, a scattering of picnic tables and grills, and a playground.

Charts indicate there should be enough water for most boaters to cruise all the way to the bridge near Essex. But keep an eye on your depthsounder. If it shows only 3 feet or so, you may want to play it safe and not venture farther upstream.

It is important to give the channel markers sufficient berth because silt deposits tend to build up around them. Insiders will tell you to stay in the middle while you enjoy this pleasantly surprising piece of the Chesapeake.

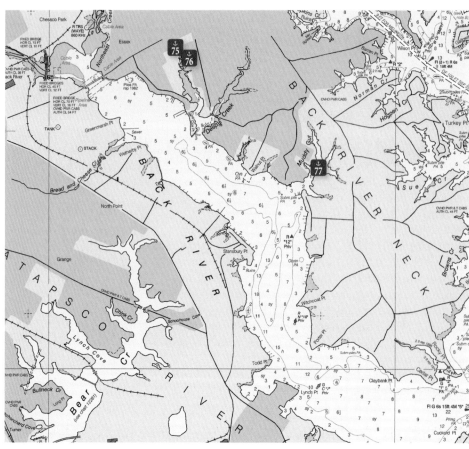

Back River; from NOAA Chart 12278—not to be used for navigation.

● On Premises
➤ Nearby

Back River

	Overnight Slips MLW	Gas	Diesel	Propane	Electric	Showers	Laundry	Restaurant	Lodging	Pool	Pump-out	Ice	Marine Supplies	Groceries	Boat Repair	Bait	Haul-out Services	Launch Ramp	Wi-Fi	Other
Riverside Marine Back R. 410-686-1500; www.riversidemarine.com	3'		➤		●	●	➤	➤	➤		●	➤	➤	●	➤	●	●	➤	●	Boat sales, service dept, repowers, parts store, lift slips
Weaver's Marine Service Back R. 410-686-4944; www.weaversmarine.net	6'	●	●		●	●	●	➤		●	●	➤	●	●	●	●	➤	●		Indoor repairs w/32' clearance; A/C specialist
West Shore Yacht Center Back R. 410-686-6998; www.westshoreyachtcenter.com	5'	●	●		●	●	●	➤		●	●	●	●	➤	●	➤	●	●	➤	Floating docks, club room, kitchen, Wi-Fi, lifts

SPOTLIGHT CRUISE

Better late (season), than never: Northeast and Elk rivers, with coffee on the Sassafras

This is my idea of a great northern Bay weekend cruise: A trip to the piney-woods-crowned top of the Bay, up the Northeast River say, with a leg-stretching stop somewhere like Charlestown, Md. Then, at day's end, dropping the hook in a brand-new anchorage, like Cara Cove on the Northeast, perhaps . . . or, even better, Piney Creek Cove around the corner on the Elk River. There you could sit on the doorstep of the C&D Canal and watch the shipping come and go.

"Let's do that," I enthused to a progression of friends and family members. "It's only November. That's not too late."

"You're nuts!" they said, one and all. "You are seriously nuts!" Finally, a volunteer stepped forward: my dog Skippy. (In truth, he doesn't know how to say "no.") So at daybreak on a bright blue Saturday in November, the Ship's Dog and I, bundled up to the teeth, cast off the Albin 28 *Journey*'s lines from JPort in Annapolis and set off for the northern Bay.

It's almost eerie to cross Annapolis harbor without having to weave through swarms of sailboats, powerboats, kayaks and the occasional Naval Academy mini-battleship. Eerie, but nice. Hooray for late-season cruising, I thought! I gave the fishing boats collected around the Chesapeake Bay Bridge a wide berth, passed through the center span and headed up into the empty upper Bay.

The sky was intensely cobalt blue and the visibility seemed infinite. I soon passed Love Point at the northern

tip of Kent Island, then Swan Point, as we followed the Tolchester Channel east to hug the shore and then north again. With a draft of just over three feet, *Journey* didn't really need to stay between the markers, but the channel was something to aim for. I kept her at the channel's edge, though, just in case I failed to see a tug and barge or 12-story RORO sneaking up behind us. (I say I, because although Skippy is a great conversationalist. That is, he lets me do all the talking; he's forever falling asleep on watch.)

Just off Worton Point, we followed the channel as it turned northeast, and three hours after we had left, we passed Howell Point at the mouth of the Sassafras River. In the distance, I could already see Elk Neck jutting out beyond Grove Point, the northern entrance to the Sassafras. Beyond that, I could just make out the low shoreline between the Susquehanna and Northeast rivers, seeming to hover just above the Flats. I love the intimacy of the upper Bay, where you can often see both sides and the top, all at the same time. It seems almost like lake boating—until you turn around and realize you can just about see clear down to Dixie.

At Turkey Point at the tip of Elk Neck, I throttled back from our get-there speed of 13 knots, and we ambled north, slowly now, hugging the steep shoreline of Elk Neck State Park to stay in deep water and avoid the Flats, now a superconductor of reflected sunlight. Skippy unfolded himself from his get-there position (wedged between the passenger seat and the cabin bulkhead) and took up his working position at the stern, on the lookout for herons and other known threats to national security.

About noon, we reached Cara Cove, the first fair anchorage beyond Turkey Point. Cara Cove sits just about opposite Carpenter Point at the entrance to the Northeast River and carries four to six feet, except along its shoreline, where it gets shallow, not surprisingly. Cara Cove is pretty open, though, for anything other than a quiet night. In any case, it was too early to stop yet. The sky was still clear and the wind negligible, and I figured we had another four hours before we'd have to drop the anchor for the night.

So we kept to the channel up the Northeast, and two miles later we were at Hance Point, another fair anchorage in a southerly or easterly blow. Just beyond that we crossed the river to Charlestown, where the docks stretch out to the edge of the channel. Skippy looked at me pleadingly from his position at the stern, so we sidled up to a dock and went ashore.

Charlestown is a nice little settlement, full of old houses and history, and the wistful air of a town bypassed by both time and the highway. Founded in 1742, Charlestown was meant to be a major port for the transport of goods and services. And it was set up as the county seat. But fate and the hurricane of 1786 changed the course of Charlestown's history by improving water access to Havre de Grace and Baltimore. The coupe de grace came when the county seat was moved to Head of Elk, now Elkton. The rest is history—or non-history. Yet, there is much to be said for the quiet life in the historical backwaters, and Charlestown's thousand or so residents consider themselves the better for the oversight.

Skippy and I enjoyed our stop in Charlestown very much, though perhaps not for the same reasons. While I chatted with people at Charlestown Marina who were industriously winterizing their boats and cursing the end of the season, Skippy found plenty of interesting smells and a satisfactory number of bushes. We both enjoyed walking down Water Street to the stone wharf, which was built over the old cribbings of the town's 18th century wharf. While I studied the various historical markers, Skip watched the seagulls feeding in the shallows. We walked back toward town and peered into the windows of the antiques shops, which were closed, and then clambered back onto the boat and onto the river.

The sun was already beginning its descent into the west, so I turned *Journey* south again, and we retraced our route until we were below Turkey Point once more. This time we rounded the point and headed up the Elk River. Three o'clock.

If this had been summer, I would almost certainly have made a beeline for Veazey Cove on the southern shore of the Bohemia River. There, we would have found shelter from the late afternoon squalls that habitually come tearing across the Bay out of the southwest.

But this was late fall—almost winter in my almanac— when the bad weather is likely to come out of the north. And for that, Piney Creek Cove, set into the north shore of the Elk,

seemed like just the ticket. Or at least that was my working hypothesis.

Piney Creek Cove is just over a mile wide and half a mile deep, from Hylands Point on the south to Oldfield Point on the north, making it a broad rectangle that, on the map, looks like an artificial construction, a harbor built to order. It's not, of course. Inside the cove, the depth varies from six feet to . . . oh, about a teaspoon, with the best water apparently toward Oldfield Point, where a ferry service once took passengers across the Elk. But shoals shift, bottoms change and part of the fun is to sound out your own personal gunkholes. Sometimes the actual depths match the charts, but just as often they don't. The trick, of course, is to find the variations that fall your way.

With that in mind, I worked in along the north shore until we were well inside. When I thought we were about as far in as prudence would allow, I pulled forward and then went up front to drop the hook. With no wind to push us back, I nudged the motor in and out of reverse to set the anchor. Done. Now we had a front row seat for the entrance to the C&D Canal. Just about a mile beyond Piney Creek Cove, the channel turns off the Elk into Back Creek and the canal. That meant that all the canal traffic would pass right under our nose.

And perhaps it did. We didn't see it. Within minutes of dropping anchor, the sun dropped below the horizon, taking the day's warmth along for the ride. Skippy and I dove as one for the relative warmth of the cabin. Shortly afterward we were burrowed deep into our respective beds and sound asleep.

The next morning, I pushed open the cabin door to find a river full of whitecaps, with a knife-sharp wind out of the northwest shoving hard against the ebbing tide. Overhead, clouds scudded fast into the east, making a strobe light of the rising sun. Out on the river, a tug pushed a loaded barge slowly upriver toward the canal; a small schooner under power fought its way downriver through the foam.

I shivered and poured out the last of my coffee. "You're nuts!" my friends had told me. "I must be nuts," I told Skippy, as he headed back inside the cabin. I knew where his get-there place was going to be today. I sighed, pulled on my watch cap, zipped up my jacket and started the engine.

An hour and a half later, we were threading our way into Turner Creek on the Sassafras. Here, I knew, we would find a refuge from the wind and a place to dock the boat for a few hours. I could make some more coffee while we waited for the wind to subside. Skippy could run off the cold and find a few bushes.

A few minutes later, sitting at a picnic table overlooking Turner Creek, I sipped hot coffee and watched the last of the clouds blow out. Things were looking up. "Hey, who's crazy now?" I asked Skippy.

—**Jody Argo Schroath**

Baltimore to the Chesapeake Bay Bridge

The Patapsco, Magothy and Chester Rivers Baltimore and Rock Hall

For most of us, the cruising lifestyle is a passion for variety. True, there are boaters who will always anchor out, and there are those who will always look for a marina with air-conditioned bathrooms, a welcoming pool and a good Wi-Fi connection. But most us fall somewhere in the middle; we pluck a little of this and a little of that from the Chesapeake's rich cruising tree. And many locals argue that nowhere on the Bay is there more cruising variety to be found than here—from Baltimore down to the Bay Bridge.

In one day, we can easily find ourselves lazing at anchor, absorbing the shimmering vistas of a Chester River tributary during a midsummer picnic onboard. Then, before nightfall—with the assistance of a spry breeze or twin Cummins diesels—we can be tied up at a Fells Point marina in the shadow of the Baltimore skyline, sipping cocktails and paying homage to the gods of the gas grill. If we want some nightlife after the sun has melted orange over the city, we can put on high heels and wingtips and revel in a performance of the Baltimore Symphony Orchestra or a funky jazz club.

Grand, isn't it?

And that scenario is just the beginning. The Chester River alone offers more than any of us could possibly enjoy in a weekend—heck, even a month. From the Corsica River, with its well-earned reputation as one of the Bay's prettiest anchorages, to the architectural and culinary charms of Chestertown, the array is dizzying. And then there's the cruiser's perennial favorite, Rock Hall, with its protected harbors, myriad marinas and service yards, busy Main Street and renowned crabhouses.

The Western Shore too has quiet charms to contrast with the bustling port of Baltimore. What about the Magothy River, a lovely sailing and boating river with tributaries of its own? There too you'll find the ever-popular Dobbins Island and the always rocking anchorage just to its north. Here too cruisers can swing gently at anchor in Broad Creek—which, coincidentally, has its own little island, great for wading.

So many destinations, so little time.

Section 2

TowBoatU.S.
LOCATIONS

A **Baltimore**
410-255-8700

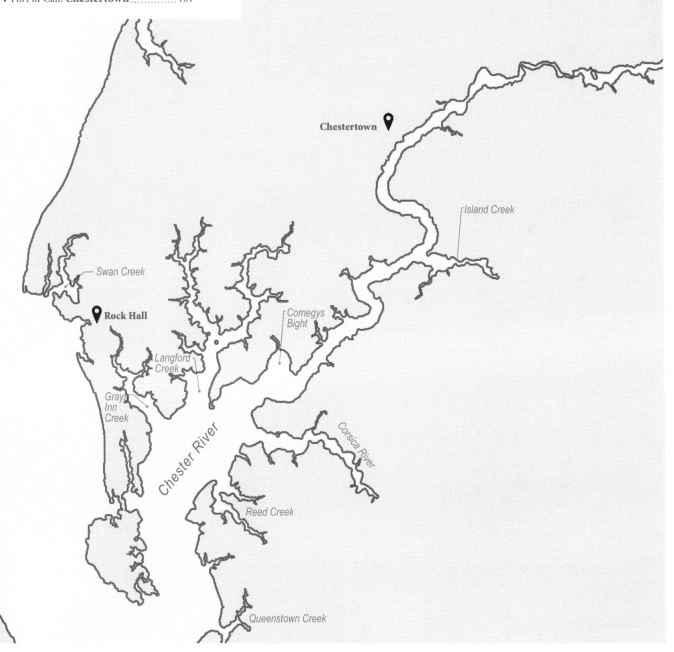

Patapsco River

Boaters who have the inclination to explore the creeks and bays of the **Patapsco River** below Francis Scott Key Bridge will find surprisingly pleasant anchorages far removed from the urban hub upriver, where the teeming port of Baltimore draws ships from all over the world.

You should have little difficulty finding the Patapsco's entrance, marked by red nun "2B" off North Point, which defines the convergence of Brewerton Channel's eastern extension and the Craighill Channel. And the line of buoys marking the shipping lanes into the city is among the most recognizable navigation aids on the Bay.

Shipping traffic is often heavy—Baltimore is one of the country's busiest ports—but the water outside the channel is plenty deep for recreational craft. Monitor VHF (channels 9 and 13) to keep track of big ships and tugs as you follow the Fort McHenry Channel. Along the way you'll pass a shoreline steeped in history, and in the process of reinventing itself as it emerges from its industrial past.

Bodkin Creek

❶ **Bodkin Creek**, the first tributary off the Patapsco, is a great one. But the channel is narrow and subject to shoaling, so diligence is required. Bodkin Point's shoals exend a considerable distance out toward the shipping channel. Skirt the shoal, as indicated on the charts, and then follow the

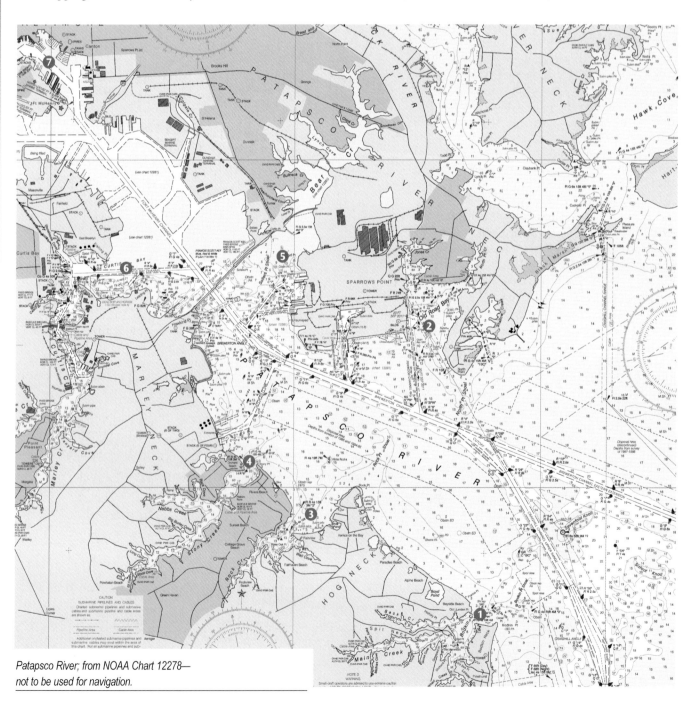

Patapsco River; from NOAA Chart 12278—
not to be used for navigation.

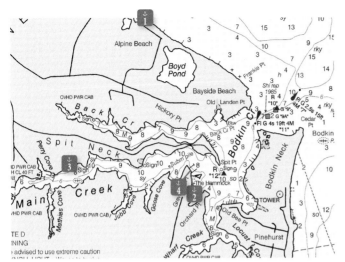

Bodkin Creek; from NOAA Chart 12278—not to be used for navigation.

PLEASURE COVE

A Suntex Marina

*L*ocated just fifteen minutes from Annapolis and Baltimore, Pleasure Cove Marina offers unparalleled services and amenities, deep water slips and ample storage in our heated and sprinkled buildings. They also specialize in service for large boats, including those up to 24 1/2 feet wide, 90 ft. long and 100 tons.

pleasurecovemarina.com
1701 Poplar Ridge Road, Pasadena, MD 21122 | 410.437.6600

marks—"3", "5" and "7"—to Bodkin's entrance. Be particularly wary of shoaling between daymark "9" and light "11". By using some care, even those boats that draw 5 feet can come in on a moderate tide with no grounding. Once inside, the depths are 7 to 9 feet, though shoaling exists in the usual places, such as off points of land.

Most cruisers recommend two anchorages on Bodkin Creek. One, on the east side of the main branch just across from Spit Point, lies in the little cove above Old Bee Point. The second is located farther upstream near the entrance to **Jubb Cove**. Both are attractive and offer good holding.

"No Wake" buoys make for much smoother water in the main branch and in **Back Creek**, the northern branch of Bodkin. Still, you probably shouldn't anchor too far out in **The Hammock**, which is a small bay just inside the entrance and a busy spot.

Fuel, basic marine supplies and repairs are available at several marinas along the main branch of Bodkin Creek and in Back Creek. Geisler Point Marina, to starboard near the mouth of Back Creek, has transient slips but few services. In exploring Back Creek, as you motor toward Hickory Point

(another favorite anchoring spot), use care—you may touch on the shoal at its eastern side, but you ought to be able to back off easily and motor upstream.

The Back Creek branch is attractive, but the shoreline narrows considerably and homes and piers crowd the water's edge. Depths are good, ranging from 8 to 9 feet, with no other serious shoals reported. Another half-mile upstream of Hickory Point, you'll find a fine anchorage at the bend of the creek.

● On Premises
➤ Nearby

	MLW	Overnight Slips	Gas	Diesel	Propane	Electric	Showers	Laundry	Restaurant	Lodging	Pool	Pump-out	Ice	Groceries	Marine Supplies	Bait	Boat Repair	Haul-out Services	Launch Ramp	Wi-Fi	Other
Patapsco River/Bodkin Creek																					
Atlantic Marina Resort Patapsco R./south of Rock Cr. 410-437-6926; www.atlanticmarinaresort.com	4'	●	●			●	●		➤		●	●	●				●	●	➤	●	Pool, beach, playground, gas, pump-out
Hammock Island Marina Patapsco R./Bodkin Cr. 410-437-1870; www.hammockisland.com	7'		➤	➤		●	●				➤	●		➤			➤			●	Sailboats only with annual contract
Pleasure Cove Marina Patapsco R./Bodkin Cr. 410-437-6600; www.pleasurecovemarina.com	8.7'	●	●	●	➤	●	●	●	●		●	●		●		➤	●		●	●	25 ft w/ 110-ton lift; repower; golf adjacent
Ventnor Marina Patapsco R./Bodkin Cr. 410-255-4100	12'	●	●	●	➤	●			➤			●	●	➤	●	➤	●	●	●		full-service, parts, certified techs, diesel-89-93 gas dock

BALTIMORE'S *Best* FULL SERVICE BOATYARD

- 75 & 35 Ton lifts ◆ 20,000 lb forklift
- Service building for vessels to 55'
- Bottom painting ◆ Fiberglass & blister repair
- Woodwork & fine interior joinery
- Electronics & equipment installation & service
- Engine & generator sales/service

- AC/DC electrical service
- Cleaning and detailing
- Mobile service in the harbor
- Dry storage to 90' (power/sail) on paved & lighted area w/year-round water & electric
- Rack storage ◆ Do-it-yourselfers welcome

All our work meets ABYC standards. We have 2 ABYC master techs and 2 electrical certified techs.

- Discount marine supply store & parts department.
- Our staff is fluent in "boat-talk" and ready to give all the assistance you need.
- Special orders handled easily - many items available next day ◆ Fully stocked parts for all major brands including:

@ Port Covington Maritime Center
321 Cromwell Street • Baltimore, MD 21230
T: 410 625-4992 • F: 410 539-3078 • www.tysc.com

Have The Most Fun
EVER AT YOUR WATERFRONT GATEWAY TO THE BEST OF BALTIMORE, YEAR ROUND.

We are...
- Midway between Harborplace and Fells Point/Canton.
- An ideal "all-weather" port.

More annual slips available — check out our slip specials, seasonal or winter-over.

Large, single loaded floating slips • 24-hour staffing • Gate/video surveillance
Boater's lounge w/TV, fireplace, heads/showers

At the foot of I-83, within 2500' of most seasonal festivities, major attractions and top restaurants!

VHF 16 to 68 • Call for reservations » (410) 625-1700
HARBOR EAST MARINA
40 International Drive, Baltimore, MD 21202-4336 • www.harboreastmarina.com • harboreastmarina@harboreast.com

Old Road Bay *continued*

As mentioned, two of the best and most picturesque anchorages are off Old Bee Point in the main body of Bodkin and on **Main Creek** at Jubb Cove. Main Creek also has several other good anchorages, including a fine one at the interesection of **Mathias** and **Perry** coves, and one of our favorites, an unnamed cove on the north shore, just upstream from Jubb Cove. Main Creek also features Bodkin's only restaurant and its largest full-service marina. Pleasure Cove Marina is located just upstream of Perry and Mathias coves.

Old Road Bay

Gathered between the steel plant on Sparrows Point and Fort Howard on North Point, ❷ **Old Road Bay** lies on the north shore near the Patapsco's entrance. At the bay's north end, North Point Creek and Jones Creek poke up like two horns. While some charts indicate otherwise, both are navigable. To enter Old Road Bay, stay close to the north side of the shipping channel until you pass North Point. The basin has 8 to 10 feet of water in most of the outer half, but stay on the safe side and watch your depthsounder.

North Point Creek (with an unmarked channel at mid-creek holding 4- to 6-foot depths) has two marinas, Markel's Boat Yard and Rudy's Marina, that offer transient slips, fuel, marine supplies, repairs and a long history. North Point Creek is tranquil, in part thanks to NORTH POINT STATE PARK on its northeast shoreline. To enter the creek, stay to the east side of Old Road Bay. Leave Jones Creek markers "1" and "2" to port. To starboard, a flashing red "4" marks North Point Creek's entry channel. From there, head northeast about eight-tenths of a mile to red flashing "2". Leave that close to

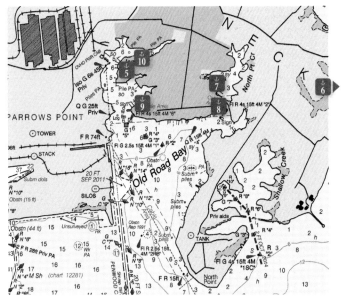

Old Road Bay; from NOAA Chart 12278—not to be used for navigation.

starboard then turn north into the creek. Watch for a sandbar mid-channel.

Jones Creek has been dredged to 7 ½ feet. Its dogleg channel begins with the markers "1" and "2". Following the corridor indicated by daymarks "3" and "4" to the west through "5" and "6" will put you inside. Despite the looming smoke stacks and perpetual thrum of auto traffic, the creek is filled with wildlife. Osprey careen overhead. Ducks and Canada geese paddle among the cattails. Transient slips may be had at Old Bay Marina or Young's Boat Yard.

● *On Premises*
➤ *Nearby*

Patapsco River/Old Road Bay	MLW	Overnight Slips	Gas	Diesel	Propane	Electric	Showers	Laundry	Restaurant	Lodging	Pool	Pump-out	Ice	Groceries	Marine Supplies	Bait	Boat Repair	Haul-out Services	Launch Ramp	Wi-Fi	Other
Atlantis Marina Patapsco R./Jones Cr. 410-477-6831	5'		➤	➤		●	●	➤	➤			➤	●	➤				●	➤		
Bill's Boatyard & Marina Chesapeake Bay/Cuckhold Point 410-477-5137	6'	●			●	●		●			●	●		●		●	●				Floating docks, full length piers, canvas, dock bar
Markel's Boat Yard Patapsco R./North Point Cr. 410-477-3445	6'	●	●		●		➤	➤			●	●	➤	●	➤	●	●	➤			Marine railway, travel lift, supplies, 89-octane gas
McCluskey's Marina Patapsco R./North Point Cr. 410-477-2446	5'	●	➤	➤	➤	●	●	➤	➤			➤	➤	➤	➤	➤	●	●	●		
Old Bay Marina Patapsco R./Jones Cr. 410-477-1488; www.oldbaymarina.com		●	➤	➤		●	●	➤	➤				➤				●	●	●		30-ton lift, boat prep for overseas shipping
Young's Boat Yard Patapsco R./Jones Cr. 410-477-8607; www.youngsboatyard.com	6'	●			●	●		➤			●						●				Protected deep water slips. 15-ton open lift

Rock Creek

Nearly three miles southwest of the juncture of Craighill and Brewerton channels are the **White Rocks**. Rising 15 feet out of the water, these gull-splattered rocks used to serve as navigation aids for Bay shipping long before lighthouses were built here. Now a light warns mariners of *their* presence.

It is best to stay near Brewerton Channel to clear the southern shoals, particularly the unmarked Rock Point Shoal, which extends from ❸ **Rock Creek**'s eastern shore. You may enter the creek on either side of the rocks. After passing green "7", aim for the rocks or for flashing red "2" at the creek's mouth.

Rock Creek affords an easy and quick stop for cruisers, with marinas offering slips, marine services and repair facilities. The Maryland Yacht Club sells ice, gas and diesel and has a pump-out. Fairview Marina, White Rocks Marina, Oak Harbor Marina and Pasadena Yacht Yard have transient slips. The creek's anchorages also serve well for a longer stay. The creek channel is well-marked to about midway, Water Oak Point. From there, stay centered. The two prime anchorages, Wall Cove and Tar Cove, are both located before Water Oak Point.

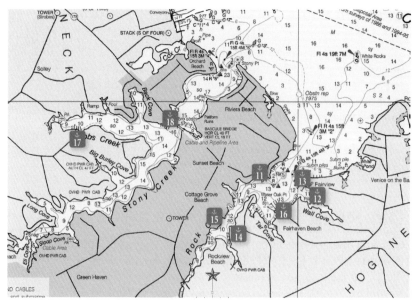

Rock Creek and Stoney Creek; from NOAA Chart 12278—not to be used for navigation.

The mouth of **Wall Cove** forms a pleasant, small, dish-shaped anchorage with low banks and wooded, residential lots that offer weather protection from the south and north. The holding ground is muddy but generally good. Since this area is bordered by marinas, boat traffic can be heavy on weekends.

● On Premises
➤ Nearby

	MLW	Overnight Slips	Gas	Diesel	Propane	Electric	Showers	Laundry	Restaurant	Lodging	Pool	Pump-out	Ice	Groceries	Marine Supplies	Bait	Boat Repair	Haul-out Services	Launch Ramp	Wi-Fi	Other
Patapsco River/Rock Creek																					
Blake's Bar Harbor Marina — Patapsco R./Rock Cr. — 410-255-5500; www.blakesbarharbormarina.com	8'		➤	➤		●	●	➤	➤			●	➤	➤	➤	➤	●	●			
Fairview Marina — Patapsco R./Rock Cr. — 410-437-3400; www.fairviewmarina.com	10'	●	➤	➤	➤	●	●	●	●	➤	●	●	●	●	➤	●	➤	●	●	●	27-ton Travel-lift, crane, aerial lift
Maryland Yacht Club — Patapsco R./Rock Cr. — 410-255-4444; www.mdyc.org	9'-16'	●	●	●		●	●	●	●	●	●	●	●	➤	➤	➤	➤	➤		●	Public fuel dock; slips for MYC, CBYCA, YCA clubs
Oak Harbor Marina — Patapsco R./Rock Cr. — 410-255-4070; www.oakharbor.8m.com	10'	●	➤	➤	➤	●	●	●	➤	➤	➤	●		➤	●	➤	●	●			40-ton lift, picnic area, grills; MD Clean Marina
Pasadena Yacht Yard — Patapsco R./Rock Cr. — 410-255-1771	12'	●	●	●	➤	●	●	●	➤	➤	●		●	➤	➤		●	●			35-ton lift 15-ton lift, gas, storage
White Rocks Marina — Patapsco R./Rock Cr. — 410-255-3800; www.whiterocksmarina.com	12'-14'	●	➤	➤	➤	●	●		●			●	●		●		●	●	●	●	25-ton and 35-ton lift, lift slips
Patapsco River/Stony Creek																					
Maurgale Marina — Patapsco R./Stony Cr./Nabbs. Cr. — 410-437-0402; www.maurgalemarina.com	9'	●					●	●		●		●		●							Deep water slips, protected hurricane hole
Stoney Creek Bridge Marina — Patapsco R./Stony Cr. — 410-255-5566	12'		●			●				➤			●	●	➤	●	●	●	●	●		

A second anchorage lies farther up Rock Creek in **Tar Cove**, where most longer-duration cruisers anchor, on good holding ground with water depths in the low teens. The cove is surrounded by wooded, residential lots on slightly higher banks. Protection is good here; but when the wind gusts from the north, a short chop can build inside the cove. In summer the breeze can be blocked, and this anchorage can become warm.

More secluded anchorages lie upstream of Water Oak Point in several snug little coves on the eastern side. Higher wooded banks lend an air of privacy.

At Rock Point, at the creek's eastern entrance, Fort Smallwood Park encompasses 100 acres with a 380-foot fishing pier, historic barracks and battery, picnic areas and a restored cedar pavilion for group rental (410-222-0087). A canoe-kayak launch permits access for non-motorized craft only. The original Fort Smallwood—along with Fort Howard, across the river at North Point—once guarded the outer waterway to Baltimore.

Stony Creek

West of Rock Creek on the Patapsco's southern shore, ➍ **Stony Creek** lies nearly five miles above Bodkin Point. Look for "4" and "5", the creek's entrance marks, and follow the channel, keeping to starboard to avoid a rock ledge at the creek's mouth. Inside, the channel carries 10 feet or more. The Route 173 draw-bridge, located less than a mile above the creek's mouth, is 40 feet wide with an 18-foot vertical clearance. Weekends it opens on the hour and half-hour on Saturdays from 11 a.m. to 7 p.m. and on Sundays from noon to 5 p.m. It's closed weekdays for morning (6:30-9 a.m.) and evening (3:30-6:30 p.m.) rush hours—except at 7:30 a.m. and 5 p.m. At other times, the bridge opens on request. Be sure to notify the bridgetender for all openings, whether on schedule or demand, on channel 13 or at 410-225-6630.

Nabbs Creek, a tributary of Stony Creek that branches off to the right just above the bridge, carries depths of 9 to 12 feet for a mile. Nabbs Creek largely boasts fairly high banks lined with attractive homes and, farther upstream, some apartment complexes. In a stiff southwesterly breeze, you might find the going quite choppy until you get in the lee of the shore.

If you're anchoring out, consider one of the several coves located on Stony Creek or on **Back Cove** (off Nabbs Creek), which has depths of 9 to 11 feet.

Bear Creek; from NOAA Chart 12281—not to be used for navigation.

Bear Creek

On the Patapsco's northern shore, just below the Francis Scott Key Bridge, you'll find ➎ **Bear Creek**, with the crumbling, forgotten and completely fascinating Fort Carroll guarding its mouth just off the shipping channel. Located about halfway between the bridge and the charted Marine Channel leading to Sparrows Point's commercial piers, the hexagonal concrete and stone fort is now a bird-nesting site and oyster reef restoration project. The deep, well-marked channel forks to the north before the Key Bridge (I-695)—beyond which the Brewerton Channel becomes the Fort McHenry Channel. From the Marine Channel, head toward "3" off Coffin Point. Here you'll generally find 7 to 12 feet. Watch for charted obstructions, though, while traversing the wide unmarked center.

Past the first of Bear Creek's four bridges (I-695, with a fixed vertical clearance of 55 feet), tiny but navigable **Clement Cove** and larger **Peachorchard Cove** lie to port. These are popular fishing and crabbing areas. In Clement Cove, the deep water lies to port; in Peachorchard Cove, it lies in the center.

Beyond "5", which marks the shoal off Long Point, and before the next bridge, you'll find **Bullneck Creek**, leading

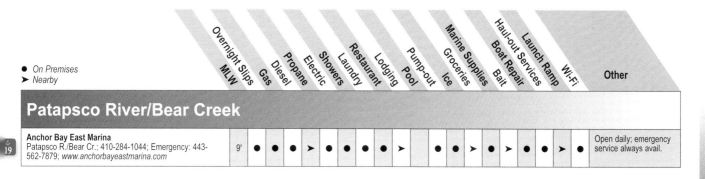

● *On Premises*
➤ *Nearby*

Patapsco River/Bear Creek	MLW	Overnight Slips	Gas	Diesel	Propane	Electric	Showers	Laundry	Restaurant	Lodging	Pool	Pump-out	Ice	Groceries	Marine Supplies	Bait	Boat Repair	Haul-out Services	Launch Ramp	Wi-Fi	Other
Anchor Bay East Marina Patapsco R./Bear Cr.; 410-284-1044; Emergency: 443-562-7879; www.anchorbayeastmarina.com	9'	●	●	●	➤	●	●	●	●	➤		●	●	➤	●	➤	●	●	➤	●	Open daily; emergency service always avail.

Bear Creek *continued*

inland to port. Inside this pleasant creek, private homes with docks line the southern shore and, opposite them, two county parks separated by a small creek. The unmarked channel here carries 7 to 9 feet. Bullneck Creek is a quiet anchorage, and the parks' docks allow dinghies.

The next bridge on Bear Creek is a bascule highway bridge (25 feet vertical clearance) that opens on request and monitors channel 13. The third, a railroad swing bridge, is generally left open during daylight hours, rarely interfering with recreational boat traffic. (The last span, a bascule bridge at the head of the creek, has only a 12-foot vertical clearance.)

Just beyond the railroad bridge on the northwest side is Anchor Bay East, a full-service marina with a restaurant, the Hard Yacht Cafe Bar & Grill. Across the creek opposite the marina, an anchored float with picnic tables and a barbecue grill is open to boaters who use it respectfully. If you're anchored in the creek, dinghy in with your food and supplies (including charcoal) and enjoy a meal. Be sure to take your trash with you when you leave.

A sharp turn to port after Anchor Bay East leads into **Lynch Cove**. Here you'll find Sheltered Harbor Marina with transient slips. Lynch, as well as two smaller coves, **Club** and **Schoolhouse**, and **Chink Creek** are all located before the final bridge and are all deep enough for exploration. Beyond the bridge, 6 to 8 feet depths continue for a mile.

Inner Harbor; from NOAA Chart 12281—not to be used for navigation.

Curtis Bay

At Key Bridge, a red-white-and-blue nun northeast of the shipping channel commemorates the spot where Francis Scott Key, held aboard a British warship, wrote the "Star-Spangled Banner" while he watched the bombardment of Fort McHenry. It's a fitting introduction to ❻ **Curtis Bay**, where the U.S. Navy's first ships were built in the late 1700s. Inside the bay, water-skiers zip around on summer weekends and anglers in small boats fish near mossy pilings and bulkheads. Curtis Bay is peppered with scrapped vessels, it is grim and grimy with industry, and, in the end, it is an utterly fascinating place.

Flowing into the bay from the southwest, **Curtis Creek** is crossed by the Pennington Avenue bridge, then the two spans of I-695. These bascule bridges have a vertical clearance of 40 feet. Farther along, a swing railroad bridge is kept open except for trains. Beyond all of these bridges sits the Baltimore Coast Guard station. Houses line the creek's west side, but the east side, running down into **Tanyard Cove** and **Marley Creek**, is rimmed with trees. There is plenty of water, and it's a good, protected anchorage.

Inner Harbor/Baltimore

Three and a half miles upstream of Key Bridge the Patapsco divides at Fort McHenry. The right branch takes you into what the charts call "Northwest Harbor," which ends in Baltimore's vibrant ❼ **Inner Harbor**. Marine facilities line the north shore from **Canton** to the Inner Harbor, where there are also tie-up facilities (the floating docks on the south shore belong to Baltimore Inner Harbor Marine Center).

The city of Baltimore's public docking on the west side has fixed piers. Signs indicate tie-up spots (color-coded cleats) along the bulkhead in the Inner Harbor. In addition, a small anchorage marked by white buoys is available right in front of the World Trade Center. Holding ground is hard mud in 20 to 25 feet of water, so be sure to let out enough scope. (Some boaters have reported anchors fouled by debris, however, and others have had difficulty setting a hook.) On weekends, it is quite crowded; leave your dinghy tied up (and locked) at the city docks. You'll find anchorage space more plentiful in Canton on either side of Anchorage Marina in depths of 10 to 20 feet. The small area on the southeast side (10 feet) of the marina is convenient if you want to make a shopping run, but the holding is not suitable for an extended stay.

The small bay to the southwest of Fort McHenry is known as **Middle Branch**, home of the South Locust Point Marine Terminal and a large cruise ship terminal. As the number of luxury waterfront homes has increased here, so has the availability of marine services. Tidewater Yacht Service (whose Inner Harbor fuel dock is located under the Domino Sugar sign) has moved its full-service boatyard to Port Covington Maritime Center on Middle Branch. Two other marinas also serve boaters on Middle Branch: Middle Branch Marina and the recently renovated Baltimore Yacht Basin, which also has a seafood restaurant.

● On Premises
➤ Nearby

Patapsco River/Baltimore Harbor Area

#	Marina	Overnight Slips	MLW	Gas	Diesel	Propane	Electric	Showers	Laundry	Restaurant	Lodging	Pool	Pump-out	Ice	Groceries	Marine Supplies	Boat Repair	Bait	Haul-out Services	Launch Ramp	Wi-Fi	Other
1	**Anchorage Marina** Patapsco R./Baltimore Harbor/Canton 410-522-7200; www.anchoragemarina.com	●	15'	➤	➤	➤	●	●	●	➤	➤	●	●	●	●	➤	➤	➤	➤	➤	➤	Slips for sale, 24-hr security, updated facilities
2	**Baltimore Marine Center at HarborView** Patapsco R./Inner Harbor 410-752-1122; www.baltimoremarinecenters.com	●	20'-25'	➤	➤	➤	●	●	●	●	➤	●	➤	●	●	➤	➤	➤	➤	➤	●	Full-service marina w/278 deep water slips
3	**Baltimore Marine Center Inner Harbor** Patapsco R./Inner Harbor 410-837-5339; www.baltimoremarinecenters.com	●	16'	●	●	➤	●	●	●	●	➤	●	➤	●	➤	➤	➤	➤	➤	➤	●	May-Nov, fuel Sun-Thurs 9am-7pm; Fri-Sat 9-8
4	**Baltimore Marine Center Inner Harbor West** Patapsco R./Inner Harbor 410-837-5339; www.baltimoremarinecenters.com	●	20'-25'	➤	➤	➤	●	●	●	●	➤	➤	●	➤	➤	➤	➤	➤	➤	➤	●	Floating piers, walking distance to attractions
5	**Baltimore Marine Center Lighthouse Point** Patapsco R./Baltimore Harbor/Canton 410-675-8888; www.baltimoremarinecenters.com	●	12'	●	●	➤	●	●	●	➤	●	●	➤	●	●	➤	●	●	●	➤	●	Full-service marina with 500 slips to 200 feet, dog park
6	**Baltimore Public Docking** Patapsco R./Baltimore Harbor 410-396-3174; www.baltimoredockmastersoffice.com	●	16'	➤	➤	➤	●	●	➤	➤	➤	➤	➤	➤	➤		➤				●	
7	**Baltimore Yacht Basin** Patapsco R./Middle Br. 410-539-8895	●	9'	➤	➤	➤	●	●		●	●		●	➤	➤	➤		●		➤		Nicks Fish House Restaurant, near stadiums
8	**Captain James Landing** Patapsco R./Baltimore Harbor/Fells Pt. 410-327-8600; www.captainjameslanding.com		20'				●		➤	●	➤		●	➤	●	➤			➤	➤	●	Waterfront pavilion for crabs & corn
9	**Center Dock Marina** Patapsco R./Inner Harbor 410-685-9055	●	10'	➤	➤		●	●	➤	➤		➤	●	➤	➤	➤			➤	➤		Picnic area w/grills, located in Fells Pt.
10	**The Crescent Marina** Patapsco R./Baltimore Harbor/Fells Pt 443-510-9341; www.coastal-properties.com	●	8'-15'				●			➤	➤		●		➤	➤				●	➤	Along harbor promenade, in Fells Point
11	**Harbor East Marina** Patapsco R./Inner Harbor 410-625-1700; www.harboreastmarina.com	●	5'-15'	➤	➤	➤	●	●	●	●	●	➤	●	●	●	➤	➤	➤	➤	➤	●	Inner Harbor Location, 200+ slips, party pad, gym
12	**Henderson's Wharf Marina & Inn** Patapsco R./Inner Harbor/Fells Pt. 410-732-1049; www.hendersonswharfmarina.com	●	20'	➤	➤	➤	●	●	●	➤	●		●	●	➤	➤	➤	●	➤	➤	●	private exclusive slips, 38-room inn, facilities for special events, Tiki hut
13	**Middle Branch Marina** Patapsco R./Middle Branch 410-539-2628	●	6'	●	●		●	●				●	●		●			●	●	➤		
14	**Thames Point Marina** Patapsco R./Balt. Harbor/Fells Pt. 410-522-7368		9'-13'		➤	●			➤	➤		➤		➤	➤			➤	➤		Water taxi, parking, walk to Fells Point, Canton, & Harbor East
15	**Tidewater Yacht Services at Port Covington Maritime Ctr** Patapsco R./Middle Branch 410-625-4992; www.tysc.com	●	18'	➤	➤	➤	●	●	●	➤	➤		●	●	➤	●	●		●	●	➤	Large yacht repairs 77-ton lift, floating docks

Port of Call

Baltimore's Inner Harbor

Baltimore's effervescence is captured in the bustling waterfront area known as the Inner Harbor. With its many shops, restaurants, museums and entertainment venues, the Inner Harbor hums day and night. So, too, do the surrounding neighborhoods, many easily reached from the waterfront and each injecting its unique personality into Maryland's largest city.

Discover a bevy of attractions along a 7 1/2-mile waterfront promenade between the south shore and the Canton neighborhood east of Inner Harbor. In a park-like setting at the harbor's mouth, Fort McHenry offers visitors a look at the fortification that inspired our national anthem. (There is no dockage, but the fort can be reached easily by water taxi or city bus.) History is also the focus at the Museum of Industry, where visitors can marvel at past industrial and maritime technology. Continuing around the harbor, you'll find the American Visionary Art Museum, which displays the imaginative works of self-taught artists, and the Maryland Science Center, offering hands-on displays, a planetarium, laser shows and IMAX screenings. Two more unique museums lie just west of the harbor: Sports Legends at Camden Yards and Geppi's Entertainment Museum, honoring pop culture. At the harbor, the *Constellation*, the last all-sail warship designed and built (in 1854) for the U.S. Navy, offers tours and often stages demonstrations of historic shipboard operations. The ships of the Baltimore Maritime Museum are also open to the public: the World War II submarine *Torsk*, Coast Guard cutter *Taney* and lightship

Chesapeake. The historic ships are berthed in the shadow of the World Trade Center, designed by famed architect I.M. Pei. Ascend to its observation level and enjoy a breathtaking view of the sprawling city below.

Visitors to the National Aquarium in Baltimore can meet marine life

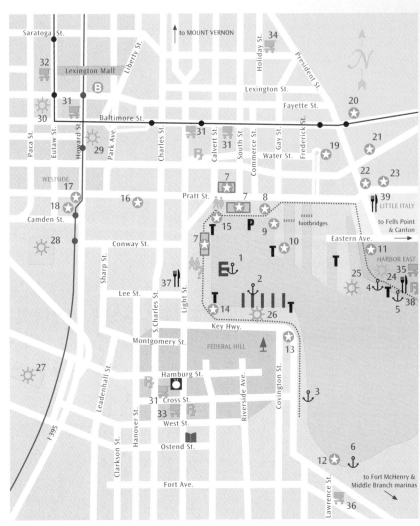

Inner Harbor

⚓ Marinas/Dockage
1 City of Baltimore Public Docking
2 Baltimore Marine Center Inner Harbor
3 Baltimore Marine Center at HarborView
4 Harbor East Marina
5 Center Dock Marina
6 Tidewater Yacht Service at Port Covington

◉ Points of Interest
7 Harborplace & The Gallery
8 World Trade Center
9 Baltimore Maritime Museum
10 National Aquarium in Baltimore
11 Baltimore Public Works Museum
12 Museum of Industry
13 American Visionary Art Museum
14 Maryland Science Center
15 U.S.Frigate *Constellation*
16 Convention Center

17 Geppi's Entertainment Museum
18 Sports Legends at Camden Yards
19 Port Discovery
20 Phoenix Shot Tower
21 Carroll Mansion
22 Reginald F. Lewis Museum
23 Star-Spangled Banner Flag House

❓ Information (Visitor Center)

☼ Entertainment/Recreation
24 Landmark Theatres (movies)
25 Pier 6 Concert Pavilion
26 Rash Field
27 M & T Bank Stadium
28 Oriole Park at Camden Yards
29 1st Mariner Arena
30 Hippodrome Theatre

🛒 Groceries
31 7-Eleven
32 Lexington Market
33 Cross Street Market

34 Farmers Market
35 Whole Foods
36 Shoppers Food Warehouse

🍴 Dining Areas
37 Inner Harbor
38 Harbor East
39 Little Italy

🏃 Public Restrooms
●— Metro System & Stations
●— Light Rail & Stops
T Water Taxi Landings
⚑ Park
📖 Library
℞ Pharmacy
Ⓑ Bus Terminal
.... Waterfront Promenade
P Paddle Boat Rentals

from around the world and marvel at the 4D Immersion Theater. Kids will be captivated by the activities at the Port Discovery children's museum or can climb through a life-size model of an underground utility system at the Public Works Museum, which explains the workings of a city's infrastructure. African-American culture and history is presented at the Reginald F. Lewis Museum, located next door to the Colonial-era Carroll Mansion and the Phoenix Shot Tower, where rifle shot was manufactured in the 1800s.

Whatever the season, sports fans can cheer a Baltimore team. The Orioles play at Camden Yards and the city's gridiron heroes, the Ravens, compete against NFL foes at M&T Bank Stadium. On non-game days, Camden Yards opens its doors for public tours that include sanctums like the dugout and the press box. Babe Ruth Birthplace and Baseball Center traces the life of the city native and baseball great. 1st Mariner Arena hosts additional sporting events, concerts and other entertainment.

Intriguing neighborhoods surround the Inner Harbor: Federal Hill, with its mix of shops and early 19th-century row houses; Little Italy, known for its bountiful restaurants; Westside, home of the historic Hippodrome Theatre; Mount Vernon, a cultural enclave of museums and theaters; and Harbor East, filled with luxury condos, restaurants and chic shops. The state-of-the-art Visitor Center is a must stop for advice on ways to tour the city, making dining and lodging reservations, and buying tickets to events and attractions.

Harborplace, a retail shopping/dining extravaganza, is housed in two glass-enclosed waterfront pavilions and a multi-tiered mall (The Gallery) on the north side of Pratt Street. It's a festive area where street performers often regale crowds. Elsewhere, some 70 dealers fill up Antique Row on Howard Street and numerous fine shops and galleries dot Mount Vernon.

You don't have to venture far to eat well or frugally: Harborplace is full of full-service restaurants and smaller cafes; Federal Hill offers a variety of ethnic eateries; Power Plant Live is a jiving night spot; Little Italy cooks up authentic Old World cuisine; and Harbor East offers some of the city's trendiest dining.

On summertime Friday nights, outdoor film festivals in Little Italy and at the Visionary Art Museum are a fun way to begin a weekend visit. No matter the season, visitors to the Inner Harbor won't lack for activities, including a variety of neighborhood festivals and dazzling Independence Day fireworks over the harbor.

Need provisions? Don't miss historic Lexington Market in Westside or Federal Hill's Cross Street Market and close-by neighborhood grocery stores. There is a Whole Foods in Inner Harbor East on the edge of Little Italy. Worth the walk is the Sunday morning farmers' market beneath Jones Falls Expressway.

Information: 877-BALTIMORE; *www.baltimore.org, www.south baltimore.com, www.mtamaryland.com* (transit information).

Bay Spotlight

Fort McHenry

National Park Service

Cruisers heading to Baltimore will pass beneath the Key Bridge, within 100 yards of where Francis Scott Key is said to have written *The Star Spangled Banner* as he watched the bombardment of Baltimore by the British in September of 1814. Every spring the U.S. Coast Guard sets a red, white and blue "star-spangled" commemorative buoy to mark the spot (the buoy is removed for the winter). Some historians question the accuracy of the buoy's location, but it nonetheless serves as a colorful reminder of the failed British attack described so deftly in our national anthem.

Fort McHenry, about three miles beyond the Key Bridge, still presides over the approach to Baltimore. Strategically situated to defend the burgeoning harbor, the fort was one of the first constructed by the new republic. It is named after James McHenry, Secretary of War under President Washington.

During the Battle of Baltimore, the fort withstood 25 hours of constant bombardment by British naval ships standing some two miles away. Fortunately, the enemy guns weren't terribly accurate from that distance, and the American cannons (with a range of only a mile and a half) could only keep the ships at bay. The naval battle was, for all intents and purposes, a stand off. Meanwhile, the British forces marching overland from North Point lost their commander to an American sharpshooter. The British second in command, a somewhat less intrepid fellow, abandoned the attack when he saw the failure of the naval strategy.

While Fort McHenry is now a national park and welcomes visitors, it has no docking facilities except those used by the water taxis that leave from Fells Point and make regular runs to and from the park site. Pedestrians can walk to the Fort from the Inner Harbor, but there is no direct connection via the Inner Harbor promenade, which stops at the Baltimore Museum of Industry. The park grounds are open from 8 a.m. to 8 p.m. during the summer. The entrance fee is $7 for adults (16 years and older). For more information visit *www.nps.gov/fomc/.*

Port of Call

Fells Point and Canton

The convivial neighborhoods of Fells Point and Canton complement the Inner Harbor's high-profile sophistication. While the Inner Harbor has Starbucks, Fells Point has Cafe Latte da; the former has McCormick & Schmick's, the latter Bertha's Mussels; the Morris Mechanic Theatre has its counterpart in Fells Point's Vagabond Players; and the Inner Harbor's high-rise luxury condos find their match in Canton's updated row houses, where traditional window screen paintings are making a comeback. Once hardscrabble ports, these historic neighborhoods have become singular destinations featuring a diverse blend of culture and style.

Fells Point has been a happening place for over 200 years, thriving first as a shipbuilding center and then as a major entry port for immigrants. Neighboring Canton served as a shipping center where sea lanes and railroad lines converged. Its industrial buildings have been transformed into condos, shops and restaurants. To get acquainted with Fells Point, take one of the Saturday morning walking tours that leave from the Visitor Center on Thames Street spring through fall. Drawing on local sites and the stories of those who once lived here, one tour chronicles Fells Point's maritime history and the other its role as an immigration center. Some contend the presence of the neighborhood's more colorful characters is still felt. See for yourself on Ghostwalks led Friday and Saturday evenings spring through fall. Near the Visitor Center is the Robert Long House (1765), the city's oldest residence. The public is welcome into the restored home and its splendid garden. Located at historic Chase's Wharf, the Frederick Douglass-Isaac Myers Maritime Park honors these two distinguished leaders and features a re-creation of the first shipyard and marine railway owned and operated by African Americans.

Ann Levelle

In Canton, visitors can stroll the waterfront park and see the Maryland Korean War Memorial. Walking inland toward the heart of the neighborhood, O'Donnell Square, you'll see signs of rejuvenation everywhere: new townhouses and condos plus old row homes undergoing renovation and spectacular churches (photo above).

Entertainment options include everything from live music and theatrical performances in both neighborhoods to the Baltimore Blast's summer soccer practice matches in Canton. The adventuresome can take a guided Segway "safari" or rent one of these two-wheeled wonders and ad-lib their own excursion.

Broadway Market (erected on the site of Fells Point's oldest marketplace, c. 1784) is filled with counter-style eateries and vendors selling fresh produce, meats, seafood and baked goods. General groceries are available at the large Safeway in Canton. Bonaparte Breads in Fells Point features fresh breads and luscious pastries; in Canton visitors will find two pastry establishments whose popularity extends well beyond the city's limits: Vaccaro's Italian Pastry Shop and Cake Love.

Both neighborhoods attracted developers who've transformed old warehouses into vibrant commercial

continued on page 84

Fells Point

⚓ **Marinas/Dockage**
   1 Public wharf

◎ **Points of Interest**
   5 Robert Long House
   6 Frederick Douglass-Isaac Myers
     Maritime Park

? **Information** (Visitor Center)

☼ **Entertainment/Recreation**
   7 Vagabond Players
   8 Thames Street Park

🛒 **Groceries/Carryout**
   9 Broadway Market
   10 H & S Bakery Outlet Store
   11 Save-A-Lot
   12 Bonaparte Breads (bakery/cafe)

⊺ **Water Taxi Landings**

···· **Waterfront Promenade**
   Shopping District

▮ **Library**

🚻 **Public Restrooms**

✉ **Post Office**

▢ **Laundromat**

Your adventures start here. Experience city boating at
Baltimore Marine Centers

BMC Inner Harbor & IH West: 410-837-5339 BMC Lighthouse Point & Boatel 410-675-8888 BMC Harbor View 410-752-1122

Annual, Transient & Winter Slips | Service Yard & Boatel | Concierge Service | Premier Amenities | Marine Fuel

BALTIMORE MARINE CENTERS

The Charms of City Boating

BMCMARINAS.COM

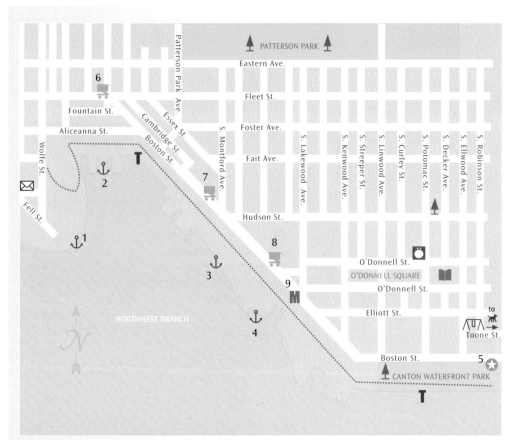

Canton

⚓ **Marinas/Dockage**
  1 Henderson's Wharf Marina
  2 Captain James Marina
  3 Anchorage Marina
  4 Baltimore Marine Center
    at Lighthouse Point

✚ **Points of Interest**
  5 Korean War Memorial

🛒 **Groceries**
  6 Royal Farms
  7 Canton Market
    Convenience & Deli
  8 Safeway

M **Marine Supplies**
  9 West Marine

⛲ **Park**
🐕 **Dog Park**
📖 **Library**
T **Water Taxi Landings**
✉ **Post Office**
Playground
  Shopping District
···· **Waterfront Promenade**

Port of Call: Fells Point and Canton continued from page 78

centers like Brown's Wharf in Fells Point and the former American Can Company building in Canton. Fells Point is noted for antiques and collectibles shops and gift and specialty stores. Canton's waterfront and O'Donnell Square retail hubs feature specialty stores and a handful of galleries.

These communities teem with excuses to dine ashore at neighborhood cafes, pubs, coffee bars—and an elegant historic hotel. Restaurant cuisine runs the gamut from seafood and raw bar fare to Greek, Italian, American, vegetarian and deli food.

Each neighborhood offers activities sure to appeal to visitors. On the first Friday on the month, galleries in Fells Point stay open late for Artloop (exhibits, events and food), and the Can Company in Canton presents happy hour and live music outdoors (June to October). On the second Sunday of the month, Fells Point hosts an Antique Market.

Fells Point comes alive with special events throughout the year: in April, Privateer Day and Pyrate Invasion; in May, the Historic Harbor House Tour; and in October, the two-day Fun Festival (music, food, vendors) and activities.

Information: Fells Point Visitor Center, 410-675-6750, *www.fellspoint.us*; 877-BALTIMORE, *www.baltimore.org*.

LOCATION...LOCATION...LOCATION...

Celebrating 30 Years

• 565 slips • Floating piers with full length finger piers
• Swimming pool
• Immaculate restrooms, showers, and laundry
• Newly renovated boaters lounge with WiFi • West Marine and Safeway supermarket less than 1 block away • Slips for sale or lease • 24-hour security • Short & long term transient rentals • Five minute walk to fabulous restaurants, shopping and entertainment in Canton and Fells Point

ANCHORAGE
MARINA

VHF Ch. 16/67

2501 Boston Street | Baltimore, MD 21224 | 410.522.7200
www.AnchorageMarina.com | ReceptionDesk@anchoragemarina.com

Magothy River

The Patapsco River can boast Baltimore as its big attraction, while the Severn River rightly claims Annapolis. Between them lies the **Magothy River**, with no big city to claim as its own. What it does have, however, is one of the Bay's most popular summer anchorages: Dobbins Island. Just beyond its narrow entrance, the Magothy opens wide; to starboard lie Dobbins and lovely Sillery Bay. As the river progresses west, it narrows considerably, sprouting creeks and coves as it goes. These in turn are flanked with new homes, neighborhood restaurants and marinas, and stretches of scenic undeveloped land.

The entrance to the Magothy River lies almost due west of Baltimore Light, with its red base and white circular house. Once inside the narrow but well-marked entrance, you'll find that the river offers much to explore. On the north shore, the private community of Gibson Island rises high above the water. Many beautiful homes cling to its steep sides, presenting a somewhat Mediterranean atmosphere. Notice that a 6-knot speed limit is strictly enforced in the Magothy's narrow entrance, between buoys "2" to "5".

Deep Creek, to port just inside the river's entrance, has depths from 5 to 8 feet for about a half mile inside. It offers protection from winds, except from the north, and is home to Deep Creek Restaurant and Marina, which offers free overnight dockage with dinner, and Fairwinds Marina, with no transient dockage, but a large selection of used and salvaged boating supplies, as well as gas and repairs.

Dobbins Island

Immediately upriver off the river's north shore stands ❶ **Dobbins Island**, less than a quarter-mile in length. High red-yellow cliffs along its southern side are being lost to erosion, adding to the shoal that extends into the Magothy. Unless your boat draws less than 1½ feet, you shouldn't approach that side of the island.

The island's real beauty lies along its north side, where the land forms a gentle crescent, making a perfect boat anchorage in hospitably deep water (10 to 12 feet) with good holding ground. The island is private property, and a chain fence was erected along the once-popular beach. After years in the courts, however, the chain was ordered removed and the beach reopened below the high water mark to cruisers.

To reach the Dobbins Island anchorage, approach from the island's east side. Once inside, you'll find the anchorage is not only deep, but well protected from strong southerlies. Be aware that on summer weekends, this spot can be a beehive of water-skiing, swimming and partying, with as many as a hundred boats at anchor.

George W. Dobbins, a Baltimore judge, bought the island in about 1840 for duck hunting excursions. Along with nearby **Little Island** (also known as Little Dobbins Island) it became a

- 182 Slips for Sale or Rent ~ Transients
- Fuel Dock (Gas/Diesel) ~ Waste Pump Out
- Secured Parking & Gate w/Key Card Entry
- Launching Boat Ramp

- Heads ~ Showers ~ Laundry
- Private Salt Water Pool
- Picnic Area/Patios
- WiFi Service

- Live WebCam
- Poolside Yoga
- Dinghy Racks
- Marine Services

MAGOTHY MARINA
~ Charted as Crystal Beach ~

360 Magothy Road
Severna Park, MD 21146

410-647-2356

www.magothymarina.com
magothymar@aol.com

Dobbins Island continued

summer retreat for his family and friends. Lately, Little Island has been embroiled in controversy after its owner built an elaborate home—complete with a mini-lighthouse—without securing the proper permits. The court battles continue to rage.

If things are too crowded at Dobbins, there are other anchorages nearby. **Cornfield Creek**, just north of Holland Point on Gibson Island, provides good water for seven-tenths of a mile from the entrance. You'll find a lovely wooded area to starboard, and protection from winds from almost all directions. This is another popular spot for water-skiers, though it quiets down after dark. Cruisers can also anchor in **Eagle Cove**, the area between Holland and Purdy points just before the Gibson Island Yacht Club. The open area is a good place to catch a breeze.

Grays Creek

If you're looking for a quieter anchorage, try ❷ **Grays Creek**. Its entrance lies a little over a half-mile north of Dobbins Island on the northwest shore of **Sillery Bay**. This snug little creek, too small for water skiers, is situated in a well-populated area, and piers line most of its shoreline. Still, it offers an intimate and peaceful anchorage.

Approaching the creek, you'll want to avoid the shoal off the north end of Little Island, a simple matter if you follow the navigation aids. Be aware that the entrance to

Grays Creek, marked by two pairs of daymarks, is one of the narrowest you'll find, and we've received reports that the entrance has shoaled to 3 feet.

Once inside, the creek opens up considerably and divides. Homes and private docks line the shores, particularly on the starboard branch. Atlantic Marina offers fuel, ice and repairs.

To port you'll find a small cove and next to it a larger one with somewhat deeper water. If your draft is shallow enough to negotiate the creek's entrance you'll have no problem in the port branch. The houses here typify this part of the Bay—mostly one-time summer cottages now transformed into permanent residences. Grays Creek remains one of those little waterways where an anchored boater can become part of the surroundings. And that's really not a bad feeling.

Broad Creek

Cruisers will find ❸ **Broad Creek** easily accessible and attractive, with several good anchorages. From the Magothy River's entrance mark, set a course to the Broad Creek entrance mark, red "2", a distance of about two and a half miles. Daymarks identify the edges of the shoals that narrow the passage. But they are easy to spot, and the channel is accommodating, so getting inside is uncomplicated.

Upstream, on a point at the northern end of a break in the shoreline that marks a little cove, you will see one of the Magothy's architectural attractions, the Glass House—a stun-

● On Premises
➤ Nearby

Magothy River/West End Bay Bridge

	MLW	Overnight Slips	Gas	Diesel	Propane	Electric	Showers	Laundry	Restaurant	Lodging	Pool	Pump-out	Ice	Groceries	Marine Supplies	Bait	Boat Repair	Haul-out Services	Launch Ramp	Wi-Fi	Other
Atlantic Marina ⚓36 Magothy R./Grays Cr. 410-360-2500	6'	●				➤			➤	➤											Ship store, boatel, fuel, pump-out, 25-ton-lift
Cypress Marine ⚓37 Magothy R./Cypress Cr. 410-647-7940; www.cypressmarine.net	8.5'	●	➤	➤	➤	●	●	●	➤	➤	➤	●	➤	➤	●	➤	●	●	➤	●	50-ton lift, 15-ton hydraulic crane, wood repairs
Deep Creek Restaurant & Marina ⚓38 Magothy R./Deep Cr. 410-757-4045; www.thedeepcreekrestaurant.com	12'	●				●				●		●	➤	➤	➤	➤	➤	➤			Sunday buffet brunch on the water
Fairwinds Marina ⚓39 Magothy R./Deep Cr. 410-974-0758 ; www.fairwindsmarina.com	7'	●	●			●	●		➤	➤		●	●	➤	●	●	●	●	●	●	25-ton lift, dry storage, lift slips, outboard parts
Ferry Point Marina & Yacht Yard ⚓40 Magothy R./Dividing Cr./Mill Cr. 410-544-6368; www.ferrypointmarina.com	10'	●	➤	➤		●	●	●	●		●				●		●		●	●	●	Ramp, dry storage, svc, waterfront restaurant
Magothy Boatel, Marina & Boatworks ⚓41 Magothy R. 410-647-0733; www.magothyboatel.webege.com	12'		●				●							●		●	➤	●	●	●		Covered boatel, Travel-lift, fork lift 7 tons
Magothy Marina ⚓42 Magothy R./Crystal Beach 410-647-2356; www.magothymarina.com	10'	●	●	●	➤	●	●	●	➤	➤	●	●	●	➤	➤	➤	➤	➤	●	●	Slips for sale, ramp, pool, fuel, pump-out, Wi-Fi, picnic area
Podickory Point Yacht & Beach Club ⚓43 Chesapeake Bay/Podickory Pt 410-757-8000; www.podickorypoint.com	5.5'	●				●	●		➤		●	●	●		●		➤	➤	➤	●	Clubhouse, boatel, tennis, beach, lift slips
Sandy Point State Park ⚓44 Chesapeake Bay/Sandy Pt. 410-974-2772; www.dnr.maryland.gov	8'		●	●		●			➤	➤		●	●	●	●	●	➤	➤		●	Park w/beach, ramps, store, food, bait, rentals

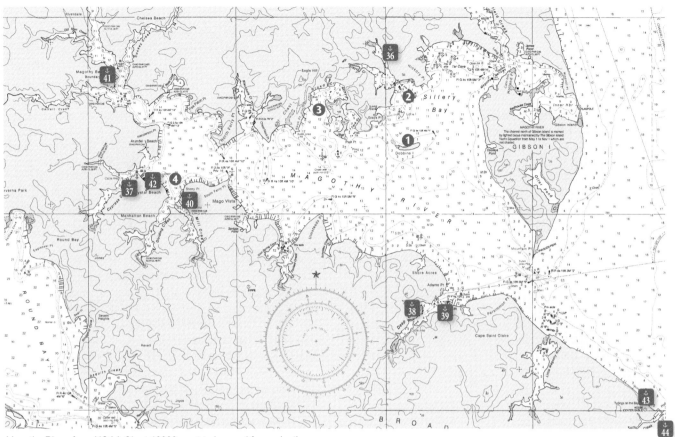

Magothy River; from NOAA Chart 12282—not to be used for navigation.

DISCOVER FERRY POINT MARINA

SLIPS UP TO 50' | COMPLETE BOAT CARE
FULL SERVICE MECHANICAL | 25 TON TRAVEL LIFT
New in 2014 - Stand Up Paddleboard

THE POINT CRAB HOUSE & GRILL
Waterfront dining 7 days a week | www.thepointcrabhouse.com

FERRY POINT
MARINA • YACHTYARD

410.544.6368
10 MINUTES FROM ANNAPOLIS | ON THE SCENIC MAGOTHY RIVER
www.ferrypointmarina.com | office@ferrypointmarina.com

*Annual & Transient Slips,
Lifts & Storage (up to 40')*

Be Our Guest!

FAIRWINDS
MARINA
Magothy River • Annapolis, Maryland

FULL-SERVICE MARINA ON THE MAGOTHY RIVER

100 FAIRWINDS DRIVE, ANNAPOLIS, MD 21409
410.974.0758 | **FAIRWINDSMARINA.COM**

Broad Creek continued

ning private residence made of floor-to-ceiling glass panels.

Give ample berth to the shoals on either side of the cove's entrance. Broad Creek makes an abrupt easterly turn upstream and reveals a small islet, which oddly is not always shown on the charts. The rather shallow water around the islet is clearly marked with white "Danger Shoal" buoys. There's plenty of water elsewhere; choose the starboard side and curve east-northeast into a small cove to find a comfortable anchorage.

On the south shore of Broad Creek, just opposite the tiny island, you'll find a pretty little anchorage. Private piers dot the southern and eastern shorelines and houses sit amidst the stands of tall trees. Several piers on the northern shore belong to a private community, and no commercial facilities are available. The small island across the way features a bit of beach (which invites a visit) and a sparse covering of stunted trees.

Broad Creek carries 10 to 12 feet of water to the islet and about 8 feet south of it. The shallowest water (just a couple of feet) is on the cove's northern shore.

Dividing/Mill Creeks

4 **Dividing Creek**, about four miles upstream from the mouth of the Magothy, is on the southern shore west of South Ferry Point. It shares a common entrance with **Mill**

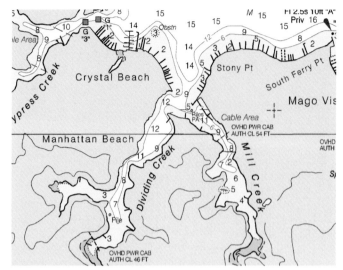

Dividing and Mill creeks; from NOAA Chart 12282—not to be used for navigation.

Creek, where Ferry Point Marina offers a full-service boatyard and a popular new restaurant, The Point Crab House. Shoals project on either side of the creek's entrance, so use caution.

Immediately inside, Dividing Creek widens into a snug anchorage with room for several boats. High banks, though breeze-stoppers in summer, serve as shelter from strong winds; and while homes cover the wooded shoreline, most are screened by thick shrubs and trees.

Both of these creeks are fairly deep and navigable nearly to their heads. However, with no aids to navigation, it's wise to follow the winding channels' center-lines while keeping an eye on depths. In Dividing Creek, once past a constricted area, the waterway splits into two unnamed prongs. The juncture, known locally as **Buckingham Cove**, has at least 7 feet.

Mill Creek is reported to have greater depths than shown on charts. Note that an overhead cable restricts passage to 54 feet about a third of the way in.

The land around Dividing Creek, in colonial days called "Bushy Neck," once thrived with tobacco-growing, and later fruits and vegetables. In the late 19th and early 20th centuries the Magothy's Ferry Point saw schooners and steamships shuttling passengers, seafood and crops. Later, an amusement park called Crystal Beach drew folks by train from Baltimore, Annapolis and Washington. Embarking at a nearby stop, visitors then boarded horse- and mule-drawn carriages for the short ride to the water. Eventually, small communities developed as summer-cottage enclaves, later growing more elaborate for year-round use. Today the old rail line is a multi-use greenway trail.

North of Dividing and Mill Creeks, the Magothy's wide coves and narrow wooded tributaries, with intriguing names such as **Cattail** and **Old Man** creeks, are worth exploring and offer a number of anchorage possibilities and facilities. Just beyond Dividing Creek, Magothy Marina at Crystal Beach has slips, a pool, fuel, ice, and on **Cypress Creek**, Cypress Marine has slips, ship's store and repairs. Farther up the Magothy, to port after **Cockey Creek**, is Magothy Boatel Marina and Boatworks, with repairs, gas, ice and supplies.

TOLCHESTER MARINA

Dock. Dine. Unwind.

FULL SERVICE MARINA
BEACH BAR • CHANNEL RESTAURANT
GORGEOUS SUNSETS • SWIMMING POOL
FUEL DOCK • FACTORY TRAINED MECHANICS
RIGHT ON THE BAY
with 6' MLW

www.TolchesterMarina.com
21085 Tolchester Beach Road | Chestertown, MD 21621 | 410.778.1400

Rock Hall

On the Eastern Shore, the stretch of land just north of the mouth of the Chester River offers several alternatives to cruising boaters. Sitting nearly on the Bay itself is **Tolchester Beach**, once a popular summer resort and now a sleepy year-round community with few vestiges of its roller coaster past. Tolchester Marina occupies the largely man-made basin that cuts into the shoreline (6 feet MLW) just north of flashing green buoy "21". A lighted beacon marks the end of the jetties that lead inside. Amenities include transient dockage, the Channel Restaurant, beach bar, repairs and the sandy beach that drew vacationers a century ago.

Below Tolchester, Swan Creek and Rock Hall Harbor provide access to one of the Shore's most charming and popular communities. Right off the Bay and only 10 miles north of the Bay Bridge, it's the weekenders' choice for a quick and easy destination. Cruisers heading north or south find the area a convenient tuck-in. And they aren't the first. In colonial times, George Washington, Thomas Jefferson, James Madison and Eastern Shore patriot Tench Tilghman rode sailing ferries between Annapolis and Rock Hall on their way to Philadelphia, New York and Boston.

The origin of the name **Rock Hall** is lost in history. Bearing in mind that Bay watermen call the huge oyster shoals that once muddled the channels of the Bay "oyster rocks," some say that a building overlooking the harbor had oyster shell piled so high around it that it was dubbed "Rock Hall." Others will tell you that Rock Hall is named for the Bay's singularly tasty rockfish. In the spring, when town fishermen brought in masses of rockfish daily, people would say, "The men sure made a rock haul today." Who knows?

Nowadays, the once busy fishing village and its environs serve as a recreational boating center with numerous full-service marinas, restaurants and B&Bs. Yachts fill slips once used by watermen, and seafood buildings and warehouses have given way to condominiums and new homes. The town's tranquil business district, which is walking distance (or a trolley ride) from most of the marinas and landings, features an expanding number of shops, inns, restaurants and three museums, including one devoted to the resort at Tolchester Beach. An intimate concert hall, the Mainstay, attracts world-class musicians for regularly scheduled concerts year round.

The town of Rock Hall sponsors several family-friendly festivals throughout the summer, including a big Fourth of July celebration and August's Pirates and Wenches Fantasy Weekend. This naturally puts slips at a premium on those weekends in particular. Reservations are advisable and should be made well in advance.

Boaters visiting Rock Hall, especially those with deeper-draft vessels, would be well advised not to cut inside navi-

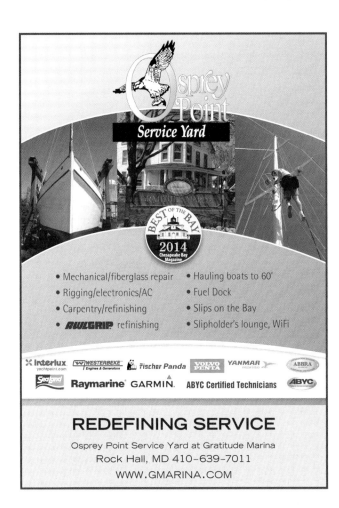

Osprey Point Service Yard

• Mechanical/fiberglass repair
• Rigging/electronics/AC
• Carpentry/refinishing
• **AWLGRIP** refinishing
• Hauling boats to 60'
• Fuel Dock
• Slips on the Bay
• Slipholder's lounge, WiFi

✕ **Interlux** yachtpaint.com   **WESTERBEKE** *Engines & Generators*   🛢 *Fischer Panda*   **VOLVO PENTA**   **YANMAR**   ABBRA
Sea Hawk   **Raymarine**   **GARMIN.**   **ABYC Certified Technicians**   ABYC

REDEFINING SERVICE

Osprey Point Service Yard at Gratitude Marina
Rock Hall, MD 410-639-7011
WWW.GMARINA.COM

Osprey Point

Inn • Restaurant • Marina

THE EASTERN SHORE'S PREMIERE RESORT MARINA

• **Floating Dock Marina**
• **Fine Dining Restaurant and Bar**
• **16 Charming Rooms**

Best Resort Marina, Best Marina for Natural Environment, Best Dockmaster, Best Restaurant for Crabcakes, Best Romantic Restaurant, Best Dog-Friendly Marina

Located on Swan Creek
Rock Hall, MD   f
410-639-2194 • www.ospreypoint.com

Rock Hall ^{continued}

gational aids marking Swan Point Bar, which stretches two and a half nautical miles south from Swan Point, across the entrance to both Swan Creek and Rock Hall Harbor. The shoal is only 3 to 5 feet deep at low tide, so it's often possible to scoot across it in a boat with a 4 ½-foot draft, staying just south of the Brewerton Channel range light, a 30-foot tall structure with a powerful flashing white beam. Boats with deeper drafts will want to play it safe and round can "3" marking the end of the shoal. (If you're approaching from the Chester River, simply get inside the shoal as you move north along the shoreline.) The channel contains 15 to 20 feet of water as far as the entrance to Rock Hall harbor, then 8 to 10 feet to the entrance of Swan Creek. At flashing red can "4" you'll have to choose between Rock Hall Harbor or proceeding into Swan Creek.

Lighted buoys mark the jettied entrance into Rock Hall harbor. Inside, shoaling keeps the channel moving between dredging operations, so don't be surprised to see the markers moved from what is shown on the charts. In fact, in 2012, the channel was straightened to make negotiating the harbor easier. A number of marinas ring the harbor. These offer transient slips: North Point Marina, Rock Hall Landing Marina and Sailing Emporium. Waterman's Crabhouse & Restaurant offers dockage to diners. Among them, these marinas offer a full range of services. Anchoring spots are limited, although a small basin with 7- to 8-foot depths northeast of Sailing Emporium can accommodate a small number of boats.

Swan Creek

Swan Creek has long been a favorite destination for cruisers because of its rural beauty and ample anchorage . . . and because it's located directly north of Rock Hall Harbor so it constitutes a kind of back door to the town. This deep, well-protected creek winds a mile or so into the Kent County countryside. On summer weekends you'll find numerous cruising boats anchored in its protected waters and others enjoying the facilities at one of its many marinas.

Sailors often refer to the creek's locale as **Gratitude**, after the old steamboat landing there. The entrance into the creek is narrow. Flashing red "6", the last marker before the bulkheading at the mouth of Swan Creek, is elevated for easier visibility. Gratitude Marina, the first of six marinas that ring Swan Creek's southeastern shore, marks the original steamboat landing. To the north are marshes and a shoal tributary, **Tavern**

Creek. Entering Swan Creek, stay in the middle as you pass the seawall near Gratitude Marina. Two red seasonal nuns near Deep Landing Point mark the shoal on the eastern side of the creek's Coke-bottle entrance. Once you pass the point, the creek opens up into **Deep Landing Cove** and, farther east, a natural basin called **the Haven**. Just beyond Deep Landing Point, Swan Creek Marina's mooring field marks the deepest water. Boaters looking to anchor in the creek's maximum depths should stay close to the moored boats and avoid the northern edge of the creek.

Two green seasonal nuns mark the shoals on the creek's northern side approaching "14". Depths are 7 to 12 feet until making the turn into the Haven toward three marinas: Spring Cove (no transient slips), Osprey Point and Haven Harbour. The well-marked channel to Haven Harbour Marina carries 6 feet MLW, while the short spur channel to Spring Cove Marina has slightly more than 5 feet MLW. (There is a small anchorage with 5-feet just northeast of green daymark "7".)

Boaters seeking a slip for the night, who need any type

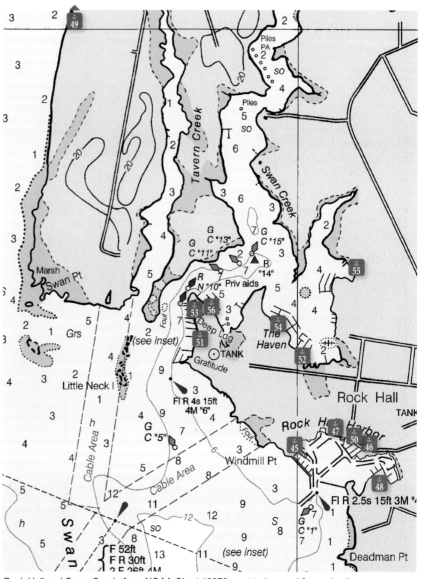

Rock Hall and Swan Creek; from NOAA Chart 12272—not to be used for navigation.

● On Premises
➤ Nearby

	MLW	Overnight Slips	Gas	Diesel	Propane	Electric	Showers	Laundry	Restaurant	Lodging	Pool	Pump-out	Ice	Groceries	Marine Supplies	Bait	Boat Repair	Haul-out Services	Launch Ramp	Wi-Fi	Other
Rock Hall/Tolchester																					
North Point Marina — Rock Hall Harbor; 410-639-2907; www.northpointmarina.net	8'	●	●	●	➤	●	●	●	➤	●	●	●	●	➤	●	➤	●	➤	➤	●	Picnic area, gas grills, covered slips, rental bikes
Rock Hall Landing Marina — Rock Hall Harbor; 410-639-2224; www.rockhalllanding.com	7'	●	➤	➤	➤	●	●	●	➤	●	●	●	➤	➤	➤	➤	➤	➤	➤	➤	Boatel, cable, bike rentals; closest to town, free Wi-Fi
Rock Hall Marine Railway — Rock Hall Harbor; 410-639-2263	5'					●	●			➤	➤		➤		➤	●		●	●			
Sailing Emporium — Rock Hall Harbor; 410-778-1342; www.sailingemporium.com	7'	●	➤	➤	➤	●	●	●	➤	●		●	●	➤	●		●	●	➤	●	Free pump-out. Transport to dining, yacht sales
Tolchester Marina — Chesapeake Bay/Buoy #21/Tolchester; 410-778-1400; www.tolchestermarina.com	6'	●	●	●												●		●	●	●		Restaurant, Beach Bar
Waterman's Crabhouse & Restaurant — Rock Hall Harbor; 410-639-2261; www.watermanscrabhouse.com	8'	●	➤	➤	➤		➤	●	➤	➤	●	➤	●	➤	➤	➤	➤	➤	➤		Free 2-hour dockage for diners
Swan Creek																					
Gratitude Marina — Swan Cr./Gratitude, Rock Hall; 410-639-7011; www.gmarina.com	6.5'	●	●	●	➤	●	●	➤	➤	➤		●	●	●		●	●			●	
Haven Harbour Marina — Swan Cr.; 410-778-6697 or 800-506-6697; www.havenharbour.com	6'	●	●	●	➤	●	●	●	●	●	●	●	●	●	●	●	●	●	➤	●	Full-service resort; two pools, waterfront bar/grill
Moonlight Bay Inn & Marina — Swan Cr.; 410-639-2660; www.moonlightbayinn.com	7'	●	➤	➤	➤	●	●	●	➤	●		➤	➤	➤	➤	➤	➤	➤	➤	●	bikes, barbecues, firepit
Osprey Point Marina Inn & Restaurant — Swan Cr.; 410-639-2194; www.ospreypoint.com	6'	●	➤	➤	➤	●	●	●	●	●	●	●	●	➤	➤	➤	➤	➤	➤	●	Floating docks, pool, gourmet restaurant/bar
Spring Cove Marina — Swan Cr./The Haven; 410-639-2110; www.springcoverockhall.com	6'				●	●				●	●	●							●		Relaxing, family owned marina on Swan Creek
Swan Creek Marina — Swan Cr.; 410-639-7813; www.swancreekmarina.com	7'	●	➤	➤	➤	●	●	➤	➤	➤	➤	●	●	●	●		●	●	➤	●	Rigging, carpentry, electronics, welding, moorings

of repairs or fuel, or who want creature comforts like private showers, a nice meal and a comfy bed at an inn will find it all on Swan Creek. Provisions are a mile's walk into town, but bicycles are available at the marinas and there's always the Rock Hall trolley.

If you prefer a quieter anchorage, head up the northern fork of Swan Creek, which is navigable for almost a mile. Depths are at least 6 feet. This area is well protected, with land shielding the anchorage from nearly every direction. The upper reaches of this fork invite dinghy exploration. Although many cruisers do anchor out in Swan Creek, others report the holding fairly poor, with thin, soft mud. The alternative is to pick up one of Swan Creek Marina's moorings.

Swan Creek is beautiful at any time of the year, with marshes stretching west toward the Bay and cornfields climbing the rolling hills to the north. But in the fall, geese, ducks and swans offer companionship on the water for the night.

MEADE A. BREESE SAILMAKER — VOTED BEST OF THE BAY EVERY YEAR SINCE 2002 — Best of the Bay 2015 Chesapeake Bay Magazine

SAILS, REPAIRS, SAIL CLEANING, RECUTS, CANVAS

rock hall, md | 410-639-2646
21295 allens lane | info@breesesailmakers.com

Port of Call
Rock Hall

Once a fishing village whose harbor was thick with working skipjacks, Rock Hall has undergone a dramatic transformation. After weathering a decline in the oyster industry, it has emerged as a vibrant, friendly place filled with marinas, interesting shops, a bevy of restaurants and a lively arts and music scene. The village proper is a bit of a walk from the shorefront, which is ringed with marinas. Two little vehicle-pulled trolleys run a circle route from various stops in town to the outlying marinas.

At the Visitor Center, located in a cheery bungalow on South Main Street, you'll learn about three town attractions that capture the local heritage: Rock Hall Museum portrays the community's economic life and social traditions; the Waterman's Museum tells the story of those who made their living from the Bay; and artifacts at Tolchester Revisited bring the once-vibrant amusement park/resort at Tolchester Beach back to life.

Visitors can book a cruise aboard *Bessie L*, a 52-foot buyboat, or at Blue Crab Chesapeake Charters. Anglers have their pick of nearly two dozen fishing charters, while sailors can enjoy the friendly competition of races held every other Friday evening in the summer. Chester River Kayak Adventures leads eco-tours and rents kayaks—as do Haven Harbour Marina and Swan Haven B&B. Hop on a bicycle and ride the six miles to Eastern Neck National Wildlife Refuge, a large island sanctuary for migrating birds and other wildlife.

For music, the Mainstay, with its down-home decor, is a popular spot to hear performing artists from around the corner and across the globe.

Browse for clothing, gifts, antiques and a variety of artisans' works in the shopping district, which includes art galleries and a charming courtyard of cottage shops. Durding's Store, a beautifully restored 19th-century pharmacy, still serves ice

Rock Hall

⚓ Marinas/Dockage
1 The Sailing Emporium
2 Waterman's Crab House
3 Rock Hall Bulkhead
4 Rock Hall Bulkhead
5 Bayside Landing & Park
  (loading/unloading)
6 North Point Marina
7 Gratitude Marina
8 Moonlight Bay Marina
9 Swan Creek Marina
10 Osprey Point Marina
11 Haven Harbour Marina
12 Spring Cove Marina

✪ Points of Interest
13 Rock Hall Waterman's Museum
14 Tolchester Revisited
15 Rock Hall Museum

🍴 Dining
 2 Waterman's Crab House
16 The Inn at Osprey Point
17 Muskrat Alley Cafe
18 Pruitt's Swan Point Inn
19 Harbor Shack
20 Dockside Cafe
21 Java Rock
22 J & J Seafood
23 Pasta Plus
24 Bay Wolf
25 New Yartmouth Restaurant

26 Passages Bar and Grill
27 The Kitchen at Rock Hall

☼ Entertainment/Recreation
28 The Mainstay
29 Swimming Pool at Bayside
  Landing & Park

🛒 Groceries/Carryout
30 Bayside Foods (supermarket)
31 Rock Hall Liquors and Deli
32 Shore Stop
33 J & J Seafood

Ⓜ Marine Supplies
34 Meade A. Breese Sailmakers
35 West Marine

🏴 Blue Heron Park
  Wetland Observation Pier

◯ Public Landings

🚲 Bicycles

🛶 Kayak Rentals

📖 Library

✉ Post Office

🅡 Pharmacy

✛ Medical Clinic

⚑ Parks/Play Areas

🍦 Ice Cream

🛏 Lodging

? Information

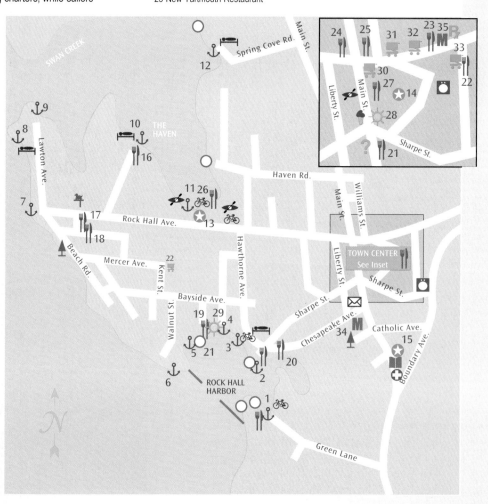

Port of Call: Rock Hall

cream cones. The Cat's Paw at the Sailing Emporium and the Ditty Bag at Haven Harbor Marina offer apparel and gifts.

Groceries are readily available at Bayside Foods supermarket, and you can pick up fresh seafood at J&J Seafood.

Restaurants feature seafood prominently on their menus, and range from burger joints to more upscale eateries. Several are within easy walking distance of most Rock Hall marinas; many serve breakfast. Osprey Point and Waterman's Crab House offer dockage for diners (Waterman's Crab House also repeatedly wins a Best of the Bay award for its crabcakes).

Rock Hall puts on a variety of family-friendly events over the course of the boating season, including an old-fashioned Independence Day celebration and Waterman's Day (including workboat contests); the Pirate and Wenches Fantasy Weekend in August; FallFest (music, food, crafts, local heritage) in September; and the Oyster & Seafood Festival in October.

Information: Kent County Office of Tourism, 410-778-0416; www.rockhallmd.com or www.kentcounty.com.

RESORT & MARINA
BOATYARD
INN AT HAVEN HARBOUR

HAVENHARBOUR.COM
800.506.6697
Chesapeake Bay
Rock Hall, MD

BEST OF THE BAY
Chesapeake Bay
Magazine

Power & Motoryacht Magazine
Top 25 Marinas Nationally

A PLACE WITH EVERYTHING?

SHORETHING

HAVEN
HARBOUR
MARINA

Chester River

There are more than a few Bay cruisers who put the lovely **Chester River** at the top of their list of favorites. They do so for the beauty of its many tributaries and for the prize to be won at the end of the long and winding trip upriver: the lively and charming village of Chestertown. The Chester begins at **Love Point** just above Kent Island. Three miles across at its widest point, the river narrows to about a quarter mile by the time it reaches Chestertown, 24 miles later. All along that way, the river maintains consistently good navigating depths in its well-marked channel.

The third-longest river on the Eastern Shore—after the Choptank and Nanticoke—the Chester is bordered along much of its shoreline by beautiful, rolling country-side and lovely estates. Hail Point, on the southeastern tip of Eastern Neck Island, is where Colonial merchant ships underwent thorough inspection before being allowed to proceed upriver to Chestertown, and above it the land quietly reflects the industry of its people.

EASTERN NECK ISLAND, a national wildlife refuge along the Chester's northern shore, is worth a visit if you travel with bicycles or kayaks aboard. There is also a boat ramp on the island's east side. (To

Chester River; from NOAA Chart 12272—not to be used for navigation.

avoid a rather extensive area of fishtraps in the vicinity of green can "7" off the island's southwest side, be sure to stay on the proper side of the marker.)

Above Eastern Neck Island, the Chester fans out in four generous, cruisable branches: Gray's Inn Creek, Langford Creek, the main extension of the Chester that leads to Chestertown and the Corsica River. All are inviting.

(NOTE: **Kent Island** *is covered in Section 3, as is* **Kent Narrows**, *the busy passageway between the Chester River and Eastern Bay.)*

Queenstown Creek

Around the mouth of ❶ **Queenstown Creek**, homeport for many watermen, you'll often see deadrise workboats trotling on summer mornings or heading in after working the river. This quiet tributary lies 7 nautical miles up the Chester, in the river's horseshoe as it turns north. It's only a few miles from the bustle of Kent Narrows, but feels more like a hundred miles and fifty years.

While some report no problems, Queenstown's channel can be tricky, especially for those with deeper drafts. Shallows lurk uncomfortably close on either side of the narrow route, not helped by the Chester's cross-currents, which contribute to shoaling as well as drift. Since the bottom is generally soft and forgiving, deeper drafts with full-keels, proceeding cautiously with one eye on the tide and the other on the current, may get in with inches to spare. But it's better to seek local knowledge to be safe. In settled weather, some avoid the angst altogether and anchor out of traffic just west of the channel entrance in about 15 feet, and then deploy the dinghy.

Approaching from the lower Chester, Queenstown

Creek's first entrance mark—red nun "2Q"—is about 2 miles east-northeast of green "9", the lighted buoy due south of Eastern Neck Island's Cedar Point. From there, a few nav aids lead eastward for less than a mile into this two-pronged tributary. Ample water will take you to the first green "3", but the skinniest stretch is between "3" and "5". Past "5" it's about 8 feet again. There you can either turn left toward the main branch leading to **Ditchers Cove**, or turn right around Coursey Point, into the shallower Little Queenstown Creek

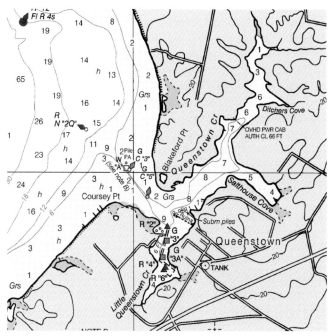

Queenstown Creek; from NOAA Chart 12272—
not to be used for navigation.

		Overnight Slips																			
● On Premises																					
➤ Nearby	MLW		Gas	Diesel	Propane	Electric	Showers	Laundry	Restaurant	Lodging	Pool	Pump-out	Ice	Groceries	Marine Supplies	Bait	Boat Repair	Haul-out Services	Launch Ramp	Wi-Fi	Other

Chester River																					
Castle Harbor Marina Kent Island/Chester R. 410-643-5599; www.castlemarina.com	6'	●	●	●		●	●	●	➤	➤	●	●	●	●	➤	●		➤	➤	➤	●	Cross-island bike trail nearby; large pool
Chestertown Marina Chester R./Chestertown 410-778-3616; www.chestertownmarina.com	6'	●	●	●		●	●	●	●	➤		●	●	➤		●		➤	●	●	●	Walk to shops & restaurants, historic homes
Grays Inn Creek Marina Chester R./Herringtown Cr. 410-693-7212; www.graysinncreek.com	6'	●					●	●	●			●										state of the art marina and climate controlled facility
Kennersley Point Marina Chester R./Island Cr. 410-758-2394; www.kennersleypoint.com	4'	●	➤	➤	➤	●	●	●	●	➤	➤	●	●	●	●	●		●	●	●		Quiet full-service marina, lift, pool, dry storage
Lankford Bay Marina Chester R./Davis Cr. 410-778-1414; www.lankfordbaymarina.net	7'	●	●	●		●	●	●	➤	➤	●	●	●	➤	●	●		●	●	➤	●	Cable, bus to Rock Hall, Wi-Fi, pool, fuel, full service
Long Cove Marina Chester R./Long Cove 410-778-6777; www.deckelmanslongcovemarina.com	6'	●	●	●		●	●	●	➤	➤	●	●	●	●	●	●	➤	●	●	➤		Full-service marina, pile driving, prop repair
Rolph's Wharf Chester R./Buoy 35410-778-6389 or 800-894-6347; www. rolphswharf.com	8'	●	●	●		●	●	●	●	●	●	●	●	●		●		●	●	●	●	Pet- and kid friendly, beach bar, RV sites avail

Chester River *continued*

and on to the port of Queenstown, established in 1707.

The northern branch is the favored anchorage, and most cruising boats drop the hook just inside Blakeford Point. It's a protected spot with a nearby sandy beach, popular in summertime. While you might have 8 or 9 feet in the creek's center, it quickly shoals outside the channel so use care when making your way around other boats already at anchor. Exploring beyond Blakeford Point is best done by dinghy if your rig won't pass under the overhead power cable (charted at 66 feet) that crosses the creek just before Ditchers Cove. To the right—forking east—vessels are limited in exploring Salthouse Cove, by its depth (less than 5 feet at the entrance).

Little Queenstown Creek, with more docks but less water than the main branch, has a marked channel leading to Queenstown's sturdy wharf. Keep away from both shores since submerged pilings, including the remains of an old steamboat landing, may lurk here. Boaters are welcome to tie up at the end of the dock in 6 feet of water, but don't block access to the municipal slips. These are rented yearly and not for transient use. Call the dockmaster (443-496-1931) about the availability of overnight accommodations. (In lieu of fees, cruisers are asked to make a donation to the local fire department.)

Queenstown, a sleepy page from the past with well-tended homes on shady streets, offers the chance to stretch and indulge in some obscure local history. The small port may never have reached the fame of Oxford, Annapolis or

Chestertown, but it was significant enough in 1813 to attract a British invasion. Near the town center is the private waterfront estate called Bowlingly which received the brunt of the attack. Historic markers nearby explain what happened.

From the dock at the foot of Second Avenue, it's a pleasant stroll to the heart of town. Just walk up the hill, past the dockmaster's home and turn right at Charity Lane leading to Main Street. You'll soon be admiring the original 1708 Queen Anne's County Courthouse, a rustic, shake-roofed, wood-and-brick structure—a busy place until the county seat was moved to Centreville in 1782. The town office (410-827-7646) will tell you when this restored relic is open.

Nearby on Main Street, a pizzaria serves lunch and dinner seven days a week. Adventure Crafters School of Coastal Kayaking, once based here, now arranges activities from the Chesapeake Bay Environmental Center in Grasonville. They offer tours around Eastern Neck National Wildlife Refuge, elsewhere in the Bay and along the Atlantic (*www.adventure-crafters.com*).

Despite neighboring golf courses and an outlet plaza, the town and creek remain tranquil with scenic wooded shores that alternate with farmland and estates. While strolling the village, watch for Queenstown's unique white squirrels, often scurrying around the old-fashioned gardens.

Reed Creek

❷ **Reed Creek** on the Chester River is considered by some cruisers as one of the finest anchorages around. But first, you have to navigate its tricky inlet. Located between Queenstown and the Corsica River, Reed Creek's entrance is marked by green can "1" about one-third mile offshore and red nun "2" where a shoal marks the opening. As you leave the green can astern and line up with the red nun, be aware that the shoal on the port side bellies out into your path. Once at green "1", find red "2" and take a course slightly to starboard; then keep your eye on the depthfinder. With a showing of shallow water, edge a little more to starboard. Once you've cleared the shoal and are about halfway to the nun, favor the port side of the channel. Maintain a distance of 100 to 150 feet from nun "2", which rests near the tip of the shoal extending from Gordon Point as you make a wide arc around it into Reed Creek, keeping the nun to starboard. Do *not* cut close to the buoy, as it is not at the tip of the shoal, but truly does mark the north side of the channel. Once south of the nun, aim for the grove of trees adjacent to the marshes on Gordon Point to stay in the best water. (If you are using an old chart, "2" may look as if it's on the wrong side of the channel, but be sure to keep it to starboard.)

You can anchor in this outer area, between Gordon Point and the little unnamed point on Tilghman Neck, or continue ahead to drop the hook in about 8 feet in the large, sheltered harbor beyond. Favor the right-hand shore, as the shoal on the other side is larger than charted. There is a truly snug place farther up where the creek narrows between wooded banks. Reed Creek is a great spot for watching migrating waterfowl, and local cruisers consider it a fine

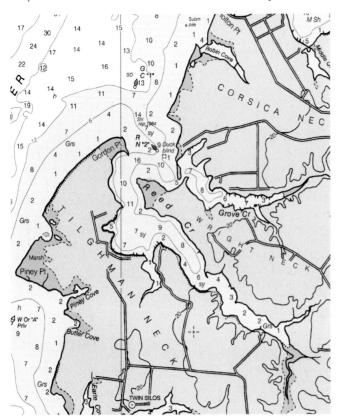

Reed Creek; from NOAA Chart 12272—
not to be used for navigation.

anchorage any time of the year.

At red "2", **Grove Creek** heads off to port. Grove Creek is navigable, but not for all craft. Its entrance is tiny and quite tricky, so proceed with care.

Grays Inn Creek

❸ **Grays Inn Creek** lies on the western shore of the Chester, almost 12 miles upstream from Love Point. Although the mouth of the creek is broad, its entry is not entirely straightforward. However, if you use the method that was prescibed 60 years ago in the first Bay cruise guide, you'll have no trouble at all. Here's how it works: The best way to avoid the long shoals on both sides of the entrance is to leave green "1" close to port and head for the end of the wharf at Spring Point on the west (port) side. Then keep 50 yards off the wharf and continue up the creek, staying in mid-channel.

Well inside, near the head of Grays Inn Creek, you'll find Herringtown Creek Marina, located on the north bank of **Herringtown Creek**.

If you want to head left and continue up Grays Inn, hold hard to the right bank and then go far enough after making the turn to have a clear view up the center of the left fork before actually making the turn. Watch your depthfinder, and be careful to give the shoal at Browns Point, just south of the fork, plenty of room.

By taking the fork to the west, you'll reach the location

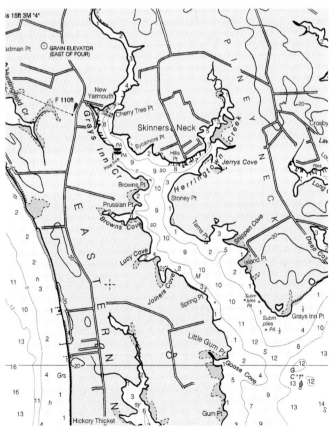

Grays Inn Creek; from NOAA Chart 12272—
not to be used for navigation.

of one of the earliest settlements on the Eastern Shore. New Yarmouth, founded in the 17th century, was the site of the first Kent County courthouse. In 1696 the court was moved to Chestertown (then known as New Town); afterwards, New Yarmouth rapidly declined then disappeared altogether.

A favorite anchorage lies just past the point of land opposite Herringtown Creek. The little cove formed here has tree-lined shores and a quiet atmosphere. In the summer, however, an anchorage off Prussian Point near **Browns Cove** may offer more breeze. For maximum protection, consider the water off Cherry Tree Point. If you're a devotee of sailboat racing, Grays Inn Creek can give you a ringside seat for regattas on the Chester. You might be treated to log canoe races or a fleet of racing Hamptons.

Corsica River

Seven miles from Kent Narrows, the Chester widens at the confluence of four tributaries (including Grays Inn Creek). And here you must pay attention or you'll shoot off up the wrong tributary—not that there actually *is* a wrong tributary in this case. As the main river channel turns northwest toward Chestertown, Grays Inn and then Langford Creek branch off to the north, while the lovely ❹ **Corsica River** strikes off to the east. The Corsica's open bays and tuck-away spots are popular with raft-ups since several groups can gather simultaneously without problems. Reports suggest, however, that there has been some shoaling at the approach. Like much of the Chester, the Corsica offers no services, unless your draft permits a trip to the top of the creek near **Centreville**. There a modern municipal dock offers a spot to tie up alongside a fleet of watermen's boats.

Green-and-red nun "CR" marks the entrance to the Corsica. If you plan to continue up the Chester, this remains to starboard, but if you're heading into the Corsica keep it to port. Boaters often cut this mark, however, since the depths are generlly 7 to 9 feet north and east of "CR".

Between Spaniard and Holton points, where the channel carries 14 to 16 feet, the Corsica's most noteworthy landmark sits to starboard facing the Chester. Summer foliage may hide all but its top floor and chimneys, but this distinctive white-trimmed, red brick mansion, c. 1920, was the home of financial executive John Raskob who financed the Empire State Building. It was bought by the Soviet Embassy in the 1970s and has been used since as dacha for employees of the (now) Russian Embassy.

Beyond it, the embassy's private beach, with its tiny green-and-white striped lighthouse, occupies Town Point where depths drop and the channel constricts. Shoals encroach from both shores here at red nun "2". Minding the mark gives you 8 to 9 feet for about 100 yards before double-digits reappear and the navigable area widens again. Be mindful of a small, uncharted piling in the vicinity of "2". It holds a green-painted water-quality sensor and is not a navigational aid. Keep it to starboard along with the nun.

Past this point, several bights allow plenty of options, then the channel swings north around Ship Point. Opposite

Grays Inn Creek continued

red daymark "4" off Wash Point is **Emory Creek** with a fairly well protected small anchorage at its mouth. The creek itself is reported to be even snugger, with 6-foot depths beyond its opening. Elsewhere, there are good depths and holding around Cedar Point and Rocky Point.

The channel narrows and curves around fixed red "6", which marks the shoal extending from a southern promontory intriguingly called Jacob's Nose. Trawlers often anchor in this area near Gunston Day School and its fleet of small boats. Charts don't always show the area beyond Jacob's Nose, but 6 to 7 feet prevail before a shallower,

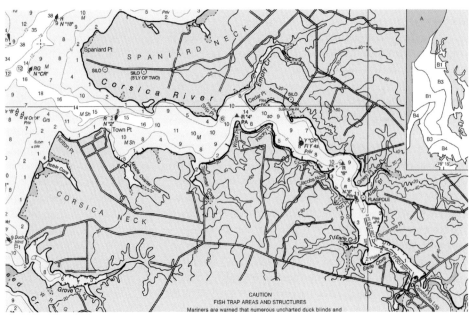

Corsica River; from NOAA Chart 12272—not to be used for navigation.

marked channel continues on toward Centreville Town Wharf—another "lost" Chesapeake port once busy with tall ships and steamboats. If your draft can't make it (the channel was reported at 3 feet in 2009), it's worth anchoring and taking the dinghy in.

Centreville's landing sits on the southern branch of the two streams that form the Corsica. Besides a public launch ramp, the wharf hosts shallow-draft workboats and fishing boats; dinghies can dock in any out-of-the-way spot. Overlooking the wharf, Captain John Ozmon's restored two-story brick store, c. 1880, is now a private home.

If you walk upstream, following the road beyond the low bridge, you'll find a peaceful boardwalk leading to a scenic overlook, one of Centreville's waterfront restoration projects. Along the way you'll pass an architecturally unique grouping of four identical Captains' Houses. These slender, three-storied, one-dormer private residences—shoulder-to-shoulder facing the creek—were built by Ozmon for the captains of his schooner fleet.

A short walk to the east from the water is Doc's Riverside Grille, a sports-friendly place with an appealing patio and menu. If you don't mind a 15-minute hike farther up the hill, Centreville's pretty town square with its historic courthouse, shops and eateries is worth the effort.

Langford Creek

Over and over again we hear cruisers say that part of the Bay's fascination lies in unraveling the mystery of what lies hidden ahead, just past that next bend. Such a place is **Cacaway Island**, an unexpected treasure tucked inside ❺ **Langford Creek**.

As you head up the Chester and come to the confusing intersection of creeks and rivers we mentioned on the previous page, you may find the mouth of Langford Creek hard to identify. The easiest way is to follow the series of green cans ("1", "3" and "5") on the western shore of the Chester. You

also can use a pink-roofed house on Nichols Point to keep you heading in the right direction. If the pink roof is on your port side, you've missed Langford and you're still in the main branch of the Chester.

Just above the entrance to Langford Creek and to the west you'll find a marked channel leading to Long Cove Marina, which has slips, fuel, marine supplies and travel lifts. Nearby there is a county launch ramp (you can obtain a permit at a local sporting goods store).

A distance of 1 mile separates green markers "5" and "7". In summer haze, "7", which marks the shoal off Drum Point, can be hard to distinguish against the green of the shoreline. If you can't see it, do this: From "5", take a heading for the lookout tower on Orchard Point until "7" gradually appears.

Beyond Drum Point, to port, you'll find another Langford tributary, **Davis Creek**, which is marked by red "2". Davis is the most protected anchorage in the Langford Creek area. Lankford Bay Marina, a full-service facility, is located on the south shore of the creek, just past the entrance. Up-creek, there's 7 feet of water for another quarter mile. Anchored here, you're in the middle of a bucolic picture: hills, fields, trees, a barn and a small, neat cottage.

If you choose to hide here from an approaching summer storm under menacing afternoon skies, listen carefully for the rumble of thunder. If it seems to be maintaining a static distance, it could be the rumble of Aberdeen Proving Ground, 25 miles to the north. The weapons testing can be heard throughout most of the upper Bay.

Cacaway Island lies beyond Davis Creek, at the junction of **West Fork** and **East Fork**. On the chart, the island looks something like an upside-down high-top boot. Its toe points northeast, and the curve formed between the toe and the instep provides the most popular anchorage. A long sandbar extends from the toe toward land, making it nearly impossible to circumnavigate the uninhabited island.

Anchoring just east of this sandbar in about 9 feet of water roughly 50 feet from the island, one cruiser swam in to discover how close to shore he could have anchored. Within 12 paces of dry land, he found 6 feet of water.

"No Trespassing" signs warn boaters to stay off the island; still, with deep water just off its eastern side, it is a well-used anchorage and swimming hole. The swimming is great because there are few sea nettles in the fresher water here.

If you decide to explore the Forks, remember to stay well off the points of land; there are no marks to indicate shoals. (Some cruisers have become inadvertently intimate with Island Point on the East Fork.) West Fork is characterized by several large, well-manicured estates, while East Fork has developments with small lots.

At the head of West Fork is old St. Paul's Church, believed to be the oldest Episcopal church in Maryland used continuously as a house of worship. (The water is only a couple of feet to a few inches deep for the last mile or two before the church.) Established by the Maryland legislature in 1692, the church stands amid oaks and sycamores that were probably already a century old when it was built. Its silver chalice and plate, bearing the date 1699, were used in the original wooden church on the same site. Thirty-four pews were constructed and rented out at so many pounds of tobacco per year. Or, one could buy an entire pew outright for 1,000 pounds of tobacco. You'll find the tomb of stage and screen actress Tallulah Bankhead in the graveyard. This and other surprises make Langford Creek an intriguing stopover.

Comegys Bight

The wide-open waters of ❻ **Comegys Bight** are particularly inviting on a hot, still summer evening when you want a long fetch of water to catch what little breeze there might be. Located 14 miles up the Chester, Comegys Bight is on the main stem of the river, just beyond the big intersection against the northern shore. To stay in the main part of the Chester River, look for the pink-roofed cottage perched on Cliffs Point. This point is on the river's northern shore and also marks the beginning of Comegys Bight. If you keep the cottage to port as you head upriver, you'll not only make the Chester, but you'll also be in a good position to enter Comegys.

The bight's west side has fairly deep water—about 8 or 9 feet—so you can head in, keeping just a few hundred feet off shore, without worrying about shoals. (If you draw over 6 feet, beware of a 6-foot lump smack in the middle of the cove.) The bottom is soft, sandy mud—good holding for either a Danforth or a plow.

The bight is a wide, round basin, with two tiny, unnavigable creeks feeding into it from the north. Its deep water is a half-mile wide and stretches a half-mile inland, creating an anchorage large enough for a fleet of boats. Comegys is rimmed with woods and a few homes, which almost become lost in the thick summer foliage. It's a good place to observe wildlife such as great blue herons, osprey and deer. As dusk

Langford Creek; from NOAA Chart 12272—not to be used for navigation.

settles, you may be serenaded by a cadence of resident frogs.

Boaters approaching from upriver should be aware of the 3-foot shoal that stretches about a quarter-mile off Deep Point on the east edge of the bight. It is marked by flashing green "23" and green can "21". Deep Point got its name from the depth of the river channel that passes by it; charts show the spot to be 56 feet, making it one of the deepest points in the Chester.

Another busy spot lies across the river, off Conquest Beach, a short stretch of sandy beach on Spaniard Neck, used by groups who gather to swim, sunbathe and play sports.

Upper Chester River

Above Comegys Bight, the ❼ Chester River snakes from buoys "21" to "41" in two long S-curves for nine pastoral miles to Chestertown. The channel, as deep as 54 feet off Melton Point and carrying no less than 13 feet, gives way to shoals along the banks, outside the well-marked course. Meanwhile, you'll pass estates, lush farmland, forests and

Langford Creek continued

hills.

Boat traffic is usually light on this part of the river. The shoreline provides enough protection from wind and weather to offer anchorages wherever you choose (outside the channel). Anchor for lunch north of Melton Point or stop for a nettle-free swim at **Devils Reach**.

The river's current flows swiftly. On a slight-breeze day, you can waft downstream with a favorable current and note the same sensation you get from a movable walkway. When the current's against you, however, you *know* you're trudging uphill, and getting anywhere will feel like a long, heavy slog.

Between Comegys Bight and Chestertown, cruisers will find only one navigable tributary—**Southeast Creek**, above nun "32". Most boats will find that there isn't enough water in Southeast Creek to anchor out, but cruisers can find services by taking a privately dredged, marked channel that leads to Kennersley Point Marina at the mouth of **Island Creek**, a tributary of Southeast Creek. Even here, though, the water is charted at 4 feet.

On the Chester and just before you get to Devils Reach, Rolph's Wharf Marina offers fuel, a launch ramp, a picnic area with grills, lodging and a seasonal beach bar. This can be a loud and happy place on weekends. As you pass Rolph's, be sure to observe the 6 knot speed limit.

If you wish to spend a quiet night away from the crowded anchorage off Chestertown's waterfront, try the south shore of the river along Devils Reach, about a mile

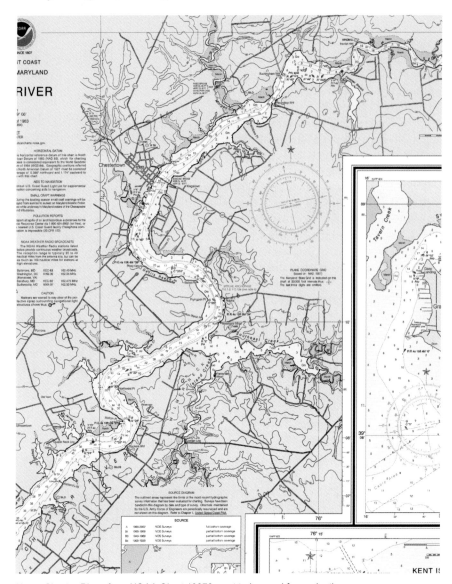

Upper Chester River; from NOAA Chart 12272—not to be used for navigation.

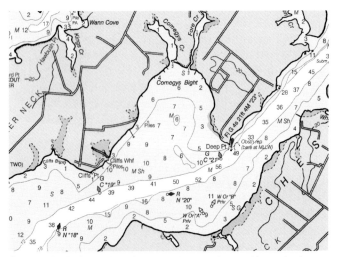

Comegys Bight; from NOAA Chart 12272—not to be used for navigation.

south of town. Bear southwest from "37A," anchoring in 12 feet of water between "37A" and "39". Here, scenic woods overlooking a sandy beach provide good protection from southerly winds. Devils Reach names an S-shaped curl in the river bed. You can just imagine how devilishly difficult it must have been for sailing ships to get around that bend as they carried freight to Chestertown!

Chestertown

Past Devils Reach, one last curve brings you within sight of **❽ Chestertown** and her lovely bascule bridge. This drawbridge (vertical clearance 12 feet), which carries Route 213 over the river, is no longer manned daily. Six hours notice is now required for an opening. Call the state highway maintenance facility (410-778-0818), and the tender on duty will accommodate you as soon as possible.

Many boaters anchor off the Chestertown riverfront, where there's good depth, but be sure to leave enough room to allow for swinging with that swift current. Two notes of

Port of Call

Chestertown

Chartered as a port of entry in 1706, Chestertown retains its historical charm. Stately colonial homes overlook the Chester River, and restored Georgian, Federal and Victorian buildings line the historic district's brick sidewalks. Add to its appeal a thriving arts community, delightful specialty shops, great restaurants and the presence of venerable Washington College and it's no wonder Chestertown is such a favorite Eastern Shore destination. Unfortunately, the town has limited docking facilities, though boats are welcome to anchor below the Chester River bridge and use the dinghy landing at the foot of Cannon Street (where the *Sultana* is berthed). Lodging in town is available at the Imperial Hotel as well as myriad B&Bs.

Chestertown's wide shady sidewalks invite visitors to explore. The Visitor Center offers several handy brochures, including a self-guided walking tour of historic and architectural landmarks, among them the Geddes Piper House. Built in the 1780s, it's open Saturday afternoons (May–October) for tours. Another publication pinpoints antiques shops, fine arts galleries and craftsmen's studios. All lie within strolling distance of the waterfront. Guided town tours are also available for a fee (for information, contact 410-778-2829 or *cliokent@yahoo.com*).

Sultana Projects, a non-profit group dedicated to maritime education and the preservation of shipbuilding skills, offers *Sultana* excursions to the public (410-778-5954, *www.schoonersultana.com*.) Berthed near *Sultana* at the foot of Cannon Street are the skipjack *Elsworth* and the buyboat *Annie D.*, both of which are owned by Echo Hill Outdoor School. You're likely to find images of vessels like these at the Chestertown Arts League's gallery, showcasing local artists' work. Art galleries and antiques stores sell everything from clothing, books and jewelry to custom-built furniture.

Entertainment is close at hand: a first-run movie theater on the

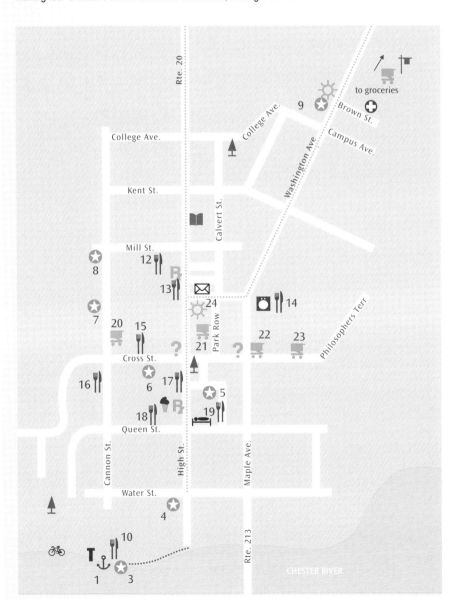

Chestertown

⚓ **Marinas/Dockage**
  1 Chestertown Marina

⊙ **Points of Interest**
  2 Kent County Historical Society
  3 Schooner *Sultana* berth
  4 Custom House
  5 Geddes Piper House
  6 Sultana Projects
  7 Chestertown Arts League
  8 Schooner *Sultana* Shipyard
  9 Washington College

? **Information**

🍴 **Dining**
  10 The Fish Whistle
  12 Washington Tavern
  13 Dunkin' Donuts
  14 Ellen's Coffee Shop
  15 Play It Again Sam
  16 Blue Heron Cafe
  17 White Swan Tavern
  18 Evergrain Bread Co.
  19 Imperial Hotel

🛒 **Groceries**
  20 Chestertown Natural Foods
  21 Farmer's Market
  22 Royal Farms
  23 Dollar General

☼ **Entertainment/Recreation**
  9 Prince Theatre
  24 Fountain Park

⚑ **Park/Playground**

🍦 **Ice Cream**

⚑ **Lodging**

🚲 **Bicycles**

℞ **Pharmacy**

✉ **Post Office**

⊤ **Water Taxi**

▭ **Laundromat**

▪ **Library**

○ **Hospital**

···• **Trolley Route**

···· **Waterfront Promenade**

⊤ **Shopping Center**

Port of Call: Chestertown

town's outskirts; concerts, lectures and films at the restored Prince Theatre downtown; bi-weekly concerts in Fountain Park during the summer; occasional live music at Play It Again Sam and other dining venues; and a variety of cultural events at the Washington College campus and the restored Customs House which overlooks the river from Water Street.

Galley provisioning is easy. Farm-fresh produce, local cheese, jams and baked goods are available at the Saturday morning farmer's market at Park Row (which also includes an artisans market) or at Chestertown Natural Foods, which sells general foodstuffs, too. More extensive shopping may require a trip to supermarkets a bit farther away, but they're accessible by taxi cab (410-778-9496).

Diverse cuisines and creative chefs are the hallmarks of the many restaurants sprinkled throughout Chestertown's business district, including at the historic Imperial Hotel and the rustic Brooks Tavern. The Fish Whistle is the only waterfront dining in town, Play It Again Sam is a popular coffeehouse/wine bar a short walk from the water. Stam Drugs, also on High Street, sports an old-fashioned soda fountain.

Shops and galleries extend their hours on First Fridays, when entertainment and activities fill the historic district until 8 p.m. To begin these special evenings, visitors are invited to a wine and cheese reception and history discussion from 4 to 6 p.m. at the Geddes Piper House. Memorial Day weekend's Chestertown Tea Party commemorates the purported uprising by colonists who dumped a ship's cargo of British tea into the river (reenactment, parade, music, food, arts and crafts). Other annual events include Independence Day festivities and fireworks, the Wildlife Exhibition and Sale (artists, carvers and crafts people) and in November, the *Sultana*'s Downrigging Weekend (visiting tallships, boat rides, and spectacular special lighting as darkness falls).

Information: Kent County Tourism Development, 410-778-0416, Kent County Visitors Center, 410-778-9737; *www.chestertown.com* or *www. kentcounty.com*.

Bay Spotlight

Schooner Sultana

On your cruise up the Chester River you might be lucky enough to catch a glimpse of the schooner *Sultana* under sail with a batch of school kids at the helm or carrying passengers out for an afternoon adventure. A meticulous reproduction of a 1768 Royal Navy revenue cutter that once patrolled the Chesapeake, the 97-foot long *Sultana* represents the sweat and effort of an entire community that came together to build a dream.

The boat was the brainchild of master boatbuilder John Swain of nearby Millington, Md., who saw the project as a way to build a sense of community and revitalize a flagging town center. Built in an empty lot on Cannon Street, the boat ultimately engaged nearly the entire population of Chestertown in the building process, with volunteers contributing over 200,000 hours of labor for her construction. Thousands of individual supporters made donations to fund her progress. By the time *Sultana* was launched on March 24, 2001, more than 10,000 people came to Chestertown to see her launch.

Sultana was built directly from a 1768 plan of the original vessel that Swain and his team acquired from the National Maritime Museum in Greenwich, England. Virtually every detail from the 1768 *Sultana* was replicated on the new vessel, including the officer's cabins below, a working brick fireplace in the galley and four-pound swivel guns on deck. Built completely from wood, the schooner is even fastened together with more

Sultana Projects Inc.

Canvas up and flag flying, the schooner Sultana (above) reaches down the Chester River on one of her many excursions around the Bay. Every autumn she hosts her own gathering of tall ships during the annual Downrigging festival in Chestertown.

than 10,000 traditional wooden treenails or "trunnels."

The highlight of *Sultana*'s sailing season comes in late October or early November with the annual Downrigging Weekend, which celebrates her last sailing day of the season before being winterized.

For more information about the schooner *Sultana*, visit *www.sultanaprojects.org* or call 410-778-5954.

Chestertown continued

caution. Beware of an underground power cable running between the Chestertown Marina and the bridge, which has caused, at times, deep grief. (The cable is not shown on older charts.) Also, it's best to use a plow anchor with lots of chain instead of a Danforth. When the current reverses, it can dislodge a Danforth; boaters too close to the bridge might find their vessels drifting upriver onto it. Many folks report having a difficult time anchoring here, and that could be why.

If the comforts and services of a marina are preferable, you can reserve a slip at Chestertown Marina, the only transient facility in town. Dinghies are welcome to tie up at a small floating dock attached to a larger dock at the foot of Cannon Street (where the schooner *Sultana* is usually berthed). You may also tie up a dinghy to the town dock at the foot of High Street (access can be difficult, though, depending on the tide) or at the bulkhead in front of the pavilion at Wilmer Park, just south of town but within easy walking distance.

What Chestertown lacks in boating facilities it makes up in sheer charm. Upon reaching Chestertown, you'll be greeted by graceful waterfront homes that have welcomed mariners for centuries. The town was a busy colonial port of entry and

became the Kent County seat in 1706 (a role it continues to serve). Since 1782 it has been home to the new nation's first chartered college, Washington College, a private liberal arts institution.

Today's Chestertown reflects its past in a handsome downtown historic district filled with architecturally interesting buildings, and celebrates its most recent claim to fame—as a haven for artists—with more than a dozen studios and galleries tucked among a fine collection of restaurants, inns and cafes. The Prince Theatre, a short walk up High Street, offers live entertainment, including symphony, jazz and folk concerts. Turn down Cross Street to find Play it Again Sam's, a charming coffee shop and wine store that often features live music and wine tastings.

Most boaters view Chestertown as the end of the line, but the Chester River is navigable for another eight miles above the bascule bridge. Continuing through the countryside, with buoys marking the most difficult curves, the river carries between 6 ½ and 22 feet all the way to **Crumpton**, where vestiges of the old landing remain. Adventurous cruisers may want to hike to the extensive Crumpton auction which takes place every Wednesday, rain or shine. Crumpton's fixed bridge (14-foot vertical clearance) will stop many boats from proceeding farther upriver.

SPOTLIGHT CRUISE

Here is a story about an escape from the wind-blown Bay that turns into a great cruise up the Chester and a night on Comegys Bight.

The *Right* Right Turn

I was muscling the Albin 28 up the Bay out of Annapolis one morning, bound for the Sassafras River but caught in a family argument between an ebbing tide and 15 knots of hot-tempered southerly. My daughter Kristen and I were not having a family argument—at least not yet. She and I had been bouncing silently along for about half an hour when I looked over and saw her hunkered down in the passenger chair, her bare feet braced against the bulkhead and her arms wrapped around her little furball of a dog, Echo, in a kind of maternal death-grip. At her feet, wedged between the base of the chair and the bulkhead, lay my dog Skipper, who at that moment raised his head and gave me a look that clearly asked the question, "Why can't you just take up knitting?" Then, after sighing the sigh of a dog who has bounced his way from the Elk River to Rudee Inlet, he went back to sleep.

What could I do? I surrendered as gracefully as I could. "Okay," I said, laughing, "I'm thinking we don't really have to get to the Sassafras today."

"Oh, it's okay," Kristen replied in the voice of one who is also considering the virtues of a quiet day spent knitting.

"Oh, no," I countered, "we'll find some place closer."

Only a few minutes earlier we had passed under the Chesapeake Bay Bridge, and we were now nearly parallel with Love Point at the tip of Kent Island. Well, here we were at the entrance to the Chester River. What could be better? We could simply cruise upriver as far as we felt the urge and then come back and settle into any one of a dozen quiet spots for the evening. With the decision made, I swung the Albin east to intersect Love Point Light.

After the bucking bronco of oncoming chop, our ride became positively prim as we turned south to enter the Chester. True, we were now headed dead into the wind, but it felt good, and the chop was now hustling us along from behind. The boat fairly hummed down the channel between Kent Island and Eastern Neck Island. The tension onboard eased as well. I eased my hold on the wheel and backed down the throttle; Skipper rolled over onto his side; and Kristen toted Echo back to the big padded seat over the engine and sprawled out on her back to enjoy the sun.

A little while later we entered the Chester's big horseshoe turn, passing Kent Narrows and then Queenstown Creek to starboard and the marshland of Cedar and Hail points to port. And then we were headed north again. But this time, in

Spotlight Cruise continued

more protected waters, the chop was minimal and the southerly was lost altogether in our forward progress. The regrettable feature of this was that the rising heat was now glaringly apparent. Early morning would soon stretch into late morning, and the summer sun—now with no mediating breeze—was becoming a force to be reckoned with.

We had just passed Piney Point on the tip of Tilghman Neck, when I turned to point out the felicitously named Fryingpan Cove to port and I noticed that Kristen had fallen sound asleep. Sigh. Isn't that the way? Here I had someone other than Skipper aboard to point things out to, and she was asleep. I looked hopefully over at Skipper, but he merely closed his eyes even tighter and snored a little for good measure. I got the point.

In silence, I piloted the Albin past Fryingpan Cove, then into the Hydra-headed portion of the Chester, where rivers and creeks come and go willy-nilly. If you're not paying attention at this point, you can end up "heading" off in the wrong direction. Reed Creek is the first, breaking off to starboard, followed almost immediately by Grays Inn Creek to port. Both are lovely creeks, deep enough for a visit and with several good anchorages each—though the entrances require a careful eye on the charts and depthsounder. After Grays Inn Creek, the main channel of the Chester turns eastward, while the entrance to Langford Creek—as broad as the Chester—lies dead ahead. Langford, too, has good deep water, even after it forks east and west a mile and a half upstream, with fine protected anchorages galore. Cacaway Island, which lies at the metaphorical fork in the creek, is the hands-down favorite anchorage on Langford. It has deep water nearly to its shoreline and the possibility of a little dry land below the private island's high-water mark when the tide is out.

On the other hand, if you swing too far east as the Chester turns at this busy intersection, you can find yourself entering the Corsica River. That's no bad thing, of course, because the Corsica, too, is an admirable river, though its most intriguing sight lies right at the entrance facing the Chester: the Russian embassy's elegant summer dacha, the red-brick former mansion of John Jacob Raskob, builder of the Empire State Building.

Having nobody to distract me, I easily found the road most traveled and continued up the Chester channel, remembering almost in time to slow down for the large 6-knot speed-limit zone off Rolph's Wharf Marina, another seven miles upstream. The sudden decrease in speed was enough to wake up Kristen . . . just long enough to turn over onto her stomach. Harrumph! Well, I was enjoying the trip, anyway.

It was not until we reversed course just above Chestertown that Kristen finally woke up for good. She dived into the cabin and returned with a couple of bottles of cold water before climbing back into her seat.

"That's nice," she said, sipping water and indicating Chestertown's elegant colonial waterfront buildings.

Ah, an opening, I thought, and immediately launched into a description of the charms of that city, with its great restaurants, wonderful bookshop, lovely old 18th-century buildings, town square and Washington College. "And that's the Sultana, a replica of an 18th-century British schooner," I concluded as we glided slowly by her berth.

As we continued downriver, I happily pointed out nearly everything I had wanted to show her on the way up. But by the time we had reached Deep Point at flashing green "23", we were both rendered speechless by the heat. The sun, now slung low on the horizon, felt like a laser beam. The morning's southerly was a desultory memory.

"Look," Kristen said with sudden enthusiasm, pointing to a trio of powerboats anchored stern to the shore. In the water, a half-dozen adults and as many children, and a single black lab, were splashing in the water along a narrow sand beach, having a wonderful time.

"Conquest Beach!" I enthused. "No dogs allowed on the beach—it's private—but if we stay below the high tide line and out of the way, we'll be all right. And happily the tide is just now starting to flood back in."

We dropped the anchor farther off shore than the other boats, but out of the channel, then I quickly changed—Kristen was already properly attired—and we grabbed some doggie bags and tumbled into the water. The dogs watched for a moment, then followed suit. I don't remember the water ever feeling any finer! We swam and paddled and splashed until we were all exhausted.

A little while later, we hauled ourselves and then the dogs back aboard. Motor restarted and anchor up, we simply crossed the river and motored into Comegys Bight, the large open bay directly across the river from our swimming hole. Comegys is about a mile wide in every direction, with reasonably deep water, especially on its western side. That makes it a lousy place for a hidey-hole, but since there were no storms in the forecast (it was that kind of summer, if you'll remember), it was perfect. We decided on a spot well out of the way but still far enough out to catch any breeze that might appear out of the south. We also put out plenty of rode. Really, forecasters have been wrong before.

The sun finally dropped out of sight, but the heat lingered on late into the evening. We ate a cold supper, then pulled our bedding up into the cockpit. Kristen, who is shorter than I, settled back down with Echo on the engine seat. I stretched out across the sole in the stern and promptly fell asleep. At about 2 o'clock I awoke long enough to feel a soft breeze that had sprung up in the south. Excellent!

Early the next morning, over coffee and kibbles, we watched a workboat commuting downriver and a few herring gulls flying overhead in search of an early worm—or whatever gulls eat for breakfast. Half-an-hour later, we pulled up stakes and shuttled off after the waterman. As we passed Langford and then Grays Inn creeks, Kristen curled up on the engine seat and went back to sleep.

Well, we didn't make it to the Sassafras, but we couldn't we have found a better place to cruise than up the Chester with a night on Comegys. I would have said so, too, but there was nobody awake to hear me.

—**Jody Argo Schroath**

Chesapeake Bay Bridge to Herring Bay

The Severn, South, West, Rhode, Miles and Wye Rivers
Whitehall, Herring and Eastern Bay and Kent Island
Annapolis and St. Michaels

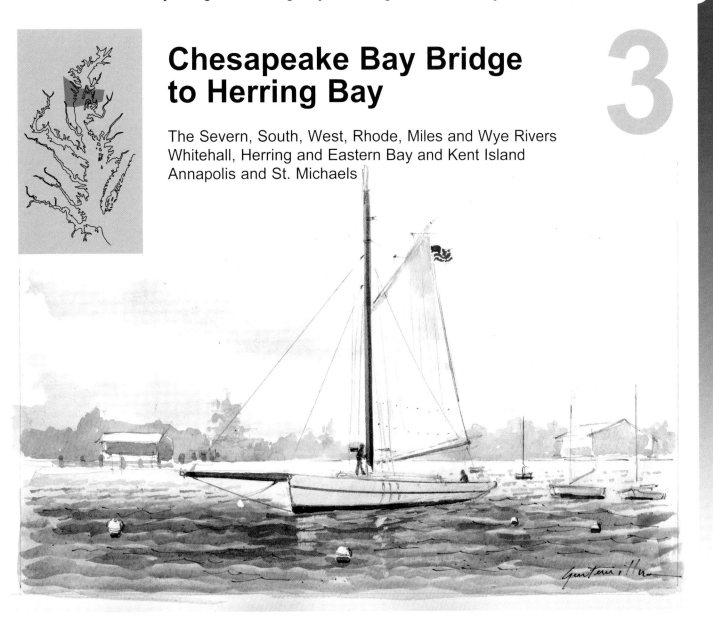

The middle Bay cruising region offers stunning vistas of pure Chesapeake country ringed with rolling farmland, densely wooded shores and picturesque fishing villages—not to mention Annapolis and St. Michaels, undisputed favorites among cruising boaters. Throughout the middle Bay you'll find remarkable dining opportunities, excellent marinas and hearty hospitality.

Between the wonders of Annapolis and St. Michaels lies the site of one of Maryland's earliest settlements, Kent Island—strategically located for commerce and easily defended against unfriendly incursions. For today's boaters, it makes a strategically convenient stopover for any Bay cruise, or a good sheltered layover for those heading north and south.

The Kent Island Narrows separates the island from the mainland by only a few hundred yards. In the past couple of decades, Kent Island Narrows—the aquatic alleyway between the Chester River and Eastern Bay—has bloomed into a destination port of its own. Today, the churning bottleneck promises no-holds-barred boating fun, along with a host of

full-service marinas, bars and crabhouses and a network of scenic hike-bike trails to stretch the sealegs.

For more serene surroundings, you can head south of the Narrows to the Wye River. Known for producing some of the Bay's biggest and sweetest blue crabs, this meandering waterway is among the Bay's least spoiled cruising grounds. The river runs around Wye Island and, while narrow in many spots, is by no means "skinny." Many of its creeks hold plenty of water for deep-draft vessels. You could spend a week gunkholing the Wye River.

Across the Bay on the West River, the hamlet of Galesville offers a different sort of solitude, with several waterfront restaurants and good places to tie up. West River was also the birthplace of one of the Bay's most storied racing sailboats, the Chesapeake 20, which dates to the 1930s. Fetch up in Galesville on a summer afternoon and you're likely to see these over-canvassed craft gliding effortlessly along through the West River waters.

Oh, there's a lot to see and do in the middle Bay . . .

SECTION 3 | WESTERN SHORE: *Whitehall Bay to Herring Bay*

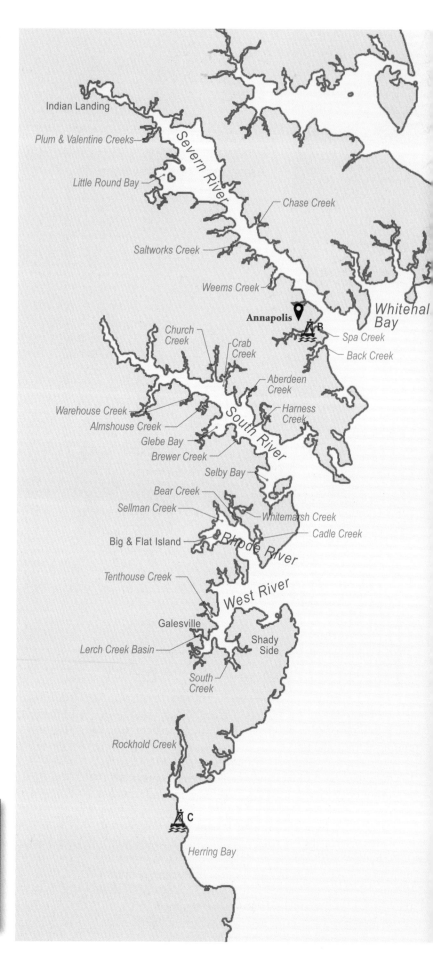

TowBoatU.S.
LOCATIONS

A Kent Narrows
410-745-3000

B Annapolis
410-263-1260

C Herring Bay
410-610-0100

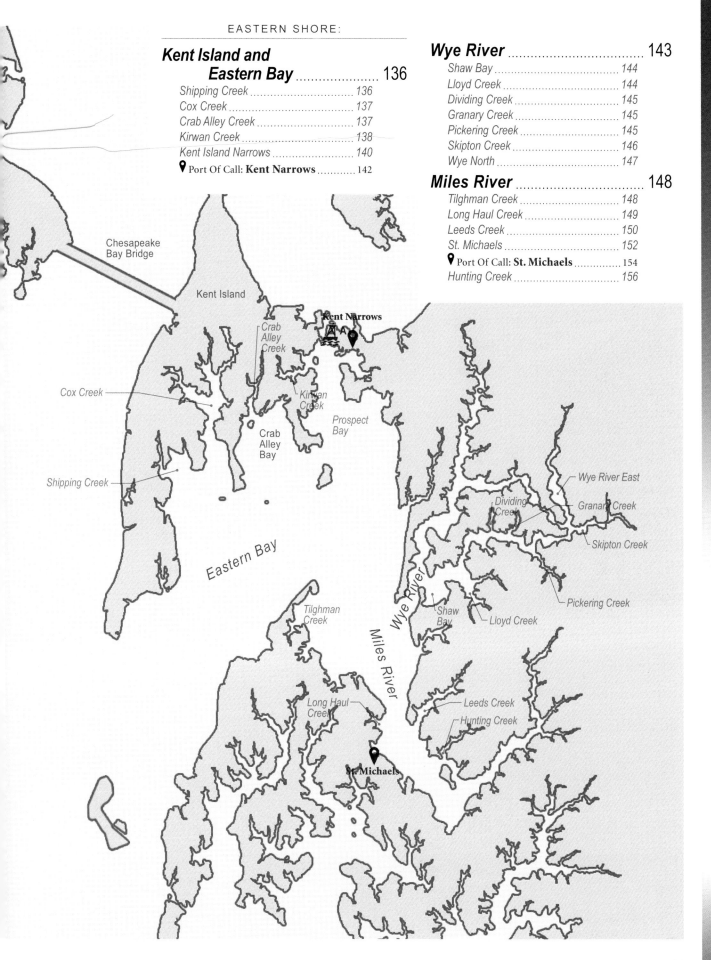

Young people changing waterskiers on Mill Creek off Whitehall Bay—This popular area still has an easy-going neighborhood feel.

Whitehall Bay

Whitehall Bay is a convenient anchorage just south of the Chesapeake Bay Bridge. An attractive destination for weekenders and club raft-ups, it's an equally appealing alternative to busy Annapolis harbor and the congestion of Spa and Back creeks. From Whitehall Bay it's an easy run around Greenbury Point into Annapolis for supplies or sightseeing.

Whitehall Bay has general depths of 6 to 13 feet. The entrance channel is about 300 yards wide between **Whitehall Flats** on the west and **North Shoal** on the east, both with depths of 3 to 4 feet. Inside the ample anchorage, manicured lawns roll down to the water's edge and expensive homes hide among old growths of trees. Because of its size, Whitehall Bay is never crowded, despite its close proximity to Annapolis.

To enter, be sure to give Hackett Point a wide berth, as the shoals here extend a fair distance south before curving westward in a hook shape to the red flashing entrance marker "2W". Stay well to port as you approach the flashing red beacon, and don't be too quick to cut east around it once inside the bay. The shoals extend north, south and east of the marker. (Be sure not to confuse the 4-second "2W" with the 2.5-second "2M" farther to port and much closer to shore, marking the entrance to Mill Creek.)

If you turn northeast to anchor directly behind Hackett Point, the water is 10 feet deep close to shore. The only thing to watch out for here is a group of pilings, evidently the remains of an old dock, which juts out into the water near the home

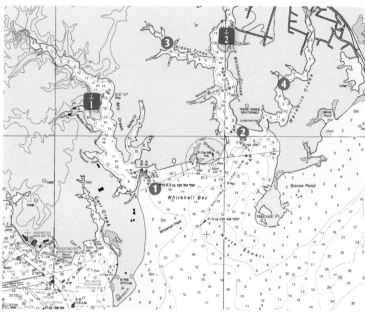

Whitehall Bay; from NOAA Chart 12282—not to be used for navigation.

	MLW	Overnight Slips	Gas	Diesel	Propane	Electric	Showers	Laundry	Restaurant	Lodging	Pool	Pump-out	Ice	Groceries	Marine Supplies	Boat Repair	Bait	Haul-out Services	Launch Ramp	Wi-Fi	Other
Whitehall Bay																					
Cantler's Riverside Inn Whitehall Bay/Mill Cr. 410-757-1311; *www.cantlers.com*	10'		●				●		●				●								Great seafood, waterside patio; dockage for diners
Whitehall Marina Whitehall Bay/Whitehall Cr. 410-757-4819; *www.whitehallannapolis.com*	11'	●											●	●							Protected deep-water slips for rent

● On Premises
➤ Nearby

on this peninsula.

Hackett Point, a privately owned estate, is almost an island, connected to the mainland only by a narrow strip of land. If you anchor near this low-lying neck, you have a wonderful view of the Bay Bridge spans forming their long, graceful arch over the Chesapeake. A boater running from a storm could not ask for a better harbor of refuge. From the first buoy marker out in the Bay, it takes only about 15 to 20 minutes at 6 knots to reach a good place to anchor.

Whitehall Bay is wide and open, yet fairly well protected from moderate winds out of the north or west. It is exposed to the southeast, and if the wind is from that quarter, or if the weather is generally rough, you can seek more protection by continuing into one of Whitehall's pretty and snug creeks.

Whitehall Bay has three creeks heading inland. To the west lies ❶ **Mill Creek**, which has a dredged and well-marked entrance. Its constricted dog-leg channel looks trickier than it is. Just follow the red and green daymarks in their proper sequence and swing wide past the last red marker. From there the creek is fairly easy to negotiate. Mill Creek is narrow but deep, with 8 to 14 feet of water along most of its length and 8 to 9 feet in the channel at MLW. Be aware, however, that a strong northwesterly can push a lot of water out of the creek. For deep drafts, it's probably best to stay closer to "2" at the entrance—and go slowly, just in case. This water can be skinny for a 6-foot draft. Mill Creek is the home of Cantler's Riverside Inn, perennially voted a "Best of the Bay" crabhouse and well worth the trip. There's a protected anchorage with good holding in front of Cantler's, as well as free dock space for patrons.

Just inside Mill Creek, the first tributary to starboard is **Burley Creek**. This anchorage is lovely but a bit snug for more than a few boats. Burley sports a number of docks with sailboats, attesting to its 10-foot depths; the narrowness of the creek provides good protection from a blow. Past Martin's Cove and Cantler's, Mill Creek takes a sharp northwest turn. Entering the turn, the channel skirts a marked but treacherous shoal. Beyond it lies a popular and well-protected anchorage. The spot is quite peaceful, although your anchor may have difficulty penetrating the thick layer of twigs and sodden leaves that covers the bottom.

Off Whitehall Bay to the north is ❷ **Whitehall Creek**, navigable for about 2 miles past Sharps Point and with its shallows clearly marked. Cruising into Whitehall Creek,

red daymark "4" will get you lined up for green "5", which marks a sharp turn to port toward red "6". In beam seas (not an unusual occurrence in this area), you could be eased to leeward out of the channel, but use care and you'll get safely around "6" into the calmer waters beyond.

Although heavily settled, Whitehall Creek offers a number of attractive anchorages. Aids to navigation mark the deep water for about a half mile until the creek forks at ❸ **Ridout Creek** (pronounced *RIDE-out*). Eight- to 10-foot depths continue along both forks almost to their sources.

Winding your way past daymark "8" and heading for Ridout Creek, you'll find that even in a fading light its entrance is easy to negotiate. In a breeze, the tall trees on both banks may be swaying and sighing in the wind, but down on the water all will be relatively calm. Ridout Creek is one of those truly beautiful creeks you'll want to revisit often.

The third tributary off Whitehall Bay, ❹ **Meredith Creek**, runs northeast from Hackett Point. While it has plenty of deep water inside, its unmarked entrance is narrow and shoal (1 foot, according to the charts). You may see big boats moored at docks inside this creek, but venture in carefully, paying close attention to your depthsounder and the tides.

Severn River

There's little doubt about the highlight of any cruise on the **Severn River**—it's Annapolis, Maryland's capital and a city whose name is synonymous around the world with boating in

International **M**arine **I**nsurance **S**ervices®

Celebrating our 28th year in business! We invite you to join the IMIS family for the super service for which we're known.

800–541–IMIS (4647)
Local: 410-827-3757
Fax: 410-827-3758
Email: mail@IMIS.pro

Wells Cove Marina
110 Channel Marker Way
Grasonville, MD 21638

Severn River continued

general and sailing in particular. Annapolis's landmarks are among the better known on the Bay: the domes of the State House and Naval Academy Chapel, the spires of St. Anne's and St. Mary's churches, and the forest of sailboat masts ringing Spa Creek. But, as anyone who has cruised farther up this lovely residential river can tell you, it also claims many delight-

ful anchorages. There are few amenities upriver of Annapolis, but quiet splendor abounds. A creek-by-creek description of the rest of the Severn River follows the Annapolis pages.

Annapolis

The entrance to ❶ **Annapolis**—though often chock-a-block with boats of every size and description, all headed in different directions—is quite easy to negotiate. As you round Greenbury Point from the north or Tolly Point from the south, be sure to stay in the main channel and follow the fairway marked by cans, nuns and lighted buoys for about three-quarters of a mile, heading, roughly for the Naval Academy campus at the mouth of Spa Creek. This will allow you to clear the long shoal projecting from Horn Point on your port side (just north of Back Creek). The shoal is marked by a lighted aid, where a pair of ospreys often have an active nest. Past that, you can turn southwest and head into the mooring field toward the downtown docking areas. Here, as you enter **Spa Creek**, you'll see the campus of the U.S. Naval Academy

continued on page 110

Severn River; from NOAA Chart 12282—not to be used for navigation.

Port Annapolis Marina

Contact us for Slips and Service!

Visit our new, fully-stocked Marine Supply Store

take time out to enjoy our café

Just

minutes from the heart of downtown Annapolis, you'll find 16 acres of resort-like setting, top notch marine services, an event pavilion, clubhouse with a pristine pool, and a café and fitness center to use as your

private retreat.

www.portannapolis.com | 410.269.1990

Annapolis continued from page 110

to starboard and then the City Dock area. To port, you'll see the maritime community of **Eastport**, linked to downtown Annapolis by the Spa Creek drawbridge. Tended 24 hours a day, this bascule bridge (15-foot vertical clearance) opens every half-hour from May through October, with rush-hour restrictions on weekdays. Off-season, the bridge opens on request.

As part of its first-come-first-served docking facilities, the city offers plenty of moorings at these locations (for boats up to 45 feet, unless otherwise noted). On Spa Creek: between City Dock and the Chart House; just above the Spa Creek drawbridge in **St. Mary's Cove** (named for the church that towers above it) for boats up to 35 feet; and farther up Spa Creek, off Truxton Park. On **Back Creek**, there are city mooring balls near Bert Jabin Yacht Yard. Before you get too settled on a mooring, though, contact the harbormaster's office at 410-263-7973 or on VHF

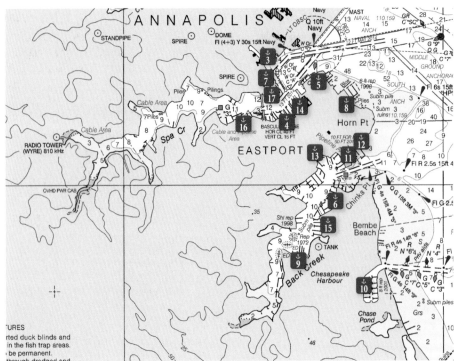

Annapolis; from NOAA Chart 12282—not to be used for navigation.

channels 9 or 17 to arrange for payment. The fee includes the use of on-shore shower facilities at City Dock. Anchoring is not permitted in these designated mooring areas. If you anchor elsewhere, observe the marked channel and stay well clear of marina fairways. Whether you have come to enjoy the comings and goings in boat-crazy Annapolis, or to watch the finish of a Wednesday Night Race near the Spa Creek bridge, arrive early for a prime spot.

Transient dock space is available along the City Dock area known as Ego Alley. Cutting into the heart of town and ending at a public dinghy dock, Ego Alley is named for the nearly endless parade of boats, often showy, that slowly navigate its tight U-turn to see and be seen. Boats may dock for a few hours or overnight, with electricity and fees charged accordingly. As you can imagine, these ringside docks are popular and tend to be at a premium. If you can't find a space right away, contact the harbormaster, who will try to advise you when something becomes available.

Boaters can register at the harbormaster's office, located in the center of the parking lot at City Dock, where you'll also find an extensive book exchange. The harbormaster and his staff patrol city facilities, collect fees, oversee anchored and moored boats, and can arrange pumpouts by the municipal pumpout boat (410-320-6852; VHF channel 17). Wi-Fi (with a fee) is available to boaters both in the harbor and on the outer moorings.

The city recommends anchoring in Spa Creek above the bridge, in certain areas of Back Creek, or in the south anchorage marked on the chart. This south anchorage is popular but has some drawbacks: heavy traffic, no protection from wind or waves, and deep water that shoals rapidly to a treacherous sand bar at Horn Point. Anchoring off the Naval Academy's seawall that faces the Bay (reserved for small naval craft) is

YOUR ALTERNATIVE TO BOAT OWNERSHIP

BOATING MADE SIMPLE!

FREEDOM BOAT CLUB

CELEBRATING 25 YEARS
1989 • 2014
OF BOATING FUN

LOCATED AT BEAUTIFUL PORT ANNAPOLIS MARINA

JOIN THE CLUB
CALL 443-458-5179

www.FreedomBoatClub.com

● *On Premises*
➤ *Nearby*

Severn River/Annapolis

	MLW	Overnight Slips	Gas	Diesel	Propane	Electric	Showers	Laundry	Restaurant	Lodging	Pool	Pump-out	Ice	Groceries	Marine Supplies	Bait	Boat Repair	Haul-out Services	Launch Ramp	Wi-Fi	Other
Annapolis City Dock Severn R./Spa Cr. 410-263-7973; www.annapolis.gov	8'	●	➤	➤	➤	●	●	●	➤	➤	➤	●	➤	➤	➤	➤	➤	➤	➤	●	Moorings and slips for transients
Annapolis City Marina Severn R./Spa Cr. 410-268-0660; www.annapoliscitymarina.com	12'	●	●	●		●	●	●	●	➤		●	●	➤	➤	➤		➤	➤	●	Complete on-water dock shop and fuel dock
Annapolis Harbor Boat Yard Severn R./Spa Cr./Eastport 410-268-0092; www.annapolisharbor.net	11'	➤	➤	➤	➤	●	●	➤	➤	➤		●	●	➤	➤	➤	●	●			Full-service repairs
Annapolis Landing Marina Severn R./Back Cr. 410-263-0090; www.annapolislandingmarina.com	9'	●	●	●	➤	●	●	●		➤	●	●	●	➤	●		➤	➤	➤	●	Cable TV, Wi-Fi, fuel, annual & transient slips
Annapolis Marriott Waterfront Hotel & Marina Severn R./Spa Cr. 410-268-7555	8'	●	➤	➤	➤	●		➤	●	●		➤	●	➤	➤	➤		➤	➤	●	Wharfside dockage only, no slips
Annapolis Maryland Capital Yacht Club Severn R./Horn Pt. 410-269-5219; www.amcyc.com	9'	●	➤	➤	➤	●	●	●	➤	➤		●	●	➤	➤		➤	➤	➤		Clubhouse w/TV, micro-wave, fridge, grill, tennis
Bert Jabin Yacht Yard Severn R./Back Cr. 410-268-9667; www.bjyy.com	9'	●	➤	➤	➤	●	●	●	➤	➤		●	●	●	●	➤	●	●	●	●	Hi-Dry boatel, ship's store, full-service marina
Chesapeake Harbour Marina Severn R./south of Back Cr. 410-268-1969; www.chesapeakeharbour.com	8'	●	➤	➤	➤	●	●	●	●	➤	●	●	●	➤	➤	➤	➤	➤	➤	●	Pvt beach, pools, tennis courts, 24-hour security
Eastport Yacht Center Severn R./Back Cr. 410-280-9988; www.eastportyachtcenter.com	12'	●	➤	➤		●	●	●	➤			●	●			●	●			●	One Minute from the Bay
Horn Point Harbor Marina Severn R./Back Cr. 410-263-0550; www.hornpointharbor.com	6.5'	●	➤	➤	➤	●	●	●	➤	➤		●	➤		➤		➤	➤		●	Quiet, beautiful, easy to access slips
Mears Marina Annapolis Severn R./Back Cr. 410-268-8282; www.mearsannapolis.com	9'	●	➤	➤	➤	●	●	●	➤	●	●	●	●	➤	➤	➤	➤	➤	➤	●	Walk downtown; pool-side cafe/tiki bar, tennis, grills
Pier 4 Marina Severn R./Spa Cr. 410-990-9515; www.pier4annapolis.com	12'		➤	➤	➤	●	●	●	➤	➤	➤	●	➤	➤	➤	➤	➤	➤	➤		Across Spa Creek from Annapolis YC. Floating docks
Port Annapolis Marina Severn R./Back Cr. 410-269-1990 or 301-261-1999; www.portannapolis.com	12'	●	➤	➤	➤	●	●	●	➤	➤	●	●	➤	●		●	●		●	●	50-ton lift, full/DIY repairs, bikes, rental car
South Annapolis Yacht Centre Severn R./Spa Cr. 410-263-1643; www.sa-yc.com	13'	●	➤	➤	➤	●	●	●	➤	➤	➤	●	●	➤	➤	➤	●	●	●	●	50-ton ultrawide lift, full-service yard, covered slips
The Yacht Basin Company Severn R./Spa Cr. 410-263-3544; www.yachtbasin.com	12'	●	●	●		●	●	●	●	●		●	●	➤	➤		➤	➤	➤	●	Wi-Fi, cable; Vessels to 240' in heart of town

not advised and requires permission from the Navy.

At the head of Ego Alley is a free landing for dinghies and tenders 17 feet or less; the restrictions are enforced. Water taxis serve boats moored, anchored or docked in Spa and Back creeks. They can also shuttle you to Eastport, the marinas on Back Creek and to restaurants. Call them at 410-263-0033 or on channel 68.

Both Spa Creek and Back Creek are chock-a-block with full-service marinas. In addition to the basics (slips, fuel, supplies and repairs), they provide varied recreational amenities like pools, tennis courts and casual dining. Marinas more distant from downtown generally have water taxi or courtesy transportation into town. Also nearby you'll find canvas and sail shops, electronic specialists and marine supplies. Note that Fawcett Boat Supplies, long a City Dock fixture, has moved to Bay Ridge Road. Stevens Hardware, another City Dock staple, closed its doors in 2012.

Spa Creek is deep enough for most deep-keeled boats almost to its head, but most cruisers prefer to anchor in parts of the creek that are shown on the chart. There is an uncrowded anchorage just off Truxtun Park (by the boat ramp), about three-quarters of a mile above the bridge, portside. Truxtun has free tennis courts, a swimming pool, nature

continued on page 116

Port of Call
Annapolis and Eastport

Yachts, sail and power, set the nautical tone of Maryland's capital. City Dock and its environs form the commercial heart of Historic Annapolis, where visitors can shop, dine and explore the port's charming neighborhoods. Located on the opposite side of Spa Creek is Eastport, the city's free-spirited "republic," where busy boatyards, friendly bars and more good restaurants abound.

Helpful attendants and a plethora of brochures at three visitor centers provide a quick orientation to this centuries-old harbor. The official Visitors Guide lists attractions, shops and restaurants, and outlines a walking tour of historic homes and museums. Even if you make Annapolis a regular port of call, this and other self-guided tours offer fascinating ways to explore the city, including its neighborhoods, public art and African American heritage. Another orientation site is HistoryQuest, where displays, artifacts and multimedia presentations offer further insight into the city. Admission to the museum is free, and here visitors can purchase tickets for guided tours and obtain a variety of audio tours.

Annapolis boasts a trove of colonial-era buildings. Prominent among them is the State House, which towers above the skyline as it has since 1779. Visitors can wander through the first floor or take one of two daily tours. Nearby are the stately former residences of some of Maryland's most prominent citizens. The Hammond-Harwood House and the William Paca House and Garden are both open to the public. The city's museums include the Banneker-Douglass Museum, a repository of African American history and culture, and the U.S. Naval Academy Museum in Preble Hall, with its marvelous model ships and collections of naval artifacts and memorabilia. The Annapolis Maritime Museum, housed in a former oyster packing plant in Eastport, reflects the city's nautical prominence with exhibits, artifacts, a film and boat tours to Thomas Point Shoal Lighthouse. One of the few Annapolis venues that offers public access to the water, the museum is a popular put-in spot for kayaks and dogs. Sailing is a vital sporting and cultural aspect of the city's love affair with the water and the National Sailing Hall of Fame is now open for business at the City Dock.

Two historic higher learning centers are located downtown. St. John's College, founded in 1696 as King William's School, welcomes visitors to its campus and its art gallery. The U.S. Naval

Academy, established as a Naval College in 1845, has a visitor center inside Gate 1, offering guided tours, exhibits and a film. Guides also conduct city walking tours based on variety of themes: history, important buildings, architecture, women's studies, the Naval Academy and even ghosts. Not all of your visiting has to be done on foot. You can arrange tours by schooner, tour boat, "pirate" ship, scooter, trolley, horse-drawn carriage or Segway.

Culture thrives in many forms here. Art galleries fill the downtown area. Performing arts venues include the Summer Garden Theatre (offering musicals and Shakespearean comedies), the Colonial Players and

Annapolis

⚓ **Marinas/Dockage**
1 City Dock
2 Annapolis Marriott Waterfront
3 Yacht Basin Company

✪ **Points of Interest**
4 HistoryQuest
5 William Paca House & Garden
6 Maryland State House
7 Banneker-Douglass Museum
8 St. John's College
9 Hammond-Harwood House
10 U.S. Naval Academy Museum
11 Naval Academy stadium

12 National Sailing Hall of Fame
13 Market House

❓ **Information**
1 Harbormaster's Office
14 Visitor Center, U.S. Naval Academy
6 Maryland State House
15 Conference & Visitors Bureau

🛒 **Groceries**
16 The Big Cheese
17 Annebeth's
18 Main Street Mini Mart
19 Graul's Market

🍴 **Dining Areas**
20 Main Street
21 West Street
22 Maryland Avenue

🍦 Ice Cream
┈ **Navy Blue Shuttle Route & Stops** (free)
Ⓑ Bus Stop
T Water Taxi Landing
○ Public Landings
🧺 Laundromat
✉ Post Office
Playground
℞ Pharmacy
Public Restrooms

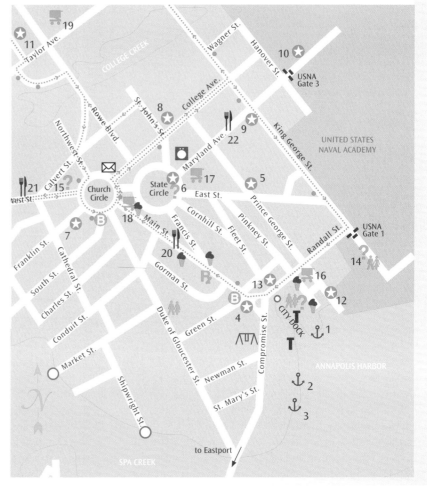

the Bay Theatre Company. Nationally known musicians entertain at the Ram's Head Tavern on West Street and local favorites like Them Eastport Oyster Boys and Calico Jack share Chesapeake lore at concerts staged at the City Dock and beyond. The Annapolis Chorale, Symphony Orchestra, Opera and Ballet hold performances at Maryland Hall for the Performing Arts, a short cab ride from the waterfront (walking distance for those anchored up Spa Creek).

Taxis can also whisk visitors to outlying attractions and businesses, while water taxis (410-263-0033 or hail them on channel 68) based at City Dock travel to and from Eastport, Back Creek and other waterways. Annapolis Transit offers bus service and free shuttles in and around town (410-263-7964 or www.annapolis.gov).

Browsers will love the small shops and upscale stores lining Main Street, but reserve time, too, for the antiques stores, galleries and boutiques on West Street, Maryland Avenue and State Circle. Boaters coming into Annapolis from Weems Creek will find casual eateries and an intriguing array of shops along Annapolis Street in West Annapolis.

Main Street Mini Mart downtown and Royal Farms and Leeward Market in Eastport can meet limited grocery needs, but from the downtown waterfront the nearest supermarket is Graul's (accessible via free trolley). There is a Giant not far from the head of Back Creek in Eastport, but it is a mile walk from the nearest marinas. Across from the Giant, you'll find Fawcett Boat Supply, West Marine, restaurants and a liquor store. At the edge of Eastport, you'll find a plaza that features a liquor store, restaurants, coffee shop and drug store. A farmers market sets up on Sundays at Annapolis City Dock.

Whether you're in search of a sandwich or an elegant meal, you'll find it mere blocks from the city's harbor and on either side of Spa Creek. Overnight lodging is available at a variety of world class hotels, including the Annapolis Marriott on Ego Alley and a variety of B&Bs (*www.bedandbreakfast.com*).

During the summer months there are Sunday afternoon art festivals with live music on West Street (May-October), U.S. Naval Academy Band concerts Tuesday evenings at City Dock (June-August), a Thursday evening concert series at the Annapolis Maritime Museum, and Wednesday evening sailboat races that finish just shy of the Spa Creek bridge.

Annual events include the Eastport Home and Garden Tour in June followed by the Eastport a Rockin' streetfest (live music, food/drink vendors). In July, the city's Fourth of July celebration (parade, re-enactors, concerts and fireworks) draws a huge fleet of boaters packing the harbor (expect a strong Coast Guard presence). In August, the Rotary Club of Annapolis holds its annual Crab Feast. Two of the biggest boat shows around—the U.S. Sailboat Show followed by the U.S. Powerboat Show—both occupy Ego Alley and fill the streets with traffic and people in October. And you can start the season with the Spring Sailboat Show. Finally, the annual Tug of War between the Easport and Annapolis waterfronts, brings a fun and friendly close to the busy season while raising money for local charities.

Information: Visitor Information, 410-280-0445; *www.visitannapolis.org, www.annapolis.gov, www.eastportcivic.org.*

Eastport

⚓ **Marinas/Dockage**
  1 Annapolis Landing Marina
  2 Port Annapolis Marina
  3 Bert Jabin's Yacht Yard
  4 Mears Marina Annapolis
  5 Eastport Yacht Center
  6 Horn Point Harbor Marina
  7 Annapolis City Marina
  8 Pier 4 Marina
  9 South Annapolis Yacht Centre

✪ **Points of Interest**
  10 Annapolis Maritime Museum

🛒 **Groceries**
  11 Royal Farms

🍴 **Dining Areas**
  12 Eastport Plaza
  13 Severn Avenue
Elsewhere
  14 Davis Pub
  15 Bread & Co.
  16 Leeward Market

🛍 **Shopping Center**
🌲 **Parks (Truxtun Park)**
T Water Taxi Landings
○ **Public Landings**
✉ **Post Office**
℞ **Pharmacy**
🏕 **Picnic Area**
🛝 **Playground**
Ⓑ **Bus Stop**

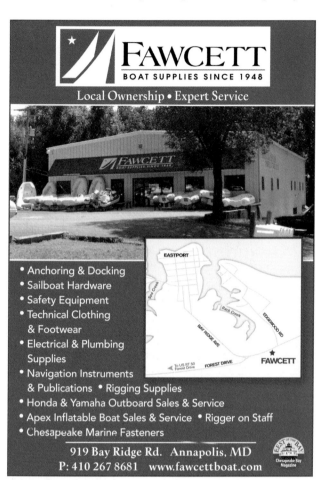

FAWCETT
BOAT SUPPLIES SINCE 1948
Local Ownership • Expert Service

EASTPORT

- Anchoring & Docking
- Sailboat Hardware
- Safety Equipment
- Technical Clothing
  & Footwear
- Electrical & Plumbing
  Supplies
- Navigation Instruments
  & Publications • Rigging Supplies
- Honda & Yamaha Outboard Sales & Service
- Apex Inflatable Boat Sales & Service • Rigger on Staff
- Chesapeake Marine Fasteners

919 Bay Ridge Rd. Annapolis, MD
P: 410 267 8681   www.fawcettboat.com

Annapolis continued from page 113

trails and picnic facilities.

On Back Creek you can anchor just off the water tank, but away from the nearby mooring balls, or you can land your dinghy at the dock next to Bert Jabin's Yacht Yard. From here, it's a mile and a half walk to Fawcett, several shopping plazas—one with a supermarket (Giant), another with a large West Marine and a very good wine and spirits store. There are also half a dozen good restaurants here. Nearby are a laundromat and library.

On the creek's north shore, at McNasby's Wharf, sits the ANNAPOLIS MARITIME MUSEUM, on the site of an old oyster packing house. The Barge House, on the museum campus, is home to the THOMAS POINT SHOAL LIGHTHOUSE INTERPRETIVE CENTER, and regularly scheduled trips leave from here to carry visitors on a guided tour of the lighthouse itself. The small musuem campus, which includes a public beach and dinghy landing, is a short stroll from several marinas. A Thursday night concert series (free) runs throughout the summer and features an international line-up of maritime musicians. Concert-goers should bring their own seating and are welcome to picnic before and during the show. Also nearby are several colorful neighborhood restaurants and pubs.

Above Annapolis, on the main stem of the Severn River, houses line the high shores, making for a pleasant trip upriv-

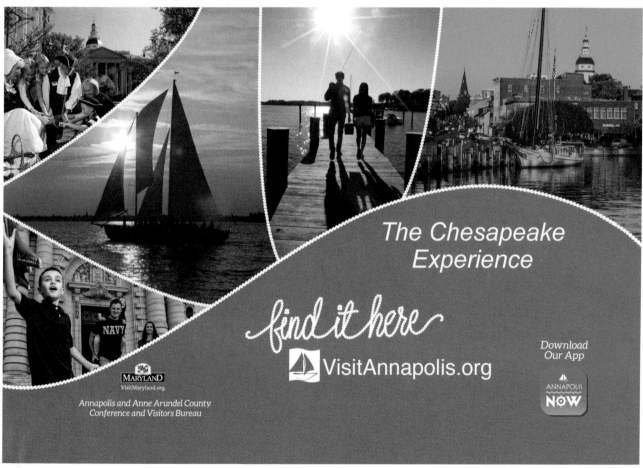

The Chesapeake
Experience

find it here
⛵ VisitAnnapolis.org

Download
Our App

ANNAPOLIS
NOW

MARYLAND
VisitMaryland.org

Annapolis and Anne Arundel County
Conference and Visitors Bureau

CHESAPEAKE HARBOUR MARINA

CHESAPEAKE HARBOUR — A RESORT MARINA

EASIEST BAY ACCESS IN ANNAPOLIS

Located on the Severn River, Chesapeake Harbour is the ideal port for exploring the Bay and enjoying the historic town of Annapolis.

While staying at Chesapeake Harbour, you can relax in style with our bountiful amenities and peaceful surroundings.

Full Service Marina • Dockage for Yachts 25' to 120'

- 4 tennis courts and 2 swimming pools
- 1800' private sandy beach with 2 fishing piers
- Fitness Facility • WiFi Access • Cable TV at each slip

- Fine dining & dockside bar at Sam's on the Waterfront
- On-site yacht management and maintenance
- Courtesy shuttle to downtown Annapolis

410-268-1969
www.chesapeakeharbour.com

Annapolis continued

er. In fact, some boaters bypass Annapolis entirely, bent on a more relaxing stay in nearby Weems Creek, just above the first bridge, or beyond.

Navigating the river is fairly straightforward, but keep track of the marks as you go, as some sandbars extend a considerable distance. The wind normally blows up or down the river, funneled along by the high banks, so sailors face either a run or a beat. Naval facilities mark the river's entrance on both sides, and boaters heading upriver sometimes have to run a kind of nautical gauntlet. The Naval Academy's "YPs" (Yard Patrol boats) are used to train midshipmen, and these gray 108-footers do a lot of stopping, backing and turning. Cruisers may also encounter fleets of novice dinghy sailors off the Academy's sail training center. This area is often used as the starting point for a variety of sailboat races as well. Things can get pretty confusing if racers are frantically trying to position for the start while you're ambling by.

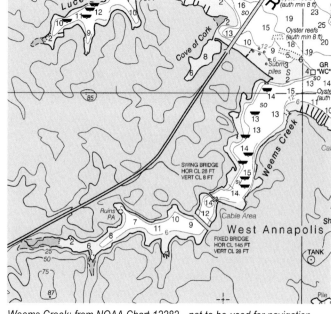

Weems Creek; from NOAA Chart 12282—not to be used for navigation.

Weems Creek

Once you've passed under the handsome Naval Academy Bridge (75-foot vertical clearance) and are heading up the Severn, don't go inside the green "1S" off Horseshoe Point. Continue to the next creek, which is ❷ Weems.

Leave the green and red channel marker "WC" at the mouth of the creek (where there's 15 feet of water) well to starboard, swing wide around the point to your left, and head on in. There's a 6-knot speed limit at the entrance. In addition to private mooring buoys, Weems contains about a dozen "hurricane moorings" owned by the Naval Academy.

Anchoring is easy, with plenty of room and good holding ground. There are no marinas in Weems Creek, but about a

half mile in on the southern shore there is a dinghy landing on a small public beach at the foot of Tucker Street (look for the waterfront condos). It's near the swing bridge. From here, you can walk a few blocks to reach a grocery store (Graul's), a pharmacy, a laundry, a deli, a bagel shop and a number of restaurants. If you can't find what you need in **West Annapolis,** you can walk into the city, which is a little over a mile—or take a cab or shuttle bus.

The main drag in West Annapolis is Annapolis Street. Formerly residential, it's now filled with restaurants, coffee shops, boutiques, antiques stores, gourmet food sellers and art galleries. There is also a gas station and professional offices. On Thursday afternoons, boaters will find a farmers market a short walk from the shopping center, on the other side of Rowe Boulevard.

The Weems Creek drawbridge opens on request from May 1 through September 30 (call the tender at 410-263-3953 or on VHF 13). Although there is 7 to 14 feet of water in the creek beyond the drawbridge, the fixed Rowe Boulevard Bridge, with a vertical clearance of 28½ feet, precludes further exploration by most sailboats. The creek runs out of water a half-mile past the fixed bridge; here the treelined shore is a scenic reminder of how this area once looked.

Chase Creek

The entire reach of the Severn River is easily navigated now that high fixed spans have long since replaced all the old drawbridges. The remains of one of these (on

Bay Spotlight

Thomas Point Lighthouse

The last of the screwpile lighthouses still in its original place, Thomas Point Lighthouse is as picturesque as it is useful to Bay pilots and yachtsmen alike. The structure marks the long shoal reaching into the Bay from the northern shore of the South River. It went into service in 1875, replacing a light structure that originally stood on a bluff at the edge of Thomas Point. More than a century later, the light remains a steadfast signal to boats moving up and down the Bay, though the high ground of Thomas Point has eroded steadily westward.

Screwpile lighthouses, so named because they are "screwed" into the Bay bottom, were economical and fairly easy to erect in the turbulent Bay water. Manned by teams of keepers whose job it was to keep the lanterns lit, they monitored Bay traffic for more than a century. When the Coast Guard began installing fully automated lights, the lighthouses being replaced were burned or dismantled. Preservationists recognized the need to save some of these historic structures. The first to be moved was the Hooper Strait Light, which serves as the centerpiece for the Chesapeake Bay Maritime Museum in St. Michaels. The Drum Point Light was eventually moved to its present site at the Calvert Marine Museum.

In 1975 Congress recognized the Thomas Point Lighthouse as a historic landmark, and it remained in place and fully staffed until 1986, when the Coast Guard automated its light. A consortium consisting of the Annapolis Maritime Museum, the Chesapeake Chapter of the U.S. Lighthouse Society, the City of Annapolis and Anne Arundel County now owns the lighthouse as a public trust. The Annapolis Maritime Museum houses lighthouse exhibits and coordinates lighthouse tours, which leave from the museum on Back Creek (*www.amaritime.org*; 410-295-0104).

Patricia Raymond

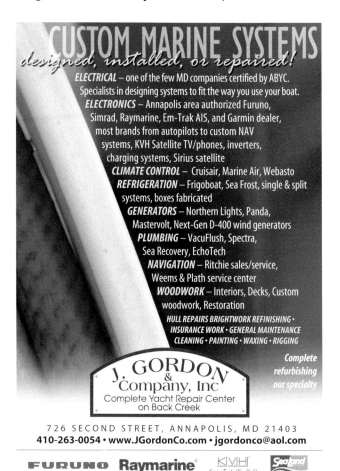

CUSTOM MARINE SYSTEMS
designed, installed, or repaired!

ELECTRICAL – one of the few MD companies certified by ABYC. Specialists in designing systems to fit the way you use your boat.
ELECTRONICS – Annapolis area authorized Furuno, Simrad, Raymarine, Em-Trak AIS, and Garmin dealer, most brands from autopilots to custom NAV systems, KVH Satellite TV/phones, inverters, charging systems, Sirius satellite
CLIMATE CONTROL – Cruisair, Marine Air, Webasto
REFRIGERATION – Frigoboat, Sea Frost, single & split systems, boxes fabricated
GENERATORS – Northern Lights, Panda, Mastervolt, Next-Gen D-400 wind generators
PLUMBING – VacuFlush, Spectra, Sea Recovery, EchoTech
NAVIGATION – Ritchie sales/service, Weems & Plath service center
WOODWORK – Interiors, Decks, Custom woodwork, Restoration
HULL REPAIRS BRIGHTWORK REFINISHING • INSURANCE WORK • GENERAL MAINTENANCE CLEANING • PAINTING • WAXING • RIGGING

Complete refurbishing our specialty

J. GORDON & Company, Inc
Complete Yacht Repair Center on Back Creek

726 SECOND STREET, ANNAPOLIS, MD 21403
410-263-0054 • www.JGordonCo.com • jgordonco@aol.com

FURUNO **Raymarine** KVH *Keeping Track of Your World* **SeaLand**

EASTPORT YACHT CENTER
On Back Creek • Annapolis

ONE MINUTE FROM THE BAY
Fixed, Floating and Lift Slips Available
New Bath House
Walk to Restaurants and Historic Eastport
Full Yacht Services Onsite

Free Wi-Fi

726 Second Street
Annapolis, MD 21403
410-280-9988
www.eastportyachtcenter.com

Chase Creek continued

the northern bank), serves as a popular fishing pier. Its submerged pilings are a favorite fishing hole for local anglers.

Boaters venturing upriver beyond the second of the river's bridges, U.S. 50 bridge (80-foot vertical clearance) will next find popular ❸ **Chase Creek** to starboard. Quick-flashing red "2A" marks a shoal off the northern and western portion of the creek's ample entrance, about a mile past the second high bridge. Otherwise, Chase Creek's quarter-mile-wide mouth presents no difficulties, with charted depths of 14 to 16 feet to the other shoreline.

Chase Creek is Y-shaped. The port branch often holds many anchored and moored boats. The starboard branch is quite attractive, with tree-lined slopes on one side while the north side is lined with pleasant-looking houses. This branch continues about 300 yards, then curls around a sandy point for another 100 yards or so. Chase Creek can provide a snug, protected anchorage where only an occasional puff of wind will find your boat as it swings on the anchor.

Chase Creek and Saltworks Creek; from NOAA Chart 12282—not to be used for navigation.

Saltworks Creek

As you explore this beautiful part of the Severn, you might want to poke your way into ❹ **Saltworks Creek**. With a terrain that resembles a small mountain lake, Saltworks is one of the prettiest and most protected havens on the Chesapeake—though you could certainly get an argument on that point from proponents of other beautiful and protected creeks that sprout all along the Severn River.

This tributary, opposite Chase Creek, is about a mile above the second (U.S. 50) bridge across the Severn. With shoaling on both sides of the entrance, the unmarked channel is easier to negotiate if traveling upriver. The key is to stay in the center, but favoring the starboard side. Once inside, locals report that deep water extends nearly to its steep shoreline. Beyond the first two boathouses, you'll find good holding in about 10-12 feet feet across from a narrow dock-studded cove. Farther along is a wider spot on the southeast side. More anchoring possibilities exist upstream before the waterway narrows, carrying about 6 feet before becoming unnavigable.

While Saltworks Creek, with its high wooded shores, offers serenity and snugness, it has plenty of good company. Neighboring creeks **Luce**, **Clements** and **Brewer** are navigable as well, and all have something special to add as you cruise your way up the Severn.

Little Round Bay

In fact, just about every creek on the Severn provides a comfortable anchorage in good deep water. The ❺ **Round Bay** area, five miles up the river, has several of its own, including **Little Round Bay** and St. Helena Island.

There's good protection all around **St. Helena Island**. Just don't anchor in the cable area directly west of the island. When the weather is really "sticky," you could drop your hook inside the protecting arm of Long Point. The shores here are well settled, but you'll be protected from any nor'wester. As in Weems and Saltworks creeks, the Navy maintains a submerged mooring system in Little Round Bay to use when severe storms threaten its small-craft fleet in Annapolis.

There are several houses and private docks on St. Helena Island, too, and legend has it that a gambling casino operated there in the distant past.

In **Browns Cove**, west of St. Helena Island, Smith's Marina offers some overnight slips, fuel, ice, repairs and haulouts. There is 7 feet of water at the fuel dock. Other choice spots to anchor are in **Hopkins Creek** and **Maynadier Creek**, south-southwest of St. Helena Island.

If you draw over 3 feet, give a wide berth to the shoal (marked by green "3") jutting out just opposite Mathiers Point. Stay mid-channel until you round the long sandspit at the entrance to Hopkins Creek, then circle around to port, where you can drop your hook. The sandbar will keep any wave action at bay while it permits the breeze to find you, even on a hot summer's night. Water depths range to 10 feet, and the shoreline has little activity.

But if you want to find a really good anchorage on a hot

summer night, turn west around Mathiers Point into Maynadier Creek (called "Cocktail Creek" by locals, who favor it for sunset cruises). The channel leading around this point is an ample 14 feet or more, and the creek opens up inside with depths of 8 to 10 feet. The bottom is soft mud and provides good holding. There are some fine homes along the shore of this bay-like creek. Extensive marshes on its south and west shores suggest a dense mosquito population, so carry insect repellent and have good screens on your companionway.

Round Bay itself is wide enough for good sailing and small enough to offer protection from heavy seas. Wednesday night racers circle the buoys during the summer, and an active batch of small boat enthusiasts, including water skiers, launch from area beaches and docks. It is a beautiful body of water, about 2 miles across at its widest point, and particularly busy on summer weekends.

Plum and Valentine Creeks

The twin creeks of ❻ **Plum** and **Valentine** lie on the western bank of the Severn about 7 nautical miles from Annapolis, 5 miles above the U.S. 50 (westernmost) bridge. They share the same mouth, and while there are no markers—the entrance is wide and uncomplicated—your depthfinder should give solid readings in the low teens.

Just inside, the waterway splits at a community beach. Plum Creek lies to starboard and Valentine to port. Both are about equal in length and lined with tidy well-kept homes.

In Plum Creek, a deck built over the water makes a good landmark to starboard as you approach the entrance. The upper reaches have no obstructions, only a navigable, reasonably wide (albeit unmarked) passage. The shore is entirely residential, with lots of private piers and small boats. The northern bank is high and heavily wooded, giving ample protection from northeast winds. An anchorage in the upper section is possible.

Heading back to Valentine Creek, turn to starboard past the sandy beach, staying at the center of the creek in 10-foot depths. Swimming buoys lie off this beach. Just beyond the beach is a tiny point to starboard, and, just above that, Valentine Creek widens slightly into a shallow cove where the community of Arden-on-the-Severn has a private beach, two piers and a small ramp. Here, trees block sounds—as well as breezes. Private mooring balls make finding a place to drop the anchor difficult, except just off the small beach, where boats occasionally stop for the night.

Upper Severn and Indian Landing

About 8 miles upriver from Annapolis, the Severn dramatically narrows. Up until 1930, a ferry at Whitney's Landing shuttled across the river, saving miles of travel on country roads. Today, the Severn River Narrows can get pretty hectic on summer weekends, crowded with small boats, swimmers along both shores, and other traffic. A speed limit is posted for parts of the Narrows.

The long, unmarked sand bar at Mathews Point above the Narrows stops most cruisers from going all the way to Indian Landing, but you'll find at least 9 feet of water at the end of the bar, and it is quite easy to follow the channel. A designated slalom water-ski area near the southern shore opposite Mathews Point draws enthusiasts. As you approach the point, carefully stay close to this ski area, because the deepest water is about 100 feet from the south shore of the river. Continue to hug the left side, where the private piers are, until you have passed Mathews Point, and then swing to starboard into the 7 and 8 foot depths that surround the easternmost of the three islands in the Indian Landing vicinity.

The first island you approach, a sandy spot with a tiny

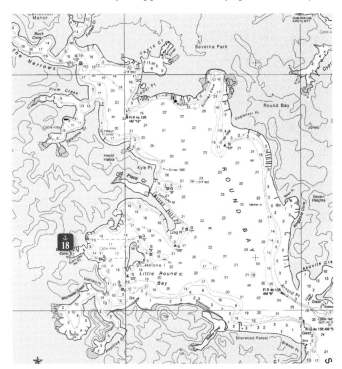

Little Round Bay; from NOAA Chart 12282—not to be used for navigation.

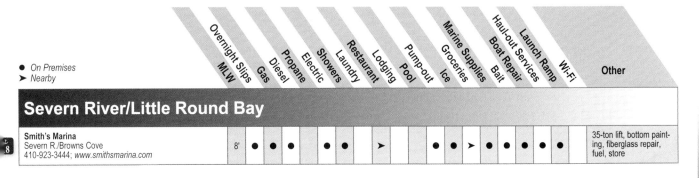

● *On Premises*
➤ *Nearby*

		Overnight Slips	MLW	Gas	Diesel	Propane	Electric	Showers	Laundry	Restaurant	Lodging	Pool	Pump-out	Ice	Groceries	Marine Supplies	Bait	Boat Repair	Haul-out Services	Launch Ramp	Wi-Fi		Other

Severn River/Little Round Bay

| Smith's Marina
Severn R./Browns Cove
410-923-3444; www.smithsmarina.com | | 8' | ● | ● | ● | | ● | ● | | ➤ | | | ● | ● | ➤ | ● | ● | ● | ● | ● | | 35-ton lift, bottom painting, fiberglass repair, fuel, store |

An abandoned cottage and outbuilding on First Island, off Indian Landing at the top of the Severn. Nearby Second Island is a popular anchorage.

Upper Severn and Indian Landing *continued*

clump of trees, was four times its present size in the 1950s. Trespassing picnickers cut its trees to roast marshmallows, and erosion did the rest. This property is called Second Island by its owners, but many people living along the river know it as Ski Island and believe it is public. It's not.

The two other islands in this little bay are properly named First Island and Third Island (though you won't find names—proper or improper—on the charts). First Island sits adjacent to Indian Landing on the southern shore and has a small summer cottage on it, while Third Island is surrounded by shallow water farther upstream. Third Island has been nicknamed Shark Island; legend has it a dead shark was once found here with a beer can in its stomach.

Northeast of Second Island is a shoal, not shown on most charts, that was once Fourth Island, according to tales told by old-timers. When choosing a place to anchor, do not stray too close to that area, although you may circumnavigate Second Island in at least 7 feet of water.

A fine anchorage lies directly east of Second Island in 8 feet of water with good holding on a mud bottom and protection from winds. The fetch is short, so waves never build to any significant height here. During storms this is an even better place to hole up than the more popular places downriver. Any place in the Narrows would also be very well protected.

Indian Landing was a shipping point during the 17th and 18th centuries. Farmers brought tobacco here to send to Annapolis, where the cargo went aboard oceangoing sailing ships for the voyage to England. Old photographs at the Indian Landing clubhouse document the landing's more recent history. They depict vessels resembling skipjacks tied up at the wharf, loading cargo.

More history is nearby. General's Highway, parallel to the river's south shore, is named for George Washington, who regularly traveled its length to meet with the nation's founders in the then-American capital at Annapolis. French troops under Comte de Rochambeau are said to have spilled seeds from their sleeping bags along that road, giving rise to the Scotch Broom plants that grow there today.

South River

The **South River**'s old reputation as the drag strip of the Chesapeake's Western Shore used to discourage some boaters from venturing here. These days the river is a quieter and gentler place. Noise restrictions and speed limits have tamed the speedboaters who once rattled windows on waterfront properties and threatened small boats in their path. The South River has fine restaurants, several marinas and is the site of historic London Town, with its refurbished Georgian house and acres of gardens.

The entrance to South River is marked by the historic Thomas Point Shoal Light, the last of the "screwpile" lights on the Bay that remains in its original location. Boaters approaching South River from points north must round the long shoal off Thomas Point, although many boats find enough water to cut inside the lighthouse. The unmarked passage between the shoal and the lighthouse shows a mini-mum of 5-6 feet, but be aware of the charted shallows, rocks and wrecks surrounding the area south of Marshy Point and Thomas Point.

South River's entrance mark, green-red "SR", lies less than a half-mile southeast of Thomas Point Light. From here, an easterly course takes you into the safest waters toward flashing red "4", a little more than 2 nautical miles away.

On the other hand, the approach to South River is more direct and deeper when approaching from the south. Proceeding to Turkey Point, the navigable course narrows at "5" and "6" to about a quarter-mile before opening up again. Constriction is repeated at "8" and "9". Depths remain good, and shoaling here is well marked along both shores.

Note, however, that an unmarked 6-foot shoal exists in the middle of the river, almost in a direct line between "6" and "8". Otherwise the main channel is easily navigable—and often busy, especially on summer weekends.

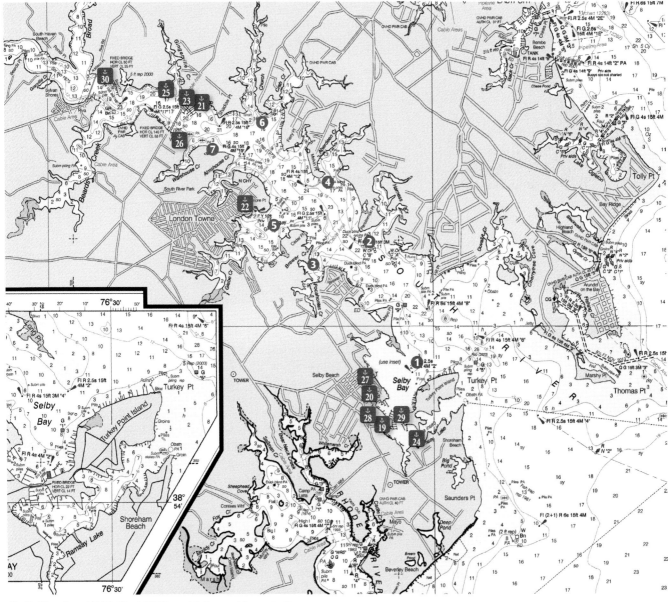

South River; from NOAA Chart 12270—not to be used for navigation.

● On Premises
➤ Nearby

South River

#	Marina	MLW	Overnight Slips	Gas	Diesel	Propane	Electric	Showers	Laundry	Restaurant	Lodging	Pool	Pump-out	Ice	Groceries	Marine Supplies	Boat Repair	Bait	Haul-out Services	Launch Ramp	Wi-Fi	Other
19	**Anchor Yacht Basin** South R./Selby Bay 410-269-6674 ; www.anchoryachtbasin.com	6'	●	●	●		●	●		➤			●	●	➤	●			●	●		Full-service, gas, diesel, boat sales, lift, repairs
20	**Holiday Point Marina** South R./Selby Bay 410-956-2208 301-261-4282; www.holidaypointmarina.com	7'	●	➤	➤		●	●	➤	➤			●	➤	➤	➤	➤	●	●	➤	●	Dry storage, machine shop, 35-ton lift, repairs
21	**Liberty Yacht Club & Marina** South R./South River Bridge 410-266-5633 or 800-971-1300; www.libertymarina.com	15'	●	●	●	➤	●	●		●	➤	●	●	●	●	➤	●	➤	●	●	➤	● Full-service, 25-ton lift; snack shop
22	**Londontowne Marina** South R./Glebe Bay 410-956-5077; www.londontownemarina.com	10'		●			●	●					●	●			●	●				Fork lift for haulout, picnic site
23	**The Marina on the South River** South R. 410-212-3214; www.marinaotsr.com	9'+		➤	➤		●			●			➤				➤	➤	➤		●		
24	**Norris Marina** South R./Ramsey Bay 410-320-1628	8'	●	➤	➤	➤	●	●	➤	➤	➤		●	➤	➤	➤	➤	➤	➤	➤		
25	**Oak Grove Marina** South R./Gingerville Cr. 410-266-6696; www.boatoakgrove.com	12'	●	●	●	➤	●		●				●	●		●		●	●	●	●	Boatel, fuel; new, used boat sales; PWC/boat rentals
26	**Pier 7 Marina** South R./South R. Bridge 410-956-2288; www.pier7md.com	10'	●				●	●		●			●	●						●	●	
27	**Selby Bay Marina** South R./Selby Bay 410-798-0232; www.selbybaymarina.com	10'	●	●	●		●	●	●				●	●	➤	●		●			●	Picnic area
28	**South River Marina** South R./Ramsey Bay 410-798-1717 or 301-261-8277; www.southrivermarina.com	6'	●	➤	➤		●	●	●	➤	➤	➤	●	●	●	●	➤	●	●	➤	●	● Full-service marina, in-water pool, picnic areas
29	**Turkey Point Marina** South R./Ramsey Bay 410-798-1369; www.turkeypointmarina.com	5'	●	●	➤	➤	●	●	●	➤	➤	➤	➤	●	●	●	●	➤	●	●	●	Full-service, lift slips, brokerage, 24-hr. security
30	**Warehouse Creek Marina** South R./Warehouse Cr.; 410-946-1880; www.multihullmarina.com/warehouse-creek-marina.html	6'	●	➤	➤	➤	●	●	●		➤			➤	➤	➤	➤	➤			●	Long term rentals for catamarans

Selby Bay

Only a few miles from Thomas Point Light, ❶ **Selby Bay** is the first deepwater tributary on the southern shore. Tucked inside Turkey Point, it's easy to slip into as the cruise day draws to a close. Despite being home-base for numerous boats, it's pretty and peaceful. Broad enough to catch a summer breeze, it's also snug enough for most conditions.

After passing through the bottleneck between "5" and "6" and turning to the southwest, be aware of the pilings of an abandoned pier off Turkey Point. Often visible, these are non-threatening as long as you don't cut the point too closely. Following Selby Bay's southern shoreline, you'll see a number of private piers and 9 to 11 feet of water not far off these docks. Red "2" will keep you away from the extensive shoaling off Long Point to the north.

Cruisers report that the best anchorage is a haven with 10-foot depths along a wooded shoreline in the northwestern corner. After turning north, watch for "4", which marks a shoal extending from another, but smaller, unnamed point to the northwest. This shoal divides the northern part of the little bay in two; boats anchor in the pocket formed between this peninsula and Long Point. The mile-long section of Selby Bay, between the two flashing nav aids of "2" and "4", is wide enough for several boats to swing at anchor without crowding.

Several marinas along Selby Bay's southwestern shore offer slips and fuel, marine supplies and services. South of here sits shallow **Ramsay Bay**, often called Ramsay Lake by locals and spelled "Ramsey" on some charts. Both access points—via Selby Bay and South River—limit the area's use to low-profile, shallow-draft vessels. The fixed bridge connecting Turkey Point Island to the mainland has a vertical clearance of 14 feet; the unmarked inlet from South River has shoals and obstructions.

Harness Creek

❷ **Harness Creek** lies on the north shore 2½ miles from flashing "4" at the entrance to South River and just short of marker "10". If you want a landmark, look for the well-groomed grassy hill with a pair of cream-colored gazebos accented with green rooftops. A three-tiered stairway leads to the water's edge. This idyllic scene is part of Quiet Waters Park (340 acres of woodland and grassy fields owned and operated by Anne Arundel County) and announces the approach to Harness Creek.

The creek's entrance is unmarked. After you bypass the 4-foot shoal on the lower point, keep fairly close to the starboard shore to avoid the shoaling off Persimmon Point. Once you are through the narrow cut, a basin opens to starboard behind the spit. Erosion has taken its toll on this modest spit, but when the tide is favorable, small craft can nose up onto it. (The bottom falls off sharply, so don't expect to beach your craft and be able to walk all the way around the spit.) On any given summer weekend, flotillas of boats frequent this harbor, and it can get crowded.

If you follow the eastern shoreline, you'll find a gap in the marsh which reveals a hidden cove, large enough for one or two boats if they raft together. This is the famous Harness Creek "hurricane hole," accessible through a slender but deep channel. Being surrounded by thickly wooded high banks and a marshy point makes this tiny anchorage safe in just about any blow. On cool fall and spring days, it can provide a private and serene back-to-nature getaway; however, on hot summer days and breezeless nights, it is a bit too protected to be comfortable.

Following the main body of Harness Creek as it meanders inland, you'll find a beautiful residential neighborhood to port and more of the sheltering tranquility of Quiet Waters Park to starboard. It is in this section (near the park's boat rental pier) that you can anchor in about 8 feet of water. Wide enough to accommodate raft-ups, the creek is deep (8 to 10 feet) almost from shore to shore, but can be

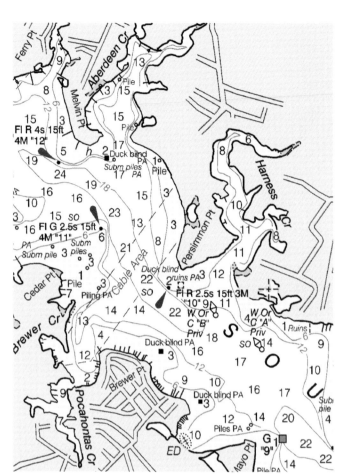

Harness, Pocahantas and Aberdeen Cr.; from NOAA Chart 12270—not to be used for navigation.

congested during summer weekends and events. Use caution since the bottom is mucky and anchors are known to drag. Be sure that yours is well set.

The park's pier, primarily for the boat rental concession, has a designated but very limited space for dinghies which fills quickly at busy times. The concession, Paddle or Pedal (410-271-7007), rents a variety of small non-motorized boats as well as bicycles for use on park trails. The park (open 7 a.m. until dusk daily, closed Tuesdays) offers many amenities, including paved hiking/biking trails, a dog-walking park and doggie beach, picnic facilities, a multi-level playground and a visitors center with art galleries and formal gardens.

On Saturday evenings during the summer, the park hosts a series of evening concerts in a natural amphitheater behind the visitors center. Bring a blanket and stake out your spot early. Call the park at 410-222-1777 for more information.

Brewer Creek

Along the southern shoreline, between Selby Bay and Glebe Bay, are two often-overlooked features. The first, about 2 nautical miles upstream of "4" between Mayo Point and Brewer Point, is **Limehouse Cove**. Not always identified on charts, it has depths of 10-12 feet but is exposed. The easternmost shore-

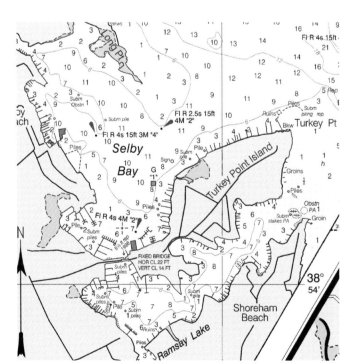

Selby Bay; from NOAA Chart 12270—not to be used for navigation.

Bay Spotlight

Historic London Town and Gardens

Any cruise of the South River should include a stop at Historic London Town and Gardens on Almshouse Creek, where the remains of a thriving colonial seaport are being unearthed. Owned by Anne Arundel County and managed by the nonprofit London Town Foundation, this 23-acre park includes meticulously maintained grounds as well as the manor house built by ferry operator and tavern keeper William Brown in 1758. Boaters wishing to tour the site are permitted to dock free, first-come, first-served at London Town's private pier (4-foot depths), but it is fairly exposed, subject to the wave action from river traffic.

Founded in 1683, the new town of London was strategically located, offering ready access for sailing ships carrying Maryland tobacco to foreign ports and importing cargoes of European and East Indian goods. The town's prosperity was short-lived, however. In 1747, in order to impose tighter control on local shipping, the state assembly restricted the number of ports allowed to inspect and export tobacco. For reasons unknown, London Town was not on the final list of state-designated sites and so quickly faded from view. Merchants packed up and moved to other enterprising zones, like Baltimore to the north. The last private owner of Brown's grand brick house

sold the property to the Trustees for the Poor of Anne Arundel County in 1828, and it was used as the county almshouse until 1965 (hence the name of nearby Almshouse Creek).

The Colonial story of London Town is steadily emerging from the soil, pot shard by pot shard, as archaeologists and volunteers carefully unearth evidence of old buildings and walkways. Current efforts focus on the excavation of Rumney's Tavern, built in the 1690s, which is thought to have served an elite clientele of merchants, planters and mariners. (To volunteer, call the county's Lost Towns Project, 410-222-1318.)

Today, the renovated William Brown House and the London Town site are open for tours Tuesday through Saturday, 10 a.m. to 3 p.m., and Sunday, noon to 3 p.m. (410-222-1919). Visitors may also wander for an additional hour through the grounds and eight acres of gardens massed with native trees, shrubs, flowers and medicinal plants. London Town is not open on Mondays and the William Brown House is closed from January through March.

If you plan to overnight in the area, you might anchor nearby, in either Almshouse, Church or Crab creeks, well protected in a blow and sheltered from the bustle of the river.

Harness Creek *continued*

line remains natural as part of a local county park. The 183-acre SOUTH RIVER FARMS PARK, primarily a maintenance facility, is open to the public for hiking, canoeing and kayaking, but is rarely visited. The other half of the small basin is occupied by private docks, among them a community marina.

Just beyond Brewer Point is ❸ **Brewer Creek**, southwest of "10", whose wide-looking entrance is deceptively tricky for deeper drafts without local knowledge. Shoaling appears to extend from both sides, despite the charted double-digits. It is unmarked, so watch carefully while keeping the pilings and charted shallows to starboard, and mindful of encroachment on the port side.

Inside to the right is shallow **Larkington Cove**. The creek itself was named for John Brewer, a prominent property owner in the earliest settlement days. Most of the original 400 acres, granted from the 2nd Lord Baltimore in 1651, and called Larkington, remained in family hands into the 1900s.

The shoreline to port, densely residential, leads to **Pocahontas Creek**, whose narrow entrance, despite its charted appearance, reportedly carries 10 feet. Inside and to starboard is Pocahontas Marine Service. Wooden boat restorers, they also offer overnight and long-term slips, haul-out and repairs.

If considering anchoring inside Brewer Creek, be aware of the charted underground cables.

Aberdeen Creek

Among the deep tributaries feeding South River, ❹ **Aberdeen Creek** is a favorite for anchoring and small raft-ups. It lies west of Harness Creek on the northern shore and, like its sister creeks, attention must be paid to unmarked entrance shoals and the shallows extending off various points.

Once past lighted "10" at Persimmon Point, and following the indented northern shoreline, you might notice a remnant of bygone days atop a large, grassy hill between Harness and Aberdeen Creeks. The structure is flanked to the west by a red-roofed outbuilding and two lower-profile modern homes, all appearing to share the same immense sweeping green lawn. Despite the manicured surroundings, the brick dwelling, c. 1800, has been unoccupied for decades. The tract, once known as "Lydia's Rest", was part of an original land grant called Middle Neck Hundred, and the home recalls the quieter agricultural times that followed London Town's heyday.

Approaching Aberdeen's entrance from the Bay is not difficult. A duck blind off Melvin Point helps define the shoal there, along with a speed-limit buoy. Just stay centered in the channel, navigating past the sturdy private dock to starboard. Inside the hour-glass-shaped creek, a large park-like property on the right, at one time a camp, is well-posted with no-trespassing signs. It makes a pretty setting for dropping the hook, however, with lots of bird activity to watch.

To port, the curve beyond Melvin Point is rimmed with handsome, sprawling homes and docks. Roomy with good holding in 15 feet, the cove's depths hold fairly close to shore. Farther upstream, the creek not only narrows but is occupied

with moorings. One can continue beyond those, to the right, toward the head of the creek and a green marker. A couple boats can anchor snugly there in 7 to 10 feet.

Melvin Point is named for the prominent Annapolis family that owned the peninsula west of Aberdeen Creek for nearly a century. The respected Judge Ridgely P. Melvin, who once served in the Maryland House of Delegates, was an avid yachtsman and long-distance cruiser. While the idyllic, "country" feel of his fruit-tree-filled acreage has now morphed into a bedroom community of mansions, he'd be pleased to see boaters at anchor enjoying the beauty of Aberdeen Creek.

On the other side of this peninsula, between Melvin Point and Ferry Point, is one of South River's shallowest tributaries. Charts don't give a name for this narrow creek which carries about 8 feet, but locally it's known as Little Aberdeen Creek.

Glebe Bay

❺ **Glebe Bay** lies on the south shore of the South River about $1\frac{1}{2}$ miles below the South River Bridge at Edgewater. At the downstream side of Glebe Bay's entrance—3 miles upriver from lighted red "4"—flashing green "11" pinpoints a considerable shoal. As you approach from downstream, don't mistake this aid as a mark intended for the north shore. It guards not only the extensive shoal off Cedar Point but also a few pilings as well (some visible, some underwater).

As you enter Glebe Bay, you'll want to favor the port side a bit. If you study the chart, you'll see why. There are more underwater pilings, right in the middle of the entrance to the bay. Once past "11", choose a course that will keep you about 150 yards offshore as you round Cedar Point.

One hazard immediately noticeable on your chart is an extensive unmarked shoal right in the middle of Glebe Bay, so don't try to cut through the middle. There's a marina on the

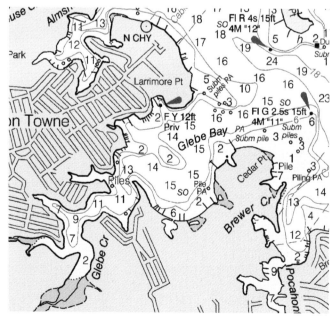

Glebe Bay; from NOAA Chart 12270—
not to be used for navigation.

Glebe Bay continued

bay that offers gas, ice and some repairs.

Although the shoreline is attractive, you may decide that just about any place you might anchor would be too exposed. In this case, head up into **Glebe Creek**. Keeping about 150 yards offshore, you can skirt the southeast shore of the bay all the way to the low-lying point of land that guards the entrance to Glebe Creek. Beyond the point is a tiny bay with 11 to 15 feet of water.

Anchoring here may not come easily, however. One cruiser reported carefully lowering the anchor, swinging delicately back on the rode, and then, when the engine was put into reverse, dragging the anchor across the lagoon—not once, but fully six times before the hook finally held. Each time the dragging anchor was retrieved it also brought up a large quantity of mud and leaves. The decaying leaves appeared to be preventing the flukes from really digging into the mud.

With the hook secure here, however, you'll find your anchorage to be attractive and intimate. Most of the shore is lined with modest but handsome homes. There are many piers along the shoreline, with the exception of the point of land on the northeast side.

Morning can bring a variety of "shore sounds." These are not of the natural variety, but the human noises such as garbage trucks, automobile engines, motorbikes and small airplanes headed in and out of the nearby airport.

Glebe Bay is attractive and Glebe Creek well protected, but you may want to bring along ear plugs.

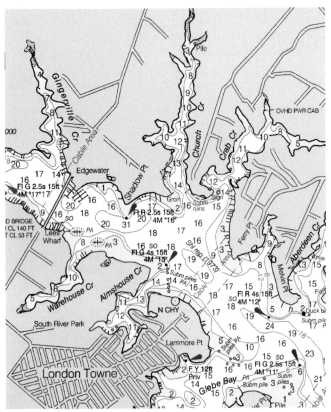

Crab and Church Ck, Almshouse and Warehouse Ck; from NOAA Chart 12270—not to be used for navigation.

Crab and Church Creeks

Past Little Aberdeen Creek, Ferry Point, at "14", is a quiet spot today. But long ago it connected London Town, the once thriving port across the river, with cities such as Boston and Charleston, S.C. It was a little like today's South River Route 2 bridge with its non-stop traffic.

Crab Creek and Church Creek—the last two tributaries on the South River's northern shore before the fixed Route 2 bridge—feel miles away from world's bustle. The two share a common mouth, good depths and protection in quiet, pleasant surroundings.

❻ Crab Creek's opening is straightforward in a northeasterly direction, but favor the starboard side to avoid shoals and a charted piling. Just inside to port is a small cove suitable for anchoring. Most prefer to continue upstream past the constriction at a sharp point on the starboard side. Private buoys mark the channel, reported to be safe for just about any draft, but caution is suggested and seeking local knowledge is never a bad idea. Depths remain 10 to 12 feet beyond the narrows and up into the right fork, before they taper off toward the creek's headwaters.

Next door, **Church Creek** shoots directly north. While its entrance is a little narrower than Crab's, it's not particularly tricky. Just inside you'll see a grouping of private community docks to port and not too far beyond is a wide spot and cove with 10 to 12 feet. The anchorage, surrounded by upscale homes discreetly tucked behind foliage, offers a sweeping view of South River with the stately William Brown House visible at London Town on the southern side. The upper reaches of the creek are narrow, but still deep with room for perhaps a dozen vessels strung along its length. Watch for shoaling at marshy points.

The church for which this pretty creek was named is long-gone and, despite lushly green banks, upstream sprawl and its impervious watershed has introduced stress.

Almshouse and Warehouse Creeks

As you cruise South River's southern shoreline toward ❼ **Almshouse Creek**, it's hard not to notice the regal-looking William Brown House, c. 1760, perched high above the water at London Town. In fact, it's clearly charted: "N CHY", for its north-facing chimneys. And one can't ignore the imposing modern dwellings that flank it. At Larrimore Point, you'll spot a striking glass and steel home, and at the mouth of Almshouse Creek, a row of tall contemporary brick homes.

You'll find more architectural contrasts inside the creek, which is unmarked but easy to negotiate. Unlike its neighboring northern tributaries, nearly every inch is developed and filled with docks. However, it is deep and protected with room for a few boats to anchor.

It's also a good place to drop the hook when taking the dinghy around the corner to access **Historic London Town and Gardens**. (A day-use pier on the South River in front of the William Brown House may accommodate up to 5-foot drafts.) Check in at the visitors center. Also, check the web site (*www.historiclondontown.com*) for concert schedules and other events at the lost town.

West of Almshouse is the last tributary on the southern shore before the bridge. Although its entrance is bordered by charted wrecks, **Warehouse Creek** is not difficult to enter. Inside it is narrow, with 8 to 10 feet, but has space for smaller boats to drop the hook and tuck in for the night.

As the name implies, this was once a local hub of commerce, where agricultural products were brought for shipping elsewhere. It was deeper then. Now, Warehouse Creek Marina, which does not offer services but snug dock space in a serene setting, sits on the northern bank.

If your boat will fit beneath the Route 2 bridge (vertical clearance 53 feet), there are two more lovely creeks—Gingerville and Beards—to explore. Several marinas with services are clustered on both sides of the bridge. If your boat will fit beneath the 25-foot fixed Riva Road bridge, you'll enjoy cruising Broad Creek and the main stem before it shallows out in marshes within sight of U.S. 50/301.

West River

If you're seeking picturesque anchorages and commercial services, you can't do better than the West River and the Rhode River. Located on the Western Shore of the Bay, 9 miles south of the Chesapeake Bay Bridge, they constitute a delightful cruising area. The main Rhode River anchorage around its islands upstream is scenic, secure and beautiful, while Galesville on the West River provides a full range of marine services, as well as restaurants. In addition, the West-Rhode Riverkeeper offers pump-out boat services during the boating season. Call 410-940-3750 or hail *Honeydipper* on VHF 71.

To reach the mouth of the ❶ **West River** from the north, drop down the Bay below Annapolis until Thomas Point Light is abeam. Then pick up the green "1A" that marks the northern corner of Curtis Point Shoal at the West River mouth.

To enter the West River from the south, proceed north up the Bay to green "1", then turn westerly to "1A" at the entrance. On hazy summer days, the marks may be hard to see against the low-

lying land to the west, but with reasonable care the entrance can be found. As you enter, there may be a little confusion with which of the "2" aids to navigation mark which river. But when you remember that the Rhode River is a branch of the West River it becomes clear. The West River's "2" is mounted on a round steel pile and flashes every 2½ seconds, while the Rhode River's "2" is on a tripod of wooden pilings and flashes red every 4 seconds.

Parish Creek and Shady Side

Also lying just inside entrance to the West River—but

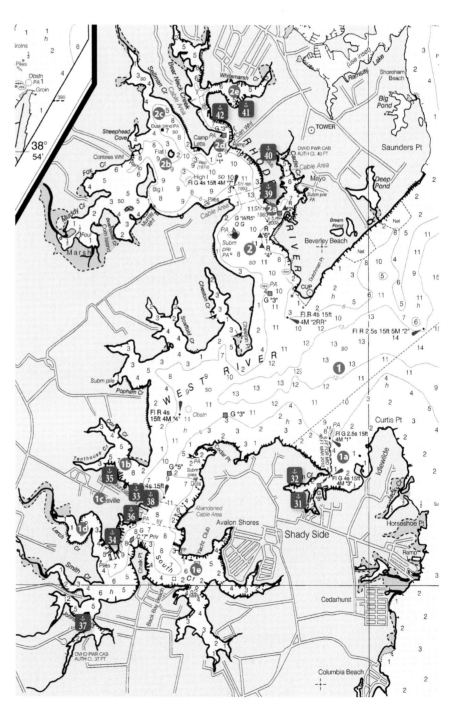

West and Rhode Rivers; from NOAA Chart 12270—not to be used for navigation.

Parish Creek and Shady Side continued

on the southern shore— are 🅐 **Parish Creek** and the town of **Shady Side**, home to several boatyards and an active community of watermen. The creek's entrance lies west of Curtis Point and is well marked, but narrow. Despite recent dredging, new shoaling has been reported, so seek local information.

The modest Shady Side home of one long-ago waterman has been preserved as the CAPTAIN SALEM AVERY HOUSE MUSEUM, accessible by dinghy or shallow-draft boat. As you head up the West River, the pier (with depths of 3 to 4 feet MLW) is located to port a half-mile east of green "3", where you'll see a large flagpole on the shore. The Captain Salem Avery House, which dates to the 1860s, is open Sunday afternoons from April to December and by appointment (410-867-4486). Its popular annual oyster festival is held the third Sunday in October.

As you head into the West River, you'll find a succession of creeks branching west into the mainland, with few homes along their banks. Much of the land bordering these creeks belongs to the SMITHSONIAN ENVIRONMENTAL RESEARCH CENTER, whose facilities may be accessed from the Rhode River behind High Island.

Tenthouse Creek

The first three of these tributaries, **Cheston, Scaffold** and **Popham** creeks, are fairly shallow, about 3 feet in depth, but on a calm night a deeper-draft boat could drop anchor at the mouth of any of these. The fourth, 🅑 **Tenthouse Creek**, is home to the fine 1756 Georgian mansion Tulip Hill, which sits at the headwaters of the creek. Be aware that at "5" the shallow water extends a bit to the south of the marker. The S-shaped channel can become congested with boat traffic

● On Premises ➤ Nearby

	MLW	Overnight Slips	Gas	Diesel	Propane	Electric	Showers	Laundry	Restaurant	Lodging	Pool	Pump-out	Ice	Groceries	Marine Supplies	Bait	Boat Repair	Haul-out Services	Launch Ramp	Wi-Fi	Other
West River																					
Backyard Boats West R./Parish Cr. 301-261-5115; www.backyardboats.com — 31	10'	●	●	●	➤	●			➤	➤		●	●	➤	●	➤	●	●	●	●	
Clark's Landing Yacht Sales West R./Parish Cr. 410-867-9550; www.clarkslanding.com — 32	5.5'		➤	➤		●			➤			●	➤	➤	●	➤	●	●	●	●	Sales and service only—no marina facilities
Galesville Harbor Yacht Yard West R./Galesville 410-867-7517 or 301-261-5135 — 33	7'	●	●	●			●		➤	➤	●	●	●		➤			●	●		Full-service yacht yard
Hartge Yacht Harbor West R./Lerch Cr. 443-607-6306; www.hartgeyachtharbor.com — 34	8'	●	➤	➤	➤	●	●	●	●	➤	➤		●	●		➤	➤	➤	●	●	y
Hartge Yacht Yard West R./Tenthouse Cr. 410-867-2188; www.hartgeyard.com — 35	6'	➤	➤	➤	➤	●	●	➤	●			➤	➤	➤	●	➤	●	●		●	Full-service yard; 25- & 30-ton travelifts, 25-ton trailer
Pirate's Cove West R./Galesville 410-867-2300; www.piratescovemd.com — 36	13'	●	➤	➤		●	●	●	●	●	●	●	●		➤		➤	➤		●	Big Mary's Dock Bar
Shady Oaks Marina West R./Johns Cr. 410-867-7700; www.shadyoakswestriver.com — 37	5'	➤	➤	➤	➤	●	●	●	➤	➤		●	➤	➤	➤	➤	●	●		●	Quiet, protected, beautiful
West River Fuel Dock West R./Galesville 410-867-1444 — 38	9'	●	●	●		●			➤			●	●	●			➤	➤		●	
Rhode River																					
Cadle Creek Marina Rhode R./Cadle Cr. 410-798-1915; www.cadlecreekmarina.com — 39	6'	●				●	●		➤			●	●	➤	●		●	●	●		
Casa Rio Marina Rhode R./Cadle Cr. 410-798-4731; www.casariomarina.com — 40	5'	●	➤	➤		●			➤	➤		●	●	●			●	●			2 lifts, launch, dry storage, painter, DIY storage
Holiday Hill Marina Rhode R./Whitemarsh Cr. 443-871-3909 ; www.holidayhillmarina.com — 41	8'	●	➤			●	●		➤	➤		●	●	●			●	●			Sailboat marina
Rhode River Marina Rhode R./Bear Neck Cr. 410-798-1658; www.rhoderivermarina.com — 42	10'	●	●	●	➤	●	●	●	➤	➤		●	●	●	●		●	●		●	Boatel, slips, lift, engine repair, fuel, pump-out

around constrictions. This is true especially on weekends and during Wednesday evening sailboat races that begin and end in Galesville.

Galesville

As you round "6", **1c** **Galesville** unfolds on the west bank of the river. More than 350 years old, this quiet, old-fashioned community is small and unimposing, with a cluster of old houses set among shady trees. Its combination of well-known boatyards, inviting antiques shops, an exceptional art gallery featuring the work of local artists, and waterfront restaurants renowned for good food and music makes the village a hit among boaters. Many cruisers like to tie up at the public dock or at one of the restaurants. Or if no dock space is available, you can drop anchor in the harbor and dinghy to shore.

Early settlers in this area were Puritans who arrived following the Act of Toleration in 1649, and West River Landing became a busy port for shipping and travel. In 1672, the West River Quaker meeting marked the beginning of organized Quakerism in the state. The village was later named for Richard Gale, an early local Quaker planter.

The GALESVILLE HERITAGE MUSEUM, located in the Carrie Weadon House, is one of the historic buildings featured in the *Heritage Tour* brochure produced by the Galesville Heritage Society (*www.galesvilleheritagesociety.org*). Copies

can be found at locations throughout the town.

The Hartge family has been an important part of the Galesville community since 1865, when Emile Hartge started building boats on the peninsula across from Chalk Point at the mouth of Lerch Creek. A small museum, housed in the 1878 home of the shipyard's founder, is at Hartge Yacht Harbor, managed by his descendants as a marina. Others in the family continue to offer full repair services at Hartge Yacht Yard on Tenthouse Creek, on the other side of Galesville; its business offices and marine store occupy the historic West River Market building a few blocks away.

Lerch Creek Basin

Just beyond Galesville, there's a quiet and somewhat secluded anchorage in the broad basin formed by **1d** **Lerch Creek** and its neighboring creeks, **Smith** and **Johns**. This large area is mostly filled with permanent moorings, but to the west and south of CHALK POINT there is room for several boats to anchor in 5 to 7 feet. The unusual array of vessels gives this area a kind of New England charm. You might see wooden sharpies, antique mahogany-hulled motorboats or several retired draketail workboats (whose sterns fan out like duck tails). Houses and woods surround this area.

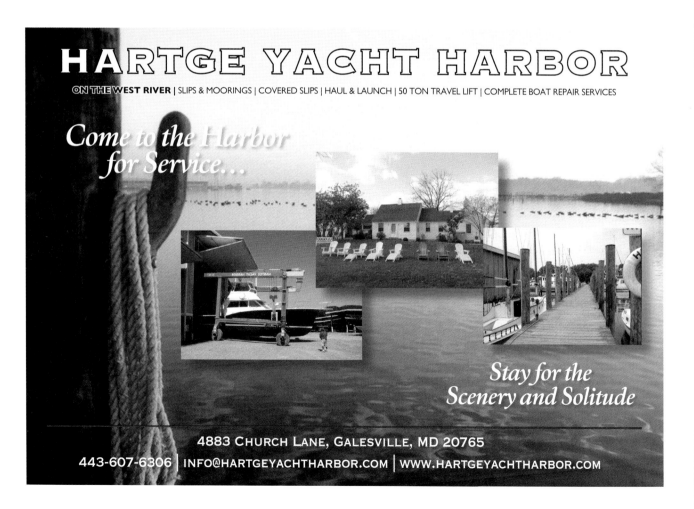

HARTGE YACHT HARBOR

ON THE WEST RIVER | SLIPS & MOORINGS | COVERED SLIPS | HAUL & LAUNCH | 50 TON TRAVEL LIFT | COMPLETE BOAT REPAIR SERVICES

Come to the Harbor for Service...

Stay for the Scenery and Solitude

4883 CHURCH LANE, GALESVILLE, MD 20765

443-607-6306 | INFO@HARTGEYACHTHARBOR.COM | WWW.HARTGEYACHTHARBOR.COM

South Creek

Chalk Point separates West River from South Creek. This slender piece of land was the site of Anne Arundel County's only Revolutionary War action: The British knocked out a cannon emplacement and burned Steward's Shipyard at the head of West River. Its legacy is explored in a room at the Galesville Heritage Museum dedicated to artifacts belonging to the Steward Colonial Shipyard Foundation.

1e **South Creek** to the east has depths ranging from 2 to 8 feet and attracts principally powerboaters with shoal drafts. The area north of Chalk Point, at the mouth of South Creek, is a popular anchorage, with depths of 7 to 8 feet.

Rhode River

The entrance to the **2** **Rhode River** is guarded by Dutchman Point. A white, two-storied building with a cupola is a good identifying feature if the "2" on the right side of the river can't be seen in the haze. The river is well marked; follow your chart and stay off the points.

In the summer, the wind on the Rhode is often out of the south or southeast, and the banks of the river act as a wind funnel to the north; but when it's out of the west or the north, it seems to be channeled down the river instead. For a sailor on the Rhode River, a reach is a rare treat.

A half-mile above the river mouth the channel opens up on the west side and forms a semicircular bay that offers good protection for anchored boats from thunderstorms, which generally travel from west to east in this area of the Bay.

Cadle Creek

2a **Cadle Creek** enters the Rhode River on the right, three-quarters of a mile above the river mouth. Its two marinas offer slips, fuel, supplies and repairs. Shallow-draft vessels will find the creek more accessible than deep-draft boats, whose skippers may be discouraged by the 4-foot bar shown on charts across the mouth of the creek. The shores are heavily populated, and the creek is too narrow for anchoring.

Big and Flat Islands

Continuing past Cadle Creek north up the Rhode River, be careful of the shoal that extends out from the western side of the river just in front of the lighted green "7" mark. Boaters tend to use the mark as a range when approaching from the south; if you don't pay attention to the relative bearing of the light, you could go aground. Continue past the light, make a turn to the left, and follow the shoreline in 10 feet of water.

After making the turn, the upper Rhode's **2b** **Big** and **Flat islands** come into view. Many charts still show three islands, but only two remain after dramatic erosion during the past

RHODE RIVER MARINA

Protected Harbour Only 7 Minutes from the Bay!

A FULL SERVICE MARINA
Fuel Dock • Pumpout
Wet Slips, Lift Slips & Boatel
Travel & Fork Lifts
Boat & Engine Repairs & Maintenance
Factory Center & Certified Technicians

YAMAHA
When you want the best
MERCURY® MerCruiser
EVINRUDE
VOLVO PENTA
FORMULA

3932 GERMANTOWN RD., EDGEWATER, MD | 410.798.1658
WWW.RHODERIVERMARINA.COM

decade. **High Island**, far from resembling its name, is now a marked shoal. Once crescent-shaped, its shallows still extend northeasterly from its core, so plot a course to avoid this area. Go slowly and watch depths carefully. The only indication of the no-longer-an-island's presence could be a few gulls looking like they're standing on water.

After navigating safely past High Island's shoal, boats generally anchor in the large cove bounded on the southwest by Murray Wharf, Big Island to the west and Flat Island to the north. The 8- and 9-foot depths here have good holding and high trees and bluffs provide beauty along with protection. Expect some weekend raft-ups, but quiet prevails on other days, with canoeists and kayakers and an occasional research vessel from the nearby Smithsonian Environmental Research Center (SERC) slowly conducting field experiments.

If draft permits, you can squeeze between Big and Flat Islands to anchor (in 7 or 8 feet) closer to Contees Wharf, once a vital link in the tobacco trade and later a steamboat landing. Screened from both wind and most of the homes lining the river's east bank, you'll sit in the shadow of some historic chimneys, all that's left of a stately mansion that stood on the rise above.

By 1673, Europeans had established nine plantations along the Rhode, with Thomas Sparrow holding some 700 acres for tobacco growing. The ruins are what remain of his early-1700s manor house. John Contee bought the property in 1828, naming it Java Plantation for HMS *Java*. (Contee served aboard the U.S.S. *Constitution* when the ship captured *Java* off the Brazilian coast in 1812.) Unfortunately, the home, with giant pilasters and hyphens and wings on either side, burned in 1890. Farther west is the SERC's 14 miles of shoreline with a launch ramp and kayak dock where small non-motorized craft are permitted to land. Besides extensive scientific projects, the center (*www.serc.si.edu*) offers public programs, a picnic area, hiking and water trails, and guided tours. Call ahead (301-238-2737) to assure space.

Big Island, owned by SERC, is not hospitable, but small boats and dinghies often land at the little beach on Flat Island's eastern side. Use extreme caution when navigating a boat of any draft in the narrow unmarked strip of water between Flat Island and what is left of High Island.

Sellman Creek

Another anchorage is north of Flat Island in the mouth of **②c** **Sellman Creek**. With 7- and 8-foot depths and sheltered from west and north, it is best approached from the south due to charted shallows between Flat Island and the mainland. Camp Letts, owned by the YMCA, is located on the neck of land between Sellman Creek and Bear Neck Creek on the northeast side of the anchorage.

Bear Neck Creek

②d **Bear Neck Creek** is worth exploring. It enters the Rhode River northeast of High Island. Its entrance is identified by

daymark "1" on the left and Carr's Wharf—a public fishing pier extending out to deep water—on the right. Beware of cutting the point off Camp Letts to port too closely, as the shoal extends out farther than the chart shows. There are services available, such as gas, ice, water and some mechanical help, on Bear Neck Creek. As you continue past the second daymark, the creek's shores become residential to starboard, but remain wooded on the Camp Letts side. Watch out for a small shoal that extends from the west side of the creek just above Rhode River Marina.

②e **Whitemarsh Creek** opens up on the right a quarter-mile above the mouth of Bear Neck Creek. It carries 5 to 6 feet, but is rarely used as an anchorage. At this point Bear Neck widens, and on the left there is room for a snug anchorage for a shallow-draft boat.

Herring Bay and Rockhold Creek

Herring Bay's first entrance mark, flashing "1" off Holland Point, lies about a mile northwest of "81A", one of the unlighted buoys that define the Western Shore's busy shipping lane. Alternately, if you are approaching from the north, look for "83A"; from there you can plot a course for Herring Bay's flashing "2", nearly 3 miles to the southwest.

Southbound skippers should note that "2" marks the southernmost edge of Long Bar, a 2-mile-long shoal with 1- to 5-foot depths. Shallow-draft vessels often take this shortcut, but locals warn of unknown snags. Likewise, northbound captains should heed the shoals that extend offshore after the main entrance to Chesapeake Beach.

Anchoring in Herring Bay is not advised, but scores of overnight slips with a variety of amenities and services lie at both ends of the bay. Two big marinas, both popular with cruisers and cruising clubs, dominate the landscape here: Herrington Harbour South, the recreational destination at the bottom of Herring Bay, and its sister facility, Herrington Harbour North, at the top. Herrington North is also a full-service yacht yard with a wide range of marine services on its large campus, including a West Marine store. Reservations for any of the area's many marinas are recommended, especially on holiday weekends.

From "2", the wide channel leads northward about 1 1/2 miles before narrowing at the jetties that funnel boats toward Herring Bay's two main tributaries, **Rockhold Creek** and **Tracys Creek**. The village of **Deale** stretches along Rockhold's shores, where there are several full-service marinas that welcome transients. Depth at these marinas is generally 7 feet MLW. Most of the docks here are clustered at the mouth, or just inside, of both Rockhold and Tracy's creeks, though two marinas lie above Deale's fixed bridge (14-foot vertical clearance).

This friendly waterfront community also hosts a charter fishing fleet and a variety of businesses with marine expertise and supplies. Deale's quaint rural character, how-

Herring Bay and Rockhold Creek *continued*

ever, also means that non-boating services can be somewhat limited. Among the town's several convivial restaurants is Skipper's Pier, which has a large deck bar as well as outdoor and indoor dining on the southeastern tip of Rockhold Creek. Petie Green's Bar and Grill, while not on the water, is a cozy casual place nearby on Drum Point Road. On the western side, and at the hub of the charter fleet near the Route 256 bridge, is fun-loving Happy Harbor, a tradition since 1933.

Calypso Bay, in Tracys Creek just below the fixed bridge, has a sand- and palm-strewn tiki bar as well as fine indoor-dining. Nearby, and worth a visit, is a growing collection of antique Chesapeake-country structures, saved from demolition and displayed at Herrington Harbour North.

Deale has no handy grocery or convenience stores, but a short hike eastward from Rockhold Creek's bridge takes you to a hardware store, post office, library and consignment shop. On Thursday evenings during the growing season, look for the farmers market in the parking lot of Cedar Grove Methodist Church, at the corner of Mason Beach Road and Deale Road.

Rockhold Creek meanders northward another mile or so beyond the bridge, where it becomes shallow and the docks are fewer,. Boaters with shoal draft and low profile may enjoy exploring those quieter upper reaches. This lush farmland is the heart of Anne Arundel's "South County."

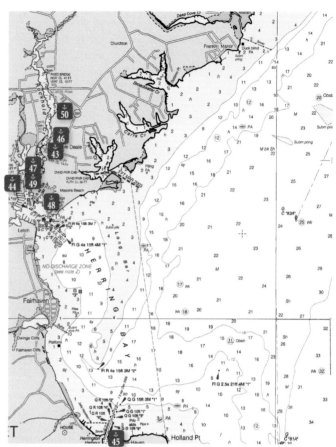

Herring Bay and Rockhold Creek; from NOAA Chart 12270—not to be used for navigation.

● On Premises
➤ Nearby

	MLW	Overnight Slips	Gas	Diesel	Propane	Electric	Showers	Laundry	Restaurant	Lodging	Pool	Pump-out	Ice	Groceries	Marine Supplies	Bait	Boat Repair	Haul-out Services	Launch Ramp	Wi-Fi	Other
Herring Bay																					
Harbour Cove Marina ⚓43 Herring Bay/Rockhold Cr. 301-867-1600; www.harbourcove.com	4'	●	➤	➤		●	●	●	➤		●	●	●			●		●	●	●	Full Service, mechanics, pool, laundry, storage
Herrington Harbour North ⚓44 Herring Bay/Tracys Cr.; 410-867-4343 or 800-297-1930; www.herringtonharbour.com	7'	●	➤	➤	➤	●	●	●	➤	●	●	●	➤	●	➤	●	●	➤	●	Marina resort, full service, DIY yard, West Marine, Wi-Fi
Herrington Harbour South ⚓45 Herring Bay/Rosehaven 410-741-5100; 301-855-8399; www.herringtonharbour.com	7'	●	●	●	➤	●	●	●	●	●	●	●	➤	●	➤	➤	➤	●	Eco-lifestyle marina resort, beachfront lodging, dining
Hidden Harbour Marina ⚓46 Herring Bay/Rockhold Cr. 410-867-9666; www.hiddenharbour.net	5'	●	➤	➤	➤	●	●	➤	➤		●	●	●	●	●	●	●	●	●	Full-service, storage, lift, parts, boat sales
Rockhold Creek Marina & Yacht Repair ⚓47 Herring Bay/Rockhold Cr. 410-867-7919; www.rockholdcreekmarina.com	6'	●	➤	➤	➤	●	●	➤	➤	➤	●	➤	➤	●	➤	●	●	➤	●	Boatel, courtesy car, full-service/DIY yard, kayaks, Wi-Fi
Sherman's Marina ⚓48 Herring Bay/Rockhold Cr. 301-261-5013	8'	●	➤	➤	➤	●	●	●	➤	➤	●	●	●	●	➤	●	➤	➤	●	In-town marina
Shipwright Harbor ⚓49 Herring Bay/Rockhold Cr.; 410-867-7686 or 301-261-5632; www.shipwrightharbormarina.com	7'	●	➤	➤	➤	●	●	➤	●	➤	●	●	➤	●	➤	●	➤	●	●	Beautiful picnic area with gazebos, grills. Dog park
Tri-State Marine Tackle ⚓50 Herring Bay/Rockhold Cr. 410-867-2398; www.tristatemarine.com	3'		●	●		●			➤			●	●	●	●	●	➤	➤	●	Fishing charters, tackle, crab supplies, nautical gifts

HERRINGTON HARBOUR SOUTH

Marina • Resort

**Protected Enclosed Harbour featuring Restaurant
Inn with Hot Tubs • Catering • Sauna
• Olympic Sized Pool • Fitness Center
• Laundry Facilities • Pumpout
• Fuel Dock • Picnic Areas • Tennis Courts
• Beach Areas • 30/50 Amp Electric
• Internet Access, Cable TV, and more.**

LAT 38° 44: 12" • LON 76° 32: 20"

1.800.213.9438

HERRINGTON HARBOUR NORTH

Marina Resort • Yacht Center

**Protected Countryside Harbour featuring Restaurant &
Dock Bar • Pool Bar • Bayside Pool • Jacuuzzi Spa
• Fitness Center • 7' MLW
• Complimentary Slip Holder Events
• Laundry • WiFi • West Marine Store • Pump Out
• Kayaks and Bicycles • Full Service/Do-it-Yourself
Yacht Yard • Customer Lounges, and more.**

LAT 38° 45: 86" • LON 76° 32: 80"

1.800.297.1930

Visit us on Herring Bay on the Chesapeake and at www.HerringtonHarbour.com

Kent Island and Eastern Bay

Across the Bay from the Rhode and West rivers lies the lower end of **Kent Island**. Cruisers will find three marinas along the island's Bay (western) shore, all located south of the twin spans of the Chesapeake Bay Bridge. These facilities—Bay Bridge, Kentmorr and Queen Anne marinas—offer slips, fuel, repair services and restaurants with front-row seats to some of the Bay's most spectacular sunsets.

Opening up to the south of Kent Island, **Eastern Bay** is a wide, reasonably deep waterway whose broad entrance lies between Bloody Point and Poplar Island. This irregularly shaped bay concludes in three sections—northerly to **Prospect Bay** and Kent Island Narrows, easterly to the Wye River and southeasterly to the Miles River.

When entering Eastern Bay from the north, give Bloody Point Light a good berth. Setting a course toward green "1", avoid the shoal that extends south almost a mile from Kent Point. Boaters also have to dodge a slew of crab pots off this point. Approaching from the south, from red "84A", head for lighted aid "1" about 2 miles north of Poplar Island. There are shoals around the island too.

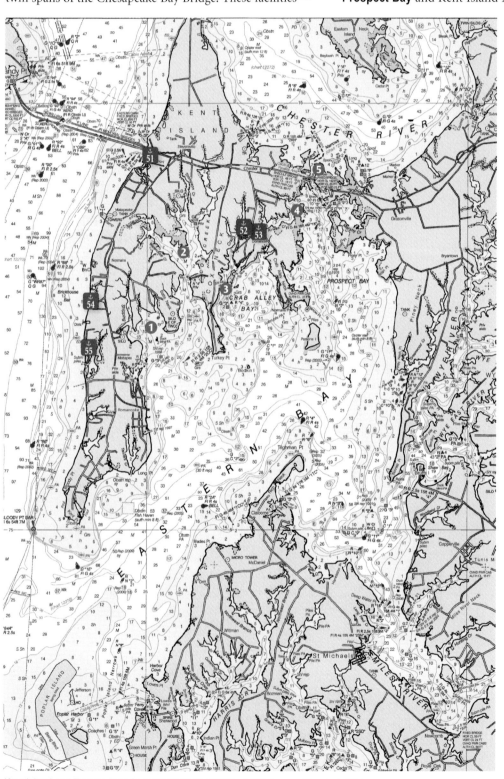

Kent Island and Eastern Bay; from NOAA Chart 12263—not to be used for navigation.

Shipping Creek

The closest shelters lie in small creeks to the north. ❶ **Shipping Creek** is the first navigable tributary on Kent Island's southeastern shore. It is about 6 miles inside Kent Point, the southernmost tip of the island, and $1\frac{1}{2}$ miles north of the little community of **Romancoke** (which was once a ferry stop).

Coming from **Poplar Island Narrows**, you'll have a clear path almost directly north into the wide mouth of Eastern Bay. You can cross the mouth and duck in along the inside shore of Kent Island. Beyond Romancoke, you'll come to the wide entrance shared by Shipping and Cox creeks, with the small **Philpots Islands** to the west and **Long Marsh Island** to the east. Green daymark "3" defines the end of a shoal

- On Premises
➤ Nearby

Kent Island

	MLW	Overnight Slips	Gas	Diesel	Propane	Electric	Showers	Laundry	Restaurant	Lodging	Pool	Pump-out	Ice	Groceries	Marine Supplies	Boat Repair	Bait	Haul-out Services	Launch Ramp	Wi-Fi	Other
Bay Bridge Marina Kent Island/Chesapeake Bay 410-643-3162; www.baybridgemarina.com	6.5'	●	●	●	➤	●	●	●	●	➤	●	●	●	➤	●	➤	●	●	➤	●	Airport, boat sales, beach, floating docks, cable
Clark's Landing Kent Island/Eastern Bay/Crab Alley Cr. 410-604-4300; www.clarkslanding.com	7'		●			●	●				●	●		●			●	●			Specializing in engine repairs; haulout, storage
Crab Alley Marina Kent Island/Eastern Bay/Crab Alley Bay 410-643-7339; www.craballeycustomboats.com		➤	➤	➤			➤	➤	➤			●	➤					●			Dry storage boat rental
Kentmorr Marina Kent Island/Chesapeake Bay 410-643-0029; www.kentmorrmarina.net	5'	●	●	●		●	●		●	➤		●	●	➤	➤	➤	●	●		●	Two beaches
Queen Anne Marina Kent Island/Price Cr. www.queenannemarina.com 410-643-2021;	5'	●	●	●		●	●			➤		●	●	●	●	●	●	●	●	●	Floating docks, ship store, fuel, pump-out, lift

off Philpots, with water depths of 1 foot. Rounding this navigational aid, be careful to avoid the long, unmarked shoal extending from BATTS NECK to the north. Continuing upstream, stay in the 10- to 11-foot unmarked channel.

Just inside Shipping Creek proper—a long, narrow creek that runs in a north/south direction along the Kent shoreline—is a somewhat confined spot where you can find a snug and quiet anchorage in 7 feet of water.

Once largely rural, the surrounding area has evolved into a small community of large homes and estates, many with piers and pleasure boats. The creek is not as isolated as it once was, but it's still a beautiful anchorage. Watermen motoring along their trotlines in the creek still provide their pleasant wake-up call just after daybreak. Inside the creek, to port, is a small, shallow cove with a public launching ramp, also a good dinghy landing.

Cox Creek

From Shipping Creek, you can head east into ❷ **Cox Creek**, which has good depths but a few unmarked shoals. Beyond flashing red "2CC" at the creek's mouth, red nun "4" is about 2 miles north. About one mile farther is green daymark "5". You'll notice the shoal on the starboard side a mile and a half upstream; at low tide, marsh grass is visible on it. Pick a wide spot in the creek to anchor or take the left fork into lovely **Warehouse Creek**, where you'll find plenty of room to anchor, either just inside or upstream near a tiny uncharted island.

Crab Alley Creek

En route through Eastern Bay to ❸ **Crab Alley Creek**, you must stay well clear of the now almost-invisible island east southeast of Turkey Point. In its larger days, the island stood as a sort of sentinel at the entrance to **Crab Alley Bay**, about 6 miles from Kent Point.

According to William B. Cronin's *The Disappearing Islands of the Chesapeake*, **Bodkin Island** comprised about 30 acres in 1899, but had eroded considerably by the time a group of duck hunters bought it in 1939. They erected a bulkhead to halt further erosion, but to little avail. Adding insult to inundation, a fire set by vandals swept Bodkin in 1985, destroying its only remaining building and most of its trees. The state of Maryland purchased the island 10 years later, planning to rebuild it as wetlands using dredge spoils from Kent Narrows Channel. The project was deemed too costly, however, and Bodkin was abandoned for good.

Shipping Creek; from NOAA Chart 12270—not to be used for navigation.

Crab Alley Creek *continued*

Most boats have no problem with Crab Alley Creek's depths of 7 to 11 feet. As you pass Bloody Point Light and head up Eastern Bay, resist the temptation to head directly toward Bodkin Island for a closer look, since the long shoals that project from its south end are unmarked. Rounding green can "1" at the northeast end of the Bodkin Island shoal, head for daymarks "3" and "4" at the mouth of Crab Alley Creek, a little over a mile away.

As you pass these marks you will see two islands ahead to starboard. The nearest, Little Island, is no more than a mound of marsh grass. The other, **Johnson Island**, is much larger, with a few buildings. Between them, a marked channel, which becomes shallow, leads up to a marina pier and a seafood house on **Little Creek**.

Crab Alley Creek lies west of Johnson Island and its surrounding shoals. Although the creek widens opposite Johnson Island, you might decide there are too many crab lines and head

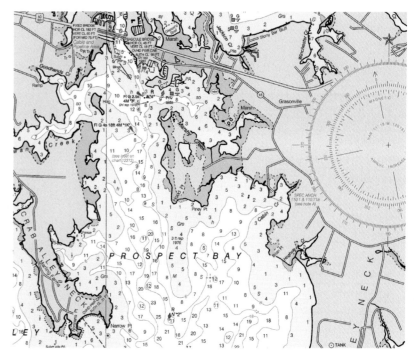

Prospect Bay; from NOAA Chart 12270—not to be used for navigation.

Crab Alley and Crab Creek; from NOAA Chart 12270—not to be used for navigation.

farther upstream—where you'll find depths of 6 feet or more for nearly another mile. Cruising boats can find a comfortable anchorage in good protected water. Marinas near the mouth of the creek offer gas, supplies and repair services.

If you anchor just northwest of the gap between Johnson Island and the mainland, you'll find a quiet shoreline with a few small, private docks.

Kirwan Creek

With the popularity of the Kent Island area, the difficult thing can be finding a quiet anchorage within easy reach of all the activity. However, there are some fine places to set the hook after a day of cruising or exploring Kent Narrows.

Marshy Creek, south of the Narrows on the east side, is deep enough for boats drawing up to about 6 feet, but it does not have good protection from winds. If the weather is settled, it is a pretty spot. An even better anchorage is Kirwan (pronounced *CUR-wun*) Creek on the west side of the Narrows.

❹ **Kirwan Creek** presents a challenge to boats trying to access its beckoning shelter. Shoaling has altered the entrance, and deeper draft boats may have trouble getting in. From the green flasher on "1K" at the southern entrance to the Narrows, stay in the middle by aiming for a point halfway between low, marshy **Hog Island** on the left and the breakwater extending from Kent Island Yacht Club on the right. When the breakwater is abeam to starboard, swing wide to port and stay in the middle to reach the junction of Kirwan Creek and its companion, **Goodhands Creek**.

From the north and the Chester River, go all the way through the Narrows, passing marker "3" and going halfway to "1K" before turning north toward Hog Island. Don't try

Bay Bridge Marina is conveniently located on the Eastern Shore of the Chesapeake Bay at the base of the Bay Bridge. It provides easy access in a short cruise time to Annapolis, Baltimore, St. Michaels and Kent Narrows.

BAY BRIDGE
MARINA YACHT
CLUB

Come for the Sunset, Stay for the Season!

357 Pier One Road Stevensville, MD 21666 I 410-643-3162 I www.BayBridgeMarina.com

Kirwan Creek *continued*

to shortcut across the sand bar south of the breakwater—the water here is very shoal, with bare spots at low tide.

Cruising experience suggests the depths are 6 feet or less between Hog Island and the breakwater, and extending into Goodhands (pronounced *GOOD-ens* locally) and Kirwan creeks. A nearby launch ramp churns out plenty of shoal-draft crab and fishing boats at seemingly all hours of the day, along with some rowdy teenage parties at night. You may prefer the south fork. By staying in the center, you might find as much as 6 feet in Kirwan Creek up to the spot where a marshy cove forms on the south shore. You can anchor anywhere in quiet comfort.

There is little boat traffic here. The south shore is undeveloped and the north shore is bordered by a large farm and an attractive waterfront community with large lots. Except for the sound of the Route 50 traffic in the distance, you can forget that the Kent Narrows business district is just around the corner. The marshes along the south shore of Kirwan Creek mean mosquitoes; you'll want screens on summer evenings.

For some fine Eastern Shore scenery, explore the upper reaches of the creek by dinghy. The dinghy can also take you to businesses located at the Narrows, if you wish. Be careful of the outboard's prop if you decide to cut between the yacht club and the breakwater. The water there is shallow (only about 3 feet) at the western end.

Kent Narrows

Kent Island, the Chesapeake's largest island, was settled in 1631 by William Claiborne as a trading post where native Americans and Europeans exchanged goods. Named by Claiborne for his British birthplace, it's the oldest English settlement in present-day Maryland. Later it became a seafood packing center, but today, in addition to anchoring the eastern end of the Bay Bridge, it's a recreational boating mecca with a variety of services available to boaters.

The waterway that separates the island from the rest of the Eastern Shore, ❺ **Kent Narrows**, is the fastest route between Eastern Bay and the Chester River. Beneath its parallel bridges—a multilane with 65-foot clearance and a drawbridge with frequent openings—is a high volume of water traffic, and a route that can be confusing on busy summer days. And then there's the shoaling . . . and the wicked current. Keep red to starboard when entering from both north and south. You are "returning" when entering from either direction.

Both approaches to Kent Narrows can get touchy, with thin water just outside the channel in many places. Despite dredging in recent years, transiting may be tense, and neither end is a place for shortcuts except for those with shallow draft.

The northern end of the Narrows was dredged in the spring of 2014, making the perennially problematic northern

SELLING YOUR BOAT?

We Sell Boats –

We Purchase Boats –

We Trade Boats –

We Invest in Your Boat –

We are open 7 days a week

We provide financing & insurance

We provide full service in 2 resort marinas

"The difference is in the details"

Contact Mike Sweeney today to see what we can do to get your boat sold.

410–382–6346 (24/7)

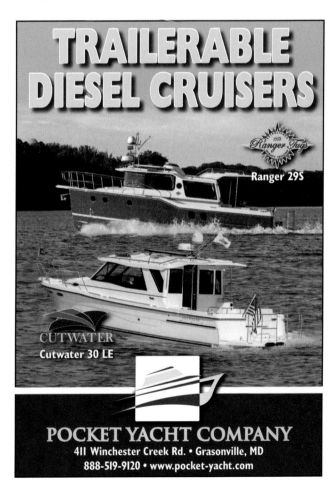

TRAILERABLE DIESEL CRUISERS

Ranger Tugs

Ranger 29S

CUTWATER
Cutwater 30 LE

POCKET YACHT COMPANY

411 Winchester Creek Rd. • Grasonville, MD

888-519-9120 • www.pocket-yacht.com

channel considerably less so—at least for the time being. But the channel remains narrow, and crowded weekend traffic and a strong tidal set can easily push boaters out of the deep water and into the sand. The northern channel is a dogleg, oriented to the northwest and the mouth of the Chester River. A large unmarked shoal lies east of the northernmost end as it joins the Chester, and depths outside the channel fall off quickly. If you are using charts that are more than a couple of years old, they may show marks such as "R4" in the wrong place. (That marker now reads "danger shoaling" and old green "3" is now a red, with a new green set in what was once outside the channel.) When entering or exiting Kent Narrows, lighted aides "1K" and "2K" are vital. On the southern side, shoaling has been reported at the mouths of Marshy and Kirwan creeks.

And that's just the markers. Mind the current as well, since it runs strong, especially around the bridges. Maintain good boat speed and keep an eye on your instruments. The drawbridge's horizontal clearance is just 48 feet, and vessels traveling with the current have the right of way. It's a good idea to check in with the bridge tender on VHF, so that other transiting boaters can hear, to determine who's got right of way. The drawbridge (18-foot vertical clearance) opens on the hour and half-hour from 6 a.m. to 9 p.m., May 1 to October 31, and on request from 6 a.m. to 6 p.m., November 1 through April 30. The draw does not open after hours. The bridgetender monitors channel 13. Give at least five minutes

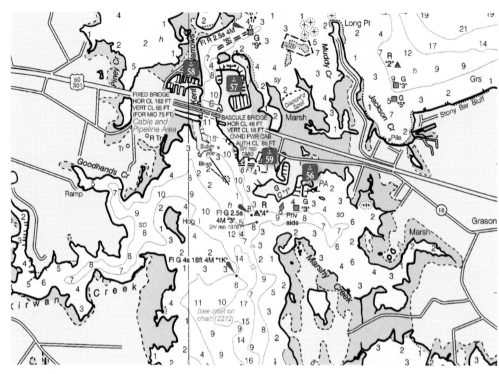

Marshy Creek and Kent Narrows; from NOAA Chart 12270—not to be used for navigation.

notice. The usual bridge horn signal will work also: one prolonged blast (four to six seconds) followed by one short blast (one second). The bridgetender may be reached by phone (410-643-5963). A speed limit of 6 knots is enforced by Natural Resources Police.

Marinas at the Narrows range from simple to elaborate, and local yards do a brisk business in maintaining and restoring boats. Excellent restaurants in all price categories, a real crabhouse, two motels, a dive shop and a visitor's center are all within easy walking distance over paved pedestrian pathways. The nightlife is lively and includes bikini contests, dancing to live bands on open-air decks, karaoke music and a variety of water-oriented events throughout the sum-

continued on page 143

● On Premises
➤ Nearby

Kent Narrows

	MLW	Overnight Slips	Gas	Diesel	Propane	Electric	Showers	Laundry	Restaurant	Lodging	Pool	Pump-out	Ice	Groceries	Marine Supplies	Bait	Boat Repair	Haul-out Services	Launch Ramp	Wi-Fi	Other
Lippincott Marine Kent Narrows/Marshy Creek 410-827-9300 ; www.lippincottmarina.com	7'	●	➤	➤	➤	●	●	●	➤	➤	●	●	●	➤	●	➤	●	●	➤	●	Full-service, storage, new/brokerage boat sales
Mears Point Marina Kent Narrows 410-827-8888; www.mearspoint.com	8'	●	●	●	➤	●	●	●	●	➤	●	●	●	➤	●	●	➤	●	●	➤	Yacht club, gym, pool bars, restaurants, kids club
Piney Narrows Yacht Haven Kent Narrows 410-643-6600; www.pineynarrows.com	7'	●	●	●	➤	●	●	●	●	●	➤	●	●	●	➤	●	●	●	➤	●	Brokerage, condo slips, sales & rentals
Wells Cove Marina Kent Narrows 410-827-3869; www.wellscovetownhomesandmarina.com	6'	●			●	●		➤	➤	●	●	●	➤						●		Floating docks, freshwater pool, free Wi-Fi

Port of Call
Kent Narrows

The narrow strip of water and land that constitutes Kent Narrows might be called the Sunset Strip of the Chesapeake Bay. Not even in Annapolis, Solomons, St. Michaels or even Hampton Roads are you likely to find so many boats in such a small area. To put it simply, on summer weekends, things can get just plain crazy here! Kent Narrows is a potent combination of dock bars, seafood restaurants (all with their own docks), marinas, yacht clubs and a basin dedicated just to watermen's workboats, all lying along the thin waterway that connects Eastern Bay, to the south, with the Chester River, to the north. But wait, there's more. To all of that we must add a bracing current, a bascule bridge as narrow as an Alpine pass, and a channel that is notorious for shoaling on its north side (but, happily, was dredged in the winter of 2014). Now we have a full portrait of a visit to Kent Narrows.

The passage separating Kent Island from the rest of Queen Anne's County was not always navigable. In fact, in the colonial days, it was known as the Wading Place, a shallow ribbon of water that meandered through acres of marshland. A causeway was built across it in the early 1800s, but was removed in 1876, when the waterway was dredged to allow boat traffic. Opening bridges replaced the causeway. For the next 100 years, the Narrows became a center for the local seafood industry, with a dozen packing houses served by hundreds of workboats. Today the packing houses are pretty much gone, replaced with marinas and res-

taurants, and the workboats are concentrated in the county Watermen's Boat Basin on the southwest side of the Main Street bridge. But you can still buy fresh fish at Fisherman's Seafood Market, near Fisherman's Inn and Marina. And you can find some of the best and freshest seafood around at the Narrows many restaurants, from the venerable Fisherman's Inn (south side of the bridges) and Harris Crab House (north side) to the new and entrancing Bridges Restaurant. And there are plenty of opportunities for kicking back and watching the passing show—like Red Eye's Dock Bar and The Jetty. Nearly all of the bars and restaurants on the Narrows have free dockage for diners. In June, the Narrows roars to the sound of powerboats during the annual Thunder on the Narrows races.

Information: kentisland.cc; kentisland.com

Kent Narrows

⚓ **Marinas/Dockage**
 1 Lippincott Marine
 2 Wells Cove Marine
 4 Harrison's Yacht Sales & Repair
 6 Angler's Boatworks
 7 Mears Point Marina
 8 Kent Narrows Yacht Club
 9 Piney Narrows Yacht Haven
 13 Kent Island Yacht Club

🍴 **Dining Areas**
 3 Jetty Restaurant & Dock Bar
 5 Fisherman's Inn
 10 Bridges
 11 Red Eyes Dock Bar
 12 Harris Crab House
 14 Big Owl's Tiki Bar

⊕ **Points of Interest**
 15 Watermen's Boat Basin

🛒 **Groceries**
 5 Fisherman's Seafood Market

℞ **Pharmacy**

Ⓜ **Marine Supplies**

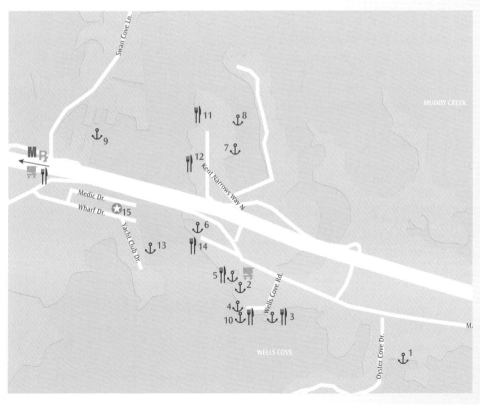

Kent Narrows *continued from page 141*

mer months. On July 4, the skies light up with a spectacular fireworks display. Generally scheduled for the first week in August, Thunder on the Narrows aptly describes the annual powerboat races sponsored by the Kent Narrows Racing Association (*www.kentnarrowsracing.com*).

Trailer-boaters will find a four-lane launch ramp under the Route 50 bridge on the west (island) side of the Narrows. Permits are available at the nearby Exploration Center. If you're planning a long stay, you'll need to find a place to store your rig; there's no overnight parking allowed.

For local color, visit the county-owned commercial docks on the west side, south of the bridge, where you'll see numerous workboats. Those with conveyor belts alongside are clam dredges; most of the others are used for crabbing, either with "pots" (wire traps) or long trotlines.

Bus service connects the Narrows to various points on Kent Island and to nearby Grasonville on the Eastern Shore. Call 410-758-2357 to let them know your location and your destination and they will help you determine a pick-up point and time. There's no service on Sundays, however. Two

taxi/courier companies also serve the Narrows: Kent Island Express (410-604-0486) and Kent Island Transportation (410-643-1500).

A large shopping complex of outlet stores is located about five miles east at the U.S. 50/301 junction. Two public golf courses are located in the area, and a growing number of paved, non-motorized trails help you forget the constant flow of traffic funneling on and off the Bay Bridge. Check out Queen Anne's County Recreation's website, *www.parksnrec.org*.

Castle Harbor Marina, about 4 miles from the Narrows just inside the Chester River, offers boaters a quieter option, far from the madding crowd. Look for the striped lighthouse.

Wye River

Secluded anchorages and a rich historical heritage are among the many charms of the **Wye River**. The river—divided into three branches—encircles Wye Island, most of which consists of WYE ISLAND NATURAL RESOURCE MANAGEMENT AREA, a 2,450-acre day-use facility with nearly 12 miles of hiking and biking trails and 30 miles of shoreline to explore.

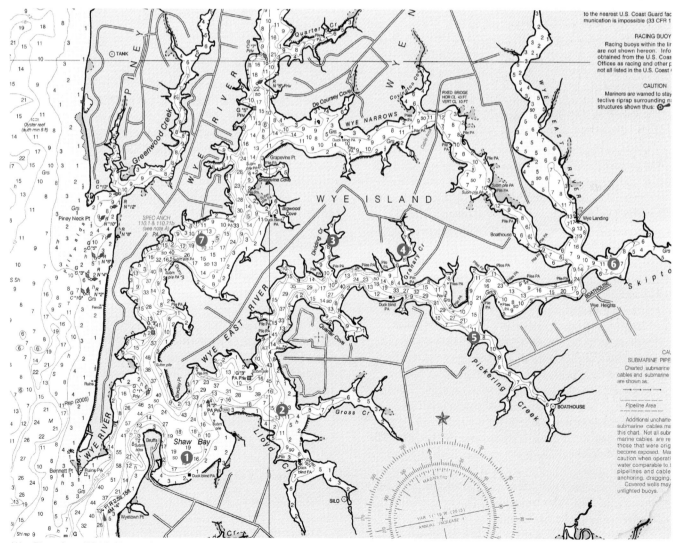

Wye River; from NOAA Chart 12270—not to be used for navigation.

Wye River continued

Boaters are welcome to land along its hospitably sloping shoreline to access its old growth forests and fields once used for agriculture. Landing sites within easy reach of popular anchorages are found in the descriptions of Dividing Creek, Granary Creek and Drum Point Cove. Another favored landing site is along Wye Narrows.

Wye River proper runs in a northerly direction, with **Wye East River** forking to the east and **Wye Narrows**, which runs along the northern and eastern sides of the island, connecting the two branches. A fixed bridge (10-foot vertical clearance) crosses Wye Narrows, connecting the island to the mainland.

The western shore of the Wye River is well developed, but its eastern shore offers more secluded anchorages. On the Wye East, large houses, many dating back to Colonial days, stand on the banks, greeting cruisers at every turn. Fields of grain roll down to the water's edge. Watermen putter around in wooden boats, trotlining for crabs. At night, owls call out in the darkness. All is serene with an air of suspended time—as if nothing had changed in 200 years. With the exception of a few newer houses and more engine-powered workboats, the modern world seems to have left the Wye East River behind.

You won't find supplies or public facilities anywhere on Wye Island. But you will find blue herons fishing along the muddy shores, white egrets that don't seem to mind the presence of boaters, families of mallards, and swans who make Wye Island their year-round residence. In addition, you sight bald eagles, whitetail deer and the endangered Delmarva fox squirrel.

The Wye is famous for producing the biggest and tastiest crabs on the Chesapeake, especially in late summer and early fall. You'll often see families out crabbing in their skiffs, many rented and launched from Wye Landing on the Wye East near the Narrows or from Schnaitman's on Skipton Creek.

The most difficult part of cruising the Wye is rounding the long shoal off Bennett Point at the tip of the narrow peninsula at the mouth. The point can be identified by a white stucco water tower shaped like a traditional circular lighthouse. (It serves no official navigational function.) About three-quarters of a nautical mile off Bennett Point, green "3" marks the long shoal. Boaters coming out of the Miles River can stay in deep water inside the shoal, but those approaching from Eastern Bay should give the point a wide berth. Also watch for a second shoal just a quarter-mile south of the Bennett Point shoal. This triangular patch of shallow water is all that remains of Herring Island.

Upstream on the Wye the water is deep almost from shore to shore, making this an ideal cruising ground. Just

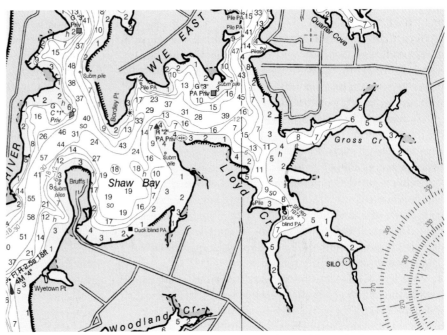

Shaw Bay and Lloyd Creek; from NOAA Chart 12270—not to be used for navigation.

watch your charts and stay off the points.

Shaw Bay

Every weekend during the summer hundreds of cruising boats make their way to the Wye River, and a great many of them drop their anchors in ❶ **Shaw Bay** on the Wye East River. It's easy to get to. Simply round Bruffs Island, now a peninsula, and head into this anchorage, which is over a half-mile wide and deep enough to accommodate any size boat.

One of the larger and more commodious anchorages of the middle Bay, it's a popular raft-up spot for cruising groups and dock buddies. The place fills up on summer and fall weekends, with boats packed in like blue crabs in a bushel basket. But be wary—Shaw Bay is open to the north and northwest, so a heavy fetch can make it a rockin' spot in more ways than one. Whether through poor anchoring techniques or bad holding ground, lee shore groundings are not infrequent on the southeasterly side of the bay.

Good holding and protected anchorages abound in Shaw Bay and, across the Wye East, along the southwestern shoreline of Wye Island. Generally, boaters can choose a spot to benefit from summer southerlies or they can tuck in for protection from heavier northerlies.

If either side of Shaw Bay is too exposed for real comfort, there are many better protected and more secure anchorages farther up the scenic Wye East.

Lloyd Creek

On the Wye East's south shore, just past Shaw Bay, a long shoal aims northwest toward Bordley Point. It's marked by red daymark "2" (which tends to blend into the shoreline). Rounding this mark, just follow the Wye East until you pass the next green, daymark "3", on the north shore. Then round gently into ❷ **Lloyd Creek**. The creek was named for the Lloyd family, who built Wye House and first settled this shoreline, prospering from slave labor that included Frederick Douglass.

Lloyd Creek has the Wye's typical beautiful shoreline of meadows and cornfields broken by wooded areas. Open to the northwest, the creek is consequently quite exposed to summer storms from that direction. However, if a northerly is threatening, just go farther upstream. Give a wide berth to the shoal on the east bank and head into the west branch where the 7-foot mark shows on your chart. The land on the north side of this little anchorage is a bit higher here and will give you one of the snuggest anchorages anywhere.

Between Lloyd Creek and Dividing Creek—the first major creek on the Wye Island side—are two anchorages of note, both on the island side. Neither has a name, but both are regularly visited by cruisers for an overnight anchorage. The two are narrow little bays, mere "dimples" in the river's shoreline, but both carry about 9 feet of water. On hot summer evenings you may find a better breeze here than on either Dividing or Granary creeks, the next two—and very popular—island-side creeks.

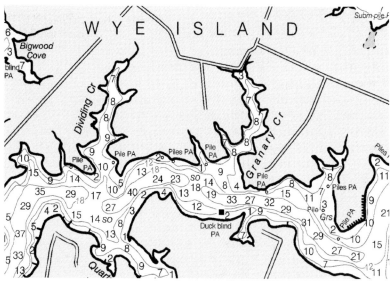

Dividing Creek and Granary Creek; from NOAA Chart 12270—not to be used for navigation.

Dividing Creek

About 1¹⁄₂ miles past Lloyd Creek on the Wye East is ❸ **Dividing Creek**, which cuts more than a half-mile into Wye Island.

Most cruising boats traveling up the Wye East River seem to end up in Dividing Creek at one time or another. A correspondent once reported motoring in past a 13-boat raft of Cal 25s followed by a 13-boat raft of Alberg 30s. At the same time, there was a scattering of individual or paired boats, making it tough to find open water to anchor in. However, the creek has good deep water practically to the shore, allowing you to find a nice spot to drop the hook, even when it's relatively crowded. Access to the Wye Island NRMA's trails is easy here, as well. As the evening shadows close in, the tranquil waters are broken only by fish feeding and the sound of tree frogs coming from the woods surrounding the area.

There's still more to explore farther up the Wye East. Across from Dividing Creek lies **Quarter Cove**. The few homes located on this bight are unobtrusive, as is typical on Eastern Shore creeks. You should favor the starboard side on entering Quarter Cove. A good location for putting down ground tackle is in the spot showing 13 feet in the mouth of the cove.

It is easy to understand why this was one of the earliest regions settled by Europeans in colonial America, when rivers were highways. The Wye's waters are deep and well-protected, and the land is fertile and high. A number of prominent Marylanders settled along the shores of the Wye in the 18th century, including the Lloyds and the Pacas. Just before the river turns north toward Wye Landing, you'll find Wye Heights, a colonial mansion and one of the oldest brick dwellings on the mainland.

Granary Creek

A bit less than a mile beyond Dividing Creek on the northern shore of the Wye East River lies ❹ **Granary Creek**, which is not quite as long or as wide as Dividing Creek. While both creeks offer quiet, rural settings, Granary usually has fewer boats in it—only six to eight can anchor here comfortably.

Granary Creek has 9 to 10 feet of water at its mouth and carries 7 feet to within several hundred feet of its end. Deep water also extends fairly close to the shores, though you should be careful of an old piling on the west side at the mouth of the creek. The wooded banks on both sides of the creek help make this a particularly snug anchorage in any type of weather.

Boaters often jump ship here to spend a few hours on the shaded trails of Wye Island NRMA, landing their dinghies or kayaks near the picnic area at the head of Granary Creek. The dirt road heads west to the multi-use trails that wind around neatly planted cornfields, through stands of osage orange trees and a forest of ancient hardwoods with trunks measuring three to four feet in diameter. One nearby trail is named for, and leads past, a revered holly tree that must be nearly 300 years old.

Granary Creek is one of the Chesapeake Bay's truly wild, undeveloped anchorages—and thanks to the state's ownership of most of the island, it looks as if it will stay that way for quite some time.

Pickering Creek

Beyond Granary Creek, the Wye East River narrows to about a quarter-mile, remaining deep from shore to shore. You can drop anchor almost anywhere and, with modest protection, enjoy the bucolic splendor of the river's upper reaches. Watch for eagles above and otters in the water around you.

As you continue upstream, the tributary appears to divide in half, with the Wye East making a northward turn

Pickering Creek continued

and ❺ **Pickering Creek** stretching out before you in a nearly straight line. Cruisers often anchor in the mouth of the creek, where the chart shows 11 feet.

If you are adventurous and have a shallow draft, you'll find beauty and protection farther upstream. Charts appear to present a benign swath with 8-to-10-foot depths, but shoals lurk left and right, constricting the unmarked channel. Once past the bulkheaded point to starboard (and the low bluff's picturesque Tidewater-colonial-style home with seven dormers), you'll need to pick your way along this zig-zag course.

One of the Bay's wilder tributaries, Pickering's thickly wooded banks alternate with low farmland. Part of the Lloyd family's vast Wye Heights Plantation in the 1600s, the old-growth forest dates to the close of the Civil War, when lack of labor left once-cultivated areas fallow. The resulting shoreline probably looks as it did when the European settlers arrived.

Boats generally anchor in the coves where smaller tributaries emerge from the woods and spill into the Pickering. At the mouth of the longest branch is Pickering Creek Audubon Center (410-822-4903) on the southern shoreline. The facility's dock and wildlife observation deck, with its small white building representing a waterman's shanty, is easy to spot. Looking down the creek from the mouth, more than a half-mile away, no other man-made structure is visible.

The 400-acre sanctuary, open daily from dawn to dusk, offers wetland and forest trails, birdwatching and public programs. Dinghies and kayaks are not permitted to tie up at the Center's dock; instead follow the shoreline to the right and use the canoe landing.

The property became a family farm in the 1890s. Almost 100 years later, its heirs began bequeathing pieces to the Chesapeake Audubon Society. Today the entire tract is the Pickering Creek Audubon Center and remains a working farm.

More recently, the Center became the permanent home for the cabin of Gilbert Byron, Eastern Shore sailor, writer and naturalist. Hand-built by Byron in 1942, it was moved from San Domingo Creek at St. Michaels. Byron not only shared the same birthday as Henry David Thoreau, but shared his belief in simplified living. For nearly 50 years, he wrote about the Eastern Shore in poems, essays, novels, and articles from this cabin.

Skipton Creek

Beyond Pickering Creek there's more deep-water territory to explore. The Wye East turns sharply north and is joined by Wye Narrows as it flows around the back of Wye Island. East of this juncture lies ❻ **Skipton Creek**.

Heading into the creek, stay in the middle between the elegant grounds of Colonial-era Wye Heights Plantation to starboard and the marshes to port. Inside the creek to starboard there's a cove that will accommodate a number of boats. Occasionally, a club will raft up here. The outer portion of the cove carries 7 feet of water, and there's 6 feet to the next point. If you draw less than 4 feet and are equipped to withstand Chesapeake mosquitoes, push on.

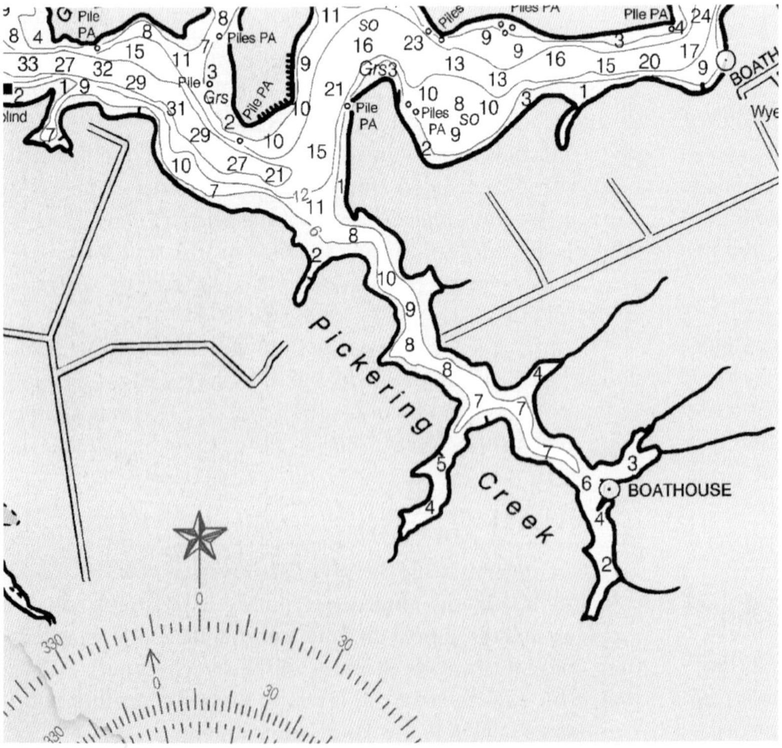

Skipton Creek and the upper end of the Wye East are prime dinghy exploration territory. Take the dink or a kayak up Skipton beyond the junction with shallow Mill Creek and you'll come close to Route 50. If you head back out of Skipton Creek and turn right, you'll pass the launch ramp at Wye Landing, where the river is navigable for a couple of miles. Stop at Schnaitman's at Wye Landing for soft drinks, some bait or a submarine sandwich. With its old signs and pinup calendars, this classic waterfront store will take you back to the 1940s.

You can anchor above Wye Landing, but the area can get pretty busy; Schnaitman's rents rowboats, which are joined by small, trailerable boats and the early morning traffic of workboats that dock nearby—especially in late summer and fall when the Wye River crabs are at their best. Instead, slip into **Wye Narrows**, the section of the river that leads to the low bridge (10 feet vertical clearance) onto Wye Island. The anchorage here is deep enough for most cruising boats.

Swimming in these waters is generally good, with fewer sea nettles in the upper Wye East than in the lower river.

Pickering Creek; from NOAA Chart 12270—not to be used for navigation.

Wye North

Even those cruisers who enjoy the companionship of others will seek out secluded anchorages. Less well-traveled than the Wye East River, the Wye River (❼ **Wye North**) proper provides plenty of privacy in its several interesting anchorages as it meanders northward above Bordley Point. And those cruisers wishing to go ashore to enjoy the beauty of Wye Island Natural Resources Management Area have a perfect landing site along a sandy beach near Drum Point.

Bordley Point marks the southwestern end of Wye Island. Be sure to locate green "1" marking a long shallow shoal from the western shore. This mark appears to be in the middle of the river, but don't overlook it. After passing green "3", favor the river's west side until you round Drum Point.

Just around Drum Point to the south is a lovely bay about half the size of Shaw Bay. This is a fine destination for a summer's day. In a light breeze following you into the river, you can drift lazily in the late afternoon's heat. The Wye River, which is as deep as 58 feet at its entrance, here measures some 40 feet deep. You will appreciate the unspoiled shoreline, part of the Wye Island NRMA. As you slowly round Drum Point you may see a sprinkling of boats already in the anchorage ahead of you. But this pleasant cove is almost a half-mile wide and has good holding ground. It always seems to be able to accommodate one more boat, so there's room enough for all. It's the largest anchorage on this portion of the Wye.

An anchorage for shallow drafts lies along the westerly side of Wye Island. It is **Grapevine Cove**, just below the entrance to Wye Narrows. This little cove is tight at its entrance and shoaling has been reported at its mouth. Once

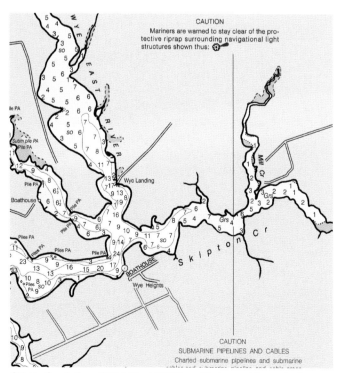

Skipton Creek; from NOAA Chart 12270—not to be used for navigation.

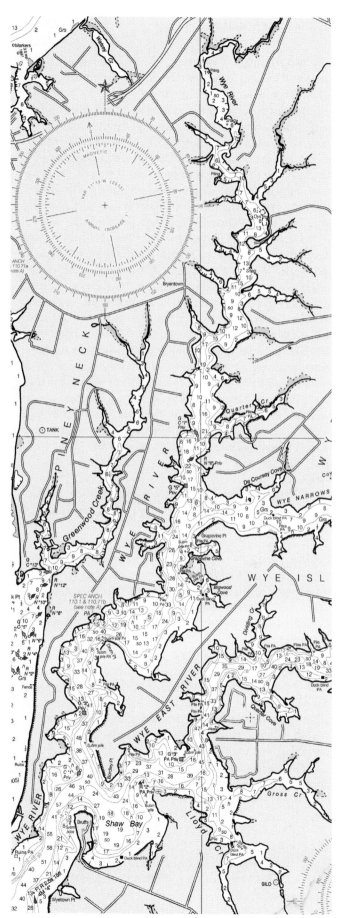

Wye River North; from NOAA Chart 12270—not to be used for navigation.

Wye North continued

you make it inside, Grapevine Cove becomes quiet and secluded, a small pocket of serenity sheltered by two points of land.

Across from the entrance to Grapevine Cove and Wye Narrows are two unnamed coves that share a common mouth. There is deep water here, but residences line the shore, and these locations are not as quiet as those spots backing into the Wye Island preserve.

Just north of the western entrance to Wye Narrows is **Quarter Creek** (not to be confused with Quarter Cove on the Wye East River). Quarter Creek, located along the east side of the northerly portion of the Wye River, is the last anchorage here that provides any flavor of woodland and farmlands. The best place to drop a hook is in the mouth of the creek in 9-foot depths, but the creek carries 7 feet of water for about half its length. It also offers good dinghy opportunities.

The point of land on the southern side of the mouth of Quarter Creek belongs to the Wye Conference Centers at Aspen Institute, whose holdings extend all the way along the eastern shore of Wye Narrows behind Wye Island. The institute provides a venue for discussing critical issues, fostering values-based leadership. This is where world leaders Clinton, Arafat, Netanyahu and Hussein met in 1999 to try to establish the building blocks for peace in the Middle East.

Miles River

If you're cruising the **Miles River** and spy what look like billowing clouds scooting along the water like tumbleweed, you've just stumbled across one of the oldest sports on Chesapeake Bay—log canoe racing. Despite what the name implies, log canoes are anything but clunky. Sleek, graceful and impressively fast, they are so sail-heavy that they require human counterweights—crew members who perch precariously on "hiking boards" on the boat's windward side—to keep from capsizing. The Chesapeake Bay Log Sailing Canoe Association hosts a June-through-September racing schedule for the dozen or so log canoes competing on the Bay. Taking in a race is really a must for Chesapeake boaters. (For the association's race schedule, visit *www.blogcanoe.com.*)

The Miles is also noted, of course, as the passageway to one of the most popular cruise destinations on the Bay, St. Michaels. It is a river of delightful harbors, quiet anchorages and lots to see and do.

The marks in the Miles may seem odd. The *Coast Pilot* says that the river flows into Eastern Bay "between Tilghman Point…and Bennett Point, two and one-third miles east-south-eastward." The mouth of the river then, is on a line between the two points.

To enter the Miles from Eastern Bay, take red "4" north of Tilghman Point as your guide. The course then follows the

increasing numbers on the markers, generally south-south-east, to red "12" north of Deep Water Point (you are still following the Eastern Bay numbers). Off Deep Water Point you will see flashing green "1". Red "2" stands off Long Haul Creek and "4" off the turn into St. Michaels, whose harbor is flanked by flashing red "2" and green daymark "3".

Beyond Tilghman Point's high bluff, the Miles River has a friendlier, more intimate appearance. Farms and woodlands decorate the shoreline as the river wends its way serenely southward.

The river has widths of about a mile for a couple of miles south past Deep Water Point before it turns northeast, where one can find at least five more miles of navigable waters that offer many quiet coves and creeks.

Tilghman Creek

At the upper end of Eastern Bay where it merges with the Miles River is Rich Neck. Matthew Tilghman, known as the "Father of the Revolution in Maryland," once lived here in stately Rich Neck Manor plantation. Rich Neck Manor Chapel, built in the 1650s, still stands on this privately owned site and is listed on the National Register of Historic Places. Rich Neck is crowned with a dense stand of tall pines which, from offshore, give it an abrupt cliff-like appearance all the way to its end at Tilghman Point.

About a mile below Tilghman Point, on the western shore of the Miles is ❶ **Tilghman Creek.** To enter this beautiful creek from mid-river, look closely to see the two outer markers, a lighted "1" and daymark "3". There are reports of shoaling here, particularly at "3" and close to "4", but your depthsounder should show 6 feet and better all the way in, on a track about 50 feet off the markers.

Once you are inside the mouth of the creek, past the third mark, a red daymark, the creek opens up significantly.

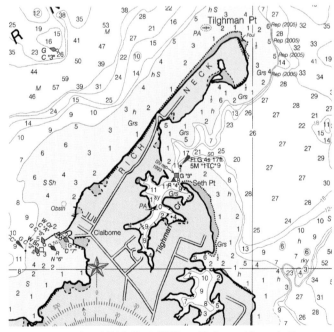

Tilghman Creek; from NOAA Chart 12270—not to be used for navigation.

The effect is startling. The rugged shoreline outside the creek's entrance gives way to more attractive, wooded banks with cultivated fields visible through the trees. You'll see a few well-finished homes here with neat bulkheads and rip-rap shorelines. There's a cozy, peaceful atmosphere evident that contrasts sharply with the hurly-burly wide-open Miles River.

Although Tilghman Creek is only about a mile in length, it contains several snug coves where several cruising groups can find room to raft up for the night. Water depths along the creek range from 8 to 11 feet at MLW, and the bottom is soft mud, which generally means good holding ground.

To port just beyond red daymark "4" is the creek's smallest cove. Although it's a little too snug for some tastes, other cruisers think it would be perfect in a real blow—although exposed to northwesterlies.

As you round red "4" and head upstream, the largest cove will appear to starboard. This sometimes is the scene of several large raft-ups. The cove offers protection from almost every direction, and water depths range from 10 to 11 feet.

A little farther upstream to port is another cove. It's snug

enough for those who prefer shelter, and yet there's room to swing with a sudden wind shift.

At the head of the creek lies Cockey's Wharf, a public landing. From here you can walk (about half a mile) to **Claiborne**, once an active summer resort and a primary destination for visitors to the Eastern Shore. You'll still see evidence of the old hotels and summer homes that graced the town. Things are quieter these days, but Claiborne does have a post office and a county boat ramp located at the old ferry dock.

Tilghman Creek is a pleasant anchorage. You can anchor here and enjoy seclusion and safety, aware that the shadows of history still linger along its beautiful shores.

Long Haul Creek

Deep Water Point is only four miles from Tilghman Point. About halfway you will see the buoys to port which mark the sunken **Herring Island.** According to members of the Herring Island Sailing Fleet, this large shoal was once attached to Bennett Point. Now all is awash and well marked to alert

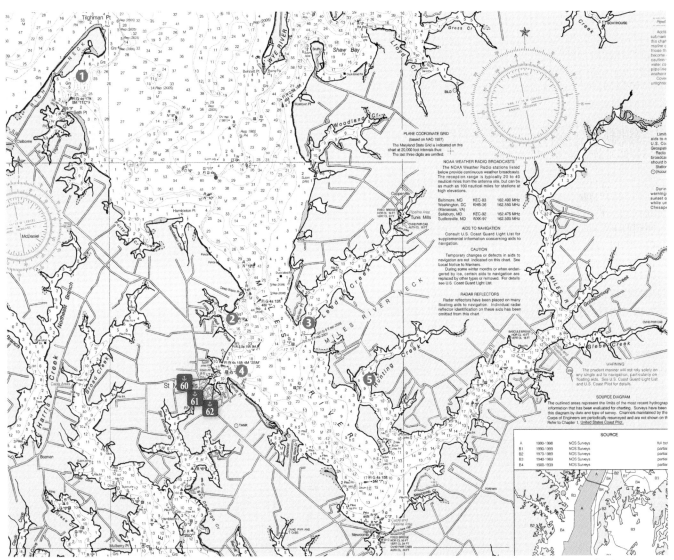

Miles River; from NOAA Chart 12270—not to be used for navigation.

Long Haul Creek *continued*

passing boaters.

Keep well away from the shoal off Deep Water Point and then honor the green lighted marker to port. Just beyond, to starboard you will see the red "2" daymark that identifies the starboard side of the entrance into ❷ **Long Haul Creek**. This quarter-mile shoal has depths of only 1 to 2 feet and thus discourages shortcuts.

Long Haul Creek is the location of the well-known and active Miles River Yacht Club, whose prominent clubhouse and piers are to port as you enter the creek. Long Haul divides into two active branches just beyond the creek's entrance. Locals recommend anchoring in the southern branch, with the best water to be found favoring the yacht club's docks. However, there may be several boats on semipermanent moorings here and larger boats might find it snug.

Motoring back to the yacht club docks and then up into the northern branch is not very far since this is a fairly narrow bit of creek also. With no moored boats here—but several docks—water depths range from 8 to 10 feet and you can put out quite a bit of rode to hold comfortably throughout the night.

If you are looking for peace and quiet, don't go into Long Haul Creek during regatta weekends, unless the log canoes are racing. The excitement of seeing these beautiful boats in competition makes this one of the highlights of a summer cruise.

Leeds Creek

❸ **Leeds Creek**'s nearness to St. Michaels gives it a special appeal when you want a nice, quiet anchorage instead of the crowded harbor scene. At flashing "1" off Deep Water Point just north of St. Michaels, continue south until green "1" is abeam to avoid the 3-foot shoal from Fairview Point. Then make your turn. Boaters report that there has been some shoaling at the already narrow entrance, so pay attention. Once inside Fairview Point, follow the left-hand shore around and into the little cove and drop your hook. If this cove is too crowded, just continue upstream until you find a

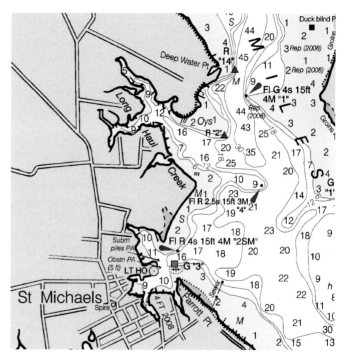

Long Haul Creek; from NOAA Chart 12270—not to be used for navigation.

pleasing spot.

A cruise up Leeds Creek is like a trip back in time. A large Georgian-style plantation looks across the creek from the right-hand side, with a boathouse and outbuildings on the unnamed creek located between the words "Leeds" and "Creek" on the chart. Farther along on the left side of Leeds you will find good anchoring in the 10-foot and 8-foot coves.

The creek opens up and splits just below the town of **Tunis Mills**. Here is good anchoring in 8-foot depths without fear of high-speed traffic. More than a century ago there was a sawmill at Tunis Mills, when timber was first harvested on the Eastern Shore and loaded onto large, three-masted schooners bound for the markets in Baltimore and Philadelphia. Nowadays, you'll see yachts instead, all up and down the creek. Several bald eagles have been regular residents here, too, and the creek begs for dinghy exploration.

● On Premises
➤ Nearby

Miles River/St. Michaels

	MLW	Overnight Slips	Gas	Diesel	Propane	Electric	Showers	Laundry	Restaurant	Lodging	Pool	Pump-out	Ice	Groceries	Marine Supplies	Bait	Boat Repair	Haul-out Services	Launch Ramp	Wi-Fi	Other
60 **Higgins Yacht Yard** Miles R./St. Michaels 410-745-9303; www.twoswaninn.com/higgins.htm	10'	●	➤	➤	➤	●	●	➤	➤	➤	➤	➤	●	➤	●	●	●	●	➤	●	Two Swan Inn B&B, vacation cottages
61 **St. Michaels Harbour Inn Marina & Spa** Miles R./St. Michaels 410-745-9001 or 800-955-9001; www.harbourinn.com	10'	●	➤	➤	➤	●	●	●	●	●	●	●	●	➤	➤	➤	➤	➤	➤	●	Exercise room, spa, pool, bikes, coffee, van
62 **St. Michaels Marina** Miles R./St. Michaels 410-745-2400; www.stmichaelsmarina.com	10'	●	●	●	➤	●	●	●	●	●	●	●	●	➤	➤	➤	➤	➤	➤	●	Bikes, cable TV, Wi-Fi

Homeport of Memories

A stay at St. Michaels Marina, for a night, or two or three, or a week, is memorable in every respect. Whether with friends or family, make us your "Homeport" for all the special times St. Michaels has to offer. And, with special attention paid to all the creature comforts cruisers deserve, the list of our impressive amenities may be the most memorable of all.

- Situated in the center of St. Michaels restaurants & shops
- Eric's Crab House, Town Dock & Foxy's Restaurants on premises
- First-class amenities with a pool kids love & no "resort fees"
- GEM cars for rent – great way to see St. Michaels, fun to ride and street legal – seats 4 adults
- Cable TV at every slip with FAST free Wi-Fi
- More than adequate power supporting 30 Amp, 50 Amp & 100 Amp services
- Fueling and pump-out at your slip for most vessels
- Pay with check or cash and get the region's best fuel prices
- And above all, customer service that strives to make your visit the best experience you'll have on the Bay

St. Michaels Marina® LLC

Maryland Certified Clean Marina

P.O. Box 398 · 305 Mulberry St. · St. Michaels, MD 21663

Reservations: 410-745-2400
stmichaelsmarina.com

St. Michaels

❹ **St. Michaels** is one of those truly unforgettable cruising spots on the Chesapeake Bay. The town began attracting recreational boaters long before cruising became the mainstay of Bay boating. Although the town was officially chartered in 1804, early accounts of trading here date back to 1631, and in the late 1600s a parish church was built where the Christ Episcopal Church now stands. As St. Michaels grew it became an important shipbuilding center especially noted for its "Baltimore Clippers," the fastest sailing vessels of their time. Today the town is better known for its maritime museum, meticulously refurbished Victorian streetscape and fine dining.

When entering St. Michaels, take a course from flashing red "4" in the Miles River to St. Michaels Harbor Light red "2" at the entrance. Pass it to your starboard, of course, and not too far off. The corresponding marker, green "3" off Parrott Point at the other side of the entrance, is off a shoal that is both extensive and shallow. Give this shoal a wide berth, for it can be a trap for the unwary. Then look for the buoys marking the fairway and anchorage as you enter the harbor. The old Hooper Strait Lighthouse

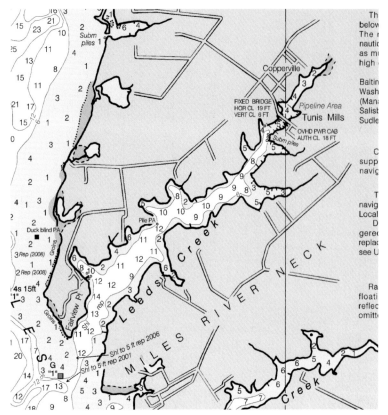

Leeds Creek; from NOAA Chart 12270—not to be used for navigation.

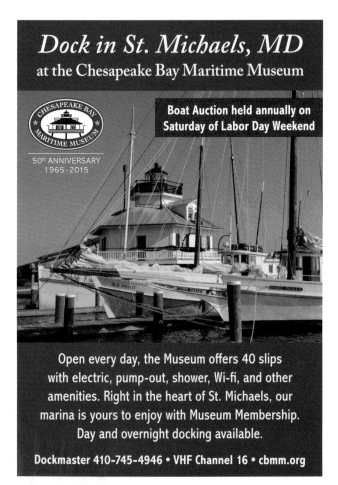

Dock in St. Michaels, MD
at the Chesapeake Bay Maritime Museum

Boat Auction held annually on Saturday of Labor Day Weekend

50th ANNIVERSARY
1965-2015

Open every day, the Museum offers 40 slips with electric, pump-out, shower, Wi-fi, and other amenities. Right in the heart of St. Michaels, our marina is yours to enjoy with Museum Membership. Day and overnight docking available.

Dockmaster 410-745-4946 • VHF Channel 16 • cbmm.org

marks the Chesapeake Bay Maritime Museum on Navy Point where crabhouses and packing plants once stood. Berthed in front of the old screwpile light, which was moved from its foundation in Tangier Sound in 1966, are two more testaments to the Bay's past: the bugeye *Edna Lockwood* and the skipjack *Rosie Parks*.

Some boats anchor in the shallower waters of **Fogg Cove** to the right of the museum. If the harbor is full, boats will anchor farther out in the Miles River—not advisable except in fair weather. A water taxi operates in season, sparing outliers too long a dinghy ride to shore.

Two marinas in St. Michaels harbor offer overnight slips and a full range of amenities to visiting boaters, but because of the area's enormous popularity, advance reservations are a must. Fuel is available at the St. Michaels Marina. The venerable Higgins Yacht Yard continues to offer repairs. An Acme store is a few blocks from the waterfront.

There is always something going on in town—whether it's a free concert staged by the local community center or a full-blown festival spilling onto the streets. If you'd prefer a quieter visit, plan to arrive in the middle of the week. There will be lots of time to chat with the local storekeepers or keep your eyes peeled for the D.C. cognicenti that call the town home.

(NOTE: There is another way to visit St. Michaels. San Domingo Creek off Broad Creek, off the Choptank River, leads boaters to the south side of St. Michaels. There are no marinas there, but it is a quieter anchorage with access to town. It is covered in the Broad Creek/Harris Creek Area in Section 4.)

Legendary Chesapeake Hospitality is Closer than You Think!

A Full-Service Marina with Resort Amenities & Award-Winning Dining

MARINA FEATURES:
- 52 Transient Slips
- Dockside Electricity and City Water
- Clean and Modern Showers
- Outdoor Pool
- Complimentary Cable Hook-up
- Pumpout Service
- Laundry Facilities
- Water Taxi Service from the Dock

ROOM AMENITIES
- Complimentary Shuttle Service around Town
- Daily Newspaper, Bicycles and Wireless Internet
- Luxurious Spa & Fitness Center
- Ship's Store
- Waterfront Dining with Indoor/Outdoor Seating
- Continental Breakfast included daily
- Outdoor Pool

SPECIAL PROMOTIONS* FOR MARINA GUESTS:
10% off all Spa Services anytime.
Terms & conditions apply, current promotions, subject to change, call for details.

JOIN US FOR DOLLAR FIFTY FRIDAYS!
Stay with us on Friday and take advantage of our $1.50 per foot rate.
No minimum. Does not apply to holiday weekends. Call for details.

We will match any advertised rate in St. Michaels Harbor. Please call 410.745.9001.
GPS 38° 47.13' N   076° 13.15' W • Monitor VHF 16

HARBOUR INN
MARINA & SPA
ST. MICHAELS

Rates subject to change without notice. Check our website for current rates.

1.800.955.9001 | www.harbourinn.com

Port of Call
St. Michaels

In St. Michaels, you can be as busy or idyllically idle as you like. There are interesting museums, diverse shops, fabulous restaurants, tour boats, spas and numerous festivals to entertain you. Though in-town dockage is limited, there are plenty of anchorages to be had and plenty of nooks and crannies to explore along the Miles River. All of this makes St. Michaels one of the most popular places on the Bay.

The Chesapeake Bay Maritime Museum is perhaps the crowning glory of St. Michaels—as far as boaters are concerned. Of the museum's many buildings, the most recognizable is the cottage-style Hooper Strait Lighthouse, overlooking the harbor and blinking out the letters C-B-M-M in Morse code. Decommissioned and moved to its present site after standing watch for 75 years at the mouth of the Honga River, it has been restored and furnished to reveal the lighthouse keeper's world. Other exhibits examine such local maritime heritage as waterfowl hunting, boatbuilding, leisure activities and oystering. Museum members are entitled to courtesy dockage during the day, but must pay for overnight stays (check out the museum's special boating membership); non-members are charged for their vessel, and each passenger must pay the museum's admission fee. (Hail the dockmaster on VHF 16 or visit *www.cbmm.org* for information.)

In addition to the maritime museum, the St. Mary's Square Museum revisits centuries of local life (open weekends, May to October). Visitors can gain further insight into St. Michaels and the seafood industry in general through narrated excursions aboard the skipjack *H.M. Krentz*. Tours are also available on board the vintage catboat *Selina II*, the *Patriot* and the St. Michaels Harbor Shuttle (for water taxi service, hail them on channel 71). Kayaks are ideal for

Talbot County Tourism

quiet explorations of the surrounding tidal creeks; rental kayaks can be delivered if you need them (Peake Paddle Tours, *www.paddletours.com*). Land-based tours are hosted by Dockside Tours and St. Mary's Square Museum.

Within walking distance of the harbor, St. Michaels Winery offers behind-the-scenes tours and tastings of its award-winning creations. For the travel-weary, spas at Five Gables Inn, the Inn at Perry Cabin and St. Michaels Harbour Inn pamper their clients with a variety of services.

Shops specializing in unusual gifts, clothing, art and antiques line Talbot Street, which runs the length of town. Amble down the town's side streets to discover other eclectic shops. Even window shopping is fascinating. Browsers will find a range of merchandise, from pottery and sportswear to books and antiques. Practical needs are addressed, too. A pharmacy, several banks and an Acme supermarket are within steps of the waterfront. Specialty foodstuffs can be found in abundance at the Village Shoppe. On Saturday mornings (May to October), shop for local produce, meats, flowers, plants, baked goods, cheeses and eggs and attend special demonstrations at the farmer's market in Muskrat Park (*www.freshfarmmarkets.org*).

Home to several of the Bay's most acclaimed restaurants, St. Michaels is a diner's delight, serving everything from nouvelle cuisine to old-style seafood dinners. Your best bet, if you want to go beyond the several dining establishments right on the water, is to stroll up Talbot Street, peruse the menus and take your pick. A St. Michaels chef once

Chesapeake Bay Maritime Museum

Richard Norwitz

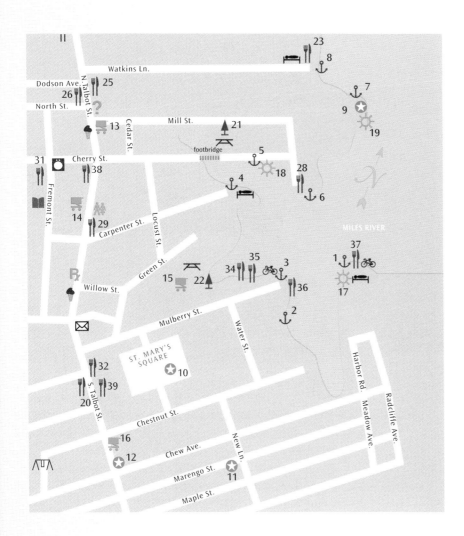

St. Michaels

⚓ **Marinas/Dockage**
1 St. Michaels Harbour Inn
2 Municipal Dock
3 St. Michaels Marina
4 Higgins Yacht Yard
5 Public dinghy dock
6 Crab Claw
7 Chesapeake Bay Maritime Museum
8 The Inn at Perry Cabin

◎ **Points of Interest**
9 Chesapeake Bay Maritime Museum
10 St. Mary's Square Museum
11 St. Michaels Winery
12 Eastern Shore Brewing

🛒 **Groceries**
13 Market House Gourmet Grocer
14 Acme Market
15 Farmers Market
16 The Village Shoppe

☼ **Entertainment/ Recreation**
17 Catboat *Selina II*
18 Patriot Cruises
19 Skipjack *H. M. Krentz*

🌲 **Park**
21 Hollis Park
22 Muskrat Park

🍴 **Dining**
20 Awful Arthurs
23 Inn at Perry Cabin
25 Key Lime Cafe
26 208 Talbot
28 Crab Claw
29 Carpenter Street Saloon
31 Blue Crab Coffee Co.
32 Bistro St. Michaels
33 St. Michaels Perk Coffeehouse
34 Town Dock Restaurant
35 St. Michaels Crab and Steak House
36 Foxy's Marina Bar
37 St. Michaels Harbour Inn
38 JoJo's Cupcakes & Creams
39 Ava's Pizzeria

🚻 **Public Restrooms**
🧺 **Laundromat**
℞ **Pharmacy**
📖 **Library**
✉ **Post Office**
🪑 **Picnic Area**
🛝 **Playground**
🍦 **Ice Cream**
? **Information**
🚲 **Bicycles**

told us that he worked extra hard to present spectacular food. Other chefs have seconded his remarks, and boaters certainly benefit from their efforts.

In addition to the marina dockage available in town, the ever-popular Crab Claw offers dockage for diners, but no overnight amenities. On-land lodging can be had at the Harbour Inn Marina or any of the local B&Bs (*www.bedandbreak fast.com*). The St. Michaels Perk Coffee House offers free Wi-Fi.

On Thursday evenings in July and August, the sounds of music and applause fill the air as Muskrat Park hosts its summer concert series. The Maritime Museum and Bay heritage figure prominently in the town's annual festivals and events, including: in April, Bay Day (the Chesapeake's own Earth Day) and the three-day St. Michaels Food and Wine Festival; in May, St. Michaels Goes to the Dogs (canine walkathon, pet-oriented activities) and the museum's Maritime Model Expo (radio-controlled and static model boats); in June, the Maritime Museum's popular Antique and Classic Boat Festival; in July, Independence Day fireworks (launched from Miles River Yacht Club), Big Band Night and the Chesapeake Folk Festival (Bay music, folkways, food and traditions); in August, the Maritime Museum hosts its Boat Auction; followed in October by its Mid-Atlantic

Small Craft Festival (boats by amateur and professional builders) and the town-wide Fall into St. Michaels celebration (including a Halloween parade and activities for kids); and in December, Christmas in St. Michaels.

Information: St. Michaels Business Association, 800-808-7622; *www.stmichaelsmd.org* or *www.tourtalbot.org*.

A beautiful home in harmony with its surroundings on upper Hunting Creek off the Miles River.

Hunting Creek

Few cruisers venture past St. Michaels, which is a shame. The Miles River is long and beautiful, well worth exploring. It offers lovely anchorages that serve as a pleasant alternative to the congestion of the harbor.

❺ **Hunting Creek** is a good option, well away from the bustle at St. Michaels. More secluded than other waterways near town, Hunting Creek is about two miles farther south, where the river makes a sharp turn northeast. To get there, skirt the shoal point that bulges out from **Spencer Creek** before aiming for the green 4-second flasher off Long Point. From the flasher, which marks the river's turning point, take a course that keeps you well off Long Point in order to avoid the submerged pilings marked on the chart. For a guide, you will be able to use a small boathouse on the southeast tip of Long Point. From there, follow the chart into the creek.

The best course is generally to stay in the center of the creek, except where you find local markers that indicate otherwise. Hunting Creek meanders north for about a mile before turning northeast. You'll find a good anchorage in this bend, just out of sight of the creek's entrance. The trees in this section of the creek come right down to the water's edge, and herons and egrets stalk the shores.

Across from Hunting Creek, on the other side of the river at the elbow's funny bone, lies the public wharf and launch ramp at **Newcomb**, just below a fixed bridge (24-foot clearance). If you can make it under the bridge, duck into **Oak Creek**. The channel runs around 5 feet with a few 4-foot humps. Stay in the center, favoring the right hand side, and

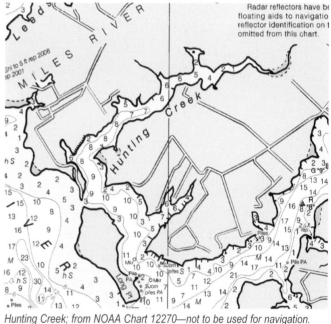

Hunting Creek; from NOAA Chart 12270—not to be used for navigation.

bear left around the point into a lovely sheltered anchorage.

Back in the river proper, cruisers can continue north and eventually pass through the drawbridge (18-foot vertical clearance when closed; opens on demand between sunrise and sunset from April through October). Above the drawbridge, the river separates into three branches. The river stem bends north, navigable for more than a mile. The other branches, **Goldsborough** and **Glebe** creeks, are navigable for maybe a quarter-mile for deep-draft boats.

Choptank River to Patuxent River

The Tred Avon and Little Choptank Rivers
Chesapeake Beach, Oxford, Cambridge and Solomons

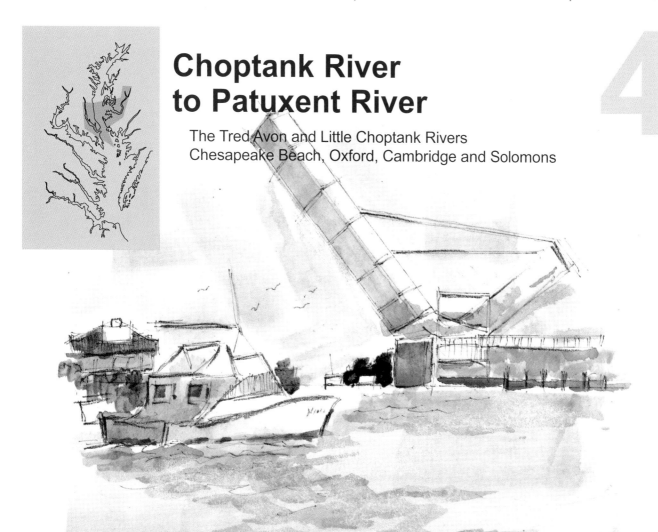

The difference between the Eastern Shore and Western Shore along this part of the Bay is palpable. Even so, each shore has an irresistible appeal to cruisers. The steep sheer of Calvert Cliffs to the west stands in vivid contrast to the low-lying terrain to the east where well-protected creeks inside the wide mouth of the Choptank River harbor pleasant coves and plenty of gunkholes. There the lush greenery provides camouflage for sunning herons, and the splash of jumping fish is apt to be the only sound you'll hear—except for conversation and laughter aboard anchored boats. Branching off to the northeast, the Tred Avon River offers even more picture-perfect anchorages, many graced by a shoreline dotted with fine country homes. From there, the wide, well-marked Choptank continues inland, traveling another dozen miles before narrowing and threading its way through a marshy landscape.

The water played a vital role in the growth and development of many towns on the Eastern Shore. Tilghman Island, for example, remains a watermen's haven where workboats share the harbor with recreational vessels, and seafood is a given on all restaurant menus.

There are any number of popular destinations along these rivers. Oxford still evinces the character of its days as a port of entry in colonial times. Cambridge, the seat of Dorchester County's government, is a city reestablishing its cultural and economic vitality. Easton's melding of history, the arts, restaurants and shopping make it well worth the walk or taxi ride from the waterfront.

The Western Shore of the Chesapeake presents a different persona to those cruising south from Herring Bay. The fabled cliffs are not only beautiful, they're a favorite destination for amateur paleontologists, who unearth fossils and shark teeth near the shoreline. Cruisers are more exposed here, with the marinas at Chesapeake Beach, Breezy Point and Flag Harbor offering the only shelter north of the Patuxent River.

Like the Choptank, the Patuxent is a welcoming river, although it provides fewer idyllic anchorages. It does offer prolific fishing grounds that support an impressive charter-boat fleet based in Solomons, a favorite Southern Maryland destination. A former seafood industry town, Solomons celebrates its past in one of the Bay's finest maritime museums, the Calvert Marine Museum.

Given their beauty and timelessness, it's no wonder the waterways of these two shores are favorite cruising grounds.

Section 4

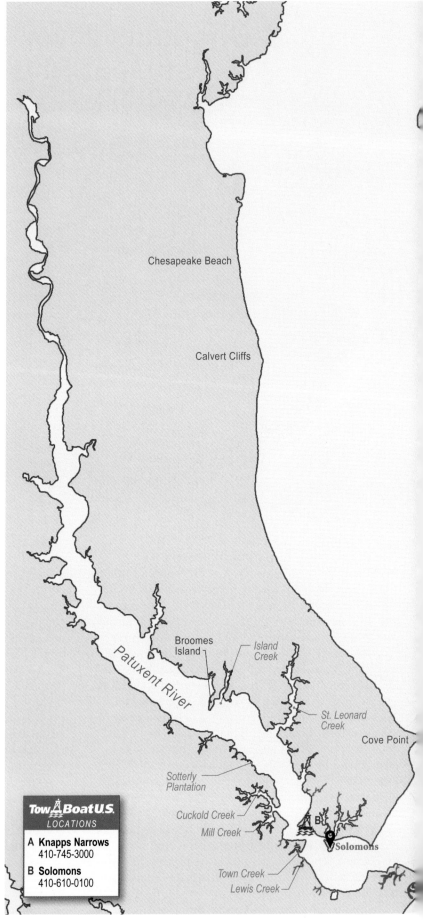

Chesapeake Beach

Calvert Cliffs

Patuxent River

Broomes Island

Island Creek

St. Leonard Creek

Cove Point

Sotterly Plantation

Cuckold Creek

Mill Creek

Solomons

Town Creek

Lewis Creek

Tow BoatU.S.
LOCATIONS

A Knapps Narrows
   410-745-3000

B Solomons
   410-610-0100

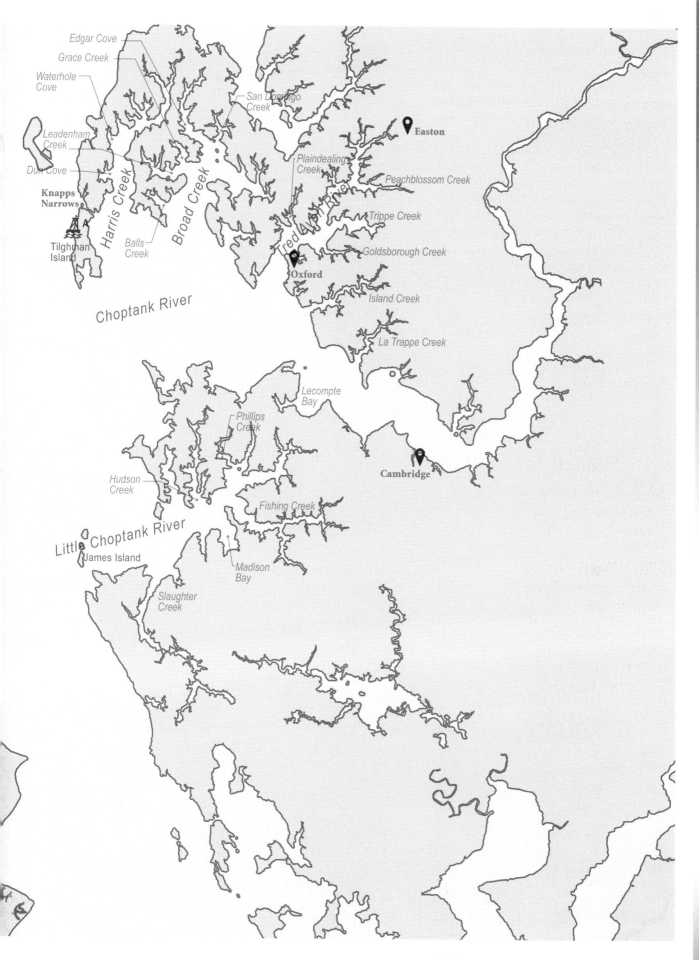

Edgar Cove
Grace Creek
Waterhole Cove
San Domingo Creek
Easton
Leadenham Creek
Plaindealing Creek
Peachblossom Creek
Dun Cove
Harris Creek
Broad Creek
Tred Avon River
Trippe Creek
Knapps Narrows
Goldsborough Creek
Balls Creek
Oxford
Island Creek
Tilghman Island
Choptank River
La Trappe Creek
Lecompte Bay
Phillips Creek
Hudson Creek
Cambridge
Fishing Creek
Little Choptank River
James Island
Madison Bay
Slaughter Creek

Lower Choptank

Although John Smith bypassed it in his explorations, the **Choptank River** has had a long and storied existence. Its unique regional culture is quickly changing, but watermen still motor out before dawn, and visitors are treated to a blend of quaint byways and touristy hubs.

On the Choptank's southern side, from the mouth eastward to Cambridge Creek and on to the fixed Route 50 bridge just past Cambridge itself, the river claims about 20 miles of shoreline compared to the more than 90 miles that outlines the opposite shore. This, combined with exposure, explains why the most protected anchorages are found in the

many tributaries along the Choptank's north side.

When traveling from the upper Bay, boaters enter the Choptank by two different routes. One, which bypasses the mouth of the river altogether and passes through Knapps Narrows, can shave six or seven miles off this leg of the cruise. But if draft is an issue, or if the often-congested Knapps route holds no appeal, proceed along the Bay side of Tilghman Island. Even then, charted depths could be as little as 7 feet (you may find more), but a course toward nun "80A" should keep you well clear of shallows. Keep an eye out for ever-present fishtraps and crabpots, though. From here, take a southeast heading to Choptank's "7".

Although the river's entrance is more than three miles

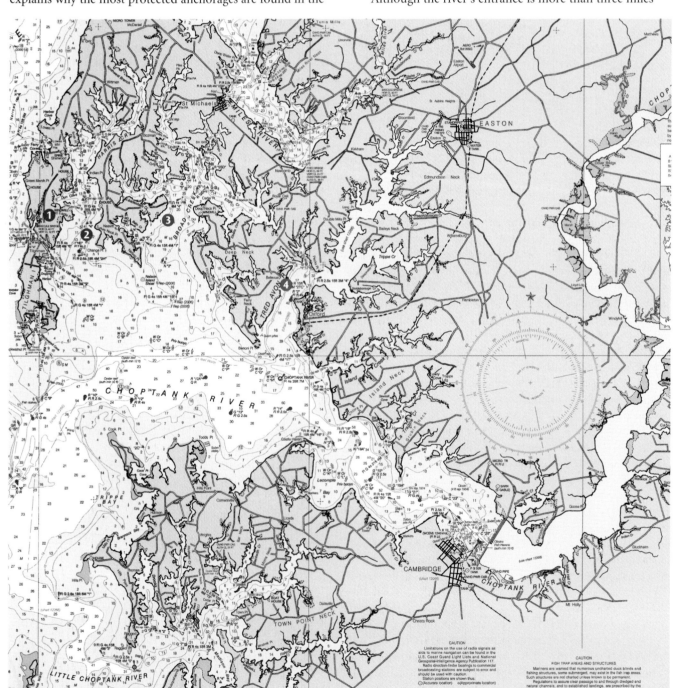

Choptank River; from NOAA Chart 12263—not to be used for navigation.

wide, the deepest water lies in the very center, in a broad swath of more than a mile. Marsh and shoals extend well beyond the points that flank each side; the shallows off Black Walnut Point alone reach out for nearly one and a half miles. Shortcuts are a bad idea. Just follow the well-marked route.

The distinctive Sharps Island Light guards the river's mouth. Damaged by ice in 1977, the tilted sentinel (erected in 1882) continues to deteriorate. In 1675, when Sharp Island was purchased from the crown by its first owner, a Quaker physician named Peter Sharp, it was nearly 900 acres. Much later, it was the site of a small community that boasted a resort hotel with a long pier for steamboats arriving from Baltimore. By 1954, however, only about 200 feet of the island remained above water. Today, nothing remains but a shoal area noted on charts as "Sharps Island" and "Subm piles" where the pier once stood.

Knapps Narrows and Tilghman Island

❶ Knapps Narrows, with its bascule bridge, is the shortest route between Eastern Bay and the Choptank River if you are coming from the north. This makes it one of the Bay's busiest passages . . . and trickiest. Follow the south shore of Eastern Bay until you reach Poplar Narrows. Crab pots could be plentiful, inevitably drifting into the channel regardless of a waterman's best efforts. Pay attention.

To the west of Poplar Island Narrows are three islands—400 hundred years ago, one complete island of about 1,000 acres. Erosion has created three: **Poplar** and **Jefferson** islands almost side by side, and **Coaches Island** to the south. In the mid-20th century, a sportsman's lodge on Jefferson Island attracted Washington's social set, including Presidents Franklin D. Roosevelt and Harry S. Truman. Poplar Island, the westernmost and largest of the three is having its erosion reversed, continuously augmented by dredge spoils. This explains the busy tug and barge traffic in the area. You are not permitted to land on any of these islands.

Due east of Jefferson Island, a 4-second flasher, north of daymark "6", identifies the channel leading into Lowes Wharf on the Bay Hundred peninsula. Depths are 5 feet at best, so proceed cautiously. Lowes has fuel, slips, a restaurant and inn.

If you're going on to Knapps Narrows, follow the peninsula's shoreline to the lighted beacons that mark its channel. Shoaling along this half-mile-long stretch is a perennial problem. Before arriving, it's a good idea to call one of the Narrows marinas for advice on how to negotiate the channel. Currents are notoriously unpredictable in the Narrows, too, because they don't always correspond to the rise and fall of the tide. Also, remember that docking is easiest when pointing into the current, and that negotiating into and out of docks perpendicular to the current can be tricky.

Note that the navigation aids have red markers to starboard as you approach the Narrows from either end. Entering Knapps Narrows is considered to be "entering from seaward" from both the Bay and the river sides, so remember the "red-right-returning" rule when coming *and* going.

To navigate the Knapps Narrows bridge (vertical clearance 12 feet MHW) you may use your horn (one long blast and one short), hail the tender on VHF channel 13, or call 410-886-2588. It doesn't take very many boats in this narrow waterway to cause a traffic jam, and winds and current can further complicate the passage. Patience and planning, along with careful boat handling, is required when you find yourself in a group of three or four boats milling about waiting for the opening. The tender is on duty 24/7.

Despite its difficulties, transiting Knapps Narrows is always worth it. The route is colorful with marinas, waterview restaurants, inns and boats of every description lining the banks. **Tilghman Island**, once occupied by the British and used as a supply base in the War of 1812, is popular among cruisers. But it's still an active waterman's village—traditional workboats go about their business, and locals still gather on the bench in front of Fairbank Tackle Shop. It's the home port of the *Rebecca T. Ruark*, built in 1886—the oldest working skipjack on the Chesapeake.

Among the island's simple frame dwellings are examples of the distinctive Tilghman style (a three-corner or "W" house) from the late 1800s. Besides fresh seafood, the island has a small grocery store and a self-service produce stand. Restaurants range from downhome crabhouse to upscale nouvelle cuisine, and transportation is often available—ask at your marina. Several B&Bs offer overnight accommodations. Also, look for the Tilghman Waterman's Museum in the old

Characters BRIDGE RESTAURANT

Tilghman Island, MD

On Knapps Narrows - Free Dockage While Dining!

410-886-1060
charactersbridgerestaurant.com

Lowes Wharf Marina & Inn

410-745-6684
LowesWharf.com   Sherwood, MD

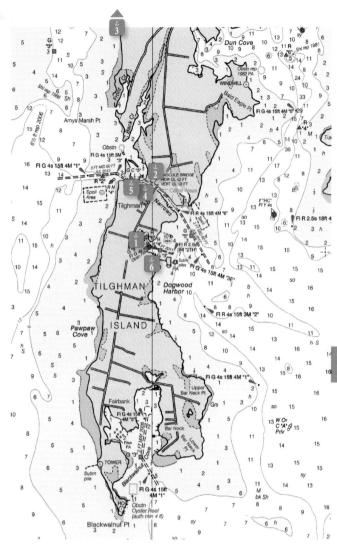

Knapps Narrows; from NOAA Chart 12266—not to be used for navigation.

Knapps Narrows and Tilghman Island *continued*

barbershop on Tilghman Island Road. It's open Saturday and Sunday in season.

South of the eastern entrance to Knapps Narrows on Tilghman Island is **Dogwood Harbor**, a popular destination despite its limited space and shallow nature. Honor the marks "2" through "7." Inside you'll find the modern Tilghman-on-Chesapeake just after entering to port, and at "5" you'll see Harrison's Chesapeake House Country Inn. The latter serves steamed crabs and homestyle meals with a large dollop of interesting history—and a menu stating: "no apologies, lots of butter." Coffee shops, antiques and a fascinating bookstore are a short walk away. Dogwood Harbor is the home base for most of the island's workboats and fishing charters. Pleasure boats are welcome to tie up for an hour or so, provided they don't block the watermen's access to the wharf for loading and unloading. Overnighting is not permitted.

Harris Creek

As you enter the Choptank, you'll be hard pressed to choose where to go next unless you've already mapped out an itinerary. One good place to begin is to the north, where you'll find ❷ **Harris Creek**, which boasts some delightful, protected coves.

Dun Cove

❷ₐ **Dun Cove** is as pretty and protected a spot as you could hope to find—which is why it is among the most popular on the Eastern Shore. Cruisers once shared Dun Cove with only one or two other boats and the cows, horses and snowy egrets

● On Premises
➤ Nearby

Knapps Narrows/Tilghman Island

	Overnight Slips	MLW	Gas	Diesel	Propane	Electric	Showers	Laundry	Restaurant	Lodging	Pool	Pump-out	Ice	Groceries	Marine Supplies	Bait	Boat Repair	Haul-out Services	Launch Ramp	Wi-Fi	Other
1 Harrison's Chesapeake House Tilghman Island/Dogwood Cove; 410-886-2121 or 410-886-2109; www.chesapeakehouse.com	●	6'	●	●	➤	●	●	●	●	●	●	●	●	●	➤	➤	●	➤	●	➤	Gift/nautical shop, fishing charters, cruisers welcome
2 Knapps Narrows Marina & Inn Knapps Narrows/Chesapeake Bay 410-886-2720; www.knappsnarrowsmarina.com	●	6'	●	●		●	●	●	●	●	●	●	●	●	➤	●	➤	●	●	➤	Full repair facility
3 Lowes Wharf Marina Inn Tilghman Island/Ferry Cove/east of Poplar Island 410-745-6684 or 888-484-9267; www.loweswharf.com	●	5'	●	●	●	●	●	●	●	●		●	●		●	●			●	●	Guest Rooms, charters, kayak/bike rentals
4 Tilghman Island Inn Knapps Narrows 410-886-2141 or 800-866-2141; www.tilghmanislandinn.com	●	3'	➤	➤	➤	●	●		●	●	●	●		➤	➤			➤	➤		pet-friendly
5 Tilghman Island Marina Knapps Narrows 410-886-2500; www.tilghmanmarina.com	●	6'	➤	➤	➤	●	●	➤	➤	●		●	●	●	●	●	➤	➤	➤	●	Boat, PWC, bike, kayak, fishing gear rentals
6 Tilghman-On-Chesapeake Knapps Narrows/Dogwood Harbor 800-735-2933; www.tochesapeake.com	●	5'	➤			●	●	●	➤	●	●	●	●	➤	➤	➤	➤	➤	➤	●	Picnic area, pool, floating docks, walk to restaurants

on shore. Now visitors will find a number of large houses discreetly tucked in behind the shoreline to the west and north, although the south shore is still mostly tree-covered, with small piers jutting into the water. On weekends, the cove is apt to hold raft-ups or idling cruisers.

On leaving Knapps Narrows, avoid the charted shoal (5-6 feet) east of the channel by continuing southeast past flashing green "3" before turning northward toward flashing green "5" in Harris Creek, about 1 1/2 miles away. At "4" and "5" the deep—but constricted—channel has nearby shoals of just 1 and 2 feet, so watch the depthsounder and give these marks a wide berth.

Beyond "5" and the bottleneck, the entrance to Dun Cove lies to port, about halfway between "6" and "7". Favor the center of the opening since shoaling may be encroaching farther than charts predict.

Holding is good inside, but deeper drafts should keep to the cove's center when choosing where to drop the hook. Its southern shores have shallows extending all around the irregular peninsula north of the windmill facing Harris Creek. On the cove's northern side, good water exists in a narrow area west of Seth Point (on some charts this is Seths Point), but serious shallows extend south and east of it.

If you are approaching Harris Creek from points east, or if you're leaving or heading for Oxford or Cambridge, note that shoaling has developed west of flashing red "2" off Change Point. Use care and don't cut too close to the mark.

Harris and Broad Creeks; from NOAA Chart 12263— not to be used for navigation.

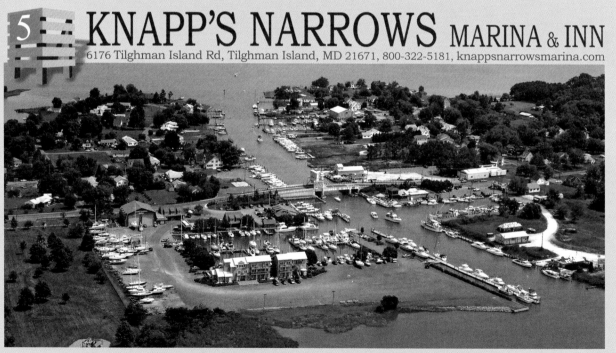

5 KNAPP'S NARROWS MARINA & INN

6176 Tilghman Island Rd, Tilghman Island, MD 21671, 800-322-5181, knappsnarrowsmarina.com

Continental Breakfast, Swimming Pool, Wireless Internet, Showers and Laundry, Pet Friendly, Kayaks, Full Service Marina 35 ton Travelift, Winter Storage, Painting and Refitting, 750 ft Transient Dock, Fuel and Pump-out, Courtesy car and bikes Waterfront dining, Conference rooms, Fishing Charters, Sailing Charters, Hunting Trips

Come for a night and stay forever!

Waterhole Cove

2b **Waterhole Cove** is another lovely anchorage with a wooded shoreline unspoiled by dense commercial development. Besides a smattering of small piers and docks, a few comfortable-looking, attractive homes are visible from the water. Open to the east and with shallows that prevent tucking in close to shore, there's no full protection in a blow, but its water is generous for rafting in settled weather.

The cove is said to have taken its name from a freshwater spring that once bubbled up from the creek's bottom. Here, ships could fill water casks without going ashore, a major convenience for colonial sailors. Well, it's a nice story.

Heading into Harris Creek from the Choptank and flashing red "2" off Change Point, follow daymarks "4" through "10" to Waterhole Cove. The sleepy village of **Sherwood**, near the cove's southern mouth, is worth a stroll and has a substantial public pier where you may tie up briefly; or you can anchor off and use the shore-end of the dock to tie up the dinghy.

Sherwood can't offer much more than quiet charm, including a couple of examples of the distinctive three-corner or Tilghman House style of 19th century architecture and the post office, which is a short walk from the landing. But if you're ambitious and hungry—and it's not too muggy and hot—you can stroll across the peninsula to the restaurant at Lowes Wharf, perhaps a mile away, on the other side of the main road leading from St. Michaels to Tilghman Island. It's a pleasant way to experience Lowe s Wharf, if your draft prohibits visiting in the usual fashion.

Broad Creek

As its name implies, **3** **Broad Creek** has a wide mouth—two miles across. Entering from the west, give a wide berth to flashing "1B" which lies more than a mile southeast of Nelson Point. This marks the shoals associated with long-gone Nelson Island, which once lay between this navigational aid and the mainland.

Due east of "1B" is **Irish Creek**, and while it may look enticing, its shifty channel remains a challenge to chartmakers and locals alike. There's a long shoal extending far into the Choptank from Holland Point with extensive shallows all along its eastern entrance and Lucy Point. The crooked narrow channel that runs between them is no longer maintained by the Coast Guard, but the DNR has set some buoys there. However, it is suitable mostly for small boats with shallow draft, and preferably with local knowledge—unless you're feeling adventurous.

Balls Creek

An alternative at this point is **3a** **Balls Creek**, with its little-used scenic and sheltered anchorage. At the juncture of the Choptank and Broad Creek, when you are safely clear of flashing green "1B", and with the bow pointed north toward red nun "2", look west for the creek's marked channel.

About a mile long, the channel leads toward the tiny, quiet waterman's community of **Neavitt** (pronounced NEV-it) on the spindly finger of land to port. While charts indicate 8-foot depths, it's reported to be just 5 feet in some spots, and the suggested path is along the channel's southern side between flashing green "1" and red daymark "2". If you take it very slowly, you can ease back out if your draft doesn't like it. Favor the north side between "3" and "4", looping north around the shoal there. Beyond this point, the center of the channel generally holds 8 feet at low tide.

A small peninsula in the center of the creek creates a well-protected anchorage along the northwestern shore in the wide basin just past it. Beyond the big boathouse and well-manicured farm, the creek begins to shoal quickly for sailboats, but there appears to be plenty of water for motorboats. On the northeastern side of the peninsula, depths vary and then drop significantly as this small branch winds toward a farmhouse.

Balls Creek possesses a special old-fashioned beauty. You're likely to see a number of crabbing boats at the small public dock near the mouth and many more tucked here and there along the creek. About halfway up the creek, the low tin roof of a crab shed identifies Richard Higgins Soft Shell Crab Company (open daily from May through October; 410-745-3175). Dinghy up to the company's dock to buy a dozen fresh soft shells and savor one of the many pleasures this part of the Chesapeake has to offer. There is also a county launch ramp here, which provides ready access to the wide Choptank River.

Leadenham Creek

On Broad Creek's eastern side, opposite Balls Creek, you'll find **Bridge Creek**. This may look wide and inviting but it's only for the shallowest of drafts. Not too far north, however, deeper-drafted cruisers will find several good options, including **3b** **Leadenham Creek**, which lies west of flashing "4" off Deep Neck Point. This tributary shares its entrance with Grace Creek which branches off to the north. Access to both is gained by passing between daymarks "1" and "2". Then bear to port for Leadenham, starboard for Grace.

One popular and well-protected anchorage with good holding is the charmingly named **Boby Owl Cove** with its 9-and 10-foot depths. Boby Owl is to starboard on Leadenham's northern side. Note that the beach on the easterly point and all the surrounding land is private.

Farther along, to starboard as well, is **Caulk Cove**, also snug with tall trees but with a bit less water (7 and 8 feet). Continuing in the main branch, anchorage possibilities in depths of 7 feet continue for about one-half mile before the water dips into the 5-foot range. Some boats drop the hook at the mouth of the shallower branch to the southwest.

Leadenham's southern peninsula, a nearly 1,000-acre prime parcel with more than 8 miles of shoreline, was once a fox-hunting preserve owned by William duPont, Jr., financier, equestrian, sportsman, and an heir to the duPont fortune. His daughter Jean Ellen duPont Shehan donated all of the land to the Audubon Society in 1997, but when the trust fund's investments—essential for maintenance, management and taxes—were hard hit by the economic downturn, it was sold. Happily, thc new owner has put a conservation easement on the property to ensure it remains undeveloped.

Grace Creek

In contrast to Balls Creek, both Leadenham and Grace creeks have channels that are straightforward and deep and that access several good anchorages. For ⓷ **Grace Creek**, after bearing right at red daymark "2", proceed north. This tributary's best anchorage, snug and out of the way of traffic, is in the small cove on the western shoreline. Holding is good in soft mud.

The marked channel continues for about six-tenths of a mile, ending at red daymark "6". Beyond that, depths drop at the creek's headwaters, which lie on the "outskirts" of the community of **Bozman**. Here you'll find the docks of P. T. Hambleton Seafood, purveyors of live crabs, ice and bait. The channel can be busy with watermen and pleasure boats, and the shoreline is dotted with homes and docks. Nevertheless, Grace Creek easily lives up to its name.

Edgar Cove

The dolphin off Deep Neck Point in Broad Creek, flashing red "4", is the only lighted navigational aid in this tributary and marks an important juncture. To the west are Leadenham and Grace creeks, with Edge Creek lying about 3/4 mile to the east beyond "2EC". The main stem of Broad Creek, however, continues northeasterly in a dog-leg fashion, becoming nearly parallel with San Domingo Creek to its east. Upper Broad Creek has good depths for about 3 1/2 miles and several good anchorages. Among them is ⓷ **Edgar Cove** along its western shore, just a little more than two miles beyond "4".

When navigating this area, which can be busy in the high season, binoculars might be helpful in sorting out all the marks, which may seem confusing. Identifying each mark and matching it to the chart should keep you going where you intend to go.

To find Edgar Cove from Deep Neck Point, head northeast toward "5" and "6", giving each a wide berth to skirt the shoals they mark. Past "7" off Mulberry Point, continue north toward "8", parallel to and west of Hambleton Island.

Hambleton Island must at one time have been either one large island or a long spindly peninsula off Church Neck south of St. Michaels. Today it is three small islands, eroded over time by waves and weather, and separated by shoal water. So while you may see boats passing by on next-door San Domingo Creek, do not be tempted to cut between these islands unless you are in a dinghy or kayak—the water there is only a foot or two deep.

Nearly past the islands, at green "9", your course will turn westerly. Being mindful of charted shoals and obstruc-

tions on both shores, look for Edgar Cove to port, about 1/2 mile beyond "9".

At the entrance to Edgar Cove is a heavily wooded shoreline to starboard that curves southward along the inside of the cove. Here you'll find a small natural landing where you can go ashore to stretch your legs. If workboats are tied up at the dock on the northwest shore, you can expect them to leave quite early in the morning, making a bit of a ruckus as they get underway. You'll rest easier too if your anchor light is lit and visible.

Beyond Edgar Cove, Broad Creek is navigable for nearly two more miles with snug anchoring possibilities. Two similar coves, one to port and one to starboard have good depths, and farther up, before depths drop to 5 and 6 feet, the chart shows good sticky mud in 7 feet.

San Domingo Creek

⓷ **San Domingo** is a quiet lovely creek, with wooded shores that hide many of the waterfront homes that nestle along its banks. The head of San Domingo Creek is about as near as you can get to the Miles River and still be in the Choptank. It also laps the backside of St. Michaels, making a visit to town easier than having to haul yourself back out into Eastern Bay and down the Miles to get to the town's busy harbor.

To reach San Domingo Creek, curl around "4" at Deep Neck Point and go past "2 EC" to daymark "3". The creek winds two miles north from here. Many cruisers choose to anchor near the mouth of the creek in the lee of Hambleton Island, but San Domingo is long enough to accommodate dozens of boats. At a quarter-mile in width, it is sufficiently narrow to provide a snug anchorage anywhere along its length except, perhaps, where Hambleton Island has eroded away, leaving the anchorage exposed. The holding ground is super, though sticky and hard to clean off the hook.

Past Hambleton Island, San Domingo is lined with homes half-hidden in the trees. About a mile and a half up, an unnamed creek meanders east, providing a secluded anchorage for several boats. About a quarter mile past it, another branch heads west. This is **Old House Cove**, where Eastern Shore poet and writer Gilbert Byron lived and wrote. His cabin is now at Pickering Creek Audubon Center.

James Michener bought a home on San Domingo Creek after writing his famous novel *Chesapeake* and lived there for some years. In his epic tale of four Eastern Shore families, Michener used the Choptank River and portions of Talbot County as his setting. The histories of St. Michaels and Cambridge were woven into his fictional village, Patamoke. Devon Island, which Michener placed in the middle of the lower Choptank River, was based on real-life islands such as Sharps, Jefferson and Hambleton, which have been, or are being, gradually erased by nature's forces.

The last branch to starboard (which residents of St. Michaels call **Back Creek**) brings the cruiser into the residential suburbs of St. Michaels. At the end of this prong is a public dock, where you can usually find a spot for your dinghy. With a shoal-draft boat, you may be able to pull all the way

San Domingo Creek *continued*

in to the nearby bulkhead to the left, but you won't be able to stay there long. Commercial watermen use the dock and bulkhead and return to it at mid-day or early afternoon, after selling off their day's catch of crabs. Courtesy dictates staying out of their way.

Deep water is to be found about a half-mile from the public pier, but cruisers should be warned that as you get closer, mounds of oyster shells will give you a "false bottom." A cruiser once reported that on a three-boat raft-up, the middle vessel was left high and dry the next morning atop a mound of shells. It provided amusement to the watermen as they headed out that morning.

Once you've reached the dock, you're at the foot of Chew Avenue, a long, shady block away from Talbot Street, the main drag through St. Michaels. Turning left will take you to the Chesapeake Bay Maritime Museum and a grocery store.

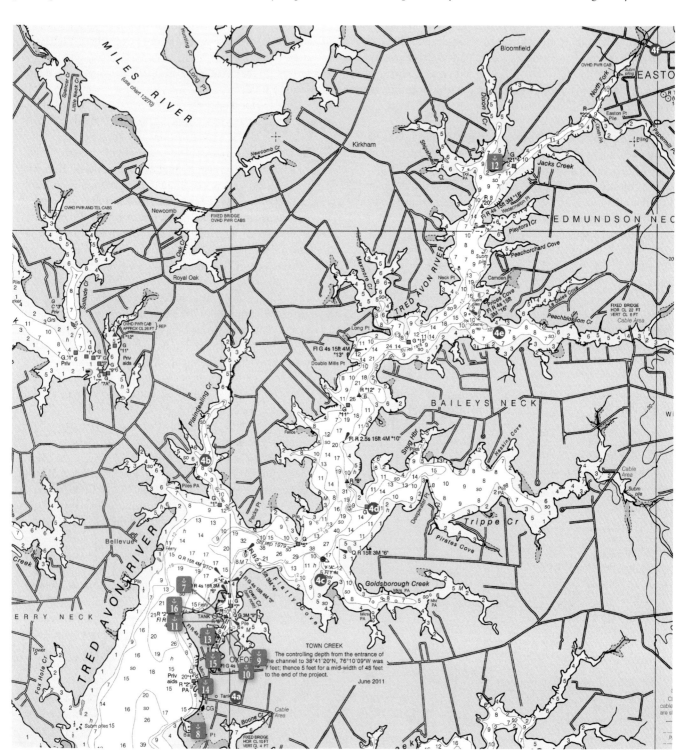

Tred Avon River; from NOAA Chart 12266—not to be used for navigation.

Tred Avon River

The **4 Tred Avon River** is most associated with the town that once bore its name, Oxford. At one time rivaling Annapolis as a commercial port, Thread Haven (as it was then known) was named an official port of entry in 1683. Some say the river and the town derived their common name because of their heavy commerce in hemp, rope and cordage. The name was corrupted into Third Haven, according to the U.S. Geological Survey, and later to Tred Avon.

Today the Tred Avon is one of the Chesapeake's most prestigious waterfront addresses, and Oxford remains an important boating center for this part of the Eastern Shore. Good-looking boats are always parading in and out of the river, many bound for the town located within view of the river's mouth.

Oxford

A little over two miles up the Tred Avon River from the Choptank River Light lies **4a** **Oxford**, cradled between **Town Creek** on the east and the Tred Avon to the west. Isolated geographically on a peninsula at the end of Oxford Neck, though not far from Easton, it is a soothing kind of place, retiring by nature. The town attracts cruisers, summer people and tourists, while resisting the type of development that would change its character. Residents maintain a balance between small-town life and some commercialism, emphasizing restoration, renovation and businesses that are compatible with its image. The result is a charming sailor's haven.

Approaching Oxford, you'll see nothing rising above the trees except the town water tank, thoughtfully labeled "Oxford" for those boaters who aren't sure where they are. There is a protected anchorage in Town Creek, but the bottom is notoriously poor holding and space is limited. You can choose from one of several marinas that offer transient slips and amenities or you can anchor overnight in one of the lovely nearby creeks.

There are public beaches along the river, the largest one bordering a roadway called The Strand, where cruisers land their dinghies, locals picnic and traffic stops for ducks crossing the road. If the weather is calm, you can anchor off The Strand, between the ferry docks and the entrance to Town Creek. Be sure to stay well clear of the traffic, especially the Oxford-Bellevue ferry, which makes regular daylight runs across the river. This is a cool anchorage that seems to catch whatever breeze might drift to the Tred Avon on a summer day, but it is open and consequently rough during a thunderstorm or a nor'easter. And the wakes can make for an uncomfortable anchorage. The holding ground here is fairly slippery.

● On Premises
➤ Nearby

Tred Avon River

	MLW	Overnight Slips	Gas	Diesel	Propane	Electric	Showers	Laundry	Restaurant	Lodging	Pool	Pump-out	Ice	Groceries	Marine Supplies	Bait	Boat Repair	Haul-out Services	Launch Ramp	Wi-Fi	Other
Brewer Oxford Boat Yard & Marina Tred Avon R./Town Cr. 410-226-5101; www.byy.com/mdmarinas/oxford	10'	●	●	●	➤	●	●	●	➤	➤	●	●	●	➤	●	➤	●	●	➤	●	Bike, car rentals; cable, Wi-Fi, 75-ton lift
Campbell's Bachelor Point Yacht Co. Tred Avon R. 410-226-5592; www.campbellsboatyards.com	9'	●	➤	➤	➤	●	●	●	➤	➤	●	●	●	➤	●	➤	●	●	➤	●	Pool, 70-ton lift, dry storage, repairs
Campbell's Boatyard at Jack's Point Tred Avon Cr./Town Cr. 410-226-5105; www.campbellsboatyards.com	6'	●	●	●	➤	●	●	➤	➤	➤	●	●	➤	●	●	➤	●	●	➤	●	56-slips; restoration, repairs, fuel, floating docks
Campbell's Town Creek Boatyard Tred Avon R./Town Cr. 410-226-0213; www.campbellsboatyards.com	6'	●	➤	➤	➤	●	●	●	➤		●	●	●	➤	●	➤	➤	➤	➤	●	40-slips, custom boat-building, restoration
Cutts & Case Tred Avon R./Town Cr. 410-226-5416; www.cuttsandcase.com	8'	●	➤	➤	➤	●	●	➤	➤	➤		➤	➤	➤	●	➤	●	●	➤	●	Full repairs, railway, yacht design, boat-building
Easton Point Marina Tred Avon R./Easton 410-822-1201; www.eastonpointmarina.com	5'	●	●	●	➤	●	●	●	➤	➤	➤	●	●	➤	●	●	●	●	●	●	Full-service, mechanic, fuel, store, to-go beer, kayaks
Hinckley Yacht Services Tred Avon R./Town Cr. 410-226-5113; www.hinckleyyachts.com	6'-7'	●			●	●	●	●	➤	➤	➤	●	●	➤	●		●	●			Full-service marina in Oxford
The Masthead at Pier St. Marina Tred Avon R./Oxford 410-226-5171	7'	●				●	➤	●	➤	➤	➤		➤	➤	➤	➤	➤	➤			Dockage for restaurant patrons
Oxford Yacht Agency Tred Avon R./Town Cr. 410-822-8556; www.oya.com	6'	●		➤		●	●		➤	➤	●	➤	➤	➤		●			➤		Tennis, basketball, park
Schooners on the Creek Tred Avon R./Town Cr. 410-226-0160; www.schoonersonthecreek.com	7'+	●	➤	➤	➤	●	➤	●	➤		●	●	➤	➤	➤	➤		➤	➤		Monitor channel 16

Port of Call

Oxford

One of Maryland's oldest towns, Oxford was a colonial port of entry and home to several heroes of the American Revolution. Today its allure is its quiet charm, its walkability and its many boating services. A compact community with shade-drenched sidewalks and charming homes, it is bordered by Town Creek and the Tred Avon River, where workboats, sleek yachts and a historic ferry go about daily their business.

A commercial listing and street map put together by the Oxford Business Association locates and describes stores, restaurants and marinas. Just as valuable is the brochure's synopsis of local history and site map of places of interest. It also lays out a self-guided walking tour of historic houses such as Bratt Mansion (c. 1848), once part of the Maryland Military Academy; Barnaby House, erected in the 1770s; Byberry, one of the area's oldest homes (records indicate it was standing in 1695); and the Grapevine House (1798), which has a grapevine planted in 1810 still growing in the front yard. All of these homes are private so the "tour" is limited to looking at their exteriors, of course. (Copies of the guide can be downloaded at *www.portofoxford.com*). Get other perspectives on Oxford's past by perusing the artifacts and displays in the Oxford Museum or taking a guided tour of the town arranged by museum staff (reservations required). And don't miss the vintage boats and maritime memorabilia on display at Cutts & Case shipyard.

Be as active or idle as you please. Enjoy water activities such as fishing and exploring by dinghy, or make use of the athletics facilities on the edge of town, including tennis courts, swings and a sports field. Sit on a small beach and watch boat traffic or take to one of the shaded benches and picnic tables in a grassy park overlooking the river.

Cyclists are familiar with the Eastern Shore's flat terrain and generally uncrowded roads. Route 333 from Easton to Oxford is a good bike route, for example, with a bike lane all the way. And Oxford itself seems to be made for cycling. If you don't have bikes on board, rent them at Brewer Oxford Boat Yard, Hinckley Yacht Services or Easton Cycle and Sport (*www.eastoncycleandsport.com*). For the adventurous who don't mind bicycling on narrow roads, extend your tour by heading to the foot of North Morris Street to take the Oxford-Bellevue Ferry across the Tred Avon. Believed to be the oldest privately operated ferry in the nation, it began running in 1683 and has operated continuously since 1836. The ferry drops you off in the countryside on a road that shortcuts the seven or so miles between Oxford and St. Michaels.

Paddlers may want to explore the nooks and crannies of nearby creeks. Easton Cycle and Sport (410-822-7433) and Eastern Shore Adventure Company (410-820-8881) rent paddle-

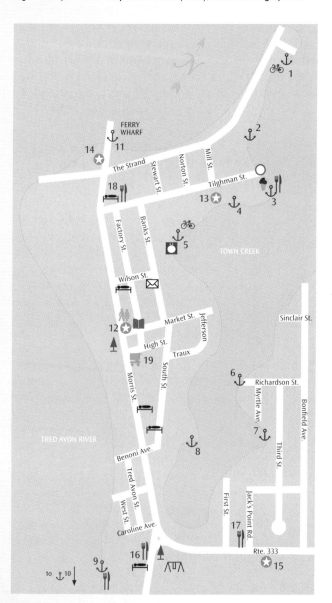

Oxford

⚓ **Marinas/Dockage**
1 Brewer Oxford Boatyard
2 Oxford Boatyard
3 Schooners on the Creek
4 Cutts & Case
5 Hinckley Yacht Services
6 Campbell's Boatyard at Jack's Point
7 Campbell's Town Creek Boatyard
8 Oxford Yacht Agency
9 Pier Street Marina
10 Campbell's Bachelor Point Yacht Co.
11 Public Dockage (no overnights)

⊙ **Points of Interest**
12 Oxford Museum
13 Byberry
14 Custom House
15 Oxford Community Center

🍴 **Dining**
3 Schooners on the Creek
9 The Masthead at Pier Street
16 Pope's Tavern
17 Latitude 38° Bistro & Spirits
18 Robert Morris Inn

🛒 **Groceries/Carryout**
19 Oxford Market and Deli

🛏 **Lodging**
🍦 **Ice Cream**
🚲 **Bicycles**
⛺ **Park**
✉ **Post Office**
📖 **Library**
🔲 **Laundromat**
⛹ **Playground/Athletic Fields**
○ **Public Landings**
🚻 **Public Restrooms**

craft and offer guided excursions.

Oxford's retail district, though small, has a few shops worth browsing. Go treasure-hunting among the antiques and collectibles at Americana Antiques (Friday-Saturday, noon-4 p.m.). You'll find used books and current titles at Mystery Loves Company, where whodunits share shelf space with books for all ages and interests. Shop for gifts, books and town memorabilia at the Oxford Museum's gift shop and small collectibles from the British isles at the Scottish Highland Creamery. Address your nautical needs in the ship's store at Hinckley Yacht Services.

Oxford Market and Deli can fill your galley supply needs. More than a convenience store, it carries produce, groceries, dairy products, sundries and even rental movies. You can also restock at the Farmer's Market held Wednesday afternoons (in summer) at the Oxford Community Center.

Seafood and hospitality characterize the local restaurant scene, and boaters will find that complimentary shuttle service is often available to and from establishments not located along the waterfront. Fine dining is key at Latitude 38 Bistro & Spirits (American cuisine served in dining rooms graced with handpainted murals), Pope's Tavern (a European style bistro in the historic Oxford Inn) and the Robert Morris Inn, near the ferry landing. More informal dining is to be had at the Masthead (a crabhouse/seafood restaurant at Pier Street Marina with free dockage for patrons) and at Schooners on the Creek (steamed crabs, live music and free dockage for patrons). The Scottish Highland Creamery (designer ice creams, sorbets, handmade fudge) is down Tilghman Street.

Talbot County Tourism Photos

Oxford's relaxed atmosphere is reflected in its fun-filled, boat-oriented annual events. Especially popular is the annual Cardboard Boat Race (contestants use cardboard to fashion vessels held together with everything from staples to duct tape) in June. The town hosts an Independence Day celebration (including fireworks), and in August the Bay's famous log canoes compete on the river in regattas hosted by the Tred Avon Yacht Club. Throughout the year, the Oxford Community Center's calendar is filled with performances by the Tred Avon Players, concerts and special programs like the annual Fall Festival (visit *www.wso.net/oxfordcc/* or *www.tredavonplayers.org*).

Information: Oxford Business Association, 410-226-5527, *www.portofoxford.com; www.oxfordmd.com;* or *www.tourtalbot.org.*

Oxford *continued*

As an alternative, good anchoring can be found across the Tred Avon River from Town Creek and just west of the entrance to Plaindealing Creek. Although open to southeasterly breezes, the water is deep enough that you can duck in to the spot on the chart where the 6-foot sounding is shown and, with caution, slightly farther.

Today Oxford retains its importance as one of the Chesapeake's principal boating centers. In addition to being a fine supply and repair port for cruising vessels, the town boasts a number of yacht brokers and dealers. The Tred Avon Yacht Club (established in 1931) is known for its summer sailing regattas, a tradition that began more or less by accident. Two weeks after the club opened as a bath house, sea nettles moved in and put an end to swimming and bathing in the river. So instead, club members organized a

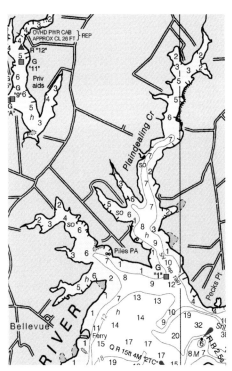

Plaindealing Creek; from NOAA Chart 12266—not to be used for navigation.

free-for-all sailboat race. This marked the beginning of the club's class racing schedule. Nowadays, you can watch the classic sailboat races from anchorages off the town and across the river.

Oxford works hard to maintain its serene, boater-friendly atmosphere and boasts a small, easily walkable downtown with enough shops, restaurants and attractions to satisfy most visitors. Daytime dockage is available at the Oxford ferry wharf (3-hour limit). Although known as a prime sailing destination, Oxford is a true gem in any boater's book.

Plaindealing Creek

In a breeze on Town Creek, you can sit up at anchor watch into the late hours, worried about whether you'll go crashing into one of the expensive boats that crowd Oxford's marinas . . . or you can try **45 Plaindealing Creek**. Located across the Tred Avon, this creek—

Plaindealing Creek continued

named for historic Plain Dealing Farm—is a better, more relaxing place to anchor in the Oxford area, and it is closer than popular **Trippe Creek**.

If you're overnighting here with other boaters and planning to have dinner in Oxford, you may want to consider using just one of them as a taxi into Town Creek, while leaving the rest lying at anchor. Motoring back to Plaindealing in the dark can be a little tricky because Plaindealing Creek has only one aid to navigation, and that one is unlighted. So you may want to plan your return before daylight fades completely.

On entering Plaindealing Creek, stay in the middle. Once inside, the creek broadens and you can pull off into the forked branch on the port side, or anywhere else you choose, to anchor. We've gotten some reports of shoaling on the approaches to Plaindealing and in the creek itself, in particular on the port side about 30 yards northwest of "1" daymark at the mouth of the creek. Shoals also seem to be encroaching on the channel from both sides, so it's a good choice to stay in the middle, where you should find 8 and 9 feet all the way in. Favoring the port hand on leaving as you approach "1" should keep you off the mud.

If you have a depthfinder with an alarm, you ought to be able to steer a safe course by setting the alarm for a depth a couple feet greater than your draft and correcting your heading according to the readings. Anyway, it would be good practice to do it a couple of times.

Goldsborough Creek

As you pass the green "5" on your way up the Tred Avon, you may see a good-sized fleet of boats anchored in **Flatty Cove**, which lies between Town Creek and Goldsborough Creek. If the hour is growing late and you don't like the look of Goldsborough Creek's narrow entrance channel on the chart, you might want to consider joining them for the evening. But the next day, be sure to look into Goldsborough Creek. It's a

delightful spot and well worth a visit.

You can't head right into the creek from "5" or you'll run aground. Instead continue northeasterly another 300 yards or so until the small cove on the north shore is abeam, then turn and head for the ④ⓒ **Goldsborough Creek** entrance. Throttle way back and keep the cove dead astern, at the same time favoring Goldsborough's port side slightly. You'll find good water as you slowly motor past the grassy shoreline.

Try anchoring just inside the entrance where the water broadens opposite a large boathouse. There are few homes or other buildings on this part of the creek, and the low banks are open to whatever faint summer breeze may be stirring. If the weather gets blowy, you can head farther upstream for a bit more protection.

A good-sized sand bar located on the eastern side of the creek, and almost awash at high tide, is a popular gathering place for local seagulls, which squawk and jostle each other for the occasional scrap of food they seem to find there. A few egrets and herons will be watching at a discreet distance.

Goldsborough's bottom is soft, sticky mud, making anchoring easy with good holding ground. As the sun sets and evening shadows turn the shoreline colors from rich greens to deep purple blues, you'll enjoy the tranquility of your surroundings.

Both Goldsborough Creek and Flatty Cove are popular with Canada geese as well as cruisers. Depending on the season, you may find great flocks in either spot, their raucous voices greeting each new flock of geese landing in both waterways.

Trippe Creek

④ⓓ **Trippe Creek**, one of the most beautiful spots on the Eastern Shore, is located a couple of miles upriver from Oxford. Its channel is deep and well marked with no surprises. A good landmark for finding Trippe Creek is the estate on Bailey's Neck, where the Tred Avon bears off to port. The white house, accented by tall columns in the grand Southern tradition, is set back from the point. Its tall flagpole can be seen for at least a mile downriver.

From daymark "1" plot a course for the mouth of aptly named **Snug Harbor**. This charming and peaceful little cove is just the right size for a couple of boats to ride out a storm. Snug Harbor is wide open to the south, which provides a cool night's sleep in a light to moderate southerly.

Trippe Creek provides other anchorages farther up, but give the western side of Deepwater Point a wide berth. On the eastern side the water is deep, almost up to the brick bulkhead that surrounds a modern, castle-like home (complete with turrets) built on the point.

Beyond Deepwater Point, Trippe Creek opens up to a wide and well-protected bay capable of accommodating a hundred or so boats. This is a favorite spot for groups cruising the area and a good alternative to anchoring off The Strand in

Goldsborough Creek and Trippe Creek; from NOAA Chart 12266—not to be used for navigation.

With three great full-service locations in Oxford, MD, Campbell's can do it all.

· Protected Slips
· Custom Boat Building On-site

Town Creek

TOWN CREEK BOATYARD
109 Myrtle Avenue
410.226.0213

· Two 70 ft. Floating Docks
· Travel Lift
· Repairs & Maintenance

Jack's Point

**CAMPBELL'S BOATYARD
@ JACK'S PT.**
106 Richardson Street
410.226.5105

· 70 Metric Ton Travel Lift
· 1.5 Acre Dry Storage Area
· Certified Cummins Dealer

Bachelor Point

BACHELOR PT. YACHT CO.
26106A Bachelors Harbor Drive
410.226.5592

CAMPBELL'S
★ BOATYARDS ★
OXFORD, MD

All the comforts of a
full-service marina plus
repairs, repowers and refits.

2 floating docks for boats to 70 ft.

Year-round and transient slips

On-site custom boat building
by Campbell's Custom Yachts

Certified Cummins Dealer

List your boat or buy the boat of your dreams through CYS.

CCY 37

Campbell's Yacht Sales will make your brokerage experience both
successful and stress-free. Benefit from our extensive background and
experience with both power and sail boats. Call us at 410.829.5458 or
410.226.5592, or email boats@campbellsyachtsales.com to find out more.

Think of Campbell's for all your boating needs!

www.campbellsboatyards.com · www.campbellscustomyachts.com · www.campbellsyachtsales.com

Trippe Creek *continued*

Oxford. In this expansive basin between Deepwater Point and the next point to the east you can enjoy a delightful swim on hot summer days, finding especially cool spots that are likely fed by underground springs.

If you explore farther up Trippe Creek, be aware that there is an extended shoal off the third northern point of land beyond Snug Harbor. That tiny thumb jutting from the main peninsula shoals out into the creek farther than is shown on the charts.

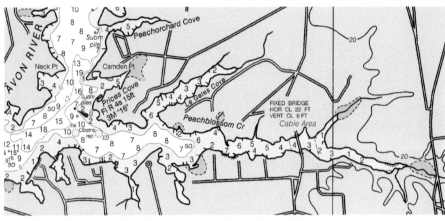

Peachblossom Creek; from NOAA Chart 12266—not to be used for navigation.

Peachblossom Creek

From the Choptank River "spider," it's about 7 miles up the Tred Avon to ④ **Peachblossom Creek**. Honor the marks "11" through "15". That last one indicates a serious shoal just past the entrance to Maxmore Creek. While approaching "16", turn to starboard into the opening of Peachblossom Creek, taking heed of all the charted shoals and obstructions. Once inside, you'll see some piers showing on the chart along the south shore. This is a perfect spot to drop the anchor and relax. Peachblossom carries 7 to 8 feet for nearly a mile, then 6 and less toward the fixed bridge (6 feet of vertical clearance).

The story goes that a man named George Robins was the first to plant peaches on the Eastern Shore, and the blossoms proved to be such a sensation that both his home and the creek were named for them. Only the creek remains today. Less verifiable lore also suggests that in the early 1700s a shipyard between Peachblossom and Trippe Creek catered to the infamous pirates of the day, until beheadings put a stop to their reign of terror.

Peachblossom Creek is every bit as lovely as Trippe or Goldsborough creeks. If weather gets really rough, go upstream past **Le Gates Cove** to where the creek broadens out again. If you draw less than 4 feet, go all the way to the little bridge. Here Peachblossom becomes more like a friendly country stream.

Across from the mouth of Peachblossom Creek there are other cruising options. Just inside the aptly named Long Point on the west shore, you'll find the narrow entrance to **Maxmore Creek**. Rounding the point, note green "15" to starboard; it marks the end of a long sandbar. Hugging the long point shoreline to port, with 7 feet of water, you should get safely inside the creek.

Just beyond the creek's mouth are the east and west forks of Maxmore, both with approximately 5-foot depths. Some of the holding ground can be weedy, so back down on the anchor to get a good set in the vegetation.

Maxmore's main east fork does not offer an isolated anchorage because of the number of homes. Inside the creek itself, there are no landings or any facilities whatever.

Easton

If you're continuing up the Tred Avon to ④ **Easton**, at "18" off Watermelon Point, watch the next two markers carefully to avoid being misled into **Shipshead** or **Dixon** creeks, although both offer safe and secluded anchoring. Shipshead (which branches off to port) and Dixon (which heads due north) can carry 7 feet behind the marshy point and within view of the stately brick mansion and terraced gardens of Ratcliffe Manor. Built by the Hollyday family in the mid-1700s, the historic plantation is now privately owned.

At green "21" the Tred Avon turns eastward. The channel narrows to about 100 yards, but maintains depths of 10 feet or more. Less than a mile farther, at red "22", you'll spot the buildings of Easton Point Marina immediately beyond. Easton Point Marina is a small, full-service facility that can handle boats up to about 5 feet in draft and has an adjacent county launch ramp (buy permits at the marina). There's no overnight parking at the ramp site, but the marina can accommodate a few rigs (call 410-822-1201 in advance). Fishing supplies, boat hardware and carry-out food are available in the marina store. From here, it's a pleasant mile and a half walk or taxi ride into Easton.

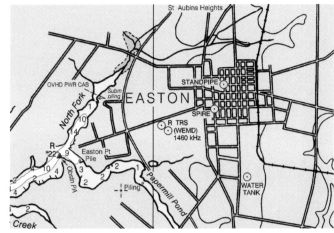

Easton; from NOAA Chart 12266—not to be used for navigation.

Port of Call
Easton

Once known as the Colonial Capital of the Eastern Shore, this historic town has become a center for regional arts and culture. Numerous art galleries, a renovated 1920s theater, gourmet restaurants and cozy inns make Easton a popular weekend destination. A former port town whose distinctive 18th- and 19th-century homes reflect that rich history, Easton now lies a mile and a half from the Tred Avon River. It's a trip well worth making.

Designated the Talbot County seat in 1710, Easton continues to serve that role today. The first county courthouse was erected in 1712 (at a cost of 115,000 pounds of tobacco) and added to in 1794. It reached its present size in the late 1950s. The town's growth is reflected in three homes maintained by the Historical Society of Talbot County: a reconstructed one-room cabin from 1670, a restored 1796 cabinetmaker's home and a restored 1810 brick townhouse, one of the town's larger dwellings of its time. Historical Society staff members lead tours through the homes and welcome visitors to wander through the adjoining Federal-style gardens. Nearby, the diminutive Third Haven Friends Meeting House, a Quaker religious center built in 1682, is acknowledged as the country's oldest framed place of worship still in use and the state's earliest dated building. A self-guided walking tour of the historic district is available at the Historical Society Museum or can be downloaded at *www. eastonmd.org*.

Easton came alive when town merchants began to stage the annual Waterfowl Festival, featuring decoy carvers and wildlife painters from around the world as well as hunting books, demonstrations and artists' workshops. Money raised annually has been used to fund conservation efforts along the Atlantic flyway. Now the arts are an integral part of the town. Its visual arts showcase is the nonprofit Academy Art Museum, which features a collection of 19th- and 20th-century works by European and American artists. Performing arts thrive in the revitalized Avalon Theatre. Built in 1921 as a vaudeville and silent movie house and restored to its art deco grandeur, the theater presents lectures, concerts, plays, recitals and dances. (Call 410-822-7299 or visit *www.*

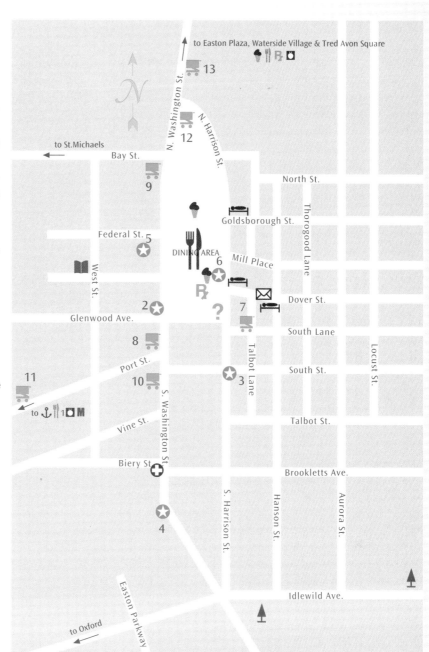

Easton

⚓ **Marinas/Dockage**
   1 Easton Point Marina

⊙ **Points of Interest**
   2 Historical Society of Talbot County
   3 Academy Art Museum
   4 Third Haven Meeting House
   5 Talbot County Courthouse
   6 Avalon Theatre

? **Information**
   Visitors Center

🛒 **Groceries**
   7 Mason's (gourmet food/deli/sweets)
   8 U5 Foods
   9 Safeway
   10 Doc's Quick Shop Market
   11 Gay's Seafood (& steamed crabs)
   12 Easton Farmers Market (Sat. 8-1)
   13 Captain's Ketch Seafood Market

🌲 **Park**
🍴 **Dining Area**
Ⓜ **Marine Supplies**
🛏 **Lodging**
🍦 **Ice Cream**
✚ **Memorial Hospital**
   Shopping District
📖 **Library**
✉ **Post Office**
🧺 **Laundromat**
℞ **Pharmacy**

Port of Call Easton continued

avalontheatre.com for a schedule.) The theater also serves as the center for the Chesapeake Film Festival every fall.

For recreation, Idlewild Park has tennis and basketball courts, ball fields, picnic areas and playgrounds. Cross-country bicyclists can follow the 2.2-mile Easton Rails to Trails path that runs from the park to North Easton Park or strike out on their own through the flat Talbot County countryside. (A suggested 35-mile loop is available at *www.eastonmd.org*.) Easton Cycle and Sports (410-822-7433) rents bikes and delivers kayaks. Kayaking is a great way to explore the upper reaches of the Tred Avon. Eastern Shore Adventure Company also rents and delivers kayaks, and offers naturalist-led tours (410-820-8881). Golfers are welcome at two championship courses, Easton Club (800-277-9800) at the headwaters of the Tred Avon and Hog Neck (410-822-6079) on the outskirts of town.

Easton's chic shops sell an array of upscale merchandise, including jewelry, gifts, decoys, books, home decor items, gourmet foods and fine fashions. Antiques lovers will treasure the town's quality shops and the Sunday open-air antiques market, made more festive by afternoon musical performances. The town is also proud of its art galleries, whose numbers are rising. Toward the edge of the retail district lies TalbotTown, the Eastern Shore's first shopping center (1955), which features about a dozen stores, including Talbot's, the women's clothiers. Farther away are Easton Plaza, Tred Avon Square, Easton Marketplace and Marlboro Plaza, which offer restaurants, specialty shops, pharmacies, grocery stores and gourmet, natural foods and Amish markets. In town, you'll find sliced meats, cheeses and specialty foods at Mason's, seafood at Captain's Ketch and Gay's Seafood, fresh-picked produce at the Saturday morning Farmers' Market on Harrison Street and a Safeway supermarket for major reprovisioning.

American, Mediterranean, European and Asian cuisine; seafood, steaks, fine wines and raw bars—you'll find them all in Easton, one of the Eastern Shore's culinary capitals. A stroll up Harrison or

Talbot County Tourism photos

Washington streets will bring you to plenty of creative and inviting eateries. Along these quiet streets you'll also find a host of charming B&Bs and the Tidewater Inn if you're seeking overnight accomodations.

On First Friday Galley Walk, many galleries, shops and attractions stay open until 9 p.m. to offer exhibits and refreshments. On other summer Fridays, bring a chair for outdoor movie nights across from the Farmer's Market (rain venue: Avalon Theatre). Easton is known as an arts showplace and its busy calendar includes the internationally acclaimed Eastern Shore Chamber Music Festival in June and the week-long Plein Air Easton arts festival in July. The Waterfowl Festival is always on the second weekend in November.

Information: www.eastonmd.org, or Talbot County Office of Tourism, 410-770-8000; *www.tourtalbot.org*

Middle Choptank

The Choptank River begins to shed its bay-like dimensions east of the mouth of the Tred Avon River, as the channel passes first Island Creek then funnels between Castle Haven and Chlora Point before winding past Cambridge and under the fixed 50-foot Route 50 bridge.

Choptank travelers headed upriver will notice the long finger of land at the tip of Castle Haven on the south shore. The earliest British settlers, seeing this as the shortest distance between two points, established a ferry here in 1690. Chlora Point, the landing on the Talbot County side, was a tract purchased from Edward Lloyd in 1666 by Clora O'Dora for

12,000 pounds of tobacco. At some point, government cartographers misspelled it, and it remains today "Chlora" with an *h*. Later, the ferry was moved upriver to Chancellor Point, more convenient to the growing port of Cambridge. Another two and a half centuries would pass before the upper and lower Eastern Shore would finally be linked by the first bridge at Cambridge, just south of Chancellor Point. With a length of nearly two miles, the span was the longest in the state at the time. President Franklin D. Roosevelt dedicated the new drawbridge by sailing through its opening on the presidential yacht *Sequoia*.

By the 1980s, beach-bound traffic on Route 50's "Sunburst Highway" created the need for a new, fixed bridge, which now

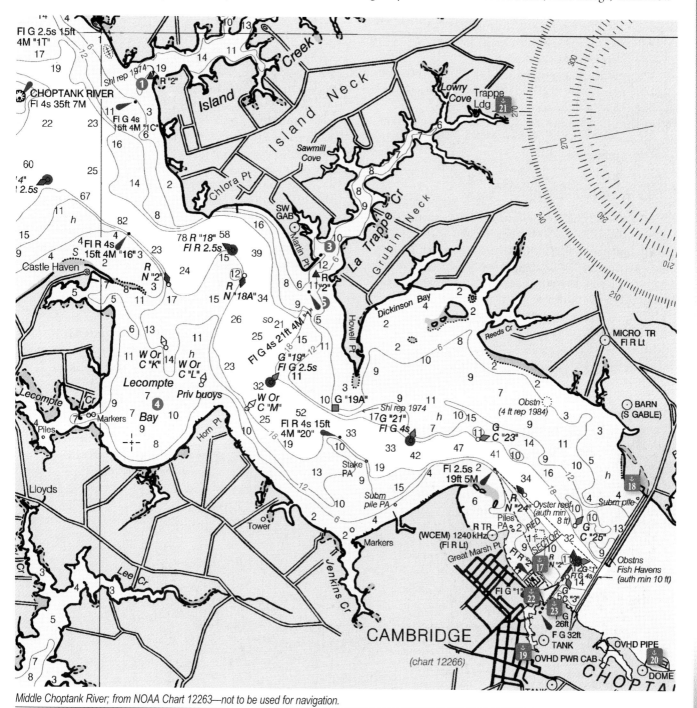

Middle Choptank River; from NOAA Chart 12263—not to be used for navigation.

Island Creek *continued*

prevents sailors with masts loftier than 50 feet from exploring the Choptank River above Cambridge.

Island Creek

❶ **Island Creek** lies just south of the mouth of the Tred Avon River, 1¼ miles southeast of the Choptank River Light. Its entrance channel—distinguished by two marks, flashing "1" and daymark "2"—runs somewhat diagonally across the mouth of the creek, with the first mark at the south or starboard bank. As you enter, keep the green "1" close to port.

The entrance is marked by a wide shoal, all that is left of an island that once stood smack at its doorway. Watch the tides and follow the markers. Many good anchorages lie on both sides of the creek. A small branch on the north side of the creek offers snug protection.

LeCompte Bay

❷ **LeCompte Bay**, the spacious body of water along the southern shore between **Castle Haven Point** and Horn Point, takes its name from the wealthy French Huguenot refugee Antoine LeCompte, who acquired 800 acres here in 1659 by land patent. (You may hear longtime locals pronounce the name *LaCount*.)

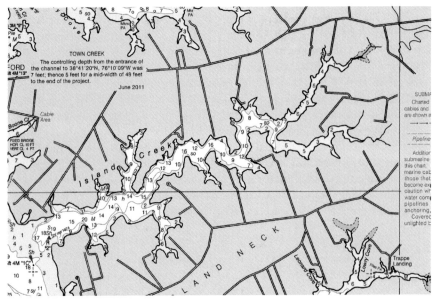

Island Creek; from NOAA Chart 12266—not to be used for navigation.

A prominent wharf and large boathouse stand along Castle Haven's eastern side, but trees hide the handsome home, which dates from 1730. The mansion has seen many owners, among them the Rt. Rev. James Kemp, bishop of Maryland, and Thomas King Carroll, governor of Maryland from 1830 to 1831. The small shallow tributary to the south of the spindly peninsula, also called **Castle Haven**, is tricky to enter and not recommended without local knowledge.

In settled weather, boats anchor in the 7- to 11-foot depths of LeCompte Bay. It is wide and exposed, however, and getting an anchor to dig in can sometimes be a problem. **LeCompte Creek** empties into LeCompte Bay at its southwest corner.

● On Premises
➤ Nearby

Middle Choptank River

	MLW	Overnight Slips	Gas	Diesel	Propane	Electric	Showers	Laundry	Restaurant	Lodging	Pool	Pump-out	Ice	Groceries	Marine Supplies	Bait	Boat Repair	Haul-out Services	Launch Ramp	Wi-Fi	Other
17 Cambridge Municipal Yacht Basin Choptank R./Cambridge 410-228-4031; www.choosecambridge.com	10'	●	●	●	➤	●	●	●	➤	➤	➤	●	●	➤	➤	➤	➤	➤	➤	●	Courtesy bikes, grocery delivery, park-like
18 Ferry Point Marina Choptank R./Route 50 Bridge 410-476-3304; www.ferrypointmarinatalbot.com	4'	●	●	●		●	●	➤	➤	➤	➤	●	●	●	●	●	●	●	➤		50-ton lift; certified techs, ships store
19 Generation III Marina Choptank R./Cambridge Cr. 410-228-2520	12'	●	➤	➤	➤	●	●	➤	➤	➤	➤	●	➤	➤	●	➤	●	●	➤		Full-service, yacht carpentry, awlgrip painting
20 Hyatt River Marsh Marina Choptank R./Cambridge 410-901-6380; www.hyatt.com/gallery/chesamarina	7'	●	●	●		●	●	●	●	●	●	●	●	➤	●	●	➤	●	➤	➤	➤	●	Golf, spa, small boat rentals, mini golf, tennis
21 Oxford Yacht Agency At Dickerson Harbor Choptank R./La Trappe Cr. 410-822-8556; www.oya.com	6'	●				●	●					➤					●	●	➤		Protected harbor; inside storage for large boats
22 Snapper's Waterfront Cafe Choptank R./Cambridge 410-228-0112; www.snapperswaterfrontcafe.com	6'	●				●				●	➤	➤		●	➤	➤	➤			Free dockage for diners, 3 overnight slips, tiki bar
23 Yacht Maintenance Company Choptank R./Cambridge Cr. 410-228-8878; www.yachtmaintenanceco.com	12'	●	➤	➤	➤	●	●	●	➤	➤		●	➤	➤	●	➤	●	●	●	➤		Complete repairs, 300-ton railway; 60-ton lift

Sandbars make this a haven for boats with shallow draft. Enter cautiously, honoring the private aids to navigation.

On October 19, 1814, a British raiding party entered the Choptank and went ashore at Castle Haven to take poultry and cattle at Kemp's farm. During the War of 1812, Charles Goldsborough, a Maryland congressman and later governor, occupied the plantation on the other side of LeCompte Bay at Horn Point. An opponent of the war, Goldsborough wrote detailed observations of the British fleet in Choptank waters.

In later years, Horn Point became a hunting preserve under the ownership of U.S. Sen. Coleman duPont, who used the original 1750 house (later destroyed by fire) as a part-time residence. Today Horn Point Environmental Laboratory, one of three labs of the University of Maryland Center for Environmental Science, occupies the property. It has a national reputation for research in estuarine, ecosystem and aquaculture studies, including restoration ecology. A tour schedule and contact information can be found at *www.umces.edu/hpl/tours*. The docks at the facility are for research vessels only and are not available for public use.

After the original LeCompte estate was divided, many generations of descendants lived along this shoreline. One, James Richardson (1906-1991)—who was descended from a long line of shipwrights—became known for the shipyard he owned and operated here. This is where he and his team of craftsmen built the full-scale reproduction of the 1634 *Maryland Dove* for Historic St. Mary's City. Recognized for his dedication to rediscovering, preserving and passing along boatbuilding methods of the past, the Richardson Maritime Museum in Cambridge was named in his honor.

Dozens of older homes along the Choptank, described

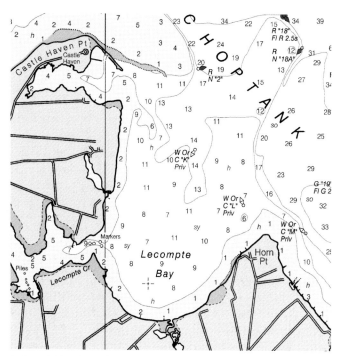

LeCompte Bay; from NOAA Chart 12266—not to be used for navigation.

eloquently in Hulbert Footner's 1944 classic, *Rivers of the Eastern Shore*, have illustrious pasts, and dominant Dorchester and Talbot families produced more than a half-dozen governors. Footner hints that from a certain vantage point in the river one might be within view of all their former homes.

La Trappe Creek

❸ La Trappe Creek's unusual entrance markers resemble little lighthouses. "1" has a green 4-second flasher; "2" is unlit and stands to the northeast, about 350 yards farther inshore.

Once inside La Trappe Creek, most boaters head immediately for the popular and protected cove (7-and-8-foot depths) to port that's formed by the sandbar extending northeast from Martin Point. The inviting spit of sand, however, is privately owned with a thicket of no-trespassing signs, so boaters must stay below the high-tide mark. Farther into the cove, depths drop to 5 feet amid the densely wooded shoreline of a smaller tributary.

Since this anchorage is popular on summer weekends, you might want to continue up La Trappe's twists and turns for other options with peaceful surroundings and good depths. Be mindful to steer clear of all points of land, where shoals may lurk. A mile above Martin Point, **Sawmill Cove** lies around the bend on the port side. With 6 or more feet at its entrance, you can anchor here off the main channel, but be aware that depths drop inside.

Like the late-18th-century farmhouse inside the cove at Martin Point, some of La Trappe's handsome homes are among the oldest on the Chesapeake—dating from Colonial days, when this tributary was known as Dividing Creek. Noteworthy is **Compton**, an eye-catching manse easily seen on the way to Sawmill Cove. With its commanding view of the lower creek, the stately brick manor occupies a peninsula

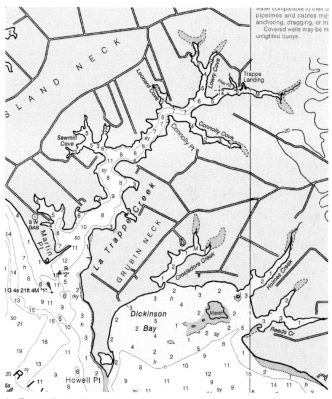

La Trappe Creek; from NOAA Chart 12266—not to be used for navigation.

La Trappe Creek *continued*

on Grubin Neck along the eastern bank.

Compton was originally a modest c.1760 home, but when Samuel Stevens inherited it from his father in 1794, the home was altered to reflect the owner's stature as an influential planter and, eventually, 18th governor of Maryland. After serving Talbot County in the House of Delegates, Stevens was elected in 1822 to the first of three terms as governor. Among his tenure's history-making events was the creation of the Chesapeake and Ohio Canal. Returning to Compton following his last term in Annapolis, Stevens gave the building its present look, adding the east wing and raising the main section to two floors.

Another historic home, north of Sawmill Cove on the western side and more hidden by trees, is **Hampden**. The earliest 17th-century dwelling here was built on a large tract owned by Thomas Martin, who arrived from England in 1663. He named his home for John Hampden, an English statesman who opposed the abuses that had forced the Martin family to emigrate and settle in Maryland. The original part of the residence, c. 1720, is said to be the oldest existing brick structure in Talbot County and retains much of the original exterior and interior detail. The Martins—a politically prominent family that included Daniel Martin, twice governor of Maryland—occupied the land for 223 years, until 1888.

Two other Martin family homes also stand west of La Trappe's waters: Beauvoir, the governor's birthplace, and The Wilderness, his home. Behind them rise a dark forest of trees reminiscent of an old English countryside.

Above Sawmill Cove the main channel narrows, straightens, and turns easterly, still with a good 7 or 8 feet of water at high tide. At Trappe Landing, a public boat ramp has replaced the dock where steamboats once unloaded goods and passengers. Here also the Dickerson Boatyard produced a line of classic boats during the 1960s and 70s. Now occupying the facility at the head of the creek is the Oxford Yacht Agency at Dickerson Harbor, a full-service boatyard. Private daymarks lead to the harbor. Beyond, the water shallows from 6 feet at the docks down to 6 inches just beyond the boatyard.

Cambridge

Established in 1684, ❹ **Cambridge** lies about 13 miles upriver from the mouth of the Choptank, just before a fixed bridge (50-foot clearance) that takes U.S. Route 50 across the river. Long portions of the old drawbridge extend from either shore and are used as fishing and crabbing piers. Shallow-draft vessels can obtain fuel at Gateway Marina on the north shore just before the bridge.

Cruisers visiting Cambridge can find modern overnight slips in a bulkheaded basin on the south shore just west of Cambridge Creek. But Cambridge Municipal Yacht Basin's expansion a few years ago has changed the entrance channel, so use an updated chart. For navigation information, you can also call the dockmaster's office (410-228-4031). The marina monitors VHF channels 16 and 68.

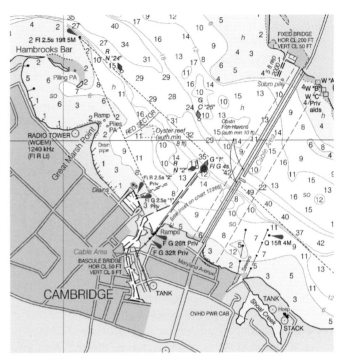

Cambridge; from NOAA Chart 12266—not to be used for navigation.

The entrance, which carries about 7 feet, serves both the town marina and the Cambridge Yacht Club, which occupies the promontory on the northwestern side of the basin. The club offers docking privileges to all. The Municipal Yacht Basin has slips to 50 feet, a fuel dock, pumpout, and other amenities for cruisers. The redesigned basin also includes a replica of the Choptank River screwpile lighthouse, which houses the dockmaster's office and a small museum. The town marina is bordered by a spacious, tree-lined public park popular for group gatherings.

If you're looking for a protected anchorage for the night, you'll find it inside **Cambridge Creek**, where oyster-dredging skipjacks and bugeyes, and cargo-carrying schooners once jammed the harbor rail-to-rail. Today, tall ships and visiting skipjacks make occasional appearances and the *Nathan of Dorchester*, a replica skipjack, runs excursions from here.

The creek is well-marked with paired buoys that extend a half-mile into the Choptank and parallel to the Route 50 bridge. Coming down the channel, follow the buoys toward the bulkheaded keyhole-like opening. You'll see a shipyard to port, then the channel turns to starboard.

Once inside, depths may show more than the charted 9 to 11 feet. While space does not allow room to let out a lot of scope, a couple of boats can anchor safely on the western side near Snapper's Restaurant or to the east near the Jim Richardson Museum's RUARK BOATWORKS. Occasionally, boats find a spot above the bridge near Generation III's boatyard, which offers limited transient dockage. Take care when anchoring anywhere on Cambridge Creek since there's quite a bit of boat traffic coming and going.

Free public docking (limit 48 hours and with no power hook-ups) is available at a long bulkhead in front of the Dorchester County Building, with depths of 10 feet toward the

continued on page 178

Port of Call

Cambridge

The elegant 19th-century homes lining Cambridge's shaded streets hail from a time when the town was an economic and social center—a heritage also proudly preserved in its maritime museum. Today, renovated downtown buildings house chic new shops and galleries as the city undergoes an exciting rebirth.

The Visitor Center at Sailwinds Park East has brochures to acquaint you with the city. The Dorchester Center for the Arts, located in the old Nathan Furniture Store on High Street, showcases visual and performing arts. The Harriet Tubman Museum and Educational Center explores the life of the fomer slave known as "the Moses of her people." Call 410-228-0401 for information). Other guided tours acquaint visitors with different aspects of this growing town, including the anecdote-filled Cambridge Historic Tours (Saturdays at 10 a.m., April-October).

Maritime history is lovingly preserved in Cambridge. The Richardson Maritime Museum, named for boatbuilder and Dorchester County native son "Mr. Jim" Richardson, honors the boats of the Bay and their builders. The museum building on High Street offers a collection of boatbuilders' tools and watermen's artifacts, as well as meticulously constructed models and diplays dedicated to Dickerson yachts and the city's long history of speedboat racing. At its Ruark Boatworks waterfront site overlooking

Cambridge Creek, visitors are welcome to watch or help build and restore traditional wooden boats.

The skipjack *Nathan of Dorchester* lies moored at Long Wharf. Visitors can sail aboard this member of the Bay's skipjack fleet, built by local craftsmen to document the techniques required to produce these traditional workboats of the Bay. The Dorchester Skipjack Committee coordinates an annual race in September for these historic vessels (*www. skipjack-nathan.org*).

Kayakers and cyclists can rent equipment or arrange for guided tours from Blackwater Paddle & Pedal Adventures (*www.blackwaterpaddle-andpedal.com*). A short trolley ride takes visitors to the Hyatt Regency Chesapeake Bay golf course, marina and resort facilities.

The business district, easily reached on foot from the waterfront, is infused with history and old-time charm. Its many galleries and shops offer antiques, home decor, jewelry, art, books and gifts.

Foodstuffs are readily available. At A Few of My Favorite Things, you can stock up on wines and cheeses from around the world as well as coffee

Cambridge

⚓ **Marinas/Dockage**
 1 Municipal Yacht Basin
 2 Cambridge Yacht Club
 3 Hyatt Regency Ches. Bay Marina
 4 Yacht Maintenance Company
 5 Generation III Marina

✪ **Points of Interest**
 6 Dorchester Center for the Arts
 7 Richardson Museum
 8 Harriet Tubman Museum & Educational Center
 9 Ruark Boatworks

❓ **Information**
 10 Sailwinds Park

🍴 **Dining**
 3 Hyatt Regency Chesapeake Bay
 11 Snappers Waterfront Cafe
 12 High Spot
 13 Jimmy and Sooks
 14 Bistro Poplar
 15 Stoked Woodfired
 16 Leaky Pete's Oyster and Wine Bar

🛒 **Groceries/Carryout**
 17 ZipMart (convenience store)
 18 A Few of My Favorite Things
 19 The Creek Deli
 20 Center Market
 21 Convenience store
 22 Kool Ice & Seafood
 23 J. M. Clayton Company (crabs)
 24 Farmers Market
 25 Pep-Up (convenience store)

☼ **Entertainment/Recreation**
 3 Hyatt Regency Resort
 26 Governors Hall

🚲 **Bicycles**

≈ **River Cruises**
 Nathan of Dorchester

🚢 **Lodging**

🍦 **Ice Cream**

⬆ **Park/Playground**

SB **Sandy Beach** (dinghy landing)

✪ **Dorchester General Hospital**

📖 **Library**   ✉ **Post Office**

℞ **Pharmacy**   ⬜ **Laundromat**

👥 **Public Restrooms**

···· **Bus Route**

···· **Historic Walking Tour**
 ★ **Starting Point**

···· **Wetlands Nature Walk**

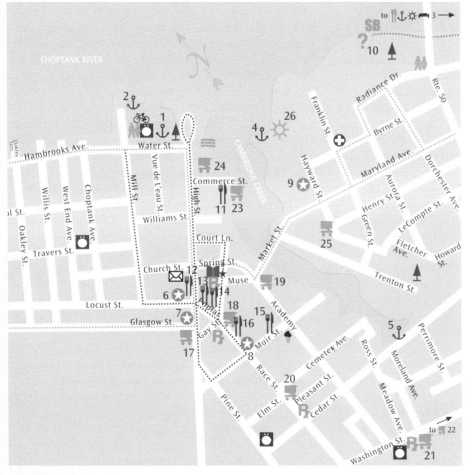

Port of Call Cambridge continued

beans and teas. Fresh produce is available at Center Market, a neighborhood grocery, or at the Farmers Market (days can change, so check for this season's schedule) on Long Wharf, adjacent to the town marina. Buy fresh-from-the-boat live crabs, steamed crabs and packed crabmeat at J.M. Clayton Company (ice available, bring a container) or pick up fresh or packaged seafood at Kool Ice & Seafood. For extensive grocery shopping take public transportation to the Super Fresh or Wal-Mart on Route 50.

Cambridge harbor was once thick with oystermen's boats, a seafood heritage still reflected in many restaurants. Snappers Waterfront Cafe offers seafood and dockage for diners. A walk up HIgh Street brings you to several enticing restaurants and coffee shops, like High Spot, Jimmie & Sooks and Bistro Poplar. The Hyatt Regency, above the Route 50 bridge, offers dockage for its four dining locations, all open to the public: Blue Point Provision Company (Eastern Shore cuisine), Water's Edge Grill, Dock's Poolside (light fare) and Eagle's Nest Bar and Grille.

On Second Saturdays, shops extend their hours while museums and galleries host special openings. Local heritage figures in many of Cambridge's annual events, which include the Heart of Chesapeake Country Heritage Day, the Groove City Jazz and Blues Fest, Taste of

Art Smith

Cambridge Crab Cook-Off, the Cambridge Classic Powerboat Regatta (hydroplane and flat-bottom boat races, photo above), the Peach Festival and Seafood Feast-I-Val. In September, the Dorchester Showcase features juried artworks. Interspersed with the city's busy calendar are concerts, events and festivals at Sailwinds Park East.

Information: Dorchester County Department of Tourism, 800-522-TOUR; *www.tourdorchester.org.* Cambridge Main Street, *www.cambridge-mainstreet.com.*

Cambridge continued from page 176

middle, less at either end. Dorchester County public buses run to Vienna, Hurlock, East New Market and the local Wal-Mart and shopping center; call 410-221-1910 to arrange pickup.

Small condos and townhouses (with private docks) occupy land once dominated by seafood processing plants, oil tanks and other industry. Several boatyards here have given way to more condos, but Cambridge is still a working port and its businesses can handle almost any marine job. Past and present blend: A restaurant adjoins the last crab-processing operation on the creek, the family-run J. M. Clayton Company, which dates to 1890. "The oldest working

crab-processing plant in the world," the company proudly declares. And who are we to argue? Certainly, Clayton's lump crabmeat is said to rival any on the Bay and is regularly purchased by many of the Bay's best restaurants.

A bascule bridge at Maryland Avenue, the town's busiest street, separates the anchorage basin from the inner creek. It opens on signal from 6 a.m. to 8 p.m. (410-228-8311; channel 13). The inner creek is deep, narrow and less than a mile long. Beyond the Maryland Avenue bridge, the once commercial shoreline now holds tall condominiums. Portside Restaurant is to port. Generation III boatyard is farther up.

On the Choptank River beyond the Route 50 bridge, the Hyatt Regency Chesapeake Bay Resort boasts a 150-slip

● On Premises
➤ Nearby

	MLW	Overnight Slips	Gas	Diesel	Propane	Electric	Showers	Laundry	Restaurant	Lodging	Pool	Pump-out	Ice	Groceries	Marine Supplies	Bait	Boat Repair	Haul-out Services	Launch Ramp	Wi-Fi	Other
Upper Choptank River																					
Choptank Marina Choptank R./town of Choptank; 410-479-8120; *www.caroline md.org/facilities/facility/details/Choptank-Marina-9*	6'	●				●			➤			●	●	➤					●		70 slips, boat ramp
Mathews Landing Choptank R./Denton 443-786-9551; *www.mathewsboats.com*	20'	●							➤							●		●	●	●	Full-service working boatyard
Suicide Bridge Restaurant and Marina Choptank R./Cabin Cr. 410-943-4689 or 410-943-4775; *www.suicidebridge.com*	5'	●	➤	➤		●			●	➤		●	●	➤					➤	●	Waterfront dining, fresh seafood, crabs, river cruises

marina with fuel. Its fixed docks are fairly well protected by a floating bulkhead. Overnight transient boaters are welcome to use the resort's pools and other amenities, including its spa and three restaurants. The resort provides limited complimentary dockage for diners as well as land transportation to and from the Municipal Yacht Basin for sailors unable to pass under the 50-foot bridge. Golfers can register in advance to play the resort's 18-hole River Marsh Golf Club (410-901-6396). Transient dockage for golfers is also available.

Upper Choptank

Beyond Cambridge, the Choptank runs long and deep, often carrying 30 feet or more, to Denton. As it winds through fields, forests and marshes, the upper Choptank and its shoreline teem with wildlife and birds, and the river is easily navigable for 25 miles above the Route 50 bridge. The only vertical hindrance you'll encounter before reaching the town of Denton—at least for the time being—is a swing bridge (10 feet vertical clearance) that carries Route 331 (Dover Road) over the river about halfway between Cambridge and Denton. Referred to on charts as the "Dover Swing Bridge," the span was named for a nearby village that no longer exists. This once-busy port of call teemed with wooden vessels that ventured upstream far enough to reach the fresh water that would kill the teredo worms—"termites of the sea"—that ravaged the wooden hulls. The old swing bridge, however, is slated to be replaced in the next year or so with a fixed bridge with a vertical clearance of 48 feet.

If you can do it, this pretty stretch of river is well worth the exploration. It was once a major industrial route for schooners, steamboats, pungies and other working craft. From Colonial times through the early 1900s, about 20 landings lay along the upper Choptank. In some places, you can still see the old wharves protruding above the water. If you plan to cruise the upper river, the CHOPTANK RIVER HERITAGE CENTER's website,

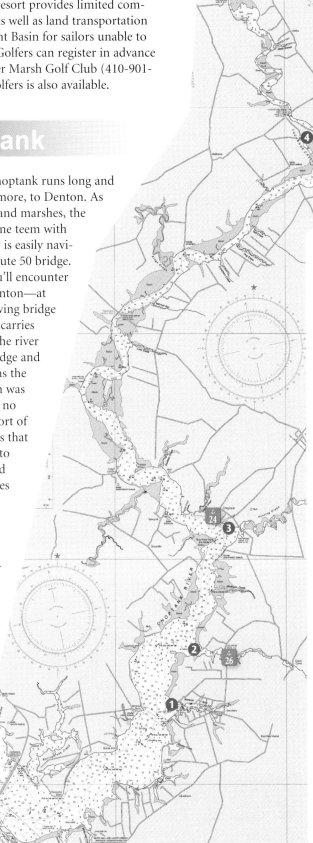

Upper Choptank River; from NOAA Chart 12266— not to be used for navigation.

choptankriverheritage.org, has historic information and maps.

With the exception of the splendidly named Pealiquor Shoal opposite the mouth of Watts Creek, navigation is easy. Shoals extend from the points, of course, and deep water follows the outside edge of the bends, usually close to shore. Buoys and daymarks designate the shoals, and your course will take you from one nav aid to the next.

Jamaica Point appears to port about a half-mile past green can "35". Across from this spot, the **① Warwick River** branches off. A narrow channel in the river leads to the town of **Secretary**, named for Henry Sewall, secretary of the province under Charles Calvert, third Lord Baltimore. Sewall was granted a few thousand acres here and settled it.

About a mile farther on, you'll find little **② Cabin Creek** (opposite flashing "38"), whose entrance is marked by a red "2". Daymarks have been added at the mouth and inside the creek, though Suicide Bridge, with a 7-foot vertical clearance, prevents most boaters from traveling farther up the creek. Legend has it a local postmaster was the first

Upper Choptank *continued*

to perish after plunging off the wooden bridge over Cabin Creek, although it's unclear precisely when the span earned its unfortunate nickname. The original bridge was built in 1888 and two more have replaced it, each retaining the tragic name. Cabin Creek is home to Suicide Bridge Restaurant, which is known for its seafood and dockside (5-feet) amenities.

A couple of miles upriver of Cabin Creek you'll find an anchorage off Bow Knee Point at green daymark "41". You can nestle into the small cove at the point's southern end in 8 feet of water with good holding ground.

Across the river is the village of ❸ **Choptank**, a charming hamlet that was home to several thriving cannery operations in the late 19th and early 20th centuries. The county-operated Choptank Marina (protected by a wooden bulkhead) sells gas and diesel fuel Friday through Sunday, May to November. Dockside depths are 3 feet MLW, and a few of their 70 slips are available for transient use.

Above the Dover Swing Bridge (hail the bridge tender on channel 13 or call 410-822-0538 or 410-770-3306), and opposite the mouth of the ❹ **Tuckahoe River**, lies Gilpin Point, where colonial residents established a ferry across the river to Price's Landing on Tuckahoe Neck. It was also the home of Colonel William Richardson, a hero of the Revolution. His tomb is here, along with all that remains of his house—one crumbling wall.

Early Bay history is more visible at Potter's Landing near the mouth of ❺ **Watts Creek**, which is home to Martinak State Park. Under a shelter within the park, you can see the reassembled remains of a Chesapeake Bay pungy schooner built between 1840 and 1880 and discovered about a century later when the state of Maryland was constructing a boat ramp on Watts Creek. Hard-working vessels in the Bay's commercial sailing fleet, these swift boats were used on the ocean as well as the Bay, serving well into the 20th century. Shallow-draft vessels can tie up at Martinak Park's pier (4-foot depths) adjacent to the boat ramp or along the bulkhead and make use of picnic tables, grills, campground, cabins, playground, restrooms and nature center. Take a kayak to discover

additional traces of history—and great scenery—along the creek near the park or up the nearby Tuckahoe River. The Tuckahoe, though long and in places deep, is full of snags and unexpected shoals, so navigation is difficult in anything larger than a kayak or small skiff.

As you approach the charming town of ❻ **Denton**, the Choptank's quiet shoreline gives way to waterfront homes. At red "80", the bridge carrying Business Route 404 into Denton comes into view. There's deep water beyond the fixed bridge,(vertical clearance 24 ½ feet). But for high rigs and sailboats, anchoring in 8 feet of water is possible to starboard immediately before the bridge. Below the bridge to port, you'll see a reconstruction of the Maryland Steamboat Company's 19th-century Joppa Wharf, part of the Choptank River Heritage Center museum complex in West Denton.

Denton is constructing a public facility for small boats above the bridge. And across the river, one of the marine facilities may have a slip. Otherwise, anchoring out is the only option for visiting this thoroughly delightful town. Be advised that the current runs strong here.

Beyond Denton, the upper Choptank meanders another eight miles or so to **Greensboro**. It's a great opportunity for a dinghy excursion.

Little Choptank River

The **Little Choptank River**, full of creeks and crannies, can be easily overlooked since it has no "destination" ports, but it more than makes up for this failing in sheer beauty, with two real gems out of history's pages: Old Trinity Church and Spocott Windmill.

Coming from the north, you should have no trouble entering the wide mouth of the Little Choptank above **James Island**. Give Hills Point and its outlying shoals a wide berth—they are marked by flashing green "1". Coming from the south, around James Island, both green "1" at the river's mouth and green "3" farther in are often hard to pick up against the wooded shoreline. On such occasions, plan to practice your navigational skills (or make good use of your chartplotter).

● On Premises
➤ Nearby

	MLW	Overnight Slips	Gas	Diesel	Propane	Electric	Showers	Laundry	Restaurant	Lodging	Pool	Pump-out	Ice	Groceries	Marine Supplies	Boat Repair	Bait	Haul-out Services	Launch Ramp	Wi-Fi	Other
Little Choptank River																					
27 Madison Bay Marina & Campground & Restaurant — Little Choptank R./Madison Bay — 410-228-4111/410-228-1108	6'	●				●	●	●	●				●					➤		●	Lounge, bar, restaurant, campground
28 Slaughter Creek Marina — Little Choptank R./Slaughter Cr. — 410-221-0050; www.slaughtercreekmarina.com	6'	●	●	●	●	●	●	●	●	➤	●	●	●	➤	●		●	●	➤	●	Restaurant, boat rentals, beer, ice, store, pool
29 Taylors Island Family Campground — Chesapeake Bay/Taylors Island — 410-397-3275	3'	●	●		●		●	●	➤	➤		●	●	●	●	●			●		

Little Choptank River; from NOAA Chart 12263—not to be used for navigation.

Hudson Creek

Farther up the Little Choptank, you will probably want to bypass the first creek you come to on the north side. **Brooks Creek** has a very narrow entrance and offers little protection from winds blowing off the Bay. But just beyond it lies, Hudson Creek, with its picture-perfect anchorage. Here you'll find a peaceful haven where you can sit on the deck of your boat and enjoy the birds and wildlife. Spring and fall are particularly pleasant for watching migratory ducks, geese and swans. While the shores are low and marshy, great groves of loblolly pines help shelter you when the wind kicks up. While you will almost always see a few yachts anchored in Hudson Creek on a summer weekend, the area is still relatively undiscovered by the cruising crowd.

Casson Point (locally pronounced *KAY-sahn*) on the northern shore of the river marks the entrance to ❷ **Hudson Creek.** Give green "7" a wide berth to avoid the shoaling off the point, and, to miss shoaling east of the point, don't head directly from "7" to green "1" inside the mouth of the creek, but instead bear off slightly to starboard.

The ideal place to drop the hook is just west of red day-

Slaughter Creek

❶ **Slaughter Creek** lies a mile due south of the Little Choptank's faxed flashing "5". It offers visiting cruisers fuel, supplies and marina service. The creek also leads to a small, quiet village inhabited by watermen and farmers.

The entrance markers guide you into a narrow channel. Sound your way in carefully. If draft is an issue, call the local marina for information, since shoaling to 3 feet has been reported, especially in the areas between "4" and "8". The general recommendation is to favor greens "5" and "7" and then to move to the middle at red "8" and green "9".

About two miles upstream, and near the bridge (vertical clearance 10 feet), Slaughter Creek Marina offers gas, diesel, supplies, lodging and other services, including haul-outs. Transient slips are available. There is anchorage room for a boat or two, but try to find a spot upstream just beyond the marina in order to avoid boating traffic. A barge at the marina houses Palm Beach Willies, an eatery and bar that's open seasonally (410-221-5111). Across the bridge, you'll find the tiny **Taylors Island** community. Here you can purchase a few foodstuffs (milk, bread) or sit down to a big cheeseburger and a real milkshake at the Island Grille.

Slaughter Creek, which divides Taylors Island from the rest of mainland Dorchester County, has the feeling of being very remote . . . even by Eastern Shore standards.

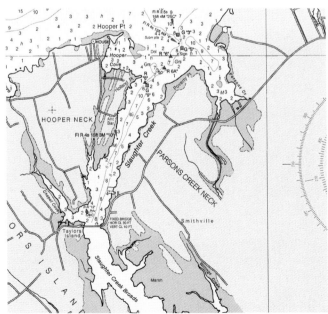

Slaughter Creek; from NOAA Chart 12264—not to be used for navigation.

Slaughter Creek *continued*

mark "2" in the cove formed by the curving arm of Casson Point with its sandy beach. When the moon rises over the trees, illuminating the sand and the water all around you, there are few prettier spots on the Bay.

However, if this anchorage is too crowded, head farther up the creek beyond green "3". (There are no markers beyond "3", but you should find plenty of water in the center of the creek.) Two unnamed coves lie on the west shore, the second being deeper and wider than the first. Both are wide enough to catch a summer breeze, and you will find at least 5 or 6 feet of water at the coves' mouths.

Most of Hudson is navigable for boats with less than 5 feet of draft if you care to explore, but there are no public landings along the creek, only some private docks. Often the residents of the creek use their small pleasure boats to go visiting after dinner, just as Bay residents did 100 years ago. These residents, as well as watermen heading home in the afternoon and evening, are usually the only traffic on the upper portion of the creek, which eventually becomes extremely narrow and marshy.

Madison Bay

Beyond Slaughter Creek on the southern shoreline, **Parsons Creek** and **Woolford Creek** are both too shallow for most cruising boats. But farther east, past Woolford Neck, lies ❸ **Madison Bay**. From the Little Choptank's "9", this long slender bay has a natural channel that begins about a half-mile to the southeast. A single mark, lighted "2", identifies the skinniest spot in its bottleneck entrance. With shoal edges and exposure, the cove isn't suitable as an anchorage except for shallow drafts under settled conditions.

Good depths of 7 to 8 feet in the center, however, lead to a dredged channel toward a county boat ramp and Madison Bay Marina in the southwest corner. Besides transient slips at the marina/campground, the adjacent bar/restaurant serves lunch and dinner. A short walk through the tiny community of **Madison** will take you to an intriguing old cemetery.

Fishing Creek

On the south shore of the Little Choptank, just beyond Madison Bay, is ❹ **Fishing Creek**. Finding its entrance is easy, since the shoal northeast of McKeil Point is marked by daymark "2", and about a half mile upstream is green daymark "3".

If you are looking for a protected anchorage, check out the Cherry Point area. Here you can skirt around the point, putting it between you and a northerly; or you can anchor north of Cherry Point, to escape anything from the south. On the other hand, if the weather is not a threat, you can launch your dinghy and take a pleasant ride along the shore. The scenery is beautiful, featuring a low shoreline covered by dense pine woods.

Above Cherry Point, there are more gunkholing opportunities as long as you keep to the middle of the road. As the charts show, you'll find only about 5 feet of water just

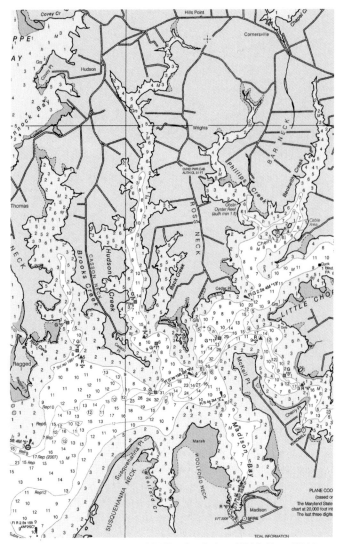

Hudson Creek, Madison Bay and Phillips Creek; from NOAA Chart 12264— not to be used for navigation.

off Cherry Point, but there ought to be plenty of depth just beyond the point, and lovely scenery to boot.

Church Creek branches off to the south about two miles from McKeil Point, but it is best suited for exploration by dinghy and kayak. Depths quickly drop off about three-quarters of a mile from the creek's mouth, becoming increasingly skinny to its head. One shallow cove to port one-half mile into the creek has swinging room, but only 3- to 5-foot charted depths.

At the head of Church Creek is the church for which the creek was named. OLD TRINITY CHURCH, meticulously restored and maintained, and still in use by an active congregation, welcomes small boats at its tiny dock, but vessels drawing 3 feet or more must anchor fairly far from it. This tiny brick church, built between 1670 and 1680, is a living reminder of the area's early heritage, with decor true to the colonial period. Its well kept cemetery, framed by ancient trees, contains the graves of veterans of every American war, Governor Thomas Carroll of Maryland and his firebrand daughter Anna Ella Carroll. Anna Ella was a political activist in her own right. Her writings largely contributed to keeping Maryland in the Union, and she later served as an

Fishing Creek; from NOAA Chart 12264—not to be used for navigation.

Chesapeake Beach to Cove Point

On the Western Shore, between Herring Bay and the Patuxent River, cruisers will find little shelter and few services. Instead, travelers find a nearly unbroken shoreline, guarded by clay-red cliffs that soar above the Chesapeake's normally flat landscape.

Chesapeake Beach

❶ Chesapeake Beach on **Fishing Creek**, about three miles south of Holland Point, is the principal exception to the rule. Its port offers both shelter and services. Early in the last century, it was a popular resort and amusement park, complete with its own railroad spur.

Flashing green "1" marks the channel into a Bay-side marina and into Fishing Creek, where the town's full-service marinas are located. The channel has been dredged to 8 feet, but creek depths are closer to 5.

The first marina, Rod 'N Reel at Chesapeake Beach Resort & Spa, sits at the entrance to Fishing Creek. The fuel dock and tackle shop at Rod 'N Reel Marina (which happens to be home to one of the Bay's largest charter fishing fleets) are open daily in season. Rod 'N Reel Marina West lies

advisor to Abraham Lincoln. The church is open to visitors every day except Tuesdays (410-228-2940).

Phillips Creek

If Hudson Creek is a little too crowded to suit you, proceed farther east to **❺ Phillips Creek**, which joins the Little Choptank at the river's last lighted mark, green flashing "13" on a dolphin off Cedar Point. The long bar (depth 2 feet) on the eastern side at the creek's entrance requires careful navigation. If you line up "13" on your stern and the tip of land to the north (where Phillips Creek swings away from **Beckwith Creek**) on your bow, you should steer clear of the long shoal.

Inside, the water has depths of 7 and 8 feet. On the east side of this little bay, where Beckwith Creek branches off to the northeast, stands **Cherry Island** (private property), conspicuous by its square tower. You can anchor on the southern and east sides of the island in about 8 feet of water or at the mouth of Beckwith Creek, where Cherry Island provides shelter from the southwest. Be sure to give the shoal south of the island (near the tower) a wide berth.

Beyond the entrance to Phillips Creek and Beckwith Creek at "13" off Cedar Point, the Little Choptank continues for another 2 miles in an easterly direction before it turns north at the fork between **Gary Creek** and **Lee Creek**. Cruisers will find good anchorage and solitude in the mouth of **Smith Cove** as well as at the fork of Gary and Lee creeks.

At the head of Gary Creek and just upstream from Smith Cove is Spocott Windmill. While it may be visible, it's inaccessible by water due to 2-foot depths and an impenetrable stretch of marsh. Built in 1972 by master boatwright Jim Richardson, this English-style post windmill is a replica of what was used to grind corn and wheat for local farmers in this once self-contained community. The millstones and steps are from the original structure, which stood on this spot until it was destroyed in an 1888 blizzard. The site includes other historic rural Dorchester buildings. (410-228-7670, *spocottwindmill.org*).

www.flagharbor.com

A Condominium Marina with on–site Marine Service

- Deep Draft Slips to 50'
- Heated/AC Bathrooms
- 30 Amp Shore Power/Water
- Gas Dock • Pumpout
- Fish Cleaning Station
- Pool • Picnic Pavillion
- Dinghy dock w/Storage
- WiFi • Access to Beach
- Restaurants, Supplies Nearby
- 20 Ton Travel Lift

Flag Harbor Condo Assoc. **(410) 586–0070** / fhca@flagharbor.com
Flag Harbor Marine Service **(410) 586–1915** / flagboatyard@gmail.com
1565 Flag Harbor Boulevard | St. Leonard, MD 20685

Flag Harbor Yacht Haven
on the bay in Calvert County

just beyond the fixed bridge (10 foot vertical clearance) and includes a launch ramp with plenty of parking. In addition to the two marinas, the 72-room resort offers luxurious suites, two waterfront restaurants and a boardwalk cafe. Farther down Fishing Creek, you'll find Abner's Crab House, with dockage for diners.

From the marinas, cruisers have easy access to the town and its grocery store, pharmacy, post office, bank, library, water park and numerous restaurants. The CHESAPEAKE BEACH RAILWAY MUSEUM, located in a renovated train station next to the hotel, is dedicated to the old amusement park and the railroad that served it (open daily, 1-4 p.m., in season).

Two public beaches, each with a fishing pier and boardwalk, lie about a mile's walk from Chesapeake Beach. Bay Front Park (known locally as Brownie's Beach) is south of town. To the north is the municipal beach at **North Beach**. Here you can tie up at the town pier and spend the day ashore, shopping and dining. North Beach pier's only protection, however, is a stone breakwater.

Calvert Cliffs

South of Chesapeake Beach, there are two more sheltering possibilities, both at marinas located in tight harbors; there is no protected place here to anchor in a storm. The first is at Breezy Point Marina on **Plum Point Creek**. The entrance is marked by green can "1". Stay east of "1" to avoid shoals that extend northeasterly from Plum Point. Once inside, the shallow channel (often as little as 4 feet, though it is dredged to 6 feet regularly) leads under fixed cables (charted 52-foot clearance) to the marina, a full-service facility with launch ramp, fuel, fishing and boating supplies.

South of Plum Point, the shoreline is impenetrable until **Flag Harbor**. This protected, man-made basin is nestled in the area called **Long Beach**, about 10 miles south of Chesapeake Beach and 2 miles north of the Calvert Cliffs Nuclear Power Plant's readily-identifiable towers. It's a challenge to find in poor visibility or at night. Approaching from the eastern side of the Bay, look for the red and white "CP" buoy, about 5 miles north of Cove Point, and proceed almost due west for about

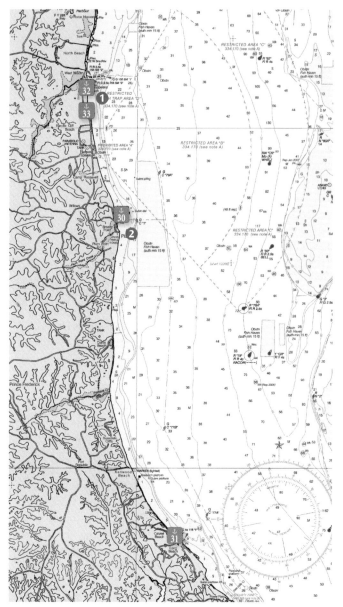

Chesapeake Beach to Cove Point; from NOAA Chart 12264—not to be used for navigation.

Legend
● On Premises
► Nearby

Chesapeake Beach/Flag Harbor

	MLW	Overnight Slips	Gas	Diesel	Propane	Electric	Showers	Laundry	Restaurant	Lodging	Pool	Pump-out	Ice	Groceries	Marine Supplies	Bait	Boat Repair	Haul-out Services	Launch Ramp	Wi-Fi	Other
Breezy Point Marina (30) Chesapeake Bay/Plum Point Cr. 301-758-9981; www.breezypointmarina.com	4.5'	●	●	●	►	●	●	►	►	►	►	●	●	●	●	●	●	●	●	●	Immediate access to Bay, 5 miles S. of Ches. Beach
Flag Harbor Marine Service & Flag Harbor Condo Assoc. (31) Flag Harbor/Long Beach; 410-586-1915—yard/repairs; 410-586-0070—slip sales/rentals; www.flagharbor.com	7	●		●	►	●	●		►	►	●	●	►	►		►	●	●		●	Condo Marina w/ separate marine service businesses
Rod 'N Reel Dock at Chesapeake Beach Resort & Spa (32) Chesapeake Beach/Fishing Cr. 301-855-8450; www.cbresortspa.com	4.5'	●	●	●	►	●	●	►	●	●	●	●	●	►	●	►	►	●	►	►	Charter fishing, restaurants, 72-room hotel & spa
Rod 'N Reel Marina West (33) Chesapeake Beach/Fishing Cr. 410-257-4392; www.cbresortspa.com	5'	●	►	●	►	●	●	►	●	●	●	●	●	●	►	●	►		●		2-ton lift; near water park, ballfields, beach

4 1/2 miles. Along the western shore, head toward green can "77A", northeast of Flag Harbor's flashing red and green entrance lights. A good landmark is the 20-foot white pylon on the beach north of the entrance channel's stone jetties.

Flag Harbor Yacht Haven is a private condominium marina that accepts transients only under special circumstances, such as an emergency or storm. In addition, space inside the basin is at a premium, with no room to anchor.

Dominating the 30-mile stretch between Chesapeake Beach and Drum Point are the imposing ❷ **Calvert Cliffs**. These Miocene-era promontories, formed when the region was covered by a warm tropical sea, became exposed after water receded millions of years ago. Ever since, the cliffs have been eroding, yielding shark teeth and other fossils. The paleontology gallery at the Calvert Marine Museum at Solomons explains the Bay's prehistoric past with detailed exhibits and fossils. Anchoring offshore to explore the cliff base is recommended only during daylight hours and in calm conditions.

Strictly enforced security zones surround both the

Calvert Cliffs Power Plant and the LNG facility about 3 miles south of it. These additions to the shoreline overshadow the picturesque and still active Cove Point Lighthouse, c. 1828. The Coast Guard requires all boat traffic to remain at least 500 yards from the liquid gas pier, which sits offshore. White buoys mark the corners of the security zone, each flashing white after dark. Entry within this security zone is prohibited.

VOTED BEST RESORT

3 YEARS IN A ROW!

Charter Fishing Capital of Maryland since 1946. Voted Best Resort Spa by What's Up! Magazine, Best of The Bay by Bay Weekly Magazine, and top ten best resorts and lodges in Maryland by About.com. Hotel with two Marinas with Transient and Annual Slips, Waterfront Dining, Charter Fishing, Water Rentals, Gaming, Salon & Spa, Live Entertainment & Family Fun Packages available.

CM.PHOTOGRAPHY

DETOTO PHOTO

Best of 2014-2015 WHAT'S UP? BEAUTY & FITNESS

CHESAPEAKE BEACH RESORT & SPA
WHERE HOSPITALITY MEETS THE BAY™

CBRESORTSPA.COM ✦ 866.312.5596 ✦ 4165 MEARS AVE ✦ CHESAPEAKE BEACH, MD

HOTEL ✦ SPA ✦ RESTAURANTS ✦ WEDDINGS ✦ MEETINGS ✦ MARINAS ✦ FISHING ✦ GAMING

Patuxent River

For some, the **Patuxent River** is synonymous with Solomons, that boaters' mecca known for its sheltered harbor, diverse restaurants and fascinating museum. But cruisers who venture up the river itself will find there's much more to discover along its big-shouldered channel, where the banks rise 100 feet in some places. The Patuxent beyond Solomons boasts snug anchorages, stunning scenery, a tidewater plantation you can tour, and one of the Bay's most unusual marinas.

Solomons

➊ **Solomons**, a one-time watermen's village and boatbuilding center at the mouth of the Patuxent has become one of the most popular cruising destinations on the Western Shore —and with good reason. Discovered by the boating crowd in the late 1970s, it has become a modern yachting hub filled with marinas offering myriad amenities. Retirement retreats and weekend residences edge a landscaped shoreline now cleared of derelict boats, crab shacks and rickety piers.

Once inside the protected, deep-water harbor, boaters have many choices for tying up or anchoring out. As a major cruising destination and a home port for recreational boaters, Solomons attracts people from all around the world.

Approaching Solomons, a mile beyond Drum Point, be aware of "the Flats," a kind of submerged island. Its perimeter is well-marked and you can pass safely on either side. Just don't try to go inside it. If taking the mid-channel path, give the lighted pier and flashing green "3" in front of Chesapeake Biological Laboratory plenty of room. Straight ahead on entering the harbor is the small, bulkheaded **Molly's Leg Island**. Mind the marks and pass it on either side.

The inner harbor forks into three channels that lead to the Narrows, Back Creek and Mill Creek. The short northwest waterway called **the Narrows** dead-ends at the causeway that brings the highway onto Solomons Island proper. The mouth of **Back Creek** lies to the north, offering anchorages a short dinghy ride from marinas, restaurants and the CALVERT MARINE MUSEUM. In the anchorage east of the museum's screwpile lighthouse, Zahniser's Yachting Center has nine moorings for rent on a first-come-first-served basis. Moored boats have full marina privileges (including pool and courtesy bikes) as well as a ringside seat for the fleet of Lilliputian remote-controlled skipjacks that race near the lighthouse every second and fourth Sunday. Zahniser's also has some services for anchored boats (dinghy landing, trash disposal, showers) for a fee. On Back Creek during World War II, troops trained for amphibious landings at what is now Calvert Marina. A few vestiges of that time remain.

Many cruisers prefer anchorages on the third split, **Mill Creek**, to the east. About one-half mile up from the island, just past lighted "3", you'll see boats snuggled against the west shore, anchored in 10 to 15 feet of water. You can drop your hook here fairly close to shore.

If this looks crowded, just go farther upstream (noting that Mill Creek makes a sharp right turn at Pancake Point while **St. John Creek** continues straight ahead). You can spend a peaceful night in the broad part of Mill Creek just past **Old House Cove**, where the bottom is hard mud. You may have difficulty keeping

Patuxent River; from NOAA Chart 12264—not to be used for navigation.

your anchor from dragging in **Leason Cove** just opposite Old House Cove. Leason can be a little tight for a larger boat, and if a sudden "duster" should spring up out of the west, your anchor may not hold in the soft mud bottom.

Although some boats choose to anchor out in the river just inside Drum Point, between the Flats and the shoreline, it may not be the best choice. The passing parade of fishing boats makes things rocky, with the result that anchored boats can get quite a jostling. The holding ground is relatively good, but a wind shift could dislodge the anchor.

For small boats, there is a county launch ramp directly alongside the Route 4 bridge with the permit office on site. No overnight parking is allowed, but Spring Cove Marina can usually accommodate parking in the storage yard (call 410-326-2161 in advance). Nearby you'll find a convenience

continued on page 194

● On Premises
➤ Nearby

Patuxent River

Marina	MLW	Overnight Slips	Gas	Diesel	Propane	Electric	Showers	Laundry	Restaurant	Lodging	Pool	Pump-out	Ice	Groceries	Marine Supplies	Bait	Boat Repair	Haul-out Services	Launch Ramp	Wi-Fi	Other
Blackstone Marina Patuxent R./Cuckhold Cr. 301-373-2015; www.blackstonemarina.com	14'		➤			●						●			●			●	● ●		
Boatel California Patuxent R./Town Cr. 301-737-1400; www.boatelcalifornia.com	6'	●				●							●		●		●	●	●	●	New/used boats, sales/ service/parts; private marina
Calvert Marina Patuxent R./Back Cr. 410-326-4251; www.calvertmarina.com	14'	●	●	●	➤	●	●	●	●	➤	●	●	●	➤	●	➤	●	●	●	●	Floating docks, covered slips, 2 restaurants, BoatU.S.
Comfort Inn Beacon Marina Patuxent R./Back Cr. 410-326-6303	12'	●	➤	➤	●	●	●	●	●	●	●	●		●	➤	➤	➤	➤	➤	➤	Picnic area, outdoor hot tub
DeSoto's Landing Marina & Boatel Patuxent R./Rt. 231 bridge 301-870-8145	5'		●			●							●			●		●	●	●		Full-service marina/boatel, MerCruiser dealer
Harbor Island Marina Patuxent R./Solomons Harbor 410-326-3441; www.harborislandmarina.net	12'	●	●	●	➤	●	●	●	➤	●	●	➤	●	●	➤	●	●	●	●	●	Storage, Charles Street Brasserie, charter fishing
Len's Marina Patuxent R./Broomes Island 410-586-0077; www.lensmarina.com	4'	●	●			●			➤				●	●	●	●	●	●	●	●		Dry storage, slips, store, full-service, boat ramp
Point Patience Marina U.S. Navy Recreation Center MM Patuxent R./Second Cove 410-326-4009; www.cnic.navy.mil	6.5'	●	➤	➤	➤	●	●	●	●	➤	●	➤	●	➤	➤	●	●	➤	➤	●	Call ahead; cabins, courtesy bikes
Solomons Harbor Marina Patuxent R./Back Cr. 410-326-1052; www.solomonsharbormarina.com	8'- 12'	●	➤	➤	●	●	●	●	●	●	●	●	●	●	●	➤	●	●	➤	●	Transient dockage to 65 ft., cable
Solomons Yachting Center Patuxent R./Solomons Harbor 866-597-6862; www.solomonsyachtingcenter.com	12'	●	●	●	●	●	●	●	●	●	●	●	●	●	●	●	➤	●	●	●	Floating piers, pool, lounge area, DIY yard
Southern Maryland Boat Works Patuxent R./Back Cr. 410-326-3256; www.drumptmarine.com	7'	➤	➤	➤	➤	➤	➤	➤	➤	➤	➤	➤	➤	➤	➤	●		●	●		
Spring Cove Marina Patuxent R./Back Cr. 410-326-2161; www.springcovemarina.com	10'	●	●	●	●	●	●	●	●	➤	●	●	●	●	●	●	●	●	➤	●	Family friendly resort, full-service marina & yard, picnic area
Town Creek Point Marina Patuxent R./Town Cr. 301-863-6854; www.towncreekpointmarina.com	8'	●				●	●	●				●	●							●	Heavy-duty piers, mobile pump-out
Vera's White Sands Beach Club Patuxent R./St. Leonard Cr. 410-586-1182; www.verasbeachclub.com	12'	●	●	●		●	●	●		●		●	●					●	●	●	Indoor/outdoor dining, veranda overlooks water
Washburn's Boat Yard Patuxent R./Back Cr. 410-326-6701; www.washburnsboatyard.com	11'	➤	➤	➤	➤	➤	➤	➤	➤	➤	➤	➤	➤	●		●	●		●		mechanical & fiberglass repair
West Basin Marina MM Patuxent R./Patuxent Naval Air Station 301-342-3573	15'	●	●	●		●	●	●				●		➤				●	●	●	Facilities for military or DOD only, must show ID
Zahniser's Yachting Center Patuxent R./Back Cr. 410-326-2166; www.zahnisers.com	14'	●	➤	➤	➤	●	●	●	●	●	●	●	●	●	●	➤	●	●	➤	●	Centrally located. Resort amenities, ABYC yard

Port of Call

Solomons

Breezes wash over Solomons, rustling the leaves on sturdy old trees and enticing sailors out of their slips with the promise of gently billowed mainsails. Formerly an island attached to the mainland in 1870 via a bridge built atop oyster shells, Solomons and its residents have long been linked to the Chesapeake. Once seafood packing and boatbuilding supported the local economy, but now tourism is its mainstay. While the town remains a fishing village (recreational and commercial), it's now also a place to escape and to learn about the Bay's past and future.

Less than 1 ½ miles long, the town has a single two-lane road traveling its entire distance. At the northern end sits the Calvert Marine Museum, dedicated to local Bay life. Exhibition Hall explores marine history, prehistory and estuarine biology in addition to chronicling regional heritage. The Bay's birth and the formation of nearby Calvert Cliffs are explained in Paleontology Hall and in the exhibit "Treasures from the Cliffs: Exploring Marine Fossils." A maritime history exhibit tells the Patuxent's story; fish and animals indigenous to Southern Maryland are the focus of Estuarine Hall. Young children will be captivated by the Discovery Room's hands-on activities, such as digging for fossils, meeting the inhabitants of a touch tank and donning watermen's clothes.

Outside, a pair of river otters delight onlookers and a raised walkway provides a perfect vantage point for observing the life that flourishes in fresh and salt water marshes. Behind the marshes, the refurbished Drum Point Lighthouse offers a window into the life of its keepers. The 1899 buyboat *Wm. B. Tennison*, the oldest Coast Guard-licensed passenger vessel on the Bay, embarks for cruises May through October. Other traditional Bay-built wooden boats are docked or displayed, and a wood-carving shop features demonstrations. One-half mile south of the museum gate, the off-campus J.C. Lore Oyster House (which operated from 1888 to 1978) displays artifacts from the local seafood and boatbuilding industries.

Follow Riverwalk, the wooden promenade, toward the south end of town, where you'll find the Chesapeake Biological Laboratory, a University of Maryland facility that does extensive estuarine research. At the welcome center on the edge of the CBL campus, exhibits, an aquarium and a video give visitors an overview of the researchers' work; 90-minute tours of the labs are offered Wednesdays and Fridays at 2 p.m. (Closed on Mondays.)

Although visitors can easily stroll downtown Solomons, there are other enjoyable ways to explore this popular Southern Maryland destination and its environs, including bicycles and kayaks, which can be rented through Patuxent Adventure Center (410-384-2770). Bicycles are also available from several Solomons marinas.

Solomons is located near some of the most bountiful fishing grounds on the Bay, and experienced charter captains are ready to take you there. You can also try your luck from shore by dropping a line off the fishing

continued on page 190

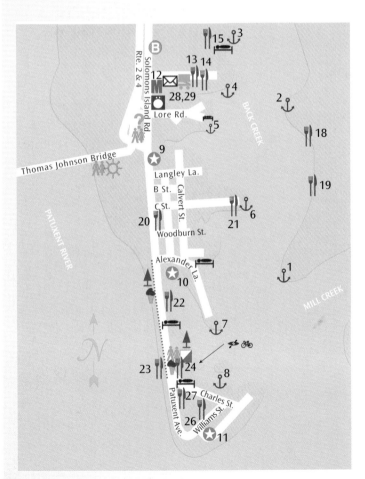

Solomons

⚓ **Marinas/Dockage**
1 Calvert Marina
2 Washburn's Boat Yard
3 Solomons Harbor Marina
4 Spring Cove Marina
5 Beacon Marina
6 Zahniser's Yachting Center
7 Solomons Yachting Center
8 Harbor Island Marina

✪ **Points of Interest**
9 Calvert Marine Museum
10 Lore Oyster House
11 Chesapeake Biological
   Laboratory Visitor Center

Ⓜ **Marine Supplies**
12 West Marine

🍴 **Dining**
13 China Harbor Seafood Restaurant
14 Jerry Subs
15 Isaac's
17 Angler's Restaurant
18 Back Creek Bistro
19 Four Winds Cafe
20 CD Cafe
21 Dry Dock Restaurant
22 Stoney's Kingfishers Seafood House
23 Solomons Pier
24 Lotus Restaurant (Kim's Key Lime Pies)
26 Tiki Bar
27 Grill Sergeant BBQ

☼ **Entertainment/Recreation**
   (Fishing Pier)

🍢 **Groceries/Carryout**

28 7-Eleven
29 Captain Smith's
   Seafood Market

🍦 **Ice Cream**

🚲 ⛵ **Bicycles/Kayaks**

❓ **Information**

▣ **Holding Tank Pump-out**

🛏 **Lodging**

Ⓑ **Bus Transfer Station**

👫 **Public Restrooms**

···· **Riverwalk**

▣ **Laundromat**

🌳 **Park**

✉ **Post Office**

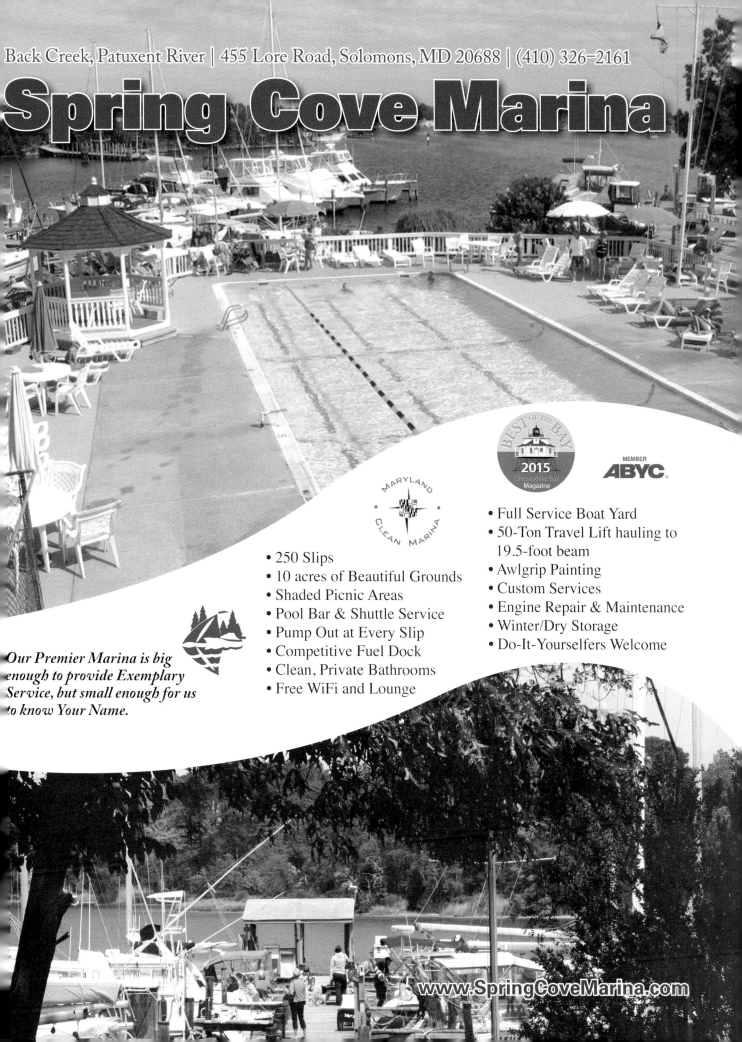

Back Creek, Patuxent River | 455 Lore Road, Solomons, MD 20688 | (410) 326-2161

Spring Cove Marina

MARYLAND CLEAN MARINA

BEST OF THE BAY 2015 Chesapeake Bay Magazine

MEMBER **ABYC**

Our Premier Marina is big enough to provide Exemplary Service, but small enough for us to know Your Name.

- 250 Slips
- 10 acres of Beautiful Grounds
- Shaded Picnic Areas
- Pool Bar & Shuttle Service
- Pump Out at Every Slip
- Competitive Fuel Dock
- Clean, Private Bathrooms
- Free WiFi and Lounge

- Full Service Boat Yard
- 50-Ton Travel Lift hauling to 19.5-foot beam
- Awlgrip Painting
- Custom Services
- Engine Repair & Maintenance
- Winter/Dry Storage
- Do-It-Yourselfers Welcome

www.SpringCoveMarina.com

Port of Call: Solomons continued from page 188

pier at Riverwalk.

Many of the town's small cottages have been converted into unique gift and clothing stores. Other shops and ship's stores are tucked into marina grounds. If you need to restock the galley, head to the north edge of town where you'll find fresh seafood, a bagel/sandwich shop and convenience stores. (Woodburn's, a longtime favorite of cruisers, closed several years ago.) Nearby supermarkets are about a mile farther north.

Many of the dining establishments on Solomons offer panoramic views of the Patuxent River or Back Creek. Fresh seafood is a menu staple. Reservatons are recommended if you plan to dine out on a weekend, especially if you're headed for the Dry Dock at Zahniser's Yachting Center. Other marinas offer eateries as well, like Back Creek Bistro and Four Winds Cafe at Calvert Marina. Stoney's Kingfishers Seafood House (a branch of the Broomes Island eatery famed for its crabcakes) is a local favorite. Angler's opened recently at the Comfort Inn, and the Solomons Tiki Bar is legendary.

The Calvert Marine Museum celebrates the first Friday of the month by offering free admission and hosting a variety of special events. Its Waterside Concert Series features performances throughout the summer by the likes of ZZ Top, Kenny Loggins, Willie Nelson and Smokey Robinson. (For a concert schedule, visit *www.calvertmarinemuseum. com.*) The town's busy calendar of events includes: the Solomons Maritime Festival celebrating Southern Maryland traditions (antique boat and marine engine show, Bay food, music and cultural activities); in July, fireworks for the Fourth, Sharkfest! at the Maritime Museum and the Screwpile Lighthouse Challenge Regatta; in September, the Calvert Waterman's Day Festival (with lots of seafood), in October, the gala Patuxent River Appreciation Days (PRAD) celebrates the river and its impact on the area (music, boat rides, arts and crafts, children's activities).

Information: Calvert County tourism, 800-331-9771; *www.calvertcountymd.us.* Solomons Visitor Information Center; *www.solomonsmaryland.com*, 410-326-6027.

Beth Walsh

CALVERT MARINA FUEL DOCK

*S*ituated between Back Creek and Mill Creek, Calvert Marina is an interesting and **affordable** stop during your cruise.

• Washburn's Boatyard • Hidden Harbour • Back Creek Bistro
• 1,000' of Transient Floating Dockage • 30 & 70 ton lifts • 30/50/100 AMP electricity • swimming pool, showers & laundry • ship's store • picnic tables & grills • BoatUS and Waterway Guide Cruising Club discounts on transient slips • new single family homes for active adults over 55

CALVERT MARINA

Dowell Rd • SOLOMONS, MD 20688 • 410-326-4251 • FAX 410-326-1035

ZAHNISER'S
YACHTING CENTER
Serving Power & Sail since 1960

FULL SERVICE RESORT MARINA
Conveniently located in the heart of Solomons Island!

Five Star Rated

WESTERBEKE
SELDÉN
Perkins
Interlux
yachtpaint.com

Universal
DIESEL MARINE ENGINES
Raymarine
YANMAR
AWLGRIP

Quality & Experience That Make The Difference

410-326-2166 • www.zahnisers.com • Solomons, MD

Solomons
continued from page 189

store, liquor store, seafood market, ATM, post office and West Marine.

Solomons is remembered for its production of fine yachts and mass-produced CruisAlong motorboats, along with schooners, pungies, bugeyes and other workboats in a heritage going back to the M. M. Davis & Company Shipyard established on Mill Creek in 1885. It officially became a town in 1870, a few years after its namesake, Isaac Solomon, established an oyster-packing house and a marine railway.

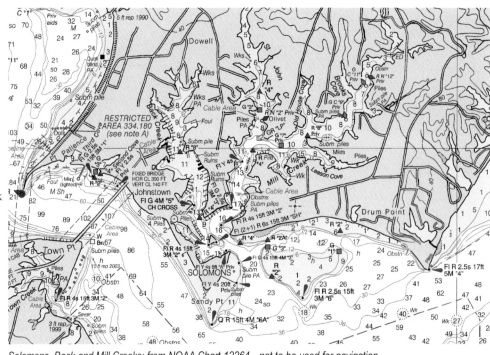

Solomons, Back and Mill Creeks; from NOAA Chart 12264—not to be used for navigation.

Lewis Creek and Town Creek

Above Solomons, the first opportunity for boaters to anchor or find dockage is just below the high Route 4 bridge, a little more than a mile upriver. South of arrowhead-shaped Town Point, the entrances to two small tributaries, Lewis Creek and Town Creek, appear to be flowing into one another as they enter the Patuxent.

While ❷ **Lewis Creek**, with thickly wooded high banks and few homes, is beautiful, its tricky entrance and marginal holding ground make it less than perfect. Charts show the entrance flanked by piles and 3-foot (1999) depths. But it has been dredged at least once since, and so may be deeper. Two small, unlit and offset buoys—a green and a red—mark the

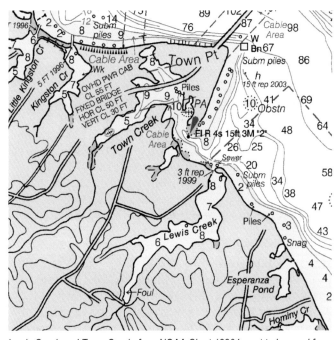

Lewis Creek and Town Creek; from NOAA Chart 12264—not to be used for navigation.

Fossils
Fish
Fun

Mention this ad for $5 off Family Membership, or $10 off a Sustaining Membership

Visit us in Solomons!
Come explore how our prehistoric past, natural environments and maritime heritage come together to tell a unique story of the Chesapeake Bay!

CALVERT MARINE MUSEUM
calvertmarinemuseum.com

OPEN DAILY:
10AM–5PM
410-326-2042

Sunset with boats and dinghy on the Patuxent River's beautiful Mill Creek anchorage. The Patuxent has two Mill creeks, this one upstream of the Rte. 4 bridge.

channel but can be difficult to spot. Approaching the outer green mark, follow the deep water that parallels a sandy spit making up the eastern side of the creek's mouth. In addition to the red and green, there are some private stakes that should keep you in the channel. In contrast to the shallow entrance, depths inside vary from 8 to 14 feet. Anchor anywhere in the middle beyond the large boathouse. The creek ends about a mile upstream.

Town Creek, right next door to Lewis, is a much better bet. With a minimum of 8 feet on approach and 7 to 12 feet inside, this one is wide and inviting, offering docking options as well as snug anchoring space. Flashing "2", marks the tip of a long shoal extending from Town Point's southernmost edge along the entrance channel. But be aware that another shoal encroaches from the south, so stay off the red mark. Look for a small private marker that indicates the edge of the shallow water there.

Inside to starboard is friendly Town Creek Point Marina with deepwater slips. On the other side of the basin, beyond a bridge that has just a 30-foot vertical clearance, Boatel California caters to power boats. With plenty of deep-water anchoring spots all around, sailboats stick to the areas near the prong just south of the bridge in 7 to 9 feet. Inside, the creek is lined with homes, many with a workboat parked at the dock.

Mill Creek and Cuckold Creek

In addition to the popular Mill Creek anchorage in Solomons, another Mill Creek lies close by—about 5 miles up the Patuxent beyond Drum Point. Along the way, the cruise upriver offers points of interest both under and over the water. The first is the 140-foot-high bridge (Route 4) linking Calvert and St. Mary's counties. It's named for Governor Thomas Johnson, Maryland's first elected governor. The house where Johnson was born in 1732 still stands on lower St. Leonard Creek. Rounding Point Patience just beyond the bridge, you'll note some of the deepest waters of the Bay beneath your hull, charted at 121 feet.

This ❸ **Mill Creek** shares its wide, deep entrance with Cuckhold Creek, and is accessed below Half Pone Point, between the Patuxent's two lighted marks "9" and "11" along the western side of the channel. Once you've made the turn to port and have passed daymarks "2" and "3", continue going left at lighted "4"; Mill Creek is the branch to the south. The deep and roomy bay here has good holding and is popular with groups for raft-ups.

North and west of this spot is a small unnamed prong known as **Placid Harbor**. Here most of the shoreline is occupied by a modern educational center offering specialized training for labor unions. Ironically, the property was

Mill Creek and
Cuckhold Creek *continued*

once the home of Fulton Lewis Jr., an ultra-conservative TV-radio commentator and news columnist of the 1930s through '60s.

Mill Creek's close neighbor, **Cuckhold Creek**, is just as lovely. Enter it from the Patuxent by turning to starboard past lighted "4". This creek and its main tributaries, **Nat Creek** and **Forest Landing Cove**, have residences along the shores but also fine anchorages.

Like Mill Creek next door, Cuckold is far less busy than Solomons, although jet skis and fast runabouts occasionally whiz by. For anchoring in Cuckhold Creek, a good spot is in Spring Cove, straight ahead where the main channel turns west. It has protection and plenty of swing room in about 9 feet. The nearby marina on the southern shore (Blackstone) doesn't have transient slips or fuel, but it does offer repair services, marine supplies and ice.

Back at the mouth of Mill and Cuckhold creeks, straddling the tip of the peninsula between them is Clarke's Landing Restaurant with slips for smaller boats, a gas dock and a launch ramp. The restaurant serves lunch and dinner, and its patio has an unbeatable view of the lower Patuxent.

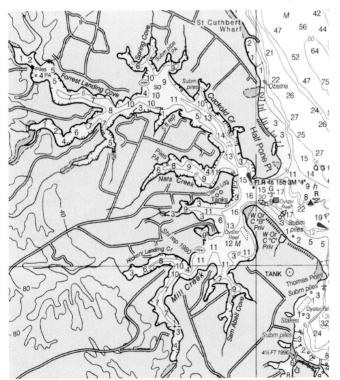

Mill Creek and Cuckhold Creek; from NOAA Chart 12264—not to be used for navigation.

Sotterly Plantation

Beyond Half Pone Point and farther up the Patuxent, the river stretches away in a straight line northwestward 12 miles before it takes a turn to north and heads off into the interior as far as busy Montgomery County. On the lower river, before shoreline turns marshy, the banks rise majestically, often to more than 100 feet.

The Patuxent is a river of history. Its manor houses played a special part in the social circle of early colonial days. Included were such estates as Robert Brookes's Delabrooke Manor, Rousby Hall, Resurrection Manor and Preston—believed to be the oldest building in tidewater Maryland, a distinction challenged only by Cross Manor on the Potomac River.

GREENWELL STATE PARK lies along the southwestern side of the Patuxent River just before Sotterley Point. The park has extensive river frontage and surrounds the estate known as Rosedale (available for special occasions). Walking trails and picnic areas are open for visitors, who can also launch a canoe or kayak at the unprotected swimming beach or use the fishing/crabbing pier. (For information, check with the ranger at 301-373-9775.)

❹ **Sotterley Plantation** is one of the best known and best kept manors in the area. It's also open to the public. Located up the Patuxent from Half Pone Point, across the river from the entrance to St. Leonard Creek, the estate's manor house looks down from high banks along the river. A modest dwelling was built here by 1717, but replaced with the much grander manor house that we see today. Its beautiful gardens, well-preserved slave quarters (of rare post-in-ground construction) and a 1757 red-brick customs warehouse all make the plantation well worth a visit. The grounds are open Tuesday through Sunday.

Although boaters are welcome, use of the plantation's private dock on Sotterley Creek (5- and 6-foot depths) is limited to reserved-tour guests. You must call ahead (301-373-2280) during office hours, Monday through Friday, 8:30 a.m. to 5 p.m., to reserve a tour time and space to tie up at the

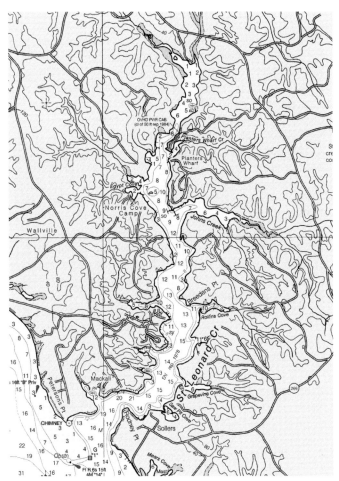

St. Leonard Creek; from NOAA Chart 12264—not to be used for navigation.

ment of the battle every September. The 560-acre state center for Chesapeake archaeology and anthropology offers tours and educational programs (410-586-8501). Boaters can access the park by landing a dinghy at any part of the beach along the river or just inside St. Leonard Creek.

If you're cruising past the park on the second Sunday in June, you'll get a front-row seat to one of the Patuxent River's rites of spring, formerly held at Broomes Island: the annual Patuxent River Wade-In led by former state senator (and Broomes Island native) Bernie Fowler. Clad in his trademark denim overalls and clasping hands with fellow citizens or visiting politicians, Fowler strides into the water until he can no longer see the tops of his sneakers. The distance is measured and compared to the 60 or so inches of visibility Fowler recalled as a young man, standing chest-deep in the river netting blue crabs. In 2010, the measurement was 34.5 inches, better than in 2009, when the measurement was a scant $25\frac{1}{2}$ inches, but still a far cry from the days when the river and the Bay were cleaner, clearer and much less polluted.

When entering St. Leonard Creek don't be confused by buoys marking the 3- to 4-foot shoal extending south from Petersons Point. Lighted red "14" is a Patuxent River mark and should be left to port on entering the creek. The entrance mark for the creek is green daymark "1", about 400 yards east of red "14"; it should be left to port on entering.

If you're approaching from upstream, head for red "14" off Petersons Point and, leaving it to port, plot a course for green "1" near the creek's mouth. Since it faces south, "1" may be hard to spot initially (edge-on to you) but head northeasterly toward the bluffs south of the creek's entrance and watch for it to appear to port. Once past it, swing north and enter the creek. Almost the entire length of St. Leonard Creek is navigable, with deep water reasonably close to shore. Many nooks and bights hold 4 to 12 feet of water.

Some cruisers like to anchor on the port side of the entrance in **Point Farm Cove**, which shows 12 feet of water (south of **Mackall**). While well-protected from the weather and fetch, it offers no protection from the wakes of powerboats heading into St. Leonard Creek and up to the marina. Nor is there room to raft up. Instead, try the eastern side of the creek, past Rodney Point, in 15-foot depths. This location is protected from the weather, with sufficient room for the boat to swing and still stay out of the main portion of the creek's channel. One spot of historical note in the small cove behind Rodney Point: High on a cliff sits Spout Farm, named for a spring where ships filled their casks before long voyages.

Other popular anchorages are **Rollins Cove** and **Johns Creek**. If you arrive too late to anchor in Rollins Cove, or if you prefer a spot where there's a better chance of a breeze, consider the area outside the cove's entrance, south of Breedens Point. The holding is good in 11 to 13 feet of water.

Cruising vessels can go quite a distance back in the creek to find an alternative anchorage, but you won't be entirely alone; homes with small docks dot the north banks.

At the mouth of Johns Creek lies Vera's White Sands Beach Club, a Bay institution. This fanciful place looks like a Polynesian island misplaced on the Chesapeake. Its for-

dock or to pull your dinghy onto the beach. From there, it's a 20-minute walk to the manor house through a beautiful network of wooded trails. Cruisers can also anchor at the mouth of Sotterley Creek, just southeast of Sotterley Point, in 5 to 10 feet of water with good holding.

St. Leonard Creek

⑤ **St. Leonard Creek**, located about 7 miles upriver from Solomons, is considered by many to be the most beautiful on the Patuxent. And it's hard to argue the point. This protected five-mile-long creek is on the river's northern shore.

A dramatic naval battle was fought at the mouth of the St. Leonard during the War of 1812. A blockading British fleet—two frigates, a brig, two schooners and a number of smaller craft—were driven off in a surprise dawn attack on June 26, 1814, by citizen-sailor Joshua Barney, commanding a small flotilla of open barges. Barney, however, was unable to follow up his advantage, and the British force later contributed troops that took part in the burning of the U.S. Capitol in Washington, D.C. Details of this battle and relics from some of the sunken ships are displayed at the Calvert Marine Museum in Solomons. In addition, many artifacts have been retrieved from the creek through the archaeological efforts of JEFFERSON PATTERSON PARK AND MUSEUM, which hosts a reenact-

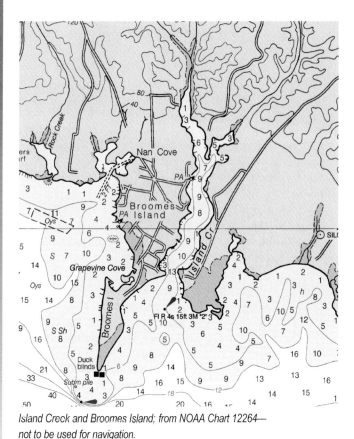

Island Creek and Broomes Island; from NOAA Chart 12264—not to be used for navigation.

St. Leonard Creek *continued*

mer owner, the late Vera Freeman, decorated the restaurant with South Sea treasures culled from her international voyages. The new owners have upgraded the marina, added a beach bar and remodeled the restaurant.

The extraordinary beauty of St. Leonard Creek captivates those who visit. The shoreline is a mix of marshes, rolling hills and wooded bluffs. Some homes are surrounded by manicured lawns that reach down to the shoreline, some are lost in the thick foliage, and others set up on the hills.

Island Creek and Broomes Island

The next deepwater tributary on the river's northern shore is ⑥ **Island Creek**, about eight miles upriver from Solomons. Flashing red "2" marks the entrance to the creek, which carries about 8 feet of water for roughly a mile before it forks into two shallower branches.

Island Creek affords good protection from summer southerlies that can churn up the Patuxent. Perhaps its biggest attraction for cruisers is **Broomes Island**, which isn't really an island at all but a skinny peninsula that juts southward into the river like the neck of a guitar. Deeper-draft vessels will have difficulty reaching the island's few commercial establishments, but if you have a taste for seafood—and for seafood lore—it's worth a visit by dinghy.

For the first half of the 20th century, tiny Broomes Island rivaled its down-river neighbor, Solomons, as a seafood processing and boatbuilding center. More than half a dozen oyster-packing plants alone once occupied the peninsula, which is bounded by Island Creek to the east and **Grapevine** and **Nan coves** to the west. Unfortunately, little trace of the industry remains. The last of the plants to close, the Warren Denton Oyster Company, which opened in 1927, stood on the peninsula's southern tip. The building has since been demolished.

The bounty that bound this community together remains, however, even if sportfishing and other recreational boats now replace the workboats that once jammed Island Creek. As you enter the creek, just past red "2", you'll see a private marina and a large lighthouse-shaped dwelling to port. Soon after, the creek narrows and a waterfront restaurant with extensive wooden decks and a profusion of table umbrellas comes into view along a cove. This is Stoney's Seafood and Crabhouse (open seasonally), which serves some of the Bay's largest, tastiest and most famous crabcakes. Stoney's has docks for diners as well.

The only facility on Broomes Island that offers overnight slips is Len's Marina, just north of Grapevine Cove on the western shore. Boats that can access the facility (4-foot depths at the outer docks) will find fuel (gas only), marine supplies, ice and groceries, including "Jerry's crabcakes." Famous in their own right, these hefty sandwiches are named for their creator, a semi-retired local restaurateur.

Past Broome's Island, the Patuxent continues north for many miles, its water deep and its shorelines wild. Most cruisers don't venture that far, but the small town of **Benedict** at the Route 231 swing bridge has a charm all its own, and BATTLE CREEK CYPRESS SWAMP PARK will make you believe you've stumbled into the Okefenokee.

Boat-Keeping Tips

- To keep your matches dry, try storing them in 35 millimeter film containers or empty plastic pill bottles.

- Use empty dried herb jars with shaker inserts in the lids as moisture-proof salt and pepper shakers.

- Make your boat its own set of tools. This way, the right screwdriver is always in the right place.

- You can remove the smell of gasoline from your hands quickly by simply rubbing them with moistened kitchen salt.

- Use empty egg cartons to make bumpers that will keep the contents of your refrigerator or shelves from shifting excessively in a seaway. Place one in front of the shelf's contents to absorb the shock of jars, etc. hitting the door.

- Sweep the deck or cabin sole with a child's play broom or whisk broom. To save space, use a small dustpan, too.

- Try a car vacuum cleaner for boat use. It can be plugged into 12-volt current.

SPOTLIGHT CRUISE: LITTLE CHOPTANK

Behind Casson Point at the mouth of Hudson Creek. Casson offers just enough protection to stop the waves but not the breeze.

Little Choptank may be winning, but the fight isn't over.

It was only a question of who would get there first, Skipper and me aboard the Chesapeake Boating Club's Albin 28 *Journey*, or Mother Nature's flying-fortress-class horseflies. Not that it really mattered. It was clear from the start that both parties would be cohabiting the anchorage on the Little Choptank River's Hudson Creek. It would be a fight to the finish.

The military-grade insects had picked us up on their radar earlier in the afternoon as we glided through the Little Choptank's still water and hot breathless air, past Hudson Creek and Madison Bay, on our way farther upriver for a pre-anchorage perambulation to Gary Creek. I had wanted to see whether one could actually see Spocott Windmill, that landmark creation of boatbuilder Jim Richardson, from there. Nice idea, but the blood-thirsty kamikazes were having none of it. This river was theirs! The squadron opened its attack from the rear, just as we slowed at the narrow passage beyond the mouth of Fishing Creek at Cedar Point. It was as if they'd known what we were going to do before we did. As I continued to steer the boat, swatting at the back-biting villains with the chart I had been studying, Skipper counter-attacked, leaping and snapping the air in the cockpit and finally cornering one on the shelf behind the settee in the cabin. One down!

Ptui! he said, quickly spitting out the kill and returned to the fray. The battle raged, with heavy casualties on both sides, until we had cleared flashing green "13" and the channel widened enough to open the throttle. It did only a little bit of good, of course, thanks to that unfortunate law of physics that allows them to fly in a boat's moving airspace no matter how fast said boat is going . . . but we did create enough wind through the open windscreen and side windows, which at least made it harder for them to land.

By now my thirst for information about seeing windmills had been pretty well squelched, so just as we reached the entrance to Gary Creek, I spun the Albin on its heel and we headed back downriver. About this time our enemies disappeared too, apparently returning to base to refuel. I knew better than to believe that they'd given up the fight. Unless a fulsome breeze cropped up this evening, we were going to be sitting ducks.

I shouldn't have been surprised. Relations between the Little Choptank River and me have never been cordial. Don't ask me why; heaven knows I've tried to make it work. But it never really has. Right from the beginning, things have gone wrong. It all started a few years ago when my sailing buddy Hal and I were bringing *Snipp*, my Albin Vega 27 sloop, back up to Annapolis from a long stretch on the Potomac. I decided that we should skip the usual stopover in Solomons and aim instead for the Little Choptank, giving us a leg up on the second day's run. In fact, I thought a night on the hook on one of the river's several creeks would be just the thing. The first creek, Brooks, has a tough entrance, but Hudson Creek looked perfect.

The trip out of the Potomac from the Smith Creek had been hot, of course, this being the ragged end of August, and also predictably short on wind. For reasons I won't go into, the Vega has a dodger but no bimini, so it was a hot, sweaty, cranky pair of sailors who wound laboriously around the markers across to enter the Little Choptank late in the afternoon. Because we'd had to motor much of the way, we were running short of fuel for the next day, so we opted to head up Slaughter Creek to the marina that lies just shy of the bridge about a mile upstream. Now we wrangled over the best route through the maze of markers, as the depth fell off alarmingly on the approach to each marker. Finally, though, we got through, found the marina easily and filled the tank. Then, lured by a loaner car and a nearby restaurant, we fatally decided to stay at the dock overnight. You will have guessed by now that we spent an airless and sleepless night without the remotest possibility (thanks to the narrow creek and surrounding boats, whose owners had the good sense to be sleeping elsewhere) of feeling the cooling breeze that might have been blowing out on the river. It was a very quiet trip back to Annapolis the next day. I don't believe Hal and I actually spoke to each other for several weeks.

I have told this story to give a sense of my troubled relationship with this river. Since that first unpleasant visit, it has not improved. Each time I tell myself that other people love this river, that they regularly stop here, and that they have a lovely time. So I try again.

On this most recent occasion, Skipper and I had left Annapolis in mid-morning, just as the last cloudbanks from Tropical Storm Lee were scudding away north and east. The Bay was flat calm and a kind of whipped-up lima-bean-julius green, but free of the storm run-off debris that was making a mess of everything to the north. As we headed southeast across the Bay, we were joined by a dozen or so cruisers, headed south as well, sails furled and motoring, taking advantage of the long-awaited break in the weather. By noon the last of the morning's fog had given way to bright blue skies. It was a beautiful day and the sunshine felt warm and wonderful after days of solid cloud-cover and rain. My bad luck with the Little Choptank is about to end, I said to myself later, as we turned south to follow the channel into the river.

Wrong. What I should have been thinking was: Two weeks of rain followed by sunshine and warm temperatures means that in low-lying marshy areas the insect population is going to explode like firecrackers on the Fourth of July; the Little Choptank is nothing if not low-lying and marshy; therefore, perhaps one would be wise to avoid the Little

"Got one!" Skipper pauses in mid-battle with the horseflies to find himself up on the shelf behind the setee of the Albin 28.

Choptank like the plague. Life is a learning process, and I am apparently a slow learner.

After our encounter with the horseflies, Skipper and I motored back downriver to Hudson Creek, licking our wounds (literally in Skipper's case, figuratively in mine) and mentally preparing for the night's rematch. At least we would have the choice of field position. Instead of heading upstream to one of the creek's several well protected little bays, we would opt for the cruisers' favorite spot, the long narrow spit that forms the west side of the creek's mouth. Known as Casson Point, this spit is now partially riprapped, but it still has its inviting sandy shoreline at the tip. This has long been a popular spot for transiting boaters because it offers protection from the long southwest fetch, but is low enough that it doesn't block the summer's prevailing southwesterly breezes. And the water behind the spit is deep—8 feet or more—nearly to the shoreline. Great for cruisers. Great for their dogs.

I dropped the anchor behind Casson Point just as the sun dropped into the Bay beyond the pines and sawgrass. A soft breeze picked up. Maybe this was going to work out after all, I thought with Neville Chamberlain-like optimism, as Skipper and I settled into the cabin for the night. Of course it didn't work out. Five minutes later, the breeze fell away. Half a minute after that, the enemy was at the gates. And they had brought their kinfolk. A lot of kinfolk. In addition to the dozen horseflies, hundreds, thousands . . . shucks, maybe millions . . . of little green-and-white striped marsh mosquitoes descended on us like Old Testament locusts. Oh, it was a massacre! Even now, with the last of the bites nearly gone, I shudder at the memory of that terrible night.

At first light, I pulled up the anchor, and we left the Little Choptank as fast as prudence would allow. I know that someday I'll go back to try again. I refuse to give up. But I'll tell you this: It's going to be on a cold day in Hell!

— Jody Argo Schroath

The Potomac River

St. Marys, Yeocomico and Coan Rivers
Washington D.C., Alexandria, National Harbor,
Colonial Beach and St. Mary's City
Smith, Mattawoman and Machodoc Creeks
Nomini Bay, Cobb and St. George Islands

Boaters familiar with the waters at the mouth of the Potomac River know that it is apt to be cantankerous when strong tides clash with high winds. Worse, it's susceptible to late summer squalls. Many a skipper has sighed in relief after passing the river's 10-mile-wide entrance.

However, those who cruise up the Potomac's 96 miles of navigable waters are in for a treat: a gently sculpted, lushly foliated shoreline interrupted by well over two dozen welcoming creeks and rivers. Places like the Coan, Yeocomico and St. Marys rivers, Smith and St. George creeks and Breton Bay offer quiet, protected anchorages where cruisers can get away from it all in serene surroundings or restock, refuel and snuggle in for the night at a marina.

Aside from picturesque backdrops, the Potomac is famous for its beguiling ports of call. Historic St. Mary's City, the site of Maryland's first settlement and provincial capital, is an 800-acre living-history museum where costumed interpreters will take you back three centuries or so to the days of the area's first European settlers. Colonial Beach was a turn-of-

the-20th-century resort where today's visitors come to stroll its neighborhoods and soak up its old-fashioned charm.

Farther upstream, Mount Vernon, George Washington's estate, unfolds along the banks of the Virginia shore. His house sits invitingly atop a hill as if to welcome those who come to explore the grounds and buildings. Visitors to nearby Alexandria will find an eclectic blend of historic sites, numerous restaurants, trendy shops and a thriving arts scene in its historic Old Town district just a stroll away from the public waterfront.

At the head of the Potomac's navigable waters lies Washington, D.C., with its acclaimed museums, awe-inspiring monuments, renowned restaurants and countless things to see and do—from attending a concert to strolling through a park to visiting one of the Smithsonian's many museums. The nation's capital is a city easier to reach than it is to leave.

Above Washington the Potomac narrows and becomes shallow and rocky. By then, however, you'll be looking forward to the trip back.

SECTION 5 | *St. Jerome Creek to Washington D.C.*

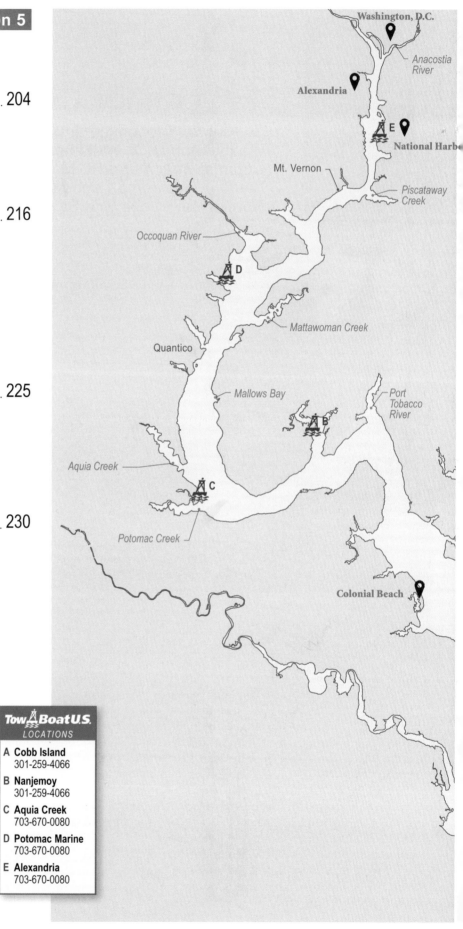

Tow⚓BoatU.S.
LOCATIONS

A **Cobb Island**
301-259-4066

B **Nanjemoy**
301-259-4066

C **Aquia Creek**
703-670-0080

D **Potomac Marine**
703-670-0080

E **Alexandria**
703-670-0080

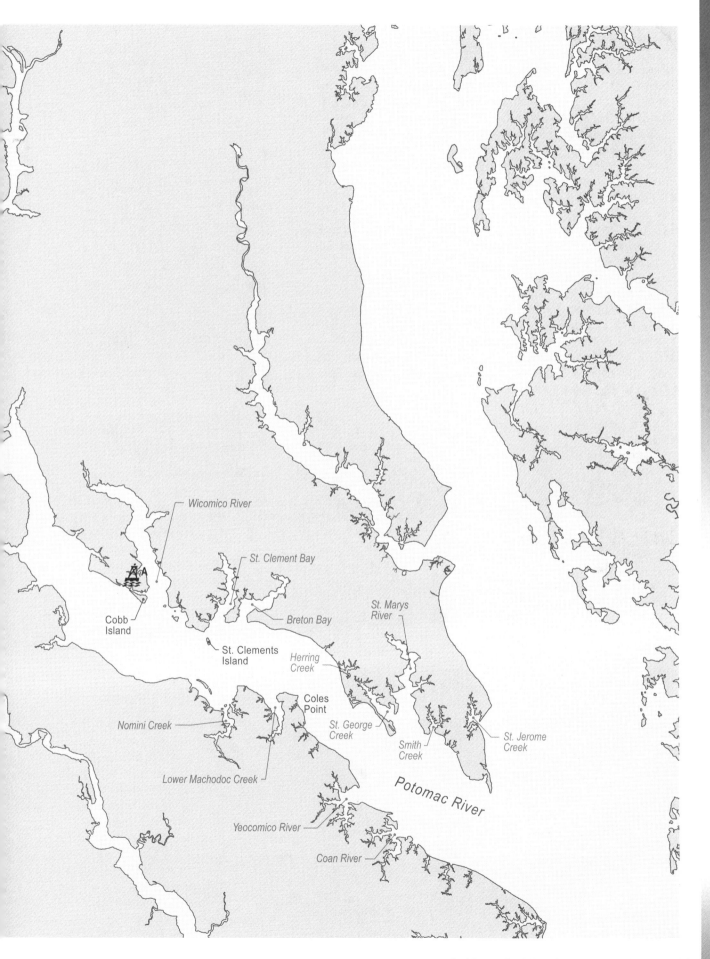

Wicomico River

St. Clement Bay

Cobb
Island

Breton Bay

St. Marys
River

St. Clements
Island

Herring
Creek

Coles
Point

Nomini Creek

St. George
Creek

St. Jerome
Creek

Smith
Creek

Lower Machodoc Creek

Potomac River

Yeocomico River

Coan River

St. Jerome Creek

We begin Section 5 five miles north of the Potomac's entrance, at **St. Jerome Creek,** which tucks into Maryland's lower Western Shore, just west of Point No Point. This attractive creek opens right onto the Bay and would be a perfect overnight stop on long cruises, *except* that perennial shoaling makes it a very tricky place if your boat draws more than 3 feet. The charts are optimistically confusing, showing enough 5-foot depths to provide hope, as well as intimidating shoals with 2- and 3-foot depths. For shallow-draft vessels, though, it can be an inviting refuge, situated some two miles southwest of the 52-foot-high Point No Point Light. If you do decide to venture in, follow the markers you see in front of you, not the markers on the chart . . . and, of course, keep an eagle eye on the depthsounder. Don't even think of going in there at night without local knowledge.

Flashing green "1SJ" marks the channel into the creek, which is by way of a narrow passage between Deep Point to the south and St. Jerome Point to the north. Rounding Deep Point, head west to pick up the next markers before turning north to follow the markers off Split Point. Here the creek deepens to 4 to 5 feet. Anchor in this area or look for Drury Marina (which has a fuel dock) on the southeastern shore of the **Northern Prong**. The second marina, Buzz's (gas, repair services, supplies), lies at the head of the **Southern Prong**.

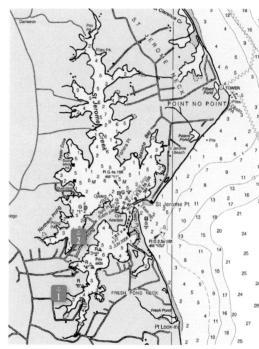

St. Jerome Creek; from NOAA Chart 12233—not to be used for navigation.

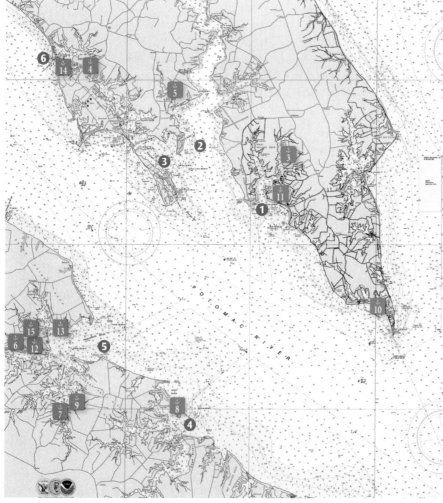

Lower Potomac River; from NOAA Chart 12233—not to be used for navigation.

Lower Potomac

POINT LOOKOUT STATE PARK occupies the very southern tip of Maryland's Western Shore. A popular fishing destination with launch ramps and piers, the park can also afford shelter for shallow-draft vessels ducking a storm on the river. The entrance to **Point Lookout Inlet** is just inside the Potomac's northern entrance and leads to **Lake Conoy**. Supplies are available, but not overnight dockage.

Smith Creek

❶ **Smith Creek,** located on the Maryland shore of the Potomac, six miles upstream of Point Lookout, is a popular destination, with marinas and small coves for anchoring and relaxing. This 2-mile-long waterway is actually two creeks in one.

The entrance into Smith Creek isn't all that tricky, but it is a bit narrow. The three entrance marks—red "2", green "3" and red "4"—form an S-curve. Just follow along and you'll be inside. You will find one more marker, "6", off the commercial docks at

	MLW	Overnight Slips	Gas	Diesel	Propane	Electric	Showers	Laundry	Restaurant	Lodging	Pool	Pump-out	Ice	Groceries	Marine Supplies	Bait	Boat Repair	Haul-out Services	Launch Ramp	Wi-Fi	Other

● On Premises ➤ Nearby

St. Jerome Creek

	MLW	O.Slips	Gas	Diesel	Prop	Elec	Show	Laund	Rest	Lodg	Pool	Pump	Ice	Groc	Mar.Sup	Bait	Boat Rep	Haul	Ramp	Wi-Fi	Other
Buzz's Marina St. Jerome Cr. 301-872-5887; www.buzzsmarina.com	4'	●	●				●	●					●	●	●	●	●	●		●	Easy acces to excellent fishing
Drury's Marina St. Jerome Cr. 301-872-4480	3.5'	●	●	●	➤	●	●	➤	➤				●	●	➤	➤	●	➤		●	

Lower Potomac River

	MLW	O.Slips	Gas	Diesel	Prop	Elec	Show	Laund	Rest	Lodg	Pool	Pump	Ice	Groc	Mar.Sup	Bait	Boat Rep	Haul	Ramp	Wi-Fi	Other
BluHaven Piers Potomac R./Smith Cr./Jutland Cr. 301-872-5838; www.bluhavenpiers.com	10'	●	➤	➤	➤	●	●	➤	➤	➤		●	●	➤	●	●	●	●	●	●	Protected cove, kayak rentals, Wi-Fi, mechanic
Cedar Cove Marina Potomac R./Herring Cr. 301-994-1155	6'	●				●	●	●	●			●			●		●	●	●	●	Full-service, 25-ton lift, transient slips
Dennis Point Marina and Campground Potomac R./St. Mary's R./Carthagena Cr. 301-994-2288; www.dennispointcampground.com	10'+	●	●	●	●	●	●	●	●	➤	●	●	●	●	●		●	●	●	●	Non-ethanol gas, rental cabin, kayaks; 75-ton lift, full service
Kinsale Harbour Yacht Club and Marina Potomac R./West Yeocomico R. 804-472-2514	8'	●	➤	➤	➤	●	●	●	●		●	●	●	●	●	➤	●	➤	➤	●	Tennis, campsites, waterfront dining, well protected
Krentz Marine Railway Potomac R./Yeocomico R. 804-529-6851	12'	●	➤	➤	➤	●	➤	➤	➤	➤		●	●	➤	●	●	●	●	●	➤	60-ton lift, customers may use facilities at Krentz's Marina
Lewisetta Marina Potomac R./Coan R. 804-529-7299	8'	●	●	●	●	●	●					●	●	●	●	●	●	●	●		25-ton open-end hoist; mechanic
Olverson's Lodge Creek Marina Potomac R./South Yeocomico R./Lodge Cr. 800-529-5071; www.olversonsmarina.com	10'	●	●	●	➤	●	●	●	➤		●	●	●	➤	➤	➤	➤	➤	●	●	Covered land boat & RV storage. Rental house
Point Lookout Boating Facility Potomac R./Lake Conoy 301-872-5688; www.dnr.state.md.us	6'		●				➤	➤				●	●	●	●		●			●	In-state park; campgrounds, full hook-ups
Point Lookout Marina Potomac R./Smith Cr./Jutland Cr. 301-872-5000; www.pointlookoutmarina.com	9'	●	●	●	●	●	●	●	●	➤	●	●	●	●	●	●	●	●	●	●	Sunset Cove Restaurant open thur-sun; courtesy car
Port Kinsale Marina Potomac R./West Yeocomico R. 804-472-2044; www.portkinsale.com	8'	●	●	●		●	●	●		●	●	●	●	●	●	●	●	●	●	●	Screened pavilion, picnic area, B&B, gas grills
Sandy Point Marina Potomac R./Yeocomico R. 804-472-3237	7'		●	●		●						●		●			➤	●	●		Fishing tackle
Tall Timbers Marina Potomac R./Herring Cr. 301-994-1508; www.talltimbersmarinasomd.com	6'	●	●	●		●	●		●	➤		●	➤		●			●	●	●	Private beach, catering, restaurant on site
White Point Marina Potomac R./Yeocomico R./Shannon Br./White Pt. Cr. 804-472-2977; www.whitepointmarina.com	8'	●	●	●	➤	●	●	➤	➤	➤	●	●	●	➤	●	➤	●	●	➤	●	Quiet; pool, courtesy car, gas grills

Wynne. Smith Creek heads directly north, carrying 15 feet or more, before shallowing gradually to 6-feet about two miles upstream. Beyond that point, deep-draft boats should watch their depthfinders closely.

North on Smith Creek, in the mile or so from red "6" to its head, there are no fewer than six delightful areas where the water has etched out small coves, sandy beaches and tranquil niches, each with its own personality. Probably the most protected anchorage on Smith Creek is in the first cove to starboard past the mouth of Jutland Creek (which forks to the right beyond Smith Creek's entrance). Here you'll be surrounded by tall trees and can rest in absolute calm. The charts clearly show the off-center entrance channel with 10-foot depths. Just beyond, to port, is a good-sized cove large enough to accommodate several rafts of cruisers.

About a half-mile from Smith Creek's entrance, **Jutland Creek** branches off eastward before turning northward also. This creek offers yet more anchoring options, as well as a couple of marinas. **Deep Cove**, to starboard just beyond Scheible's Fishing Center, is the "side door" entrance

Smith Creek *continued*

to the summer station of the Corinthian Yacht Club of Washington, D.C. Private docks line both sides of the cove, but it would be an excellent anchorage in a hard blow. Cruisers will find quieter and more remote anchorages farther up Jutland Creek.

Upstream to starboard is **Fox Harbor**, an attractive little creek. The entrance is broad without significant outlying shoals. Tall pines and hardwoods at the water's edge will protect you from fierce winds on the Potomac. If you anchor here, expect a few workboats to rumble by near dawn.

Along most of both Smith and Jutland creeks, the banks are tree-lined with many indentations where boats anchor in comfort and safety. The creek bottom is the sort of soft mud that allows the anchor to set deeply and firmly.

Point Lookout Marina on Jutland Creek specializes in boat repairs and service. It also offers slips for transients, fuel and a popular restaurant, Spinnakers. Quiet Bluhaven Piers Marina, farther upstream, has kayak rentals and occasionally dock space for transients. Closer to Smith Creek's entrance you'll find Courtney's Restaurant and, on the creek itself, Scheible's Fishing Center, home of a fleet of charter fishing boats, a restaurant and a motel. Scheible's offers free dockage for diners and motel guests at its 500-foot pier.

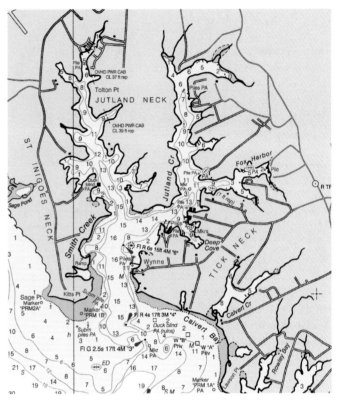

Smith Creek; from NOAA Chart 12233—not to be used for navigation.

46555 Dennis Point Way | Drayden, MD 20630 | 301–994–2288 | www.dennispointmarina.net

Cruising the Potomac and St. Marys rivers?

Point Lookout Marina offers a beautifully landscaped setting on 24 acres, just six miles from the Bay. Marina guests can enjoy the pool, playground and picnic areas. The marina has 160 slips, and can accommodate vessels up to 200' and pleasure cruises of 30 to 40 boats. Waterfront restaurant on-site. Full service and emergency repairs.

We are your marina destinations!

Dennis Point Marina & Campground

is just three miles from historic St. Mary's City, and has 80 deep-water slips on scenic Carthagena Creek. Visitors can enjoy the entire 50-acre property which includes a swimming pool, playgrounds, cabins, kayaks, canoes, paddle boards, restaurant and outdoor bar overlooking the creek. Full service, hauling boats to 75 tons with max beam of 24'.

16244 Miller's Wharf Rd | Ridge, MD 20680 | 301-872-5000 | www.pointlookoutmarina.com

St. Marys River

2 **St. Marys River** is the second tributary (just after Smith Creek) on the northern shore of the Potomac. Anyone who has sailed up the St. Marys can understand why, of all the many beautiful places on Chesapeake Bay, this attracted Maryland's first permanent English settlers. Hills along the river banks offer protection from heavy winds, yet there nearly always seems to be enough breeze rolling down the slopes to keep the sails full. The exception to this rule is perhaps during the finish of the annual Governor's Cup race from Annapolis to St. Mary's City, when the wind traditionally dies at the mouth of the river, leaving exhausted crews to drift helplessly with the tide. But that anomaly aside, the wind is good, the river deep and anchorages plentiful. In short, it's a *beaut* of a river.

In 1634, Governor Leonard Calvert led a band of settlers in the *Ark* and the *Dove* up the river to what is now Church Point on the eastern bank. They had first landed farther up the Potomac on St. Clements Island, where they planted a cross, then sought a permanent location. When they found friendly Yaocomico Indians in the present St. Mary's City area, they purchased the site.

The river's mouth is wide and deep—just avoid the shoals off **St. George Island** to the west and Kitts Point to the east. The scenery doesn't look as if it has changed much since brigantines sailed these waters. You'll see rolling farmland with an occasional hilltop mansion. If you're lucky, you may spy the *Maryland Dove* on one of its sails; this is the vessel built as a representation of the supply boat that accompanied the *Ark* to Maryland with that first load of colonists. The *Dove* is not licensed to carry passengers, but does a frequent "turn-around" cruise into the river and back, reversing its mooring, so the boat weathers evenly.

After you pass St. George Creek, you'll next see, also to port, **2a** **Carthagena** (*KAR-thuh-GEEN-uh*) **Creek.** This peaceful and protected creek offers several good anchorages as well as the only marina on the St. Marys River. Tucked behind Josh Point, Dennis Point Marina and Campground is a full-service facility, with a restaurant—Riverside Bistro— acres of campgrounds, gas and diesel, hauling, repairs, and a small but useful ship's store. The marina's new owners have done a lot of work sprucing up the docks and grounds.

On the eastern side of St. Marys River, opposite Carthagena Creek, a large Navy installation occupies a significant portion of St. Inigoes (*INN-i-goes*) Neck. Along its northern border, **2b** **St. Inigoes Creek** is easy to enter as the only shoal, on the south bank at Priests Point, is clearly marked by lighted "2". Stay in the middle until you reach the two branches. The creek bends to the north and then east again. On your starboard side is a prominent sandy point with a charted wreck on the far side. Give this point a wide berth and hug the docks to port till you reach the deep open area where you'll be able to anchor in safety.

The St. Inigoes Coast Guard station is located in **Molls Cove.** Their jurisdiction stretches from Point No Point in the Bay to Smith Point at the southern tip of the Potomac and up

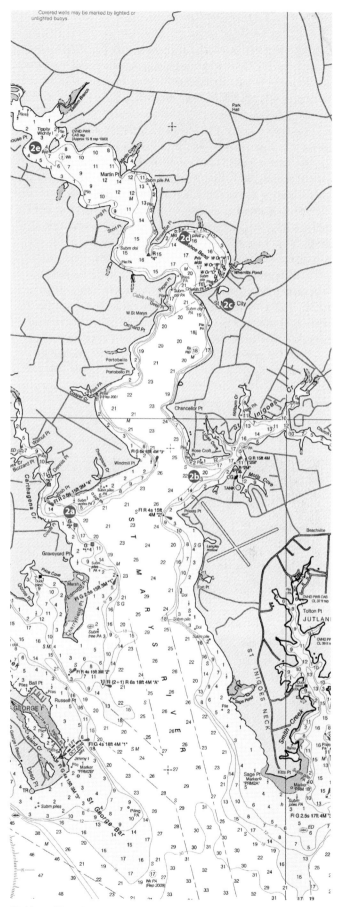

St. Marys River; from NOAA Chart 12233—not to be used for navigation.

St. Marys River *continued*

the Potomac to the Route 301 highway bridge.

Above the Coast Guard station are secure and lovely anchorages along both sides of St. Inigoes Creek. On the northerly side are **Lucas Cove** and **Milburn Creek**, with **Church Cove** on the southerly side. St. Inigoes opens out after the point between Lucas and Milburn creeks, beckoning cruisers to explore and enjoy in depths of 7 to 17 feet.

Cross Manor, a beautiful brick structure on the south side of St. Inigoes Creek, has been identified as one of the oldest homes in Maryland, having been completed, some say, in 1644. It stands on original manor land granted to Thomas Cornwallis. Cross Manor was a historical restoration project undertaken by television newsman Ted Koppel and his wife, who brought the buildings and gardens back to their original 17th century lines and appearance. Remnants of other venerable manors sit along the river's western shore. Their names—Carthagena and Porto Bello—were significant in their time, celebrating the Caribbean cities where the British (and American colonials) fought the Spanish in the 1730s.

As you continue upriver, the heights of **2c St. Mary's City** come into view. The spire of Trinity Episcopal Church, built in the 19th century on Church Point, can be seen above the river, and, below it, the golden and brown hull of the *Dove*. The *Dove* is maintained by the Historic St. Mary's City Commission as part of the exhibits commemorating the first settlement in the Maryland colony. Also above the *Dove*'s dock stands a replica of the 1676 State House, built in 1934 for Maryland's Tercentenary. The State House and Trinity Episcopal Church contain much of interest. In the church cemetery stands an obelisk marking the place where Governor Leonard Calvert is supposed to have met the Native Americans under a mulberry tree to bargain for the land now known as St. Mary's County, the mother county of Maryland. Maryland Day ceremonies are held annually in March to commemorate the colonists' arrival in 1634.

A very fine anchorage lies in **2d Horseshoe Bend**, about 5 miles up the St. Marys River between Church Point and Horseshoe Point. The water is deep almost up to the sand bar that forms Church Point. Motor around the bar, which is often in use by sunbathers and swimmers, and you're in Horseshoe Bend, a large bay-like basin about three-quarters of a mile wide and 16 to 20 feet deep, almost to shore. The anchorage is very well protected. Surprisingly, only northwesterlies—blowing from the source of the river—give boats any trouble here, according to local residents.

Forty or 50 boats can anchor in Horseshoe Bend without anyone feeling claustrophobic, but the only time the anchorage really tests its capacity is the weekend of the aforementioned St. Mary's College of Maryland Governor's Cup Race, traditionally the first weekend in August. This popular race

MARYLAND
VisitMaryland.org

Where the Potomac and the Chesapeake meet!

st.mary's county, md.

Find inspiration, relaxation and new adventures.
Full service marinas, great dining, wineries and water trails, plus historic sites, lighthouses and state parks—all on the water.

visitstmarysmd.com

Bay Spotlight

Historic St. Mary's City

Along the southern edge of Horseshoe Bend in the St. Marys River, you'll find St. Mary's College of Maryland, a small liberal arts school with a first-class sailing program. Visiting boaters are allowed to tie up at the college's pier (during daylight hours only) or land a dinghy on the beach to visit Historic St. Mary's City, which is only a short walk from the campus. In 1968, the Historic St. Mary's City Commission was given the responsibility for rescuing and preserving this abandoned historic site by creating an outdoor museum.

As the fourth permanent English settlement in North America, the founding place of Maryland and the state's first capital, St. Mary's City was an experiment in religious tolerance. Lord Baltimore, a Roman Catholic, and fellow religious dissidents hoped to establish a colony in the New World where they were free to prosper and worship as they chose. St. Mary's City became the colony's first settlement in 1634 and served as Maryland's capital until 1695, when it was moved to Annapolis, a Protestant stronghold.

Appropriately, the town was centered on two buildings: a State House, built in 1676, and what was described as a "good brick chappell," believed to be an imposing structure that balanced in size the government building. The State House and the Brick Chapel are among the reconstructed buildings at the site today.

In addition to the State House and a representation of the colonists' vessel, the square-rigged *Maryland Dove*, Historic St. Mary's City includes the Godiah Spray Tobacco Plantation, a Woodland Indian Hamlet, Smith's Ordinary and Cordea's Hope. These recreated 17th-century settings as well as costumed interpreters bring the old city to life. At the Visitor Center, an introductory video and an archaeology exhibit will get you started.

Since 1971, the Historic St. Mary's City archaeological program has recorded well over 300 sites within the grounds. At one site, a significant amount of lead type, typical of that used in the 1600s, suggested the location of one of the first printing presses in the English colonies. The recreated Print House now stands on the original building's post holes and holds a reproduction printing press. The St. John's Site Museum, which opened in fall of 2008, examines how researchers learn about the past. It preserves the foundation of the 17th-century home where Maryland's legislators first met.

With several new and expanded exhibits, as well as special events and tours, Historic St. Mary's City is open 10 a.m.–5 p.m., Wednesday–Sunday, from mid-June through the end of November. For spring and fall hours and other information, call 240-895-4990 or *visit www.hsmcdigshistory.org.*

When you're done visiting Historic St. Mary's City, you can stroll along miles of walking trails, admiring the river views that Lord Baltimore and his followers once beheld.

Above: Costumed interpreters portray the lives of Maryland's first colonists at Historic St. Mary's City. Right: Visitors try their hand at the windlass aboard the Maryland Dove.

St. Marys River *continued*

attracts hundreds of boats and is the oldest overnight race on the Bay.

St. Mary's College owns most of the big brick buildings on the east side of Horseshoe Bend. The school was founded in 1840 as a monument to religious tolerance in colonial Maryland, beginning as a boarding high school for girls. It became a junior college in 1926 and a coed, four-year liberal arts college in 1969. In 1992 it became Maryland's only legislatively mandated Honors College. In addition to its strong academic program, St. Mary's College has a consistently strong sailing program, with its teams among the top-ranked in the nation.

The college has a 150-foot pier north of Church Point where cruisers can dock for a few hours on a first-come-first-served basis. Visitors must be off the pier by nightfall. It's free, but the school welcomes donations to the St. Mary's College Foundation. You can top off your water tanks for free as well, but no other services are available. Be sure not to block the college's boats when you tie up. You can also take a dinghy ashore to a 300-yard public beach just north of the college pier.

While there is no real town or city here, visitors are welcome to wander the campus and browse through the college's Campus Center. Besides a convenience store, book store and a campus pub, visitors are welcome at the full-service dining hall, which offers breakfast, lunch and dinner. It's one of the Bay's best food bargains. Call 240-895-4220 to confirm dining hours. The Athletic and Recreation Center (ARC) with an indoor pool is a short walk from the waterfront and open to the public ($5 one-day use fee). For pool and gym hours, call the ARC Welcome Desk at 240-895-4295. On June and July weekends you can anchor off the pier about mid-afternoon Friday and dinghy in to enjoy the college's River Concert Series that evening (free lawn seating) along with a meal from one of the vendors. Concerts begin at 7 p.m. (240-895-42956)

The premier attraction here is Historic St. Mary's City—Maryland's reemerging earliest settlement. But if sightseeing and shore expeditions are not your choice, try cruising about

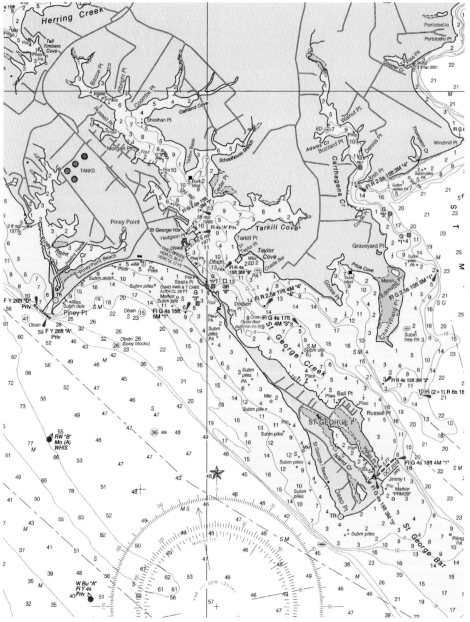

St. George Creek; from NOAA Chart 12233—not to be used for navigation.

a mile upriver from Horseshoe Bend. Anchoring along the southern side of an island with the intriguing name of ②e **Tippity Wichity** might make a nice addition to the ship's log.

St. George Creek

To port entering the St. Marys River you'll find ❸ **St. George Creek**, 8½ miles from Point Lookout. From the red/green buoy two miles off the St. Marys River entrance, head northwest toward flashing red "A" then look to the west for flashing "2". The latter, at the mouth of St. George Creek, marks the shoals off Cherryfield Point. On the left, teardrop-shaped St. George Island has a marked channel at its eastern tip leading to shallow **Island Creek.**

St. George Creek's channel is well-marked. **Price Cove,**

A 180-degree panoramic view of a cove near the top of Kingscote Creek on the Coan River. This nearly idyllic anchorage is open to breezes off the Potomac and Judith Sound, just beyond the trees, yet protected from all but the worst blows.

to starboard, is a popular anchorage with a long sandy beach, but stay mid-channel when entering since a shoal at Goose Point is barely awash at low tide. Past this cove, a pair of lighted markers are spaced about a half-mile apart. Watch your line between "3" and "4" since the channel narrows, curving to port. Stay well off the marks, especially at low tide. Opposite "6", green daymarks show the entrance to the channel between island and mainland. The fixed bridge (17-foot vertical clearance) allows shortcuts from here to the Potomac for low-profile, shallow-draft boats. (Shoaling is reported on both sides of the bridge.)

Seeming out of place among the tall pines and low sandy beaches are the multi-story buildings of the Paul Hall Center. Offering a Coast Guard-approved curriculum (and safety and firefighting courses), the Harry Lundeberg School of Seamanship has an associate degree program and opens to the public the first Sunday of the month (301-994-0010). Guests may tour the grounds and visit the center's library-museum.

At the nearby PINEY POINT LIGHTHOUSE MUSEUM AND PARK, visitors are welcome to come and stay a while. Accessible by boat, the park offers a sturdy handicap-accessible pier that connects to a wooden boardwalk that circles the lighthouse grounds. Benches and picnic tables are available for visitors who want to linger and enjoy the panoramic view.

The museum offers several displays of note, among them a small fleet of classic Chesapeake workboats on permanent loan from the Paul Hall Center: the 67-foot skipjack *Joy Parks*, the 84-foot bugeye *Dorothy A. Parsons*, a log canoe and a Potomac River dory boat. Piney Point's six-acre site is accessible daily, sunrise to sunset, but the museum buildings, gift shop and photogenic lighthouse are only open Friday-Monday, May-October. (Call ST. CLEMENT'S ISLAND MUSEUM, 301-769-2222, for info.) Displays include the story behind the World War II submarine lying in 90 feet of water off Piney Point. The wreck, designated as Maryland's first historic shipwreck preserve, is marked from April to December with a blue-and-white mooring buoy.

Most boating activity centers on St. George's low bridge, and a convenient anchorage for visiting both the Lundeberg School and Piney Point Lighthouse lies southeast of the parade grounds and gigantic training crane on Hodgson

Point, Here you'll find good holding and fairly good protection in 11- to 13-foot depths. Then take the dinghy under the bridge to the museum's sturdy dock near the tip of Piney Point. After a self-guided tour (informative plaques explain the area's unique history), choose a bench or stroll the sandy beach. The quaint Keepers Quarters is a private residence and not part of the tour.

Other anchorage possibilities lie beyond the tall modern buildings. Due east is **Tarkill Cove** with 7 to 9 feet at its entrance but shallowing dramatically where it narrows. **Schoolhouse Branch**, just to the north, has a tight unmarked channel but affords some room to drop the hook.

Sparsely settled St. George Creek is navigable for nearly a mile beyond Schoolhouse Branch with 7 to 10 feet of water. Loblolly and longleaf pine, farmland and bright white beaches make this a picturesque cruise.

Coan River

The ❹ **Coan River** appears to be a close sibling of its next-door neighbor, the Yeocomico, but although there is a strong family resemblance, the two have a very different feel to them.

From the Bay, the Coan is the first river to port on the Virginia side of the Potomac, about 15 miles from Smith Point Light (if you approach the Potomac from the south) and 7 miles from Point Lookout (if you approach from the north). Green "7" in the Potomac channel is northeast of the river's entrance. From there run southwest to green "5" off Travis Point, where the summer houses of Lewisetta line its Potomac shores.

Next, there's a short dogleg south to red "6", a most significant aid, because without it, you'd stand a good chance of grounding on the 2-foot shoal east of Lewisetta. The mouth is quite wide here, and you may be tempted to cut across—*don't.* It is fairly shallow, and there is a submerged jetty as well. At "6", turn west through a forest of brush stakes and poles to red "8" off Honest Point. Once there, you'll find three lovely paths from which to choose—Kingscote Creek to the northwest, The Glebe straight ahead to the west, or the Coan itself, which winds southward another four miles to Nokomis.

Coan River continued

If you need supplies or fuel, you have two options. North from "8" is the full-service marina at **Lewisetta** on the southern tip of Travis Point. There are 8-foot depths at the long fuel pier, with limited space for transients. At Lewisetta General Store, you can generally find a few groceries and boat supplies—and the latest local news.

The other transient marina, Coan River Marina, is opposite "13" at Walnut Point in a cove on the southeast side of Stevens Point. This area tends to shoal, so keep an eye out. Turn to starboard at the red-and-white vertically striped marker, then follow the private aids to the marina. To approach the fuel dock at the base of the second pier, try to stay close to the pier.

4a **Kingscote Creek** offers 8- to 9-foot depths. The area is predominantly a community of watermen's homes and summer cottages, but as the creek turns to the north, it becomes less populated, and you'll have a lovely view over the marshes of **Judith Sound** all the way across the Potomac to St. George Island off the Maryland shore.

Kingscote Creek is unmarked, and there are long shoals extending from either shore, but the channel is much less difficult than it appears. Look for a distinct, dark patch of trees to the left of a conspicuous white ranch-style house inside the creek. From this position, the channel is obvious, with crab pots on either side of the open water entrance.

4b **The Glebe** provides numerous scenic anchorages and, with higher banks, is more protected. Heading for The Glebe from the Coan River entrance channel, keep red "8" to port. (Note that "8" is a channel marker for the Coan, not the Glebe.) There are numerous Glebe Creeks and Glebe Coves on the Chesapeake Bay. The name hails from the old English custom of assigning a portion of land to the benefit of a church rector, who could farm or let it as he pleased and live off the proceeds.

A large cove to starboard named **Fisherman's Cove**, according to local residents, lies about a half-mile upstream. At the mouth of the cove on the east side, a bit of a shoal

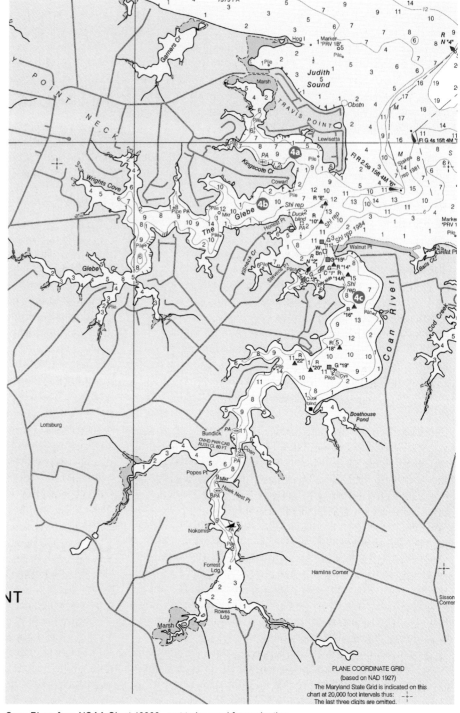

Coan River; from NOAA Chart 12233—not to be used for navigation.

pushes out toward The Glebe's midchannel; marked by brush stakes, it is easy to avoid. Purple martin houses line the shore, suggesting (but hardly guaranteeing) the possibility of a low mosquito population. There's a pleasant anchorage at the mouth of the cove and a smaller anchorage almost out of sight around the corner—a snug spot in which to ride out a storm or high winds. Depths range to 10 feet.

In earlier times, many small boatbuilding yards dotted the landscape. Until about 1960 the Headley brothers maintained a yard here, established by their father in about 1898.

In 1945, they built the *Sea Cloud*, a 30-foot skipjack that later sailed the Potomac, crewed by Sea Scouts under the leadership of Frederick Tilp, author of *This Was Potomac River.*

If you head farther up The Glebe, a privately maintained green aid identifies the shoal on the south shore that extends well beyond midchannel. On the south shore a bit farther past the marked shoal is another pleasant anchorage, **Kanes Cove**, which is open but provides a good spot for a calm night.

Beyond the cove, with no further marks, stay mainly in the middle of the channel, taking a left turn beyond the "finger peninsula" to port into Glebe Creek. You can then head south a half mile to the narrow passage between two points of land and, squeaking through in 6-foot depths, turn west and anchor for lunch in the first cove to starboard. It's one of those special private spots that allows enough room for just one boat, but it's seldom occupied.

Back on the Coan River itself, **4c Walnut Point** has a small sandy beach ideal for picnicking and swimming. The point is interesting historically. In the late 1800s, a summer resort hotel stood here, and later the community included a packing plant for seafood and vegetables. Now, amid lush green fields, the aging remnants and sagging roofs of deteriorating structures are all that remain of more prosperous times. On still nights, you'd swear you can hear the echo of laughter.

Once past the bottleneck area at Walnut Point, it's easy to follow the Coan's daymarks. Depths in the main branch range from 7 to 14 feet, with several snug anchorages and fairly undeveloped banks. The areas around "18" and "20" are roomy and popular spots for cruising groups, so you may have company if you anchor there on your own on a weekend. On the peninsula north of "20" and "22" are buildings belonging to Cawart Seafood Corporation, an oyster-packing enterprise.

Less than a mile beyond the Coan's last mark, red "22", an overhead power cable (charted at 60 feet) spans the narrowed shores. A grain storage depot is on the righthand shore, and you may see trucks making deliveries from nearby farms. Come late summer, be prepared to encounter a tug pulling a laden grain barge on its way to market.

Until the mid-1930s, two communities—Bundick on the western shore and Coan on the eastern shore—were connected by a cable ferry. A bustling tourist hotel and store in Coan fell into ruins and eventually disappeared. It seems remarkable that this was a town-site decreed by the Virginia House of Burgesses more than 300 years ago. It must have seemed then, when roads were few, that navigable waterways and a seemingly endless supply of fish and shellfish would ensure a town's continued viability.

Beyond the overhead cable, a small western fork has 6 feet at the mouth, but soon becomes shallow. The main branch, however, continues south with 7 to 9 feet beyond Hawk Nest Point for about a half mile toward **Nokomis**. You can anchor here and explore the river's shallow headwaters by dinghy or kayak. The closest town is charming **Heathsville**, about two miles from Rowes Landing, which is farther along the tributary.

Listed on the National Register of Historic Places, Heathsville has a restored hotel with a tavern/restaurant, working blacksmith forge and a very nice library. A grocery store is located at the Eastern edge of town.

Yeocomico River

With numerous branches and anchorages, good depths and marinas, the **5 Yeocomico** (*yuh-KAHM-eh-ko*) **River** never seems crowded. Like the fingers of an outstretched hand, the five-mile-long stream's several branches split further into creeks and coves, and its wooded shores offer beauty and serenity.

The river, nearly 12 miles up the Potomac from the Bay, is not difficult to negotiate, though its entry mark, red "2" (known locally as the "birthday cake" for a larger marker that was lost many years ago in a storm), can be devilishly hard to spot against the afternoon glare. From "2", run nearly two miles to flashing green "3", which may also be tough to see against the dark shoreline. From here, you can choose your branch: north into Shannon Branch, ahead into the West Yeocomico and **Kinsale**, or to port into the South Yeocomico.

To enter **5a Shannon Branch**, turn northwest after flashing green "3" into the first wide tributary; the first is actually short and shallow **Parkers Creek**. Honor flashing green "5", which marks a shoal south of White Point. As you enter this branch you'll see an oyster house to port and a sprinkling of modest homes along the starboard shoreline. Continuing to port leads you into **White Point Creek**, home of the peaceful and protected White Point Marina with complete facilities for the cruiser. Besides pool, tennis, ice, fuel, engine and hull repairs, a courtesy car is available for supplies and groceries.

Back at the mouth of the Yeocomico, the course to Kinsale, three miles west, begins with a dog-leg around Horn Point and into the **5b West Yeocomico.** If you honor red "2" off the point, there'll be no trouble with the long shoal that extends to menace the unwary. (Brush stakes abound here and elsewhere in the river are puzzling to newcomers. They denote oyster beds and are not aids to navigation.)

For a pleasant anchorage, look to port after clearing **Mundy Point** shoal. **Wilkins Creek**, with wooded shores and a few substantial homes, is a favorite. Broad and deep with 7 to 8 feet of water almost to its head, Wilkins has only a hint of a shoal at its entrance, most prominently on the western side and clearly marked by a duck blind.

Port Kinsale Marina, situated in **Allen Cove** on the West Yeocomico's north shore, suffered a serious fire in January 2015. We advise you to call ahead to check on the availability of various facilities. The *Virginia W*, a 1904 Virginia-built skipjack listed on the National Register of Historic Places and once moored at Port Kinsale, is now being restored across the Bay in Cambridge, Md.

Continuing west, **Great House Point**, near Kinsale on the chart, has an interesting early history. For many years the Bailey home, known as the Great House, has maintained the tradition of keeping a bright light in an upper dormer

Yeocomico River *continued*

window as a nighttime guide for mariners. In 1813, several British vessels entered the Yeocomico and attacked the *USS Asp* just offshore of the Great House. During the ensuing battle, the *Asp*'s young commander lost his life and was buried in the Bailey family cemetery, where a small cannon and a plaque still mark his grave. If you anchor overnight east of Great House Point (10 feet of water with good holding) you'll be able to see this long-standing tradition for yourself.

Just to the north, beyond the nearby grain elevator where the West Yeocomico becomes significantly narrower, you'll find Kinsale's waterfront and the fixed docks of Kinsale Harbor Yacht Club and Marina. No marine services or fuel are available, but the facility offers transient slips, a pool and dinghy docking space. From here, a pleasant stroll takes you to the heart of the tiny village.

Named for the Irish town from which her early settlers came, Kinsale was initially a customs port. When regularly scheduled steamboat service began in 1855, Steamboat Landing became a dynamic hub filled with stores, taverns, warehouses and a hotel. Today, among the lovely old homes surrounding the village green is Kinsale Museum. Worth a visit, it attractively chronicles the area's once-bustling past. Open Fridays and Saturdays, the museum also has walking tour maps.

During harvest time, the normally sleepy street leading to the waterfront is packed with trucks full of local bounty, waiting to off-load their cargo to barges. North of the village and farther upriver, a low fixed bridge (8 feet vertical clearance) halts most vessels, but 5- to 7-foot depths continue.

South of Great House Point, the **Hampton Hall Branch** spills into the West

Yeocomico offering protected anchorages. The first one, a cove to starboard with 8-foot depths, is opposite a sharp point of land. Another nook with charted depths of 8 feet lies on the other side of this promontory.

The **5c** **South Yeocomico** offers good anchorages in Cornish Creek, Palmer Cove, Dungan Cove, Mill Creek and Drum Cove on the north shore of Mill Creek. From daymark "2" off Horn Point, head southward favoring the Mundy Point side (starboard) to avoid the shoal off Tom Jones Point.

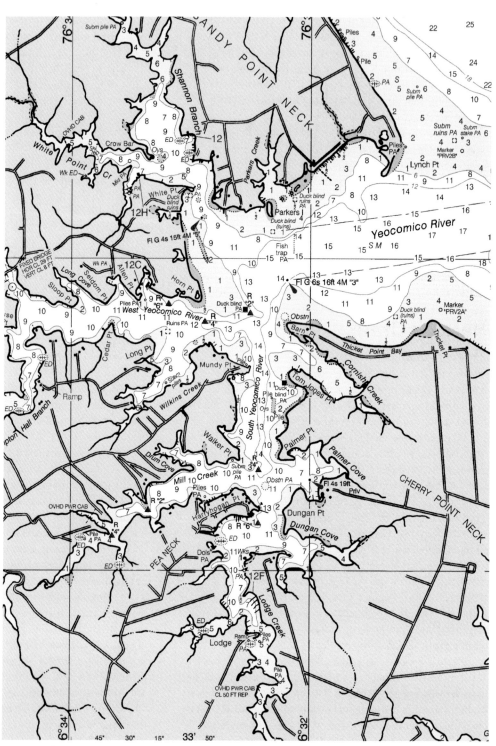

Yeocomico River; from NOAA Chart 12233—not to be used for navigation.

Opposite Mundy Point and southeast of daymark "2", **Cornish Creek** is a quiet anchorage with 5- to 7-foot depths in its center. You'll find a few homes and private docks here, but also a full complement of oyster stakes and floats.

Drum Cove, inside **Mill Creek** on the South Yeocomico Branch, is snug and quiet. After rounding daymark "4" at Walker Point, continue westward until opposite the cove's entrance to starboard before continuing in. There should be 7 to 8 feet at the entrance and inside, but be mindful of the shallows on the eastern side of the opening.

Another pretty anchorage on the South Yeocomico is **Palmer Cove** opposite the mouth of Mill Creek. The entrance is about 400 yards wide with plenty of room inside for a group of boats. The bottom is soft mud, so make sure your anchor is well set before you settle in for the night.

The river splits at **Harryhogan Point**, home of the well-known shipyard established by Herman Krentz where one of the last working skipjacks on the Bay was built in 1932. Krentz Marine Railway/Harryhogan Marina remains in operation there today. Opposite and southeast of "6", you'll find a lovely place to drop the hook at the mouth of **Dungan Cove** (about 7 feet inside).

Continuing southward you'll find **Lodge Creek** and Olverson's Lodge Creek Marina. A large, homey facility, it caters to both power and sail, offering gas and diesel, showers, boaters lounge, courtesy car and pool. Some slips are wide enough to handle catamarans. Lodge Creek, like other forks of the Yeocomico, once had a steamboat landing.

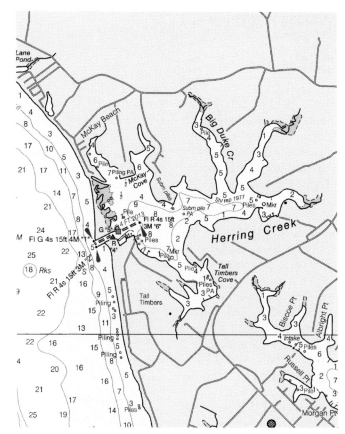

Herring Creek; from NOAA Chart 12233—not to be used for navigation.

Herring Creek

⑥ **Herring Creek** is often referred to as "Tall Timbers," because of the community and marina there. Herring is a fair-sized, almost landlocked body of water on the Maryland shore of the Potomac, about three miles upstream of Piney Point and approximately 15 miles from Point Lookout.

After you pass Piney Point, Herring Creek is the next waterway on the Maryland shore. Its entrance is a subtle indentation, little more than a hollow spot in the verdant shoreline.

As you arrive offshore of the creek's entrance, you'll find a pair of handsome stone jetties with tall, 4-second flashers (a green "1" and a red "2") at the outer ends. These were built by the Army Corps of Engineers in the 1960s, who also dredged the creek's entrance channel is dredged to 9 feet. But it is subject to shoaling (you can probably count on finding 5 to 6). At the inner end of the jetties is a red "4" daymark and a green "5". The end of the channel is marked by a flashing red "6". Directly to starboard is Tall Timbers Marina, a full-service facility with gas, diesel, transient slips and a restaurant, The Reluctant Navigator. (Don't turn toward the marina until you've cleared "6"!)

As you pass into the creek proper, you'll be struck by the sheer beauty of the place as it spreads out before you. Lovely lawns and tended fields bordered by lush, deep-green woodlands (tall timbers, if you will) frame an idyllic setting. There's room here for several modest-sized raft-ups.

From this point, several prongs split from the creek. To port is **McKay Cove**, a bit open when the winds are blustery and with less water than the other prongs. To starboard is **Tall Timbers Cove**, with depths of 7 feet at the mouth, dropping to 5 and 4 feet inside. The shoreline of this cove is more wooded, offering more protection in a blow.

From the entrance, the main branch of Herring Creek runs directly ahead and carries 8 feet of water or more for about a mile. Expect to find 7 feet all the way to **Big Duke Creek** (5 feet inside), which may remind you of Dividing Creek on the Wye River. Dense woods growing right up to the shoreline provide a cool, shaded spot. You'll find a dandy place to anchor at the mouth of Big Duke, just out of the traffic.

Beyond Big Duke is a creek known locally as Little Duke. The head of Herring Creek also has a nickname (**Cedar Cove**) and is home to Cedar Cove Marina, with 6 feet of water at its dock and offering transient slips, gas, showers, a laundry, repair services and some supplies. Its small restaurant is open weekends for lunch and dinner.

Edwin Beitzell, in *Life on the Potomac River*, says that Herring Creek got its name from the great herring runs during spawning season, which still occur here. Frederick Tilp's *This Was Potomac River* notes that a deed of 1649 shows the name as "Herring Creek" although an 1841 chart calls it "Heron Creek." The creek was said to have been a favorite of smugglers during the Civil War and Prohibition, due to the continually changing channel and shoaling at the creek's hidden entrance.

Middle Potomac

Coles Point

Bordering Lower Machodoc Creek on the east is ❶ **Coles Point**, a beautiful promontory named for its long-ago owner, Richard Cole, the early settler who owned a 1,350-acre parcel of land here. Today the most prominent enterprise is Coles Point Marina, located on the Potomac River side of this neck of land, just downstream of Ragged Point Light. The marina's breakwater is a good landmark for cruisers, who will find 6 feet of water in the entrance channel. Transient boaters are welcome at this charming resort, which recently changed hands and has seen a lot of updates and improvements—with more in the planning. The marina offers gas and diesel, a small ship's store, new restaurant—The Landing Restaurant and Waterfront Bar—a new boat ramp and one of the nicest beaches around. It is also dog- and children-friendly. In addition, there are walking trails through the woods, and a large freshwater pond that's stocked with bass (no gas-powered boats allowed) and home to Japanese grey geese and white swans. The 340-acre resort also has a large wooded camp-

ground, new rental cottages and a large events building.

On your way around the top of Coles Point, you'll see a ramshackle tavern on pilings built out over the river. This is Coles Point Tavern, and, yes, it's open for business. Boaters can tie up right beneath the tavern. The food is good, area musicians are frequently featured, and it's a popular place with locals.

Lower Machodoc Creek

❷ **Lower Machodoc** (*muh-SHO-duck*) **Creek**, 11 miles upstream from the Yeocomico River, is a great place to explore and its upper reaches a peaceful place to drop the anchor. But first you need to learn how to get in. The approach up the Potomac is fairly straightforward. Simple compass and shoreline navigation will bring you to Ragged Point near the Lower Machodoc's entrance, marked by a platform with an automated light and a sprinkling of riprap on its western side. From there a gentle curving course around Coles Point brings you to the creek entrance.

You may find several gill nets along the eastern shore here. If you see a flag (usually red) on a stick, look around for its partner; they signal an underwater net, sometimes 200

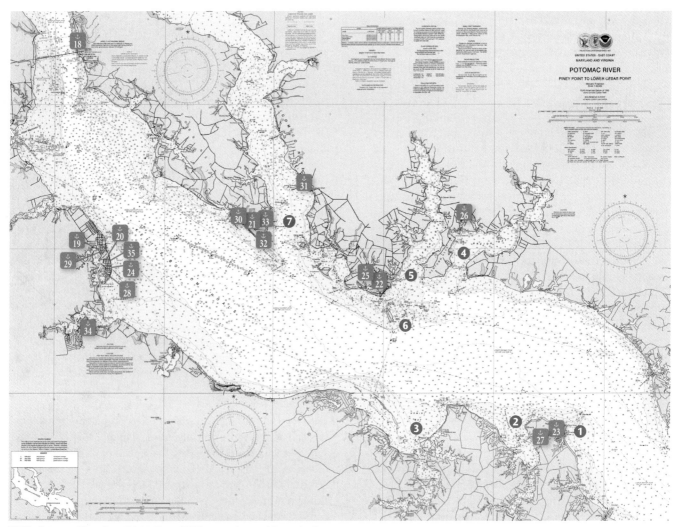

Middle Potomac River; from NOAA Chart 12286—not to be used for navigation.

to 300 feet in length. Although the nets are weighted to keep them near the bottom, its always a good idea to give them a wide berth.

Flashing "1LM" and two other unlighted marks, green "1B" and red "2", lead you into the creek. To starboard, private aids show the way to channels for **Cabin Point Creek** and **Glebe Creek** farther south. Both are shallow and subject to shoaling.

To port is **Branson Cove**, where the village of Coles Point is largely centered. To get there, round green daymark "1B" and then turn east. Closer to shore, two green marks identify Branson channel. Unfortunately, because of a failed develop-

● On Premises
➤ Nearby

Middle Potomac River

Marina	MLW	Overnight Slips	Gas	Diesel	Propane	Electric	Showers	Laundry	Restaurant	Lodging	Pool	Pump-out	Ice	Groceries	Marine Supplies	Bait	Boat Repair	Haul-out Services	Launch Ramp	Wi-Fi	Other
Aqua Land Marina & Campground Potomac R./northeast side Route 301 bridge 301-259-2572	4'	●	●	●	➤	●	●	➤	➤			●	●	●	●	●	●	●	●	●	
Bayside Marina Potomac R./Colonial Beach 804-224-7570; www.baysidemarina.org	4'	●	➤	➤		●	●		●	➤				➤	➤						Block from downtown, 5-star restaurant, trolley stop
Boathouse Marina Potomac R./Monroe Cr./Colonial Beach 804-224-7644	7'	●	➤	➤	➤	●	●	●	➤			●	➤	➤	●	●	●	●	➤	●	
Capt. John's Marina Potomac R./Neale Sound/Cobb Island 301-259-2315; www.cjcrab.com	6'	●	●	➤	➤	●						●	●	●	●	●	➤	➤	●	●	Brand new docks built in 2013!
Cather Marine Potomac R./St. Patrick Cr. 301-769-3335; www.cathermarine.com	5'	●	●	➤		●		●				●	●	➤	●	➤	●	●	●		30-ton lift, factory-authorized repairs; surveyors
Cole's Point Marina and Boatyard Potomac R./Ragged Point 804-472-4011; www.colespointmarina.com	7'	●	●	●	●	●	●	●	●		●	●	●	●	●	●	●	●	●	●	Beach, store, cottages, pavilion, campsites, trails
Colonial Beach Yacht Center Potomac R./Colonial Beach 804-224-7230; www.cbycmarina.com	10'	●	●	●	●	●	●	●	➤		●	●	●	●	●	●	●	●	●	●	Trolley, protected harbor, beach, golf carts
Coltons Point Marina Potomac R./St. Patrick Cr. 301-769-3121; www.coltonspointmarina.com	5'	●	●	●	➤	●	●	●	➤		●	●	●	●	●	●	●	●	●		30-ton lift, pavilion, lounge, big screen TV
Combs Creek Marina Potomac R./Breton Bay/Combs Cr. 301-475-2017; www.combscreekmarina.com	8'	●	➤			●	●	➤	➤		●	●	●	●	●	➤	➤	➤	●		Covered slips, PWC drive-on docks; well protected, boat lifts
Harding Marine Railway Potomac R./Lower Machodoc Cr. 804-472-2698	7'								➤			➤	➤	●	●	➤	●		➤		Railway for boats to 80 ft/60 ton; woodwork
Monroe Bay Marina Potomac R./Monroe Cr./Colonial Beach 804-224-7544 or 804-224-9560; www.monroebaymarina.com	5.5'	●				●						●							●		
Nightingale Motel & Marina Potomac R./Monroe Bay/Colonial Beach 804-224-7956	6'	●	➤	➤	➤	●	●	➤	➤	●		➤	➤	➤	●	➤	➤	➤	➤		
Pirate's Den Marina & Restaurant Potomac River/Neale Sound/Cobb Island 301-259-2879; www.piratesdenmarina.com	16'	●	●			●	●	●	●			●	●	●	●			●	●	●	Tiki bar, live entertainment, karaoke
Quade's Store Potomac R./Wicomico R. 301-769-3903	6'		●							●			●		●				●		Crabcakes, soups and burgers
Saunders Marina Potomac R./Neale Sound 301-259-2309	3'	●	➤	➤	➤	●			➤			●	➤	➤	➤			●	●		Camper sites with electricity & water, picnic area
Shymansky's Marina Potomac R./Neale Sound 301-259-2221	6'	●	●	●	●	●	●	●	●		●	●	●	●	●	●	●	●	●	●	Restaurant on site, breakfast, lunch, dinner
Stepp's Harbor View Marina Potomac R./Mattox Cr. 804-224-9265; www.harborvu.com/	6'	●	●	➤	➤	●			➤		●	●							●		Covered slips, pool, picnic area, low rates
Winkie Doodle Point Marina Potomac R./Monroe Cr./Colonial Beach 804-224-9560	5'	●				●						●							●		

Lower Machodoc Creek *continued*

ment, there is no longer anywhere to dock in Branson Cove—once lively with marinas, restaurants and seafood plants. Still, it's well worth the exploration if you choose to drop anchor and dinghy in.

For years, this guide has suggested that an exploration of Coles Point start at the town's tiny post office. It's still a fine place to start. The problem in recent years is that you will have a problem finding a place from which to start. There are no longer any marina slips for transients. The best plan is probably to anchor nearby and dinghy in. There are still several stops for your Coles Point itinerary. One of them, however, may or may not be open. If it is, sit down and enjoy a great meal. The problem is that the every-popular Driftwood Restaurant has been opening then closing at irregular intervals over the past few years. Across the street, however, you'll still find Jordan's Store, a fascinating old general store. Be sure to ask about the rocking chair behind the cash register. On Branson Cove itself, you'll find Harding Brothers Marine Railway, with its array of interesting boats under repair—occasionally even a Navy landing craft on the rails for a once-over. From Branson Cove, you can walk the mile or so to Cole's Point Marina through a wooded area rumored to harbor pirate treasure. Blackbeard frequented this stretch of the Potomac, and local lore has it that some of his plunder may be hidden along the trail.

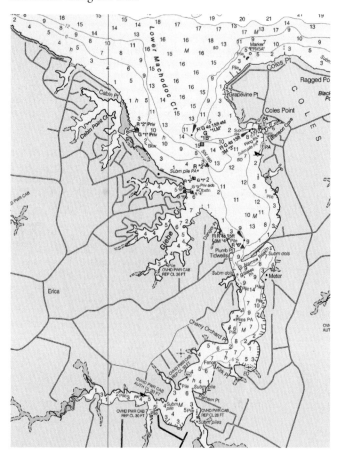

Lower Machodoc Creek; from NOAA Chart 12286— not to be used for navigation.

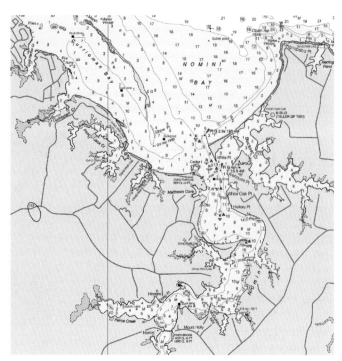

Nomini Creek; from NOAA Chart 12286—not to be used for navigation.

The hillside along the eastern shoreline of Lower Machodoc Creek offers some lovely countryside. Charming homes tucked into clusters of trees overlook well-tended green lawns and fields. Many cruisers anchor overnight in the entrance area between Branson Cove and **Narrow Beach** (known as **The Narrows**), a long, thin strip of land that juts well into the creek from the eastern shore.

Continuing upstream, flashing "4" and daymark "6" help define the channel as it squeezes toward Plumb Point and Narrow Beach, but from there on its all guesswork. Follow the local brush stakes and you should find enough water. But motor cautiously, watching the depthfinder. Generally, a line of brush stakes parallels the starboard shoreline, and a second parallel line of stakes does the same to port. Follow the starboard stakes for 100 yards or so and turn into the middle of the creek to find 8 to 9 feet of water for anchoring, or motor upstream and explore this beautiful creek. Nearby on the western bank is historic St. James Episcopal Church in **Tidwells**, dating to 1890. If not for the large cross on its waterfront lawn, you might miss this tiny church, nearly hidden among the trees. It's said that in the days when the church was being built, services were held under a sail stretched between the trees. Today St. James hosts a blessing of the fleet every June.

Exiting Lower Machodoc Creek is relatively easy if you follow these instructions from local gill netters on how to find the deepwater channel: Motor between the two rows of brush stakes that form a pathway to the end of Narrow Beach. The stakes mark oyster beds, not necessarily shoals. Then swerve to port to honor the little cluster of brush stakes and follow around the two red marks out to the main part of the creek. Using this route, you should find 8-foot depths the entire way.

Nomini Creek

❸ **Nomini Bay** on the Potomac's south shore is full of pleasant surprises: stunning 150-foot-high cliffs, an island studded with prehistoric shark's teeth and Nomini Creek, a deep, picturesque waterway that offers cruisers shelter and solitude.

Nomini Bay's wide mouth is marked by green can "13" in the main channel of the Potomac. Inside, depths vary from 10 to 15 feet, quickly dropping near each shoreline. To the west is **Hollis Marsh**, a private sandbar-like island nicknamed Shark's Tooth Island by locals. The island is privately owned and open to members. You'll find contact information posted on a sign on the beach.

To enter **Nomini Creek**, at the bottom of the bay, look for flashing green "1" and daymark "2". The entrance channel is fairly narrow, but widens once you're in the creek. As you wind upstream several miles, you'll see on a bluff along the southern shore the Mount Holly House. Built in 1876, when Nomini Creek was filled with commercial landings, boatyards, oyster houses and canneries, this three-story frame house was a popular steamboat stop. Now closed, it served as a restaurant and inn until recent years.

Breton Bay

About 16 nautical miles beyond St. Marys River on the Potomac's north shore is ❹ **Breton Bay**, separated from St. Clements Bay to the west by Newtown Neck. Off the beaten path, both bays offer deep water, great fishing and fine anchorages. To enter either, the safest, deepest approach is east of **St. Clements Island**, between red-green nun "HI" (marking the eastern side of Heron Island Bar) and flashing "2" at the mouth of Breton Bay.

Breton Bay, with just one unobtrusive commercial enterprise at Lovers Point—a quarry operation with barges—is otherwise pastoral, with most coves carrying deep water nearly to shore. About 2 miles from "2", **Combs** (*kooms*) **Creek** on Breton Bay's western side is the site of small and friendly Combs Creek Marina, which offers snug slips. If you draft 6 feet or more, enter Combs carefully since its narrow opening could hold only 7 feet at high tide. Inside, however, a protected anchorage carries 8 to 9 feet.

At the head of Breton Bay, beyond a sharp turn west at "11", **Leonardtown** welcomes boaters to its rejuvenated waterfront. The new brick wharf and promenade, dotted with cleats, have about 4 to 5 feet alongside and a terraced canoe-kayak landing. However, reports of underwater obstructions here indicate that this is not a good place for vessels with a draft of 4 feet or more. On the other hand, anchoring space abounds in the surrounding waters, with 8 to 10 feet, good holding and protection. Dinghy in to enjoy the center of town, just a short walk up the hill. Established in 1708, Leonardtown was once an important tobacco-shipping and steamboat port. Displayed at the 1858 jail, now a museum, is a cannon from the *Ark*, one of two ships carrying the first colonists to Maryland. Nearby, Tudor Hall, c. 1744, is also open to the public. Leonardtown's lush Town Square, rimmed with shops and eateries, stages special events.

St. Clements Bay

Rounding Newtown Neck to enter ❺ **St. Clements Bay**, look for the charted white beacon that marks a shoal off the neck. From here pick up the lighted red "2" to starboard off Long Point, and about a half-mile upstream is the entrance of **Canoe Neck Creek**. The creek is fairly wide with an easy-to-negotiate entrance. Be very aware of the shoal off the northern shore, however, which in one spot extends about a third of the way across the creek. The unwary will find the depths there change quickly from 8 feet to ½ foot.

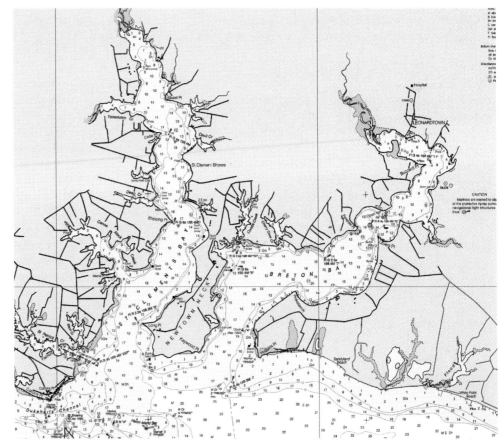

Breton Bay, St. Clements Bay and St. Clements Island; from NOAA Chart 12286—not to be used for navigation.

St. Clements Bay continued

The two branches at Morris Point are well populated with attractive homes and boat docks. At the point, to port, sits Morris Point Restaurant, a casual family eatery (dockage for diners, including overnighters). Favor the port side of the channel until you are opposite the entrance to the first large cove on the north shore. At the mouth of this cove there is an extensive shoal out from the starboard shore, so keep to port.

Typically, the summer evening stillness here is punctuated by the screeching of herons and other avian voices. The large number of great blue herons in this area provides interesting watching as they compete for fish and wade along the shore. As you drift up to the head of the creek, you'll note several more spots that would make good places for an overnight stay. You may find yourself in the company of another boat or two, but more often you'll have this scenic creek to yourself.

Most of St. Clements Bay is broad and deep, with beautiful surroundings and without obtrusive shoals. Several small creeks offer protected anchorages, the first being **Deep Creek**, with a narrow entrance and 8 or 9 feet of water inside.

As you head out St. Clements Bay toward Dukeharts Channel, to starboard—marked by flashing red "2"—lies serene, protected **St. Patrick Creek**. Somewhat narrow, the creek carries about 14 feet at its mouth, dropping to 5 feet at its head. You'll find a number of coves suitable for anchoring as well as two marinas, a waterfront campground and a B&B. Cather Marine provides slips for transients, gas, supplies, repair services, parts and a 30-ton lift. Coltons Point Marina offers gas and diesel, supplies, repairs and service, and picnic facilities.

St. Clements Island

It is difficult to imagine what ❻ **St. Clements Island** must have looked like more than 300 years ago when settlers led by Leonard Calvert arrived in early spring after their long voyage across the Atlantic. At that time, the island measured almost 400 acres (it is now only 40) and was no doubt a welcome sight to the colonists as their two small ships dropped anchor. They named the island for St. Clement, the martyred saint cast into the sea with an anchor fastened around his neck.

This name was later changed to Blackiston's Island, after the family who owned it for 200 years. Over time a farm with several buildings was established, along with a lighthouse and a small hotel. In 1962, the name St. Clements was restored. The land is now operated as ST. CLEMENTS ISLAND STATE PARK.

Time has erased all evidence of the original buildings. However, a replica of the old Blackistone Lighthouse, which stood on the island's southern tip from 1851 until it burned a century later, has recently been erected near the site of the original and is open by appointment (call 301-769-2222). The island's other landmark is a 40-foot cross erected by the state of Maryland in 1934 to celebrate the tricentennial of the colonists' first landing. As you approach the island, the huge white cross stands dramatically against the skyline.

A long shoal projects from the northwest end of the island

into **Dukeharts Channel** toward **Heron Island Bar**, a couple of sandy islands visible only at low tide. Those navigating these waters have a choice between circling north of Heron Island Bar and coming into St. Clements Island from the direction of Newtown Neck, or taking the more direct route by way of the channel between the two islands. This channel is quite wide and not the least risky, but from a distance you may have a hard time spotting the buoys that mark the shoals on either side. As you approach the second can ("5"), the park's large dock will be easy to see. Nearly 200 yards long, it can accommodate quite a few cruisers but since the park is for day use only, boats may not stay overnight.

St. Clements is an interesting place to go ashore, so don't miss the opportunity. In addition to the lighthouse, you'll find walking trails, sheltered picnic areas, grassy expanses and a nice beach on the Potomac side. To protect the island from erosion, the state has placed riprap around much of the shoreline. (Storms have shifted a lot of sand around the island; be aware that chart depths may not be accurate.)

At Coltons Point across Dukeharts Channel, a summer cottage has been converted into the ST. CLEMENTS ISLAND MUSEUM, which offers water taxi service to the island on weekends, Memorial Day through September. Visitors can see many historical mementos as well as a turn-of-the-century photograph collection of the hotel and farm buildings. The museum is the scene of an annual historical pageant and blessing of the oyster fleet, which takes place in the fall. There is also an annual jazz and seafood festival on the site.

Wicomico River and Cobb Island

Fishing is the main draw on the ❼ **Wicomico River**, which has numerous shoals and few sheltered anchorages. At the mouth of the river, however, **Cobb Island** is a favorite overnight stop for boaters traveling up or down the Potomac. The island sits snugly off the end of Cobb Neck, about 33 miles from the Bay. Less than two miles long and a half-mile wide, it is separated from the mainland by Neale Sound, a calm, narrow harbor with a front door (onto the Wicomico) and a back door at its northwest end, where a channel has been cut through the shoal. A fixed bridge (vertical clearance 18 feet) links the island near its midpoint to the mainland.

Depth is not an issue approaching **Neale Sound**'s eastern entrance, where the Wicomico's mouth is marked on the north side by 18-foot-high flashing "1W" at the end of Cobb Point Bar. Between "1W" and Cobb Point itself stands the remainder of Cobb Point Light, a screwpile lighthouse dating from 1889 that was destroyed by fire in 1939. Called the "spider buoy" by locals, it is not a navigation aid and is not lit at night, so boaters absolutely should not cut inside "1W".

Just beyond lighted green "3W", the entrance to Neale Sound lies to port where flashing red "2" is followed by daymark "4", since a straight shot to the bridge from flashing red "2" will put you on a shoal. (Long shoals lie in wait all through these waters. They're well marked, but boaters do get fooled. If it happens to you, kill the engine and call the Boat/U.S. dispatcher at 800-391-4869.)

Cobb Island was nearly a peninsula a century ago, but the dredged channel at the northwest end of the sound now allows shallow-draft boats to sneak through. The cut is about 5 feet deep at high tide, 3 feet at low. (When the wind has been blowing from the northwest for a few days, though, all bets are off.) Boaters entering Neale Sound through this northwest end should note, in addition to the limited depth, that navigational aids change at the bridge; no matter which end you enter, it's "red right return."

Along this stretch of the Potomac, storms barreling down from the northwest can be quick and dirty, but between Cobb Island and the mainland it's nearly always calm and you'll find good-holding anchorages on both sides of the channel.

Though small, Cobb Island has everything a boater might need: marinas, a repair yard, rental skiffs, restaurants, post office and a small grocery, plus an art gallery/coffee shop. Most businesses are clustered near the bridge or a short walk away. Three marinas on the mainland side have slips for transients, with two—Shymansky's and Capt. John's—providing fuel; the smaller Saunders Marina is a little farther north, on the upriver side of the bridge. South of the bridge on the island side is Pirate's Den Marina, with overnight slips, gas and diesel, and a restaurant, and Scuttlebutt Restaurant and Marina.

Perhaps the only negative about this neighborly place is its proximity to Dahlgren U.S. Naval Weapon Laboratory, just upstream on the Virginia side. When the range is "hot," and the wind isn't cooperating, islanders are serenaded with the booms of artillery being fired into the Potomac. Testing is announced on VHF 16, or boaters can call 877-845-5656 for the schedule; when the range is active, patrol boats will direct you to the safe route, indicated by yellow markers.

Each June, islanders celebrate their rich history with Cobb Island Days. One source of community pride is that in December 1900, a team of scientists led by Reginald Fessenden accomplished the first voice radio transmission here. The famous words were: "Is it snowing where you are?" The answer was yes, since Fessenden's message was transmitted only a mile, from one 50-foot mast to another in Neale Sound. One of the houses in which the scientists and their

families stayed, Vickers House, a Victorian grande dame with two turrets, is now a prominent landmark overlooking the sound just south of Pirate's Den Marina.

Captain James Neale purchased the island in 1642, and it's said that the place got its name from the confiscated Spanish coins he brought back from the West Indies. The gold and silver, crudely cut into "cobbs" or "cob money," was used by early settlers.

Colonial Beach

About halfway between Point Lookout and the Wilson Bridge, **Colonial Beach** makes a convenient waypoint and a lively stop along the Potomac. This Northern Neck resort, founded in the late 1800s, lost momentum when the Bay Bridge opened, luring beachgoers to Atlantic shores. Recently rediscovered, boaters and daytrippers now enjoy its sandy beach—the second longest in Virginia—along with its shops, art galleries and interesting restaurants

Nearly opposite Cobb Island on the Maryland side, Colonial Beach can be approached from the river's main channel around lighted buoy "17". Set a course for the first entrance mark, flashing "2", about 4½ nautical miles west of there. Deeper drafts will want to mind the depth-sounder as they approach this area and while heading for the next mark, "4", also lighted. Charted depths can be as

continued on page 224

CAPTAIN JOHN'S CRABHOUSE
COBB ISLAND, MD

SEAFOOD RESTAURANT & MARINA
Our 52nd Year!

Great Safe Harbor to Have Dinner & Spend the Night
All New Boat Slips for 2013. Transients, monthly and anual slip-holders welcome. Fuel dock with gas and diesel, electricity, water, pumpout, and free WiFi. Access to remote security cameras.

ActiveCaptain
1st Choice Marina
2013/2014

COBB ISLAND, MD
301-259-2315
WWW.CJCRAB.COM
WWW.FACEBOOK.COM/CAPT.JOHNS

BoatUS COOPERATING MARINA

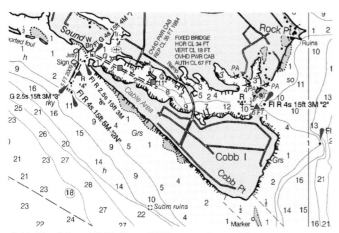

Cobb Island; from NOAA Chart 12286—not to be used for navigation.

Port of Call

Colonial Beach

Although its wild casino days are long gone, they are not entirely forgotten. Today, however, Colonial Beach attracts a different crowd—those in search of a getaway from life's hectic pace. Sandy beaches, a long boardwalk and a pier beckon visitors to the riverfront, while shaded streets with their shops, vacation cottages and stately Victorian homes invite a leisurely stroll.

Boaters have several options for getting around the peninsula that separates the Potomac and Monroe Creek: walking, riding the sightseeing trolley that makes a loop around town during summer months (nominal fee, 804-224-0175) or—the favorite mode for many—renting a golf cart (marina delivery, 804-761-1594).

Among the local attractions is the Museum at Colonial Beach, whose exhibits and videos chronicle the town's lively history, including bloody feuds between Maryland and Virginia (dubbed the Oyster Wars) over seafood harvesting rights, and the Virginia town's days as a gambling center, when casinos were strategically built *over* the Potomac (waters owned by Maryland) to sidestep Virginia's anti-gambling laws. Visitors also should not miss the World War II veterans' memorial.

For recreation, there are playgrounds, beaches, town commons and a community stage. Charterboats depart from the waterfront on fishing trips and scenic cruises.

Virginia's Northern Neck is rich in history, and Colonial Beach is a good base from which to hire transportation for a visit to nearby sites. Downriver from Monroe Creek is Wakefield, the reconstruction of George Washington's birthplace. Also south are Westmoreland State Park with its stunning Horsehead Cliffs (3-foot depths MLW at the small boat dock) and Stratford Hall Plantation, the birthplace of Robert E. Lee.

The shopping district is a compact compilation of just enough gift, antiques shops and art galleries to keep browsers happily occupied on a lazy afternoon. You can provision (and get excellent sandwiches) down-

continued on page 224

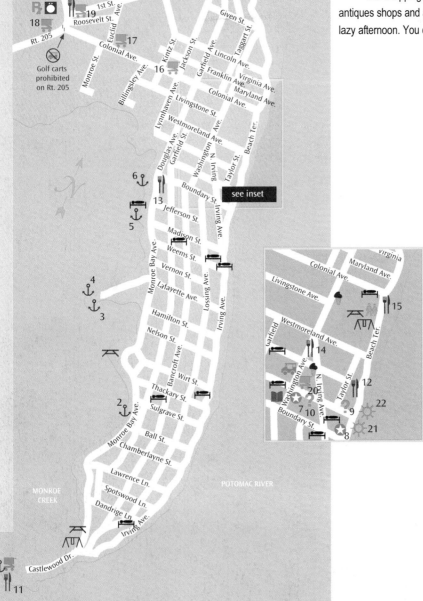

Colonial Beach

⚓ **Marinas/Dockage**
 1 Colonial Beach Yacht Center
 2 Boathouse Marina (formerly Stanford's)
 3 Winkie Doodle Point Marina
 4 Monroe Bay Marina
 5 Nightingale's Marina
 6 Bayside Marina

◎ **Points of Interest**
 7 Museum of Colonial Beach
 8 World War II Memorial

❓ **Information**
 9 Visitors Center
 10 Chamber of Commerce

🍴 **Dining**
 11 Dockside Restaurant & Blue Heron Pub
 12 High Tides on the Potomac
 13 Lighthouse Restaurant
 14 SeaSide French/Thai Restaurant
 15 Riverboat on the Potomac

🛒 **Groceries/Carryout**
 16 7-Eleven
 17 Dollar General
 18 Food Lion
 19 Get & Zip
 20 Denson's Grocery

☼ **Entertainment/ Recreation**
 21 Town Pier (fishing)
 22 Tour boats/fishing charters

🍦 **Ice Cream**
⛺ **Lodging**
🛵 **Golf Cart/Scooter Rentals**
🚻 **Public Restrooms**
⛱ **Picnic Area**
🎠 **Playground**
📖 **Library**
℞ **Pharmacy**
🧺 **Laundromat**
···· **Boardwalk Promenade**

VIRGINIA CLEAN MARINA

The Town of NO BOAT TAX

Visit the tranquil shores of the historic Northern Neck of Virginia

Located in a safe, year-round harbor

Last deep water port until Washington, DC

Dockside Restaurant on-site - serves local seafood and daily specials

1787 Castlewood Drive | Colonial Beach, VA 22443 | 804.224.7230 | mail@cbycmarina.com

cbycmarina.com

Colonial Beach Chamber of Commerce

Port of Call Colonial Beach *continued from page 222*

town at Denson's. There is also a 7-Eleven, Get & Zip and a mini-mart inside Dollar General; grocery stores lie just beyond the permissible cart driving limits. Marine supplies are as close as the ship's stores at Boathouse Marina and Colonial Beach Yacht Center.

Like the town, you'll find dining in Colonial Beach relaxed and unpretentious. Several restaurants are well within walking distance of the marinas and make the most of their waterfront locales. Dockside Restaurant (seafood, steaks) and its Blue Heron Pub (British-style tavern) are located at Colonial Beach Yacht Center, and, built out over the river. Riverboat on the Potomac offers seafood and steaks (as well as off-track betting). A number of other establishments are a stroll away, including High Tide, SeaSide French & Thai Restaurant and Lighthouse Restaurant.

Art flourishes locally as evidenced by the Colonial Beach Artists Guild, which presents Second Friday Art Walks, when galleries and craft shops stay open late to exhibit and sell the works of local artists. On the fourth Saturday of the month, Town Hill Park becomes the setting for Market Days (a farmers' market) and a concert series (both held May to November). A gala three-day Potomac River Festival in June features music, arts, crafts, a parade and fireworks. Independence Day festivities include a big fireworks display. International Jet Ski Races tear up the Potomac in July, and a Rockfish Tournament is held in November.

Information: Colonial Beach Tourism Council, 804-224-0732 (Friday through Sunday); Chamber of Commerce, 804-224-8145 (Wednesday through Friday), *www.colonialbeach.org*; Town of Colonial Beach, 804-224-7181, *www.colonialbeachva.net*.

Colonial Beach *continued from 219*

low as 6 and 7 feet, and shoals of 1 and 2 feet extend off Gum Bar Point.

Note: The yellow nuns and cans on both shores in this stretch of the Potomac define the "Middle Danger Area," Dahlgren Naval Surface Warfare Center's testing range. When firing is in progress, range control boats fly red flags and monitor VHF 16 and 14 to assure safe passage for all water traffic with minimal inconvenience.

At "4", south of Gum Bar Point, a sharp turn to starboard leads into the snug harbor between two skinny strips of land. The channel carries 8 feet but watch for strong currents that can run through the narrow cut. This tributary, **Monroe Creek**, is named for James Monroe, the country's fifth president who was born and raised nearby. Locals prefer to call the lower section "Monroe Bay."

Inside to starboard, several marinas offer transient slips and most waterfront restaurants have courtesy dockage for diners. Colonial Beach Yacht Center, to the right just inside Gum Bar Point, has repairs and fuel (gas and diesel). Outside of the dredged channel expect as little as 2 to 4 feet, but any vessel needing more depth to anchor will find room for a few boats around marks "10" and "12" where 8 feet is reported.

The municipal pier along the Potomac side, like much along this entire peninsula, was rebuilt in recent years following tropical storm damage. Reserved for fishing charters and tour boats, and exposed to river turbulence, recreational vessels may not dock here. Two concrete boat launching ramps are available for public use in Monroe Creek.

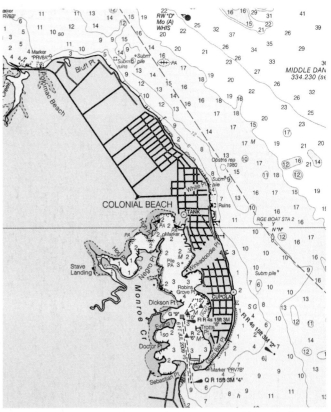

Colonial Beach; from NOAA Chart 12286—not to be used for navigation.

Upper Potomac

Above Colonial Beach and Cobb Island—and beyond the U.S. 301 bridge—the mighty Potomac begins its transition to a narrower, less daunting body of water. But as it makes its broad S-turn (known locally as The Hoseshoe), the river also leaves behind its long deep tributaries, with their many safe anchorages, for the shorter, shallower creeks that lie upriver. And as its deep-water channel switches from one side of the river to the other, it also loses its character as a great sailing river. Here the sails are often sacrificed to the cause of forward progress . . . unless, that is, the wind happens to be favorable, in which case the Upper

Potomac becomes a splendid ride through American history. At its first turn, the river offers up a short but beautiful tributary.

Port Tobacco River

Although the ❶ **Port Tobacco River** is small (about three miles long), its natural beauty matches anything on the Bay. There are panoramas of green and tan river banks and small, sandy beaches. The feeling of solitude you'll experience while cruising these sparkling waters—especially at midweek—defies description. At the river's head lies the town of Port Tobacco, which played an important role in colonial times.

The mouth of the river is located just $6\frac{1}{2}$ miles above the Governor Harry W. Nice Bridge, which carries Route 301 across the Potomac between Maryland and Virginia. A word of caution here: As you enter the river and the companion cove of Goose Creek, the depths fall off rapidly. Off Windmill Point is a particularly extensive shoal marked by green "1". Stay in the well-marked, deep-water channel, particularly during low tide, as some cruisers report the river appears shallower than shown on the charts. Also, be mindful at dusk of the numerous crab pots in the area. When north and west winds are blowing they'll move a lot of water out of this river, too.

Goose Creek (or Goose Bay) is a sheltered cove near the junction of the Port Tobacco and Potomac rivers. It's a good spot to go ashore for a picnic or a walk along the sandy beach. There is a full-service marina located here with a campground and another marina at the head of the Port Tobacco River offering transient slips, gas, a small store and repair services.

Leaving Goose Creek and heading back into the river, you will see St. Ignatius Roman Catholic Church (1798) with its inspiring white steeple visible high on a hill on the eastern shore at Chapel Point. Behind the church sits St. Thomas Manor, built in 1741. The manor's land deeds date to 1662 when 4,000 acres were turned over to the Jesuit Order by Thomas Matthews. Under a high bluff at **Chapel Point**, you will find a fine anchorage or refuge from a nor'easter and a sandy beach, part of CHAPEL POINT STATE PARK.

Upper Potomac River; from NOAA Chart 12288—not to be used for navigation.

Legend: ● On Premises ➤ Nearby

Upper Potomac

	MLW	Overnight Slips	Gas	Diesel	Propane	Electric	Showers	Laundry	Restaurant	Lodging	Pool	Pump-out	Ice	Groceries	Marine Supplies	Bait	Boat Repair	Haul-out Services	Launch Ramp	Wi-Fi	Other
36 Aquia Bay Marina & Marine Works — Potomac R./Aquia Cr. — 540-720-7437; www.aquiabaymarina.com	4'-8'	●	●	●	➤	●	●	●			➤	➤	●	●	●	●		●	●		35-ton lift, hydr. trailer, complete repairs
37 Belmont Bay Harbor — Potomac R./Occoquan R. — 703-490-5088; www.belmontbay.com	7'	●	●	●		●	●	●	➤	➤		●	●	●	➤	➤		●	➤	➤	Golf course, brokerage, ample parking
38 The Breakwater at Leesylvania State Park — Potomac R./Bouy 47/opposite Mattawoman Cr. — 703-730-8205	4'						●					●							●	●	Storage, fishing pier, picnic area, fuel dock
39 E-Z Cruz Marina — Potomac R./Neabsco Cr. — 703-670-8115; www.ezcruz.com	5'	●	●			●	●	●	➤	➤		●	●						●	●	●	Gas dock open 24 hours with credit card
40 Fort Belvoir Marina MM — Potomac R./Ft. Belvoir, Va. — 703-781-8282; www.belvoir.armymwr.com	4'	➤	➤	➤	●	●	➤	➤	●	➤	●	●	●	●				●	●	●	Under 40' lift; scenic marina
41 Ft. Washington Marina — Potomac R./Piscataway Cr. — 301-292-7700; www.coastal-properties.com	4.5'	●	●	●		●	●		●			●			●				●	●	●	Indoor & outdoor dining, floating docks, kayak rentals
42 Goose Bay Marina — Potomac R./Port Tobacco/Goose Cr. — 301-934-3812; www.goosebaymarina.com	5'	●	●	●	●	●					●	●	●	●				●	●	●	Campground, picnic area; gas, diesel, propane
43 Hamptons Landing Marina — Potomac R./Neabsco Cr. — 703-221-4915; www.hamptonslandingmarina.com	5'	●	●	●		●	●	➤	➤	➤		●	●	●	➤				●	●	●	TowBoatU.S. and BoatU.S. co-op marina
44 Hoffmaster's Marina — Potomac R./Occoquan R. — 703-494-7161; www.hoffmasters.com	6'	●		➤		●	●		➤	➤		●	●	●	●	➤		●	●	●	●	Service, Cobalt, Bennington and Chaparral
45 Hope Springs Marina — Potomac R./Aquia Cr. — 540-659-1128; www.hopespringsmarina.com	5'	●	●	●		●	●	●											●	●	●	300-rack boathouse, beach, picnic area w/ firepits
46 National Harbor Marina — Potomac River/Base Wilson Bridge — 301-749-1582; www.nationalharbor.com	9'	●	●	●		●	●	●	●	●	●	●								●	Slips to 120-ft., restaurants, shopping, water taxi
47 Occoquan Harbour Marina — Potomac R./Occoquan R. — 703-494-3600; www.occoquanharbourmarina.com	8'	●	●	●		●	●	●		●	➤		●	●	➤	●	●	●			●	Floating Docks
48 Pilot House Marina — Potomac R./Neabsco Cr. — 703-670-6900; www.thepilothouse.com	8'	●	●			●	●							●	●	●	●		●			BoatU.S. towboat Potomac Marine
49 Port Tobacco Marina and Restaurant — Potomac R./Port Tobacco R. — 301-870-3133; www.porttobaccomarina.com	3'	●	●			●			●			●	●	●	➤	●		●		●		Port Tobacco Restaurant, full-service marina
50 Prince William Marina — Potomac R./Occoquan R. — 800-216-2628; www.pwmarina.com	5'-6'		●	●	●	●			●	➤		●	●	●	➤	●		●			Sea Ray sales, slips & dry storage boatel
51 Quantico Marina MM — Potomac R./Quantico, Va. — 703-784-2359; www.quantico.usmc-mccs.org	6'	●	●		➤	●	●	●	➤	➤	➤	●	●	●	●	➤				➤	Free pump-out to military, others $5
52 Smallwood State Park/Sweden Point Marina — Potomac R./Mattawoman Cr. — 301-743-7613; www.dnr.state.md.us	6'	●	●			●	●	●									●		●		
53 Tantallon Marina — Potomac R./Swan Cr. — 301-651-7016; www.tantallonmarina.com	6'-8'	●	➤	➤	➤	●	●	●	➤			●	➤	➤	➤		➤	➤	➤		Floating docks, 100 amp service w/ 110/220 volts
54 Tyme N' Tyde Marina — Potomac R./Occoquan Bay — 703-491-5116; www.tymentyde.com	4'		●			●	●		➤	➤	➤	●	●	●	●	●	➤	●	●		Larson boats & Mercruiser sales/service
55 Willow Landing Marina — Potomac R./Aquia Cr. — 540-659-2653; www.daverino.net	3'		●			●	●					●	●					●	●	●		All gas engine repair, ramp

Port Tobacco River *continued from page 225*

As you continue up the Port Tobacco River, there are numerous historic buildings and sites inland. The Port Tobacco Courthouse, a fine example of Georgian architecture, has been restored and is used as a museum by the Society for the Restoration of Port Tobacco. Several old homes originally built by colonists and patriots are fully restored and currently occupied as private dwellings.

Although the town of **Port Tobacco** did indeed deal in exporting tobacco during colonial times, it was not named for this reason. The original inhabitants of the area were Piscataway Indians, who named this area "Potopaco," which means "the jutting of water inland." The present name seems to be an anglicization of the Indian name.

Mallows Bay

Past the Port Tobacco River and Nanjemoy Creek, the Potomac heads west for about 10 miles before making its swing northward. Halfway, the channel narrows between Riverside (another "lost" summer resort) and Metomkin Point, sending the current zipping through the turns. Stay in the deepest part of the channel, if the tide is with you, and you'll pick up a couple of extra knots.

As the river begins its final turn north, two tributaries— **Potomac** and **Aquia** creeks enter to port. Both are largely shallow and cater to powerboats, with 3- to 5-foot depths. Both are lovely. Aquia has several marinas.

Heading north now, the current hugs the eastern shore, with deep water nearly to the water's edge. About three miles north of the mouth of Aquia Creek, you'll find a modest shelter for the night in **Wades Bay**. Two miles farther upriver, at nun "40", you'll see the river's most unusual sight. ❷ **Mallows Bay** is the final resting place for a fleet of wooden ships built during World War I. Part of an ill-conceived plan to counter German attacks on Allied shipping, the vessels were finally scuttled, unused, and are known to this day as the "ghost fleet of Mallows Bay." You can see their outlines, bristling with weeds, lining the shore.

There is a small park and launch ramp here for a dinghy landing, but don't venture in with your boat. With all the wrecks and debris, it would be like playing Russian roulette with your prop.

Mattawoman Creek

Located about midway between Port Tobacco River and Washington D.C., ❸ **Mattawoman** (*MAT-uh-WOE-mun*) **Creek** is a waterway blessed with unspoiled beauty and plenty of tempting anchorages. Bluffs are topped with oaks, maples and poplars, another flotilla of yellow pond lilies, which also go by the curious and playful name of "spatterdock."

If you're heading into Mattawoman Creek after dark, play it safe and head to flashing green "45" before turning toward the creek's mouth. This takes you close to the south shore to daymark "1". Carefully pick your way to green "3"

off Deep Point, and then to green "5" on the north shore. This will keep you clear of the shallows off Sweden Point. (Note that green "5" on the north shore almost disappears in the shoreline, but don't miss it! To avoid the shoals, take it very close aboard before heading for red "6".)

At Sweden Point, to starboard about a mile from the creek's entrance, is **Smallwood State Park**, a memorial to William Smallwood, a Revolutionary War general and Maryland's fourth governor. The park's Sweden Point Marina offers transient and long-term dockage, bathhouse, picnic areas and six launch ramps. (Call 301-743-7613 to reserve a slip in advance.) A marked channel shows the way in. The channel carries 6 feet of water under normal conditions (i.e. unless strong winds or exceptionally low tides are a factor). On the creek front you'll find a pier and fuel dock (gasoline only), where a small shop (open seasonally) sells fishing gear and licenses, ice, sodas and sandwiches.

The cove next to this facility is shallow and full of water lilies. A graceful arched bridge crosses this cove to higher ground and Smallwood Park. From here, you can walk the 100 or so yards to Mattawoman Creek Art Center, a volunteer-run gallery that features the works of local and regional artists. In the park, charcoal grills and picnic tables are scattered through the woods along a path up to the reconstructed Smallwood's Retreat, the general's plantation home (open Sunday afternoons from May to early October, 301-743-7613). Docents offer tours of the mansion, which is full of Federal period antiques. Outside, William Smallwood's grave is marked by a large monument.

Mattawoman Creek hums with the lively traffic of small powerboats, and the creek is known for its excellent bass fishing (several tournaments are held here annually). About halfway upriver, you enter a no-wake zone, and from here on the channel hugs the creek's northern side. About a mile past the boat ramp at Mattingly Park (formerly known as Slavins Ramp) is an area called the Dunes, a popular spot for boating rendezvous and rafting up. Deep water runs right up to the edge, letting you put the bow up on the beach.

Occoquan River

Boaters visiting the ❹ **Occoquan** (*AHK-uh-kwahn*) **River** on the Virginia side of the Potomac have no lack of facilities where they can find fuel, food and service: four marinas on the river, one on Occoquan Bay and three more on **Neabsco Creek**, on the western shore of the mouth of **Occoquan Bay**. The channel was dredged in 2005 to a depth of 9 feet for six miles from the river's mouth to the town of Occoquan, with its numerous attractions. Check your charts if you visit, noting the fixed bridges (the lowest with a 44-foot vertical clearance).

The Occoquan River bellies out into **Belmont Bay** to the north and Occoquan Bay to the south. Near the Occoquan's headwaters, where it tumbles from the mountains, lies **Occoquan**, a former mill town and center for river commerce.

Despite Occoquan's long riverfront, ample bulkheads, deep water, several marinas and a small public park, there are precious few slips for transients. Belmont Bay Harbor marina,

Occoquan River *continued from page 227*

to port just before red "12", and Occoquan Harbour Marina, just beyond the fixed railroad and U.S. 1 bridges (65-foot vertical clearances) offer overnight slips, but it's best to call ahead to check availability. Most slipholders are local power-boaters, who enjoy the fact that the Occoquan is only about an hour from downtown Washington. (The fixed bridges and heavy weekend boat traffic on this narrow river discourage many sailors from going very far upstream.)

Occoquan looks like a classic New England mill town, tucked along the narrow river beneath a steep hill that rises to the west. At first, it appears to be nothing more than a small cluster of shops. Not so. Though downtown lacks many services, these are located outside the historic area. Restaurants, gift stores and artisans' shops (the town hosts two major crafts shows) fill the historic district. Don't miss the MILL HOUSE MUSEUM and one of the Occoquan's most interesting historic buildings, Rockledge, a Georgian mansion perched above town. It's a setting for weddings and catered dinners.

Mount Vernon

The Potomac's shores finally become more intimate—but still a mile apart—above Hallowing Point, where a second and much smaller S-turn leads northeastward toward the marked channel for ❺ **Mount Vernon Estate and Gardens**, George

Washington's historic plantation high above the western bank. The majestic home of the nation's first president and roughly 500 acres of his former 8,000-acre estate have been preserved as they existed in 1799.

Visiting by boat involves docking on the north side of a single pier at Mount Vernon Landing. Use plenty of fenders or, better yet, a fender board, because tour boats come and go from the south side, setting up a roisterous wake. Docking is on a first-come, first-served basis, so it's wise to radio ahead on channel 16 or 13. Cost is $2/foot plus the regular admission fee. There's no overnight dockage here, but this is an unforgettable way to visit this beautiful estate.

Anchoring off Mount Vernon is also an option and dinghy dockage is permitted. (No dinghies may land on the beach, however.) To anchor, follow the dredged channel toward the dock, which starts in the Potomac at green can "71". Turn to starboard toward the marked channel leading to **Little Hunting Creek**, and anchor anywhere off the channel in reported depths of 6 feet. For more information about Mount Vernon call 703-780-2000.

National Harbor

Heading farther upriver on the Potomac, you'll pass lovely but shallow ❻ **Piscataway Creek**, where a narrow 5 1/2-foot channel leads to Fort Washington Marina. The channel swings

continued on page 230

Port of Call
National Harbor

MamaGeek-Own Work

Take a quiet bay far up the Potomac River—nearly as far upriver as Alexandria and Washington, D.C.—and add millions of dollars and and a rather remarkable vision, and what do you get? National Harbor, 300 acres of multi-use waterfront development on Smoots Bay, just south of the Woodrow Wilson Bridge. Add a marina with floating docks and you have a destination like no other on the Chesapeake Bay. A destination that's still growing. In addition to the dramatic Gaylord Convention and Hotel, six hotels, dozens of restaurants, offices, retail shops, condominiums, and entertainment plazas, National Harbor now also boasts a 180-foot ferris wheel that provides extraordinary bird's-eye views of downtown Washington. This new attraction sits at the end of the marina's main pier. At the other end, there's now a 35-foot carousel as well as a sculputure of a giant emerging from the sand beach called the Awakening. Farther uphill from the river, past the shops and restaurants, is the Children's Museum, which opened in 2012, but isn't done growing yet either. Offsite, there are the Tanger Outlet shops and a permanent pavilion for Cirque du Soleil. Coming within the next several years is a huge MGM Grand casino.

For boaters, National Harbor is an inviting destination, with the Potomac's deepwater channel making the long trip upriver easy. On the way, you pass a number of historic sites, including Mount Vernon and Fort Washington, before National Harbor comes into view. The channel into National Harbor from the river is well marked—but be sure you have charts that are new enough to include the National Harbor channel. On the way in, you may share the channel with the water taxis and excursion boats that make regular trips across the river to Alexandria and on game nights, up the Anacostia to Diamond Teague, an easy walk from the Nationals stadium. The slips lie behind the breakwater, which also holds the fuel dock. The marina office, as well as the restrooms, laundry and showers are a bit of a hike up the docks to Waterfront Street.

Watch the National Harbor website, *nationalharbor.com* for events such as the culinary and wine festivals, ice sculpture exhibition and an annual Beatles festival, Abbey Road on the River. On the waterfront, you can rent paddleboards, kayaks and canoes or hire a fishing guide.

National Harbor

⚓ **Marinas/Dockage**
  1 National Harbor Marina
  2 Marina Office

⊙ **Points of Interest**
  3 Awakening
  4 Plateau
  5 Plaza entrance
  6 Carousel
  7 National Children's Museun
  8 Capital Wheel
  9 Gaylord Convention Center

🍴 **Restaurants**

❓ **Information**
  14 Public Safety Office
  18 Welcome Center

✉ **Post Office**
  12 UPS Store
  15 Post Office Services

$ **ATM**

℞ **Pharmacy**

M **Metrobus Stop**

T **Water Taxi**

National Harbor continued from page 228

north again at the prominent Fort Washington Light (flashing red) on the eastern shoreline. About four miles past Fort Washington and just below the Woodrow Wilson Bridge, you'll come to **Smoots Bay**, lying to starboard just beyond Rosier Bluff. Approaching from the south, look for the channel markers after red "87" and before red "90". Red daymark "2" and flashing green "3" indicate the beginning of the channel into Smoots Bay, now better known as home to the ever-expanding **National Harbor** complex. The channel carries 11 feet at low tide. The marina at National Harbor offers transient and hourly dockage, fuel, shower and laundry facilities, and access to the 300-acre retail/residential community's restaurants, shops and hotels. Water taxis make regular stops at the marina's pier and provide cruisers with access to Alexandria, Mount Vernon and Georgetown. Transient space is at a premium during the boating season, so be sure to call ahead to arrange for a slip.

Urban Potomac

Alexandria

Ahead lies one of the world's largest bascule bridges, Woodrow Wilson Memorial Bridge, which carries Interstate 95 and the Capital Beltway over the Potomac. Its twin spans form a gateway to ❶ **Alexandria** and the nation's capital. The bridge has a vertical clearance in midchannel of 76 feet MHW, which allows most recreational and commercial water traffic free passage. For vessels requiring more clearance, night-time openings can be arranged in advance at 703-370-0992.

Just beyond the bridge, to port, lies Alexandria. The City Marina at the foot of Old Town (the historic heart of town) offers pleasant facilities and a convenient base from which to explore the area. Adjoining the marina is a large courtyard with a restaurant, food pavilion, several shops and the vast Torpedo Factory Art Center.

A little more than a mile upriver of Alexandria, the Washington Sailing Marina sits on the west shore below Reagan National Airport, offering a safe refuge and plenty of amenities for cruising boaters. To enter, head west off the main channel toward the large stacks of the power station at flashing green "1" and red daymark "2"; then turn north to follow the west shoreline through markers "4", "5" and "6". Stay to port past "WR6A", which marks a partially submerged wreck, and continue up the channel. At "13" and "14", the channel makes a 180-degree turn around the point to enter the facility's basin. You can also anchor out north of the basin or contact the dockmaster (703-548-9027) for a temporary berth on one of the

Urban Potomac River; from NOAA Chart 12289—not to be used for navigation.

finger piers. Beware of the rocky ledge directly in front of the clubhouse inside of green "7". You may tie up temporarily at the dock, but be careful not to drift down on the ledge. The deep-water channel continues north less than a quarter of a mile, with shallow water on each side, so use caution.

Anacostia River

Washington, D.C., is a city of two rivers, the Potomac and its little sister, the ❷ **Anacostia River**. Once a busy trade route when tobacco was king, the Anacostia became polluted, heavily silted and largely unused by boaters. In the 1990s, activists pushed to reclaim the river, sponsoring clean-up days, planting trees, taking polluters to court and lobbying for government assistance. As a result, the Anacostia is already a cleaner waterway, and the District and Maryland have pledged $7.5 million to clean and restore the river.

At its wide confluence with the Potomac at Washington Channel, the mouth of the Anacostia greets boaters with the city's dramatic skyline. It's a busy place; runabouts, cabin cruisers and sailboats scurry across the water, and large party boats float guests on elegant dinner cruises. Overhead you'll hear the roar of air traffic at nearby Reagan National Airport and from the constant stream of helicopters buzzing into and away from the city.

continued on page 232

Port of Call
Alexandria

In the 18th century, Alexandria was a gathering place for patriots restless with the high cost of allegiance to England. It was also a bustling port of entry and later became a critical military district for Union forces during the Civil War. Homes and artifacts surviving the centuries are seamlessly woven into today's vibrant cityscape. In Old Town Alexandria, restored dwellings are tucked between private residences and a historic apothecary sits comfortably amid modern boutiques.

The first complex you encounter after docking at the city marina is the Torpedo Factory Art Center whose three floors provide studios for 165 artists. Each studio is a combination work area/gallery where resident artists gladly take time to talk with visitors. The complex also houses five galleries, an art school and the Alexandria Archaeology Museum. The museum displays objects from local digs and reconstructs newly unearthed items in its laboratory.

Two blocks inland lies the Visitor Center at Ramsay House, located in the 1724 home of a city founder. Here you can obtain brochures about such local points of interest as the Lyceum (a city history museum), the Athenaeum (Robert E. Lee's bank of choice, now an art gallery) and the 1774 Friendship Firehouse (home of the city's first volunteer fire company). Maps and the *Official Visitors Guide* locate and describe attractions, restaurants, shops and a self-guided walking tour of the historic district. Guided excursions can be taken on foot or by boat, horse-drawn carriage and even pedaled rickshaw.

Daily tours can be taken of Gadsby's Tavern Museum (*www.gadsbystavern.org*). A favorite haunt of George Washington, the tavern was a social and political gathering place in colonial times. Haunts of a different kind, along with local lore, are explored on ghost and graveyard tours that leave in the evening from the Visitor Center (*www.alexcolonialtours.com*). As you meander, you may notice the George Washington Masonic Memorial towering above Old Town at the western end of King Street, a mile from the river. Visitors can tour the building and enjoy awe-inspiring views from its observation deck.

Entertainment options are within walking distance (albeit a healthy one) of the waterfront at the Little Theatre of Alexandria (community theater) and MetroStage (professional productions). The Old Town Theater treats patrons to first-run movies; and live productions are staged at the Masonic Memorial. Taxis can take you to country, folk and other musical concerts at the Birchmere and performances by the Alexandria Symphony Orchestra. Many restaurants offer live entertainment. Find out more in the *Gazette Packet* newspaper, the city's visitors guide and at *www.alexandria guideonline.com*.

Alexandria is a convenient base from which to explore

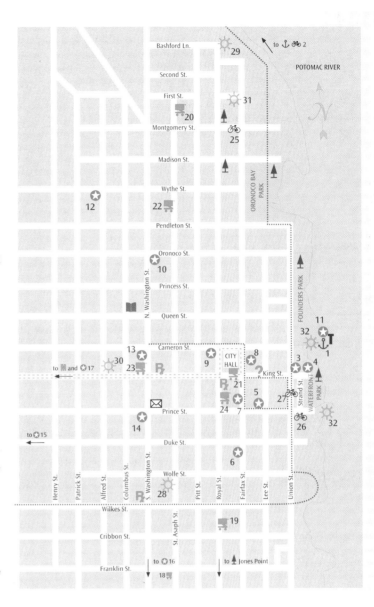

Alexandria

⚓ Marinas/Dockage
1 Alexandria City Marina
2 Washington Sailing Marina

◎ Points of Interest
3 Torpedo Factory Art Center
4 Alexandria Archaeology Museum
5 The Athenaeum
6 Old Presbyterian Meeting House
7 Stabler-Leadbeater Apothecary
   Shop Museum
8 Carlyle House
9 Gadsby's Tavern
10 Lee-Fendall House
11 Alexandria Seaport Center
12 Black History Museum
13 Christ Church
14 The Lyceum
15 Freedom House Museum
16 Mt. Vernon
17 George Washington Masonic Memorial

❓ Information
Alexandria Visitors Center
at Ramsay House

▣ Groceries/Carryout
18 Balducci's (specialty food store)
19 Safeway
20 Giant Food
21 Farmer's Market (Saturday mornings)
22 Trader Joe's
23 Le Pain Quotidien (organic foods)
24 Grape & Bean (gourmet market)

⑃ Bicycles
2 Washington Sailing Marina
25 Wheel Nuts
26 Big Wheel Bikes
27 Bike and Roll

☼ Entertainment/Recreation
28 Little Theatre of Alexandria
29 MetroStage
30 Old Town Theater
31 Tennis courts
32 Tour boats

- - - **King Street Trolley** (weekends)
· · · · **Historic Walking Tour**
· · · · **Bike Path**
✉ **Post Office**   ◼ **Library**
🛆 **Park**   ℞ **Pharmacy**
Ⓜ **Metro Station**   T **Water Taxi**

Port of Call: Alexandria

nearby attractions. Take the Metro subway to Washington, D.C., or visit Mount Vernon, George Washington's estate, via excursion boat or the 18.5-mile Mount Vernon Trail (hike, jog or bike). Water taxis also shuttle visitors to National Harbor and Georgetown, while a free trolley connects the waterfront with the city's Metro station

Information: Alexandria Convention & Visitors Association, 800-388-9119 or 703-746-3301; *www.visitalexandriava.com.*

Anacostia River *continued from page 230*

Just off Fort McNair, green "1" marks the beginning of the Anacostia channel, which carries 15 feet at this point. James Creek Marina to port has slips, gas and diesel fuel, showers and picnic facilities. Just upriver, Buzzard Point Marina also offers slips. A good place to begin your Anacostia journey is Washington's new waterfront Nationals baseball stadium, less than a mile from the Washington Channel. This glass, steel and concrete structure, which opened in 2008, is the centerpiece of a planned riverfront entertainment district. Just upstream of the stadium sits the historic Washington Navy Yard, home of the NAVY MUSEUM and the USS *Barry*, a 418-foot decommissioned destroyer that rests as a floating museum at the yard's wharf. There are no public docking facilities; to schedule a visit, call 202-433-4882.

Leaving the Navy Yard astern and heading upstream, watch out for the river's growing fleet of rowers. As the ramparts of the former baseball park, RFK Stadium, come into view, boaters approach the upper section of the Anacostia, where thickening woods along the river begins to mute the sounds of the city. Due to a low-lying railroad trestle with an unmarked channel beyond, the upper Anacostia is best explored in shallow-draft vessels. Five other bridges with vertical clearances ranging from 16 to 40 feet further discourage anything but low-profile vessels. Those who can make this 10-mile trip up-river will revel in the upper Anacostia's offerings. Around a few bends lies the NATIONAL ARBORETUM, 440 acres of formal gardens and collections. (Boaters can tie up to its small floating dock.) Just up-river is 32-acre **Kenilworth Marsh**, lush tidal wetlands teeming with wildlife. A jewel for paddlers, accessed through a cut in the marsh, is KENILWORTH AQUATIC GARDENS—a sanctuary of exotic water lilies and lotus

continued on page 234

● On Premises
➤ Nearby

Urban Potomac River

	MLW	Overnight Slips	Gas	Diesel	Propane	Electric	Showers	Laundry	Restaurant	Lodging	Pool	Pump-out	Ice	Groceries	Marine Supplies	Bait	Boat Repair	Haul-out Services	Launch Ramp	Wi-Fi	Other
56 Alexandria City Marina Potomac R./Alexandria 703-838-4265; *www.alexandriava.gov/Marina*	6'	●	➤	➤		●	●		●	➤		●	➤			➤		➤			
57 Belle Haven Marina Potomac R./Alexandria 703-768-0018; *www.saildc.com*	5'		➤	➤		●			➤	➤		●	●	➤	➤	●			●		Boat rentals, sail instruction, explore Dyke Marsh
58 Buzzard Point Marina Potomac R./Anacostia R./Washington DC 202-488-8400	8'	●	➤	➤		●	●		➤	➤	➤	➤	➤	➤	➤	➤	➤	➤			
59 Capital Cove Marina Bolling AFB MM Potomac R./Washington, D.C. 202-767-4651	6'	●	●		●	●	➤	➤	●	➤	➤	●	●		●	●	●	●	●	●	Across from Washington Sailing Marina
60 Capital Yacht Club Potomac R./Washington Channel/Washington DC 202-488-8110; *www.capitalyachtclub.com*	20'	●	➤	➤		●	●	●	➤	➤		●	●	➤	➤	➤	➤			●	Short walk to attractions and DC Mall
61 Columbia Island Marina Potomac R./Pentagon Lagoon 202-347-0173; *www.columbiaisland.com*	14'-18'	●	●			●	●		●	➤		●	●						●		Parks nearby
62 Gangplank Marina Potomac R./Washington Channel/Washington DC 202-554-5000; *www.gangplank.com*	20'	●	➤	➤	➤	●	●	●	➤	➤	➤	●	●	➤	➤	➤	➤	➤	➤	➤	Near subway/DC attrax.; winter bubbler
63 James Creek Marina Potomac R./Anacostia R./Washington Channel 202-554-8844, 866-554-8844; *www.jamescreek.com*	6'	●	●	●	➤	●	●	➤	➤	➤		●	●	➤	●		●		➤		US park property, floating docks, picnic area
64 Washington Marina Potomac R./Washington Channel 202-554-0222; *www.washingtonmarina.com*	9'-12'	●	➤	➤	➤	●	●		➤	➤		●	●	➤	●		●	●			Full service marine facility with floating docks
65 Washington Sailing Marina Potomac R./Alexandria 703-548-9027; *www.washingtonsailingmarina.com*	8'	●				●	●	●	➤	●	➤		●	●	●		●		●	●	Gift shop, marine store

Port of Call
Washington, D.C.

I t's easy to think of Washington simply as the nation's capital. There are government buildings, many quite impressive, and grand monuments, but they just scratch the surface. D.C. also has a thriving cultural life and plenty of less-formal sites to see. Most of Washington's major attractions are within walking distance of the Washington Channel marinas, but those that aren't can be reached by Metro, bus or taxi.

No matter how much time you have allotted for your visit, it won't be enough to take in all the city has to offer. Of the numerous government buildings, the White House, the Capitol and the Supreme Court should be tops on your must-see list. The Washington Monument and the Jefferson, Lincoln and Franklin D. Roosevelt memorials are stately tributes to past presidents. Fallen heroes and martyrs are honored at the stirring World War II, Vietnam and Korean War veterans memorials, the Holocaust Museum, the Navy Museum and the Women in Military Service Memorial. On the Mall, the museums comprising the Smithsonian Institution are dedicated to air and space exploration, art, industry, natural history, African American and Native American heritage, as well as U.S.

history. Get an enlightening look at the origins of printed money at the Bureau of Engraving and Printing. Take a guided tour of the Library of Congress and you'll see not only the nation's library, but the richly ornamental buildings in which it is housed.

The city has many art galleries, concert venues and theaters. Among them is Arena Theater, just two short blocks away from the Washington Channel. Farther away is the Kennedy Center for the Performing Arts, elegant host of symphony concerts, opera, dance and theater performances, and film screenings. Washington has enthralling botanical gardens and the popular National Zoo.

Recreation is close at hand. East Potomac Park at Hains Point has two 9-hole courses, mini golf, tennis courts and a playground. Paddle boats can be rented on the Tidal Basin. Stroll along a 7-mile path that follows the banks of the Potomac, part of the city's many miles of walkways and trails. The Washington Nationals play in their state-of-the-art baseball park on the Anacostia waterfront and D.C. United takes on soccer rivals at RFK Stadium. Team tennis is located right behind Gangplank and Capital Yacht Club.

The magazine *Where* lists attractions, entertainment, nightlife,

Washington, D.C.

⚓ **Marinas/Dockage**
1 Washington Marina
2 Capital Yacht Club
3 Gangplank Marina
4 Columbia Island Marina
5 James Creek Marina

⚙ **Points of Interest**
6 Bureau of Printing and Engraving
7 International Spy Museum
8 National Gallery of Art
9 Jefferson Memorial
10 Lincoln Memorial
11 Vietnam Veterans Memorial
12 Washington Monument
13 World War II Memorial
14 U.S. Capitol

15 White House
16 White House Visitor Center
17 Holocaust Museum
18 National Archives
19 National Postal Museum
20 Korean War Veterans Memorial
21 FDR Memorial
22 Air & Space Museum
23 Hirshhorn Museum & Sculpture Garden

24 Smithsonian Castle
25 Sackler Gallery/Museum of African Art
26 Freer Gallery of Art
27 Museum of Natural History
28 Museum of American History
29 U.S. Botanic Garden
30 U.S. Supreme Court
31 Library of Congress
32 National Portrait Gallery/ Museum of American Art
33 Convention Center
34 Corcoran Gallery
35 National Museum of the American Indian
36 Tomb of the Unknown Soldier
37 The Newseum

🛒 **Groceries/Carryout**
38 Farmer's Markets (Fridays, June–Oct.)
39 Maine Avenue fish markets
40 Safeway at Waterside Mall
41 Eastern Market

♻ **Entertainment/ Recreation**
42 National Theater
43 Warner Theatre
44 Arena Stage
45 Kennedy Center
46 Ford's Theatre
47 Union Station (movie theaters)
48 Sylvan Theater
49 Verizon Center
50 Constitution Hall
51 Potomac Spirit (tour boat to Mount Vernon)
52 Folger Shakespeare Library (plays, readings)
53 Shakespeare Theatre Company
54 Nationals Park

Ⓜ **Metro Station**
▓ **National Parkland**

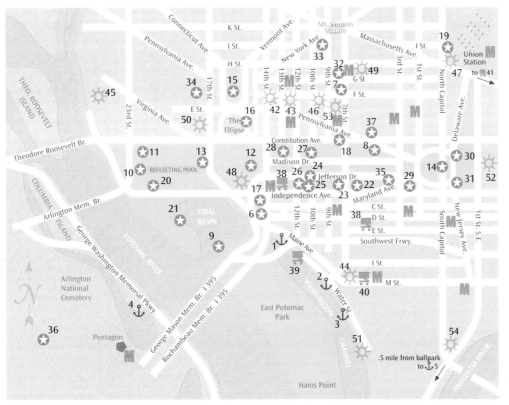

sports events and more, and the *Washington D.C. Official Visitor Guide* also offers historical tidbits, descriptions and profiles of neighborhoods like Georgetown, Dupont Circle and Capitol Hill. (Both available at the Visitor Information Center in the Ronald Reagan Building, 1300 Pennsylvania Ave.) Guided walking, bicycle, Segway, scooter, trolley, bus, boat, "Duck" and other tours focus on topics ranging from history to scandals to popular landmarks. Or you can take a free narrated cell phone tour of a dozen city landmarks (see *www.mobiletours.org* for a toll-free number and list of sights). DC Circulator buses shuttle visitors along popular center-city routes (*www.dccirculator.com*).

In addition to the shopping districts of Georgetown, Capitol Hill and downtown D.C., you'll find malls at Union Station (an Amtrak terminal and Metro stop), L'Enfant Plaza and, across the river in Virginia at Pentagon City. The Smithsonian and other museums have their own gift shops featuring many unique items.

Groceries are easy to find. Fresh and cooked seafood is sold from barges along the waterfront that have long been a part of the city scene and a Safeway supermarket is an easy stroll away. A short trip on Metro's blue and orange subway lines will get you to historic Eastern Market. On weekends, other vendors join regular merchants there for a big farmer's market and on Sundays there's a colorful flea market, too.

As befits an international city, Washington restaurants represent a spectrum of ethnic and regional cuisines. In addition to dining opportunities along the waterfront, the neighborhoods of Georgetown, Dupont Circle, Capitol Hill, Chinatown and Adams-Morgan are noted for an abundance of good restaurants. Visitors guides have compiled information on many of these establishments, including a general description of their menus, price ranges and closest Metro stop (where applicable).

The city's signature event is the National Cherry Blossom Festival and Parade. Mother Nature willing, the pink-blossomed trees reach their peak during the two-week celebration in late March/early April. The city's calendar is packed with other fun-filled festivals, celebrations, concerts and special events, including the Dragon Boat Festival in May. The Smithsonian's two-week American Folklife Festival straddles the Fourth of July weekend.

Please note that the waterfront and marinas along the Washington Channel are in the midst of a multi-year redevelopment project. So call ahead for space availability.

Information: Destination DC, 202-789-7000; *www.washington.org*; Metro Transit Authority, *www.wmata.com*.

Anacostia River *continued from page 232*

spread in a mosaic of shallow ponds and dikes.

Washington, D.C.

From the Woodrow Wilson Memorial Bridge over the Potomac, a clearly marked channel, averaging 20 feet in depth, can take you up the ❸ **Washington Channel** inside Hains Point to the waterfront of the nation's capital.

After passing the Wilson Bridge, just past historic Fort McNair on the starboard side, you'll find a waterfront lined with floating docks, restaurants, the Capital Yacht Club and several other marinas, nightclubs, an open-air seafood market, marine repair facilities and the commercial docks of excursion boats. Be aware that all of that is under extensive reconstruction, so check with the marina of your choice to be sure it has transient space available. This includes the docks at Gangplank Marina and Capital Yacht Club. Riding on the hook at an anchorage (fair holding ground) on the port side of the channel off EAST POTOMAC PARK remains an option. The deep channel can handle the largest cruising yachts. The Metropolitan Police Harbor Branch (202-727-4582), with headquarters at a municipal pier next to the excursion pier, has authority over the anchorages located in protected water along the west side of the channel. Contact them on VHF channel 17 for permission to stay up to a week at an anchorage. (Two anchors and a 32-point white anchor light are required.) Washington Marina at the head of the channel (beyond a fixed bridge, vertical clearance 37 feet) also generally offers transient slips, has full marine repair facilities and replacement parts service.

From your slip or anchorage on the waterfront, you can easily reach the myriad attractions of the nation's capital.

The city's subway system, Metro, can take you virtually anywhere you want to go. The stops nearest the waterfront are L'Enfant Plaza, served by four of the city's five subway lines, and Waterfront/SEU, on the Green Line. There is a Safeway a couple of blocks away and miles of lovely walking (and dog-walking) opportunities.

The Washington Channel ends at the **Tidal Basin** with no access back into the deep ship channel. To go farther up the Potomac, you must go back around Hains Point and head for the series of low, fixed bridges. The charted clearance here is only 18 feet, which prevents sailboats and other high-aspect craft from venturing any farther. Past Thompson Boat Center (rental canoes, rowboats and kayaks; 202-333-9543) on the starboard side is **Georgetown**. This famous neighborhood is filled with restaurants, clothing and gift shops, gourmet markets and two large retail/dining complexes.

Above the bridge, the river channel deepens and the water becomes very swift, particularly in the spring. At Key Bridge, on the Georgetown side, you'll see the Washington Canoe Club's 1904 shingle-style boathouse. University and high school crew races are held in this area between **Three Sisters Islands** and Thompson Boat Center. This is a popular launching spot for canoes and kayaks, and often there is considerable small boat activity.

Above Georgetown the 96-mile navigable channel comes to an end. Above Key Bridge and the fall line is the rocky, dangerous channel that includes Little Falls, Chain Bridge and Great Falls—an area not recommended for recreational use, though whitewater kayakers are attracted to the rough and tumble waters. Georgetown also marks the start of the Chesapeake and Ohio Canal, a 185-mile system of locks and channels that once carried lumber, coal and grain to the markets of the world. Now that historic and scenic path is a popular hiking and biking path.

The Hooper Islands to Cape Charles

The Honga, Nanticoke, Wicomico, Big and Little Annemessex and Pocomoke Rivers; Smith, Tangier and Deal Islands Salisbury, Crisfield, Pocomoke City, Onancock, Kiptopeke and Cape Charles; and the creeks of the Eastern Shore of Virginia

As you journey along the eastern side of the lower Chesapeake, you'll enter a world of authentic fishing villages, scenic anchorages, glorious beaches and stunning sunsets. You'll also enter a world of narrow winding channels through miles of shoal water.

There are gorgeous rivers like the Nanticoke, Wicomico and Pocomoke, where your splendid isolation is shared only with shorebirds and eagles. There are protected harbors like the one at Deal Island. There are cities and towns like Salisbury, Pocomoke City and Crisfield that are loaded with history, Eastern Shore culture and steamed blue crabs. There is quiet charm and stark beauty on Smith and Tangier islands, both places that time hasn't forgotten but perhaps neglected to spoil. Both have easy approaches, good docking and fine accommodations. Here you will find friendly people who are tied closely to the water and

whose speech has a rhythm and idiom of its own.

The Eastern Shore of Virginia sustains that leisurely pace. Creeks like Onancock, Pungoteague and Occohannock are beautiful, with wide marshes and protected anchorages. The town of Onancock, with historic homes, antiques shops and fine restaurants, is well worth a visit. Cape Charles, with its proud Victorian houses, is a gem to be treasured.

At the tip of the shore is a gem of another kind, the lovely public beach and bird-watcher's paradise of Kiptopeke State Park. You can anchor here safely, thanks to a line of concrete ships that form an artificial harbor. You might then dinghy ashore, walk up to the bird sanctuary and, in fall and spring, watch and listen for songbirds or catch hawks or eagles in flight. Or you can simply stroll the beach at sunset and reflect on your lovely journey on the Bay.

A young crabber at Goose Creek Marina on the Manokin River shows how it's done—old style.

A workboat heads out of Anns Cove on Pocomoke Sound. The islands and shallow waters of the lower Eastern Shore still belong to the watermen.

Smith and Tangier Islands

Connected to the mainland only by ferry boat, Smith Island and Tangier Island are true watermen's communities, whose relative isolation simply adds to their appeal.

From the mouth of the Potomac River, Smith Island lies about 13 miles east and Tangier Island about 18 miles southeast. These islands remain home ports to extensive fleets of workboats. Soft-shell crab pounds, shanties and workboat slips line the major waterways.

Skiffs, often with a dog keeping lookout in the bow, skim to and fro. Workboats come and go, maneuvering with enviable expertise. From May to November, if you overnight (in a slip or at anchor), be prepared for flurries of activity around 11 p.m. and 3 a.m. (soft-shell crab culling), from predawn till 7:30 a.m. (workboats leaving), and from noon till 4 p.m. (workboats returning). A measure of tranquility descends on Sundays when the workboats take a well-earned rest. Both islands are busy, fascinating ports to visit.

Cruise boats from Crisfield, Onancock, Reedville and Point Lookout State Park regularly bring visitors to the islands, most running only during the warm-weather season (May to October), with a few offering year-round service. If you're planning an overnight stay at one of the inns on the islands

during the tourist season, it's best to reserve a room in advance.

According to *Chesapeake Kaleidoscope* by Anne Hays and Harriet Hazleton, the two islands were once joined, but years of erosion have left one vast shoal and a sprinkling of marsh that, today, all but connects the two. The Virginia-Maryland state line cuts through Smith Island. The towns of Ewell, Rhodes Point and Tylerton are in Maryland; the marshes, at Smith Island's southern end, and Tangier Island belong to Virginia.

The islands were first explored in 1608 by Captain John Smith, who, legend has it, named them Russell Islands after Walter Russell, the physician accompanying him. The larger, now called Smith Island, measures 9 miles by 4 miles and was first settled in 1657 by dissenters from St. Clements Island. Tangier was first settled in 1686 by a Cornishman, John Crockett, and his sons. During the Revolutionary War, most of the people on both islands were British sympathizers. Some, called "picaroons," were infamous as raiders and pirates throughout the Bay. During the War of 1812, British troops by the thousands were quartered on Tangier, and it is said that Tangier, at the time, was stripped of its native trees in order to repair British naval vessels and to build a fort on the southern tip of the island.

Today, environmental factors seriously threaten the two islands and their inhabitants' unique way of life. Recent estimates show that Smith Island has lost nearly 3,300 acres of wetlands in the last 150 years. Tangier's land mass, report-

Smith and Tangier Islands continued

edly only a third of what the first English settlers found, now dwindles at the rate 16 feet a year on its western side and 3 feet a year along the east. Erosion has wiped out many of the natural barriers and submerged vegetation that once protected their shorelines, and rising sea levels exacerbate the situation. In addition, the land itself is sinking, settling after thousands of years of continental shifts. All these factors increase the destructive power of waves and storm surges. Both islands have seen a sharp downturn in population as well: Smith Island's 900 habitable acres now have well under 300 residents, and Tangier fewer than 500 inhabitants on its 128 "upland" acres.

Smith and Tangier each have two entrances—one from the Bay, the other from **Tangier Sound**. If you approach the islands from the west (the easier entrance for both islands), be aware of the U.S. Navy target ships (reduced to mounds of rust) just offshore. There is another target ship west of Kedges Straits to the north of Smith Island, about five miles offshore, and three bombing targets west of Tangier at distances between 1 ½ and 3 miles. These are easy to spot and are marked on charts within a large restricted area. (For full meanings of "restricted" and "prohibited" areas, refer to the *U.S. Coast Pilot*. The target areas can be dangerous and should be avoided.)

Smith Island

The best time to enter **Smith Island** is at mid-tide or higher, particularly if your boat draws over 5 ½ feet. The entrance is protected by two stone jetties with lighted aids. Unless visibility is poor, you should have no trouble finding these marks, but favor the port side of the channel.

From the Bay side, the entire channel into **Ewell** (the largest of the island's three villages) is well marked; it runs generally easterly for about three-quarters of a mile before turning south. Water depths here are now reported at least 6 feet throughout, except for a bump of 5 feet just west of "2A". Watch for markers placed by watermen as the channel shifts. The ferry uses this route regularly.

Tidal current is another factor to keep in mind, particularly when docking at Ewell. Here the current flows with a velocity that can make maneuvering difficult.

As you turn east after "15", you will see, on both sides of the channel, several shedding houses for soft-shell crabs. Then at daymark "16" a small workboat basin opens to starboard. Depths in the basin are reported at 2 to 3 feet. Controlling depth into Ewell from the west is 5½ feet at low tide. From Tangier Sound through the back-door channel, **Big Thorofare**, the depth is 6 feet though shoaling is all too common. The eastern approach is a four-mile-plus winding route that can be a little unnerving, particularly with a cross current or cross wind.

Once you've reached Ewell, dockage is limited. After the tour boats leave in mid-afternoon, you can tie up at the dock in front of Ruke's Store (410-425-2311) at the western end of the boat basin for the day or overnight. A word of caution

here, though: Although water depths on the channel side of the pier are 6 to 8 feet, depths on the inside—the land side—are 2 feet or less.

Short-term (two hours or less), full-day and overnight dockage is also available at Smith Island Marina. The marina, which monitors channel 78, has six slips and can handle boats up to 60 feet; to reserve one in advance call 410-425-4220. The marina also offers free bicycles to guests. Ewell's fuel dock is open Monday through Saturday from 8 a.m. to 5 p.m.; avoid holding up the watermen by fueling up at midday.

Beyond the entrance to Big Thorofare, a 6-foot channel has been dredged, but there really isn't enough swing room to anchor there. If no tie-up is available and it's getting late, a small anchorage is located east of flashing "9" at the end of the first leg of the western approach to the island. It is exposed to wind, however, and inconvenient for going ashore.

Ruke's serves lunch, including sandwiches, crabcakes, soft-shells and a local speciality, Smith Island cake (the official state dessert of Maryland, by the way), which consists of ten pancake-thin cake layers with icing slathered between each. The store also sells groceries, ice and antiques. (Alcohol is not sold on the island.) Ice can also be bought at the fuel dock and at the Bayside Inn restaurant, which offers a more extensive lunch menu. The restaurant rents bikes and golf

Smith Island; from NOAA Chart 12231— not to be used for navigation.

carts, too.

Across the street from Ruke's, the museum at the SMITH ISLAND VISITOR CENTER (open daily, noon to 4 p.m., May through October) highlights the area's heritage and culture with a fascinating video and exhibits. Visitors can obtain a walking tour map of the island here. If you've rented a bicycle, enjoy a pleasant one-and-a-half-mile ride to **Rhodes Point**. Originally called Rogue's Point, the hamlet is said to have been a home to pirates. One of the point's homes is a late 19th-century dwelling, the oldest on the island.

A highlight in Ewell in the summertime is the sight of many flowering pomegranate bushes. They seem to be everywhere, and their glossy, dark green foliage and brilliant red-orange blossoms add a cheerful note to the tidy, tree-shaded yards. The lanes of Ewell are just one car in width, and the concrete markers along the sides protect those yards with hefty enforcement.

The third community on Smith Island, **Tylerton**, down on **Tyler Ditch**, can be reached only by boat. You may want to approach this pretty and remote little village by way of dinghy, kayak or other shallow draft craft. The waterway around Tylerton is busy with crab shedding pens and houses, and with workboats bustling about. Here you'll find the Drum Point Market and the Smith Island Crabmeat Co-op on Wharf Street. Call 410-968-1344 for days and hours.

Tangier Island

Tangier Island, a third the size of Smith, is fully its equal in charm. It's also a more bustling place, with a slightly bigger population. In the early morning, you can watch the watermen parade out to their fishing grounds.

Like Smith, Tangier has two entrances. The wide eastern entrance from **Tangier Sound** was dredged in 2014, the narrower Bay side channel has been dredged to 9 feet.. Entering from Tangier Sound, from flashing bell buoy "5" set a course

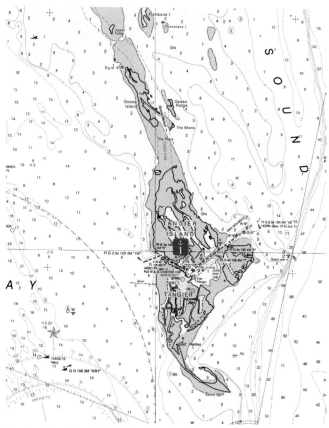

Tangier Island; from NOAA Chart 12228—not to be used for navigation.

for flashing green "1", which marks the entrance to the thoroughfare leading into the town of Tangier. To your left, you'll see **Port Isobel**. Here the small enclave of buildings is an environmental education center operated by the Chesapeake Bay Foundation. Ahead, a water tank and a church steeple rise above the rooftops.

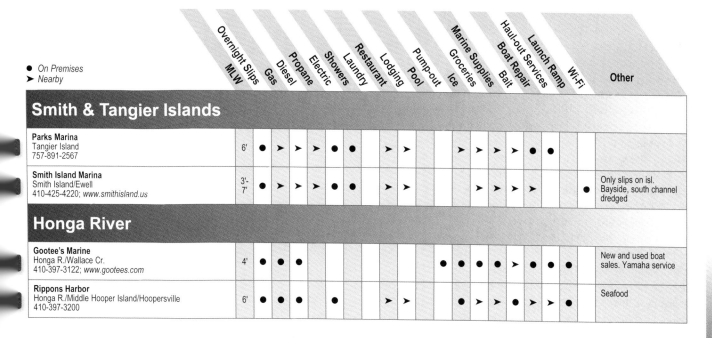

● *On Premises*
➤ *Nearby*

	MLW	Overnight Slips	Gas	Diesel	Propane	Electric	Showers	Laundry	Restaurant	Lodging	Pool	Pump-out	Ice	Groceries	Marine Supplies	Bait	Boat Repair	Haul-out Services	Launch Ramp	Wi-Fi	Other
Smith & Tangier Islands																					
Parks Marina Tangier Island 757-891-2567	6'	●	➤	➤	➤	●	●		➤	➤			➤	➤	➤	➤	●	●			
Smith Island Marina Smith Island/Ewell 410-425-4220; www.smithisland.us	3'-7'	●	➤	➤	➤	●	●		➤	➤			➤	➤	➤	➤				●	Only slips on isl. Bayside, south channel dredged
Honga River																					
Gootee's Marine Honga R./Wallace Cr. 410-397-3122; www.gootees.com	4'	●	●	●								●	●	●	●	➤	●	●	●		New and used boat sales. Yamaha service
Rippons Harbor Honga R./Middle Hooper Island/Hoopersville 410-397-3200	6'	●	●	●		●			➤	➤			●	➤	●	●	➤	➤	●		Seafood

Tangier Island *continued*

Entering from the Bay, you'll find crab shanties and piers to port. To starboard, slips for workboats line the first section of the channel, which also carries 8 feet. Immediately beyond the workboats, Parks Marina has transient space, with 25 slips and a small face dock. It isn't always easy to reach Milton Parks by phone (757-891-2567) or VHF, and cell signals are notoriously sparse here, but persistence often pays off. If all else fails, call out to the first person you see in the vicinity of the small white building with black shutters on the face dock (the marina's showers and bathrooms are here). Parks' ability to accommodate beamier vessels is limited, so call ahead. Also note that docking can be tricky in the strong current.

Besides the current, this channel is busy with workboats and tour boats maneuvering around, especially mid-morning and mid-afternoon. The tour boat dock, the third pier from the bayside entrance, is also the island's only fuel dock (gas and diesel). On the second long peir, Charnock's sells ice.

Because of the constricted waterway and heavy traffic, anchoring anywhere along the channel is not advised. **Cod Harbor** at the southeast tip of Tangier is another option, with access to a long sandy beach for swimming and sunning. Both anchorages, however, are exposed and suitable only for settled weather.

There are three roadways on Tangier, running parallel north-south: Main Ridge and West Ridge and Canton Ridge. Between them is a gut that cuts through the marshes and a series of small bridges that connect the three roads. Most yards are enclosed by chain-link fences, and it is not uncommon to see front-yard graves, since dry land is hard to come by. Explore the marshes by dinghy or kayak/canoe to best appreciate their exquisite beauty and abundant wildlife.

Tangier's out-island, small town flavor is endlessly charming to visitors. Golf cart tours present unique tidbits of its history, and bike rentals are available if you're heading for the beach on the southernmost tip, but the island is entirely walkable. A grocery store on Main Ridge has essentials, but one thing you can't buy on Tangier is alcohol.

Hilda Crockett's Chesapeake House is the island's oldest and most famous inn/restaurant, serving family-style meals. It's a short pleasant walk along Main Ridge from the docks. You may share the route with bikes, golf carts and cats that weave carefully among the pedestrians. Other dining options include Fisherman's Corner and Four Brothers Crabhouse and Ice Cream Deck, which has an ATM. Other lodging options are Sunset Inn and Bay View Inn.

On Main Ridge, among its gift shops and between Spanky's Place ice cream parlor and the Chesapeake House, is the TANGIER HISTORY MUSEUM AND INTERPRETIVE CULTURAL CENTER. In addition to its treasure-trove of island memorabilia, the center has a new exhibit about Tangier's role in the War of 1812. It also offers water-trail maps and the free use of canoes and kayaks (first-come first-served).

If you can't reach Smith and Tangier in your own boat, you can take a ferry from Crisfield, Md., or Reedville, Va., or do what the locals do and take the mailboat from Crisfield.

Honga River

When cruising along the eastern side of the mid-Bay's ship channel between Cedar Point and Point No Point, you're likely to spot Hoopers Island Light about 3 miles west of the Hooper islands. First lit in 1902, it is one of only 11 of its kind in the United States—an iron caisson foundation sunk into the Bay bottom using a pneumatic process. Taller than other Maryland "spark plug" lights, it is now owned and preserved by the U.S. Lighthouse Society.

Below the lighthouse, the **Honga River** snakes between Maryland's low-lying lower Eastern Shore and a spindly peninsula south of Taylors Island that ends in the three Hooper islands—Upper, Middle and Lower. With scantness of both harbor depths and services, neither cruisers nor developers have paid much attention to this region. While the area lacks the allure of Smith and Tangier islands, or the amenities of Crisfield and Onancock, the wetlands' austerity and the population's tenacity are worthy of respect. Folks are friendly and quick to help those in need, but boaters should arrive with ample fuel, water, provisions and up-to-date charts.

Upper Hooper and **Middle Hooper islands** connect to the peninsula by road, but marshy **Lower Hooper**—known locally as Applegarth Island and once inhabited—has been bridgeless since the Great August Storm of 1933. Island land grants date

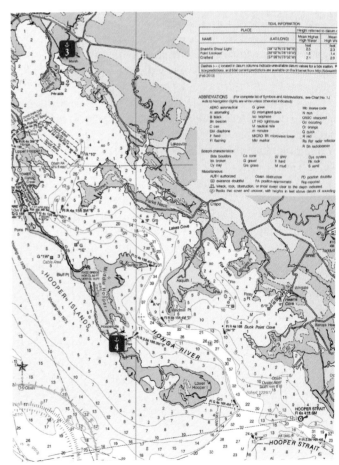

Honga River; from NOAA Chart 12230—not to be used for navigation.

to 1659, with Henry Hooper among the first settlers arriving from the fledgling St. Mary's City across the Bay.

While a northern entrance to the Honga exists for shoal-draft low-profile vessels (a 24-foot fixed bridge links Meekins Neck to Upper Hooper Island), it's best left for those with local knowledge and a clear understanding of the various stakes that mark the channel. This forever-shoaling serpentine route—the **Barren Island Gap**—traverses shallow **Tar Bay**, doglegs northeast into the marked channel under the bridge in **Fishing Creek**, and ends in the northerly, and exceedingly shallow, reaches of the Honga.

East of the bridge, shallow-draft boats continuing northeastward—instead of turning south from Fishing Creek's bridge—can carefully navigate the shoaly waters past Keenes Point into **Wallace Creek**, where a privately maintained channel leads to Gootee's Marine. This family-run facility caters to small vessels with fuel, slips, marine supplies and repairs. Its marked channel carries 4 feet at the top of the tide but just 2 ½ feet at low.

Boats turning southeast from the bridge head toward lighted "10" and into the Honga's deeper waters. South of "10" and west of flashing "8", a marked channel leads into **Back Creek**, the main harbor for Upper Hooper and the village of Fishing Creek. A watermen's haven carrying 4 to 5 feet, Jones Marina offers limited services for cruisers. On Back Creek's western shore, visitors are welcome to dinghy in and walk across the main road to Old Salty's restaurant (410-397-3752) or, farther up the road, to the islands' only market (which also serves meals). South of Back Creek, the Honga continues to widen and deepen; some Fishing Creek charter captains choose this longer, scenic route back and forth from the Bay.

Boats arriving from the south should give a wide berth to bell buoy "1", 6 ½ miles southeast of Hooper Island Light, and set a course for nun "2" on the western edge of Hooper Strait. From there, follow the chart, watching for the few but lighted marks identifying shoals. About 4 miles northwest of Hooper Strait Light, two lighted red navigational aids lie about a mile apart. The eastern one marks Windmill Point; the western one marks the beginning of the channel leading to **Hoopersville**, another watermen's outpost with charted

depths of 5 ½ feet. The community (6 miles by road from Fishing Creek) offers well-protected slips, fuel and the bonus of fresh crabs steamed or picked at Rippons Harbor, where Windmill-brand crabmeat has been packed by three successive generations. Dining facilities consist of a park pavilion or your own boat.

East of Hoopersville, a narrow channel leads to the watermen's community of **Wingate** on the mainland. Intrepid explorers will find a landing there but no services to speak of.

With low marshy topography, the Honga may not have snug, all-weather anchorages, but boats can anchor away from traffic at **Flag Cove** on the eastern side of Middle Hooper Island, or upriver in 7 to 8 feet east of the channel in **Lakes Cove** along the mainland. Keep a constant eye on your depthsounder. This is fabulous kayak water. Only the lowest of profile and shallowest of drafts can boast of circumnavigating the wild, unspoiled Hooper islands.

Nanticoke River

For those who like out-of-the-way cruising destinations, the **Nanticoke River** is a delight. This 40-mile-plus river is so lightly developed that in places you can go for long periods without seeing any houses or other evidence of human habitation. Almost all you get to see are beautiful heavily forested shorelines with tidal and freshwater marshes, cypress swamps, cultivated flatland, and miles and miles of lily pads.

Because of the Nanticoke's pristine condition, several conservation groups have identified it as one of Maryland's healthiest rivers and Delaware's last "wild river." Providing habitat for an abundance of wildlife and plants, it flows southwest from its headwaters in Seaford, Del., meandering into Maryland between Dorchester and Wicomico counties for many miles before it empties into Tangier Sound.

In the Nanticoke, there are still places to drop anchor or drift and be completely alone. It has long been a favorite of anglers, and its tributaries are ideal for canoes and kayaks.

If you're cruising up the Nanticoke, be aware that fuel is hard to find until you reach Seaford. Nor does the river have deep water in a lot of its harbors, further reducing its appeal

● On Premises
➤ Nearby

	MLW	Overnight Slips	Gas	Diesel	Propane	Electric	Showers	Laundry	Restaurant	Lodging	Pool	Pump-out	Ice	Groceries	Marine Supplies	Bait	Boat Repair	Haul-out Services	Launch Ramp	Wi-Fi	Other
Nanticoke River																					
Cedar Hill Marina Nanticoke R./Bivalve 410-548-4870; www.cedarhillmarina.com	5'	●				●	●		➤	➤		●	●	➤	➤	➤	➤	➤	➤	●	Pavilion, park/nature trails, basketball, tennis
Nanticoke River Marina Nanticoke R./Seaford Del. 302-628-8600; www.nanticokerivermarina.com	8'	●	●	●		●	●	●	➤			●	●	➤	●		●	●	●	●	40-ton lift; yacht club; walk to Seaford, DE
Vienna Municipal Marina Nanticoke R./Vienna 410-376-3442; www.viennamd.org	8'	●				●				●					➤						

Nanticoke River continued

to deep-draft cruisers. But it does have a well-marked channel ranging from 7 to 52 feet deep. With proper planning, the Nanticoke is worth the trip to explore its history, meet its people and experience its wild beauty. These suggestions will help you better plan your cruise:

1) Be sure to get the latest edition of NOAA Chart 12261, which contains details not in chart books and cruising guides.

2) The river has currents, both flood and ebb, of up to 2 knots. If this concerns you, you need to know that the NOAA current tables (as commercially published) have only three offsets for the Nanticoke River, two near the mouth and one at Chapter Point less than one-fourth the way up the river.

3) The river is wide and deep enough for any boater. Tugs and barges traverse the river at least daily, going all the way to Seaford. This implies that you should not anchor in the main stream of the river. With a shallow-draft boat (say, 5 feet or less), you can anchor way off to one side if you wish. In addition, there are a few other places to overnight.

4) There are two fixed bridges over the Maryland portion of the river (at Vienna and Sharptown), both with 50-foot clearances.

Two and a half miles east of 44-foot Sharkfin Shoal Light at the eastern end of Hooper Strait, flashing green "1", a bell buoy, marks the Nanticoke's entrance. Entering the river you'll find a huge marsh to your left for the first nine miles, with the right side being mostly wooded with occasional clusters of homes and at least one mansion. Just beyond Roaring Point lies historic ❶ **Nanticoke**, once a popular resort boasting several hotels and a beach. What remains today are neatly kept Victorian homes and manicured lawns. Extensive jetties shelter the harbor entrance, which has a controlling depth of 5 feet. The harbor is used primarily by work-boats, but cruisers can tie up temporarily to escape bad weather. The village is one of three along the river's eastern shoreline, each with a post office but little else.

Farther north, above Ragged Point, is ❷ **Bivalve**, named in recognition of the area's chief resource. The channel into Cedar Hill Marina at Bivalve is flanked by long rock jetties. Although it lacks fuel and supplies, this county facility does have restrooms and showers and sits in the middle of a delightful 85-acre park perfect for strolling. The marina has slips capable

Nanticoke River; from NOAA Chart 12261—not to be used for navigation.

of handling vessels drawing up to 5 feet (check with locals; depths have been reported as low as 4 feet MLW). Transients are welcome. To reserve a slip, call the harbormaster (410-548-4900, ext. 131). In settled weather, you can anchor off the marina basin and dinghy in to use the park's picnic grounds and nature trails.

There is a large shoal in the middle of the river just off Bivalve, with deep water on both sides. You'll often see workboats on the shoal as local watermen fish the shallows. With much of the Nanticoke's surrounding land preserved by the Nature Conservancy and Maryland's FISHING BAY WILDLIFE MANAGEMENT AREA, bald eagles and other wildlife thrive.

❸ **Wetipquin Creek** is about seven miles from the mouth of the Nanticoke. At the entrance to Wetipquin, a little bridge is visible beyond. You can head straight toward the finger of land near the creek's mouth and anchor on the outside in 9 feet of water. (Shoaling has been reported inside the creek, so seek out local information.) The bottom is solid, but not hard, and holding should be good. There's a little park where you can land a dinghy at the foot of Tyaskin Road, which dead-ends at the anchorage. The tiny village of **Tyaskin** has no amenities for cruisers, but it is quiet, charming and friendly—well worth a visit.

Those who enjoy watching the sun sink into the water, its afterglow streaking the purple marshlands with ribbons of soft light, or love viewing stars beyond number, should definitely spend a night anchored along the lower Nanticoke. Row up Wetipquin Creek to enjoy the marshland experience: fish scurrying away, their fins breaking through the shallow surface, and birds being flushed out of cover, pumping hard for altitude as they weave through a curtain of reeds.

For the next several miles above Wetipquin Creek, the Nanticoke twists back and forth while going up a marshy valley. There is very little development, with just the occasional house appearing along the shore. You'll find two possible anchorages here, both to starboard. Boaters can drop the hook along the south shore of Chapter Point at **Dorman Ditch** (between "14" and "15") or run up above Penknife Point and into **The Inlet**, a nar-

row, picturesque creek that is quite deep and very protected.

A few more miles and you'll reach ❹ **Vienna**, almost 20 miles up the river, but you'll be able to see the huge power plant located here long before you arrive. Though small, the historic town is truly charming and offers some amenities. Adjacent to the public launch ramp, a long metal bulkhead provides 6-10' for temporary tie-up. The restored waterfront also includes a boardwalk and several sturdy floating docks for daytime and overnight transient use. A two-block walk up the street will bring you into town, where you can get gas and diesel fuel, stock up at a convenience store, buy sandwiches or visit Millie's Roadhouse, a friendly place serving inexpensive, homestyle meals. Miles of flat country roads allow great bicycling to BLACKWATER NATIONAL WILDLIFE REFUGE to the west.

Vienna, formally established in 1706, has many beautiful and historic buildings, as much of its early architecture remains intact, including the tiny 1768 Customs House at Church and Water streets. The VIENNA HERITAGE MUSEUM was started several years ago in a restored 1920s filling station, which is open during the town's special events. Walking tour maps are available at a kiosk outside the Vienna Heritage Museum or at the Tavern House B&B.

Upriver of Vienna's 50-foot fixed bridge, the Nanticoke becomes narrower and straighter. From this point on there are wide swathes of water lily pads lining each side of the river, and in late summer the marsh mallows along the shore explode into vibrant white and pink blossoms.

After a very pleasant run of some four miles, the Nanticoke's main tributary, ❺ **Marshyhope Creek**, will appear to your left. Enter it from flashing red "38", turning to port and heading straight in. Stay in the middle of the wide, wooded entrance to avoid shoals on both sides. Beyond the entrance, Marshyhope is deep to its banks, with 7- and 8-foot depths that provide ample room for anchoring.

An additional two miles brings you to **Sharptown**. Settled in the mid-1700s, the town was once well known as a shipbuilding village. In the early 1800s, Matthew Marine founded Sharptown Marine Railway, which built three- and four-masted schooners for coastal and transatlantic trade. The four-masted *Anandale*, one of the last great, large sailing vessels made

Nanticoke River, from NOAA Chart 12261—not to be used for navigation.

Nanticoke River continued

on the Chesapeake, was built here in 1919. About this time, shipbuilding came to an end in Sharptown, as steamboats took business away from schooners. By 1921, steamers ran the river twice weekly, carrying passengers and freight.

There are several ways to come ashore here: anchor outside of the main channel and land the dinghy anywhere from the north side of the old drawbridge/fishing pier up to the beach at CHERRY BEACH PARK; tie up at high tide at Cherry Beach's dock (four-hour limit); or dock at the bulkhead on the south side of the drawbridge in 8-foot depths—or 6 in a northwesterly blow—No overnight docking is permitted at the bulkhead. A seafood market sits next to the drawbridge, with a service station selling gas and diesel two short blocks away. A nearby tackle shop also sells some groceries.

A few miles above the Marshyhope, and after a significant S-turn in the Nanticoke, you'll find another major tributary, **❻ Broad Creek**, which spills in from the east. The large, marsh-fringed and thickly forested area on the right, adjoining the south side of the Broad Creek's mouth, is PHILLIPS LANDING RECREATION AREA, which has launch ramps. Just inside the creek you should find 8- to 12-foot depths and room to anchor.

Broad Creek winds about four miles upstream to historic **Bethel, Del.**, with at least 7 feet of water up to a 30-foot-high fixed bridge. Here, years ago, Lewisville Marine Railway produced the famed flat-bottom Chesapeake rams. A store at the end of Main Street now sells gas and groceries. On Broad Creek as on other largely unmarked Nanticoke tributaries, water lilies are useful markers to keep you in the deep-water channel and off mud banks. They're not visible until May, however, so if you're going in early spring, take care.

Broad Creek continues another couple of miles to **Laurel, Del.**, where a new boat ramp at RIVERVIEW PARK allows small-boat access to the upper reaches of the creek.

Continuing up the Nanticoke, another bit of river history appears a couple of miles past Broad Creek at **Woodland, Del.**—the Woodland Ferry, whose origins date to 1793. This state-run ferry operates on demand from sunup to sundown seven days a week, weather permitting. It runs along a cable stretched tight across the river. Between ferry trips the cable goes slack and lies on the bottom of the river, giving clearance to tugs and barges. Boaters must give way when the ferry is moving (a red-flashing light on the dock will alert you); let it come to a complete stop before crossing over its cables.

Unfortunately, there is no public place where you can moor your boat to visit Woodland, but you can anchor and dinghy in. Another waterfront village with an interesting past, it's worth a stroll.

A mere three miles more will bring you to **Seaford, Del.**, effectively the end of the river. A floating city dock offers free dockage for up to two nights. Also on the south side of the river, next to the Nanticoke River Yacht Club in

Blades, Del., is the 87-slip Nanticoke River Marina, with floating docks, gas and diesel fuel, a service lift, pump-out station, showers and restrooms, laundry facilities and a ship's store. It's also within walking distance of several restaurants, a convenience store and the SEAFORD MUSEUM. (Slip reservations are strongly recommended for transients; call 302-628-8600.)

Seaford offers visitors a slice of Americana: tree-shaded streets, old houses, an old-timey hardware store, a paved riverfront promenade and a museum that celebrates the city's rich heritage.

Wicomico River

Few cruising boats travel up the **Wicomico River** (*wye-KAHM-eh-ko*)—a long, deep stream that winds from Tangier Sound to Salisbury—but it's splendid for solitude and natural surroundings. Sparsely settled with pretty homes, the Wicomico's shores are alternately marshy and wooded.

Low-powered boats should plan to travel with the current, which runs at up to 2 knots and changes within an hour after high and low water. Tide tables are a good guide for timing the trip. Watch for barge traffic hauling petroleum and gravel to Salisbury, and monitor VHF channel 13, communicating with tugboat captains if you are unsure which way they intend to pass.

The Wicomico's entrance, due east of the Nanticoke, begins at 37-foot Great Shoals Light. From there its well-marked channel courses crookedly north-northeast, bypassing two large but shallow bays—**Monie** and **Ellis**. Southeast of daymark "19", a marked channel leads to manmade **Webster Cove** where a county-maintained dock has annual slip rentals for small craft, but no dockage or services for transients.

At Deep Point, about 4 miles above its mouth, the Wicomico narrows then swings north toward the tiny village of **Whitehaven**. One of the Bay's original tobacco ports, it served as a respected shipbuilding center and later a popular steamboat stop. Its Whitehaven Hotel, miraculously enduring decades of neglect, has been carefully restored and transformed into a fine B&B. Restoration work revealed the original walls of the 1810 tavern and uncovered artifacts that are now on display. Better yet, you'll find a recently expanded dock where you can tie up while you visit. (877-809-8296) Nearby Whitehaven Marina, however, was for sale at the time we went to publication and no longer offering dockage.

Between the hotel and marina, a busy three-car cable ferry (service here dates from 1685) runs during daylight hours. Before passing up river, you *must* first get permission from the operator. Call the ferry captain on channel 13, and he'll drop the cable and give you the go-ahead.

Incorporated in 1753, Whitehaven is a lovely little village. One plantation house, Bolton, dates to the 1750s, and several of the lovingly tended Victorian homes are on the National Register of Historic Places. Whitehaven Hotel guests, like those once arriving on horseback and by boat, still savor the twilight views and breezes from the colorful landmark's porch.

Locals and tourists alike enjoy dinner at the rustic Red Roost, which is located about three miles away in a former chicken house. In addition to their famous chicken, specialties include steamed crabs, seafood, steaks and ribs. Boaters can call the restaurant for reservations and transportation from Whitehaven (410-546-5443). The Red Roost also has a dock (2 feet at low tide) for small boats near flashing green "23" on the northern shore halfway between Webster Cove and **Shiles Creek**. Guests can either walk the half-mile or request a ride from the restaurant. Use caution when anchoring in the river since it shoals dramatically beyond the edges of the channel and the current is swift.

Wicomico Creek

Nearly 2 miles above Whitehaven, just past flashing green "29", **Wicomico Creek** enters from the east. At this confluence, just beyond the creek's two fixed, unlit aids (a red and a green), the Wicomico Yacht Club sits on the northern shore. It offers fuel and friendly local knowledge, but no other services for non-members—a boon since fuel is scarce here. Entering with a deep draft, stay in the center as you approach the green daymark, and aim toward the docks. Inside, the creek has a minimum of 10 feet and is deeply navigable for a couple of stunning miles through tall grassy marshland with water as much as 20-plus feet to the shoreline.

Boats often drop the hook just inside the creek. With a tidal range here of about 2 feet, becoming 3 upstream, boats at anchor will lie to the current rather than the wind.

Less than two miles up Wicomico Creek, Wikanders Marine Services has slips for transients (6 foot depths) and repairs, but no fuel. Both creek and river are peacefully remote with miles of marsh and farmland—and abundant food and habitat for egrets, eagles and assorted wildlife. Also up the creek, you'll fine Bordeleau Winery, where you can tie up while you visit the tasting room.

Upper Wicomico

Above the confluence with Wicomico Creek, the Wicomico River remains scenic and deep, narrowing with increasing signs of civilization as it approaches **Salisbury**. Since tugs and barges use this river, watch for them at river bends and listen on channels 13 and 16.

continued on page 247

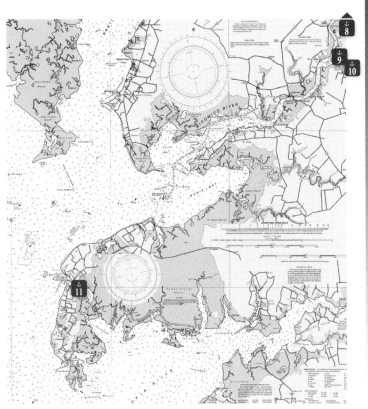

Wicomico River and Deal Island; from NOAA Chart 12261 and 12231—not to be used for navigation.

	MLW	Overnight Slips	Gas	Diesel	Propane	Electric	Showers	Laundry	Restaurant	Lodging	Pool	Pump-out	Ice	Groceries	Marine Supplies	Bait	Boat Repair	Haul-out Services	Launch Ramp	Wi-Fi	Other
Wicomico River																					
Port Of Salisbury Marina Wicomico R./Salisbury 410-548-3176; www.ci.salisbury.md.us	7'	●	●	●	●	➤	●	●	●	●	➤		●	➤	➤	➤	➤	➤	➤	●	cert. clean marina, dockage for 100-ft plus boats
Wicomico Yacht Club Wicomico R./Wicomico Cr. 410-219-5248; www.wicomicoyachtclub.org	6'		●	●		●	●	●	●		●	●	●	➤	➤		➤	➤	➤		Public welcome at fuel dock, slips members only
Wikanders Marine Services Wicomico R./Wicomico Cr. 410-749-9521; www.WikanderYachtYard-Brokerage.com	6'	●	➤	➤		●	●					●	➤				●	●	●		Relaxed setting; walking dist. to Bordeleau Winery
Deal Island																					
Scotts Cove Marina Tangier Sound/Deal Island Harbor 443-783-5857	4'	●		●		●							➤	➤	●	●	●	●	➤		All new expansion and bulkheading

● On Premises
➤ Nearby

Port of Call

Salisbury

Government center, college town, commercial hub—Salisbury's multiple roles keep this vital Eastern Shore city humming. But for cruisers, Salisbury also remains a relaxed port of call. Visiting boaters can stretch their legs along scenic walkways, explore the city's historic districts and attractions or simply unwind in a pleasant park.

Use the *Architectural Walking Tour of Downtown Salisbury* brochure as a self-guided introduction to the city. Begin at the Wicomico County Courthouse, a Victorian Gothic-style structure erected in 1878, then head west on Main Street. Past the courthouse, a two-block length of West Main Street comprises the Downtown Plaza Historic District, an open-air mall lined with benches, trees and landscaped plant beds. Diverting a block south down Market Street brings you to Camden Street and the Gallery Building (c. 1890), home of the Art Institute & Gallery, a showcase for local artists. Intrepid visitors can take a self-guided walking tour of the Newtown District, an enclave of historic homes, many exemplifying fine Victorian architecture. Among them is the restored Poplar Hill Mansion (c. 1805), which is open to the public.

From Newtown, head south on Poplar Hill Avenue to Broad Street and the Chipman Cultural Center (c. 1838), the region's oldest standing African-American church and school, now a cultural center and museum. Then head south past Main to the prettiest trek in town. The narrowing branch of the Wicomico meanders upstream past the marina, making a quiet backdrop for Riverwalk, a footpath. At City Park, the waterway is not much more than a stream, but it's postcard-lovely. There are bridges, tennis courts, playgrounds, picnic sites and the Salisbury Zoo (admission is free). This 13-acre site's gardens and naturalistic enclosures are home to a wide variety of mammals, reptiles, waterfowl and other birds. Children will enjoy Ben's Red Swings, a special playground near the zoo entrance.

Beyond hiking distance from the water, but accessible by cab are other local treasures. The Ward Museum of Wildfowl Art houses the world's largest collection of decorative bird carvings. (A scenic oyster shell nature trail leads from the museum to a nearby pond.) Beautiful Pemberton Park features 4 miles of nature trails and an 18th-century manor house, Pemberton Hall, while the Adkins Historical Museum brings Salisbury's Revolutionary War days to life.

The Chamber of Commerce's visitor center (open 9–5 Monday through Friday) offers brochures, maps and local bus schedules (including service to Crisfield and Ocean City) to get you started.

Basic groceries and sundries can be found within walking distance of the city marina at Royal Farms. Or you can sample the Bay's bounty at Chesapeake Treasures and Captain Henry's Seafood carryout markets. Extensive reprovisioning requires a short taxi ride to Sav-a-Lot market.

From the city marina, you're only a stroll away from a satisfying meal at one of the city's many restaurants. Brew River (brew pub with live music on weekends) offers dockage for diners.

On weekend mornings, browse at Park and Flea, a flea and farmer's market.

Salisbury's small-town roots are reflected in many of its annual events. The Ward World Wildfowl Carving Competition takes place in April. In September, Riverfest (music, food, water activities along the Wicomico riverfront) and Unicity Music & Performing Arts Festival take center stage. The Chesapeake Wildfowl Expo at Ward Museum (featuring a market place, competitions, demonstrations and free museum admission) draws art and wildfowl lovers alike in October.

Information: Salisbury Chamber of Commerce, 410-749-0144, *www.salisburyarea.com*; Wicomico County Convention & Visitors Bureau, 410-548-4914 or 800-332-8687, *www.wicomico tourism.org*.

Salisbury

⚓ **Marinas/Dockage**
 1 Port of Salisbury Marina
 2 Public Boat Ramp

○ **Points of Interest**
 3 Art Institute & Gallery
 4 Wicomico County Courthouse
 5 Newtown District
 6 Downtown Plaza
   Historic District
 7 Poplar Hill Mansion
 8 Salisbury Zoo
 9 Ward Museum of Wildfowl Art
 10 Pemberton Hall & Park
 11 Chipman Cultural Center

? **Information**
 1 Port of Salisbury Marina
 12 Chamber of Commerce

🍴 **Dining**
 13 Market Street Inn
 14 Brew River
 15 Sushi de Kanpai

🦐 **Groceries**
 16 Chesapeake Treasures
   (seafood)
 17 Royal Farms

☼ **Entertainment/Recreation**
 18 Arthur W. Perdue Stadium

🚩 **Shopping**

⚓ **Park**

🛝 **Playground**

📖 **Library**

○ **Hospital**

···· **Riverwalk**

℞ **Pharmacy**

✉ **Post Office**

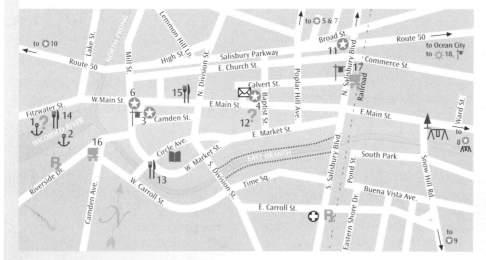

Upper Wicomico *continued from page 243*

Opposite flashing red "32" is a feature worth noting: a church whose east gable, mostly hidden in foliage, faces the river. This is Green Hill Church, c.1733, which formed the nucleus of Green Hill, once a thriving official port of entry that faded into obscurity as commerce moved elsewhere.

Less than a mile beyond an overhead cable (75-foot clearance) at flashing green "43" is **Upper Ferry**. Like Whitehaven's, this cable-operated ferry only runs during daylight hours. The apparatus is suspended at or near the water's surface, so signal the ferry captain to lower it for safe transit. Use either one horn blast or VHF channel 13. Proceed with caution and never attempt to pass a moving cable ferry.

At Salisbury, some five miles farther upriver, Port of Salisbury Marina offers dockage, good food at Brew River next door and a quaint nearby Main Street to explore on foot.

Deal Island

If you happen to be leaving the Wicomico River and dropping south into Tangier Sound around Labor Day weekend, you might be fortunate enough to spot the graceful bowsprit and raked mast of an old wooden skipjack on its way to or from Deal Island's Skipjack Races and Festival—an annual event that showcases the Chesapeake's dwindling oyster-dredging fleet. It's a fitting sight for an area that once produced so many of the Bay's skipjacks.

The entrance to **Deal Island**'s main (north) harbor is only two miles from Sharkfin Shoal Light. (Note: A potentially hazardous condition exists at Sharkfin Shoal Light. The installed riprap, not visible at MLW, extends about 100 feet from the light. There is also a charted wreck in the area.)

If draft is an issue, enter both the main harbor at Chance and the southern harbor at Wenona at the highest tides. If you approach Deal Island from the south, the green "1" entrance marker for the northern harbor is approximately 13 miles north of the Janes Island Light off Crisfield.

The channel into the main harbor at **Chance** is straightforward, but shoaling has taken its toll on the depth, so proceed with caution if you draw more than 4 feet. In fact, the most recent NOAA charts note the depth at 3 feet in August 2010. We're not saying it can't be done, just advising caution and a good high tide.

The channel runs straight for 600 yards or so from "1", then makes a right-hand turn

at red "4" inside a stone jetty to starboard. Stay close to the marks, then head toward the bulkhead before rounding up to an anchorage. Shallow-draft boats can access Scotts Cove Marina, tucked in a channel on the north side of the harbor.

To the east, the harbor is bordered by a fixed highway bridge (25-foot vertical clearance) that connects Deal Island to the mainland. If you can pass under that—and draw only 1½ feet—it's possible to explore the waters of **Upper Thorofare**. But at anchor you can get a clear view under the bridge of the marshes to the east. If you look west, across Tangier Sound, you can see the shores of Bloodsworth Island and Sharkfin Shoal Light.

The harbor is well protected, with room enough for most cruising groups. The harbor was once the home port for a half-dozen working skipjacks, and you are likely to see at least one, with more to the south. One of them, the *Ida May*, usually occupies the harbor's north side at Chance. Built in 1906 and fully restored, she is one of the oldest of this vanishing breed. Three more skipjacks are generally berthed to the south at Wenona.

Corbin's Crabs is located on the highway a short walk from Deal harbor—look for the sign. Here you'll also find Lucky's Last Chance General Store and Paradise Grille.

At Deal Island's southern end in the shallow harbor of **Wenona**, cruisers will find workboats and an old timey general store that carries snacks and watermen's supplies.

Big Annemessex River

The **Big Annemessex** and its neighboring rivers, Little Annemessex to the south and Manokin to the north, comprised the heart of the boatbuilding industry for the booming oyster-dredging business in the early 1900s. As you head into the Big Annemessex, try to imagine what this river must have

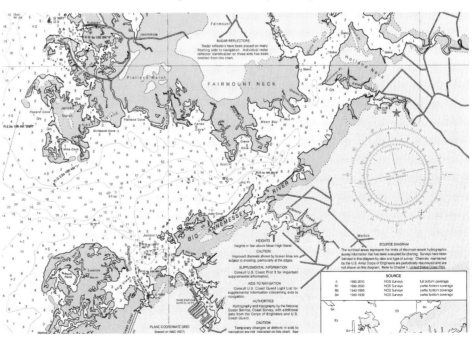

Big Annemessex River; from NOAA Chart 12231—not to be used for navigation.

Big Annemessex River *continued*

been like when John Branford and other boatbuilders were busy making dredge boats. While you may not see skipjacks here today, the Big Annemessex is a good place to anchor and ponder their history. To the north, a few skipjacks still call Deal Island home, and, to the south, Crisfield has a museum dedicated to the Bay's maritime industry.

Despite all the obvious reasons for visiting this quiet river, it may be happenstance that first brings you here. Cruising the middle Bay near the Eastern Shore as the hour becomes late, you may wonder where to anchor, especially in a boat with a draft of 4 feet or more. The lower Eastern Shore is notorious for its many shoals and barely visible (and sometimes invisible) islands. It is then that you may make the wise choice and head for the Big Annemessex River.

From the Bay, head toward **Kedges Straits**, a narrow body of water connecting the Chesapeake with Tangier Sound, with South Marsh Island to the north and Smith Island to the south. Boaters approaching these straits should be aware of the Navy-maintained restricted zone located several miles west of the straits (and marked on charts). Bombers use an old Liberty ship here for target practice; the ship is sunk in shallow water and is surrounded by debris, so stay well clear of the area.

The best visual aid for making Kedges Straits is Solomons Lump, a 47-foot light tower atop a caisson foundation that once held a lighthouse. The light marks shoals off Smith Island that can get as shallow as 2 feet.

As you exit Kedges Straits and enter Tangier Sound, a 5-foot shoal is marked by a flashing green bell buoy "5". You can navigate to either side, but the deeper water is south of the buoy. A straight course almost directly east from Kedges Straits will take you to the mouth of the Big Annemessex. You'll find at least 8 feet of water along the way, with the exception of the one 5-foot shoal. In fact, the water gets as deep as 70 feet in the Tangier Sound channel.

The mouth of the river can be a little difficult to identify from the sound because most of the land is marshy and low. Eventually, you'll be able to distinguish a sandy beach and marshes on the north side. Beyond is a community of one-story homes that blends in with the environment. In fact, it can be easy to confuse a series of poles for masts until you realize you are looking at the tallest objects on land: a long row of telephone poles. (Flashing green "1" at the river mouth also can be hard to pick out from Tangier Sound.)

After entering the river, you'll spot a series of red buoys heading off to starboard. They lead to the **Daugherty Creek Canal** (also called the **Annemessex Canal**), which connects the Big and Little Annemessex. (The canal's 2011 charted depths are 3.6 to 7 feet.)

The mouth of the river is wide, and the river becomes even wider for about two miles beyond its mouth. Then, it narrows considerably where Long Point juts out from the southern shoreline, leaving a navigable channel only about one-eighth of a mile wide. Long Point is marked by a flashing red "6". You can cruise for another mile or two beyond Long Point if you stay in the center of the river, but watch out for a 2-foot sand-

bar that juts out off Sandy Point on the north shore. Beyond Moon Bay, which lies inside Sandy Point, the river depths drop to 3 feet and less. It was here in the shallow waters, off the community of **Fairmount**, that a dozen or so skipjacks were built in the early part of this century. But skipjacks have a draft of 3 feet or less, so if you draw more, you may want to turn around and head back to deeper water.

Moon Bay looks like a well-protected anchorage but is shallow. Boats drawing 4 feet or more are better off dropping the hook just off the channel and not venturing too far in.

Continuing back toward Tangier Sound, other anchoring possibilities lie farther west along the northern shore of the Big Annemessex. **Fords Cove, Flatland Cove** and nearby **Shirtpond Cove** are all very shallow, but at their mouths provide good holding and a great sunset view in 5 to 8 feet.

Little Annemessex River

Crisfield lies six nautical miles east of Smith Island, across Tangier Sound. Because of its convenience and scruffy charm, it's a favorite landfall for both cruisers and snowbirds making an inland waterway passage. Families are attracted to Crisfield's many summer weekend festivities, and history buffs are lured by the opportunity to discover a part of Maryland's (and the seafood industry's) history.

Its sheltered Somers Cove Marina owes its existence to Maryland's Waterway Improvement Fund, which paid to dredge the cove and build the piers and 450 slips that rim it.

Deep-draft boats must access **Somers Cove** by way of the Little Annemessex River, but shoal-draft vessels have the added option of using dredged channels that cut north and south through the swamps around Crisfield, connecting the harbor with both Tangier and Pocomoke sounds. The Daugherty Creek Canal cuts north behind **Janes Island** and leads from the Little Annemessex River to the Big Annemessex River and Tangier Sound. Broad Creek cuts south into Pocomoke Sound. It was charted at 4 feet in 2011. Seek local knowledge and check the tides.

From Tangier Sound, the entrance into the Little Annemessex River is well marked by Janes Island Light, a skeleton tower on a cylindrical base. From the light, the path to Crisfield is well-buoyed, and the channel carries 8 feet of water or more right to the town dock and observation deck, which is impossible to miss.

To enter Somers Cove, keep the town dock to port as you head for the "cut" or narrow, bulwarked channel. Evans Seafood remains to starboard, opposite new condos close to the water. Inside, to port, is the J. MILLARD TAWES HISTORICAL MUSEUM. If you're looking for fuel or a slip, continue up the cove to the marina dock, where the 100 transient slips are adjacent to or near the gas dock. The marina can be reached on VHF channel 16, or you can stand off the fuel dock and hail the office. They'll assign you a spot and assist with docking lines.

To anchor, head to starboard as soon as the cove opens up and before you pass the Coast Guard Station on the south

continued on page 250

Port of Call
Crisfield

www.visitannapolis.org

Condominiums now line the former commercial harborfront, and tourists stroll streets that once were the domain of watermen and seafood processors, but in Crisfield you can still dine on steamed crabs and mouth-watering crabcakes. Visitors are treated to more than delectable seafood; they're also invited to glimpse all aspects of local life, from the workings of a seafood plant to an examination of regional history and culture.

The area's first known residents, Algonquin Indians, were supplanted by English planters who eventually turned to fishing, especially harvesting oysters. In the late 19th century, a railroad was extended into town (thanks in large part to John W. Crisfield) to transport the delectable bivalve to far-off markets. The local economy boomed as a result. Steamships and railroad cars laden with tons of oysters departed weekly, linking the community with destinations around the Bay. Photographs, displays and artifacts capture this and the watermen's story in the J. Millard Tawes Historical Museum located on the grounds of Somers Cove Marina. The museum is also the starting point for a guided walking tour whose highlight is a behind-the-scenes visit to the MeTompkin seafood processing house. By appointment, visitors can also see the workshop of Lem and Steve Ward, siblings whose craftsmanship elevated decoy carving to an art form, and the library of former governor J. Millard Tawes, which is located in his boyhood home. (For tour information and appointments, call 410-968-2501 or visit *www.crisfieldheritagefoundation.org*.)

The water, once a vital element in the town's economic fortunes, still plays an important role in daily life. Crisfield's harbor remains a bustling place where pleasure craft mingle with watermen's workboats as well as supply, mail and school boats that shuttle between the town and Smith and Tangier islands. Visitors can board one of the passenger boats that depart the harbor regularly for these captivating communities.

Outdoor and sports enthusiasts will find more activities than time permits: You can charter fishing trips, take a short bus ride to destinations such as Ocean City or the Great Hope Golf Course and arrange for guided kayak and canoe excursions from Crisfield Kayak and Canoe (410-968-0333, www.crisfieldkayaking.com) and Adrenaline High (410-749-2886, *www.adrenalinehigh.com*). Janes Island State Park on Tangier Sound (accessible by taxi) rents kayaks, too, perfect for exploring the water trails encircling its pristine shores. Janes Island park offers miles of hiking trails and stretches of beach where the observant may spy a piece of frosted sea glass or a fragment of clay pipe left behind by earlier inhabitants. Guests of Somers Cove Marina have access to a swimming pool, fish cleaning stations, pavilions and a playground. South of the marina, you can glimpse indigenous wildlife at Cedar Island Marsh Sanctuary, home to terrapins, hawks and a variety of waterfowl. The southern edge of this 330-acre marsh borders Jenkins Creek, where watermen and their crab shanties are still in evidence. Jenkins Creek also served as the heart of the once-thriving terrapin industry, when turtle soup was the height of culinary elegance.

Crisfield

⚓ **Marinas/Dockage**
 1 Somers Cove Marina
 2 City Dock
   (loading/unloading only)

⊙ **Points of Interest**
 1 Smith Island
   excursion boat
 2 Tangier Island
   excursion boat
 3 J. Millard Tawes
   Historical Museum
 4 U.S. Coast Guard Station

 5 MeTompkin Bay Oyster Co.
 6 J. Millard Tawes Library
 7 Cedar Island
   Marsh Sanctuary

❓ **Information**
 8 Visitor Center

🍴 **Dining**
 12 Watermen's Inn
 13 Gordon's Confectionery
 14 Crisfield Crab House
   & Tiki Bar
 15 Capt. Tyler's Crabhouse

🛒 **Groceries/Carryout**
 17 The Sweet Shoppe
 18 Big Willey's
 19 The Crab Place

🍦 **Ice Cream**
🛏 **Lodging**
⊙ **Hospital**
🏠 **Laundromat**
📖 **Library**
℞ **Pharmacy**
✉ **Post Office**

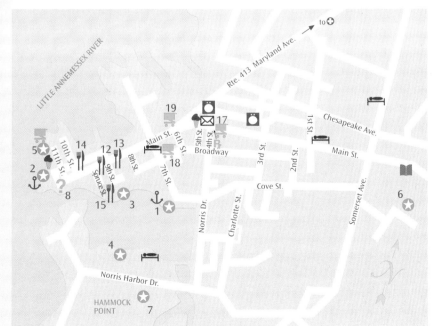

Port of Call Crisfield continued

Main Street's businesses range from trendy gift boutiques to a crab pot manufacturer. These ventures are being joined by a growing number of galleries featuring the works of local artists.

Cruisers can buy fresh catch at local seafood outlets such as Linton's Seafood, The Crab Place (in the former Fresh Pride building) and MeTompkin Bay Oyster Company. Not far from the marina, Big Willey's—a homegrown 7-Eleven—sells snacks, beer, wine and sodas (delivery also available). The Sweet Shoppe's assortment of pies, cookies, rolls and other bakery items includes a regional treat, the multi-layered Smith Island Cake.

As you might expect, fresh seafood stars at most Crisfield restaurants, many of which are clustered in the easily walkable blocks nearest the town wharf. The Watermen's Inn is deservedly a perennial favorite, and crabs are good and plenty at the Crisfield Crab House & Tiki Bar and Capt. Tyler's Crabhouse—all within an easy walk of the marina. The commodious Somers Cove Marina itself is the site of frequent boat club gatherings, and Crisfield is a town known for throwing good parties. Celebrations of seafood figure prominently on the town's calendar of events and include the Soft Shell Spring Fair in May and the J. Millard Tawes Crab and Clam Bake in July. The three-day Labor Day weekend includes the world famous National Hard Crab Derby and Fair, an activities-packed waterfront bash that traditionally includes a parade, crab skiff races and docking competitions, crab-picking contests, live entertainment, fireworks, food and Crisfield's answer to the Preakness—a time-honored highly competitive race between a mess of feisty claw-snapping blue crabs.In October, the Waterman's Festival offers all-you-care-to-eat seafood and entertainment.

Information: Somerset County Tourism, 800-521-9189 or 410-651-2968, *www.visitsomerset.com*; Crisfield Heritage Foundation, 410-968-2501; Crisfield Chamber of Commerce, 800-782-3913 or 410-968-2500, *www.crisfieldchamber.com*.

Little Annemessex River continued from page 249

side. You'll find plenty of water here—8 to 10 feet—and the anchorage is off from the traffic that flows continuously in and out of the marina and seafood plants.

If you take a dinghy ashore to the marina dock, be prepared to pay a small fee to tie up. The fee entitles you to use of the bathhouses and showers, laundry facilities and pool. You can also picnic ashore at the barbecue grills. The marina has a fishing center where anglers can find out where the fish are biting and can clean their catch at the end of the day. A dry storage boatyard is adjacent to Somers Cove Marina.

Crisfield is an interesting town with an equally interesting history. Originally known as Somer's Cove, it was built on a 1663 land grant to John Roach and Benjamin Somers. Unfortunately, few of the town's older buildings remain, lost to a number of devastating fires some decades past. From *Chesapeake Kaleidoscope* you'll learn that the last commercial sailing schooner on the bay, the *Anna and Helen*, sank in Crisfield's harbor in 1958.

The bounty of the Chesapeake has served Crisfield well. Crabbing as an industry began here about 1873 when a shipment of soft crabs was sent to Philadelphia, and the shells of millions of harvested oysters formed the foundations of the crab-picking and oyster-shucking houses. Sadly, the seafood plants are less active these days, although workboats still chug in and out of Crisfield's harbor. Condominiums have begun to sprout at the water's edge, altering the shorescape and lending an air of uncertainty about Crisfield's future.

Crisfield is one of the few towns in the Chesapeake Bay area with a hospital that has access from the water. To get there, head into the Daugherty Creek Canal north of town to daymark "16", enter the red-buoyed hospital entrance channel (5-foot depth) and tie up at the dock.

You can widen your boating lore by chatting with your fellow slipmates in Somers Cove, where you may share a dock with cruisers from Maine, Massachusetts or Canada. Crisfield is an annual stopover for many of these boaters, who have traditionally been able to find restaurants, hardware and marine supplies, a liquor store and a drugstore all within a two-block distance. (There is, however, no access for repairs to deep-draft boats. Small-boat and dinghy-engine repairs can be accommodated at Sea Mark Marine on the other side

		MLW	Overnight Slips	Gas	Diesel	Propane	Electric	Showers	Laundry	Restaurant	Lodging	Pool	Pump-out	Ice	Groceries	Marine Supplies	Bait	Boat Repair	Haul-out Services	Launch Ramp	Wi-Fi	Other
● On Premises ➤ Nearby																						
Little Annemessex River																						
12	**Sea Mark Marine** Tangier Sound/Little Annemessex R. 410-968-0800; *www.crisfield.com/seamark*	4.5'	➤	➤	➤	●		➤	➤	➤						➤	●	➤	●	●	●	Full-service yard, 50-ton lift, prop repairs
13	**Somers Cove Marina** Little Annemessex R.; 410-968-0925 or 800-967-3474; *www.somerscovemarina.com*	8'	●	●	●	➤	●	●	●	●	➤	➤	●	●	●	➤	➤	➤	➤	➤	●	●	$1.25/ft transient, picnic area, grills, bikes, pet friendly

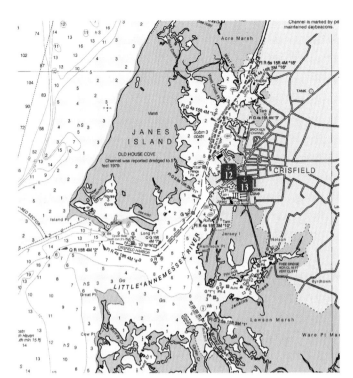

*Little Annemessex River; from NOAA Chart 12231—
not to be used for navigation.*

of the little peninsula from Somers Cove.)

To really appreciate local culture, board one of the mail-boats at City Dock and take it to Smith and Tangier islands. Unlike a tour boat, the mail boat allows you to share the passage with mail and merchandise on its way to the islanders—lawn chairs, fertilizer bags, flats of bedding plants—as you chat with island residents.

Pocomoke River

Appearing almost primordial in places, the **Pocomoke River** offers some of the most remarkable scenery of any river on the Bay. It meanders along a 30-mile course from Pocomoke Sound, flowing through salt marshes, forests and thick stands of exotic cypress to just a few miles, as the crow flies, from Chincoteague Bay. With readings of between 10 and 29 feet, the Pocomoke is unusually deep for its width.

The intricacies involved in reaching its entrance may intimidate some would-be explorers, but when you round the hairpin turn at **Shelltown** and start to wind your way upriver, you'll feel that the peace and lack of crowds, even at summer's peak, have made your careful navigation worth the effort. Two cautions are worth mentioning, however. First, keep a close eye out for tug-and-barge traffic because you'll want to meet them on the straights rather than the curves. Check in on VHF 13 to track their movements. Second, it would be wise to fill up before starting your trek up the river. Fuel, though it *can* be had by arrangement in Pocomoke City, is not readily available.

Cruises to the Pocomoke are generally launched from either Crisfield or Onancock. From Crisfield, there is a short-

cut, **Broad Creek**, that runs between the Little Annemessex River and Pocomoke Sound, but only if you can get by with 3½ to 4 feet of water. From Crisfield, through the creek, it's about 10 miles to the river's entrance channel. Otherwise, you will have to head down Tangier Sound to round the south end of Watts Island (nearly to Onancock Creek) before turning to enter Pocomoke Sound. From Onancock, it's a run of about 17 miles up Pocomoke Sound to the entrance channel.

Follow the marks carefully through the northern section of **Pocomoke Sound**. Crab pots abound. As you approach the entrance to the river, prepare for the 3½-mile run through the channel that leads behind Williams Point. You should find depths of 10 to 12 feet, with a short span of 6 to 8. Be especially alert and maintain a maneuverable speed in order to heave-to if the narrow channel is occupied by a larger vessel or barge. Green "23" at the entrance of the river itself is the last mark you'll see until reaching Shad Landing.

Now you can relax a bit and savor the beauty of this unique waterway. If you want to start fresh in the morning, you can anchor for the night in ❶ **Pitts Creek**, to starboard just beyond the hairpin turn, 14 miles downriver from Pocomoke City. By favoring the starboard side of the creek on entering, you'll find 7 feet of water in this lovely, lonely spot.

On the eastern shore, about four miles upriver near the state line, the historic colonial mansion Beverly of Somerset rests on a low bank quite near the water. It is currently occupied and not open to the public. The architecture features a curious wrought-iron filigree trim over the entrance and dentils along the eaves. The dentils probably account for its former name, Thrum Capped ("thrum" is an older word meaning "fringe"). You'll also admire the serpentine brick bulkhead.

The enticing aura of the stream beckons you on past the first clumps of feathery cypress. Cattle graze nearby, standing knee-deep in the shallows with cattle egrets perched on their backs. The winding curves of the river begin to narrow as the tiny hamlet of ❷ **Rehobeth** appears on the port side. You may be able to tie up in 7 feet of water at the small landing at Rehobeth and stroll a short distance up the street to the site of what was perhaps the oldest Presbyterian church in the country, founded and built by Francis Makemie in 1705. Beyond it stand the crumbling remains of Old Coventry Episcopal Church, built in about 1784. A trio of enormous sycamores, mantled in ivy, stands guard over the ruins and ancient cemetery.

Past Rehobeth and the marshlands of the lower Pocomoke, the banks become more deeply forested, punctuated now and then by poultry farms. Keep an eye peeled for floating logs and tugboat traffic. In warm weather, watch for numbers of diamondback terrapins sunning themselves on fallen trees along the shore. The water, nearly fresh, looks dark—stained tea-colored by cypress bark. (An Indian word, "pocomoke" means "black water.")

Once you reach the extensive sand and gravel pits on an inlet to starboard, it's another four miles to ❸ **Pocomoke City** and the three bridges that span the river: a railway bridge (normally open), an interesting old bascule bridge (tended 6 a.m. to 10 p.m. daily, call 410-957-2980) and a modern, fixed

Pocomoke River *continued*

highway bridge (35-foot clearance). Either before or after the bascule bridge—and before the fixed bridge—you can tie up at the long city dock bordering CYPRESS PARK. Convenient to the new Riverside Grill, shops and attractions, the town offers visiting boaters two free nights of dockage, which includes restrooms and showers. Register at City Hall (410-957-1333). Groceries and sundries are a short walk up Market Street or across the bridge, as is gasoline. Diesel can be ordered delivered to the docks.

Beyond Pocomoke City, masses of wildflowers bloom along the banks of the river, particularly the exquisite cardinal flower whose spikes of brilliant red blossoms attract hummingbirds. Bald eagles, herons, kingfishers and rare varieties of flycatchers create a bird-watcher's paradise. It's said that no Atlantic inland area supports a greater variety of species.

There are two separate areas of POCOMOKE RIVER STATE PARK, set amid a state forest noted

for its loblolly pines and cypress swamps. A few miles past Pocomoke City, on the north bank, you'll find MILBURN LANDING AREA with a small dock and a launching ramp; farther upriver, on the opposite shore, is the clearly marked entrance to SHAD LANDING AREA. Its 23-slip marina, located on a wide canal, is open from Memorial Day to Labor Day; transient slips can be reserved in advance (410-632-2566), and there is a fuel dock plus a launching ramp. The park offers nature trails, picnic facilities, restrooms, canoe and rowboat rentals during the summer months, and 200 campsites—an inducement to those with trailerable boats. The Atlantic beaches are only a short drive away. (Pets are not permitted in the Shad Landing Area.)

Picturesque **Snow Hill**, a town with lovely homes and a small museum, lies four wandering miles upriver from Shad Landing. Two parks along the way offer temporary dockage: BYRD PARK with 250 to 300 feet of bulkhead, and STURGIS PARK near the small drawbridge with 400 feet of bulkhead. Groceries, hardware, beer, wine and sundries are all within walking distance and the town also has a handful of restaurants, a pharmacy, a B&B, an art gallery and a country store.

The Pocomoke is navigable by boats with shallow draft for another two miles past the drawbridge. You'll need to give the part-time tender advance notice (24 hours on weekends, if you can) to open the bridge (410-632-0511).

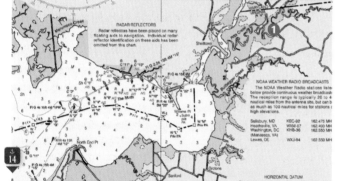

Pocomoke River; from NOAA Chart 12230—*not to be used for navigation.*

Pocomoke River

	Overnight Slips	MLW	Gas	Diesel	Propane	Electric	Showers	Laundry	Restaurant	Lodging	Pool	Pump-out	Ice	Groceries	Marine Supplies	Bait	Boat Repair	Haul-out Services	Launch Ramp	Wi-Fi	Other
Deep Creek Marina and Boatyard Deep Cr./Chesapeake Bay/Above Onancock, Va. 757-787-4565	●	4.5'	●			●									●		●	●	●		Dry storage, 25-ton lift; wood, engine repair
Pocomoke City Municipal Dock Pocomoke R./Pocomoke City 410-957-1333; www.cityofpocomokemd.gov	●	7'	●	►	►	●	●	►	●	►		●	●	●	►				●	►	2 days free docking, Near downtown
Shad Landing Marina/Pocomoke R. State Park Pocomoke R./Corkers Cr. 410-632-2566; www.dnr.state.md.us	●	7'	●	●		►	●	●	●	►	●	●	●	●	●	►	●		●	●	boathouse, 2 bath houses, pool upgrades

● On Premises
► Nearby

Port of Call
Pocomoke City

If you're cruising up the serpentine, cypress-lined Pocomoke River, historic Pocomoke City is well worth a visit. Its public dock offers ample room for visitors (unless there's a hurricane brewing; then the dock is crowded with watermen coming upriver for shelter). This peaceful port, 14 miles from the Bay, has always been proud of its heritage, but with the addition of an imaginative regional museum exploring the forces that shaped growth and settlement here, the city has even more ways to share the river and its legacy with visitors.

The Delmarva Discovery Center is an essential part of any visit. There's nothing staid about this museum—multimedia and hands-on exhibits engage your senses as you explore the Pocomoke's natural wonders and the lives of its settlers, from native peoples to shipbuilders, woodcarvers and oystermen. Berthed at the Center's dock, the *Bay Queen* offers narrated tours of the river and the Great Cypress Swamp.

The Discovery Center and the city's historic attractions lie within a few blocks of the City Dock. The Information Center can direct you to sites such as the Costen House, listed in the National Register of Historic Places. Once the home of Dr. Isaac Costen, the city's first mayor, this Victorian house has been restored and now serves as a cultural center and museum. Adjacent to it is the beautifully landscaped Hall-Walton Memorial Garden. Gain insights into local African American history at the restored Sturgis One-Room School Museum (c. 1900), originally a school for African-American students. The 1850 Heritage House next door opens a window into late 19th-century daily life. The

Mar-Va Theater (c.1927), a 700-seat art deco movie house, serves as a performing arts center/old-time film venue. In addition to performances, the theater opens its doors for tours by appointment (410-957-2752).

Adjacent to City Dock, beautiful Cypress Park offers recreational and picnic facilities for cruisers who want to enjoy some time ashore. A public nine-hole course is located nearby at Winter Quarters Golf Club and bicyclists can avail themselves of the scenic 100-mile Viewtrail, which passes through the city. SouthEast Expeditions offers guided tours and kayak rentals (757-331-2680, *www.southeastexpeditions.net*).

Centrally located on the Delmarva Peninsula, Pocomoke City is a convenient base from which to venture afield, too. A local rental agency will deliver cars to the public dock (call 410-957-2222).

Most shops are located on Market Street within a few blocks of the waterfront. Here you'll find almost all of the essentials, including a hardware store, a bank and a barber shop. For gift shopping, the store at the Discovery Center has a unique selection of books, jewelry and artworks. Spring through fall, fresh produce is sold on Monday through Saturday at the Farmer's Market. Milk and beverages can be found at River Market just beyond the bridge into town. The Route 13 retail centers—a good hike away—have pharmacies, convenience stores and a Wal-Mart.

Those eating ashore will find a new restaurant located right at City Dock. Riverside Grill opened last year and has been getting great reviews.

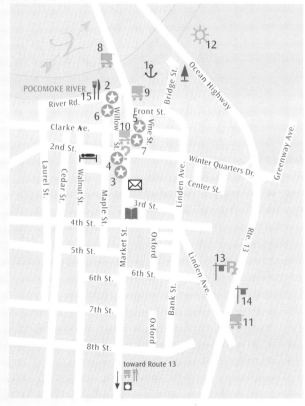

Pocomoke City

⚓ **Marinas/Dockage**
  1 City Dock

✪ **Points of Interest**
  2 Delmarva Discovery Center
  3 Costen House
  4 Hall-Walton Memorial Garden
  5 Mar-Va Theater
  6 Sturgis One-Room School Museum
    & 1850 Heritage House
  7 City Hall

❓ **Information**
  Pocomoke City Information Center

Groceries/Carryout
  8 River Market (carryout)
  9 Farmer's Market (Mon.-Sat.)
  10 Discount Variety (convenience section)
  11 Rite Aid Foodmart

⚓ **Park**

✿ **Recreation**
  12 Winter Quarters Golf Club (public)

Shopping
  13 Pocomoke Plaza
  14 Wal-Mart

🍴 **Dining**
  15 Riverside Grille

▢ **Laundromat**   ■ **Library**
✉ **Post Office**   ℞ **Pharmacy**

Major annual events celebrate the Pocomoke River and regional culture. These include two gala events: in June, the Cypress Festival (traditionally featuring food, rides, midway games, a plastic duck race along the riverfront, live music and fireworks); in August, the Great Pocomoke Fair (an old-fashioned fair with a little bit of everything: livestock exhibits, games such as sack races and a greased pig contest, carnival rides, harness racing, tractor pulls, entertainment, food and a fireworks display).

Information: Chamber of Commerce, 410-957-1919, *www.pocomoke.com*; Pocomoke City, *www.cityofpocomoke.com*.

Eastern Shore of Virginia

Below the Pocomoke River lies the Eastern Shore of Virginia. Forming the southern tip of the Delmarva Peninsula, this quiet region has an appealing mix of meandering creeks, wild marshes and small villages. While short on facilities for boaters, its isolation and rural character are definitely part of its charm, helping to preserve an era in Chesapeake history that has been erased along much of the rest of the Eastern Shore.

Onancock Creek

The entrance to **Onancock Creek** (*uh-NAN-cock*) is quite easy to spot—especially if you are coming from the north. The three lighted marks and daymarks stand out against the low shoreline. If you are near the 45-foot Tangier Sound Light at the southern entrance to the sound, you're only seven miles from the beginning of the well-marked four-mile, deep channel (controlling depth 8 feet) that leads up the creek to the Wharf at Onancock, the town dock.

Along the way, you'll pass gentle countryside and working farms dotted with lovely houses, old and new. The second oldest port in Virginia, Onancock was designated an official port of entry in 1680. Its deep-water harbor still serves as

the main port for oil and gravel in the area. Indeed, you may meet a tug and tow in the creek. To fishermen and recreational boaters, the harbor is considered one of the Eastern Shore's better storm holes.

After you pass Ware Point and Parkers Marsh on the port side, the shores become more wooded. **Parkers Creek**, to starboard past "12", is best entered only with local knowledge, and the entrances to the other tributaries of the creek are too shoal for most cruising boats.

Two favorite anchorages are off **Cedar Creek** next to "26" and farther up in a small bay just off the channel near "34". You can also anchor in the little cove to starboard near the town wharf and red "37", but there's limited space here and the holding is not that good. (Set your hook with care and let out lots of scope before jumping in the dink and heading for town.)

Just beyond "36" and "37", Onancock Creek forks into the North and South branches. Straight ahead lies historic Hopkins & Brothers Store at the town wharf, which now houses a lovely waterfront restaurant with an outdoor bar (in season). A refurbished harbormaster's office is across from the store, on the other side of the public ramp. Cruisers are strongly advised to call ahead for reservations at the wharf, which has about a dozen slips. Water and electric hook-ups are available. Amenities include new showers and restrooms. Gas and diesel fuel are available at the oil company dock across the creek, but arrange this through the town wharf. To contact the harbormaster about slips or fuel, call 757-787-

continued on page 256

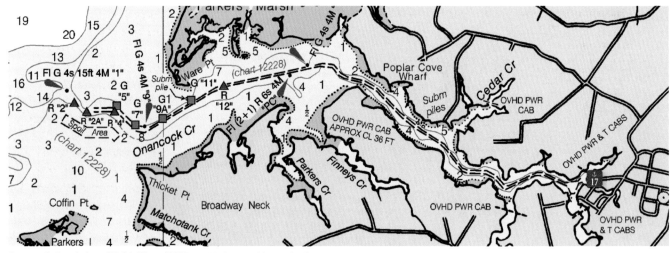

Onancock Creek; from NOAA Chart 12225—not to be used for navigation.

- ● On Premises
- ➤ Nearby

Onancock Creek

	MLW	Overnight Slips	Gas	Diesel	Propane	Electric	Showers	Laundry	Restaurant	Lodging	Pool	Pump-out	Ice	Groceries	Marine Supplies	Bait	Boat Repair	Haul-out Services	Launch Ramp	Wi-Fi	Other
The Wharf at Onancock Onancock Cr./Onancock 757-787-7911; www.onancock.com	8'	●	●	●		●	●	➤	●	➤		●	●	➤		➤	➤		●	●	walk to restaurants, galleries, shops, historic sites

Port of Call
Onancock

www.Burnham Virginia.com

Nestled on a peninsula at the head of Onancock Creek, this small town (established in 1680) charms visitors with its scenic waterfront and historic buildings. The main drag, Market Street, starts where the creek's north and central branches divide; the "liars bench" next to the boat ramp is usually occupied by overseers of the comings and goings of small boats and anglers at the wharf. The harbor yields to a neighborhood of houses graced by expansive porches and a business district filled with an increasingly sophisticated mix of shops and restaurants.

Historic Onancock comprises many 18th- and 19th-century buildings, the best known being Ker Place, home of the Eastern Shore of Virginia Historical Society. Now restored, it houses a museum that opens a window onto life in the 1800s, regional history exhibits and the restoration of the 45-foot-long batteau *Annie C.* Self-guided downtown walking tour maps can be picked up at Town Hall (weekdays). Explore nearby creeks on a guided kayak tour from SouthEast Expeditions (*www.southeastexpeditions.net*; 757-331-2680). Rent a bike from

GardenArt. Excursion boats to Tangier Island depart from the town wharf. Star Transit buses can shuttle you to shopping centers and nearby towns. This regional system provides regular weekday service and door-to-door service on request (757-665-1994).

There are two entertainment venues downtown: the Roseland Theater shows first-run movies on weekend evenings and an International Film Festival the second Thursday of the month; North Street Playhouse offers a number of productions each season.

The compact business district's restored buildings include showcases for regional artists and settings for an array of exceptional dining experiences. Fresh Pride and Food Lion (best reached by bicycle or bus) have general groceries. Aromas wafting from the Corner Bakery beckon visitors to treats inside. Mallards at the Wharf is the only waterfront venue in town. Several homes have been converted to charming and gracious B&Bs.

During Second Friday art strolls, galleries and shops stay open late to offer art demonstrations and special activities. On the second weekend in September, Harborfest features music, food, small boat races and a bake-off.

Information: Town of Onancock, 757-787-3363; *www.onancock.org*.

Onancock

⚓ **Marinas/Dockage**
  1 The Wharf at Onancock

⊕ **Points of Interest**
  2 Tangier Island cruises
  3 Hopkins & Bros. Store
  4 Ker Place

🍴 **Dining**
  5 Mallards at the Wharf
  6 Inn and Garden Cafe
  7 Corner Bakery Cafe
  8 Bizzotto's Gallery Caffe
  9 Charlotte Hotel and Restaurant

  10 Blarney Stone Pub
  11 Janet's Onancock General Store

🛒 **Groceries**
  12 Corner Mart
    (at Chevron Station)
  13 North Street Market

☼ **Entertainment/ Recreation**
  14 North Street Playhouse
  15 Roseland Theater

🚣 **Kayak Rentals**
  16 SouthEast Expeditions

? **Information**
🏳 **Shopping**
🍦 **Ice Cream**
🌳 **Park**
◼ **Library**
℞ **Pharmacy**
✉ **Post Office**
🧺 **Laundromat**
🚲 **Bicycles**

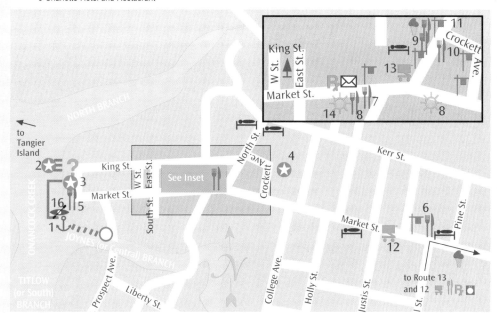

Onancock Creek continued from page 254

7911 or hail him on channel 16. The office is open from mid-March to mid-November.

The village of **Onancock**, which radiates from the wharf, is one of the three main towns on Virginia's Eastern Shore. Over the last decade this lovely old town has undergone a revival of sorts as artists and retirees have discovered its charms. Its restored Victorian homes rival those in St. Michaels and Oxford farther north. Fine restaurants and attractive shops have taken over abandoned shop fronts, and the town has a jaunty new confidence. When you walk down the street, people smile and say hello, and when you ride a bike, people in passing cars wave. It's pet friendly here, too. Onancock's out-of-the-way location, deep and scenic approach, and fine harbor make this a delightful destination for cruisers. A complete history of the town can be found in Anne Nock's *Child of the Bay*.

Pungoteague Creek; from NOAA Chart 12225—not to be used for navigation.

Pungoteague Creek

If you're looking for something new and different in an anchorage, **Pungoteague Creek** (*PUNG-uh-teeg*), south of Onancock Creek, might catch your eye. Its approach, although exposed, is deep and well-marked. You'll find a quick flasher about a mile offshore of Pungoteague's entrance and a red 4-second flasher about a half mile inshore of that.

Rounding the outer quick flasher, you'll see the nearby remains of the former mark—a tilted concrete caisson that will remind you of the pair of marks at the entrance to LaTrappe Creek on the Choptank River. Once inside the mouth, Pungoteague's channel gently curves right before making a left and then another right toward the anchorage at flashing green "13", about three and a half miles upstream. The channel, however, has few lighted aids to navigation, and although its depths are adequate for most drafts, deviation from the channel could put you quickly aground. In addition, the channel is reported to have plentiful crab pots as well as shoaling (especially on the north side at "5" and "9"), so caution is the key word.

At "13", the creek is broad but shoals along the shoreline. Boaters with greater than 4-foot draft should remain toward the center. Note that **Underhill Creek** on the north shore before "13" only has charted depths of 1 foot at its entrance. Another anchorage, closer to Harborton and just off the channel beyond "15", can be found where the river splits. You should find about 5 feet of water there at low tide and a stunning sunrise the following morning.

Pungoteague Creek is more beautiful than you might expect. Once a large, busy port that handled shipping, it is much quieter, though still used by pleasure boaters and watermen. Since a pulpwood yard went out of business, the only commercial vessels to use the creek are occasional tugboats pushing a barge of fertilizer.

The creek is largely rural until reaching the settlement of **Harborton** on the southern shore, marked by a cluster of homes. Its seafood houses and dock now lie unused.

In the early 20th century, schooners sailed as far inland as Evans and Boggs wharves beyond **Taylor Creek** and, during the steamboat era, Harborton's wharf was a regular stop. It consisted of an unusual bridge-type structure connecting the shore to the steamboat wharf several hundred feet into the river. Alongside the bridge, the town's businesses were built on pilings. But like many Eastern Shore rivers, the Pungoteague has silted in. Today boaters will often find 4 feet or less beyond "14". Nonetheless, plenty of water remains at the town dock (about 12 feet), where cruisers may tie up for a bit.

In season and out, you'll find Pungoteague Creek idyllic and pretty much empty. An old pulp mill wharf has been converted to a small-boat ramp, but otherwise even the docks behind the homes in the area are largely devoid of boats. Youngsters in sailing dinghies may be your only company on the water.

Occohannock Creek

Do your cruising dreams involve sitting idly, reading a good novel under a warm sun, with a gentle breeze bringing the fragrant scents of nature across your cockpit? If so, **Occohannock Creek** (*AHK-uh-HAN-nock*) can certainly provide the reality for your dream. This 6-mile-long creek lies 18 miles north of Cape Charles harbor.

Shallow water is so ubiquitous along the creeks of the lower Eastern Shore that you might understandably be skeptical about visiting *any* of them. Studying the depth numbers for Occohannock Creek, for example, could well give you a case of the willies as you note the large shoals on both sides of the creek's entrance. And, of course, the shoals of the Eastern Shore tend to shift unpredictably, especially after strong storms. Relax. On a rising tide, you can certainly visit this lovely body of water. Just keep one eye on the depthsounder.

The land along this section of the Eastern Shore is low with stands of tall trees and few distinguishing landmarks. Therefore, you should be able to spot green flasher "1" at a distance of approximately four miles. Its green color stands out surprisingly well, even in summer haze, against the darker background of the tall trees ashore.

If you draw 5 feet or better, you'll want to check your tide tables carefully before planning your visit. The channel is well marked as far as Morley Wharf, opposite Davis Wharf, about four miles upstream. **Tawes Creek**, across from red "10A", is fine for boats drawing less than 4 feet. It is exposed, however, to the southwest. The low and marshy surrounding landscape does not afford much protection. In the right weather it makes a good place to drop the hook for the night and to make a quick getaway in the morning.

If the weather is out of the southwest, you might try going a short distance farther, across from green "13", near **Johnson Cove**. Four feet of water, at low tide, can be carried halfway between the mark and the shore.

The shipping channel passes only four miles off the entrance to Occohannock Creek, and from the anchorage near "13" you've got a wonderful view of the parade of massive cargo vessels that steadily travel up and down the Bay. You're likely to see huge container ships, a freighter or two, or maybe even a nuclear submarine.

About one mile farther up the Occohannock on the north shore, behind Pons Point, is the first of the more protected anchorages. The deeper water is about 100 yards northeast of red "16". Here, boats with drafts up to 5 feet can anchor, raft and feel safe. On the north shore past "17" a sprawling white farmhouse perches on a hill with a broad lawn sloping down to the creek. This is Bay View Waterfront (757-442-6963), a small bed-and-breakfast inn with a dock for guests arriving by water. The three original sections of this Eastern-Shore-style home date from about 1800.

A larger and more protected anchorage is located

Occohannock Creek; from NOAA Chart 12225—not to be used for navigation.

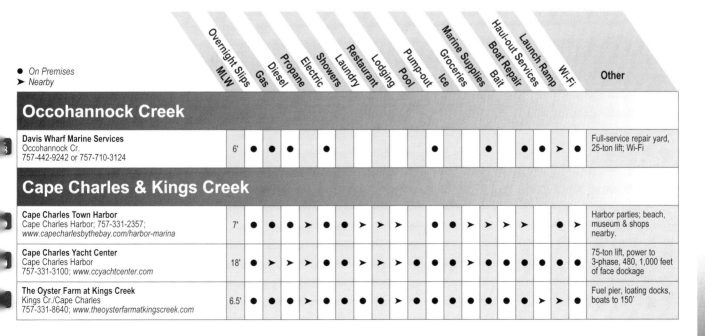

● On Premises
➤ Nearby

	MLW	Overnight Slips	Gas	Diesel	Propane	Electric	Showers	Laundry	Restaurant	Lodging	Pool	Pump-out	Ice	Groceries	Marine Supplies	Boat Repair	Bait	Haul-out Services	Launch Ramp	Wi-Fi	Other
Occohannock Creek																					
Davis Wharf Marine Services Occohannock Cr. 757-442-9242 or 757-710-3124	6'	●	●	●		●						●			●		●	●	➤	●	Full-service repair yard, 25-ton lift; Wi-Fi
Cape Charles & Kings Creek																					
Cape Charles Town Harbor Cape Charles Harbor; 757-331-2357; www.capecharlesbythebay.com/harbor-marina	7'	●	●	●	➤	●	●	➤	➤	➤		●	●	➤	➤	➤	➤		●	➤	Harbor parties; beach, museum & shops nearby.
Cape Charles Yacht Center Cape Charles Harbor 757-331-3100; www.ccyachtcenter.com	18'	●	➤	➤	➤	●	●	➤	➤	➤	●	●	●	➤	●	●	●	●	●	●	75-ton lift, power to 3-phase, 480, 1,000 feet of face dockage
The Oyster Farm at Kings Creek Kings Cr./Cape Charles 757-331-8640; www.theoysterfarmatkingscreek.com	6.5'	●	●	●	●	➤	●	●	●	●	●	➤	●	●	●	●	●	●	➤	➤	●	Fuel pier, loating docks, boats to 150'

Occohannock Creek *continued*

another mile up the creek, due south of green "19". It offers excellent protection as the land is at least 50 feet high. A long, sandy beach on the southern shore is about 300 yards from a state-controlled boat ramp at MORLEY WHARF. The small village of Wardtown is less than a mile from the landing, but it has no provisions.

Across the creek from Morley Wharf lies Davis Wharf Marine Services, a full-service repair yard offering slips for transients, gas, diesel fuel, pumpout facilities, marine supplies and the services of a 25-ton lift and excellent mechanics. You will see a workboat or two at their docks, where you'll find about 6 feet of water at low tide. There are no restrooms or showers, but you'll find a friendly offer of a ride into town for parts or supplies.

If you head out to explore the upper reaches of the creek, be aware that there are no marks beyond "19". By staying in the middle of the creek and giving points of land a wide berth, you'll find, at high tide, 6 feet of water all the way up to **Shields Wharf**. If your boat can make it that far, you will be treated to one of the most scenic and well-protected anchorages anywhere. What looks like a Civil War-era mansion sits in majestic beauty at least 75 feet above the water. The setting is well worth the trip up the creek.

Cruisers here consistently marvel at the way nature and man have combined to preserve this unspoiled setting. Houses are fairly sparse along Occohannock Creek from its entrance all the way up to **Belle Haven**, a small community near the fixed bridge (4-foot vertical clearance), and visiting boaters revel in the splendid privacy and natural beauty of the area.

Recreational anglers should note that fish seem to be all over the place, breaking the water or jumping. The number of flights of birds overhead demonstrates that this is a well travelled part of the Eastern flyway and a terrific place to observe migrating waterfowl in the fall. If you are patient and look long enough, you'll undoubtedly see all sorts of wildlife along the shores of this tranquil creek.

Cape Charles

The town of **Cape Charles**, 9 miles north of the true tip of Cape Charles, is working hard to position itself as a prime cruising destination on Virginia's Eastern Shore. With an expanded and upgraded town dock, a marina resort on Kings Creek, and, most recently, a marina dedicated to megayachts, it's attracting more visiting boaters, especially in spring and fall as cruisers heading north or south pause for a touch of Virginia hospitality away from the bustle of Hampton Roads.

The first of the navigation aids marking the channel to Cape Charles is the Old Plantation Light. Marked "A", this flashing light is charted as being 19 feet tall, replacing the former 39-foot-tall flasher built on the site of the original manned lighthouse. North of the light, flashing green "1CC" marks the north side of the channel entrance. Water on either side of the marked channel is adequate for most yachts, a good thing to keep in mind if you encounter one

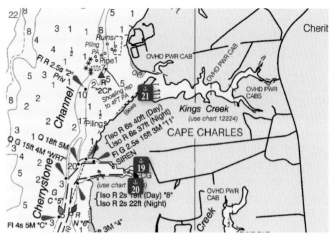
Cape Charles; from NOAA Chart 12221—not to be used for navigation.

of the railroad barges that make daily round trips between Little Creek and Cape Charles.

Follow range "A" (situated on the shoreline northeast of Old Plantation Light) until the channel turns northeast toward the entrance jetty of Cape Charles's busy harbor, about 2½ miles ahead. As the next range "B" appears to port on the end of the northern harbor jetty, you should see the entrance ahead at just under three nautical miles.

The harbor is bisected by the Coast Guard Station. On the north side is the town-owned dock, where cruisers and workboats mingle side by side. It has 95 slips, with electricity and water, and a bulkhead. You'll find gas and diesel fuel, showers and restrooms. The harbor has been dredged to accommodate drafts up to 7 feet. Stay close to the fuel dock as you enter the harbor to avoid a shoal patch on the east side.

Transients are welcome at Cape Charles Town Harbor, where discounts are available for weekly or monthly stays. To secure a slip, contact the harbormaster on channel 16 or by phone at 757-331-2357. For short tie-ups, there is a dock right next to the boat ramps with about 5 feet at low water. Anchoring space is limited to the area just south of the breakwater at the entrance. (The Coast Guard and the tugs that pick up rail cars from the terminal are rather picky about where you drop the hook.) Downtown is a quick walk from the town docks.

Cape Charles serves as the southern terminus for the raillines that run from the farmlands of the Eastern Shore to the railheads in Norfolk. A prosperous town in the days when the railroad carried passengers and freight to awaiting ferries, Cape Charles is undertaking a renaissance The 1884 Hotel Cape Charles, in the heart of downtown, has reopened as a modern, upscale, 16-room inn. Some rooms are designated pet-friendly. The hotel is close to the beach, restaurants and specialty shops. The town museum/welcome center is a few blocks away. The nearby restored Historic Palace Theatre is active year-round, hosting classes and productions in dance, drama, music and the visual arts.

As you stroll around town, you'll notice that a number of the city's late-Victorian and turn-of-the-century homes

continued on page 260

Port of Call

Cape Charles

The charms of Cape Charles are reminiscent of a tropical island or the Florida Keys: waves lapping a pristine beach, gorgeous sunsets that draw appreciative spectators, a stress-free atmosphere where relaxation is contagious. Once a thriving rail center through which passengers and freight moved, the Delmarva Peninsula's southernmost city is now a popular destination for cruisers and other visitors.

Once you're tied up at the town dock or at King's Creek Marina just north of town, exploration is easy. Cape Charles is quite walkable from the downtown dock, and King's Creek can arrange for transportation to town, which lies about a mile away.

The downtown business center is only a few blocks long and hugs the waterfront. Beyond it lies a grid of streets first laid out in the early 1880s and now lined with well-kept homes. The historic district encompasses many of these preserved late 19th- and early 20th-century structures, more than four dozen of which—including Sears kit houses, tropical cottages and the former mansions of prosperous businessmen—are identified in a self-guided walking tour. Copies of the tour brochure are available at the Cape Charles Museum and Welcome Center, which is housed in a former power plant on the outskirts of town. The museum

complex holds a trove of historic artifacts, including antique farm equipment, rail cars and a mammoth diesel engine. Nearby is a town landmark, the water tower, modeled after the Cape Charles Lighthouse built on Smith Island off the Atlantic shore in 1893.

Bay Creek Resort (adjacent to King's Creek Marina) has two public golf courses, designed by Arnold Palmer and Jack Nicklaus. Visitors have their pick of other activities as well. Hop on a bicycle, scooter or golf cart and explore the countryside; go kiteboarding, miniature golfing or take advantage of the public tennis courts located at Central Park.

For cultural diversion, take in a performance at the Historic Palace Theatre, operated by Arts Enter. This art deco-style theater with its beautiful murals debuted in 1941 and has been restored for the enjoyment of a new generation of theater-goers. The Stage Door Gallery, located around the corner, also displays some of its visual arts collection in the theater.

Art galleries and gift shops stand shoulder to shoulder with the linchpins of any town—a post office, bank, pharmacy and Chamber of Commerce. The Gull Hummock Gourmet Market offers specialty foods and wine.

If you're docked at King's Creek Marina, you'll find almost anything a cruiser desires at the small retail enclave nearby. And you'll find two restaurants, Aqua (seafood, regional cuisine) at King's Creek and Coach House Tavern (light fare) at next door Bay Creek Resort.

The downtown's mix of cafes, pubs, restaurants and sandwich shops has now been supplemented by the welcome addition of a restaurant located on the town's beautiful new dock complex. The Shanty specializes in locally caught seafood.

The beach and the view can be entertainment enough in Cape Charles. Sunsets are the inspiration for Harbor Parties, held once a month in May, June and August, featuring music, food, dancing, wine and beer—all for a small admission fee. Other town celebrations include an Independence Day gala and, in September, Cape Charles Day (featuring arts and crafts) and the Eastern Shore Birding and Wildlife Festival.

Information: Cape Charles by the Bay, *capecharlesbythebay.com.*

Cape Charles

⚓ **Marinas/Dockage**
 1 Cape Charles Town Dock
 2 The Oyster Farm at
   King's Creek Marina
 13 Cape Charles Yacht Center

⊕ **Points of Interest**
 3 Cape Charles Museum and
   Welcome Center

? **Information**

🏖 **Beach**

🍴 **Dining**
 2 Aqua; Coach House Tavern
 4 Kelly's Gingernut Pub
 5 Cape Charles Coffee House
 6 Hook U Up Gourmet
 7 The Shanty
 11 Brown Dog Ice Cream

🛒 **Groceries/Carryout**
 2 Purple Pelican
 8 Gull Hummock
   Gourmet Market

☼ **Entertainment/Recreation**
 2 Bay Creek Resort (golf)
 9 Historic Palace Theatre
 10 Fishing pier

🍦 **Ice Cream**

🚲 **Bicycles**

🚻 **Public Restrooms**

✉ **Post Office**

📖 **Library**

🛝 **Playground**

🚙 **Golf Cart Rentals**

Cape Charles continued from page 257

remain. A charming boardwalk, with a fishing pier, follows a long strand of beach north of the harbor. From the boardwalk or a long jetty along the same shoreline, you can look westward across the Bay and watch the sunset. On the east end of town, in an old power plant, the CAPE CHARLES MUSEUM AND WELCOME CENTER offers a look at the hearty souls who once made a living on the peninsula's rugged barrier islands.

Two tributaries lie north of the Cape Charles jetty: Cherrystone Inlet, about 2 miles beyond, and **Kings Creek**, closer to town. The latter leads to King's Creek Marina & Resort, an upscale golf and waterfront community that welcomes transient boaters. To get there, continue on the Cape Charles Harbor Channel, keeping the jetty light to starboard. Depths are 6 feet or better until you reach "5". Here shoaling is encroaching from the green (left) side, so the dockmaster advises favoring the red (right) side of the channel until you reach red "6". After that, stay in the center. The channel is narrow (80-feet wide) and the current can be strong, so be sure to keep track of your drift by sighting the marker behind you as well as the one in front. If you are uncomfortable about making the trip in, the dockmaster will either come out to guide you through or talk you through. (Hail him on channel 16 or call him at 757-331-8640.) In addition, the marina has replaced old markers and added some new ones to help boaters keep track of the channel.

Besides gas and diesel fuel and floating docks, King's Creek's amenities include two world-class golf courses. Pedestrian-friendly grounds lead to casual and fine dining. Excursions into town (about a mile away) can be made with King's Creek's rental bikes, golf carts and shuttle van.

Kiptopeke Beach

Kiptopeke Beach boasts a state park with swimming and fishing facilities, but it's also known as a fine anchorage. A row of partially sunken concrete ships off the beach provides the first shelter to anyone arriving from the Chesapeake Bay Bridge-Tunnel Channel (or from Norfolk and/or Virginia Beach). They're near the northern end of the Bridge-Tunnel, about three miles north of Fisherman Island and four and a half nautical miles south of the Cape Charles Channel entrance mark green "1".

At first, all you may see is an unbroken line of sandy beach. Soon the view will shift. The contours of the land will grow more angular and separated from the water. Then the shore seems to snap in half, part of it receding and the other part taking shape as the row of concrete ships you have expected. The dun-colored ships blend with the tans of the sandy beach and the gray haze and water. When you pass the gap between the two rows of concrete vessels, you'll see the old Kiptopeke ferry dock.

As you head north of the line of ships, then between them and the land, you'll find immediate shelter—an anchorage with good depths and good holding. (Mind the current, though, it's strong here.) The nine World War II Liberty ships

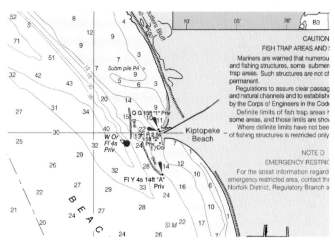

Kiptopeke Beach; from NOAA Chart 12224—not to be used for navigation.

lie about 1,500 feet from shore in 20 to 30 feet of water. The water at the end of the Kiptopeke pier is about 15 feet deep. Boaters can pick their anchorage according to the prevailing wind. (Beware that anchored vessels will rock when the wind and current are opposed.) Officials ask that you stand well off the marked swimming beach north of the boat ramp.

This old ferry terminal was abandoned after construction of the Bay Bridge-Tunnel in the 1960s and fell into disrepair. Then the Commonwealth of Virginia bought the site and developed it into KIPTOPEKE STATE PARK. Upgrades here have included bulkheads, a rock jetty and dual boat ramps (4 ½-foot depths MLW). Improvements were also made to the 24-hour fishing pier, which extends from the old ferry dock and is quite well-lit and very well-used—something to keep in mind when dropping the hook for the night. These amenities are available to cruisers, who can dinghy ashore to stretch their legs along elevated walkways through the marsh grass and stroll the park's beaches (a half-mile north of the pier and a quarter-mile south).

Located on a major migratory route, the park is also the site of a hawk observatory and a bird-banding station. The popular Eastern Shore Birding Festival in early October allows visitors to tour park areas that are generally closed to the public. For additional information on festival activities and the observatory, call the park at 757-331-2267.

The beach was named by the Virginia Ferry Corp. for Kiptopeke, the brother of an Accomack Indian chief who befriended early English settlers. The name means "Big Water." To cross that "Big Water," a ferry ran between Kiptopeke and Virginia Beach. When the Eastern Shore terminus opened in 1950, the pier was touted as the world's largest and most modern. Its successor, the Bay Bridge-Tunnel, has taken its rightful place as yet another engineering marvel.

Fishermans Island

A few miles from Kiptopeke is the southernmost tip of the Delmarva Peninsula. Just offshore sits Fishermans Island, a National Wildlife Refuge and off-limits to humans, except for one or two "visiting days" each year.

Smith Point to Rappahannock River

The Great Wicomico, Little Wicomico and
Rappannock Rivers; Fleets and Little Bays
Reedville, Kilmarnock, Irvington and Urbanna
The Bayside creeks of the Northern Neck

The Rappahannock River is the dominant feature of this region, but don't overlook the Little and Great Wicomico rivers and the deep tidal creeks that drain the Bayshore end of Virginia's Northern Neck. This land of quiet coves, great blue herons, ospreys and watermen has much to offer enterprising cruisers who live to anchor out.

Most of these waterways have lively currents flowing through narrow mouths, with the trickiest being the channel between the jetties at the mouth of the Little Wicomico (known locally as "Little River"). Once you're inside them, however, creeks such as Mill, Dividing, Indian, Dymer, Tabbs and Antipoison, south of the Great Wicomico, exhibit the pastoral charm for which the Chesapeake has long been famous. They make good places to hide from a storm, but you may choose to explore them for their beauty as well.

The Great Wicomico is an expanded version of these creeks, with a protected anchorage behind Sandy Point that has long been a favorite among groups and cruisers. Cockrell Creek, its big northeastern tributary, houses Reedville, with its menhaden processing plant, graceful "Menhaden Gothic" Victorian houses and the excellent Reedville Fishermen's Museum.

The Rappahannock is the Chesapeake's fourth largest river, flowing down the eastern slopes of the Blue Ridge Mountains. It's navigable all the way to Fredericksburg,

though most cruisers concentrate on the lower reaches, especially Carter Creek (home of The Tides resort), the old port town of Urbanna, and the sprawling Corrotoman River, the tidal Rappahannock's largest tributary. Carter Creek and Urbanna offer modern amenities, while the Corrotoman offers solitude in wooded coves with houses sprinkled along the shore.

Upriver are smaller, more secluded creeks for shallow-draft adventuring: LaGrange and Parrotts on the south shore; Deep, Mulberry and Lancaster to the north. Go farther to explore Totuskey Creek, buoyed and deep for about 3 miles into Virginia's Northern Neck. On the other shore is narrow Piscataway Creek which winds and twists through several miles of pristine marshland.

Tappahannock is a charming riverfront town. Like Urbanna, Port Royal (25 miles upstream) and Fredericksburg (50 miles), Tappahannock was a major port with a customs house during colonial times.

Until bridges spanned the Potomac and Rappahannock rivers, the Northern Neck (nearly 100 miles long) was almost isolated, dependent on goods that could be delivered by water. In the 1800s, steamships made frequent stops along all of the peninsula's rivers and creeks. Though most of the steamboat wharves are gone, it is still easy to picture one of these vessels chugging majestically into port.

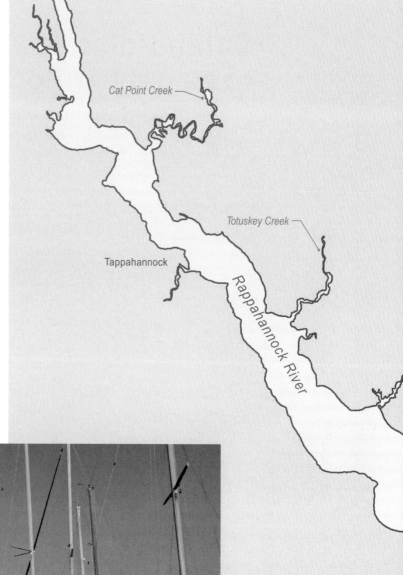

Sunset on Carter Creek

Tow BoatU.S.
LOCATIONS
A **Ingram Bay**
804-725-0453

Little Wicomico River

Great Wicomico River

Horn Harbor — Reedville

Balls Creek

Cockrell Creek

A

Mill Creek

Dividing Creek — Hughlett Point

Western Branch

Eastern Branch

Corrotoman River

Indian Creek

Carter Creek — Dymer Creek

Fleets Bay

Urbanna

Rappahannock River

Windmill Point

Urbanna Creek

Antipoison Creek

Pelicans make the most of a ready-made meal provided by a pound net located between the Great and Little Wicomico rivers. Pound nets in this area are plentiful and often located well away from shore, providing an unwelcome surprise to the unwary boater.

Little Wicomico River

The entrance to "the Little River," the **Little Wicomico** (*wye-KAHM-eh-ko*), is dredged regularly to 10 feet—most recently in 2014— because it shoals regularly. Before you go, check with one of the river's two marinas, Cockrell's Marine Railway (804-453-3560) and Smith Point Marina (804-453-4077), or the splendid Smith Point Rescue organization (804-453-4600) for the latest navigation information.

Whether you're coming from up or down the Bay, approach the entrance from the southeast. Once you can align "2LW" with red "4" on the entrance's northern jetty, turn northwest. Using these marks as a range, proceed toward the jetties and leave "2LW" very close to starboard. Oh, and of course, remember to keep an eagle eye open for pound nets, which abound in this area.

A word of caution about transiting the jetties. At full ebb

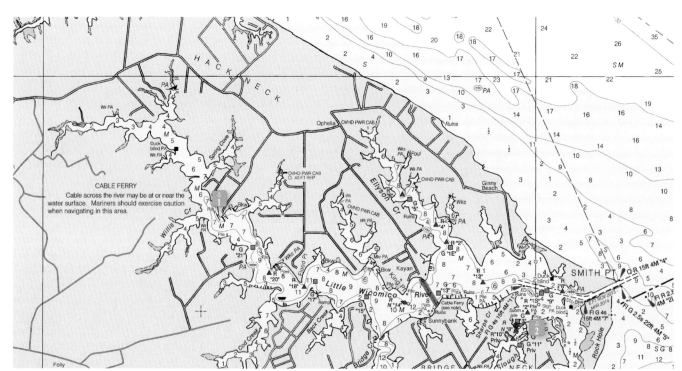

Little Wicomico River; from NOAA Chart 12233—not to be used for navigation.

and flood, a powerful current flows in and out of this narrow channel. Good power may be needed to maneuver in the river's entrance. The mouth of the river is also a favorite fishing spot for local anglers. You may find several small boats anchored or drifting between the jetties. Be prepared for some tricky maneuvering.

Once you're inside, the river is well marked. Look for each mark carefully and honor all of them. Note that at "7" the channel makes a slight turn to starboard. To the left of green "9", about 50 yards south, is green "1S", the entrance to **Slough Creek**, home to Smith Point Marina and a K.O.A. campground. You turn to port hard at its entrance and ahead is red "2". Once past red "2" look for green can "3A" and then daymarks green "3", green "5" and green "7"—all to port in a long fishhook-like curve. The channel starts to narrow at green "3", and between green "5" and "7" you will be very close—25 to 30 feet—to the western shore of the creek. Strangers often come to grief because they don't look hard enough for the marks, or don't believe what they see.

As you pass between green "7" and red "8" you will be heading straight for Smith Point Marina's gas dock. The creek's winding channel has about 4.5 feet MLW. If you need help getting in, hail the marina on VHF 16 or call them.

Smith Point Marina has 98 slips, 10 of them for transients. In addition to fuel, the marina also has a bathhouse, a laundry and a ship's store, and offers repair services. Slightly up-creek, the K.O.A. campground has slips in about 4 feet of water, along with shower, laundry and recreational facilities.

Northwest of Slough Creek is **Ellyson Creek**, the most commodious and longest of the Little Wicomico's tributaries, with charted depths to 8 feet and beautiful protected anchorages. Boaters will find transient slips about 2 1/2 miles beyond Ellyson Creek at Cockrell's Marine Railway, a full-service boatyard near green "21". Founded in 1929 by Dandridge Cockrell Sr., it originally serviced and built boats—including skipjacks—for local watermen. Today, with recreational boaters outnumbering fishermen, the fourth generation of Cockrells fills that need, too. The Cockrell's boatyard has 63 slips, shower facilities and a fuel dock (gas and diesel).

If heading beyond Ellyson Creek, be mindful of the ferry crossing between Kayan and Sunnybank. Its cable may be at or near the surface, so don't transit until you've communicated with the ferry captain on channel 13.

Great Wicomico River

Most of the Bay's rivers and creeks have many beautiful and snug anchorages, although sometimes you have to do a bit of exploring to find them. The **Great Wicomico** (*wye-KAHM-eh-ko*) **River** is no different. The chart, at first glance, teases you by showing lots of creeks with plenty of water inside; a second glance reveals that many of them have shoals across their entrance. Nevertheless, there really are many fine anchorages. The river is a beautiful one, quite broad and very inviting. Attractive farms, lush green woodlands and comfortable homes line the shores.

A 42-foot spider marks the river's entrance. This steel skeletal tower, like others of its kind around the Bay, stands on the foundation of an old screwpile lighthouse. The river's gently winding course is 15–25 feet deep; aids mark prominent points where shoals reach out beyond the norm. The biggest issue with the approach to the Great Wicomico is the presence of several sets of pound-nets. These extensive structures jut well out into the water just before the entrance to the river, surprising the unwary and forcing boats to go out and around to make their approach.

Cockrell Creek

For several miles off the coast of the Northern Neck of Virginia, boaters can spot the houses on Fleeton Point and the imposing old brick stack once used in the processing of menhaden in **Reedville**. The one remaining processor, Omega Protein, recently removed its stack after it installed a $20-million scrubber, which has made the famously heady Reedville air considerably sweeter. Omega's fleet of menhaden fishing boats, all over 100 feet in length, call Reedville, on ❶ **Cockrell Creek**, home port. These rugged, blue ships are an impressive sight close-up. Often you'll share the entrance channel of the Great Wicomico River with one of them. While you're in the area, keep a good look-out because these ships can come up fast and trail a sizeable wake.

Daylight navigation for entering the Great Wicomico is straightforward: from the light to red "4" to red "6". The entrance to Cockrell Creek sits north at green "1". At the tip of Fleeton Point, you may notice a small lighthouse perched at the end of a pier. It's a reproduction of the old screwpile lighthouse

		MLW	Overnight Slips	Gas	Diesel	Propane	Electric	Showers	Laundry	Restaurant	Lodging	Pool	Pump-out	Ice	Groceries	Marine Supplies	Bait	Boat Repair	Haul-out Services	Launch Ramp	Wi-Fi	Other
Little Wicomico River																						
Cockrell's Marine Railway Little Wicomico R. 804-453-3560; www.cockrellsmarinerailway.net		6'	●	●	●		●	●						●	●	➤	●	➤	●	●	●	●	65-ton covered railway. 25-ton lift, lift slips
Smith Point Marina Little Wicomico R./Slough Cr. 804-453-4077; www.smithpointmarina.com		4.5'	●	●	●	●	●	●	●	➤			●	●	➤	●	●	●	●	●		VA Clean marina, fishing charters, BoatU.S. disc.

● On Premises
➤ Nearby

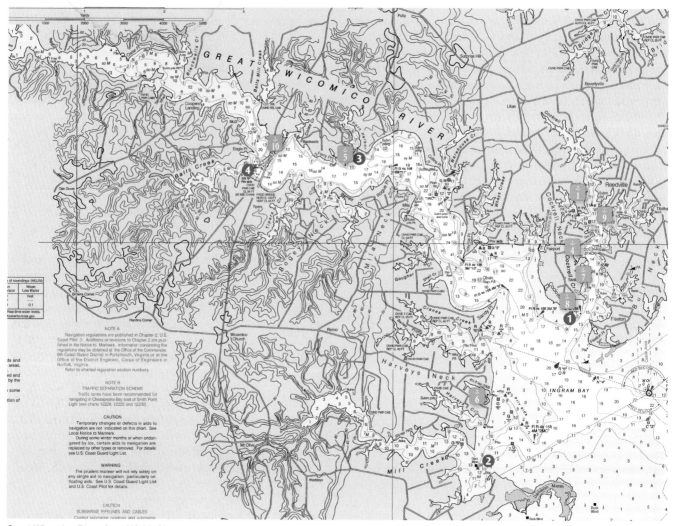

Great Wicomico River; from NOAA Chart 12235—not to be used for navigation.

Cockrell Creek continued

that once marked the entrance to the Great Wicomico.

To enter the Great Wicomico at night, keep red "4" well to starboard and be sure you locate red "6", a quick-flasher whose light is sometimes obscured by an osprey nest. Consequently, many visitors pick up the red light (4-second flasher "8") off Cockrell Point, mistaking it for "6". Confusing these two navigation aids can result in grounding off Fleeton Point.

Just inside Cockrell Creek, Pittman's Bait & Tackle offers fuel and ice. As you continue up the creek, west of the tall brick smokestack is Fairport Marina, where you can get fuel and a nice meal at Leadbelly's Restaurant. Next door to Fairport Marina is Jennings Boatyard. Both have overnight slips for transients.

Omega Protein's menhaden fishing fleet crowds most of the northern harbor here, but snug anchorages abound farther up Cockrell Creek beyond the bottleneck— around the fish-factory ruins to port and old brick smokestack to starboard. A grassroots effort a few years ago raised money to save and restore the old stack. Cockrell Creek splits at the

peninsula filled by Reedville, with Reedville Marina at its tip offering slips, fuel, ice, and the Crazy Crab Restaurant.

Both branches hold pleasant spots to drop the hook, but watch for points where shoals encroach. A popular, protected place is the eastern side of Reedville, with 12- to 14-foot depths and good holding.

In the first cove to starboard after passing the tall chimney you'll see the dock (8-foot depths reported) of Cockrell's Creek Seafood and Deli on the point east of Reedville. Besides deli specialties, their eat-in/carry-out menu includes fresh and quick-frozen seafood—steamed crabs to lobster tails.

To the west of Reedville are good depths as well. Deep in this cove is the Reedville Fishermen's Museum with the restored working buyboat *Elva C* and skipjack *Claud W. Somers* at its small dock. Among the museum's permanent and changing displays, which weave the town's and its commercial fishing legacies together, is a new land-based exhibit, a recreation of Captain John Smith's "discovery barge" called the *Spirit of 1608*.

Main Street, with elegant architecture of a prosperous past, is worth a leisurely stroll. Restored mansions of former fish-factory magnates and successful sea captains dot

"Millionaires' Row." Reedville amenities are limited, but its interesting history and rural charm make it a favorite stop, and local marinas usually help guests with transportation to the museum, restaurants and grocery stores. If anchored on the eastern side of the peninsula, you might find a dinghy landing along that shoreline, but be sure to ask permission.

When visiting Cockrell Creek, keep in mind that Reedville houses a fish processing plant whose smoke, even with the new scrubber, can discourage even the most avid cruiser if the wind is blowing your direction. So choose a spot upwind for your anchorage.

Reedville has a long history in the Atlantic menhaden industry and is still a busy commercial harbor. During the summer months catches of these small oily fish are most plentiful in the Chesapeake, and you're likely to see several boats daily, working the Bay. Purse-seining is the most efficient way to gather menhaden, a method legal in Virginia and in other coast states but outlawed in Maryland. Each "mother ship" carries one or two "purse boats" and is usually in contact with spotter planes, used to locate the schools. The purse boats are then sent out to encircle the school and "bring 'er in." On hazy or rainy days, spotting is done from the crow's nest.

Mill Creek

❷ **Mill Creek** is one of those exquisite cruising spots savvy boaters love to visit. But if you're new to the area, Mill Creek may not grab your attention at first. Its 3-mile length has high bluffs that offer protection from the ugliest weather,

deep water that will bring you to within a coin's toss of the treeline, and cruising privacy invaded only by the local fauna. There are few workboats on the creek to rouse you in the early morning hours.

From the Great Wicomico's 42-foot spider, head for red "2MC" (about 1 1/2 miles southwest) and follow the markers in. As you enter Mill Creek proper, red "4" perches on a sand bar that breaks the rough waves from the Bay. You can anchor in the bight south of "4" in 11 feet of water, although it is sometimes hard to set anchor in the soft bottom here.

Once inside the creek, keep away from points of land, and pick any cove which looks inviting to you for an anchorage. The few houses visible on Mill Creek are nestled deeply into the trees that blanket both sides of the creek. Deep water lets you tuck in close to the woods, and later in the day you are perfectly situated for sunset as herons quietly wade nearby.

The creek's assets also include tall banks, which rise to 80 feet as you travel farther upstream, where you'll find an abandoned gray building rising above the trees. Some visitors mistakenly believe this is the source of the creek's name; but rather than a mill, it was a grain storage and loading facility. Today, it is easy to forget that areas such as the Northern Neck lacked paved roads until the 1940s: the water was the roadway. Mill Creek's defunct grain depot is a window to the region's past, when small tugs and barges routinely traveled the area's rural creeks.

After the old grain facility, the creek continues west. Where the land rises high up to a grassy field is another fine

● *On Premises*
➤ *Nearby*

Great Wicomico River/Northern Neck Creeks

	MLW	Overnight Slips	Gas	Diesel	Propane	Electric	Showers	Laundry	Restaurant	Lodging	Pool	Pump-out	Ice	Groceries	Marine Supplies	Bait	Boat Repair	Haul-out Services	Launch Ramp	Wi-Fi	Other
Buzzard Point Marina Great Wicomico R./Cockrell Cr. 804-453-2628; www.tangiercruise.com	6'	●	●	●		●	●		➤	➤	➤	●	●	➤	➤	➤	●	●	●	●	Tangier Island cruises, boatel, picnic area, grills
Fairport Marina Great Wicomico R./Cockrell Cr. 804-453-5002	12'	●	●	●		●	●		●			●	●		➤	➤	➤	➤	➤		Leadbelly's Restaurant
Great Wicomico Marina Great Wicomico R. 804-580-0716	8'	●		➤	●	●	●	●	●	●	➤		●	●		➤	●	➤		●	Horn Harbor Restaurant open Fri.–Sun.
Ingram Bay Marina Great Wicomico R./Towles Cr. 804-580-7292; www.ingrambaymarina.com	7'	●	●	●		●	●	●		●	●	●	●		●	●	●		●	●	Courtesy car, picnic area, lounge, pet friendly
Jennings Boatyard Great Wicomico R./Cockrell Cr. 804-453-7181	8'	●	➤	➤			●	●	➤	➤		●	➤	➤	●	➤	●	●	●		DIY welcome. 35-ton lift, custom boatbuilding, floating docks
Pittman's Bait & Tackle Great Wicomico R./Cockrell Cr. 804-453-3643; www.genepittmancharters.com	6'		●	●								●			●						
Reedville Marina Great Wicomico R./Cockrell Cr. 804-453-6789	14'	●	●	●	●	●	●		●	➤		●	●	➤	●	●				●	Ship's store; Boat U.S. marina; Crazy Crab
Tiffany Yachts Great Wicomico R. 804-453-3464; www.tiffanyyachtsinc.com	10'	●	●	●	➤	●	●		➤			●	●		●	➤	●	●	➤	●	Full-service, 2 railways, 80-ton lift, ships store

Port of Call
Reedville

Picturesque scenery and Southern hospitality are reasons enough to lay over in Reedville. Its former downtown slowly vanished, but the village retains its grand old homes and tidy watermen's cottages—vestiges of a prosperous fishing center. Strolling Main Street is like revisiting the late 1800s, when a transplanted New Englander's ingenuity and hard work built the town.

Sea captain Elijah Reed did a brisk business carrying lumber from Maine to Virginia. During his travels, he noticed schools of menhaden in the Chesapeake. These small oily fish were commercially harvested in New England, but not in the Bay. With Yankee determination, he purchased land on Cockrell Creek and established a fish processing factory there in 1873.

As the menhaden industry grew, the community prospered. Fortunes were made and grand Victorian mansions were built along a stretch of Main Street known as Millionaire's Row. By 1912, Virginia's Northern Neck had 15 large menhaden factories and about 60 ships to supply them. Reedville had become the center of the industry and was considered to be one of the wealthiest towns, per capita, in the country. The Great Depression did not spare the region, however, and Reedville never recovered its enviable status.

During the summer, some 35- to 45-foot boats continue to work the Bay for menhaden the larger fleet is searching for menhaden out in the Atlantic, just outside the Bay. Local watermen are also busy early in the morning working the pound nets in the waters off the mouth of the Great Wicomico. They return to Reedville to unload in the early morning—generally between 7 and 9 a.m., sometimes selling part of their catch from the docks in Cockrell Creek. Get there early; it goes fast.

The history of local watermen and the impact their industry has had on the village are preserved in Reedville's first-rate Fishermen's Museum.

It chronicles the town's fishing legacy from the time Native Americans taught colonists to use menhaden as fertilizer to modern-day processing of the fish into soaps, stains, linoleum, high-protein feeds and other products. This rich heritage is also captured in an 11-minute movie shown upon request.

The museum's restored William Walker House (c. 1875) is the oldest structure in town, reflecting a typical fisherman's home of its day. Behind it, the Covington Galleries building contains a gift shop and display space where artifacts, models, paintings, photographs and an enormous ship's wheel recount the growth of the menhaden industry and Reedville's beginnings. An open shed houses small craft, while the *Elva C*, a 55-foot workboat once used for pound-netting, rides proudly in her slip across the pier from the 42-foot skipjack *Claud W. Somers*. Two other vessels round out the museum fleet: *Spirit of 1608*, a replica of Captain John Smith's discovery barge, and *Foggy River*, a locally built chunk-stern deadrise (currently being restored by vounteers from the museum's boat shop). In the Model Shop, Reedville and neighboring towns are captured in miniature in an intricately detailed model train layout whose HO-scale trains run during the winter holiday season.

To explore the area yourself, pick up a copy of the museum's self-guided walking/biking/driving tour brochure.

A few shops offer gifts and souveniers (including The Fishermen's Museum and the Crazy Crab). Several residences have been converted to B&Bs. General foodstuffs are within reach by bicycle at nearby Barnes Grocery. Reed Square convenience store sells snacks and beverages.

In this long-time fishing village, seafood and regional cuisine remain menu staples. Tommy's is located in a renovated 19th-century building that once housed Reedville Market. Order crabs at Cockrell's Creek Seafood Deli, which is accessible by boat, as is the Crazy Crab at Reedville Marina (dine indoors or on a deck overlooking the waterfront). Head for Chitterchats Ice Cream & Gossip Parlor for ice cream or coffee.

The Fishermen's Museum is the focal point of the town's annual events, which include occasional Sunday afternoon concerts, a Family Boat Building Workshop (reservations required), and an Antique and Classic Boat Show (September). Would-be oyster gardeners can attend an Oyster Gardening Workshop (oyster float construction and operation). In November there is an Oyster Roast, and in December, Christmas on Cockrell's Creek features a unique house tour along the Reedville waterfront.

Information: Northern Neck Tourism Council, 800-393-6180, *www.northernneck.org*; Fishermen's Museum, *www.rfmuseum.org*.

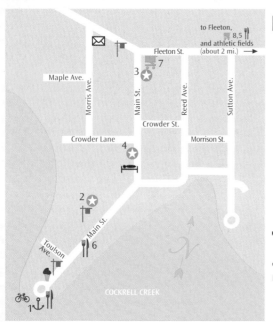

Reedville

⚓ **Marinas/Dockage**
  1 Reedville Marina

⊙ **Points of Interest**
  2 Reedville Fishermen's Museum
  3 Festival Halle
    (special events venue)
  4 Millionaire's Row

🍴 **Dining**
  1 Crazy Crab (at Reedville Marina)
  5 Cockrell's Creek Deli & Seafood
  6 Tommy's

🍦 **Ice Cream**

🛒 **Groceries/Carryout**
  5 Cockrell's Creek Seafood Deli
  7 Reed Square (convenience store)
  8 Barnes Grocery

🛏 **Lodging**

🛍 **Shopping**

🚲 **Bicycles**

✉ **Post Office**

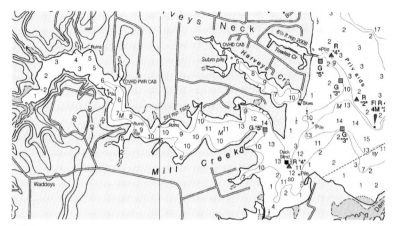

Mill Creek; from NOAA Chart 12235—not to be used for navigation.

Mill Creek *continued*

anchorage with good protection on either side in about 10 feet of water. This depth carries just around the bend beyond the field but soon tapers to about 6 feet before the creek's last mile, which is only dinghy depth. With a rising tide, you can dinghy all the way to the end and share the marsh with nothing but beaver, swans and other wildlife. You'll find Mill Creek quiet and peaceful. Few anchorages are perfect, but as you'll discover, Mill Creek comes pretty close.

There are no services on Mill Creek, but Ingram Bay

Marina on **Towles Creek** just to the north has overnight slips, gas and diesel, marine supplies, repairs and other amenities.

Most cruising groups bypass Mill Creek and head upstream for Sandy Point. The bight behind the point is popular because of its beauty, its accessibility, its ease of entry and its excellent protection. You'll carry 16 to 22 feet of water in a roomy, easily read channel. Head upriver about two miles to flashing green "9", taking it wide to avoid reported shoaling around the marker. Then head southwest into the wide bay that lies beyond the point. Once a well-defined beach, Sandy Point is now a small private spit with a long sandbar extending from its tip. At the far western end of the bay, the markers denote a state-owned oyster reef.

Horn Harbor

There are two Horn Harbors on the Chesapeake's lower western shore, one off the Bay to the south and the other on the Great Wicomico. Both are lovely, snug spots for idling away a blissful day and a serene night.

❸ **Horn Harbor** on the Great Wicomico is just plain special. About 2 1/2 nautical miles up the river from Sandy Point, almost invisible from the river, it's a tight gut in the north bank with a switchback channel that leads to one of the

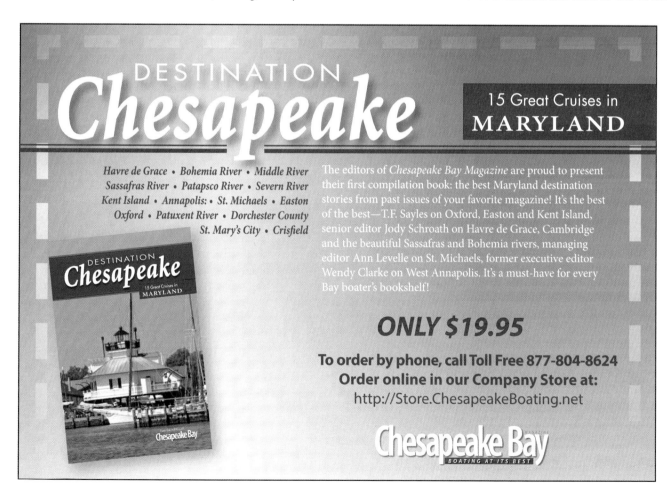

DESTINATION *Chesapeake*

15 Great Cruises in **MARYLAND**

Havre de Grace • Bohemia River • Middle River
Sassafras River • Patapsco River • Severn River
Kent Island • Annapolis: • St. Michaels • Easton
Oxford • Patuxent River • Dorchester County
St. Mary's City • Crisfield

The editors of *Chesapeake Bay Magazine* are proud to present their first compilation book: the best Maryland destination stories from past issues of your favorite magazine! It's the best of the best—T.F. Sayles on Oxford, Easton and Kent Island, senior editor Jody Schroath on Havre de Grace, Cambridge and the beautiful Sassafras and Bohemia rivers, managing editor Ann Levelle on St. Michaels, former executive editor Wendy Clarke on West Annapolis. It's a must-have for every Bay boater's bookshelf!

ONLY $19.95

**To order by phone, call Toll Free 877-804-8624
Order online in our Company Store at:**
http://Store.ChesapeakeBoating.net

Chesapeake Bay
BOATING AT ITS BEST

Horn Harbor *continued*

most protected anchorages on the Bay. If it is blowing hard on the river or the weather promises to turn rowdy, this is your haven. The slight adrenaline rush experienced on entering is immediately slowed by the serenity of its shores.

The entrance is approached just past green "11", at the tip of Rogue Point. When you spot the opening at the mouth of the creek be aware the eastern 1-foot shoal extends farther than charted and round it with an eye on the depthsounder.

The area is peppered with oyster stakes and crab pots, but there's ample water going in, with 6 feet reported over the entrance bar at MLW. A clear dogleg entrance by day, Horn Harbor is a chancy choice in the dark for the uninitiated.

The mouth of Horn Harbor has overlapping bars from both port and starboard, so you have to snake your way in. Passing the port shoal first, favor the starboard shore. Then favor the port shore to avoid the starboard shoal. After that, stay in the middle of the creek and head toward the eastern shore for best water depths.

If you anchor just north of the sand spit at the entrance, you can swing with the wind shifts to within a dozen yards or so of the beach. Even at low tide, you should show 7 feet. This is a tiny, but perfect, spot: high, wooded banks, a couple of houses hidden away in the trees, and you. The only sounds you'll likely hear will be those of birds: green herons carrying on a springtime dialogue, or an osprey patrolling the creek, shopping for supper. From your cockpit, you can see across the river and watch the occasional boat sail past. If you want to explore further, the head of the creek is accessible by dinghy.

Great Wicomico Marina is tucked along the river's northern bank, just beyond Horn Harbor. This friendly little place has a fuel dock (gas only), showers and laundry and 40 slips. Part of the homey complex is a 13-acre campground on its wooded hillside. At water's edge, the Horn Harbor House Restaurant has been pleasing diners for decades with seafood, steaks and seasonal fresh local vegetable dishes. While the marina's inner docks have 6 feet or less depths, the T-head carries about 10.

Beyond Horn Harbor, on the eastern side of Glebe Point before the bridge, sits Tiffany Yachts, which offers gas and diesel as well as overnight slips. Tiffany Cockrell and his father, Odis C.W. Cockrell, founded the company in 1934 when they began building Chesapeake deadrise workboats. After Tiffany returned from serving in the Navy during World War II, pleasure boats became the focal point of the business. Tiffany died in 2011, but the Cockrell family maintains the tradition, specializing in building one-of-a-kind yachts with elegant interiors from 30 to 80 feet. Tiffany Yachts also offers full repair service with a 60-ton lift and two marine railways. The company rebounded after fire destroyed their principal work building in 2010, with a 13,000-square foot structure, as well as new restrooms for boaters.

Balls Creek

Connecting Glebe Point to the Great Wicomico's other shore is a bridge with 55 feet of clearance, followed immediately by an overhead power cable with 54 feet at mid-channel. Boats able to venture beyond these vertical obstacles will find ❹ **Balls Creek** opening up invitingly to port. It has ample depths with 10 to 12 feet, but also plenty of fish stakes around the entrance. The middle of the channel is clear, however.

Balls Creek carries 7 and 8 feet for about a half-mile above its mouth with only a couple of points of land to be wary of, notably one to starboard just inside. High tree-covered banks crowd its shores, making it an ideal anchorage in foul weather. The few homes are so well-hidden by tall oaks and pines that one is hardly aware of their presence. Beyond Balls Creek, cruisers will find more deep water and pretty landscapes to explore for another couple of miles with several anchoring possibilities. Here you'll find protection from just about any point of the compass.

Hughlett Point to Windmill Point

Below the mouth of the Great Wicomico River, there are several intriguing creeks along the Northern Neck's eastern shore. Beginning with Dividing Creek and ending with Antipoison Creek off Little Bay, these waterways, while offering only a few services for the cruising boater, nonetheless provide protected anchorages in the event of rough weather on the Bay. Even if you're not beating a rapid retreat from an approaching storm, take time to explore them; your reward is likely to be splendid solitude and gorgeous scenery.

● On Premises
► Nearby

Hughlett Point to Windmill Point

	MLW	Overnight Slips	Gas	Diesel	Propane	Electric	Showers	Laundry	Restaurant	Lodging	Pool	Pump-out	Ice	Groceries	Marine Supplies	Bait	Boat Repair	Haul-out Services	Launch Ramp	Wi-Fi	Other
Chesapeake Boat Basin Northern Neck/Indian Cr. 804-435-3110; www.chesapeakeboatbasin.com	12'-14'	●	●	●	►	●	●	►	►	►	●	●	●	►	●	●	●	●	●	●	Floating docks, close to town, clean restrooms
Windmill Point Marina Windmill Point 804-436-1818	5.5'	●	●	●		●	●	●	●		●	●	●	●	●					●	Floating docks, pool bar with food service

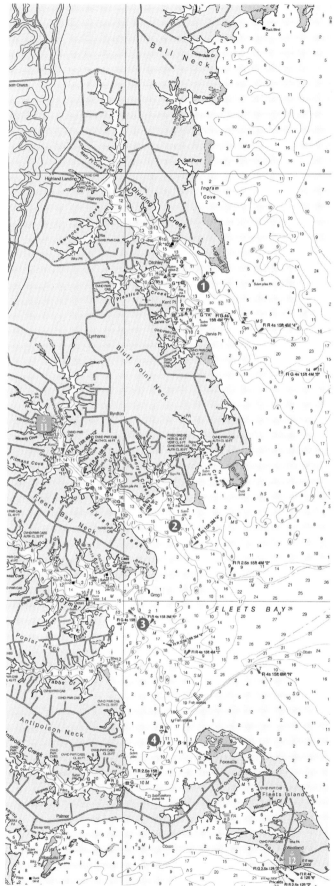

*Hughlett Point to Windmill Point; from NOAA Chart 12235—
not to be used for navigation.*

Dividing Creek

❶ Dividing Creek, with no services for boaters, offers pleasant anchorages along with a lovely nature preserve. Captain John Smith's maps showed this as Wiccomico Indian territory, and stone tools and arrowheads discovered at Hughlett Point confirm this. In addition, its upstream banks hold early colonial connections to families who eventually influenced not just the Chesapeake but the nation.

Dividing Creek's approaches are well-marked. From points north, locate flashing green "1GW" off the Great Wicomico River, plotting a course for "3", a 15-foot green flasher nearly six miles to the southwest. This, the creek's first mark, will keep you away from shoaling that extends about a mile off Hughlett Point. From the south, head past Fleets Bay toward channel junction light "B", one and a half miles southeast of Bluff Point. From there, Dividing Creek's "3" is about two miles to the north.

Dividing Creek's entrance lies between hook-like Jarvis Point to the south and Hughlett Point on the northern peninsula. HUGHLETT POINT NATURAL AREA PRESERVE's 200-plus acres of upland forest, tidal wetlands and undeveloped beach support critters from bald eagles to a tiny threatened insect called the Northeastern Beach Tiger Beetle. Since rare shorebirds nest along these low dunes, boat landing and beach walking are prohibited during specific times of year. If no signs are posted, then you may certainly land a dinghy and enjoy the

MODERN AMENITIES IN A RELAXED ATMOSPHERE —
JUST 1.5 MI. OFF THE CHESAPEAKE BAY!

Chesapeake Boat Basin

Transients welcome!

No personal property tax on boats 5-tons and greater

BEST OF THE BAY 2015 *Chesapeake Bay Magazine*

CHESAPEAKE BOAT BASIN

Kilmarnock, VA
804-436-1234

1686 WAVERLY AVE, KILMARNOCK, VA 22482
WWW.CHESAPEAKEBOATBASIN.COM

Dividing Creek *continued*

trails, woodland boardwalk, wildlife viewing platforms and interpretive signs. Swimming and sunbathing are permitted.

Once past "7A", a small, unmarked shallow bay and marked-but-tricky Jarvis Creek lie to the south. Shoal drafts and local knowledge are recommended here. Stakes marking shallows and oyster beds come and go and cannot be depended upon for navigation.

Dividing Creek's main channel, however, has good water for a couple miles. Stay in the center since shoals encroach from every point. The last aid, daymark "10", is just north of **Prentice Creek** and the peninsula charted as Ditchley. To enter Prentice Creek, note that "1" lies between two shallow areas so use care while heading for offset "2". Holding in Prentice Creek is reported to be fine.

Ditchley, one of the Northern Neck's most historic plantations, was patented in 1651 by Richard Lee, the progenitor of the Lee family of Virginia. Illustrious descendants include Light Horse Harry Lee, President Zachary Taylor, and Robert E. Lee. The mansion, begun in 1762, was occupied for most of the 1800s by the Balls, relatives of George Washington's mother. Neither accessible by nor visible from the water, the manor house was purchased in 1932 by Jesse Ball duPont, who grew up in the Northern Neck, and her financier husband Alfred I. duPont. The couple used the estate as a summer home. In 2012, ownership was transferred to the Alfred I. duPont Foundation.

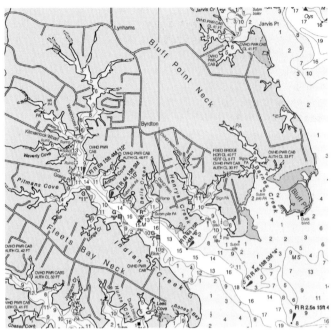

Indian Creek; from NOAA Chart 12235—not to be used for navigation.

Near the shores of Prentice Creek is the brick-walled Lee family cemetery, whose oldest grave is that of Col. Lee ("the emigrant"), dated 1664. While open to the public, it's not easily accessed from the water. The burying ground, once part of Cobbs Hall (noted on charts as "Harveys"), now stands alone. For thirteen generations, the Harvey family—Lee descendants—resided here. Only in recent years did the homestead pass to outside ownership. The manor's four brick chimneys may still be visible despite foliage and new development.

Above "10", a good anchorage is to be found in **Lawrence Cove**. Although unmarked and narrow, a popular spot is just inside. Even better on a hot quiet night, anchor at the cove's entrance. Almost opposite the cove, a yellow house sits on the main branch's northern shore. Part of the home, serving Hardings Wharf in the 1800s and early 1900s, was a general store and post office when steamships called here daily. Beyond Lawrence Cove in the northernmost branch, two small tributaries make suitable anchorages at their mouths.

As you leave Dividing Creek, be aware that there is an uncharted wreck of an old barge about a mile off shore. It's easily seen during the day, but invisible at night.

Indian Creek

2 Indian Creek is the northernmost of several lovely tributaries that empty into broad **Fleets Bay**. It is nearly 15 nautical miles south of Smith Point Light. The deep, mile-wide mouth of Fleets Bay lies between Bluff Point and North Point, the northern tip of Fleets Island—which is not really an island, though it might well have been in the past. Fleets Island is, in turn, bounded by Windmill Point and the mouth of the Rappahannock on the south.

Fleets Bay's channel is defined by two flashing marks: "B"

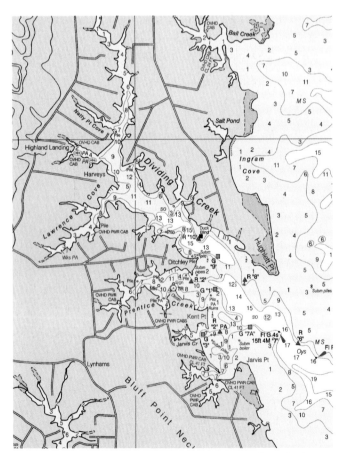

Dividing Creek; from NOAA Chart 12235—not to be used for navigation.

to the north and "N" to the south. This juncture joins directly with Chesapeake shipping channels and is used by tugs with barges going to and from the grain elevators near the head of Indian Creek.

The entrance to Indian Creek is straight-forward, its channel running northwest and deep for nearly its full length. The first entrance mark, "2", lies about one and a half miles almost due west of "B". Picturesque, lined with trees and pleasant homes, it offers many options for anchoring. Heading upstream, you'll first pass Indian Creek Yacht and Country Club, which sits in a cove just northwest of Bells Creek, opposite daymark "9". Next, you're likely to notice grain elevators for some distance away. They occupy the tip of what was once Kilmarnock Wharf, about three miles upstream of entrance mark "2". Kilmarnock Wharf is gone, but the silos remain, making an excellent landmark for locating the site's occupant, Chesapeake Boat Basin. The Boat Basin is the only transient facility between Hughlett and Windmill points. This hospitable full-service facility offers overnight slips, marine supplies and repair service, as well as floating docks and a pool. Chesapeake Boat Basin is also the only fuel stop (gas and diesel) along the western shore between Reedville and Deltaville. And since Indian Creek is roughly halfway between Norfolk and Solomons, hearty mile-makers find this the ideal stopover as well.

The nearby village of **Kilmarnock**, once an Indian trail crossroads, was given its name in 1784 by an early Scots immigrant. You'll find it about a mile and a half from the historic wharf. The busy steamboat era abruptly ended here when the entire landing was destroyed in the Hurricane of 1933. The town—an easy bike ride (a marina stay includes courtesy bikes) and not a bad walk along a rural road from Chesapeake Boat Basin—is worth a visit. Cruisers will find restaurants, gift and antique shops, galleries with local art and home furnishings, and a quaint little museum along its newly revitalized streets. Some restaurants provide transportation to transient marina dockers.

If you choose to cruise Indian Creek beyond the former Kilmarnock Wharf and Warehouse Point, the longer and more serpentine northern branch is navigable for almost a half-mile. While narrow, it has 8 to 9 feet nearly to its shores in some places. With each sharp turn, a new charming view appears through wooded banks with homes hidden among foliage; wooden boathouses add to the natural beauty. Remember that it's unmarked, so use care. You may find a snug anchorage tucked into a bend, but pick a spot out of the channel yet with enough room to swing.

On the way back down the creek, the most popular anchorage is in protected **Pitmans Cove** which enters Indian Creek from the southwest. The approach is easy between daymark "11" and flashing "12", and you'll find at least 9 feet for about a quarter-mile inside. Like other tributaries, you may find trap marks and stakes; also like many, its banks are no longer unspoiled. New development has appeared along the southern shore, but the other side is still agricultural and wooded. So perhaps the wild turkey gobbles coming from the thick curtain of trees around the small cove to starboard can still be heard while lying at anchor. While it's snug here, use caution when setting the hook since holding is reported to be difficult in some spots.

Farther downstream on the opposite shore is **Bells Creek**. Its channel is narrow and a bit tricky with shoals to port and starboard. Go slowly, using care and the tides. The first cove on the right is a good spot, and some boaters like to continue a little farther, beyond the two points on either side.

Henrys Creek, open to the south and closest to Indian Creek's entrance, has some nice attributes. About a half-mile from flashing daymark "4", its mouth may look wide and inviting but be advised that unmarked shoals surround it. Staying dead center is always the best bet, and seeking local knowledge is strongly suggested.

Keep in mind, too, that stakes, if present, can't always be counted on to mark shallows; they often identify oyster beds. So study the chart, and pick your way in and around this creek with an eye on the tide and the depthsounder.

Henrys Creek will reward you with pleasant shores rimmed with waterfront homes—new ones intermingling with well-maintained older ones. The waterway forks just above a sharp sandy point to starboard. Some boaters say the mouth of the western branch, deeper but more exposed, is a suitable anchorage. A more snug spot might be found in the eastern branch.

Indian Creek continued

It's reported that the tributary has an elegant sign reading "Henry's Creek." In charming tradition, locals are said to have an annual dedication ceremony for the sign each spring, to mark the arrival of a new boating season.

Dymer Creek

❸ **Dymer Creek** is another lovely Northern Neck tributary flowing into Fleets Bay. While unmarked beyond its entrance, Dymer is easy to navigate and offers several pleasant anchorages. After locating channel junction mark "N" north of Windmill Point, you'll be looking for flashing red "2" almost due west and less than a mile away. Then just follow the three flashing marks—"4", "6", and "7".

Shoals extend from every point and peninsula here, especially in the general vicinity of what was once **Grog Island**. This north entrance to Dymer Creek is an example of the effects of bay erosion, and how each year winter storms take a bit more of the shrinking real estate. What was once a marshy hook hanging from the tip of Fleets Bay Neck, and then a lovely uninhabited island, is now just another shoaly bit of water.

Entering Dymer Creek and approaching "7", be mindful of the waterway's constriction here, also that ex-Grog Island's surrounding shoal may be encroaching the channel's northern edges. Depths off the channel here are 3 feet or less, so favor the green side. If you stay within the boundaries defined by offset "6" and "7" where there is plenty of water, you shouldn't go wrong.

Rones Bay, the little harbor once formed by Grog Island, was once a popular anchorage, but now is suitable only in settled weather. But on a hot summer night, with no

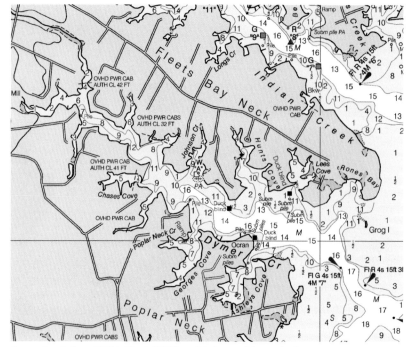

Dymer Creek; from NOAA Chart 12235—not to be used for navigation.

thunderstorms forecast, you'll have a full view of the bay's horizon and the parade of boat traffic beyond Dymer. And who knows, in a particularly low tide, you may even find a bit of a beach to wade around.

Cruisers may may find mazes of oyster stakes in the area, which can be befuddling but have no bearing on navigation. Unfortunately fewer stakes probably means fewer oysters. Wherever you go, it's best to know the tides, have a good chart, proceed slowly and cautiously and seek local information whenever possible. There it is: the best cruising advice in a nutshell.

Heading past Rones Bay, **Hunts Cove** also lies on the north shore, about three-quarters of a mile beyond "7", Dymer's last mark. Be aware that shoals invade its entrance to port and starboard. In addition, a charted submerged pile lies in its center, so use care when navigating here. A spot indicating 10 feet on the chart is reported to be a good one for an overnight anchorage, offering a pleasing wooded shoreline, broken here and there by cornfields and homes. But remember, that sticky mud bottom that holds the anchor fast can hold your hull just as well.

When leaving Hunts Cove to go upriver, a charted duckblind, to starboard off the peninsula, guides you away from the shoal there. Going past **Johnson Creek**, the main

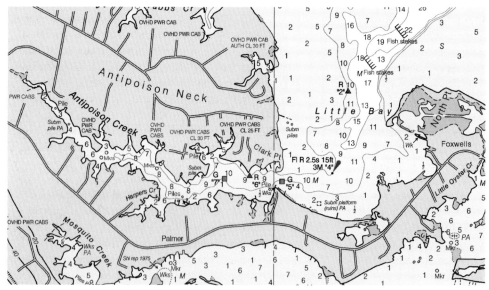

Antipoison Creek and Little Bay; from NOAA Chart 12235—not to be used for navigation.

The inviting beach along North Point inside the entrance to Little Bay.

branch has good water for another mile or so with several anchoring possibilities. Along the north shore an unnamed cove with about 8 feet is said to be snug. Besides protection, you might enjoy the horses and sheep grazing at the farm across the creek. Whinnies and bleats in company with the squawks of a blue heron can make for a surprising symphony during an otherwise quiet anchorage.

Along the southern shore, almost due south of Johnson Creek, are the docks of Dymers Creek Seafood and Winegar's Marine Railway, a small old-time operation dwarfed by the new mega-mansion that occupies the tip of this peninsula.

Continuing south, **Georges Cove** comes next, which, despite its narrow entrance, is fairly easy to manage with 7 and 8 feet inside. As usual, watch the charts and depth-sounder, stay in the center, scan for crab pots and enjoy the rural scenery. Ocran Boat Shop Marina, with a couple of slips with 5-foot depths, offers some repairs.

Ashleys Cove, the southeastern-most of Dymers tributaries, is not quite as narrow, carrying 7 feet and a shoreline dotted with stunning homes. The ruins of an old fish factory are nearby, one of many such processing plants that were once a major part of the Northern Neck's landscape and livelihood.

South of here, **Tabbs Creek,** tucked between Dymer and Antipoison creeks is only for the most shallow draft vessels. A significant bar intrudes on its entrance—a shame since it looks so snug and inviting. It would, however, be an ideal place to lull away an afternoon in a dinghy or kayak.

Both Dymer and Tabbs were names of early fur traders in the area. With the decline of the seafood industry, there is still agriculture, but the major resource today seems to be its real estate.

Antipoison Creek

The southernmost waterway on the Northern Neck, curiously named ❹ **Antipoison Creek**, offers quiet seclusion, wooded shores and little boat traffic. It also benefits from its location, well shielded by Fleets Island. It was near Fleets Island that local Indians are said to have saved the life of Captain John Smith by medicating a wound he'd received from a ray. Hence, legend has it, the name of the creek.

Antipoison Creek is well marked, and its entrance off **Little Bay** is easy to navigate. Be on the lookout for the poundnet poles outside the entrance, though. From the channel junction mark "N" in Fleets Bay, you can spot red daymark "2" about a mile to the southwest, due west of the northwest tip of Fleets Island. You then have to take a slightly arced course between "N" and "2" to avoid fish weirs that extend from the shoals off North Point into the navigable waters of Little Bay. Red "4" lies three-quarters of a mile south of "2". Give "4" plenty of room as you make your turn and head for the creek's entrance. It's best to favor the north shore somewhat, since there's a shoal to port at the opening.

Just inside the entrance, on the starboard side, lies a small cove with plenty of anchorage room for cruisers. To port, in a cove just before **Harpers Creek**, lies an abandoned herring packing plant, and on the starboard side, where the creek swings northwest, you'll see an oyster-shucking and fish-processing plant. You'll find a fine anchorage, with 7 feet of water, about 500 yards farther upstream. Be aware of a shoal that projects from the eastern side of the cove's entrance. There's sometimes a local mark that indicates the shallow spot.

It's a lovely "safe harbor" on a gentle creek. You're protected by trees and the water is nearly unruffled. If you hear a ship's horn at sundown, it's probably a commercial fishing boat returning to the dock.

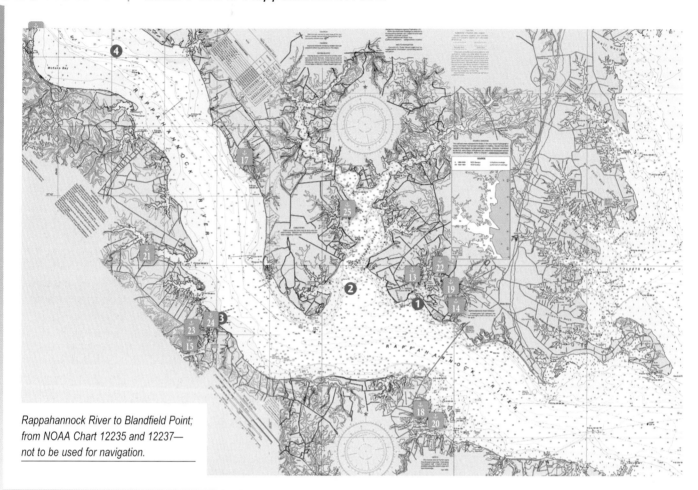

Rappahannock River to Blandfield Point; from NOAA Chart 12235 and 12237— not to be used for navigation.

Rappahannock River

*(Please note that **Broad Creek**, on the south side of the Rappahannock just west of Stingray Point, is covered in the Deltaville Area in Section 8.)*

The **Rappahannock River** slices deep into the Virginia countryside, at one point coming within six or seven miles of the Potomac River (between Leedstown and Port Royal). Less celebrated than its northern counterpart, the Rappahannock was nonetheless an important steamboat route in the days when the Northern Neck relied on both rivers as its connection to the outside world. Today's cruisers will find a fine resort marina on the river, small towns that make interesting ports of call, splendid deepwater anchorages, and here and there vestiges of the river's history.

The Rappahannock's gentle mouth is a 5-mile-wide smile. Even though storms can make her entrance surly, they don't seem to match the intensity of tempests on the Potomac and York rivers. Entering the Rappahannock from the north is not difficult, but orienting yourself to the 36-foot **Windmill Point Light**, which stands well offshore, is important before turning westward. With good visibility and smooth water, you may cut immediately west of the light and cross the Rappahannock Spit in 7-foot depths. However, there may be some pound nets, and crab pots are usually numerous in-shore, so some skippers

feel the shortcut is not worth the nuisance. Approaching the Rappahannock River from the south, keep well east of Stingray Point Light as you round Stingray Point. The Rappahannock's broad waters run on a generally northwest course to the Robert Norris Bridge (vertical clearance 110 feet), a fixed bridge about eight miles upstream.

Carter Creek

About 10 miles from Windmill Point and just above the Rappahannock River Bridge is ❶ **Carter Creek.** Lighted red "2" marks the beginning of its easy, straightforward entrance on the north shore. Named for the legendary Carters of Virginia, this was once the heart of the family's Colonial empire. Today the creek is home to several marine facilities offering transient slips, including The Tides, an acclaimed resort-complex at the head of the tributary. Its red-tiled roof might be glimpsed as you turn into Carter Creek. If anchoring out is your choice, protection from all quadrants can be found at various spots along its turkey-foot-shaped prongs, each with ample depths.

The first branch to starboard, **Yopps Cove**, offers a pretty anchorage beyond a spit of land. Watch the depth-sounder. There's plenty of room in the channel, but shoals project from both
sides, especially at points of land along the south shoreline.

Past Yopps Cove, lovely homes and deeply wooded shores line the wider **Eastern Branch**, which winds for about a mile past a lighted aid. Longer with good depths and popular with raft-ups, it also offers places to tuck in, such as narrow **Bridge Cove**, for challenging weather.

On the other side of the creek, the western branch is called **Carter Cove**. Once strictly commercial, with an occasional cruising boat finding shelter in its 6- to 10-foot depths, this modest branch holds an unusually diverse representation of boats from the last half century—big and small, working and pleasure. Two of the old businesses remain on the northern bank, giving this compact cove a special flavor. First is Ampro Shipyard and next door is Kellum Brothers Seafood. You'll find something interesting to see at both commercial docks, especially the Kellum's gleaming green and white buyboat, *Capt. Ellery.* Just beyond these muscular docks, a former family-run oyster operation is now an eye-pleasing contemporary facility for pleasure craft. Carter's Cove Marina, with 34 slips, 5- to 8-foot depths and modern laundry and showers, warmly welcomes both transient and long-term dockers.

In the 1880s, as the age of sail was winding down, the Weems Steamboat Line established a stop in Carter Cove near the site of the old plantation wharf, and a thriving village bearing the Weems name developed on the peninsula. Today **Weems** is a sleepy, rural community with no provisioning opportunities available for cruising boaters.

Carter Creek and its branches have lost all traces of their plantation and steamboat days except for HISTORIC CHRIST CHURCH, a stately brick structure a few miles from the water that was completed in 1735. Beautifully restored with its original high-backed box pews and rare triple-decker pulpit, it is worth a visit, and any of the marinas along Carter Creek will assist you in arranging transportation there. Both grounds and building are impressive, and a guided tour will bring the era to life. Adjacent to the church, a renovated gift shop and expanded gallery feature artifact displays, storylines and interactive exhibits for visitors along with an excellent film about the Carter's Colonial influence and significance.

● On Premises
➤ Nearby

Rappahannock River

	MLW	Overnight Slips	Gas	Diesel	Propane	Electric	Showers	Laundry	Restaurant	Lodging	Pool	Pump-out	Ice	Groceries	Marine Supplies	Bait	Boat Repair	Haul-out Services	Launch Ramp	Wi-Fi	Other
Carter's Cove Marina — Rappahannock R./Carter Cr.; 804-438-5299; www.carterscovemarina.com	6'-8'		➤	➤	➤	●	●	●	➤	➤	➤	●	●	➤		➤	➤	➤	➤	●	Quiet, Wi-Fi, picnic area, dog walk, wide piers
Custom Yacht Service — Rappahannock R./Carter Cr.; 804-438-5563; www.customyachtsvc.com	9'															●		●	●		Full service yard, 50-ton lift, transients welcome
Dozier's Port Urbanna Marine Center — Rappahannock R./Urbanna Cr.; 804-758-0000; www.doziermarinegroup.com	9'	●	➤	➤	➤	●	●		➤		●		➤			➤				●	40-ton lift; In Town
Garrett's Marina/Harborside Storage — Rappahannock R./Bowlers Wharf; 804-443-2573; www.garrettsmarina.com	3'	●										●		●	●	●	●	●			Service, drystack, boat sales, dockside gas
Greenvale Creek Marina — Rappahannock R./Greenvale Cr.; 804-462-0646	5'	●	●	●	➤	●	●	●				●	●		●	●	●	●	●	●	Covered slips to 45', non-ethanol fuel; repairs
Locklies Marina — Rappahannock R./Locklies Cr.; 804-758-2871	5'-6'	●	●	●		●	●		●	➤		●							●	●	Home of Rapp. River Oysters; fishing charters
Rappahannock Yachts — Rappahannock R./Carter Cr.; 804-438-5353; www.rappyachts.com	12'	●	➤	➤	➤	●	●	➤	➤	➤		➤	➤		●		●	●		➤	Full-service yacht yard. Yacht sales, 30-ton lift
Regent Point Marina — Rappahannock R./Locklies Cr.; 804-758-4457; www.regentpointmarina.com	7'	●	➤	➤	➤	●	●	●	➤	➤		●	●	●	●	➤	●	●	●	●	Park-like; sailboats & trawlers; full-service ABYC yard
Remlik Marina — Rappahannock R./LaGrange Cr.; 804-758-5450; www.remlikmarina.com	5'	●	●	➤		●	●		➤	➤	●	●	●	●	●	●	●	●		●	
The Tides — Rappahannock R./Carter Cr.; 804-438-5000; www.tidesinn.com	6'-7'	●	●	●	➤	●	●	●	●	●	●	●	●	●	●	➤	➤		➤	➤	Tennis, spa, golf, bicycles, full resort amenities
Urbanna Creek Marina at the Bridge — Rappahannock R./Urbanna Cr.; 804-740-1813;			●	➤	➤	➤	●	●		➤			➤			➤		●		●	easy walk to downtown
Urbanna Town Marina at Upton's Point — Rappahannock R./Urbanna Cr.; 804-758-5440; www.urbanna.com	3'-10'	●	➤	➤	➤	●	●	●	➤	➤	➤	●	●	●	➤	●	➤	➤	➤	●	Free dinghy landing, free Wi-Fi, free cable
Yankee Point Marina — Rappahannock R./Corrotoman R./Myer Cr.; 804-462-7018; www.yankeepointmarina.com	9'	●	●	●	➤	●	●	●	●	●	●	●	●	➤	●	●	●	●		●	Non-Ethanol fuel! wet/dry slips; cafe, full service

Carter Creek
continued

John Carter, sailing from England in 1635, first settled near Norfolk, but around 1652, after relocating to Lancaster, he began to develop his Rappahannock plantation called Corotoman (spelled with one *r*, while the river has two). His friend Governor Berkeley appointed him leader of the local militia, to deal with disputes between English and Native Americans. He was later selected as a member of the Crown Council. While best known as the father of Robert King Carter, it was John who founded Christ Church, its frame structure completed in 1670.

Son Robert later masterminded the rebuilding of this church into the remarkable relic it remains today. Robert also added to his father's estate. At his death in 1732, the *American Weekly Mercury* reported his holdings at 300,000 acres with an inventory that included 734 slaves on Carter's 48 "quarters" or plantations. He is buried near one of the cruciform-shaped walls of Christ Church, with his first and second wives with whom he had 12 children. The families into which they married

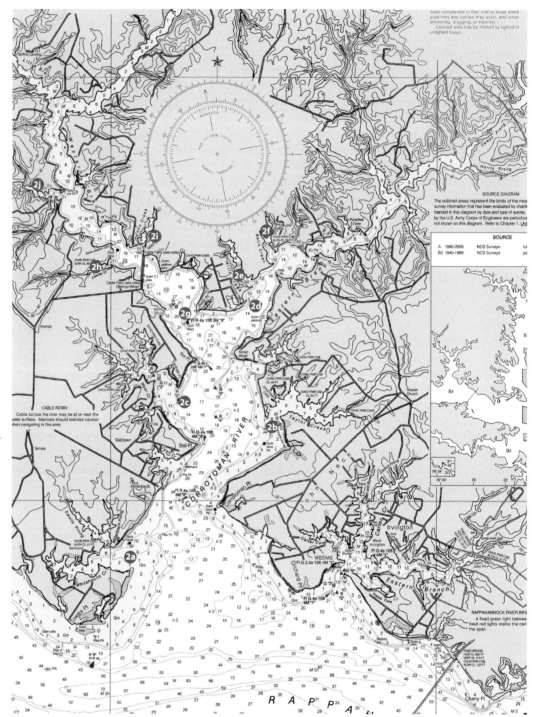

Carter Creek and Corrotoman River; from NOAA Chart 12235—not to be used for navigation.

are among the most famous names in Virginia. Descendants include three signers of the Declaration of Independence, two U.S. presidents (the Harrisons), four governors of Virginia and Robert E. Lee.

Heading farther up the main branch of Carter Creek, to starboard you'll find the Rappahannock River Yacht Club, then Rappahannock Yachts (a full-service boatyard with repairs and transient slips) and Irvington Marina.

Before 1947, all that stood at the head of this creek was a ramshackle farm, but once remodeled into a 40-room hotel,

The Tides Inn soon became world renowned. Further renovations saw it grow to over 100 rooms, several fine restaurants and 60 deepwater slips. Its elegance has long had a special allure for Bay boaters who enjoy the resort's full range of amenities. Included with dock fees, guests have access to kayaks, bicycles, pool, tennis, golf, fitness center and spa, as well as van and water taxi service. Premier Sailing School is also located here.

Tides Inn offers "101 things to do" with special events for all holidays, including a Labor Day chardonnay and croquet tournament (*www.tidesinn.com*). Visitors will often bike the short distance to the village of **Irvington** to visit its quaint upscale shops, fine eateries and Steamboat Museum. The nearby Dog and Oyster Winery and its Hope and Glory Inn (*www.hopeandglory.com*) hold tastings, offer accommodations and are within walking distance to The Tides. The first Saturday of the month is the Irvington Farmers Market, featuring fresh produce along with local artisan's wares.

Part of The Tides occupies the peninsula formed by **Church Prong** to the right and **Dead and Bones Cove** to the left. Both of these small tributaries have about 7 feet of water and are suitable anchorages.

Whether you're seeking a secure anchorage or slip for the night, repair services, resort facilities or a touch of history, you'll find it in Carter Creek.

Corrotoman River

Just upriver from Carter Creek lies the ❷ **Corrotoman River**, a pristine, out-of-the-way cruising area that proves that good things come in 3s. First, the river lies 3 miles beyond the Rappahannock's Robert O. Norris Bridge (vertical clearance 110 feet). Second it's 3 miles from the Corrotoman's mouth to West Point, where the river splits into the **Western Branch** and the **Eastern Branch**. Finally, both these branches carry enough water for about 3 more miles. The only marine facility on the river is Yankee Point Marina on Myers Creek. The Corrotoman is so quiet, out of the way, and special that perhaps you'll choose to stay awhile. This area offers tranquil scenery, solitude and many anchoring choices, both snug anchorages for spring and fall and more open spots for those warm nights of summer when a breath of air is hard to find. The shores are deeply wooded; signs of habitation, for the most part, are hidden away in the trees. It's a river for all seasons and so inviting that it's always hard to decide which lovely anchorage to choose this time.

There's even more here than meets the depthfinder. If you have a dinghy or kayak, you can anchor the mother ship and open up even more adventures by exploring the enticing narrow entrances with a sounding pole. A veritable buffet of coves and creeks and even a prong or two are accessible to the patient gunkholer.

The river is pronounced *cor-rah-TOE-man*, a name that has descended from the Indian nation that Captain John Smith transcribed as "Cuttatawoman." As well as losing a syllable, the name has undergone a sex change.

Cruisers who anchor at the foot of a bluff in a tiny cove may feel as though they've found another Eden, far from the pressures and sounds of city living. Several such spots on the Corrotoman will spark your interest.

A small cable ferry, one of the few still run by the state, glides purposefully between Merry Point and **Ottoman Wharf** on the Western Branch. Just below Punches Cove, on the Eastern Branch, the low, white buildings high on the bank are those of a former egg farm. Sandy Point, opposite Bells Creek on the Eastern Branch, offers a popular beach for swimming and picnicking.

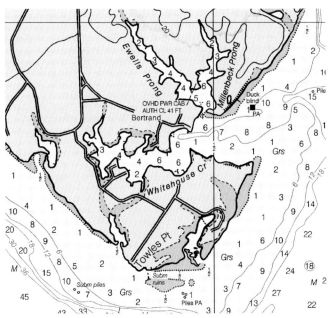

Whitehouse Creek; from NOAA Chart 12235—not to be used for navigation.

Both branches offer miles of dinghy exploration, but, if you want to add in a little extra Northern Neck history, head up the Western Branch to the first bridge. About a mile's hike west will take you to tiny, historic Lancaster Court House and the interesting Mary Ball Washington Museum. Three hundred years ago significant land holdings bordered both sides of the Corrotoman. If you had sailed upriver at that time, George Washington's grandfather, William Ball, might have waved a welcome from his dock on the western shore. Perhaps King Carter would have invited you to visit his plantation, Corotoman, on the eastern shore. These were the river barons, Carter owning (at the time of his

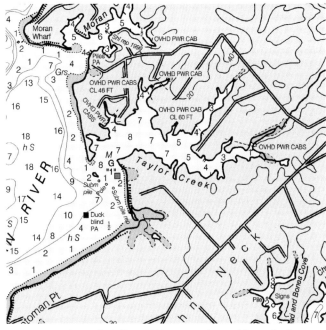

Taylor Creek; from NOAA Chart 12235—not to be used for navigation.

Corrotoman River continued

death) one percent of present-day Virginia. In those long-ago days, trading ships plied the river, carrying grain and tobacco to England, returning with furniture, clothing and household goods for the early colonists. Little evidence of that time remains (though it's fun to scan the banks for traces of old roads on which barrels were rolled to the river). The gently curving shores and today's tranquility make it nearly impossible to imagine British raiders here in the War of 1812 or slave ships with their hapless cargoes. Serenity reigns.

2e **Whitehouse Creek** lies on the western shore near the entrance to the Corrotoman. The shallow, sprawling bar off Towles Point prohibits all but the shoalest draft boats from entering directly from the south, and the bar north of the creek is also somewhat forbidding. To avoid grounding on entering, look for the privately maintained green mark near the 5-foot spot shown on the chart at the northern tip of the shoal that surrounds Towles Point. Subsequent pilings with painted tops indicate the 6-foot-deep channel into the creek.

Sand beaches line both sides of the entrance with only a few houses visible. Farther up the creek, more houses cluster around the small fishing village of **Bertrand**. Beyond Bertrand the water is reported to be a bit deeper than the 4 to 6 feet shown on the chart. There's a pleasant anchorage about 100 yards off the end of a large boathouse on the north shore of Towles Point in the horseshoe-shaped cove opposite Bertrand.

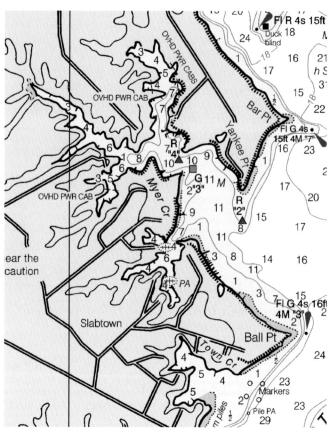

Myer Creek; from NOAA Chart 12235—not to be used for navigation.

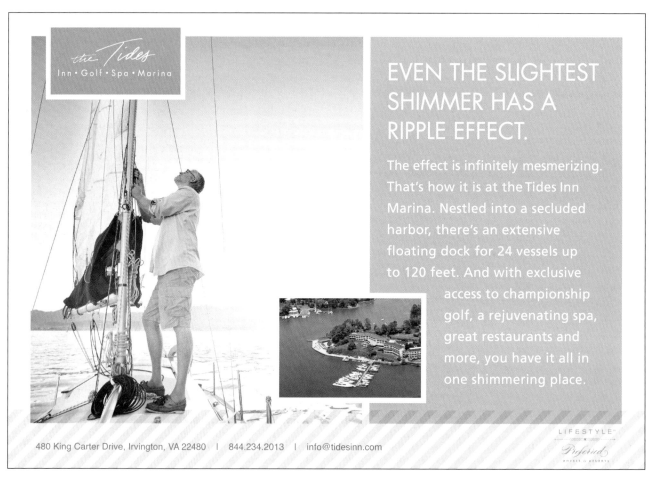

the Tides
Inn • Golf • Spa • Marina

EVEN THE SLIGHTEST SHIMMER HAS A RIPPLE EFFECT.

The effect is infinitely mesmerizing. That's how it is at the Tides Inn Marina. Nestled into a secluded harbor, there's an extensive floating dock for 24 vessels up to 120 feet. And with exclusive access to championship golf, a rejuvenating spa, great restaurants and more, you have it all in one shimmering place.

480 King Carter Drive, Irvington, VA 22480 | 844.234.2013 | info@tidesinn.com

LIFESTYLE
Preferred
HOTELS & RESORTS

It's tempting to explore Millenbeck and Ewells prongs on the creek's north shore. If you want to try sneaking through the narrow cut with 4 feet of water, a secluded spot awaits you. Stay well to port on your way through the cut. **Millenbeck Prong** shows 6 feet of water for almost a quarter mile. **Ewells Prong** isn't as deep, and you may be barred by an overhead power cable that has a charted clearance of 41 feet.

Whitehouse Creek has lost the residence that prompted its name. Built on a promontory above the creek, the house was finished in stucco that contained enough ground oyster shell to make it sparkle in sunlight.

On a voyage to the Corrotoman, you may want

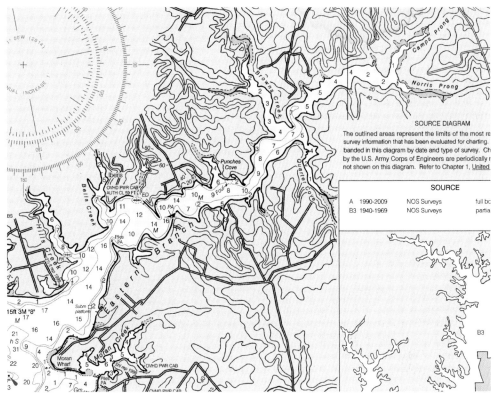

Eastern Branch of Corrotoman River; from NOAA Chart 12235—not to be used for navigation.

to challenge the entrance to **2b** **Taylor Creek**. This little tributary is lovely, but the entrance is daunting—a confusion of crab pot floats, shallow water and submerged piles. Follow the local marks and you should have no problem. Be sure to give a wide berth to the sandbar to starboard as you enter. The holding is reported good and the anchorage is a protected one. *Note: Here are the traditional directions for entering the creek, but since we haven't done this ourselves in several years, we make no promises. Here they are:* The entrance marker, green "1", may be hard to see from the channel of the Corrotoman because of its surroundings. Past red "2" on the Corrotoman and just before reaching Ball Point to starboard, look to the east. You'll notice a decided notch in an otherwise smoothly curving tree line. Head toward this notch to enter Taylor Creek, staying well to the right of the green "1" near the shore. To the left is a submerged island, and at low tide there is little more than a foot of water in places over it. The small DANGER mark locates the site of the submerged stump of an old

utility pole. Continue toward the tree-line notch until you are on a line that extends from Corrotoman Point (off your starboard quarter) and green "1". You should then be able to line up on the four privately maintained posts marking the channel into the creek, two greens and two reds. Once the main course of the creek is abeam to starboard, turn and head up into it. You'll find 8 to 10 feet up to the sandy bluff where the creek divides, and 5 to 6 feet in the main branch

A charming cottage nearly touches the shore on one of the Corrotoman River's creeks.

Corrotoman River *continued*

to starboard. Note the power cables crossing all the coves on the north shore. The cable shown with 60 feet of vertical clearance has beneath it a phone line that's considerably lower.

On the other side of the Corrotoman, and opposite Taylor Creek, you'll find **Little Taylor Creek**. It was here that Queenstown (c. 1691), the earliest port on the Corrotoman, was founded. However, the place never lived up to expectations, and by the 1740s its harbor depths were deemed "dangerous." Lancaster Court House became its successor.

Beyond Ball Point, and sharing an entrance with Taylor Creek, **2c Myer Creek** enters the river about 2 nautical miles upstream from the mouth of the Corrotoman. The north shore of Ball Point itself makes a fine anchorage in southerlies. On entering Myer, the first mark is red "2" to starboard off Yankee Point. Daymarks "3" and "4" seem to be reversed as you approach them, but remember the Three R's of "Red Right Returning," and you'll slalom in without grief.

Yankee Point Marina, the only marina on the river, lies just beyond these marks on the creek's northern shore. This facility offers transient slips, a ship's store, fuel, complete yard services and haul-outs. World on the Water and a poolside cafe serve meals and snacks along with beer and wine. A ride to the local country store can often be had for the asking.

The best anchorages are found on the left branch of Myer Creek just northeast of green "3" and west of red "4". The banks are densely wooded, and your depthsounder should show 7 to 8 feet of water.

Following the **2d Eastern Branch** all the way up to **Brownes Creek**, you can find a good anchorage and leisurely explore the creeks and coves off this branch of the river.

There are no marks on the Eastern Branch. Deep water extends fairly close to the banks on both sides. A favorite anchorage in the branch itself is opposite Bells Creek in the bight with 10 feet of water almost to the shoreline and good bottom. Known locally as Sandy Point, it has a beautiful beach, usually filled with swimmers and picnickers in the summer. In the event of bad weather, you'll find hideaways nearby, and there are any number of protected lee shores.

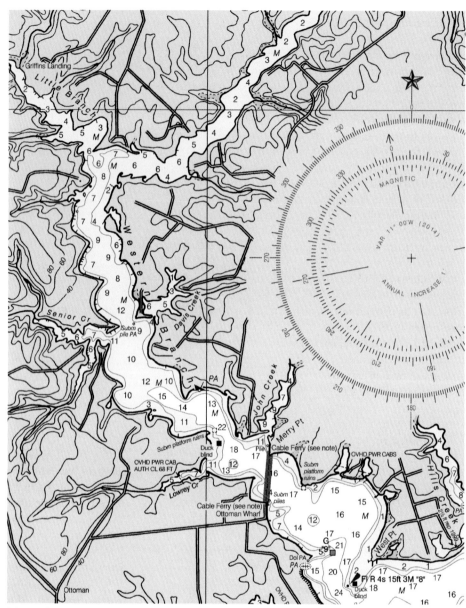

Western Branch of Corrotoman River; from NOAA Chart 12235—not to be used for navigation.

A privately maintained green mark indicates the shoal on the port side of the entrance to **2e Hills Creek**. There is ample water in the channel. Once inside, you'll probably find numerous stakes, crab pots and a few private piers, but there's enough room to swing comfortably at anchor. Houses peek through the trees. You can settle about a quarter mile up the creek in 6 feet of water.

Favor the left of center on entering **2f Bells Creek**. A dense growth of trees crowds the shoreline so that both boats and houses have a sense of privacy. This creek provides just the protection needed on a blustery night. Sailors, take note of the overhead power cable just past the first promontory to starboard. Charted clearance is just under 59 feet.

The Eastern Branch is navigable with at least 6-foot depths for a mile or so before shallowing to 4 feet and then much less. Farther along are the two prongs that form this branch: **Camps** and **Norris**. Both are worth exploration by dinghy. Once inside, you'll be enveloped in a wonderful silence, save for the sounds of nature.

Heading up the **2g** **Western Branch** past the duck blind, then red "8" and green "9", you'll find a horseshoe-shaped basin that may remind you of the small bay off St. Mary's City. If you anchor here at sunset, you can watch the Merry Point ferry cope with rush-hour traffic—a four-car line-up at Ottoman Wharf. If you are continuing upstream and the ferry is crossing, be sure to give it plenty of room ahead and astern to avoid running afoul of the cable. Merry Point is a jolly name, and it's a happy circumstance that the name of this former port was changed in the 19th century from Cotton Warehouse.

The Western Branch, like its eastern neighbor, offers many deepwater anchorages close to pleasant, wooded lee shores. Boat traffic is minimal, but if waters become choppy and you want more protection, two or three creeks offer haven.

2h **Lowrey Creek** is found on the western shore across from Merry Point. Anchor just outside, or find your way inside by avoiding the shoal off the point of land to the south, then turning south to dodge the shoal off the point to the north. The northern point extends well past the middle of the entrance, so favor the southern shore. Lowrey Creek carries at least 6 feet for a quarter of a mile. A power cable, charted at 68 feet, is about halfway up the creek.

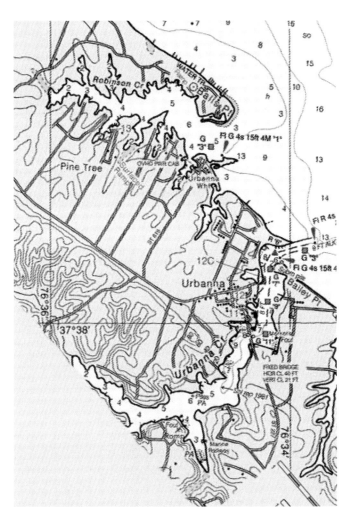

Urbanna Creek; from NOAA Chart 12237—not to be used for navigation.

2i **John Creek** on the eastern shore is located just west of the ferry landing at Merry Point. All but dinghies will be deterred from this creek by a bar across its entrance. Cruisers here report lead-line soundings of only 2 ½ feet.

2j **Senior Creek** on the western shore, is a little more than a mile above Merry Point. It has 7-foot depths, good protection and presents no problem on entering. There are a few more houses here than in other areas of the Western Branch, but it's still a pretty, quiet spot. The only sound you may hear at dawn is the overhead honking of a skein of geese.

The Corrotoman deserves a leisurely visit, not just a brief stopover. For more information, see *A Cruising Guide to the Corrotoman River* by Richard Dickson, available at Yankee Point Marina and shops in the area.

Urbanna Creek

Moving to the southern shore of the Rappahannock, **3** **Urbanna Creek** lies approximately 16 miles upstream from the Windmill Point spider. You'll be tempted to add Urbanna Creek to your cruising plans, because the historic and charming town of **Urbanna** is not to be missed. Here you can walk the compact streets, conveniently restock your galley and enjoy a mouth-watering dinner ashore. The fields and farms that once bordered the eastern side of the creek have given way to boat slips and condo development, so the ambiance of the creek has changed rather markedly over the last few years. Nevertheless, it remains a wonderful place to visit, especially on cook's night out.

From the Rappahannock River Bridge, head for red buoy "6" off Towles Point, about four miles upstream. Once past Towles Point, you can set a course for the creek's entrance jetties, which are another three miles beyond Towles Point. You can find the channel by aiming for the townhouses that stand prominently on the western shore at the creek's entrance.

The channel, which is subject to shoaling—and what channel isn't—at last report was carrying at least 7 feet into the creek, which is well defined by flashing red "2" and green daymark "3". Stay to the center and avoid the shoals along the shoreline.

Inside, the Coast Guard has added navigational aids "7" (off Bailey Point), "9" and "11" (near the bridge) and states that boats are supposed to anchor behind these marks, creating a much reduced anchorage. Except during Urbanna's Oyster Festival on the first weekend in November, you likely won't be asked to move if you anchor inside these marks. However, cruisers report only fair holding at the anchorages.

One pleasant anchorage is near the fixed bridge (21-foot vertical clearance) in 7-foot depths; another is near the high, wooded banks on the far side of the bridge. You can also anchor inside the creek off Bailey Point in 8 to 9 feet of water and row ashore to explore. The upper reaches of Urbanna Creek are enticing for dinghy exploration.

Several marine facilities line the west bank of the creek, offering full services to visitors and easy access to the town. Urbanna's trolley service is also helpful for getting around.

Port of Call
Urbanna

Long a favorite destination for boaters who enjoy Urbanna Creek's protected anchorage and numerous marinas, this town has broader appeal as well. Visitors will find historic attractions, modern shops, fine restaurants and friendly people.

Established as an official port in 1680, Urbanna thrived as a colonial tobacco shipping center and point of entry for British goods. Several buildings from that era survive and are featured in a self-guided walking tour available at the town office: the Tobacco Warehouse (1766), which now houses a visitors center; Gressitt House, (1750), thought to be the harbormaster's residence; the Customs House (c. 1755), the Old Middlesex County Courthouse (c. 1747), which served its judicial role until 1852 and is now home to the Middlesex Woman's Club, and privately owned Lansdowne (1740s), the Georgian-style home of Arthur Lee, a

Courtesy of the Southside Sentinel

diplomat for the Continental Congress.

Toward the entrance to Urbanna Creek lies the site of Fort Nonsense, where, legend has it, town leaders thwarted the British during the War of 1812. Believing a British attack was imminent, the town masqueraded as a formidable foe by mounting "cannon" (actually logs) in front of a "fort" (really a house overlooking the river). The ploy worked; the British sailed on with nary a shot fired.

The downtown is walker-friendly with most shops, restaurants, Middlesex Art Guild and a park just a stroll from the waterfront. From Memorial Day to Labor Day, a trolley makes a circuit around the business district and to destinations such as mini-golf and a country store. Cost is just 25 cents, but exact change is required.

Nestled inside cottage-style houses, charming shops offer an array of jewelry, gifts, apparel and antiques.

Restock the galley at Urbanna Market (which also carries prepared salads and entrees) and BayBerries (gourmet items). On second Saturdays from May to October, a Farmer's Market sets up within an easy walk of marinas. Something Different Country Store and Deli, which specializes in home-roasted peanuts, smoked meats and coffee, is now located in town.

"Diverse" and "relaxed" best describe the local dining scene. Consider the variety of restaurants within an easy walk of the boat: Virginia Street Cafe (local seafood), Angelo's Colonial Pizza (Greek and Italian), Cross Street Cafe (sandwiches, salads), Marshall's Drug Store (breakfast/lunch counter, soda fountain), Something Different Deli (ribs, barbecue, smoked meats, sandwiches). For a relaxing afternoon treat, make reservations for tea at Atherston Hall (804-758-2809) or sip a cup of coffee at Hingley's at the River (coffee, muffins).

Urbanna plays host to several festive events each year, including Art on the Halfshell, a juried outdoor art show and sale, in May, and a boat parade and fireworks on the Fourth of July. The Urbanna Oyster Festival, featuring seafood (see photo above), the Virginia State Oyster Shucking Contest, parades, entertainment and an arts and crafts sale, draws thousands to town in early November.

Information: Town Office, 804-758-2613; *www.urbanna.com.*

Urbanna

⚓ **Marinas/Dockage**
   1 Urbanna Town Marina
     at Uptons Point
   2 Port Urbanna Marine Center
   4 Urbanna Creek Marina
     at the Bridge

⊙ **Points of Interest**
   5 Old Middlesex
     County Courthouse
   6 Lansdowne
   7 Arthur Lee grave site
   8 Fort Nonsense site
   9 Old Tavern site
  10 Customs House
  11 Old Tobacco Warehouse
  12 Middlesex Art Guild

❓ **Information**
  11 Old Tobacco
     Warehouse Visitors Center

🍴 **Dining**
  14 Virginia Street Cafe
  15 Angelo's Colonial Pizza
  16 Cross Street Coffee
  18 Marshall's Drug Store

  19 Something Different
     Country Store & Deli

🛒 **Groceries**
  19 Something Different
     Country Store & Deli
  20 Urbanna Market
  21 Payne's Crab House
  22 Farmer's Market
     (second Saturdays)

Ⓜ **Marine Supplies**
  23 Urbanna Auto – Marine

🌲 **Park**
🍽 **Picnic Area**
🍦 **Ice Cream**
🏷 **Shopping**
🛏 **Lodging**
℞ **Pharmacy**
📖 **Library**
✉ **Post Office**
🛝 **Playground**

Today, the town's commercial activity remains centered on the river. Watermen provide a steady supply of crabs and fish and a less-steady supply, of late, of the famous Rappahannock River oysters. Now that the old grain elevators are gone from the waterfront, the town's focus is on tourism.

Upper Rappahannock

Adventurous cruisers will find more to explore on the **❺** upper Rappahannock. **Belle Isle State Park**, on the river's northern shore about eight miles upriver from Urbanna, is a 739-acre facility with seven miles of shoreline. It has picnic pavilions, restrooms, bicycle and canoe rentals, hiking trails, a public boat ramp and free docking during daylight hours on **Deep Creek**. This well-marked but misnamed tributary carries only 2 to 3 feet of water at its entrance. The park is part of a vast plantation once owned by George Washington's aunt and uncle. The manor house in which they lived still stands, but is privately owned. Nearby, a riverside plaque tells of the long-gone days when armed guards in watch houses trained their spotlights in search of poachers invading

Rappahannock, Richardson Creek to Cat Point Creek; from NOAA Chart 12237—not to be used for navigation.

Urbanna Creek *continued*

On the eastern bank is a subdivision and condominium yacht club with transient slips.

The first marina to starboard is Urbanna Town Marina, located at Uptons Point. Destroyed by Isabel in 2003, it has been completely rebuilt with modern showers and laundry facilities. Payne's Crab House, where you can watch crabs shedding in an outdoor tank, is past the marina. One cruiser reports finding the best holding (although not great) across from Urbanna Town Marina in 9 to 10 feet of water.

A short walk up the hill behind the marina and the crabhouse takes you into town and past the restored 1766 Tobacco Warehouse on the left and old customs house on the right, now a private home. The town has reopened an old brick warehouse as a visitor center, usually manned by volunteers on Fridays and Saturdays. Stop by to learn more about the building's historic past, when tobacco casks were rolled down Virginia Street (then called Prettyman's Rolling Road) to waiting ships.

Urbanna is one of the four remaining towns of the 19 ordered built in 1680 by the General Assembly of the House of Burgesses. Within the town limits stand some of the buildings from those early years, including the Old Middlesex County Courthouse and the Old Tavern, where Patrick Henry is said to have delivered one of his stirring speeches. Nearby is Rosegill, built in 1650, home of a colonial governor, and Hewick, where many colonial statesmen gathered. Somewhere near here, in 1720, two pirates were hanged.

In the early 1900s, Urbanna was a port of call for commercial vessels and steamships from Baltimore and Norfolk.

Upper Rappahannock *continued*

local oyster beds under cover of darkness.

Past red "30", lies the town of **Tappahannock**, on the Rappahannock's southern shore. Attempting to land here in 1608, Captain John Smith was driven back by Indians. A Colonial port town, it was burned by the British in the War of 1812 and shelled by the Union during the Civil War. Today, visitors will find the town's historic district filled with antiques shops and a dozen or so preserved 18th- and 19th-century buildings. It is also home to the graceful riverfront buildings of St. Margaret's, a private Episcopal school for girls, founded in 1921.

Below the 50-foot fixed Downing bridge across the Rappahannock, boaters enter Hoskins Creek, which has a marked channel with a controlling depth of just under 6 feet (deeper in mid-channel). Inside there is a small turning basin and a municipal dock, usually occupied by a tour boat. There is also a small motel/marina here. From Hoskins Creek, it's a short walk to a shopping center and, going the other way, to the old downtown. There are restaurants both directions. The only other marina in Tappahannock is Parker's Marina, just past the bridge, but the depths are shallow. Downriver, cruisers can buy gas at Garrett's Marina, which also offers repair services, marine supplies and ice.

Michael Wootton

Bay Spotlight

Captain Smith's Rappahannock

A major artery on the Captain John Smith Chesapeake National Historic Trail, the Rappahannock both challenged and fascinated its famous explorer/cartographer. Smith first saw this beautiful river in the winter of 1607-08 while a captive of a Pamunkee chief, and when he tried to return in July 1608 he suffered his infamous encounter with a stingray at the river's mouth.

Yet Smith and his crew returned a month later, taking their boat up to the river's head of navigation (present-day Fredericksburg) and back. Smith's extraordinarily accurate 1612 map based on that voyage guided the English colonists who settled along the Rappahannock 40 years later. Over the intervening centuries, farmers tilled large tracts along the tidal river, which served as the highway for shipping until roads superseded river transportation after World War II.

Today, the Rappahannock remains farm country, with sweeping pastoral views and two spectacular sandstone bluffs inhabited by eagles: Fones Cliffs between Tappahannock and Leedstown, and Horsehead Cliffs between Leedstown and Port Royal. For modern-day explorers following in Captain Smith's wake, the Rappahannock offers lots of still-natural "John Smith views," especially above Tappahannock, where the river narrows and reveals some of the best scenery on the Bay.

The well-marked channel is quite deep, but currents are swift and marinas are non-existent above Tappahannock. Clearance under the bridges at Tappahannock (Route 360) and Port Royal (Route 301) is 50 feet to accommodate the tugboats that still push barges to and from Fredericksburg.

At Tappahannock, there is no dockage for deep-draft boats, but lots of space and good holding ground to anchor. June Parker Marina (804-443-2131), just above the bridge on the south bank, allows dinghies to tie up. The walk to the center of town is about a quarter-mile. Lowery's Restaurant (804-443-2800) is a landmark that serves fresh local seafood.

Fredericksburg, about 60 miles beyond Tappahannock, is a charming city that will in time host cruisers on the John Smith Trail. Until its boating facilities are completed, the best place to tie up is about 30 miles downriver at Westmoreland Berry Farm, whose dock can hold one or two large boats (call to make sure there's room, 804-224-9171). The farm offers pick-your-own fruit in season, a store and a snack bar serving tasty barbecue sandwiches and sundaes with fresh fruit. Visitors can tour nearby Ingleside Plantation Winery. Call 804-224-8687 to arrange for pickup from the berry farm.

—John Page Williams

Deltaville to York River

8

The Piankatank, York, Perrin, Mattaponi and Pamunkey Rivers
Milford Haven and Gwynn's Island; Deltaville and Yorktown
Mobjack Bay and Back Creek

etween the marinas of Deltaville and the battlefields of Yorktown lie the beautiful Piankatank River, the four rivers of Mobjack Bay and the powerful York, the fifth largest river in the Chesapeake. In between them are working waterways like Milford Haven (the reach that separates Gwynn's Island from the mainland), a long wild Bay-shore beach that stretches from the Hole in the Wall (the narrow channel at Milford Haven's east end) to New Point Comfort, and the marshes of Gloucester County's Guinea Neck.

Once a boatbuilding center, Deltaville is now noted for its marinas and boatyards. The river on its south side, the Piankatank, is fed by Dragon Run, a wild and beautiful cypress swamp that reaches the tidewater about 15 miles above the river's mouth. The Piankatank's riverbanks are steadily growing houses, but they retain their charm and they shelter some of the Bay's most scenic anchorages. Along the south shore between Hills Bay and Cobbs Creek, you'll notice several shoals with daymarks. They are oyster reefs built by the Virginia Marine Resources Commission (VMRC) to help rebuild the Piankatank's oyster stocks.

The Hole in the Wall is fascinating to explore in a small boat, but in a cruising vessel, take great care if you try the marked channel. The Bay-shore beach stretching south to

Winter Harbor and the lagoon behind it are just right for sea kayaks and fishing skiffs, but not for big boats. Horn Harbor offers a better channel for workboats and anglers.

Mobjack Bay's rivers offer the charm of the Piankatank but in smaller packages (you'll notice VMRC oyster reefs in three of them). Moving counterclockwise, the East River stretches up to the village of Mathews, the county seat. The North and Ware are quiet, with the latter reaching up almost to Gloucester Court House. The sprawling, marsh-filled Severn—largely a watermen's river—is less sheltered than the others, but equally peaceful.

The York River runs straight and wide from West Point past the the U.S. Naval Supply Center and Yorktown on the south bank and the Virginia Institute of Marine Science (a large laboratory that is part of the College of William and Mary) on the north. The river is fed by two powerful, wild tributaries, the Mattaponi and the Pamunkey, that reach far into the woodlands of central Virginia.

By road, Yorktown serves as the gateway to Virginia's busy lower peninsula, which stretches west to Williamsburg and south to Hampton. Cruisers, however, will like its Watermen's Museum and Yorktown Victory Center, whose excellent exhibits focus on the British surrender in 1781.

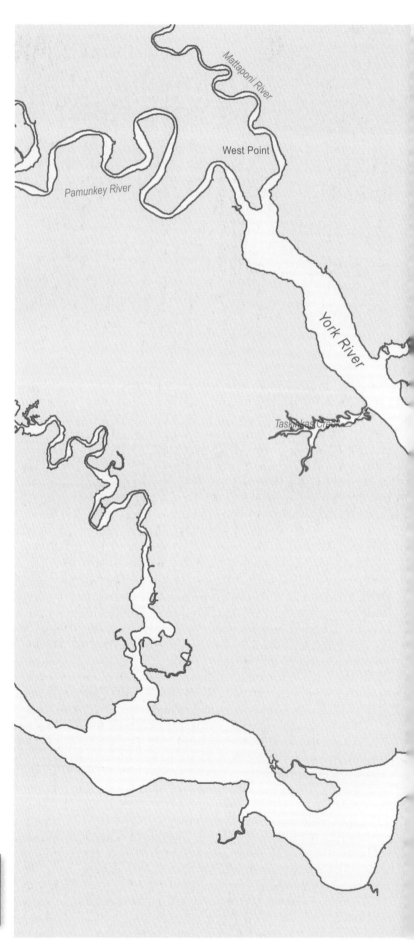

Tow BoatU.S.
LOCATIONS

A **Gwynn's Island**
804-725-0453

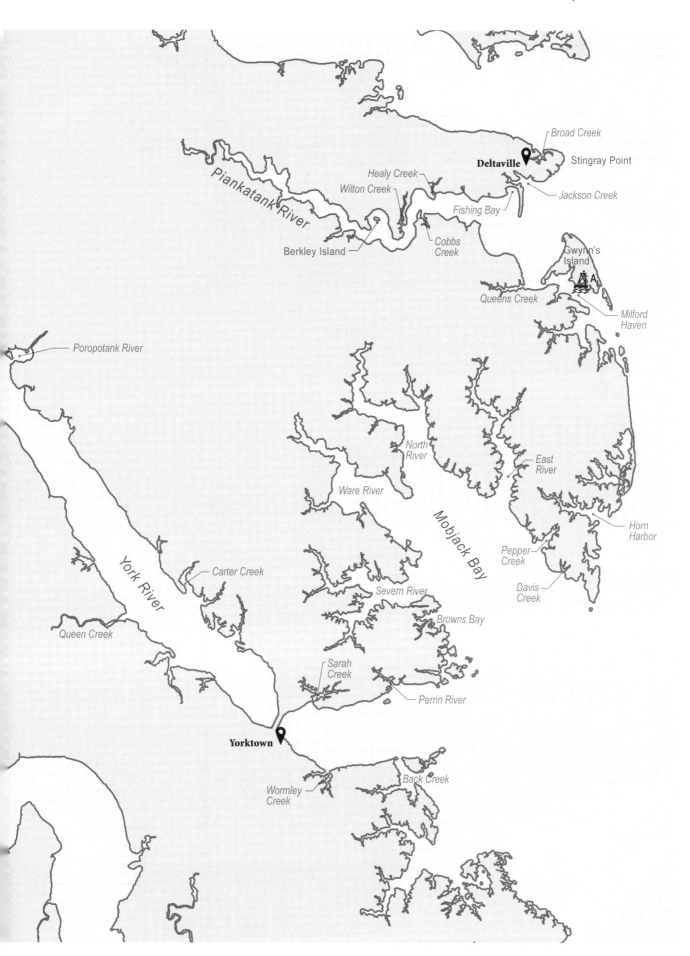

Broad Creek

Deltaville

Stingray Point

Healy Creek

Wilton Creek

Fishing Bay

Jackson Creek

Cobbs
Creek

Berkley Island

Gwynn's
Island

A

Queens Creek

Milford
Haven

Piankatank River

Poropotank River

North
River

East
River

Ware River

Horn
Harbor

Mobjack Bay

Pepper
Creek

Carter Creek

Davis
Creek

Severn River

York River

Browns Bay

Queen Creek

Sarah
Creek

Perrin River

Yorktown

Back Creek

Wormley
Creek

Deltaville

Cruisers who want to visit **Deltaville** on the western shore of the Chesapeake Bay have two ways of doing so. Because the village covers the tip of the Middle Peninsula that is bordered by the Rappahannock and Piankatank rivers, it has an entrance by water from both rivers. Either way you arrive, Deltaville appears to be more marina than town because nothing of the central town is visible.

Once the "Boatbuilding Capital of the Bay," Deltaville increasingly finds itself in a new role. Commercial boatbuilding here has become a thing of the past. Simple working boatyards have been turned into full-service marinas, clubs and yachting resorts with swimming pools, tennis courts, boat motels and landscaped grounds.

Deltaville's permanent population is nearly 800, but that number swells to several thousand in the summer. What traffic there is can be found mostly on the surrounding creeks, rivers and bays, where thousands of boats are berthed. Boaters in the area quickly learn to follow charts and be aware of shoals and sandbars.

Even with more development, the area will remain a boating, fishing and gunkholing paradise in a beguiling part of the Chesapeake. Little, laid-back Deltaville is a family

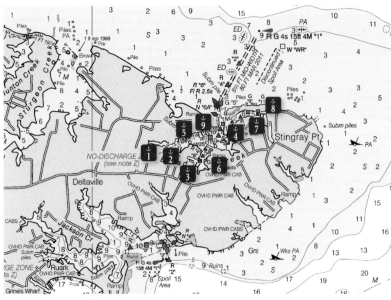
Broad Creek; from NOAA Chart 12235—not to be used for navigation.

oriented center of marine activity designed by nature and enhanced by maritime development to attract recreational boaters and anglers. Despite a devastating fire in 2012, the **Deltaville Maritime Museum**, located at Holly Point Nature Park, has reopened and continues to preserve the boatbuild-

● On Premises
➤ Nearby

	Broad Creek	MLW	Overnight Slips	Gas	Diesel	Propane	Electric	Showers	Laundry	Restaurant	Lodging	Pool	Pump-out	Ice	Groceries	Marine Supplies	Boat Repair	Bait	Haul-out Services	Launch Ramp	Wi-Fi	Other
1	**Chesapeake Cove Marina** Rappahannock R./Broad Cr. 804-776-6855; www.chesapeakecovemarina.com	5'	●	●	●	➤	●	●	●	●	➤	➤	●	●	●	➤	●	➤	●	●	➤	●	Merc, Volvo, Yanmar, 30-ton lift, prop sales/ svc, kohler, westerbeke
2	**Coastal Marine** Rappahannock R./Broad Cr. 804-776-6585; www.coastalmarinerepairs.com	6'					➤										●	●					Mercury O/B, Crusader engine sales & srvc;
3	**Deltaville Yachting Center** Rappahannock R./Broad Cr. 804-776-9898; www.dycboat.com	6'	●	●	➤	➤	●	●	●	➤	➤	●	●	●	➤	●	●	●	●	➤	●		Full-service ABYC yard, 50-ton lift, boatel, sales
4	**Dozier's Regatta Point Yachting Center** Rappahannock R./Broad Cr. 804-776-8400; www.doziermarinegroup.com	7.5'	●	➤	➤	➤	●	●	●	●	●	●	●	●	●	●	➤	➤	●				BoatU.S. marina; Wi-Fi, floating docks, courtesy car
5	**Norton Yachts** Rappahannock R./Broad Cr. 804-776-9211, 888-720-4306; www.nortonyachts.com	6'	●	●	●	➤	●	●	●	➤	➤	●	●	●	➤	●	●	●	➤	●			Sailing sch., charters, full-service yard, boat sales
6	**Norview Marina** Rappahannock R./Broad Cr. 804-776-6463; www.norviewmarina.com	6.5'	●	●	●		●	●	●	➤	➤	●	●	●	➤	●	●	●	●	●	●		boathouse, 82-ton lift, boatel, Zimmerman marine onsite
7	**Stingray Point Boat Works** Rappahannock R./Broad Cr. 804-776-7070; www.stingraypointboatworks.com	6'+	➤	➤	➤	➤	●	●	●	➤	➤	➤	➤	➤	●	●	●	●			●		Full-service boatyard
8	**Stingray Point Marina** Rappahannock R./Broad Cr. 804-776-7272 ; www.stingraypointmarina.com	6.5'	●	➤	➤	➤	●	●	●	➤	➤	●	●	➤	➤	➤	●	➤	➤	➤	●		Replica of 1858 Stingray Point Lighthouse; annual slips only
9	**Waldens Marina** Rappahannock R./Broad Cr. 804-776-9440	8'	●	●	●	●	➤	●	●	➤	➤	➤	●	●	●	●	●	●	●	➤	●		Extensive marine parts. Bar/Restaurant next door

ing history and skills that made the community famous.

If you arrive by boat, it's easy to get a ride into town, even though there are no taxis. Most of the restaurants will provide a marina pick-up and return. You can also walk, and some marinas supply bicycles. Likely as not, though, when locals spot you strolling into town they'll offer a lift. If you want to reprovision at a local market, chances are good that you'll be able to hitch a ride back to the marina with their shopping bags. Deltaville is that kind of place.

Broad Creek

Broad Creek is the Rappahannock River entrance to Deltaville. This sheltered, almost hidden basin is just inside a long, straight-forward entrance channel to the creek at the mouth of the Rappahannock. The outermost end of the channel is marked with a flashing green 4-second light. Daymarks at convenient intervals lead to a flashing red 4-second light at a turning area at the mouth of the creek.

Dredging in 2010 has opened the channel to at least 8 feet, so shoaling problems—at least for the next several years—should be alleviated and deeper-draft vessels should have no problems here. Inside, the sheltered harbor is ringed with marinas, so there's plenty of traffic coming in and out. But as always, keep one eye on the channel and one on the depthsounder. Upstream at daymark "11" Broad Creek makes

a sharp turn to the west.

In the early 1960s, the yards along Broad Creek were still catering to pleasure and commercial boats built of wood. But as seafood harvests began to decline and fiberglass gained popularity, a surge in recreational boating came into play. By the late 1960s as the "yachting" market gained strength, these working yards began evolving into first-class marinas, some in lovely expansive park-like settings, catering to the needs of visiting boaters who come from all over the world to sample a bit of the southern hospitality that makes the area famous.

Nauti Nells

Deltaville's Unofficial Welcome Center
Mall de Mer

Unique Nautical Gifts for All Ages

Used Equipment & Boats Taken on Consignment • 30 Years Experience

Turn your used nautical items into CA$H
Call or email nautinell@verizon.net

visit us at **www.nautinell.com**
Deltaville, VA: 804-776-9811

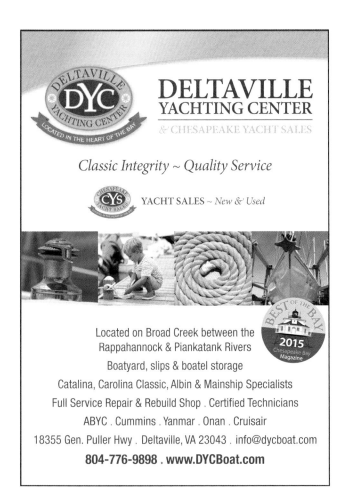

DELTAVILLE YACHTING CENTER
& CHESAPEAKE YACHT SALES

Classic Integrity ~ Quality Service

CYS YACHT SALES ~ *New & Used*

Located on Broad Creek between the Rappahannock & Piankatank Rivers

Boatyard, slips & boatel storage

Catalina, Carolina Classic, Albin & Mainship Specialists

Full Service Repair & Rebuild Shop . Certified Technicians

ABYC . Cummins . Yanmar . Onan . Cruisair

18355 Gen. Puller Hwy . Deltaville, VA 23043 . info@dycboat.com

804-776-9898 . www.DYCBoat.com

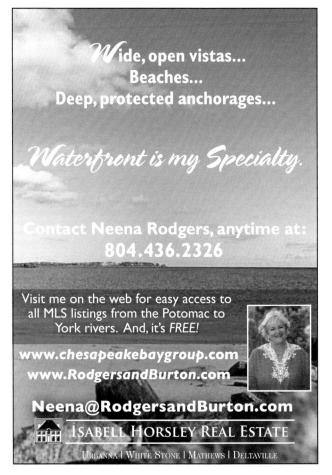

Wide, open vistas...
Beaches...
Deep, protected anchorages...

Waterfront is my Specialty.

Contact Neena Rodgers, anytime at:
804.436.2326

Visit me on the web for easy access to all MLS listings from the Potomac to York rivers. And, it's *FREE!*

www.chesapeakebaygroup.com
www.RodgersandBurton.com

Neena@RodgersandBurton.com

ISABELL HORSLEY REAL ESTATE
URBANNA | WHITE STONE | MATHEWS | DELTAVILLE

Port of Call
Deltaville

Easy-going Deltaville is all about boats. Once home to more than 20 boatyards, the town has lost many of its master boatbuilders, yet the boating emphasis remains. Many residents still earn their livelihood from maritime trades, marina operations or the sportfishing business. Although there is no town center as such, Route 33, the main street, has a smattering of shops, markets and restaurants a mile or so from the marinas. To reach them, boaters can take advantage of courtesy transportation or enjoy a leisurely stroll. Deltaville's friendliness, protected harbors like Jackson Creek, and convenient location make it a popular port and a favorite seasonal stop for the fleet of snowbirders moving north and south.

In 2012, a fire destroyed two of its buildings and many artifacts, but the Deltaville Maritime Museum is again in full swing, thanks to loyal friends and staunch supporters. With new buildings, exhibits and programs, the all-volunteer, non-profit organization dedicated to local watermen and boatbuilders continues to convey the area's rich maritime history. The museum's schedule of events includes outdoor concerts,

socials, festivals and Saturday morning farmers' market. Situated on Mill Creek on the grounds of Holly Point Nature Park, the site features a nature trail, gardens, picnic area and fish-shaped wildflower meadow. There's a dinghy dock on the creek and a kayak landing that boaters may use while visiting the park or attending special events.

Local waters reward anglers with many triumphs and tales to tell, and Deltaville's charter fishing captains are ready to whisk you to the area's prime fishing grounds. Numerous area coves and creeks invite dinghy exploration and nature expeditions. The area's flat terrain and undeveloped countryside make biking a popular activity as well. In town, there's a recreation area equipped with basketball, tennis and volleyball courts, and an inviting children's playground. Visitors will also find a public library close at hand.

Businesses run the gamut from fun to functional. In the first category, you'll find Crabby Couple (nautical and marine artwork), Nauti Nell's (maritime gifts and used marine equipment on consignment), Latitudes (jewelry, gifts, home accessories), and Carter's Cottage Consignments (antiques, collectibles, home furnishings). Shoppers will also enjoy the area's gift shops. You'll find marine supplies at West Marine, Hurds True Value, Ullman Sail Loft and several marina ship's stores.

Deltaville

⚓ Marinas/Dockage
1 Dozier's Regatta Point Yachting Center
2 Stingray Point Marina
3 Stingray Point Boat Works (boatyard)
4 Norview Marina
5 Deltaville Yachting Center
6 Chesapeake Cove Marina
7 Rivertime Marina
9 Timberneck Marina
10 Norton's Marina, Inc.
11 Walden Marina

12 Deltaville Marina & Deltaville Boatyard
13 Public pier
14 Powell's Marina
15 Ruark Marina, Inc.
16 Fishing Bay Harbor Marina
17 Chesapeake Boat Works
18 Porpoise Cove Marina

⊕ Points of Interest
19 Deltaville Maritime Museum (see text above)

Ⅿ Marine Supplies
24 Hurd Hardware
29 Nauti Nell's Gifts & Nautical Consignments

30 West Marine

🍴 Dining
20 The Railway
25 Taylor's
26 Toby's
34 Cafe By the Bay
35 Galley

🛒 Groceries
27 7-11 Convenience Store
28 J&W Seafood
19 Farmer's Market (4th Sat.)
23 Chris Mart (at Shell Station)
31 Merry Vale Farm
33 Great Valu

☼ Entertainment/Recreation
37 Deltaville Community Association complex (swimming pool, tennis courts, playground)

📖 Library

✉ Post Office

🍦 Ice Cream

🛏 Lodging
22 Deltaville Dockside Inn

🏳 Shopping

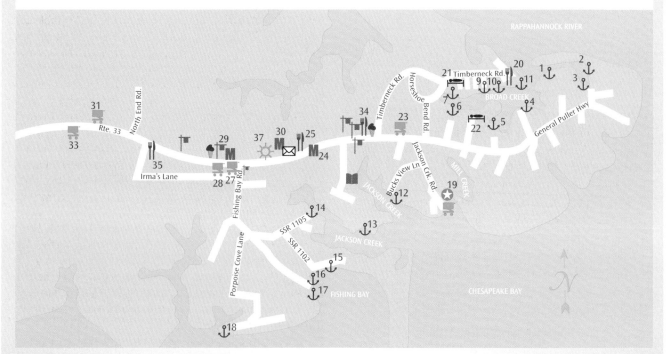

Piankatank River

Some of the best anchorages between Hampton Roads and the upper Bay lie between the Rappahannock and York rivers on the **Piankatank River**. (This river serves as a border for the Virginia counties of Mathews and Middlesex.) Captain John Smith, in records of his travels in the Chesapeake, described the Piankatank as a "little river." Although it is comparatively small, the Piankatank compensates for it by providing all-around beauty, cruisability and friendliness.

Jackson Creek

Whether you approach the Piankatank from the north or from the south, the 34-foot Stingray Point Light provides a landmark off the river's entrance. Handy marks for finding the entrance to ❶ **Jackson Creek** are "1P" and "2", southeast of the light, which identify the beginning of the Piankatank River channel.

Continue southwesterly into the Piankatank toward quick-flashing red "6", just east of Stove Point. From here turn north to Jackson Creek's entrance markers: flashing green "1" and daymark "2".

The L-shaped narrow channel leading inside is well marked but tricky, especially if vessel draft is any issue. The very center is reported to carry at least 8 feet. However, the edges can be quite shoal and outside the channel depths drop quickly to 2 feet or less. Green "5" and red "10" are often mentioned as trouble spots. Seek local knowledge when you can. Also, some of the marks were shifted after the 2011 dredge to reflect the changing channel.

Port of Call: Deltaville

Groceries are available at convenience stores and Great Valu supermarket. Fresh catch is available at J&W Seafood and fresh produce at Merry Vale Farm (seasonal). On the fourth Saturday of the month (April to November), fresh produce is also available at the Farmer's Market held at the Deltaville Maritime Museum.

Most of the town's restaurants offer courtesy transportation to visiting boaters. The Railway (formerly Cocomos) is the only waterfront restaurant in town (on Broad Creek).

Deltaville's sense of community and Bay ties are reflected in a variety of events hosted by the maritime museum: Sunday boatbuilding workshops, a summer concert series, Waterman's Appreciation Day (May) and Family Boatbuilding Week (July). The town puts on the dog for Heritage Day on the Fourth of July (parade, music, food, fireworks). In October, Holly Point's Art & Seafood Festival closes out the season.

Information: Community Association, *www.deltavilleva.com.*

At "10" Jackson Creek divides into two branches. The north branch houses a marina within eyesight of daymark "10". Deltaville Marina and Boatyard offers slips, gas and diesel fuel, repair services and a variety of amenities to local and visiting boaters. There is also ample room for anchoring just beyond the marina—but be sure to keep to the middle to avoid the shoal just upstream.

Deltaville has several restaurants, groceries and marine supply stores, along with a hardware store. Most of these businesses will provide transportation to and from marinas when called.

The southern branch of Jackson Creek is home to the Fishing Bay Yacht Club, located on the southern shore. When entering this branch of the creek, stay close to "10" and then be sure to stay in the middle of the channel to avoid the long shoal that extends off the first point to starboard past "10". Keep off all the points, especially the shoal one off the second point to starboard. The creek carries at least 6 feet almost to the end.

The southern branch also offers anchorages, marinas and the public pier, where you can tie up your dinghy. The walk to town (just follow the main road) is about a half mile, past nice homes and friendly people. In earlier days there was a lot of workboat activity on the creek; today only an occasional workboat gives a reminder of those times.

You'll find some of the most attractive anchorages on the northern fork of Jackson Creek's southern branch. Lovely homes on tree-lined shores make this a cozy and protected place to spend the night. Pick a spot, drop the hook and enjoy; in the fall you may even hear the eerie cries of another visitor—the loon.

Fishing Bay

The Piankatank River near Deltaville has earned a reputation as one of the loveliest spots on the Bay. The broad mouth of the river is well marked and easy to enter. Often the whole area surrounding Stove Point Neck is crowded with the small fishing boats of weekend residents and vacationers. The homes on Stove Point are lovely, and the residents are among the fortunate few who can watch moonrise and sunrise to the east and sunset and moonset to the west, all over the water.

To reach ❷ **Fishing Bay**, don't cut any markers beyond flashing green "5" off Cherry Point. Proceed in a straight line southwest from "7" to "8", which marks the 2- to 4-foot bar extending southeast from Stove Point Neck. Continue to "8A" before making the turn into Fishing Bay. Often the southeast bar has people on it at low tide, possibly clamming, crabbing, wading or swimming.

Proceed to "10" and "10A", giving these marks off Stove Point a wide berth as you eventually head north into the deep water of Fishing Bay. Tucking into either the northeast or northwest corner as much as possible provides fairly good protection from southerlies despite the feeling of openess. Here too you can set the hook in 16 feet of water with plenty of scope to swing comfortably.

Besides this huge anchorage, cruisers will find overnight slips, gas, diesel and repairs. Additionally, Fishing Bay Harbor,

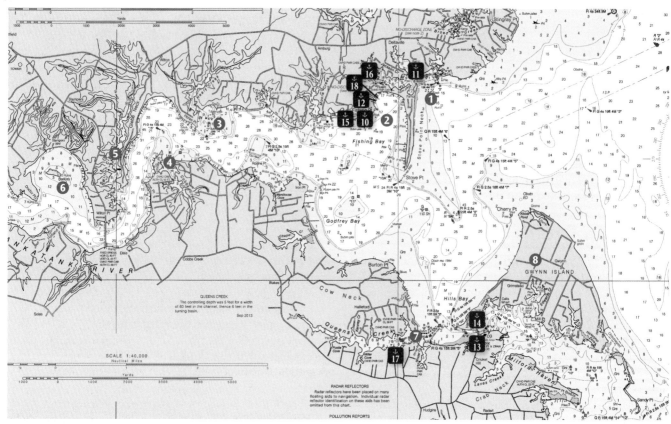

Piankatank River; from NOAA Chart 12235—not to be used for navigation.

● On Premises
➤ Nearby

Piankatank River

	MLW	Overnight Slips	Gas	Diesel	Propane	Electric	Showers	Laundry	Restaurant	Lodging	Pool	Pump-out	Ice	Groceries	Marine Supplies	Boat Repair	Bait	Haul-out Services	Launch Ramp	Wi-Fi	Other
Chesapeake Boat Works — 10 Piankatank R./Fishing Bay 804-776-8833; www.chesapeakeboatworks.com	15'	●	➤	➤	➤	●	●	●	➤	➤	➤	➤	➤	➤	●	➤	●	●		●	Boatyard, all repairs, dry storage
Deltaville Marina & Boatyard — 11 Piankatank R./Jackson Cr. 804-776-9812; www.deltavillemarina.com	9'	●	●	●	●	●	●	●	➤	➤	●	●	●	➤	➤	●	●	●	➤	●	Full-service marina/ boatyard with amenities, ABYC techs
Fishing Bay Harbor Marina — 12 Piankatank R./Fishing Bay 804-776-6800; www.fishingbay.com	15'	●	●	●	➤	●	●	➤	●	●	●	●	●	●	●	➤	➤	➤	➤	●	Deepwater dockage, lounge, Wi-Fi, cable
Morningstar Marina — 13 Piankatank R./Gwynn's Is. 804-384-9698; www.gwynns-island.morningstarmarinas.com	6'	●	●			●	●			●		●	●	●	●	●	●		➤	●	Non-ethanol gas, weigh station, BoatU.S. marina
Narrows Marina — 14 Piankatank R./Gwynn's Is. 804-815-8897	6'	●	●	●	➤	●	●						●	●		●	➤		➤		Tennis, playground
Porpoise Cove Marina — 15 Piankatank R./Porpoise Cove 804-854-8227	5'		➤	➤	➤	●	●	●	●	➤	➤		●	➤	➤	●	➤	➤	➤	●	Beach
Powell's Marina — 16 Piankatank R./Jackson Cr./Western Branch 804-776-0081; www.powellsmarina.com	7'					●	●													●	On well-protected deep-water creek
Queens Creek Marina — 17 Piankatank R./Queens Cr. 804-240-8670	6'	●				●	●						●	●							Picnic area, clubhouse, 7' MLW, raised roof boat shed
Ruark Marina — 18 Piankatank R./Fishing Bay 804-776-9776; www.ruarkmarinas.com			●			●			➤			●			➤						

Fishing Bay continued

for a fee, offers services for anchored boats and helps their guests with transportation to meet whatever needs they have.

Fishing Bay provides pretty good protection from the north, east and west. It also has other attributes. On a stifling mosquito-laden summer night in settled weather, you can get a blissful night's sleep under the stars in the open cockpit by anchoring from the stern and catching the light wisp of a southwesterly that is nearly always present—and bug-free.

Fishing Bay is a popular anchorage for many boats transiting the Bay and is an annual stopover spot for various races up and down the Chesapeake. Anchor lights can be seen twinkling in Fishing Bay nearly every night during the boating season, but there is always ample room. Whether you use Fishing Bay and its facilities as a harbor of refuge, a vacation destination, a place for rest or a place for a party, the area will not only "fill the bill" but also will bring you back again and again.

Healy Creek

The upper reaches of the Piankatank are lovely, with an almost mystical quality. Though there are many new homes here, the river remains scenic, narrow—almost serpentine—with gentle overhangs in places. Pay close attention to chart 12235 to avoid three major shoals. Two are located on the south shore, the first at Roane Point, marked by green "13", and the second at Ginney Point at green "15" just past Cobbs Creek. The reason these are hard to spot is that the shoals they mark extend more than halfway across the river, and thus the marks are not where you expect to see them. Unmarked shoaling extends on the north shore all around the entrance to ❸ **Healy** *(HAY-lee)* **Creek**; also west of the creek's entrance, daymark "14" marks the shallows around Horse Point.

In heading upriver, note that the Roane Point shoal at green "13" extends beyond the mark; as you reach "13", beware of heading directly for "14". Maintain your northwest course for another 400 yards before bearing southwest. To avoid the shoal on the north shore, proceed another 400 yards then turn toward "14" or the entrance to Healy Creek.

The marks to Healy Creek are less than a mile beyond green "13". If you study your charts, Healy may not appear so inviting. The entrance is shown with a pair of privately maintained marks and a questionable-looking channel, all of which might tend to turn you off, but the creek is worth a visit. First a green mark and then a red, bordered by a scattering of oyster stakes and crab floats, lead you through a narrow opening in the shoreline and into the quiet waters of Healy Creek.

There's plenty of water in the middle of the creek as you pass several impressive homes and large boathouses. As you head upstream, the banks are high on either side promising complete protection in a blow. Farther upstream the creek splits and the water appears to get a little thin.

Pick a broad spot in the creek, make a slow, wide circle, coast to a stop and let the anchor slip quietly into the water;

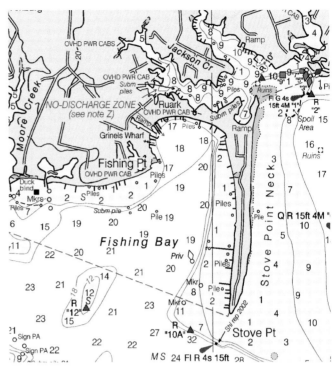

Fishing Bay; from NOAA Chart 12235—not to be used for navigation.

on both sides of the creek the wooded banks rise steeply and a flood of mountain laurel and sweet honeysuckle pours down.

Upstream where the creek divides you'll see a series of docks. These belong to the community of Chick Cove, a former name for Healy Creek.

Cobbs Creek

The entrance into ❹ **Cobbs Creek** is reminiscent of Fairlee Creek in the upper Bay, where deepwater almost up to the shoreline takes you through a keyhole tight entrance that opens up into a broad open anchorage. Entering Cobbs Creek, two daymarks lead you parallel to shore until you are almost onto Ginney Point, a finger of land jutting out from the western side of Cobbs Creek's entrance. Just when it seems you will go aground, the creek opens a narrow entrance to port and you can slip through in around 8 feet of water.

Inside, a small branch forks off to starboard, where you'll find Ginny Point Marina, a 25-slip marina once serving transients that is now closed. The main body of Cobbs Creek runs southeasterly, creating a good, well-protected anchorage with depths of 6 to 8 feet. There are several large old homes and some newer condominiums on the shores here, with a fair amount of wooded cover to shield them from view. The bottom offers good holding (thick, sticky mud that's devilishly hard to clean off your anchor).

Farther upstream about 500 yards, the creek opens into another small bay, giving an anchored boat more room to swing, but offering only 5-foot depths, which may be a little on the shallow side for you. In addition, there is very little breeze in this anchorage because of the height of the land and the heavy foliage. On a still night, you will probably be more comfortable out nearer the entrance.

Wilton Creek

West of Cobbs Creek, the river makes a 90-degree turn south around Ginney Point and with another turn west flows under the Piankatank River Bridge before winding its way another 10 miles and disappearing into marshlands. Glebe Neck separates ❺ **Wilton Creek** from the meandering Piankatank. The creek's snug anchorages are just the spot to ride out a storm.

The best way to enter Wilton Creek (since it is not marked) is to avoid cutting any corners. Don't attempt to turn in until you have the middle of the entrance dead abeam. At one time brush stakes indicated the shoals; now you'll see black-and-white "danger" signs. Give this end a wide berth and you should be okay.

Wilton Creek is narrow but carries 5- to 8-foot depths for almost a mile north. The shores are high and heavily wooded, reminding the visitor of a mountain lake. The high banks cut down on the breeze, but even if there is no air stirring when you anchor, the trees should keep the creek pleasantly cool even on hot evenings.

There's a group of boat slips around the second bend to port and a second group of slips farther up-creek. These belong to "The Coves at Wilton Creek," a tasteful and unobtrusive condo development. Many fine homes are tucked away in the trees all along the creek. Drop your hook just around the first big bend to starboard. As the thunder booms around you, the lightning flashes and the rain pelts, you'll be in a fine spot to weather the turmoil.

Berkley Island

❻ **Berkley Island** lies approximately 7 miles up the Piankatank River about a mile northwest of the Piankatank River Bridge (vertical clearance 43 feet). From the bridge, set a course to avoid the end of Wilton Point and the somewhat trickier shoal to port off Holland Point. Berkley Island is actually two smaller islands, separated by a tidal marsh. The western island is the larger.

Swing around the east side of the island, but be careful. The charts show that there is a prominent shoal extending eastward from the island about 300 feet. There are often a couple of stakes in the water to guide you, so just give this end a wide berth and you'll be okay.

The favorite anchorage is just opposite Stampers Wharf in 9 feet of water. The island is uninhabited most of the time, but there are two small piers if you should wish to go ashore. One dock is just opposite Stampers Wharf, and the other is at the island's western end. Berkley is beautiful and wild. Its elevated western end accommodates a cluster of trees. From there, the ground falls away to a grassy flat with another smaller clump of woods. This turns to marsh at the island's eastern end.

Berkley Island, owned by the Virginia Baptist Mission Board, is often used as summer camp for children. Through the years the mission board has permitted individuals, including boaters, to visit the island on days when it is not being

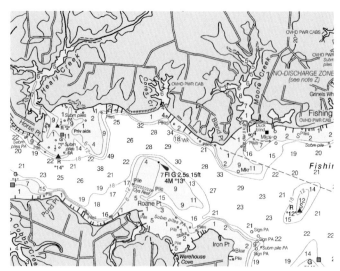

Healy Creek; from NOAA Chart 12235—not to be used for navigation.

used by campers. (Instructions on how to obtain permission to spend the night are posted on the island. For more information, call 804-776-9552.) Visitors are encouraged to use good stewardship when using the island.

Anchor to windward of the island where the river bottom is soft mud, and the high ground behind Stampers Wharf will provide you with ample protection from northerlies. There are few homes in the area to disturb the peace of this anchorage. The Piankatank carries deep water quite a way farther upstream, but it's doubtful you'll find any more attractive spot than in these quiet waters behind Berkley Island.

The 21-mile-long river culminates at its headwaters, the almost primordial cypress swamp known as **Dragon Run**. This brackish stream, deemed one of the most pristine bodies of water in all of Virginia, is well worth exploring by canoe or kayak for its exotic beauty.

Queens Creek

Back on the Piankatank, this beautiful tributary was off limits to boats drawing more than 3 feet for some time, but since ❼ **Queens Creek** was dredged in 2010, vessels are assured—at least for now—a minimum of 5 feet, according to the local TowBoatU.S. captain. The channel also has new nav aids, but remains narrow, so caution is still advised. You can call the TowBoatU.S. base at Gwynn's Island for the latest conditions (804-815-8907).

As you seek out Queens Creek, Stingray Point Light atop its spider platform at the mouth of the Piankatank River can be seen easily whether you are arriving from the north or south. From the south, you will enter the channel about two and a half miles from green "1". That navigation marker is more than a mile farther out into the Bay than Stingray Point Light, but would be the preferred mark for visitors arriving from the Eastern Shore. Hills Bay and the entrance to Queens Creek lie just ahead as you pass Stove Point to starboard.

Unlike those on many creeks you visit, homes along

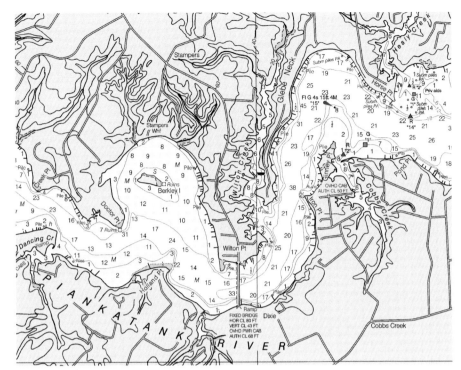

Cobbs and Wilton Creeks and Berkley Island; from NOAA Chart 12235—
not to be used for navigation.

Piankatank River, and a swing bridge connects the island's western tip to the mainland. ❽ **Milford Haven** is the bay-like body of water between the two land masses, offering a long fetch of quiet waters. Every summer the island population swells as vacationers come to enjoy its boating and fishing opportunities. Hugh Gwynn and his family were the first English settlers here in 1642 after moving from Jamestown.

A note on the name: You'll find "Gwynn" Island on some charts, but "Gwynn's" and "Gwynns" Island on others. Many years ago, this guide and sister magazine polled the island's residents. They preferred Gwynn's hands down, and so we have always deferred to their wishes.

It's fairly easy to enter Milford Haven through **Hills Bay**, its northwest entrance. From flashing red "8" and red nun "8A" that guard the southeast tip of the Stove Point Neck bar, turn south and head for the bay's first entrance mark, green "1", located a mile and a quarter south. From that point a series of navigational aids will lead you through the swing bridge (vertical clearance 12 feet), which opens on request. (Hail the bridge tender on channel 13 or call 804-725-2853.) Boats use the north side of the swing span going both ways.

The current steel swing bridge was built in 1939. The tender works around the clock out of an unusual, small house attached to the top of the bridge. It is considered one of the busiest drawbridges in Virginia.

Most boats that anchor here do so between "5" and "6" outside the channel on the north side. You can also follow the channel northeast past Callis Wharf and halfway to red daymark "8", then slip up into **Edwards Creek**. Many workboats moor here, but there's plenty of room to drop a hook with security. Unless there's wind from the northeast quadrant, **Lanes Creek**, across the main Milford Haven channel from

the shoreline of Queens Creek are farther apart and many sit atop grassy knolls. There are many small piers with vessels of all sizes and descriptions moored to them. The sandy beach immediately to starboard inside the last two daymarks carries 5 feet to the shore and is likely to be filled with children and their parents picnicking and frolicking in the water. This area is prime gunkholing for powerboats.

Upstream to port is Queens Creek Marina, which welcomes transients as space permits. Boaters not seeking the full services of a larger marina, will find plenty to enjoy here, including clean bath houses, a picnic area and a cozy club house in pleasant, quiet surrounds.

There is an anchorage just east of a small peninsula between **Kenney Creek** and a small creek without a name. The bottom is mud and your anchor should set well in 6 feet of water. From here, it's easy to occupy a couple of hours in your dinghy traveling the shoreline and two creeks that empty into Queens Creek from the north.

Both Kenney Creek and the other, unnamed one seem to have 5 feet of water all the way to their ends. Trees overhang the water at the shoreline.

The music of nature's musicians in the trees will sweeten your anchorage. Listen for the hoot of an owl somewhere in the distance and the call of Chuck-will's-widow, as the only lights you see are the stars overhead and the reflections on the water of a few house lights under the canopy of trees surrounding them.

Milford Haven

Gwynn's Island sits at the southern side of the mouth of the

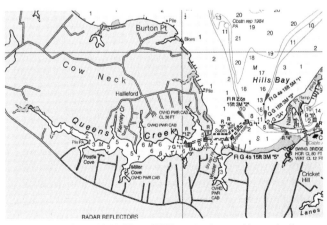

Queens Creek; from NOAA Chart 12235—not to be used for navigation.

Milford Haven continued

Edwards Creek, offers a nice spot to tuck in.

The Narrows Marina is just north of the bridge. If you decide to stay at one of the marina's slips, there are two important things to keep in mind. The first is that a strong current flows perpendicular to the line of slips. The second thing to note is that daymark "4", directly across the marina, marks 1- to 2-foot depths. Ask the limits of the navigable channel when you check in.

The Milford Haven Coast Guard Station sits at the south side of the bridge, across from the Narrows Marina, and will respond to boaters for advice on local conditions (channel 16 or 804-725-3732).

The island has a restaurant, Seabreeze, just inside the bridge near the public landing. For provisions, the Island Market and Deli is a pleasant walk away, less than a mile down the main road (Route 633) from the restaurant.

The GWYNN'S ISLAND MUSEUM (*gwynnsislandmuseum.org*) is housed in an old schoolhouse on Route 633, about a mile from the bridge and a little beyond the market. It contains Native American and Colonial-era artifacts unearthed from the mud and rock crevices along the shore. Watermen who have dredged up such rare items as a whale's vertebrae and a mastadon tooth are contributing their finds to the collection.

Many visitors to the area find entertainment at an unassuming country-music hall about two miles into the mainland. Talented area musicians perform for "Virginia's Lil' Ole Opry" every other Saturday night at Donk's Theater (*www.donkstheater.com*), located in an old movie theater in Hudgins. There's no local taxi service, however, so you'll need to check with a marina for transportation options.

Tales of Tidewater hospitality abound in these parts. One cruiser reported that after his electric fuel pump failed with no spare on board, he was met in Hills Bay just between Stove Point and Cherry Point by a very accommodating mechanic, who towed him into the Narrows Marina. The marina did not have the pump in stock, however, so the same mechanic drove "up-town" to secure the part, then installed it late on a Friday afternoon well after closing time.

At the eastern end of Gwynn's Island is another entrance to Milford Haven from the Bay through the natural gap between Gwynn's Island and its small neighbor to the south, Rigby Island. Appropriately called the **Hole in the**

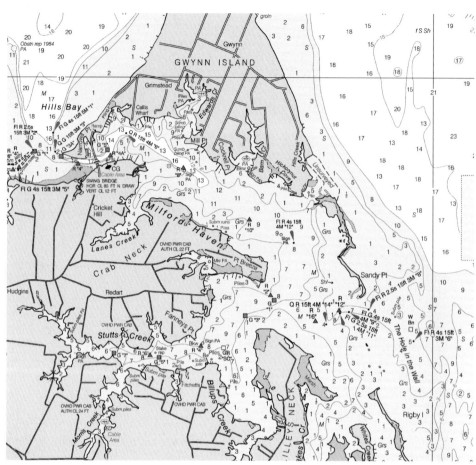

Milford Haven; from NOAA Chart 12235—*not to be used for navigation.*

Wall, this entrance is unusual indeed. A long and narrow channel twists and turns its way in and out among several marshy 2- and 3-foot shoals and sand bars. This entrance is about five miles shorter than going around the northern tip and down through Hills Bay and the swing bridge, but it's much trickier and more shallow—with as little as 3 feet of water at low tide.

From the Bay side, the entrance is easy to find, marked by flashing green "1MH" about 4 miles offshore and then a changing series of markers indicating the best water through the shoals.

Hole in the Wall gets a good bit of use by watermen, but it isn't the recommended entrance for cruisers. The best time to take a chance is on midtide with the water rising. Coming in through Hole in the Wall the numbers go from "3" up to "16" and then down from "12" to "4A" and "5" at the bridge. Look at your chart carefully. Be sure to have a new one, and for areas like Hole in the Wall, get NOAA chart 12235.

Consider a stop at Callis Wharf, which once was a bustling steamboat stop. Today the wharf is falling into disrepair, but remains an interesting spot to visit.

From Callis Wharf, follow the marked channel down to the entrance of **Stutts Creek**. You will note that if you enter through Hole in the Wall the marks switch over beyond "16"—that is, from that point on through the drawbridge you leave the red marks to port as if you were leaving a harbor.

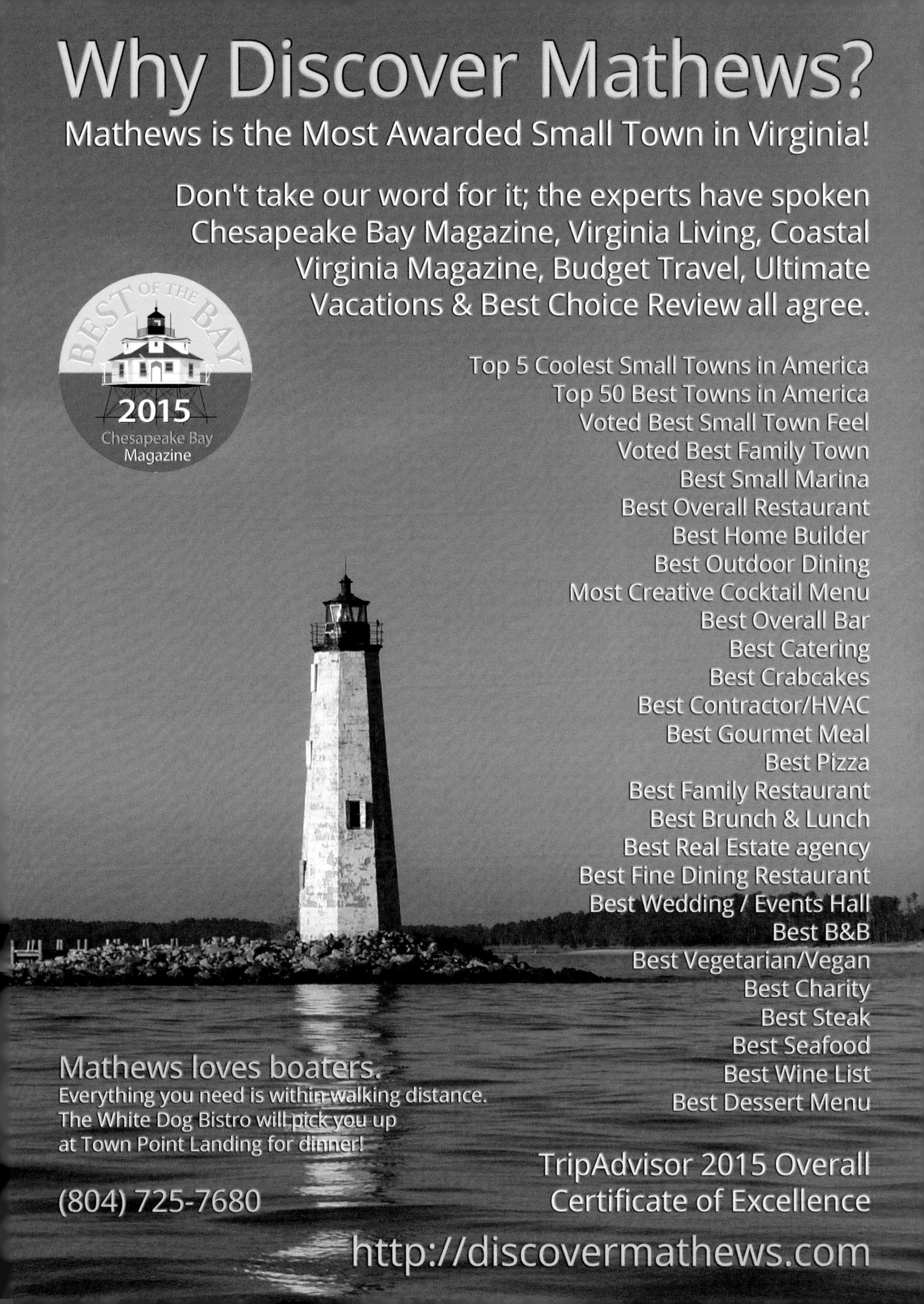

Why Discover Mathews?
Mathews is the Most Awarded Small Town in Virginia!

Don't take our word for it; the experts have spoken
Chesapeake Bay Magazine, Virginia Living, Coastal
Virginia Magazine, Budget Travel, Ultimate
Vacations & Best Choice Review all agree.

2015 Chesapeake Bay Magazine

Top 5 Coolest Small Towns in America
Top 50 Best Towns in America
Voted Best Small Town Feel
Voted Best Family Town
Best Small Marina
Best Overall Restaurant
Best Home Builder
Best Outdoor Dining
Most Creative Cocktail Menu
Best Overall Bar
Best Catering
Best Crabcakes
Best Contractor/HVAC
Best Gourmet Meal
Best Pizza
Best Family Restaurant
Best Brunch & Lunch
Best Real Estate agency
Best Fine Dining Restaurant
Best Wedding / Events Hall
Best B&B
Best Vegetarian/Vegan
Best Charity
Best Steak
Best Seafood
Best Wine List
Best Dessert Menu

Mathews loves boaters.
Everything you need is within walking distance.
The White Dog Bistro will pick you up
at Town Point Landing for dinner!

(804) 725-7680

TripAdvisor 2015 Overall
Certificate of Excellence

http://discovermathews.com

Milford Haven *continued*

The entrance to Stutts Creek is clearly marked by red and green daymarks appearing as a gateway to the beautiful creek inside. The creek is well marked and carries 7 feet or better all the way to the last marker. There are many nice anchorages either between Point Breeze and Fanneys Point or up inside the creek itself.

The first cove to starboard after Point Breeze is inviting, with few signs of civilization; the presence of many oyster stakes and crab pots in this area, however, are daunting and can keep you from getting very far out of Stutts Creek's open main channel.

To port lies **Billups Creek**. This can be a good choice for a summer night's anchorage, though the channel is a bit narrow going in, and the marshes along its banks have the potential of harboring hungry insects, but cruisers have reported finding few pests and good holding. In early spring or fall, you can safely head upstream to anchor in 5 feet of water in the cove just west of Fanneys Point.

At the Mathews Yacht Club, beyond red daymark "6", a small private marina facility has ice and gas available.

On its upper reaches the creek's shores are heavily wooded and the deep water is well protected for anchoring—a serene setting. Older homes dot the shore on both sides of the creek, and development on the south shore blends with the natural setting.

Leaving Stutts Creek, "16" marks the beginning of the tricky Hole in the Wall channel. To exit from here and go into the Bay, honor "14" as you make the turn for "12" and "11". In this area, charted depths range from 4 to 8 feet, with

Mobjack Bay

Mobjack (*MAHB-jack*) **Bay** is one of the most beautiful bays on the whole of the Chesapeake. Here the air seems sweeter, perfumed by surrounding farmland and marsh. Here the sailing is special and the rivers that empty into it beautiful. Time seems to have stopped as you cruise upriver into history. The bay opens up to the northwest on Virginia's Middle Neck, between the Rappahannock and the York rivers. Its four major tributaries—the East, North, Ware and Severn rivers—run into quiet, wooded countryside, past small fishing villages, well-manicured farms and gracious former plantations. There are no major cities and only a handful of marinas. What you *will* find are gunkholes galore, secure and secluded anchorages, abundant wildlife and constant reminders of the past.

On the western side of its mouth, the **Guinea Marshes**—the islands at the easternmost part of Guinea Neck—present an indistinct shoreline. The eastern side of Mobjack Bay's mouth is marked by lighted aids "2" and "4", south of the decommissioned New Point Comfort Light. This white sandstone landmark, completed in 1805 and the third oldest Chesapeake lighthouse still standing, is visible for miles and a welcoming sight for visitors to Mobjack Bay. It was relit in 1999, but is not an aid to navigation, so don't confuse these at night. "2" is a red-flashing 20-foot high mark nearly a mile southeast of the tower; "4" is a 15-foot red flasher about one-half mile to the southwest.

As you cruise past the tall tower, all of Mobjack Bay spreads out before you—a large body of water some 7 miles in length and at its broadest width measuring about 4 miles.

● On Premises
➤ Nearby

Mobjack Bay & Horn Harbor

	MLW	Overnight Slips	Gas	Diesel	Propane	Electric	Showers	Laundry	Restaurant	Lodging	Pool	Pump-out	Ice	Groceries	Marine Supplies	Bait	Boat Repair	Haul-out Services	Launch Ramp	Wi-Fi	Other
Compass Marina Mobjack Bay/East R. 804-363-6811; www.compassmarina.com	8'	●				●	●	●				●								●	In-slip pump-out, Wi-Fi, cottage, floating docks
Holiday Marina Mobjack Bay/Severn R./Rowes Cr. 804-642-2528	3.5'-4'		●	●	➤	●	●	➤					●	➤	●		●	●	●		60-ton lift and forklift
Horn Harbor Marina Horn Harbor/north of Mobjack Bay 804-725-3223; www.hornharbormarina.com	5'	●	●	●		●	●				●	●	➤	●		●	●	●			Full-service yard, friendly, quiet, sheltered
Marina on Davis Creek Mobjack Bay/Davis Cr. 804-725-3343	5'	●	●	●	➤	●	●	●	➤	➤	➤		●	➤	➤	➤	➤	➤		●	➤ non-ethanol gas, diesel on demand w/cash or check
Mobjack Bay Marina, Inc Mobjack Bay/North R./Blackwater Cr. 804-725-7245 or 804-695-4848	6'	●	●	●	➤	●	●	●	➤	➤	➤		●	●	●	➤	●	●	●	●	Picnic area; full service boatyard, pet friendly, mom&pop marina
Severn Yachting Center Mobjack Bay/Severn R./Willets Creek 804-642-6969; www.severnyachtingcenter.com	7'	●	●	●	➤	●	●	●	➤	➤	●	●	●	➤	●		●	●	➤	●	Large yacht capacity, fixed; floating slips, 75-ton lift
Zimmerman Marine Mobjack Bay/East R. 804-725-3440; www.zimmermanmarine.com	6'	●		●		●	●			➤	➤		●	➤	➤	➤	●	●		●	Boatyard, all repairs, custom boatbuilders

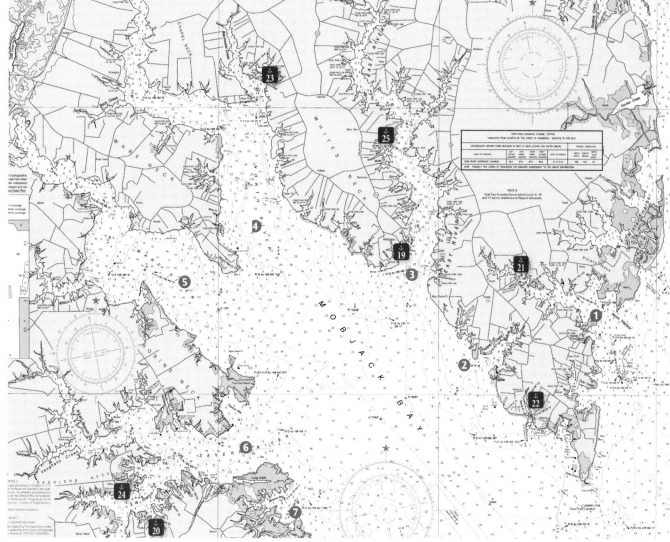

Mobjack Bay; from NOAA Chart 12238—not to be used for navigation.

If you're entering at night, be mindful of the fish traps that are often found just outside of the bay's mouth.

When choosing an anchorage on still nights, remember those ubiquitous Mobjack Bay marshes and the mosquitoes and flies that live in them, even into early fall. On the other hand, the jellyfish go away in September, dolphins and pelicans are common companions here, and loons in their winter plumage visit in the fall. (Also expect to see numerous gannets making spectacular dives into the waters off Mobjack Bay in the spring.) The smell of giant magnolias mingles with the salt breezes of the nearby ocean. You, too, will be delighted with the quiet of the area.

Horn Harbor

New Point Comfort Lighthouse sits at the tip of a peninsula bounded on the south by Mobjack Bay and the north by **❶ Horn Harbor**. This Horn Harbor (not to be confused with the snug tributary of the same name on the upper reach of the Great Wicomico) is accessible to craft with a 5-foot draft

or less. Because of frequent changes here, it's a good idea to seek navigation advice—and the folks at Horn Harbor Marina will be happy to oblige.

The entrance marks are lighted aids and clearly visible, day and night. You begin to enter Horn Harbor at Morse A "HH" below Wolftrap Light, just above New Point Comfort. The well-marked dredged channel carries about 6 feet at normal low tide. It starts at "HH", which stands 19 feet tall and at night signals the Morse letter "A" (• —). The next two sets of daymarks are probably the most important since they mark the lower portion of the shallow bar that separates the Bay from Horn Harbor. From "HH", head west toward flashing red "2" and then toward the two sets of marks—green "3" and red "4", then green "5" and red "6"—typically a troublesome spot. A lot of boaters report being snagged here. From there, turn north to green "7" and then "7A". Beyond that, locals advise turning northwest toward red "8" fairly soon to avoid a shoal that extends from "8".

Once clear, head for red "10", where the channel takes a hard turn to port and is well marked. From there you'll look

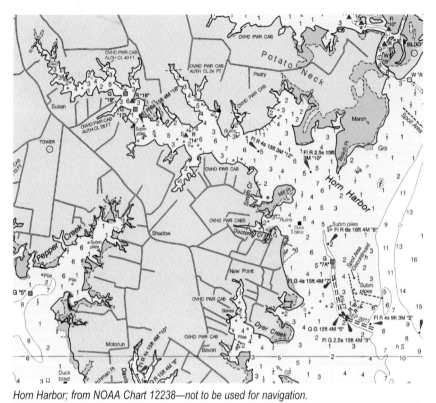

Horn Harbor; from NOAA Chart 12238—not to be used for navigation.

Horn Harbor *continued*

upstream to the crossroads community of **Port Haywood**.

Between "14" and "16", stakes are sometimes present to help identify the center of the channel. The shallowest depths here are reported to be around 5 1/2 feet, but only for a short distance. From "16" you will carry about 6 feet all the way to the Horn Harbor Marina just beyond the last daymark, green "19". Transients will find slips (with dockside depths of 5 to 12 feet), gas and diesel, repair service and a warm welcome here.

If your boat draws less than 4 feet, you can find some really secluded anchorages beyond the marina in the lovely and scenic upper reaches of Horn Harbor. There is 7 feet of water on the south side of the channel between "18" and

"19", where holding ground is excellent—a composition of hard mud and sand.

As you explore upper Horn Harbor you'll find a few homes along the shoreline, but not a lot of boat traffic. You'll be able to sit back and listen to the peaceful sounds of nature.

Davis and Pepper Creeks

❷ **Davis Creek** is about a 1 1/2 miles past New Point Comfort on the northern shore of Mobjack Bay. This small creek is home to an active fleet of workboats. Although there appears to be room to drop a hook inside, it is really too confined to allow enough anchor scope for the 10-foot (or more) water depth in the main basin (especially since its rather silty bottom provides a poor holding ground). But as an emergency stopover or harbor of refuge, Davis Creek's proximity to the Bay is important to boaters.

Green "1", a 15-foot mark, denotes the entrance to Davis Creek. The channel is straightforward but remarkably narrow and shallow. NOAA gives the channel dimensions as 1/2 foot by 80 feet, sounded in 2009, with the east half of the channel 4 1/2 feet and the

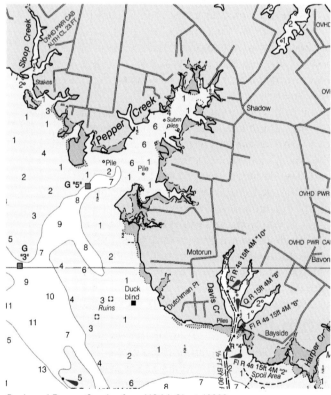

Davis and Pepper Creeks; from NOAA Chart 12238— not to be used for navigation.

Mobjack Bay Marina

BEST OF THE BAY 2015

Open Slips Available • Full Service Marina & Boatyard

20 Ton Railway, VALVTECT Non–Ethanol Gas & Diesel

454 Marina Rd., North, VA • 804–725–7245

804–695–4848 • Lat: 37° 25′ 40″ Lon: -76° 24′ 3″

MobjackBayMarina.com

west half only 1/2 foot.

About halfway up the left branch is Marina on Davis Creek, a facility that caters mostly to watermen and recreational anglers. Here you can obtain gas and diesel.

The activity in Davis Creek tends to be brisk in the early morning hours as the workboats head out for the day's catch. There's an authentic charm to the spot as well as some friendly folks. Longtime cruisers fondly remember a first visit to Davis Creek years ago when they received permission to tie up to a private bulkhead to spend the night. The bulkhead's owner, Morris Snow, ran a dredge boat out past the Bridge-Tunnel at the mouth of the Chesapeake Bay, where he fished for horseshoe crabs to be sold as eel bait.

North of Davis Creek, larger **Pepper Creek** is marked by "2P" about 1 1/4 mile south of its mouth. After green "3" and "5", the channel is unmarked. The creek carries 4 feet and a little more. It's used mainly by local watermen. (PVC poles inside the entrance denote an oyster bottom.)

Pepper Creek is exposed to the southwest. If you choose to explore its waters, you may stumble on a bit of local history. A half-mile inside the creek, an old wooden building is all that remains of the marine railway founded by legendary area boatbuilder L.R. (Lennie) Smith.

East River

Though the smallest of Mobjack Bay's four major tributaries, the ❸ **East River** is sure to be a favorite. The approach across Mobjack Bay is generally accessible, but stay to the center and mind the shoals on both sides. Boaters report that shoaling has extended beyond R "2".

The once bustling village of ❸ᵃ **Mobjack** is on the west side of the entrance. The most prominent feature of this quiet community is the beautiful church, sparkling in the afternoon sun, a striking scene as you enter the East River. At green "5", a channel (8 feet MLW) leads to Compass Marina, tucked in a cove to port. This jewel-box facility offers slips for transients, in-slip pump-outs, bathhouse and laundry.

The crumbling remains of Diggs Wharf to starboard will remind you that regular steamboat lines once connected this beautiful bay and its villages with Baltimore and Norfolk. Steamboats played a vital part of late 19th-century life here, providing essential transportation of goods and people.

A popular anchoring spot for cruisers is located off the channel just north of green "7" near Sharp Point in 8 feet of water. You can anchor on the other side of the river here, too, depending on what kind of protection you need.

The charts show that ❸ᵇ **Tabbs Creek** on the

eastern shore has enough water for most cruising boats. The mouth carries 7 feet, which drops quickly to 6 and 5 feet. You should find the deepest water along the north shore.

A couple of miles upstream of the community of Mobjack is a prominent landmark on the eastern shore at the mouth of ❸ᶜ **Weston Creek**. This is the stately, columned Poplar Grove manor, birthplace of Civil War heroine Sally Tompkins. The founder of a military hospital that saved the lives of a remarkable 95 percent of its patients, "Captain

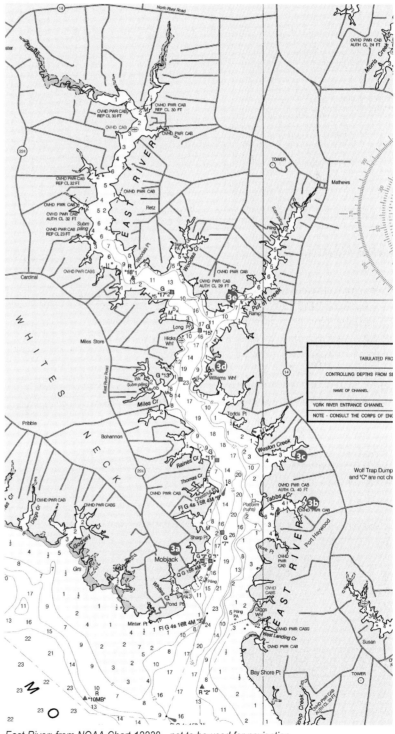

East River; from NOAA Chart 12238—not to be used for navigation.

East River continued

Sally" was believed to be the only woman commissioned as an officer in the Confederate army. Poplar Grove features one of the few remaining tide mills on the Bay. Built in 1774 and now restored, the small wooden building with its huge waterwheel sits quietly at the water's edge these days, but well into the 1900s it used the tidal flow to grind grain.

Farther upstream to port just past green "13" is Zimmerman Marine, a full-service yard for yacht repairs, custom yacht building and brokerage. This bustling yard was originally owned and operated by Tom Colvin, who designed and built several classes of steel sailboats here. It has recently expanded its operations to Deltaville and Herrington Harbor, as well as Southport, N.C. The facility does not accommodate transient boaters, however.

Opposite Zimmerman, to starboard, is **3d** **Williams Wharf Landing.** In other days, this was a major steamboat stop and one of the busiest seafood docks in the area. Now the Mathews County Land Conservancy has developed a facility for motorless boats. Ongoing activities include crew and rowing lessons and regattas, canoe/kayak excursions, small sailboat racing and performances on a small floating stage. What was once a boatyard dating to the Revolutionary War now

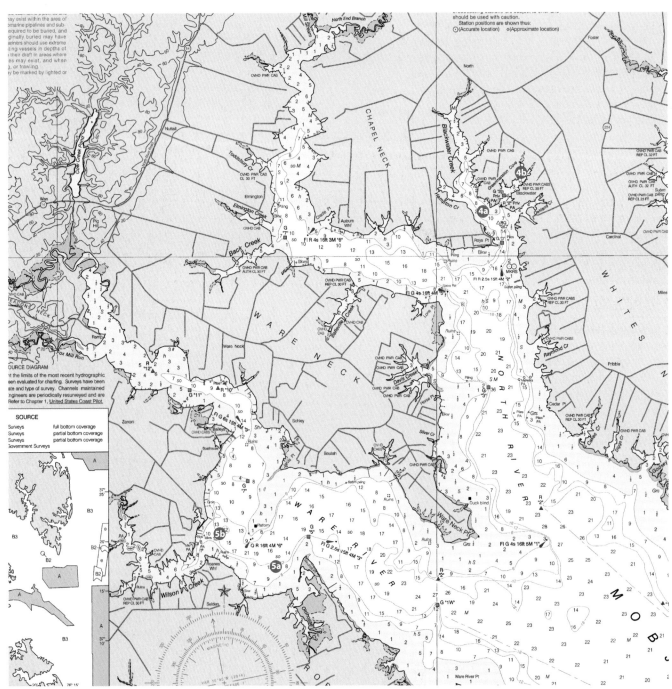

North and Ware Rivers; from NOAA Chart 12238—not to be used for navigation.

boasts an award-winning crew team and two floating public docks for launching boats.

The charts indicate a wreck a half-mile or so beyond, between Hicks Wharf and Long Point. These are the remains of the *Munnatawket*, the last steamboat on the East River and probably to Mobjack. She burned in the summer of 1935, marking the end of an era.

Opposite Long Point is the entrance to **3e** **Put In Creek** (often called "Puddin' Creek" locally). You may see stakes at a slight bend where shoals are encroaching from port. Just follow the chart, watch your depths and stay in the middle.

Put In Creek has modest homes with private piers and a feeling of wooded intimacy. There is a launch ramp, Town Point Landing, on the starboard shore; if you anchor just above that, you shouldn't be bothered by boat traffic.

Unfortunately Put In Creek has silted in, making it impossible to dinghy all the way to the welcoming little town of **Mathews**. The shops, restaurants and museums there (including the MATHEWS MARITIME MUSEUM & FOUNDATION) are now only accessible to boaters who choose to hike or bike the two or three miles from Town Point Landing.

After Put In Creek, the main part of the East River narrows and becomes quite protected. Beyond Williams Wharf Landing the river is narrow enough to furnish a protected anchorage. In the summer, a little open area is usually welcome to gather a little evening breeze. The East River continues for some distance through beautiful countryside, carrying 9 feet or more for over a mile and at least 6 feet for another half mile or so. You can anchor near the mouth of any of dozen little coves along the way.

North River

The **4** **North River**, which empties into the head of Mobjack Bay, is broad, but has some good-size shoals (well marked) along its first several miles. Just watch the marks carefully. The first, flashing red "1" is nearly a mile offshore of Ware Neck Point. Once you are inside the mouth of the river, the marks are easy to follow.

There are no notable protected anchorages here until you reach **4a** **Blackwater Creek,** about three miles upstream. Beautiful homes line the banks, with plenty of trees and some high ground. As the North River's largest tributary, it's the only one with enough water to allow deeper draft vessels to explore.

A half-mile up the creek to starboard is **4b** **Greenmansion Cove**. Mobjack Bay Marina is just inside the mouth of the cove on the right as you go in. If you enter this tributary after passing right of red-and-green daymark "GC", it will give you the best approach. Favor the mouth's right side to avoid a shoal encroaching from the west. Inside, shoaling is also reported around daymark "2". Once in, if you're looking for supplies and ice, circle to the left of the main dock, then take a right to tie up. For fuel, go down the right side of the main dock, staying close to the docks till you get to the boathouse at the end of the pier. Then swing to starboard to the fuel pumps (gas and diesel). Depth along the face dock is about 5 feet.

Greenmansion Cove was named for a plantation on the north bank of the cove. During its prime it must have been something—two stories plus dormer windows in the attic, four chimneys, a large back porch facing the water and a long pier with a gazebo at the end.

While there is room to anchor in Greenmansion Cove, some cruisers will prefer to anchor out in Blackwater Creek. The whole creek is well protected, with deep water almost to the end. A popular anchorage is around the 7-foot marks on your chart (note that the mud bottom is very soft).

The North River veers westerly at the intersection of Blackwater Creek, running another two miles to Cradle Point, where it turns northward once more. This stretch of the river is impressive and attractive, with beautiful homes and farms. Many of the homes are quite large, done in a style that has not diminished the wooded shoreline's beauty. On the western shore, just above the elbow of the turn, is Elmington, one of the loveliest estates on the Bay.

Ware River

Another broad, beautiful waterway is the **5** **Ware River**, which runs northwest from Mobjack Bay. Even in bad weather and poor visibility, the river's marks are easily followed.

About halfway up the river, a long 1-foot shoal projects from the starboard shore at Jarvis Point. There is good protected anchorage in the bight between Windmill Point and the ruins of Roanes Wharf (another former steamboat landing). In the spot just to the west of **5a** **Oldhouse Creek** in 7 to 9 feet of water there's quite a bit of room and good protection from the south and southeast.

There is a duck blind on the Jarvis Point shoal surrounded by a low-lying grassy beach. In mist and rain it takes on the look of the Civil War ship *Monitor*, an eerie apparition in the half-gloom of twilight.

Just past Roanes Wharf is **5b** **Wilson Creek**, a delightful spot to anchor and spend the night. On the chart, the entrance might deter visitors because of its narrow channel and lack of markers. It's possible to feel your way in by hugging the docks along the starboard side; more recently, cruisers have reported private aids outlining the port side as well. Water depths here are at least 6 feet, and the channel appears wide enough for almost any boat.

Inside Wilson Creek you'll find a number of homes and private piers (no commercial facilities). The scene is that of a comfortable little village—peaceful and intimate with well-cared-for lawns, cozy wooded areas and majestic magnolias. It has a mix of pleasure and workboats. As an anchorage, Wilson Creek is charming and welcoming.

When exploring the Ware River north of Roanes Wharf (opposite "6"), be aware of the 4-foot shoal mid-river, west of Jarvis Point. A green daymark on its eastern side suggests the safer route. You may find this shoal outlined with sticks, planted by those with local knowledge.

Use extreme caution going from "7" to "9". A 1-foot shoal makes out from the east side, and the shoal on the west side, south of marker "9", extends farther east than is apparent on

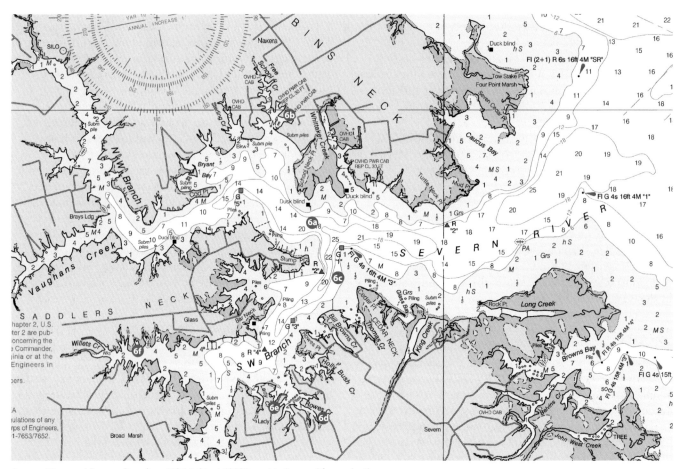

Severn River and Browns Bay; from NOAA Chart 12238—not to be used for navigation.

Severn River *continued*

the chart. Both shoals often are identified with "danger" signs.

To starboard at **Schley** is the commercial fuel dock of J. C. Brown and Company. Although the water is pretty shallow here, the long fuel dock has 10 feet of water on its south side— a reminder of the days when gas barges were regular visitors to the pier. This dock is for private use only, but visiting boaters who arrive on week days may find a congenial welcome.

The Ware River carries 6 feet of water or more for another mile or so, with no protected anchorages but with some beautiful homes scattered along a wooded shoreline somewhat higher than that of the lower Mobjack area. Over the years, the Ware has been a favorite spot for small one-design racing, and few sights are lovelier than a flock of sails on the Ware.

Severn River

Along the southwestern shore of Mobjack Bay, about due west of New Point Comfort, lies the ⑥ **Severn River**. Its entrance is broad and inviting. While the other three rivers are densely wooded, the Severn is more low-lying with extensive marshes.

A couple miles from its mouth, the Severn divides into the Northwest and the Southwest branches. Along the ⑥ᵃ **Northwest Branch** is a favorite anchorage just inside the arm

of School Neck Point, well sheltered to the north. This is a great place to ride out a northeaster, close to the northeast shore behind a stand of trees on higher ground. If the bad news here is a heavy mosquito population, the good news is that there is no major land mass to cut down any light breeze that might be stirring on a hot summer evening.

To stay in the deepest water, put your stern on the long pier on Stump Point and head due north toward the white fence at the house to the west of the entrance to ⑥ᵇ **Free School Creek**. Mind the shoal off School Neck Point. Free School Creek is a pleasant place to explore by dinghy.

Farther up the Northwest Branch, about the only choice you have is to anchor in the channel. Since there is plenty of room and little traffic, it would seem safe to do so. This whole branch has higher shores than the Southwest Branch, with some well-kept homes along the banks. There are no services on the Northwest Branch, but close to its head—accessible by dinghy—sits Warner Hall, the home of George Washington's grandparents. Now restored, the Inn at Warner Hall (800-331-2720) welcomes guests and serves elegant dinners Fridays and Saturdays.

The ⑥ᶜ **Southwest Branch** has a little more of a woodsy feel and a few modest homes. Don't be confused by the numbering of the marks at the fork. Lighted green "3" is a river mark; green daymark "1" marks the entrance to the Southwest Branch. There is a bit of shoaling to about 5 feet near red "2", but there's more than 20 feet of water approximately 100 feet from the mark.

On the right just past "2" is an open anchorage with plenty of water. On hot summer nights, it is open to breezes but has some shelter to the south and west where most thunderstorms materialize.

Red "4" is the last marker for the Southwest Branch itself. On the south shore the next marker, red "2", is for 6d **Rowes Creek**. A well-marked channel (be sure to stay in it) with about 6 feet of water leads to the small basin at Holiday Marina, which offers diesel fuel, ice, marine supplies and repair facilities. Depths at its fuel dock are 3 ½ to 4 feet.

You can also anchor just off 6e **Lady Creek** in 8 feet of water. Other anchorages are located farther upstream in a nice open stretch of water—a good choice on hot, calm nights.

Severn Yachting Center, offering overnight slips, fuel, pumpout, marine supplies and repairs, is located to starboard at the mouth of 6f **Willets Creek**.

Browns Bay

7 **Browns Bay** is a favorite stop for cruisers who want a place to get away from everyone. There's nothing here really to attract the crowds. Browns Bay does have a public dock, but it is used mostly by crab, oyster and fish boats to offload their catch. Cruisers are welcome to buy fresh catch,

but no overnight dockage is available here. If you choose to go in to the pier, follow the charted markers. Pass "4", the last mark, and turn right toward the pile shown on the chart. It is painted white. Treat the unmarked pile as a red mark—i.e., leave it to starboard going in. From the pile turn straight toward the dock. The approach has about 5 feet of water up to the dock, and there is at least that much along most of the pier. Shackleford Seafood operates a wholesale fish house next to the public pier.

A preferred anchorage with plenty of water and swinging room is located south of "4". Be sure to go as far south as your draft allows so that you will be clear of the workboats coming and going.

A word of caution: Don't go into Browns Bay in the summer if a calm night is expected; the mosquitoes will carry you away. The two points of land that form the bay are marsh. The bay is also exposed to the north and east and would not make a suitable anchorage if the wind is blowing from that quadrant.

On **John West Creek**, off the southern edge of Browns Bay, the chart shows TREE on the southern shore. There are several clumps of trees there, but no lone tree that stands out. It's most likely gone now, but it must have been one big tree to earn a spot on the chart. The creek's navigable water has gone over the years, as well, leaving it suitable only for shallow dinghies.

Bay Spotlight

The Final Battle

Every school kid knows that when Charles, Second Earl of Cornwallis finally surrendered his troops after an agonizing siege at Yorktown, the American Revolution was over and won. If they watched the movie *Revolution Revisited*, they would have seen Al Pacino send British regulars scrambling over the rocky boulder-strewn coastline that represented the beleaguered peninsula where York River touches the Bay. And technically, they've got it right (except for the boulders). Cornwallis was indeed pinned between American patriots and the deep blue sea. Too exhausted to fight his way out by land and abandoned by the British navy, Cornwallis thought it prudent to give up before winter settled in. On October 19, 1781 he waved the white flag, and the war was over.

But it really wasn't that simple. The Americans had luck and the French on their side, two factors that weighed heavily in favor of the American victory. Cornwallis hadn't exactly been abandoned by the British navy. Under the command of Admiral Thomas Graves,

said force had actually been hightailing it to the Chesapeake Bay in order to bolster British efforts and resupply the troops which had congregated in Yorktown in early August. They never made it.

Instead, they were met at the mouth of the Bay by a line of French ships commanded by Rear Admiral Francois J. P. de Grasse who proceeded to pound the Brits into oblivion. With six ships badly damaged, Graves turned for New York, leaving Cornwallis to his fate. The Battle of the Capes, as the ruckus came to be called, effectively snuffed any hopes Cornwallis might have had of vacating the Tidewater under more victorious circumstances.

Lower York River

While it may not offer as many gunkholing opportunities as Mobjack Bay, its northern neighbor, the **York River** has several of the same attributes—beautiful scenery and lots of history—and the added feature of a major destination (Yorktown) and more marinas.

In places, however, the York is as remote as any place on the Chesapeake. Marsh grasses glide by just a few feet away from your boat, while your depthsounder shows 10, 15, even 20 feet of water. Great blue herons and egrets perform their stiff-legged walk along the edge of the mud bank. Osprey and other birds, including the occasional bald eagle, wheel overhead. You feel truly alone.

Many boats visit the lower York River, often simply as a stopover on a longer cruise up or down the coast, some staying long enough to visit the nearby historic areas of Yorktown, Jamestown and Williamsburg. Visitors to the area rarely go upriver. Perhaps they don't know the charm of the area, or perhaps they are fearful of shallow water. They needn't worry. Deep-draft keel-boats and large powerboats can easily go up the York, although its main channel can be narrow in spots. After all, ships go to West Point at the head of the York to load cargo, and there is ample depth in the Pamunkey and Mattaponi rivers for any pleasure boat. The advantage to having a shallow-draft boat is having other cruising opportunities along the way and fewer worries about shallow anchorages.

What the upper York, the Pamunkey and Mattaponi lack however, are facilities. There are, in fact, none. So a trip upriver is all about anchoring out—and sometimes you just have to make it up as you go along. Ah, cruising at its purest.

At its mouth, however, the York has several tributaries on each shore with full-service marinas. Large marinas in Sarah Creek and the Perrin River cater extensively to visiting boats. There are also good marinas in the York's Back and Wormley creeks and on the Poquoson River, all within easy reach of Yorktown. All of these tributaries, other than Wormley Creek, also have anchorage areas.

Heading from the north or south, look for red "14", a gong, part way up the entrance channel to the York River. The channel is easily followed from there.

If you are approaching the York from the north, you may wish to take the shortcut across the York Spit. About a mile south-southeast of the Guinea Marshes there is a natural channel that cuts across the 3-foot-plus York Spit. The opening is defined at its narrowest point by flashing green "3", followed by daymarks "2" and "1" in the York River. This **Swash Channel** shortcut in 5 to 7 feet of water will save a couple of miles.

Perrin River

Flashing red-green "PR" in the middle of the York River identifies the ❶ **Perrin River** on the north shore. The approach to the Perrin is well marked and very easy to follow. The entrance

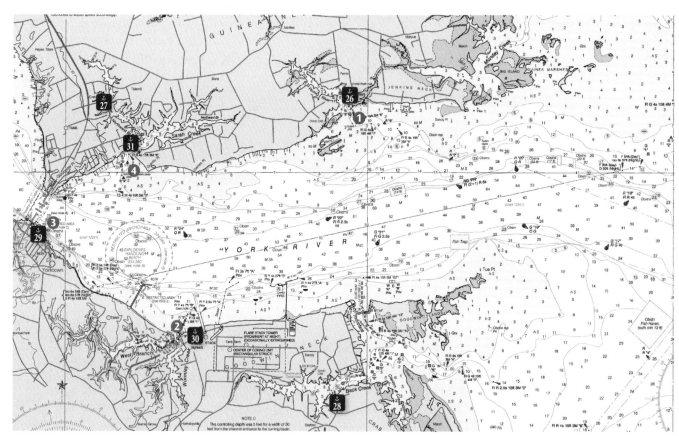

Lower York River River; from NOAA Chart 12238—not to be used for navigation.

is three-quarters of a mile northwest of the nearby red "2". Respect this mark on the north edge of the York River ship channel; it stands sentinel to a large sand bar south of Jenkins Neck. Note the fish traps which line the lower York River; clearing them is no problem if you stay in the marked channel.

Once clear of red "2" you will quickly spot "4" and daymark "6" in the entrance to the Perrin River to starboard. These aids are well placed and provide the visiting cruiser with the first glimpse of the natural beauty of this Tidewater estuary. There is 7 to 10 feet of water in the channel, but adhere to it because locals warn that it shoals quickly to the sides.

Marker "7" warns mariners of a large sand bar to port. Powerboaters may be able to traverse the bar, but there isn't enough water there for sailors. If you love clamming, anchor just off the bar's southern point and you may be able to fill a bucket with some of the southern Bay's succulent clams.

Locals advise boaters to bear hard to starboard after red "8" to avoid a grounding by going straight. After "9", stay in the middle of the channel past the crab docks to starboard. As you pass them you become aware of a widening in the river farther up. Once clear of them you will see green daymark "11" as well as yachts of all sizes at the marina about 200 yards above the crab docks.

Crown Pointe Marina, a full-service facility on the Perrin River and home of the Colonial Yacht Club, is located just off the York River about 5½ miles by water from Yorktown. Transients are welcome (slips have up to 7 feet of water);

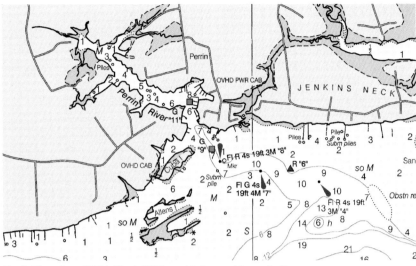

Perrin River; from NOAA Chart 12238—not to be used for navigation.

there's gas and diesel fuel, pump-out facilities, a ship's store, showers, laundry facilities and a service yard as well.

If you want to anchor out, turn to port just past green "11" to travel up a small branch of the river. If you stay in the middle, you'll carry 4 feet for about a half mile.

Wormley Creek

❷ **Wormley Creek** is the forgotten harbor on the lower York River. It competes for visitors with Sarah Creek and the Perrin River, both with well-known marinas. Wormley Creek is in the shadow (literally) of a BP oil refinery and a major Dominion Power Company generating plant. To the first-time visitor, it is all too easy to go across the York

● *On Premises*
➤ *Nearby*

	MLW	Overnight Slips	Gas	Diesel	Propane	Electric	Showers	Laundry	Restaurant	Lodging	Pool	Pump-out	Ice	Groceries	Marine Supplies	Bait	Boat Repair	Haul-out Services	Launch Ramp	Wi-Fi	Other
York River & Back Creek																					
Crown Pointe Marina York R./Perrin R. 804-642-6177; www.crownpointemarina.com	7'	●	●	●	➤	●	●	●	➤	➤	●	●	●	●	●	●	●	●	●	●	Non-Ethanol fuel, gas grills, picnic porch, free Wi-Fi
Jordan Marine Service York R./Sarah Cr./Northwest Branch 804-642-4360	4'-6'	➤	➤	➤	➤	●	●		➤	➤		➤	➤	●			●	●			100-ton rail, 60-ton lift, glass work, carpentry
Mills Marina Back Cr. 757-898-4411; www.millsmarina.com	7'	●				●	●	●	➤		➤		●	●	●	●			●	●	Owner lives on premises
Riverwalk Landing Marina York R./Yorktown 757-890-3800; www.riverwalklanding.com	30'	●	➤	➤	➤	●	●	●	●	➤	●	●	➤	➤	➤	➤	➤	➤	➤	➤	Free transportation to historic sites; moorings
Wormley Creek Marina York R./Wormley Cr. 757-898-5060; www.wormleycreekmarina.com	6'	●	●	●		●	●	●	➤	➤	➤		●	●	●	●	●	●	●	➤	Crane, 37.5 ton lift, wood & F/G repairs
York River Yacht Haven York R./Sarah Cr. 804-642-2156; www.yryh.net	8'	●	●	●	●	➤	●	●	●	➤	●	●	●	➤	●	●	➤	●	●	➤	●	Courtesy car; repairs, transport to Yorktown

Wormley Creek *continued*

to the known harbors. If you like places off the beaten path, your curiosity about Wormley Creek will be rewarded with the discovery of a new cruising destination. The skyline is dominated by the generating station's smokestacks, but the plant coexists with cruisers well—it is easy to forget they are there.

The smokestacks offer excellent guideposts to the creek's entrance. They are visible easily from anywhere between Coleman Memorial Bridge up-river and the mouth of the York River. The entrance channel into Wormley Creek is thoroughly marked, beginning with a flashing green "1", and it carries at least 5 feet. Just inside the creek on the left is Wormley Creek Marina, across from the Coast Guard Training Center. Transient boaters will find overnight slips here in 6-foot depths and a small (one- to two-boat) basin nearby with about 6 feet as well. The marina offers fuel, a pump-out facility, showers, boat supplies and repair services.

The dredged channel turns to the right here, up the **West Branch**, and directly to starboard at the split is a beautiful, sandy shoreline whose point juts out into West Branch. There

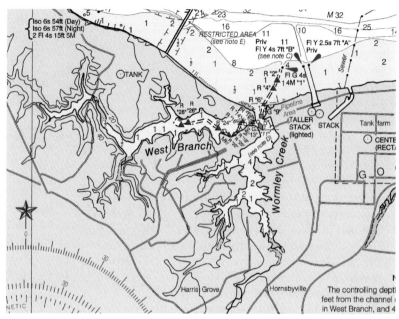

Wormley Creek; from NOAA Chart 12238—not to be used for navigation.

are plenty of daymarks here also. Follow them closely to avoid going aground, or poke along their perimeter and snuggle into an anchorage.

The channel of West Branch ends about a half-mile up-creek at the piers of the Coast Guard Training Center on the north side of the creek. The center, occupying 150 acres of this western peninsula at Wormley Creek's mouth, has a small flotilla of vessels used to teach the basics of seamanship to new recruits. The creek may be quiet during your visit, but it's apt to be quite noisy each morning when those diesels roar to life for daily training.

Though it looks narrow in places, there is plenty of room in the channel for two boats to pass. Remember, though, that the other boat may be under the command of a student, so give it plenty of room.

The main branch of Wormley Creek runs south from the marina and has depths of 3 to 4 feet. The scenery is beautiful, with high, heavily wooded tree-lined shores and quiet residential neighborhoods. There is a boat ramp near the marina, on the east side of the creek. Along most of the creek the power plant is hidden behind the trees.

Most visitors will find that their drafts will limit them to staying at the marina. There is very little room to anchor elsewhere if your draft is more than 3 feet. For shallow-draft boats, however, Wormley Creek does provide a back entrance to YORKTOWN BATTLEFIELD. Heading farther up the West Branch, is National Park Service land, wooded and wonderfully quiet.

Yorktown

Along the south shore of the York River, about 12 miles from York Spit Light and just upstream from Wormley Creek, a significant moment in American history took place. Buried in the mud along these banks are the rotting remains of the beleaguered British supply fleet, sunk during the last major

York River Yacht Haven is a full-service marina in Gloucester Point, VA, located at the mouth of Sarah Creek, opposite Yorktown. We are a family-oriented destination which is dedicated to providing the finest facilities and service to our fellow yachtsmen including deep water slips, full-service boatyard, marine store, new restaurant, pool and much more!

*NO COUNTY BOAT TAX

York River Yacht Haven
8109 Yacht Haven Rd. | Gloucester Pt., VA 23062
www.yorkriveryachthaven.com | **804-642-2156**

battle of the Revolutionary War fought here at Yorktown. As you move past these peaceful shores, it's hard to envision what must have been brutal and savage combat. Today a tall monument stands to commemorate the battle, and the YORKTOWN VICTORY CENTER educates tourists about the waning days of Colonial America.

The approach to ❸ **Historic Yorktown** takes you past the refinery and the Coast Guard Training Center pier on the river's southern shoreline to a point just below the Coleman Memorial Bridge. Here, visiting boaters can tie up for the day or overnight along the concrete floating piers of Riverwalk Landing, the modern marina and retail center at the foot of Yorktown's Ballard Street. Its long, wide pier, with dockside depths ranging from 27 to 50 feet, greets visiting cruisers, as well as tall ships, tour boats and large recreational vessels. A second smaller pier is located between it and the Coleman Bridge to accommodate smaller craft. Mooring balls, east of the two piers, provide other options for visiting boaters. For mooring and dock information, hail the dockmaster on VHF or call 757-890-3370. Be aware that the current here can be daunting. But call the dockmaster and ask for help with your lines. They'll have you safely tied up in no time.

From the docks, the National Park Service's historical interpretive center and battlefield, as well as the village's refurbished homes, shops and restaurants, are a short walk from the marina. Besides various attractions and frequent events, visitors enjoy strolling the small sandy beach just below the new waterfront. A long lovely pathway runs along the river in both directions, giving you access to the FISHERMEN'S MUSEUM and the battlefields.

Sarah Creek

Occasionally, Riverwalk's exposure to wind and weather can make tying up at the marina there an uncertain proposition. (In fact, the Riverwalk dockmasters will be the first to send you off to better shelter.) In those cases, many boaters opt to enjoy the sights of Yorktown, then cross the river to overnight in ❹ **Sarah Creek**. Directly across the river from Yorktown, the entrance into Sarah Creek looks fairly straightforward according to the chart. But as you turn at the outer marker, flashing "2", it may not look all that clear. The marks appear to lead right up to the sandy shore, then stop. Forge

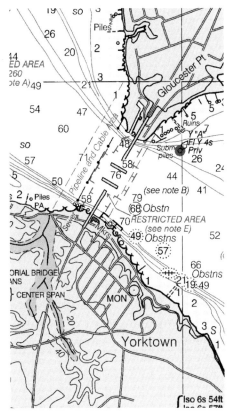

Yorktown; from NOAA Chart 12238—not to be used for navigation.

ahead. Locals advise keeping a boat-length off flashing red "8" to avoid the shoaling up to the mark. After that, the channel veers northeast to the narrow neck of the creek.

To port beyond green "9" is York River Yacht Haven, a full-service facility with a fine restaurant, River's Inn. Past the marina, the creek splits into two branches, both deserving further exploration. Upstream on the **Northwest Branch** is the venerable Jordan Marine Service, offering major marine repairs, though the depth here may be too shallow for deeper draft vessels.

Sarah Creek lies in a triangle of historic landmarks, and York River Yacht Haven can arrange transportation to the nearby YORKTOWN VICTORY CENTER, JAMESTOWN, COLONIAL WILLIAMSBURG and BUSCH GARDENS. They will also arrange rides to local restaurants, grocery stores and another nearby attraction, the VIRGINIA INSTITUTE OF MARINE SCIENCE (VIMS), whose visitor center has eight aquariums and an outdoor teaching marsh. The research facility welcomes visitors (weekdays only) and offers guided tours (804-684-7846).

Just off the marina's gas dock is a popular anchorage used by many area cruising and racing groups. Alternatively, you can proceed upstream on either the **Northwest** or **Northeast Branch** and find several small but appealing anchorages.

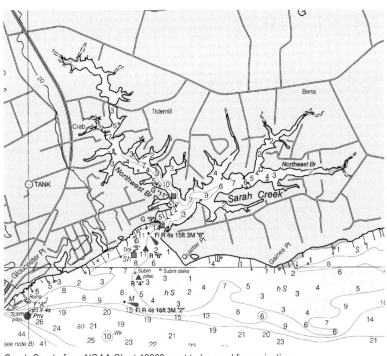

Sarah Creek; from NOAA Chart 12238—not to be used for navigation.

Port of Call

Yorktown

History runs deep in this port town, which was founded in 1691. It was here that watermen, merchants and maritime tradesmen prospered and witnessed the culmination of the Revolutionary War. While much of Yorktown's appeal is in its history, visitors will also find this a pleasant destination for shopping, dining and enjoying the redeveloped York River waterfront.

An important trade and commerce center in the early 1700s, Yorktown became the most productive colonial port between Charleston, S.C., and Philadelphia. It is best known, however, as the site where American and French forces defeated Lord Cornwallis and his British troops, ending the Revolutionary War in 1781. The victory at the Battle of Yorktown is commemorated at two sites. To the east of town is Yorktown Battlefield Visitor Center at Colonial National Historical Park, run by the National Park Service. Displays, exhibits, an orientation film and a replica of a quarter section of a British warship—complete with slanted floors, cramped quarters, swinging hammocks and creaking hull—tell the story of the war. The adjacent battlefield adds a dramatic dimension to the tale. On the opposite side of town, the Yorktown Victory Center captures the war experience from the combatants' perspective, including a re-created military encampment outside the center.

Between these two sites lies Yorktown itself, an easy stroll from end to end. (A free trolley also makes a circuit around historic and commercial areas in town.) Markers identify historic buildings like the Custom House (c. 1721), three-centuries-old Grace Episcopal Church and Moore House,

site of pre-surrender negotiations. Explore such sights on your own (maps and brochures available at the York Hall Visitor Center and at retail shops) or take guided tours led by the Park Service. York Hall is a font of information, offering an orientation video, daily events listings and a museum that chronicles the town's evolution. Then delve into more local lore at the Historical Museum's annex to York Hall, Museum on Main.

Yorktown's maritime heritage is duly honored too at the Watermen's Museum. Its main building showcases shipbuilders' tools, boat models and fishing displays and explores the watermen's life through photos and memorabilia. Outside, visitors can view a three-log canoe, engines, dredges and a working boatbuilding shed.

Nearby is Riverwalk Landing, a retail complex that is a destination of its own. It features shops, eateries, a small outdoor performance stage and dockage for tour boats, visiting tall ships and daytime and overnight space for recreational boaters. A waterside brick walkway about one mile in length links Riverwalk Landing to the Victory Center and the Battlefiled Visitor Center.

Yorktown is close to other attractions as well. Rent a car and take the scenic Colonial Parkway to Jamestown and Colonial Williamsburg, visit Busch Gardens theme park and the shopping outlets near Williamsburg, or tour Hampton Roads. From March through October another transportation option is the Yorktown-Williamsburg-Jamestown shuttle. The schooner *Alliance* offers scenic and sunset sails daily from Riverwalk (May–October).

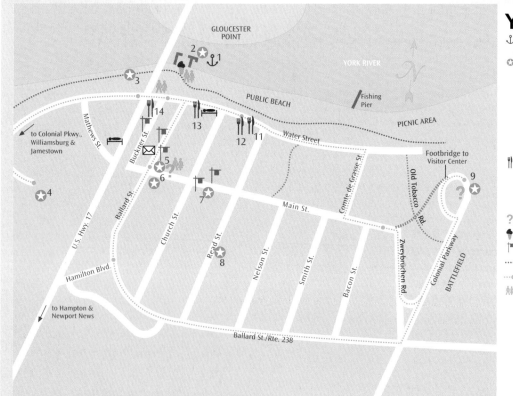

Yorktown

⚓ **Marinas/Dockage**
  1 Riverwalk Landing docks

✪ **Points of Interest**
  2 Schooner *Alliance*
  3 Watermen's Museum
  4 Yorktown Victory Center
  5 York Hall (gallery & museum)
  6 Swan Antiques
  7 Museum on Main
  8 Poor Potter Site
  9 Yorktown Visitor Center

🍴 **Dining**
  11 Yorktown Pub
  12 Beach Delly
  13 Water Street Grille
  14 Riverwalk Restaurant

❓ **Information**

🍦 **Ice Cream**

🛍 **Shopping**   ✉ **Post Office**

···· **Riverwalk**   ··· **Footpaths**

··●· **Trolley Route & Stops**

👫 **Public Restrooms**

There's more to Yorktown than colonial history as you'll see if you explore the shops, galleries and antiques stores occupying restored homes and cottages in town and the eclectic array of boutiques at Riverwalk Landing. In town you'll find antiques shops as well as 17th- and 18th-century-style gifts and furnishings. Contemporary crafts and art are on display at the Nancy Thomas Gallery. Riverwalk Landing shops sell a range of merchandise, from hand-crafted jewelry to colonial-themed gifts and needlework supplies. The Victory Center, Visitor Center and Watermen's Museum all have gift shops, as does York Hall, which specializes in works by local artists. For local produce, fresh meats and seafood, drop by the Saturday morning farmer's market (seasonal). Several homes and inns in town offer lodging or operate as B&Bs.

Diversity describes Yorktown's tempting restaurants, most of which offer water views. Riverwalk Restaurant is located at Riverwalk Landing. Casual restaurants like the Beach Delly are tucked along Yorktown's main streets, where you'll also find a Ben & Jerry's.

Riverwalk becomes the venue for a number of outdoor events including movie nights, occasional Friday evening concerts (June–August), "Shagging on the Riverwalk," (beach music, dancing, Shag lessons, food), its fall counterpart, "Rhythms on the Riverwalk," and Yorktown Market Days, a Saturday morning farmer's market which begins in June. (For a complete schedule, visit *www.riverwalklanding.com*).

Yorktown celebrates its heritage with several annual events, including an Independence Day celebration (family activities, patriotic music and fireworks) and the Watermen's Heritage Celebration at the Watermen's Museum (workboat races, blessing of the fleet, museum tours, music, food) in July. In October, Yorktown Victory Weekend features military demonstrations at the Victory Center along with battlefield tours. In November, local citizens re-enact the York Town Tea Party revolt in 1774.

Information: York County, 757-890-3300, *www.yorkcounty.gov;*

York County

Yorktown Victory Center, *www.historyisfun.org;* Colonial National Historic Park, *www.nps.gov/colo.*

Note: The Yorktown Victory Center and Jamestown Settlement are operated by the Jamestown-Yorktown Foundation. Admission to these living history museums can be purchased separately or in combination through a discount ticket offer. Visitors can also buy Historic Triangle ticket packages for Jamestown, Colonial Williamsburg and Yorktown attractions at www.historyisfun.org.

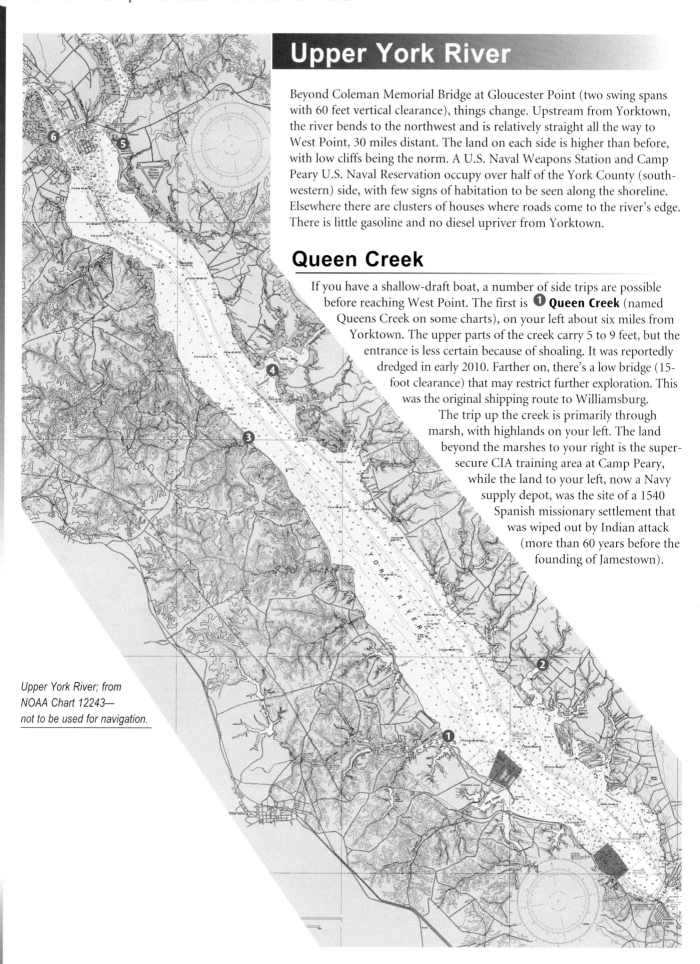

Upper York River

Beyond Coleman Memorial Bridge at Gloucester Point (two swing spans with 60 feet vertical clearance), things change. Upstream from Yorktown, the river bends to the northwest and is relatively straight all the way to West Point, 30 miles distant. The land on each side is higher than before, with low cliffs being the norm. A U.S. Naval Weapons Station and Camp Peary U.S. Naval Reservation occupy over half of the York County (southwestern) side, with few signs of habitation to be seen along the shoreline. Elsewhere there are clusters of houses where roads come to the river's edge. There is little gasoline and no diesel upriver from Yorktown.

Queen Creek

If you have a shallow-draft boat, a number of side trips are possible before reaching West Point. The first is ❶ **Queen Creek** (named Queens Creek on some charts), on your left about six miles from Yorktown. The upper parts of the creek carry 5 to 9 feet, but the entrance is less certain because of shoaling. It was reportedly dredged in early 2010. Farther on, there's a low bridge (15-foot clearance) that may restrict further exploration. This was the original shipping route to Williamsburg.

The trip up the creek is primarily through marsh, with highlands on your left. The land beyond the marshes to your right is the supersecure CIA training area at Camp Peary, while the land to your left, now a Navy supply depot, was the site of a 1540 Spanish missionary settlement that was wiped out by Indian attack (more than 60 years before the founding of Jamestown).

Upper York River; from NOAA Chart 12243—not to be used for navigation.

Carter Creek

Directly opposite Queen Creek you will find ❷ **Carter Creek**. Red "2" marks the entrance to the creek north of the main York River channel. Depths start shallow—3 to 4 feet—dropping steadily as you go. It's really suited only for a dinghy or very shallow-draft boat, but following the creek will lead you to the remains of ROSEWELL MANSION, a 1741 house that was home to, among others, a former governor of Virginia. Rosewell is said to be the place where Thomas Jefferson wrote the Declaration of Independence. The chimneys of the huge brick house can barely be spotted through the tree tops.

The lofty Rosewell Mansion commands respect even as it crumbles. Mann Page, whose family was one of the earliest to settle in Virginia, began work on the house in 1725. Sadly, Mann Page did not live to see his house completed. His widow oversaw completion of the project, which took nearly 13 years from start to finish. Ultimately, a 3,000-acre plantation supplied the family's needs and provided the wherewithal for the grand balls and lavish parties that entertained

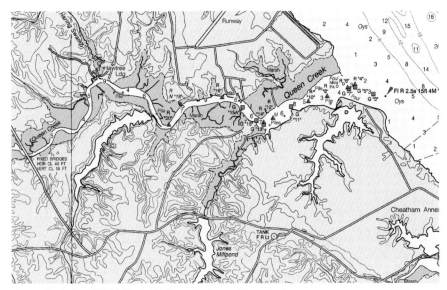

Queen Creek; from NOAA Chart 12243—not to be used for navigation.

colonial dignitaries. Mann Page's grandson (and future governor) John attended William and Mary College where he met young Thomas Jefferson. They became fast friends, and Jefferson was a frequent visitor to Rosewell. Some say Jefferson retreated to the peace and quiet of Rosewell in order to contemplate the task of writing the Declaration of Independence.

According to the book, *Some Colonial Mansions and Those Who Lived in Them* by Thomas Allen Glenn, the Page family sold the Rosewell property in 1838, and the new owner stripped it of anything that could be sold: the marble underpinnings of the family tombs, the stately cedar trees that lined the driveway, the mahogany wainscoting from the interior walls, the lead roof. When he had recouped his investment (and more) he sold the building and moved on. Time and the ensuing unpleasantness between the North and South resulted in the building falling farther into disrepair. Fire ravaged the mansion in 1916. It was never rebuilt.

Though it has been uninhabited for nearly a century, visitors swear it remains occupied by several of its earlier inhabitants. A spectral lady sometimes graces the front steps, sometimes the sounds of a harpsichord drift through the air, and there's that eery feeling you get when you nudge in close to shore just at twilight. The very real and living members of the Rosewell Foundation now oversee the site, where archaeologists and historians are trying to uncover details of life at the estate.

Taskinas Creek

There are no significant opportunities for even the shallowest of drafts to leave the river for another eight miles, until you come upon ❸ **Taskinas** *(TASK-i-NASS)* **Creek** on your left. This creek does not have a bar as such—you simply have to cross hundreds of yards of extremely shallow river to reach its mouth; and this should be done only early in the high half of the tide. But once inside, you can enjoy the deep and meandering waters of the creek as it heads back into the hills,

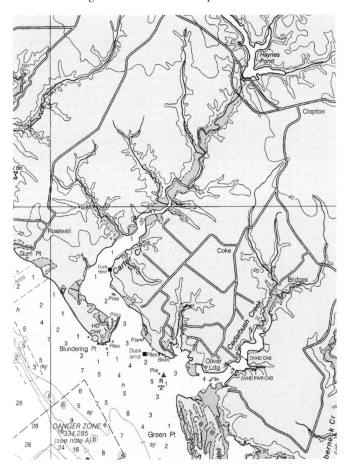

Carter Creek; from NOAA Chart 12243—not to be used for navigation.

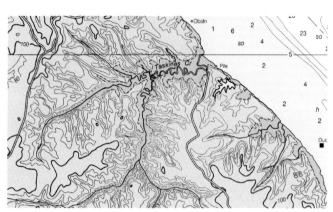

Taskinas Creek; from NOAA Chart 12243—not to be used for navigation.

Taskinas Creek *continued*

its shores almost devoid of any sign of human habitation.

YORK RIVER STATE PARK, with a pier on the creek, is an interesting place to visit. A colonial-era tobacco plantation and warehouse once stood here, its remnants preserved at a historically significant archaeological site at Croaker Landing within the park. The park's nature trails (complete with exercise stops) let you stretch your legs. The visitor's center has films about the Chesapeake; the environmental displays are particularly enjoyable. As a perhaps better alternative to entering the creek, you may visit the park by anchoring out in the York and dinghying ashore to the small beach.

Poropotank River

Another favorite side-trip is to cruise the ❹ **Poropotank** (*po-RO-po-tank*) **River**, which is across the York River and slightly upstream of the park. **Morris Bay**, at the mouth of the Poropotank, provides a picturesque anchorage for those who can cross the bar into the deeper river water. Favor the east side and watch the bush stakes that mark the twisting and narrow channel.

At lighted marker "20" aim for the point of land with a large white radio beacon (north side of the entrance). Anchor in 5 to 7 feet of water just behind the protective spit. Although there is an unmarked channel of deep water, most of the bay is very shallow. Care should be taken when crossing it in a dinghy with a motor.

A trip up this river is worth a half-day's extension to your cruise, which it will require. The Poropotank is a meandering river, with occasional clusters of cottages or houses, finally ending in a marshy valley with a deep, narrow channel twisting from side to side.

Mattaponi River

The York River forms about 7 miles above the Poropotank at the confluence of the Pamunkey (*pa-MUNK-ey*) and the ❺ **Mattaponi** (*mat-a-pon-EYE*) rivers. On the tip of the peninsula between these two tributaries is the small town of **West Point**.

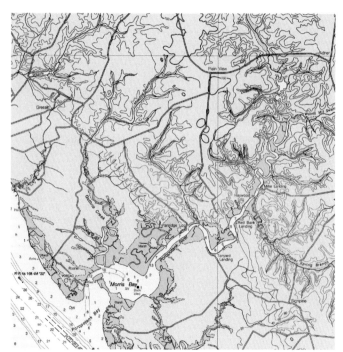

Poropotank River; from NOAA Chart 12243—not to be used for navigation.

An original port of entry in 1705, it's a charming place, reminiscent of Onancock on Virginia's Eastern Shore. However, the town currently has no boating facilities to speak of, though future waterfront development plans still include dockage and shoreside amenities for visiting boaters.

The Mattaponi enters the York River on the northeastern side of West Point. The Lord Delaware Swing Bridge there has been replaced with a fixed span with 55-foot vertical clearance. Nearly a mile north beyond the bridge is another overhead obstacle, a power cable at 62 feet. For those who can clear these, there's a fascinating river to be explored, one that snakes northward, deep and wide through marshland for more than 20 miles to the fixed bridge at **Walkerton**. There are no facilities on the Mattaponi, and the current is swift, but the adventurous cruiser can find a quiet bay in which to drop anchor, or even a stout tree to serve as a temporary piling since deep water often runs up to the banks.

Pamunkey River

The ❻ **Pamunkey** enters the York River to the southwest of West Point where a new drawbridge opened in 2007 (vertical clearance 56 feet in the closed position), replacing the Eltham Bascule Bridge. But high-profile boats planning to cruise up this river should be aware of an overhead cable with a charted clearance of 60 feet, a little more than a mile past the bridge.

The Pamunkey is, in a word, beautiful. You find yourself in a valley with impressive cliffs on each side. The floor of the valley is composed entirely of marsh. The river snakes across the valley, crisscrossing through tall marsh grasses. Other than the occasional distant train whistle, there are few signs of civilization. The water is deep enough for a destroyer, making moderate sailing possible if the wind is at all favorable.

The constant turning of the river means you can always find a nice place to anchor. If it is hot and you want ventilation, you can pick a spot which is aligned with the wind. If it is squally and you want protection, simply anchor where the wind is at right angles to the river.

Depths in the Pamunkey will allow you to go very close to the shore to avoid an opposing current. This ability to travel nearly within an oar's reach of the shore can be worth your while, since the currents are stronger here than down in the York. The Pamunkey is one of the few places you can anchor with the current so strong that it can hold your boat stern to the wind in a raging rainstorm.

Unless you have a small boat, the practical limit of navigation on the Pamunkey is established by the low railroad bridge that spans the river on the upstream side of the Pamunkey Indian Reservation. (A nice place to visit, the reservation includes the PAMUNKEY INDIAN MUSEUM and a pottery school that has operated since the 1930s; call 804-843-4792 for information.) This bridge is almost 30 miles upriver from West Point, but less than 15 miles as the bird flies.

Back Creek

On the south shore of York River's mouth is **Back Creek**, tucked behind the uninhabited **Goodwin Islands**. It can be reached from the north by way of the shallow and narrow **Thorofare Channel** from York River, or one could take a deeper route from the Bay following a serpentine line, with the islands to starboard and Green Point to port. Be alert for shoals and crab pots in this whole area.

The numbering system for these two interconnecting channels begins on the Bay side at red flashing "2" and increases until the route exits at flashing red "GT" in the York River, east of the prominent refinery docks. Conversely, when entering from the north, the numbers diminish.

Both channels converge at the mouths of two creeks: Back Creek, the tributary that enters from the west, and smaller **Claxton Creek** to the south. Easily accessed from the Bay, the latter is reported to have good holding in 6 feet, but is shallow at its mouth. Enter slowly. Green "7" marks a 2-foot shoal, so leave it well to port as you enter. Without homes or traffic, it's a serene spot, with the low marshy peninsula of Green Point reducing most chop.

To enter Back Creek, look for green flasher "1", west of daymarks "7" and "8" in the converging channels. The creek's depths are reported at a 7-foot minimum for about a mile after leaving the main channel; depths then become 5 feet and less as the river narrows. In the deeper section, Mills Marina is on the port side, past "7"—the last navigational aid on the creek—and beyond the commercial

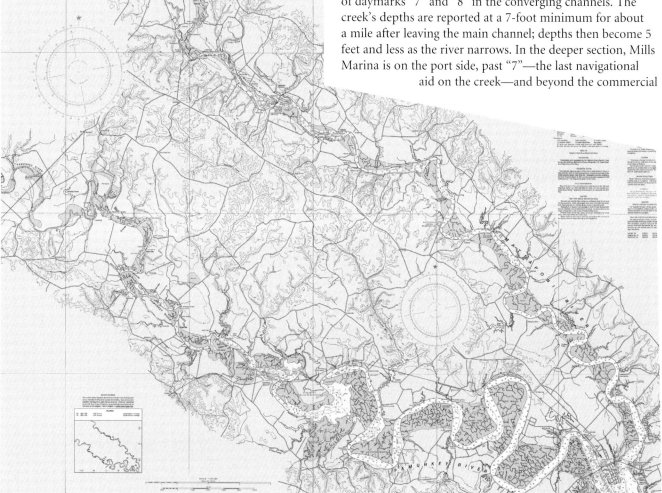

Mattaponi River and Pamunkey River; from NOAA Chart 12244—not to be used for navigation.

Two ships from the Seaford Scallop Company's fleet lie at the dock on Back Creek.

Back Creek *continued*

docks of the Seaford Scallop Company. In business since the 1920s, this is now one of the largest scallop producers on the East Coast.

Mills Marina reports 6 feet dockside, 40 slips and a marine store with ice, some supplies as well as a boat ramp for trailer vessels.

Farther upstream in a cove to starboard is Seaford Yacht Club, a fun-loving organization with an active membership. Just upstream on the same side is the 26-acre BACK CREEK PARK with floating docks, ramps, restrooms, picnic and play area, and tennis courts.

The creek borders part of the U.S.C.G. Training Center, the Coast Guard's largest training command, on the former site of a Navy Mine Warfare School.

The peninsula, **Goodwin Neck**, is the ancestral home of the family by that name. In 1668, James Goodwin, son of a London merchant and shipbuilder, purchased about 2,000 acres from the heirs of Samuel Chew who had received this grant from the King of England. Goodwin grew corn and tobacco, and served as a major in the local militia from 1657 to 1662; in 1658 he represented York County in the House of Burgesses.

The Goodwin homestead, a two-story imposing structure facing Goodwin Island on the Thorofare, was torn down shortly after 1900. The patriarch's first wife is buried in what is now the community of **Dandy**.

This whole area was strategically vital to Cornwallis during the siege of nearby Yorktown, as well as to Confederate General John Magruder some 80 years later. Both British and Confederate troops built earth redoubts on the land around Dandy, which is noted on charts toward the tip of Goodwin Neck. The Goodwin Islands are now used as a research reserve, managed by Virginia Institute of Marine Science and owned by the College of William & Mary in Williamsburg. The 777-acre archipelago of salt-marsh islands is also part of the VIRGINIA BIRDING AND WILDLIFE TRAIL SYSTEM. The extensive wetland and cover serve as nursery, spawning and foraging habitats for finfish, birds and other animals.

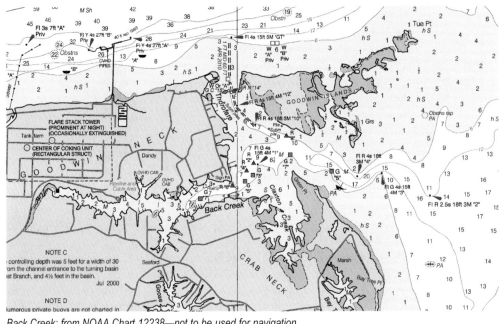

Back Creek; from NOAA Chart 12238—not to be used for navigation.

Poquoson River to James River to Rudee Inlet

Back, Hampton, James, Chickahominy and Elizabeth Rivers
Willoughby Bay, Little Creek and Lynnhaven Inlet
Hampton, Smithfield, Portsmouth and Norfolk
The Albemarle Canal and Dismal Swamp Canal

9

As you cruise the lower Bay you can feel its intimate connection to the open sea. Navy ships, cargo ships and cruising vessels of every kind hug their berths or ride their anchors. Some will be bound for the blue waters of the Atlantic, some for the Intracoastal Waterway.

The pace is palpably quicker than the quiet laid back ways of the Bay just to the north. Here you find waterfront restaurants, glitzy nightlife, upscale shops, walking tours and much more to enjoy. There are festivals and art shows almost every weekend in summer. Norfolk has its historic battleship *Wisconsin* and its Nauticus museum and science center. Portsmouth has its beautiful Olde Towne filled with antiques shops and historic churches. Virginia Beach boasts its oceanfront boardwalk and Marine Science Museum. Up the Hampton River you'll find the Virginia Air and Space Center with nearby restaurants and shops. Newport News offers the incomparable Mariners' Museum and Peninsula Fine Arts Center. There's something to do everywhere you turn.

Yet, if it's peace and quiet you're searching for, you can find it just around the bend in tucked-away marinas where the atmosphere is definitely down-home. The Poquoson River, Salt Ponds and Hampton River all have quiet harbors far removed from the bustle of Hampton Roads. Willoughby Bay has restful accommodations, and so does Little Creek. If height restrictions are not a concern, and the Atlantic is calling your name, head into Lynnhaven Inlet or around Cape Henry to Rudee Inlet for first-class dining and other shoreside amenities.

This is a region steeped in history and legend. A journey up the James River will take you to Smithfield, a town with Colonial roots, brimming with Southern hospitality. Or stop at Jamestown, where English settlers first took root in the New World. The long winding James meanders past a bevy of plantation homes before reaching the bustling city of Richmond.

Best of all are the peaceful anchorages where boaters can drop the hook, catch a breeze, read or snooze. The Poquoson and Hampton flats, Willoughby Bay, the Lynnhaven River, the Pagan—all invite cruisers and weekenders alike to soak up the stillness of a secluded gunkhole where ducks, pelicans and skimmers might be your only neighbors, and where eagles and osprey slice through the sky above you.

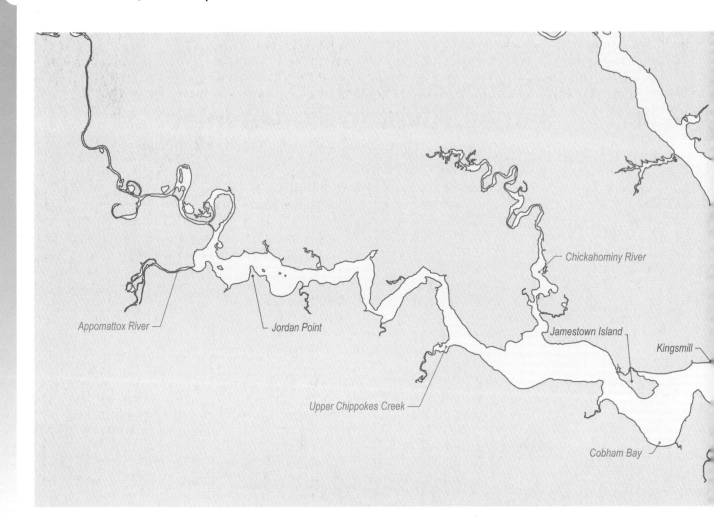

Appomattox River

Jordan Point

Upper Chippokes Creek

Chickahominy River

Jamestown Island

Kingsmill

Cobham Bay

Section 9

Tow ⚓ Boat U.S.
LOCATIONS

A Hopewell
757-582-7194

B Poquoson
757-582-7194

C Virginia Beach
757-426-3222

D Norfolk
757-582-7194

E Portsmouth
757-582-7194

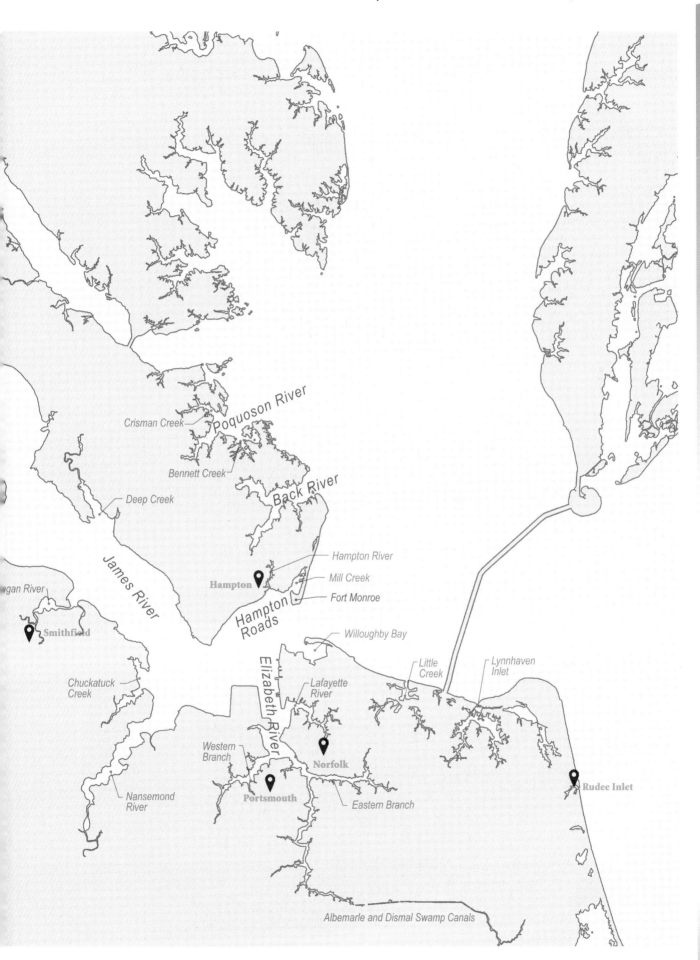

Crisman Creek

Poquoson River

Bennett Creek

Back River

Deep Creek

Hampton River

Mill Creek

Hampton

Fort Monroe

Hampton Roads

James River

...gan River

Smithfield

Willoughby Bay

Little Creek

Lynnhaven Inlet

Elizabeth River

Lafayette River

Chuckatuck Creek

Western Branch

Norfolk

Nansemond River

Portsmouth

Eastern Branch

Rudee Inlet

Albemarle and Dismal Swamp Canals

Poquoson River

With three major branches, the **Poquoson River** (*puh-KO-son*) offers cruisers a lot of shoreline to explore along Virginia's lower peninsula. Two of its creeks, Chisman and Bennett, are ideal places to find protected anchorages. You'll also find quiet working marinas, a few restaurants and fuel.

The river's entrance lies three and a half miles west of the York Spit lighted spider tower and is marked by a green-over-red fairway buoy "P". As you follow a well-marked channel down the wide mouth of the river, good water extends for at least one-half mile to the east and more than a mile to the west of the channel. At red "10" the water narrows to about one-half mile.

There are few landmarks ashore on the wide expanse of the low marshy Poquoson River between red "2" and red "10". But the huge marsh southeast of its mouth is Plum Tree Island National Wildlife Refuge, where it's not unusual to spot turtles, deer, raccoons and a variety of birds. The refuge was once a munitions testing site, and the adjacent shallow waters could still contain unexploded shells. Check your chart, because some of this area is restricted.

At "10" the Poquoson River splits, with the mainstem making a dogleg at "15" to avoid the shoal off Hunts Point. After that there is good water all the way to "17". Anchorages are good here, even though they are exposed to a chop from the northeast wind. The fetch down the river is unbroken to the north but in fair weather the beauty of the spot makes the stopover worthwhile.

For better protected anchorages, choose either Chisman Creek, which splits off to the northwest between "14" and "15", or fascinating Bennett Creek, which meanders off to the southeast after red "10".

Chisman Creek

Chisman Creek is to starboard after you pass red "10" entering from the Bay. Its wide mouth, not clearly visible until you round York Point, is to the northwest. The red-and-white smokestack at the oil refinery can be seen almost dead ahead. Give red "2" extra room. The 2-foot (at low water) shoal has reportedly spread beyond the daymark.

The creek is navigable for two miles and is bordered by the attractive communities of Seaford to the north and Dare to the south. At the few marinas here, you'll find slips, gas and repairs.

If you're anticipating a quick departure the next morning, consider a convenient, sheltered anchorage just inside the mouth of Chisman Creek behind York Point, in toward the docks at the residences that line the shore. A slow approach and knowledge of the normal 2½-foot tides will allow for a secure anchorage in good holding ground within 300 yards of

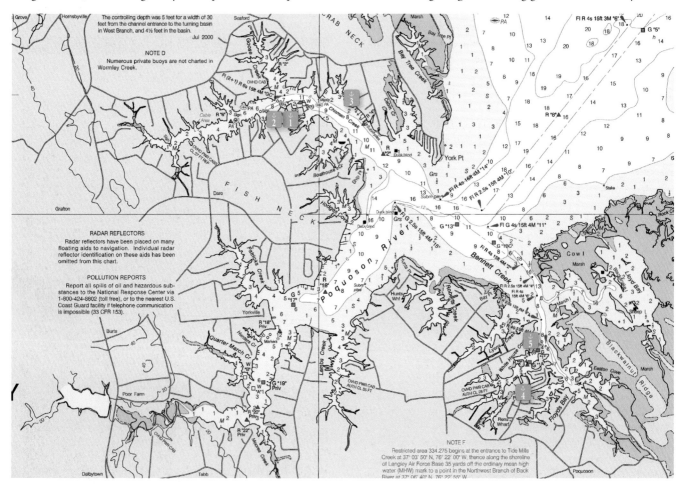

Poquoson River; from NOAA Chart 12238—not to be used for navigation.

● *On Premises*
➤ *Nearby*

	MLW	Overnight Slips	Gas	Diesel	Propane	Electric	Showers	Laundry	Restaurant	Lodging	Pool	Pump-out	Ice	Groceries	Marine Supplies	Boat Repair	Bait	Haul-out Services	Launch Ramp	Wi-Fi	Other
Poquoson River																					
Dare Marina and Yacht Sales Poquoson R./Chisman Cr. 757-898-3000; www.daremarina.com	5.5'	●	●	●		●	●						●	●		●			●	●	New and used boat sales, paddleboard rentals, sales
Smith's Marine Railway, Inc. Poquoson R./Chisman Cr. 757-898-8736	12'	➤	➤	➤	➤	●		➤	➤	➤			➤	➤	●	●	➤		●	●	
Thomas Marina Poquoson R./Chisman Cr. 757-880-3636	4.5'	●	➤	➤	➤	●	●					➤		➤	➤	➤	➤	➤	●		New docks
Whitehouse Cove Marina Poquoson R./Bennett Cr. 757-508-2602; www.whitehousecovemarina.com	8'	●	➤	➤	➤	●	●	●	●	➤	●	●	●	●	●	●	➤	➤	●	●	Floating docks, Wi-Fi, charters, storage, covered slips
York Haven Marina Poquoson R./Bennett Cr. 757-868-4532	7.5'	●	●	●	➤	●	●	●	●	●	➤	➤	➤	●	➤	●	●	●	●	●	50-ton lift, boats to 60 ft.; wood, engine repairs

shore for a boat drawing 5 feet or less.

Other anchorages abound on either side of the channel and at the mouths of several coves. If you draw 4 feet or less, you can find quiet anchorages in the smaller creeks farther up. (Note the overhead power cables with clearance of only 27 feet in the upper reaches of Chisman Creek.)

The shores here are as tranquil as any on the southern Bay. At night the quiet descends on the water, the sounds buffered by the heavily treed shoreline.

Bennett Creek

By turning to port at red "10" you enter the channel to **Bennett Creek**. The channel is narrow, but easy to navigate, assuming all of its navigation aids are in place (they tend to go missing after storms). Just go all the way to "10" before heading for green "1"; the water is too shoal to cut the corner from the river. Give a wide berth to the area southwest of "1". Depths are less than 6 feet close aboard the marker. Once cleared, the rest of the creek is no problem.

A mile beyond, at "10", you will see the large expanse of marsh behind Cow Island on the port hand. The area was named Poquoson by the Indians who were living there when the English settled it. The word means "Great Marsh," and the community of **Poquoson** has the distinction of being one of the oldest in Virginia to have its original name.

BIG SALT MARSH, part of a 3,500-acre refuge, is a habitat for waterfowl. With its history as a bombing range, unexploded ordnance remains. Consequently, the entire refuge and its surrounding shallow waters are closed to the public. Cow Island, however, allows "permitted hunting" in season, since it was not part of the range.

Beyond "10" the channel is not marked. Just remain in the center as you leave "10" to starboard. Water depths of 8 to 9 feet are found all the way to **Floyds Bay**. Anchorages are good on the southwestern side of the center, near a small

island, about 400 yards beyond "10". There are some private moorings in Floyds Bay, but the area will also accommodate a raft of six or eight boats and is out of the main flow of traffic from three marina facilities in White House Cove.

White House Cove does not have suitable anchorages for gunkholers, but does not lack for marina facilities. Boats

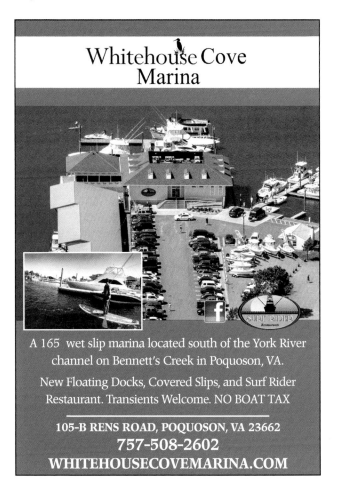

Whitehouse Cove Marina

A 165 wet slip marina located south of the York River channel on Bennett's Creek in Poquoson, VA.

New Floating Docks, Covered Slips, and Surf Rider Restaurant. Transients Welcome. NO BOAT TAX

105-B RENS ROAD, POQUOSON, VA 23662
757-508-2602
WHITEHOUSECOVEMARINA.COM

Bennett Creek *continued*

drawing 6 feet regularly transit these creeks. To port, you'll find recently redeveloped White House Cove (formerly Poquoson Marina) with slips and a restaurant. Across the cove are Owen's Marina Restaurant (daytime dockage for diners) and York Haven Marina, with slips, repairs and fuel (gas and diesel). Farther up the creek there are 4- to 5-foot depths and a small marina.

Boatyards on both Bennett (York Haven Marina) and Chisman creeks (Smith's Marine Railway) are national treasures for discovering and learning about the Bay's old workboats and the craftsmen who made them.

Back River

Back River has long been popular with powerboaters because there are so many facilities available. There are three public boat ramps, two on the north shore and one on the southwest branch that has an adjacent bait and tackle shop along with the only fuel dock on the river. Back River also has two marinas that welcome transients.

As soon as you enter Back River, be prepared for a surprise. You'll find yourself right in the shadow of Langley Air Force Base. Although there are many fine exploring opportunities here, even with only a few airplanes flying the night you visit, you'll probably hear every one of them go overhead.

LANGLEY AIR FORCE BASE, despite its noisy daytime activities, has its attractions including the NASA Research Center, which has an exciting exhibit detailing the history and activities of NASA, especially the role played by Langley and the personnel of the NASA Research Center.

Back River is home to a number of small commercial fishing boats. Many of these fishermen sell their catch at the packing house on Messick Point.

The entrance from the Bay to Back River is surrounded by areas where fish traps are allowed, ecept in the buoyed entrance channel. So keep an eye out as well for the stakes that support gill nets, especially if you're taking a shortcut.

Northend Point at the river's mouth is a long sandy beach with deep water right up to the shore on its north end. Some

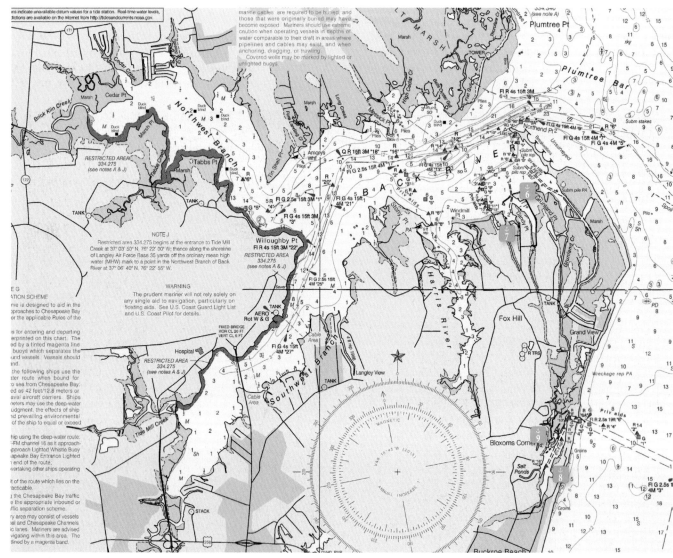

Back River; from NOAA Chart 12222—not to be used for navigation.

● *On Premises*
➤ *Nearby*

	MLW	Overnight Slips	Gas	Diesel	Propane	Electric	Showers	Laundry	Restaurant	Lodging	Pool	Pump-out	Ice	Groceries	Marine Supplies	Boat Repair	Bait	Haul-out Services	Launch Ramp	Wi-Fi	Other
Back River																					
Bell Isle Marina Back R./Wallace Cr. 757-850-0466; www.bellislemarina.com	6'+	●	➤	➤	➤	●	●	➤	➤	➤		●	●		●	➤	●	●	➤	●	Dry storage, 55-ton lift, forklift, repairs, rigging
Dandy Haven Marina Back R. 757-851-1573; www.dandyhavenmarina.com	5'					●	●					●						●	●		Dry storage
Salt Ponds Marina Resort Salt Ponds/south of Back R. Chesapeake Bay; 757-850-4300 or 888-881-0897; www.saltpondsmarinaresort.com	7'	●	●	●	➤	●	●	●	●	●	●	●	●	●	➤	➤	➤	●	➤	●	On the Bay, 2 pools, private beach, VHF 16
Southall Landings Marina Salt Ponds/south of Back R. 757-850-9929 ; www.SouthallMarina.com	6'	●	➤	➤	➤	●	●	●	➤		●	●	●	➤	●		➤	➤	➤	●	No boat tax, fixed docks, 30/50 amp service, transient slips

locals call it Factory Point, though no one knows why; apparently, there has never been a factory anywhere nearby. In the summer, powerboaters can run right up on the beach and step ashore for a picnic. Access is by boat or foot only. The point is part of the city of Hampton's Grandview Nature Preserve. There is a locked gate about two miles south of the point, so if you come by car, you must go the last two miles on foot.

The first channel on the southern shore is a private canal that runs from green daymark "7" through the preserve into a residential neighborhood. The chart shows a dredged depth of 5 feet, and residents say there is generally 5 to 6 feet except for a few shallower spots. The canal offers little to see and no room to anchor, so you may want to take their word for it.

The second privately marked channel leads to Bell Isle Marina, which offers slips and repairs. On the other side of the channel, Wallace Bait and Tackle sells fuel and supplies. A public boat ramp is next door. The approach to these facilities

POQUOSON, VIRGINIA IS
THE PLACE

EnjoyVA.Com
Download the EnjoyVA App
Iphone & Android Compatible
Providing Poquoson
Visitor Information.

To Chart Your Next Coastal Adventure

• Full Service Marinas & Slip Rentals
• No Boat Tax
• Paddle Boarding
• Kayaking
• Airboat Tours & Sunset Cruises
• Free & Accessible Boat Ramps
• Fishing Charters & Sport Fishing
• Jet-Ski Tours & Fishing
• Convenient Restaurant & Merchant Areas

Give us 15 Minutes...
And We'll Give you the Chesapeake Bay.

Poquoson is just 7 miles from I-64 on the Virginia Peninsula; 20-30 Minutes from Colonial Williamsburg & Busch Gardens. Lat 37.1332° N, Lon 76.3739° W.

Back River *continued*

is about 5 to 6 feet.

The third channel begins about 100 yards past marker "10" and takes you to Dandy Haven Marina, which also has slips and repair services. The channel depth is about 6 feet.

Pay attention to the shoals out in the middle of the river. Shoaling south of the main channel and in privately marked areas can be made worse by storms. Since the Coast Guard neither monitors nor maintains the channel, local knowledge is the only reliable guide here. Shallows may lurk anywhere, so go slowly, watch your depths and follow the channel marks.

Along the northern shoreline there is plenty of room to anchor between Messick Point and Amorys Wharf. Large raft-ups are easily accommodated in good holding ground and are well protected except for an easterly.

About four miles south of Back River is the protected haven of **Salt Ponds**. The entrance jetty, three miles north-north-west of Thimble Shoal Light, is marked by red flasher "6". The channel was dredged in 2013, but shoaling is a perennial problem. Salt Ponds, however, has a lot to offer, with transient facilities, gas and diesel, restaurants and recreational opportunities.

Hampton Roads

The term **Hampton Roads** has been around since the 1600s to define the protected waters where several rivers pour toward the Atlantic. When the area was a struggling English outpost, the colonists at Jamestown designated an administrative center in the region, near the mouth of the Chesapeake, which they called Elizabeth Cittie in honor of King James' daughter. On the other hand, the new town, the tributary on which it was located, and the nearby watery intersection were all named Hampton after the 3rd Earl of Southampton, one of the founders of the Virginia Company of London and its staunch advocate.

One of the largest natural harbors in the world—and known for its strategic importance to shipbuilding, commerce and the military—Hampton Roads has long been one of the busiest harbors in the world. What exactly is Hampton Roads? On the charts, Hampton Roads is delineated as it was originally: the waters between Old Point Comfort on the north and Sewell's Point on the south. In 1755, the Virginia General Assembly designed the Roads as encompassing the mouths of the Elizabeth, James and Nansemond rivers. Today's maps put Hampton Roads between the two bridge-tunnels that connect the communities of Hampton-Newport News with Suffolk-Portsmouth-Chesapeake and Norfolk-Willoughby-Virginia Beach. In general terms, the name has come to describe the wider geographic and metropolitan areas.

Imagine you are sitting on your boat in the center of Hampton Roads, trying to get your bearings. Scanning your surroundings counterclockwise, here is what you'll see:

Looking north toward Hampton, you'll see two small tributaries that are divided by the Hampton Roads Bridge-Tunnel, which sends traffic under the 60-foot-deep Norfolk Harbor entrance channel. Replacing vehicular ferries in 1957, the Hampton Bridge-Tunnel was the first such complex in the world. Mill Creek is to the right, tucked between the bridge-tunnel and Old Point Comfort, home to Fort Monroe. And to the left, Hampton River, which goes into the heart of the old city.

Looking straight down Hampton Roads to the west, you'll find the mouths of the James and Nansemond rivers. Then you'll see the entrance to the Elizabeth River, dominated on the west side by Craney Island—the U.S. Army Corps of Engineers' spoil disposal area—and on the west by the U.S. Navy.

● On Premises ➤ Nearby

Hampton River

	MLW	Overnight Slips	Gas	Diesel	Propane	Electric	Showers	Laundry	Restaurant	Lodging	Pool	Pump-out	Ice	Groceries	Marine Supplies	Boat Repair	Bait	Haul-out Services	Launch Ramp	Wi-Fi	Other
Bluewater Yachting Center & Yacht Sales Hampton R./Sunset Cr. 757-723-6774; www.bluewateryachtsales.com	12'	●	●	●	➤	●	●	●	●	➤	●	●	●	➤	●	●	●	●	●	●	Shuttle to downtown, bts to 200', floating docks
Customs House Marina Hampton R. 757-636-7772; www.customshousemarina.com	12'	●	➤	➤	➤	●	●	●	➤	➤	●	●	●	➤	➤		➤	➤	➤	●	Free Wi-Fi, pool access at adjacent hotel
Downtown Hampton Public Piers Hampton R. 757-727-1276; www.hamptonpublicpiers.com	12'	●	➤	➤	➤	●	●	➤	●	●	●	●	●	➤	➤	➤	➤	➤	➤	●	Shops, restaurants summer bus & rental car near
Joy's Marina Hampton R. 757-723-1022	6'	●	➤	➤	➤	●	●	➤	➤	➤		●	➤	➤	➤	➤	➤	➤	➤	●	Dockside parking, no bridges, no personal prop. tax
Old Point Comfort Marina Hampton R./Mill Cr./Fort Monroe 757-788-4308; www.oldpointcomfortmarina.com	15'-20'	●	●	●	➤	●	●	●	●	➤	➤	●	●	➤	●				●	●	Open to the public, adjacent to Ft. Monroe
Sunset Boating Center Hampton R./Sunset Cr. 757-722-3325; www.sunsetboatingcenter.com	10'	●	●	●	➤	●	●	●	●	➤	➤	●	●	●	●	●	●	●	●	➤	Boat U.S. marina, fuel & transient discounts

Farther east, you'll find the wide mouth of Willoughby Bay, which opens into the heart of Hampton Roads, between Norfolk Naval Base and Willoughby Spit. This skinny peninsula attaches the southern end of the Hampton Roads Bridge-Tunnel.

As you can see, Hampton Roads is a very busy place!

Mill Creek and Fort Monroe

The entrance to **Mill Creek**, as we mentioned, is squeezed between the man-made island that anchors the northern end of the Hampton Roads Bridge-Tunnel and Old Point Comfort to the east. A charted landmark to starboard is the Chamberlin Hotel. This grand, brick structure with its two large square towers is easy to spot from a good distance and sits at the edge of **Fort Monroe**, which occupies a large part of the point. The water is deep around the point, whether you are approaching from the north or south, which makes it possible to avoid the ship traffic funneling into the Roads.

The mouth of the Mill Creek channel often has small fishing

boats anchored or drifting, but depths are good and the channel is well-marked. Inside to starboard is Old Point Comfort Marina, protected by wooden breakwaters. The marina, previously only for military personnel, welcomes all mariners now that Fort Monroe has been decommissioned. To port, north of "3", is a wide anchorage with depths ranging from 7 to 13 feet. The bridge offers no protection in a strong west wind, but holding seems fine for settled weather.

In 2012, Fort Monroe was designated a National Monument. It's open to the public year-round, with a variety of new programs scheduled. (*www.nps.gov/fomr*) The Casemate Museum within the fort is open daily (except major holidays) and admission is free.

Surrounded by a moat, this early 19th century stronghold is the largest stone fort in the country. It sits on the site of smaller fortifications dating to the earliest English settlement. According to legend, Captain Smith assessed the peninsula as "a little isle fit for a castle," and a welcome landfall for weary voyagers. Afterwards it was called Cape Comfort or Point Comfort. While "New Point Comfort" later showed up on the charts 20 nautical

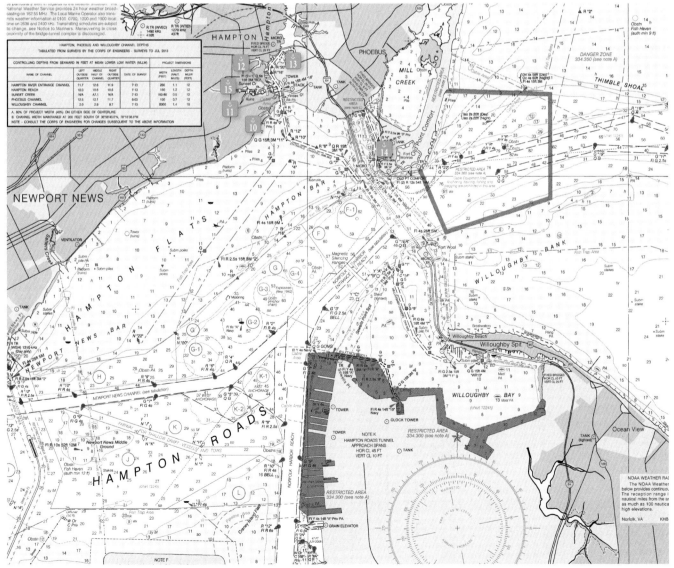

Hampton Roads; from NOAA Chart 12222—not to be used for navigation.

Mill Creek and Fort Monroe continued

miles to the north, Old Point Comfort was always an important defensive position for the harbor.

Fort Monroe was constructed following the War of 1812, when British ships had been able to enter the Chesapeake unchallenged. It was named for the fifth U.S. president, and completed in 15 years. Around to help supervise its completion in 1843 was the young engineer Robert E. Lee, fresh out of West Point, who lived in the fort, was married and saw his first child born there.

Meanwhile, entrepreneurs marketed the adjacent sweeping beach as a resort, building several hotels. The Chamberlin sits on the site of one built in 1820 and used as a hospital during the Civil War. Another hotel replaced it, and when that burned it was followed by the Chamberlin in 1920. The Chamberlin is no longer a hotel, but apartments for active seniors. It also has two elegant, water-view restaurants that are open to the public. Call 757-637-7200 for information.

For some time the tallest structure on the peninsula was the 54-foot Point Comfort Light built in 1802. Today, it stands behind a large cement breakwater near a public fishing pier, lost among the surrounding—and taller—clutter. The Bay's second oldest lighthouse, it's the oldest still operating. Only when a new light was built off Mobjack Bay, on another Point Comfort, did this one become "Old." British forces under Admiral Cockburn during the War of 1812 used it as an observation post. It also

witnessed the world's first modern naval engagement, the Battle of the Ironclads in 1862, when the USS *Monitor* and the CSS *Virginia* squared-off in Hampton Roads.

There was no clear winner at that time, but Fort Monroe remained in control of the Union Army. Three years later, at the end of the war, the President of the Confederacy Jefferson Davis, accused of treason, was held here for 18 months until freed on bail. He was never brought to trial.

Besides its military significance, the fort holds important African-American history as well. The same piece of land where traders first brought enslaved people to the fledgling colony is also where slave labor was used to construct the moat and granite walls. Then, shortly after the Civil War began, it became a refuge for thousands seeking freedom. The situation demonstrated the need for Lincoln's Emancipation Proclamation of 1863.

Post-war, freed African-Americans settled in the area, eventually forming the community of **Phoebus** (FEE-bus) and Hampton University, which fronts the nearby Hampton River. While Phoebus's center on Mellon Street is inviting, the waterfront has only commercial docks with large fishing boats and no apparent safe access for dinghies. On the other hand, the fort, abandoned batteries, lighthouse, beach and its environs are fully attainable. The Casemate Museum and the restaurants in the Chamberlin Hotel are within walking distance of the marina, but bicycles are recommended for other explorations.

continued on page 330

Best marina on the lower Chesapeake Bay!

SALT PONDS MARINA RESORT

Salt Ponds Marina Resort is the **perfect stopping point** whether you are traveling south through the ICW or heading for points north of the Bay.

Year-Round • Floating Docks Up To 110'

Long-Term & Transient • Gas & Diesel

Pumpout • Water & Power Hookups

Waterfront Restaurant • Poolside Cabana Bar

Bathhouses • Laundry • Swimming Pools

Ship's Store • Ice, Drinks, Gifts

Boater's Lounge • Beaches

11 Ivory Gull Crescent • Hampton, Virginia 23664 • (757) 850-4300
www.saltpondsmarinaresort.com

Port of Call
Hampton

Sea and sky are running themes in this city founded by ocean-voyaging colonists and now home to NASA Langley Research Center and the Virginia Air & Space Center. There are few historic buildings to see because the city was burned to avoid its seizure during the Civil War. Only colonial St. John's Church survived. But local heritage is celebrated in other imaginative ways, the annual Blackbeard Pirate Festival being one of the more colorful. With ample amenities (including lodging at the Hampton Marina Hotel) and a tranquil anchorage, Hampton is a friendly port of call, where most attractions are close at hand. You'll even find a Neil Pryde Sailmaker on the town's main street.

The Visitor Center, in the Hampton History Museum, is a perfect place to get acquainted with the city, but be sure to explore the museum before visiting modern-day Hampton. One must-see attraction is the acclaimed Virginia Air & Space Center, whose roofline suggests wings in flight. Engaging exhibits and state-of-the-art displays delve into the world of aeronautics. Marvel at a three-billion-year-old moon rock, view 3-D IMAX films or try the F/A-22 flight simulator.

On the waterfront, the former Cousteau Society building, reminiscent of a lighthouse, is now the Hampton Maritime Center, part of Hampton's Public Piers, and offers a gathering place for local and visiting boaters. Nearby, the 1920s-vintage Hampton Carousel delights children of all ages.

The arts thrive in Hampton. Hampton University Museum showcases a fine collection of African American, Native American, African and Asian artworks; the Taylor Arts Center presents contemporary art in a variety of media; and the nearby Phoebus Arts Factory welcomes visitors to its complex of studios, galleries, classrooms and performance space. Nationally renowned performers take the stage at Hampton Coliseum.

Stretching along the river banks is Hampton University, founded in 1868 to advance the education of freed slaves. Six National Historic Landmarks and the acclaimed museum are located on its rolling green campus. If sports are your passion, Hampton obliges with NASCAR races at Langley Speedway most Saturday nights, and the public Woodlands Golf Course and Hampton Tennis Center.

To reach the sports venues, Hampton Coliseum and other beyond-downtown attractions, ask the dockmaster about taxis, car rentals and public transportation. (Courtesy bicycles at local marinas and a water taxi for Bluewater Yachting Center guests can also help you get around.) The *Miss Hampton II* offers tours past maritime landmarks such as Fort Wool and Norfolk naval base.

At Blue Skies Gallery, over 70 local member artists rent space to showcase and sell their works. Also tucked among the office buildings in Hampton's compact downtown are a smattering of specialty and gift shops. A short ride from the waterfront is Coliseum Central, an enclave

continued on page 330

Hampton

⚓ Marinas/Dockage
1 Downtown Hampton Public Piers
2 Customs House Marina
3 Bluewater Yachting Center
4 Sunset Boating Center
5 Joy's Marina

⊙ Points of Interest
6 Taylor Arts Center
7 Hampton Maritime Center
8 Hampton Carousel Park
9 Virginia Air & Space Center
10 Blue Skies Gallery
11 Hampton History Museum

🍴 Dining Areas
12 Settlers Landing
13 Queen's Way

🍖 Groceries/Carryout
14 7-Eleven
15 Miller Mart (convenience store)
16 Swami Food Store/Murry's Steaks
17 La Bodega Hampton (wine; deli)
18 Farmer's Market

? Information
Hampton Visitor Center

☼ Entertainment/Recreation
19 *Miss Hampton II* tour boat
20 Hampton Coliseum
21 Woodlands Golf Club & Hampton Tennis Center

M Marine Supplies
Neil Pryde Sailmakers

🍦 Ice Cream
🛏 Lodging
🌲 Park
✉ Post Office
℞ Pharmacy
✛ U.S. Veterans Hospital
Ⓑ Bus Bus Station
T Taxi Stand
∧⊤∧ Playground
Old Hampton

Hampton Roads continued from page 328

Hampton River

Just west of Mill Creek's entrance is the start of the channel that leads into the **Hampton River** and the city of **Hampton**. The path cuts across the northeast corner of **Hampton Flats**, so mind the channel markers to be sure to avoid the 2-foot shoals that make up the **Hampton Bar**.

If approaching Hampton Flats from the James or Nansemond rivers (via the Newport News Channel) there's a marked course, from southwest to northeast, with charted 7- to15-foot depths, which joins Hampton Reach Entrance Channel at lighted "11". Just make a turn to port there, keeping daymarks "10" and "12" to starboard.

Inside the Hampton River, Hampton University with its chiming clock-tower occupies the east bank. The school has an interesting history, and its museum, one of Virginia's oldest (founded in 1868), is also the country's oldest African American museum. On the wooded campus is the venerable EMANCIPATION OAK, under which Lincoln's executive order was publicly read for the first time in the South. Just before "16", narrow Jones Creek forms the southern border of the college where the sailing team's fleet is maintained.

Sunset Creek comes in on the opposite shore. Besides deep water, transient slips, floating docks, fuel and full ser-

Port of Call: Hampton continued from page 329

of stores, restaurants and entertainment venues. For fresh produce and other goodies, visit the Saturday morning Farmer's Market held at Carousel Park.

A variety of restaurants are within easy reach of the waterfront, many along Settlers Landing Road or Queen's Way. Hungry visitors can enjoy seafood, sushi, burgers, Italian, Cajun and home-style meals. Java Junkies, a coffeeshop adjacent to the public piers, offers free Wi-Fi along with light fare.

Families will especially enjoy Fridays in and around Hampton, when Carousel Park hosts Family Fun events like puppet shows. Summer evenings are filled with Sunday beach music concerts, Tuesday outdoor movies at Buckroe Beach and Saturday nights at Summer Street Fest, when Queen Street (the main street) comes alive with music and partying. The city's annual celebrations are numerous and include the Crabtown Seafeast in April; the Blackbeard Pirate Festival (usually in May); the Afrikan American Festival and Hampton Jazz Festival in June; a Fourth at the Fort gala with fireworks at Fort Monroe; hydroplane racing at the Hampton Cup Regatta in August; and in September, Hampton Bay Days to raise awareness about the Chesapeake.

Information: Hampton Visitor Center, 800-800-2202; www.visithampton.com.

vices, the two marinas here have transportation available. Bluewater offers a pool and restaurant, and Sunset Boating Center focuses on boat storage and fishing.

Past the Hampton Yacht Club, which sits at the mouth of this smaller tributary, the Hampton River's channel continues for about another half-mile, angling to the northeast toward a fixed bridge with a vertical clearance of 29 feet. Customs House Marina and Hampton Public Piers are to port, adjacent to the VIRGINIA AIR AND SPACE CENTER. Look for the contemporary cousin of the classic screwpile lighthouse on the waterfront between the two facilities, which houses Hampton's dockmaster office and visitor information center. These friendly facilities are within walking distance of sights and restaurants. Besides courtesy bicycles and other amenities, the municipal marina's special rates may entice you to extend your stay.

Public Piers also offers complimentary services for anchored visitors: water, trash disposal, internet and bicycle use. Showers are also available for a small fee. Just check in with the dockmaster.

Anchoring in the river can get creative and is recommended only for settled weather. Some find room between "18" and "20" near the yacht club. Boats also anchor farther north in the small areas near Joy's Marina on the eastern shoreline. Choose a spot across from the public piers and out of the channel in about 12 feet. But be aware of charted and uncharted obstructions, and stay clear of traffic. The *Miss Hampton*, which takes visitors around Norfolk Harbor and to Fort Wool, needs maneuvering room.

Hampton and its river are well worth exploring, and the city hosts many special events throughout the year.

Willoughby Bay

Next to Old Point Comfort, the traffic plying I-64 disappears into a small artificial island and reappears about a mile due south at Willoughby Spit, the eastern boundary of **Willoughby Bay**. The tiny man-made island here, **Fort Wool**, was created in 1818, long before any such underwater high-speed contraption was ever thought possible. Built upon a shoal, it's basically a big pile of rocks, originally part of Fort Monroe's defense complex. First called Fort Calhoun, it's still seen on some maps as Rip Raps Island. At one time a "submarine net" even closed off the area between the two forts. This abandoned isle found new purpose in 1957 when the Hampton Roads bridge-tunnel was designed. Now the tour boat *Miss Hampton* makes excursions there.

Willoughby Bay, locally called "Little Bay," contrasts sharply with the narrow, busy Hampton River; there's plenty of space for anchoring, but less water under the keel. It can be a convenient jumping off spot for those heading north or south, but the entire body of water is only 7 to 11 feet deep. Shoaling is also being reported in various areas, and the two narrow, shoal-prone channels leading into Willoughby Bay can be tricky. The key for deeper keels is to enter slowly while carefully observing all marks. There's moderate protection from the north in an area with a smattering of

Downtown Hampton Waterfront

PEOPLE HAVE *Explored* HERE FOR OVER 400 YEARS.

THIS IS
Hampton
VIRGINIA

COME HAVE AN ADVENTURE. 800.800.2202 VisitHampton.com

Hampton River *continued*

private mooring balls, outside the beefy cement cylinders that form a breakwater. This is the boundary for a protected basin that shelters two laid-back marinas, both of which offer floating docks for transients, but no fuel, repairs or room to anchor.

Entering from the Elizabeth River, Willoughby Bay's southern channel is maintained by the Navy. It runs west to east before angling into prohibited areas belonging to the Naval Air Station that dominates the southern shore. The northern channel, parallel to I-64 on the all-civilian side, is wider and deeper but more subject to shoaling. Watch tides and your depthsounder closely. This channel ends at the juncture leading into the snug northwest corner of **Little Bay** and the basin where the marinas are located. On race nights, you'll see an impressive parade of sailboats coming and going.

The hospitable Rebel Marine Service, to port on entering the basin, has some transient slips. It is also the home of the famous "tugantine" *Norfolk Rebel*, a one-of-a-kind 51-foot auxiliary sail-powered tug, which was designed by the legendary Lane Briggs as a tug assist for tall ships. The late Captain Briggs used her for many years as a goodwill ambassador. His son David now runs the marina and remains involved with the annual Great Chesapeake Schooner Race, which his father was instrumental in starting. The marina is full of stories and often sea chanties. More prosaically, it also has new showers, hot tub and a cozy fireplace. Nearby services are limited, but folks along the docks are often willing to offer recommendations or help with particular needs.

Just east of Rebel Marine is the larger Willoughby Harbor Marina, accommodating boats to 80 feet as well as multihulls. On site is a lounge, laundry facilities and a small dockside restaurant.

While there's not much in the neighborhood, a Willoughby Bay stopover is an opportunity to experience Willoughby Beach, a long strand of clean sand perfect for walking or watching the variety of boats transiting the mouth of the Bay. The beach and a convenience store are a short stroll from either marina. If it's necessary to leave the boat for personal business or to tour the area, the airport isn't far and Enterprise delivers.

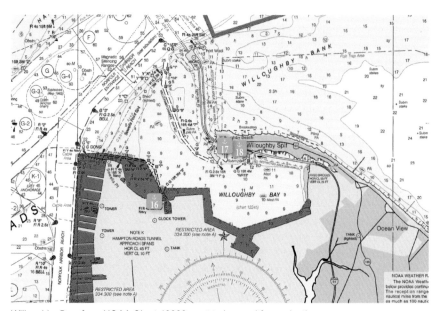

Willoughby Bay; from NOAA Chart 12222—not to be used for navigation.

Lower James River

The **James River** is not only one of the largest tributaries of the Chesapeake, it is the first explored and settled by the English colonists. Today's cruising explorers, however, often pass it by, perhaps because of its proximity to modern, industrialized Hampton Roads. Head upriver, though, and you're in a different world. It is impossible to cruise the James without thinking of those first settlers and wondering how the shoreline must have looked 400 years ago.

One change you can appreciate is the large number of markers set to guide you through the twisting channel. From Hampton Roads to Richmond, the James is characterized by shoals and bends. Today it is easily navigated, but think how deceptively inviting the broad mouth—about five miles wide—must have appeared to early explorers. The mouth of the James has plenty of water on the north side (closest to Newport News). Depths in the main channel from the Tidewater area to near Richmond vary from 25 to 80 feet.

The James River Bridge, which carries traffic along Routes 17/258 at Newport News, is a high lift bridge that opens to accommodate superstructures of military and commercial ships. It has a 60-foot vertical clearance at high tide when closed. With a normal tidal range of 2 to 3 feet and the occasional high high tide, tall sailboats will need to plan accordingly. Call the bridge tender (757-247-2133) if you have concerns. The bridge will often open on demand; however, a two-hour notice is expected. Call 757-247-2118 to request an opening.

Nansemond River

The ❶ **Nansemond River** offers a quiet, generally unspoiled peace that is hard to find so close to the beaten track. The mouth of the river opens right up into Hampton Roads and is only a few miles from most of the local marinas. Once past the Mills E. Goodwin fixed bridge (vertical clearance 65 feet) though, the Nansemond seems almost unpopulated. The Nansemond's only marina is in Suffolk, near its head.

You enter the river at the west end of Hampton Roads, where the James and the Nansemond converge. A prominent landmark for entering the Nansemond is the Monitor-Merrimac Memorial Bridge-Tunnel between Portsmouth and Newport News, which connects Pig Point (at the mouth of the Nansemond River) and Newport News Point.

The approach to the river is easy, with flashing green "5" at the entrance. The channel is wide and deep; just follow the markers. Before the fixed bridge, you'll spot a large cottage on stilts in the middle of the river. The house originally sheltered the guard for the private oyster beds here. Another guard house is located about a mile upstream. Both are now used as weekend homes.

Like most waterways on the lower Bay, the Nansemond has alternate shoal and deep areas. (There are reports of shoaling on the channel side of daymark "12" just past the 96-foot-high overhead power lines.) For several miles past the bridge there is plenty of room to anchor outside the channel. Then for about a mile the channel is dredged through a shoal, with more deep water past green daymark "13". Beyond Ferry Point the channel is dredged, and there is shoal water on either side. The dredged channel runs all the way to **Suffolk** (about 13 miles from the fixed bridge). Just before a swing bridge (vertical clearance 7 feet) near the mouth of Cedar Creek you'll pass Sleepy Hole Point, home of Suffolk's Sleepy Hole Park.

There are no protected anchorages on the Nansemond. You can just anchor out of the channel, though, happy to be in an open area to catch the breezes. Do not block the channel because there is some commercial traffic going to and from Suffolk. Most nights you will have the river to yourselves.

Constant's Wharf Public Park and Marina is located in historic downtown Suffolk near the Suffolk Hilton Garden Inn and Conference Center. From the marina, visitors can walk to restaurants, shops and historic attractions.

Chuckatuck Creek

Just north of the Nansemond is ❷ **Chuckatuck Creek**. The approach to the creek through **Batten Bay** is long and the creek is without services, yet it is a good choice for a quiet, relaxing evening with no company; choose some Brazilian jazz from your iTunes collection in tribute to Chuckatuck's most famous native son, musical legend Charlie Byrd, and enjoy.

● On Premises
➤ Nearby

	MLW	Overnight Slips	Gas	Diesel	Propane	Electric	Showers	Laundry	Restaurant	Lodging	Pool	Pump-out	Ice	Groceries	Marine Supplies	Bait	Boat Repair	Haul-out Services	Launch Ramp	Wi-Fi	Other
Willoughby Bay																					
Norfolk Naval Sailing Center and Marina MM Willoughby Bay 757-444-2918; www.tinyurl.com/NavySailingCenter	10'	●	➤	➤		●	●	●	➤	➤	➤	●	●	➤	●	●	➤	➤	●	●	Well protected basin; military and DOD only
Rebel Marine Service Willoughby Bay 757-580-6022; www.rebelmarina.com	8'	●	➤	➤	➤	●	●	➤	➤	➤	●	●	➤	➤	➤	➤	➤	➤	➤	●	Surveys, free Wi-Fi, courtesy cars, boater lounge
Willoughby Harbor Marina Willoughby Bay 757-583-4150	9'	●	➤	➤	➤	●	●	●	➤	➤	●	●	➤	➤	➤	➤	➤	➤	➤	●	Boat U.S. marina, floating docks, cable, cat. pier
Lower James River																					
Bennett's Creek Restaurant & Marina James R./Nansemond R./Bennett Cr. 757-484-8700	10'					●			●			●							●	●		
Brown's Marina Pagan R./ Jones Cr. 757-357-4459	6'		●	●		●	●											●	●			
Constant's Wharf Park and Marina James R./Nansemond R./Suffolk 757-514-7250	7'-14'	●	➤	➤	➤	●	●	➤	●	●	➤	●	➤	➤	➤						28 slips in the heart of downtown Suffolk
Deep Creek Landing Marina James R./Deep Cr./Newport News 757-877-9555; www.deepcreeklanding.com	5'+	●	●	●		●	●	●	➤	●	●	●	●	●	●	●	●	●	➤	●	Floating docks, banquet facility, full-service marina
James River Marina James R./Deep Cr./Newport News 757-930-1909; www.jamesrivermarina.com	8'	●	➤	➤	➤	●	●	➤	➤			➤	●	➤	●	●	●	●			Haul & block to 32', 14K lbs; MerCruiser cert.
Kingsmill Resort James R. 757-253-3919; www.kingsmill.com	7'	●	●	●		●	●		●	●	●	●	●	●	●				●		Golf, tennis, spa, gym, pools; near Busch Gardens
Leeward Municipal Marina James River Bridge; 757-247-2359 or 757-247-2376; www.nnparks.com/boating_leeward.php	7'	●	●	●		●	●	●	➤		●	➤	➤	➤	➤				➤		Mall and recreational facilities nearby
Smithfield Station James R./Pagan R. 757-357-7700; www.smithfieldstation.com	7'	●	➤	➤	➤	●	●	➤	●	●	●	●	➤	➤	➤	➤	➤	➤	➤	●	Shopping, bathhouse, bar, crabcakes, Best of Bay winner 2014

Nansemond River
continued

Nearby, just north of Batten Bay, is RAGGED ISLAND WILDLIFE MANAGEMENT AREA. With more than 1,500 acres of river marsh, scattered woody hammocks and sandy beach, this unspoiled area offers trails, viewing platforms and interpretive signs. While access is mainly land-centered from parking lots off U.S. 17 (the southern end of the James River Bridge), several creeks—including Ragged Island Creek, from Batten Bay, and Capper Creek, from the James—allow for easy exploration by dinghy or kayak.

Batten Bay is a large and extremely shallow flat that lies between the James River and the mouth of the Chuckatuck. The marked channel may seem to meander, but follow it carefully, proceeding with the assumption that you may run aground before arriving at the creek's deep entrance at Pike Point. Farther inside beyond red "10", fish net stakes may help to define the channel more clearly.

The small island west of Pike Point is connected to the shore by a mud flat at low tide. If you approach at low water, expect to see a clump of grass surrounded by mud here.

There is a small shipyard at Crittenden that can do repairs on boats of about any size, but the river has no other marine facilities. A pier at Crittenden on the southern shore is used by a small commercial fishing fleet. Drop your hook anywhere the water is deep enough for your draft. Space is a bit tight, but the anchorage is well protected. Just after Crittenden there is a fixed bridge with a vertical clearance of 35 feet.

Pagan River

Heading up the James River, you can pass close by red "12" as you round the Newport News coal piers to watch the fascinating process of loading coal from gigantic piles into waiting colliers. Fountains of water are sprayed over the coal piles to keep down the dust, giving the area a surrealistic glow.

Also on the northern bank of the river is huge Newport News Shipbuilding (formerly Northrup Grumman and now part of Huntington Ingalls), where you'll often see nuclear-powered aircraft carriers and submarines in various stages of construction or repair. Avoid the temptation to get too close for an inspection, because the area is vigilantly patrolled.

Once you are through the James River Bridge, the shore-line changes abruptly from industrial to residential. To the

James River, Newport News to Jamestown; from NOAA Chart 12248— not to be used for navigation.

north, large homes surrounded by lush green trees line the water's edge. The southern banks seem uninhabited, with thick, dark forests as far as the eye can see. (Be mindful that **White Shoal** splits the channel 2^1/$_3$ nautical miles north of the James River Bridge, but is well marked.)

The ❸ **Pagan River**'s flashing green entry light "3" is roughly three miles from the James River Bridge. **Smithfield**, one of Virginia's best preserved colonial seaports, is upriver about two miles from the mouth of the Pagan River and seven miles from the James River Bridge. This relatively protected, uncrowded and beautiful spot is only about 21 miles from the entrance to Hampton Roads. Its channel is dredged to 10 feet.

As you round the marker at the mouth of the Pagan, head west. Do not be lulled by the surrounding expansiveness into taking a short cut. Depths are shallower than you might expect so far from the shore, so stay in the channel. Once you have entered the Pagan, the course zigzags constantly, but daymarks keep the channel well marked.

Take note of **Jones Creek** on the southeast shore off flashing green "13". It is home to Brown's Marina, which has slips for transients and is the only place on the river to purchase gasoline and diesel. From "13" to "2" stay close to the portside point to enter the creek.

After Jones Creek is Battery Park, a colonial village formerly home to a large oyster shucking house. Here the channel narrows suddenly; give "14" plenty of room to starboard. The deep channel sweeps wide at this point, and a

shoal of only a few feet lies between the channel marker and the marshlands ahead of it.

For the next couple of miles upstream, the channel is wide, deep and straight up the middle. At Bob Shoal between "15" and "17" the channel is narrow, but dredging has deepened the area to a minimum of 6 feet at low tide. Past "17" the channel widens again.

When you reach marker "18" you may think that the river is coming to an abrupt end, but continue to follow the channel and, after several more turns, the marina complex at the edge of Smithfield will come into view. Smithfield Station (an inn, restaurant and marina complex) is hard to miss; the docks are flanked by a large main building that replicates an old Atlantic life-saving station and an exact copy of the screwpile lighthouse that once guarded Hooper Strait.

The Pagan is delightful. Sweeping grasslands. Strikingly attractive homes and yards. Enchanting scenes at every turn and twist of the narrow river. It is a mixture of old and new. While residential development has become a prominent feature on the southern shore, farther upriver elegant old mansions top the high river banks to port, and vast marshlands to the north and south provide lovely views.

At one time, the riverbanks also supported an abundance of nut trees. According to legend, curious early colonists asked local Native Americans about the name of the nut. The answer sounded something like "pagan," hence the name of the river.

continued on page 337

SMITHFIELD STATION

Waterfront Inn, Restaurant, & Marina

BEST OF THE BAY 2015 Chesapeake Bay Magazine

15% Off Hotel Stay! Code: Bay15

(877) 703-7701 | Smithfield, VA on the Pagan River | SmithfieldStation.com

Port of Call
Smithfield

From the expansive campus of Smithfield Foods to the pork dishes served at local restaurants, this town's relationship to ham is omnipresent. Yet there's more to Smithfield too, as suggested by its motto: "hams, history, hospitality and heART." The lovingly preserved historic downtown attests to its heritage, and the gracious welcome extended to visitors bespeaks Smithfield's sociable nature.

At the Visitor Center on Main Street, you can get an overview of Smithfield from a short video and set your own itinerary with brochures and

Smithfield & Isle of Wight Convention & Visitors Bureau

Smithfield

⚓ **Marinas/Dockage**
1 Smithfield Station

◯ **Points of Interest**
2 Isle of Wight County Museum
3 Old Courthouse of 1750
4 Visitor Center/Arts Center @319
5 School House Museum

🍴 **Dining**
1 Smithfield Station
6 Smithfield Inn and Tavern

7 Smithfield Ice Cream Parlor
8 Smithfield Gourmet Bakery
🍦 **Ice Cream**

🛒 **Groceries/Carryout**
8 Smithfield Gourmet
   Bakery & Beanery
9 Smithfield Farmers Market
10 Genuine Smithfield Ham Shoppe
11 Food Mart (convenience store)

☼ **Entertainment/Recreation**
12 Tennis courts
13 Wharf (fishing)

⚓ Parks
···· Historic District
   Walking Tour
℞ Pharmacy
📖 Library
Ⓜ Marine Supplies
? Information
🛏 Lodging
Laundromat
✉ Post Office

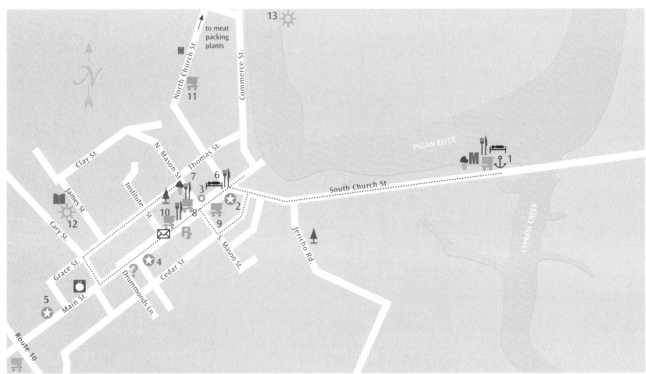

a self-guided walking tour of historic sites. These include the renovated Isle of Wight County Museum (site of a re-created general store), the Schoolhouse Museum, a one-room school built in 1932 for the African American community), the Old Courthouse of 1750 and many architecturally diverse 17th- and 18th-century homes. Guided tours of the historic district can be arranged for groups (fee, two-week notice). Or take the Historic Walking Tour of the downtown district.

Smithfield's cultural attractions include The Arts Center @319, where visitors can observe artists at work and browse the galleries, and Smithfield Little Theater, where plays are presented in fall, winter and early spring. For recreation, try the public tennis courts, go fishing at Clontz Park or work on your stroke at a nearby golf course. Relax with a stroll down Hayden's Lane, a former driveway transformed into a lovely sitting garden and brick walkway.

Within a short drive are: Historic St. Luke's Church (1632) with its Gothic-style buttresses and charming wicket door; Fort Huger, a Civil War era site; Fort Boykin Historic Park, where the Ghost Fleet of the Atlantic is visible from the bluffs; Bacon's Castle, a 1665 manor house; and the restored Boykin's Tavern. The visitor's center has a CD and map for a narrated area driving tour and rental cars can be arranged (call Enterprise at 757-357-9711 in advance of your visit).

The brick sidewalks, old-fashioned street lamps and diverse mix of retail businesses in the historic downtown will appeal to browsers and serious shoppers. Antiques shops and art galleries abound. There are also gift shops, a Christmas shop, a pharmacy, a boating supply store, and a place to buy authentic Smithfield ham (and peanuts, too). On Saturday mornings (May-Aug.) farmers sell produce and other items at the Smithfield Farmers Market.

In Smithfield, good food—and, of course, ham—are served with a side of Southern hospitality, and all within easy walking distance. On the upscale end of the food roster are the Smithfield Inn & Tavern (Southern and regional cuisine) and Smithfield Station restaurant (seafood, steaks, pork). More casual dining can be had at the IBX Bar and Grille at Smithfield Station marina (entertainment Wednesday evenings), Smithfield Gourmet Bakery & Cafe (sandwiches, soups, desserts) and Smithfield Ice Cream Parlor (subs, wraps, deli fare). For sweets, head for Three's Company (coffee bar) on Main Street.

June through August, local musicians give free concerts on the lawn in front of the *Smithfield Times.* This tight-knit sense of community is reflected in other events, among them Olden Days (parades, old-fashioned activities and a Pagan River homemade raft race) in June and in October, Town and Country Day (celebrating the city and nearby farms and vineyards).

Information: Smithfield & Isle of Wight Convention & Visitors Bureau, 800-365-9339; *www.visitsmithfieldisleofwight.com.*

Pagan River continued from page 335

Those nuts are still popular today; we call them pecans.

At Smithfield, some cruisers choose to anchor at the edge of the channel. You'll find a good anchorage off ROBERT S. CLONTZ PARK, the small community park south of the fishing pier. The river is deep here and generally uncrowded, and the park provides space to land a dinghy or kayak.

Transient slips are available at Smithfield Station marina, just be mindful of the current when docking. Here you'll have the use of a swimming pool and showers, not to mention the prospect of a fine meal. The marina-inn complex is on the eastern edge of the town's historic district, within easy walking distance of all of Smithfield's historic homes and attractions. Those arriving by water have the added advantage of being able to enjoy a "back door" view of the colonial and Victorian homes that is unavailable to visitors who travel by land.

This quaint town is known as home to the internationally famous Smithfield ham. (The company was purchased in 2013 by an international corporation based in China). Visitors can enjoy a walking tour highlighting two centuries of architecture and the ISLE OF WIGHT MUSEUM, which features a delightful reconstruction of a country store. Of special interest in town are two life-size bronze statues donated to the town by a local businessman. One depicts an elderly couple, very much in love, seated on a park bench. The other is a strikingly lifelike image of Benjamin Franklin reading a copy of the U.S. Constitution. (Franklin was postmaster for the region and founded a post office in Smithfield.)

Deep Creek

❹ **Deep Creek** lies on the northern shore of the James River about five miles upriver from the James River Bridge.

Coming in off the James, the entrance is long, deep and well marked. Depths should run 8 to 10 feet in the main channel, which is flanked by shoal banks. Although there may be sufficient depth out of the channel, it is unwise to cut corners in this section of the James for there are many broken-off stakes and pilings waiting just under the surface.

The entrance to Deep Creek is between a low, grassy spit on the right and the white city jail on a bluff to the left. Once inside, the creek opens into a small harbor, and you will see James River Marina immediately to starboard. The south end of the harbor is filled with workboats. Since watermen begin their work before daylight, it's preferable to anchor at the north end near Deep Creek Landing Marina. The marina has a small travel lift and offers a range of repair services. They also have a fuel dock. Nearby, Warwick Yacht and Country Club's casual outdoor restaurant is open to the public.

There's not much here by way of shopping, but you can visit attractions such as Colonial Williamsburg, Busch Gardens, the Mariners' Museum in Newport News and the NASA Visitor's Center in Hampton by rental car from nearby Patrick Henry Airport. In the fall, all will be quiet here, with oyster boats tied up across the creek and a few lights at the

Deep Creek continued

marina docks.

Next to Deep Creek lies the larger but less used **Warwick River**. Although well-marked up to a boat ramp beyond Lucas Creek, it's shallow and can be difficult to navigate without local knowledge.

On the other side of the James River's main channel—due west of Deep Creek and the Warwick River—is **Burwell Bay** and a ghostly collection of mothballed Navy and merchant ships. The oldest of eight original National Defense Reserve Fleets, it is currently one of three still in operation. Its dwindling number of obsolete vessels are awaiting disposal by the government. North of the fleet, on river right, is the restricted area of the U.S. Army's Fort Eustis.

Kingsmill

One of the river's popular destinations is ❺ Kingsmill Resort & Spa near Williamsburg. Its marina, off red "40", offers slips, showers, fuel, a sandy beach, a dockside eatery and access to the elegant Kingsmill complex, which includes five other restaurants, three championship golf courses, a tennis center, a spa and a health club. The dockmaster can arrange for reservations and transportation to dining and nearby attractions, like Busch Gardens and Colonial Williamsburg, making the resort an excellent place to spend a long weekend.

Across the river from Kingsmill is HOG ISLAND WILDLIFE MANAGEMENT AREA and the Surry nuclear power plant.

Cobham Bay

❻ **Cobham Bay** is a quiet anchorage, if somewhat exposed. In the hot summer months it's a good spot to catch whatever breeze is stirring. The bay can be ideal for a weekend getaway. Anchor in 4 to 5 feet of water just 50 yards from shore. Walk on the smooth, sandy bottom to explore the shoreline. Nearby is CHIPPOKES PLANTATION STATE PARK, one of the oldest working farms in the United States.

Jamestown

❼ **Jamestown** was the first permanent English settlement in the New World. Its island setting offered ample notice of threats from downriver and a barrier to possible Indian attacks from the mainland. The river was deep right up to the shore, so settlers could off-load their ships easily.

Today at JAMESTOWN SETTLEMENT, adjacent to the ferry landing at Glass House Point, you can tour a replica of the original settlement. Museums there and at nearby HISTORIC JAMESTOWNE interpret the site and its archeological excavations, and artisans demonstrate early crafts such as glassblowing.

There are no landing facilities for boats or dinghies at Jamestown, but Jamestown Yacht Basin on **Powhatan Creek** is within walking distance of the settlement. To get there, you must be able to squeeze under two fixed low bridges (11 and 14 feet MLW) and have a draft that doesn't mind 3-foot

Bay Spotlight

James River Plantations

Push your finger up a chart of the James River and look closely at the area around Charles City and Hopewell. You'll see names like "Berkeley," "Westover" and "Shirley." Jamestown's settlers knew their fortunes would come from hard work and tobacco. Pushing up the river, they started plantations, some of which supported stunning houses. A handful survive today and are open to the public. Although not many docks survive, it's still possible to tie up or dinghy in to tour some of these grand homes.

Perhaps the most spectacular is privately owned and still used as a residence: Westover. The 1730 Georgian brick mansion is open only in late April during Historic Garden Week and Westover Church's Autumn Pilgrimage in the fall, although the grounds are open daily from 9 a.m. to 6 p.m. Built by William Byrd II, the founder of Richmond, Westover is noteworthy for its architectural details, secret

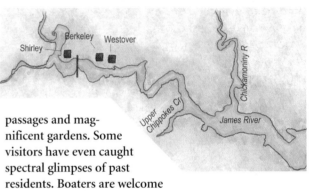

passages and magnificent gardens. Some visitors have even caught spectral glimpses of past residents. Boaters are welcome to use its dock, but are asked to call in advance (804-829-2882). Boats drawing over 3 feet are advised to anchor off and dinghy in. Westover uses an honor system, asking visitors to donate $5 for a brochure offering a self-guided tour of the grounds and outbuildings.

Within walking distance (albeit a two-mile hike) of Westover is Berkeley Hundred and its 1731 manor house. Boaters who call ahead can tie up at Westover on a limited basis and use it as a starting point for their tour. Berkeley was the ancestral home of presidents William Henry Harrison and his grandson Benjamin. It was also where "Taps" was first composed and played, when Lincoln's Army of the Potomac was camped here in 1862.

A few miles upriver from Westover is Shirley Plantation, which has no suitable river access. Tie up at Jordan Point Yacht Haven near Hopewell and take a short cab ride to the plantation. Still owned by the Hill-Carter family, it is one of the oldest and most gracious plantations on the James. The original plantation house was built in 1670 and the existing mansion in the early 1700s. Its most renowned peculiarity is a "floating" staircase that winds it way up three stories with no visible means of support.

depths. If your boat can do all that, by all means go on in. In addition to slips and gas, the marina rents bikes, kayaks, canoes and paddleboards. There's also a launch ramp for trailerable boats. Those who can't make it in, can anchor in the James and dinghy in. A $5 dinghy landing fee entitles you to day use of the marina's facilities.

The Jamestown-Scotland ferry crosses the river every 20 minutes on weekends (every 30 minutes on weekdays) between Scotland and Glass House Point. The landings are marked on the charts. You can anchor in the river north or south of the Glass House Point ferry terminus.

Chickahominy River

The ❽ **Chickahominy River** is among the most beautiful and haunting rivers on the entire Chesapeake—shoot, make that *anywhere*! It enters the James River on the north shore, not far beyond the Scotland-to-Jamestown ferry crossing. Its entrance is well marked and easy to follow. Before rounding Barrets Point, you'll pass numerous large homes and a clubhouse, all part of the Governor's Land at Two Rivers waterfront community. A new fixed bridge with 52 feet of clearance opened in 2009, replacing the old swing bridge. Unfortunately, this now prevents tall sailboats rigs from visiting this remarkable waterway.

Like the smaller tributaries at the mouth of the James, the Chickahominy is a quiet place. CHICKAHOMINY WILDLIFE MANAGEMENT AREA occupies a good portion of the western shore opposite Shields Point. Farther up, the river twists and turns to reveal one gorgeous scene after another, with cypress trees wading out into the water to stand beside the channel, wild marshes alternating with wood-covered bluffs, and everywhere herons, ospreys and bald eagles.

There are few facilities along the sparsely populated river. The first marina you'll encounter comes 9 miles above the bridge, after rounding Big Marsh Point. This is River's Rest Marina, which offers deep-water slips, gas and diesel fuel, and the Blue Heron Restaurant.

Four miles farther upriver, a sharp bend at Wilcox Neck leads to a stand of cypress in the river. This is what remains of **Smith Island**, where Captain John Smith was supposedly captured by Chief Powhatan's warriors. Behind the island is Colonial Harbor Marina, offering slips, marine supplies and repair services, gas, ice, a great restaurant and some of the friendliest folks you'll find anywhere. Anchoring

is good just above Smith Island in about 20 feet of water.

A few more miles up the Chickahominy brings you to Walker Dam, which spills water from shallow Lake Chickahominy into the river. The hand-operated locks work well and will accommodate a 30-foot boat with a 4-foot draft. Most of the lake is less than 6 feet deep, but it extends for many miles and is easily explored by dinghy.

Upper Chippokes Creek to Jordan Point

Above the Chickahominy, ❾ **Upper Chippokes Creek** lies on the southwestern shore of the James near marker "67". A channel of sorts, defined by stakes, winds beyond its wide, shallow mouth along the southern bank. Navigating this tributary, however, is best with shoal drafts and local knowledge.

If you decide to explore the 17 miles of the James River between the Chickahominy and Jordan Point, you will find the river itself much as the settlers did: "navigable upp into the country deepe." You won't find snug overnight anchorages, and the only services are at Jordan Point, but you will find the river's sweeping turns impressive with history at every bend.

As the colony of Virginia's main highway, the James was once chock-a-block with plantations, each with its own landing, where hogsheads of tobacco were rolled to waiting ships. After wharves were established, trading posts grew around them and many of today's townships along the river bear the

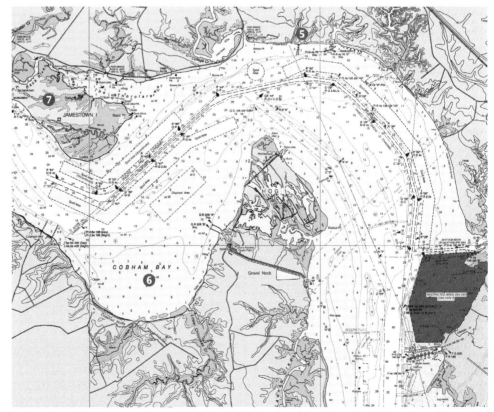

Middle James River; from NOAA Chart 12248—not to be used for navigation.

Upper Chippokes Creek to Jordan Point
continued

names of these once-bustling landings. Plantation owners and their offspring—Harrisons, Carters, Byrds, Randolphs—became social, economic and political leaders.

Later, Civil War activity up and down the James saw many of these properties occupied by both Union and Confederate forces. One skirmish occurred off Fort Powhatan on the James's southern shore. While long-abandoned, some foundations remain. Ruffin Wharf, on the north bank, belonged to the agronomist and Southern nationalist Edmund Ruffin, said to have fired the first shot at Fort Sumter.

On the southern side, FLOWERDEW HUNDRED is among the earliest plantations in the New World, dating to 1619. Two and a half centuries later, Grant's and Sheridan's troops camped in this same place before the siege of Petersburg. Remarkably, the Army Corps of Engineers constructed a pontoon bridge in a matter of hours to convey troops from north to south. The bald cypress tree that anchored the bridge reportedly still stands.

Past Windmill Point, nearly 14 nautical miles from the Chickahominy, one chart feature along the northern shore conjures images of a colonial punishment: Ducking Stool Point. Another mile upriver is WESTOVER, the first of a cluster of surviving grand plantation homes. You can anchor north of the channel in 10 feet, admiring the beauty of this stately manor and pondering the past.

Just below the lift bridge at ⑩ **Jordan Point** (closed clearance 50 feet), islands begin to appear, altering the river's character. Jordan Point Yacht Haven, at the bridge's southeast end, offers slips, fuel and repairs.

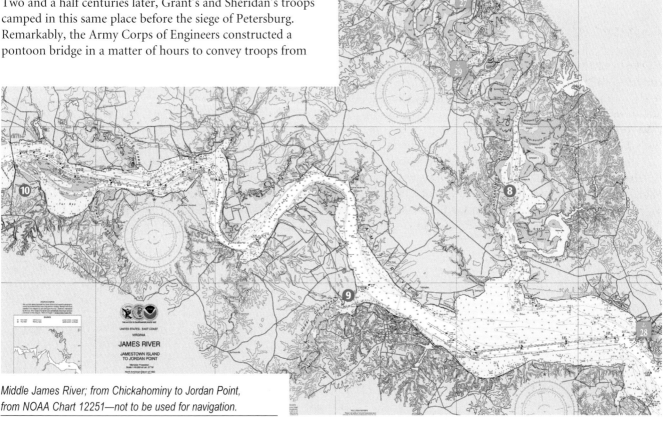

Middle James River; from Chickahominy to Jordan Point, from NOAA Chart 12251—not to be used for navigation.

● On Premises
➤ Nearby

	MLW	Overnight Slips	Gas	Diesel	Propane	Electric	Showers	Laundry	Restaurant	Lodging	Pool	Pump-out	Ice	Groceries	Marine Supplies	Bait	Boat Repair	Haul-out Services	Launch Ramp	Wi-Fi	Other
Middle James River																					
Colonial Harbor Marina James R./Chickahominy R. 804-966-5523; www.colonialharbor.com	8'	●	●	●	➤	●	●		●			●	●	●	●	●	●	●	●		Discount marine store, Hi & Dry storage
Jamestown City County Marina James R./Powhatan Cr.; 757-565-3699; www.jamescity countyva.gov/recreation/parks/james-city-county-marina.html	3'	●	●			●	●					●			●		●	●	●		Covered, full-service yard, next to Jamestown
River's Rest Marina & Resort James R./Chickahominy R. 804-829-2753; www.riversrest.com	12'	●	●	●	➤	●	●	●	●	●		●	●	●	➤	●	●	➤	➤	●	Near historic sites, Williamsburg 20min. Plantations 15, boat rental

● On Premises
➤ Nearby

Upper James River

	MLW	Gas	Diesel	Propane	Electric	Showers	Laundry	Restaurant	Lodging	Pool	Pump-out	Ice	Groceries	Marine Supplies	Boat Repair	Bait	Haul-out Services	Launch Ramp	Wi-Fi	Other
Jordan Point Yacht Haven James R./Jordan Pt. 804-458-3398; www.jordanpoint.com	5'	●	●	●	●	●	●	➤	➤		●	●	●		●	●	●	●	●	25-ton lift, non-ethanol gas, floating docks
Kingsland Reach Marina James R./Richmond 800-348-5735; www.kingslandreachmarina.com	4'	●			●	●	●	●				●	●	●						Picnic area; Sea Doo dealer
Rocketts Landing Marina James R. 804-222-3555; www.rockettsvillage.com	5'	●	●	●		●	●		●	➤		●			➤				➤	Closest to Richmond. Slips to 50'. New fuel dock

Appomattox River

Hopewell City Marina—primarily a boat-launch area—sits on the ⑪ **Appomattox River**, above the Route 10 bridge (vertical clearance 40 feet). The small facility no longer offers fuel, and other transient services are limited. The town of **Hopewell**, however, does have a hospital nearby and a sandwich shop within easy walking distance of the marina.

It's a longer walk to APPOMATTOX MANOR, a plantation home overlooking the James and now managed by the National Park Service—but it's worth the trek. The land, patented in 1635 by Francis Eppes, remained in the family until 1979. The family was absent, however, during the Union's occupation during the Civil War, when General Grant used the property as headquarters during the siege of Petersburg, the longest military event of the war. Near the manor house is the general's one-room log cabin. Grant chose to live and work as his subordinates did, rather than in the more comfortable plantation home. While City Point served as supply center during the 10-month seige, it was one of the busiest seaports in the world.

The Appomattox has a marked channel with a controlling depth of about 7 feet to the dam above the city of Petersburg and then through a diversion canal. There is a small-boat marina with some slips along the way.

Upper James

As you leave Hopewell and head up the James toward Richmond (about 20 miles away), BERMUDA HUNDRED is on your left. Settled by Captain John Rolfe in the 1600s, this was the largest tobacco port in the New World. Only a trace of the homes remain, and there is no access from the river.

Farther upriver the main channel loops around the PRESQUILE NATIONAL WILDLIFE REFUGE, an island about two miles long and a mile wide. Boats drawing less than 6 feet can circumnavigate the island, which offers several quiet anchorages.

Just north of the I-295 bridge and to your left is HENRICUS PARK, which sits high on a bluff overlooking a manmade channel called **Dutch Gap**. Water depths of 15 feet allow easy dockage at a floating dock below the park, which is a re-created village of what is known to have existed in 1619.

Farther north is the Dominion Power Dutch Gap Station, and about a mile above that is Kingsland Reach Marina (closed Sundays and Mondays), which offers ice, marine supplies, beer and snacks.

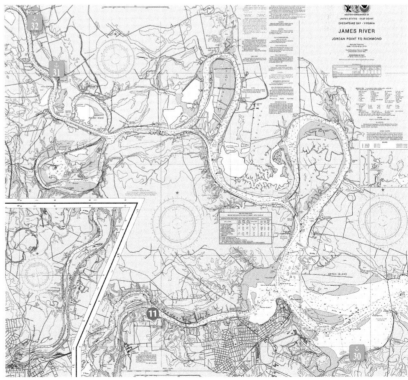

Upper James River, Jordan Point to Richmond; from NOAA Chart 12252— not to be used for navigation.

Upper James *continued*

During the remaining 6 miles to **Richmond**, you'll pass Fort Darling on Drewrys Bluff to port. This Civil War defensive site is not accessible from the water, but you may see the giant cannon at the top of the bluff. Richmond's skyline soon becomes visible as well. At the waterfront, the first phase of the new marina at **Rocketts Landing** is open, with floating slips and a fuel dock. Restaurants and shops are nearby, and museums not far.

Elizabeth River

Although it carries commercial and military traffic, from tugs to cargo ships and from aircraft carriers to submarines, the **Elizabeth River** also is a popular waterway for recreational boaters. And, importantly, it is the portal to the INTRACOASTAL WATERWAY. The Elizabeth is graced by the vibrant waterfronts of Portsmouth and Norfolk, rebuilt with boating visitors in mind. En route to the Elizabeth from Hampton Roads, you'll pass the sprawling Norfolk International Terminal to port and the Army Corps of Engineers' ever-expanding **Craney Island** dredge-spoil impoundment to starboard. Yet even on this industrial waterway, you can find means of escape from the hustle and bustle.

Lafayette River

Not long after entering the Elizabeth River, you'll come to the entrance to the **❶ Lafayette River**. Although the Layfayette lies just north of busy Norfolk and Portsmouth and south of Hampton Roads, Naval Station Norfolk and Norfolk International Terminal, you'll find it protected and surprisingly tranquil. It's a good spot to wait out stormy or choppy Bay conditions. The river is residential and picturesque with osprey, pelicans and sailors-in-training. Yet above the trees you'll spot reminders that a first-class port is not far away—the towering cranes used for loading and unloading cargo from some of the world's largest cargo ships.

While the Lafayette's mouth appears roomy,

shoals lurk south of Tanner Point and along the marshy southeastern side of the entrance. In making the turn northeast toward the Lafayette's daymarks from the main channel of the Elizabeth River, the safest path for deeper drafts lies somewhere between bell buoys "19" and "21". With plenty of water in its well-marked center, the Lafayette's channel follows a straight course for a mile before jogging due east.

The Lafayette, named in honor of the famous Revolutionary general, is home to Old Dominion University Sailing Center and its nationally ranked collegiate team. Also on the river, near the right turn at flashing "11", is the HERMITAGE FOUNDATION MUSEUM, with 12 acres of formal gardens, forest and wetlands on a small peninsula along the north shore. The museum showcases art from around the world and exquisite wood carvings. It has no facilities for docking, but you can beach the dinghy there and lug it to higher ground.

Also to port, just before the fixed Hampton Boulevard Bridge (vertical clearance 26 feet), sits the sprawling Norfolk Yacht and Country Club. Boats anchor west of the complex or opposite it—south of the channel near "14" in about 10 feet, where several "permanently" moored boats occupy much of the space. It shoals quickly outside the channel, so watch your depthsounder.

There are no marinas on the Lafayette and no fuel, unless you have reciprocal yacht club membership, so it's a good idea to arrive with topped-off tanks for both the mothership and dinghy. That dinghy will come in handy if you aren't

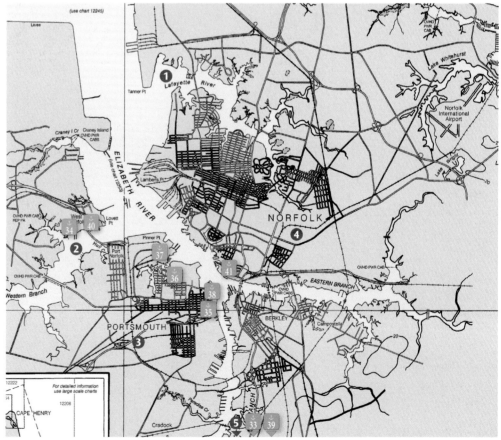

Elizabeth River, from NOAA Chart 12207—not to be used for navigation.

able to navigate under the fixed bridge. Beyond it, the Lafayette is stunning and navigable for about three more miles with depths of 7 to 15 feet.

One popular anchorage is around flashing "22". At "24" is **Knitting Mill Creek**, a pleasant side trip, though there's no room to anchor and the piers are private. At the end of the creek, O'Sullivan's Wharf Restaurant has a small floating dock and friendly service. In the neighborhood you'll also find a laundromat and a convenience store.

Beyond the Granby Street Bridge (vertical clearance 22 feet) depths drop significantly, but exploration is still worthwhile with dinghies, kayaks and similar shallow drafts. In the Southern Branch, occupying 60 acres along the shore to starboard, VIRGINIA ZOOLOGICAL PARK is perhaps the only world-class zoo in the Chesapeake region accessible by water. Land visitors gain entrance via Granby Street, about a mile south of the bridge, but small boats may use a public ramp and small dock situated next to the zoo at the foot of LaValette Avenue. Note: As is true with vehicles of any sort in any metropolitan area, locking the dinghy (and its engine) makes good sense.

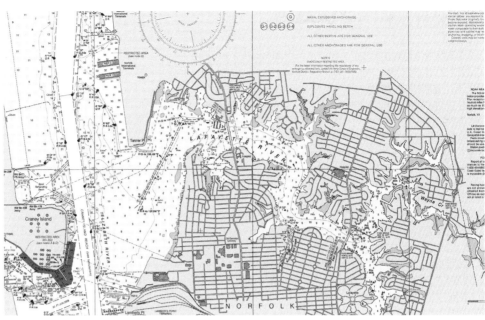

Layfayette River; from NOAA Chart 12245—not to be used for navigation.

● On Premises
➤ Nearby

Elizabeth River & ICW

	MLW	Overnight Slips	Gas	Diesel	Propane	Electric	Showers	Laundry	Restaurant	Lodging	Pool	Pump-out	Ice	Groceries	Marine Supplies	Bait	Boat Repair	Haul-out Services	Launch Ramp	Wi-Fi	Other
Atlantic Yacht Basin ICW/A&C Canal mile 12 757-482-2141; www.atlanticyachtbasin.com	12'	●	●	●	➤	●	●	●	➤	➤		●	●	➤	●	➤	●	●	➤	●	Full-service, freshwater covered storage
Nautical Boats Marina Elizabeth R./Western Branch 757-483-6148	19'	●			●	●						●	●		●			●	●		Dry storage 50-ton lift
Ocean Marine Yacht Center Elizabeth R./Mile Marker Zero 757-399-2920; www.oceanmarinellc.com	25'	●	●	●	➤	●	●	●	●	➤	➤	➤	●	●	➤	●	●	●	➤	●	Floating docks, indoor dry storage, parts, yacht sales
Portsmouth Boating Center Elizabeth R./Scott Cr. 757-397-2092	8'	●	●	●	●	●	●	●	➤	➤	●	●	●	●	●	●	●	●		●	70-ton lift, dry & land storage, Boat U.S. discount
Scott's Creek Marina Elizabeth R./Scott's Cr. 757-399-2628 ; www.scottscreekmarina.com	12'	➤	➤	➤	➤	●	●			●	●	●	●			➤	➤			●	Lending library, free laundromat & pump-out ($5)
Tidewater Yacht Marina Elizabeth R./Mile Marker Zero 757-393-2525 or 888-390-0080; www.tyamarina.com	10'	●	●	●	➤	●	●	●	●	●	●	●	●	●	●	●	➤	●	●	➤	●	500' Megayacht dock, fast fueling, 100amp 1/3 phase
Top Rack Marina Elizabeth R./Chesapeake, Va. 757-227-3041; www.toprackmarina.com	14'	●	●	●		●		●		●			●		●		●			●	Premium fuel avail. Amber Lantern Restaurant
Virginia Boat & Yacht Elizabeth R./Western Branch 757-673-7167	6'	●																●	●			
Waterside Marina Elizabeth R./Norfolk/Mile Marker 0 757-625-3625; www.watersidemarina.com	20'	●	➤	➤	➤	●	●	●	●	●	●		●	●	●	➤		●	➤	➤	●	Near Nauticus, USS Wisconsin, theaters & mall

Western Branch

For those not familiar with a commercial waterfront, the Portsmouth Marine Terminal provides a convenient opportunity to observe the stevedore's art. Naval Station Norfolk is home to a large assortment of naval vessels, including submarines, destroyers, auxiliary ships and aircraft carriers. The downtown waterfronts of Portsmouth and Norfolk are only a short distance along the Elizabeth River.

❷ **Western Branch** channel turns southwest off the main Elizabeth River channel at red "30". The most prominent landmark is the Navy Degaussing Station just west of "30". The cranes at Portsmouth Marine Terminal (on the tip of Pinner Point) are also easy to spot. Daymarks clearly delineate the Western Branch channel.

Two marinas on the northern shore have transient slips. The first, Virginia Boat and Yacht, is before the fixed West Norfolk Bridge (vertical clearance 45 feet). Nautical Boats Marina is located west of the bridge. Farther up, Route 17 crosses the Western Branch with 38 feet of clearance. The area between these spans is suitable for anchoring. All the bottom is soft mud and furnishes fair holding ground. The anchorage is quite protected except when a stiff breeze blows from due east.

Farther up the Western Branch is PORTSMOUTH CITY PARK (just west of **Baines Creek**). No pier is available for docking, so access is limited to a dinghy or shallow draft boat that can be beached. In addition to the usual picnic facilities, the park features a miniature railroad, tennis courts, nine-hole golf course and three-pier boat ramp.

Charted soundings in the river are generally accurate, but deeper draft boats should proceed with caution outside the marked channel. The numerous small creeks off the Western Branch will tempt curious gunkholers. However, all but the shallowest of vessels are advised to stay in the river since they are not even charted.

Do not plan on restocking the larder here as groceries are not readily available. Western Branch is the place to relax and do nothing. Worry about shopping another day.

Portsmouth

Once past the Western Branch, you can easily miss **Scott Creek** among all the larger-than-life distractions in this megaport. But the tributary can be a quiet, economical place to dock while you explore the area's many attractions by rental car. Although surrounded by industry, Scott's Creek Marina, near the mouth on the north shore, is family-friendly with a pool and small ships store for essentials. Farther inside the creek, on the other shore, Portsmouth Boating Center offers fuel, haul-out and repairs. Pharmacy, ATM, and convenience store are less than a mile away, and the colonial port's historic center another half-mile.

❸ **Portsmouth** is a popular stop for snowbirds traveling the Intracoastal Waterway. South of Scott Creek and Hospital Point, the cove near bell buoy "36", west of the channel, is a reasonably-protected but wake-prone anchorage. Incessant traffic and the closeness of large commercial vessels make this a bouncy place, so be sure the anchor is well set and allow extra scope. You'll fall asleep to the whistle of tugboats "talking" to one another as they move ships around.

Adjacent to the anchorage, near ICW Mile Zero, Tidewater Yacht Marina has 100 deep-water transient slips behind a breakwater. Amenities include a floating pool. Tidewater's full-service boatyard offers a complete range of repairs, and the marine store can meet most needs, from perishables to charts. From here it's a short walk to restaurants, shops, museums and the visitor center, where you can plan a tour of Olde Towne. In the evening, enjoy both dinner and first-run movie at the restored art deco Commodore Theatre.

Defining the other end of Portsmouth's waterfront is Ocean Marine Yacht Center, which has fuel, floating slips and repairs. It's also within walking distance of Olde Towne's attractions and next door to nTelos Pavilion, the large outdoor music venue at Harbor Center.

On summer weekends and during special events, a water taxi, which docks at Tidewater, serves the anchorage and marinas (757-439-TAXI; VHF 16). Free, short-term dockage may be available in one of two small basins—North Landing and High Street, the ferry piers from which folks are shuttled back and forth to Norfolk.

Cruising this section of the Elizabeth River puts you in close proximity to the impressive BAE Systems Ship Repair on the Norfolk side. Their two immense floating drydocks

Stay informed about happenings around the Chesapeake Bay

... breaking news, notices to Chesapeake mariners, Bay-wide events, special offers, and more.

✓ Sign Me Up

Chesapeake Bay Magazine's Talk of the Bay

for Chesapeake Bay Magazine's free monthly e-newsletter.

go to:
www.ChesapeakeBoating.net/Pages/Newsletter

Port of Call
Portsmouth

Virginia Tourism Corporation

Portsmouth's evolution has been tied to the sea. The Naval Shipyard, founded in 1767, now services nuclear-powered vessels, and this portion of the Elizabeth River remains as busy as ever. Ocean-going container ships load and unload at Portsmouth Marine Terminal, and Coast Guard vessels ply the waters near their home base here. Echoes of the city's past welcome those who walk the quiet streets of historic Olde Towne. Joined by a seawall, these two distinctive portions of the city convey its proud heritage.

Olde Towne comes to life on docent-led lantern tours and horse-drawn carriage rides (call 757-636-5315 for a schedule). There is also a Path of History walking tour that leads past 45 downtown and historic district sites, and an Olde Towne Walking Tour with over three dozen sites. These homes, museums and other buildings bear witness to the area's local heritage.

Water taxis also offer guided tours of this active port (757-439-TAXI). Near the water, the Naval Shipyard Museum chronicles naval history from the Civil War, the Lightship Museum (housed in a 1915 lightship) preserves the restored vessel's legacy, and visitors can marvel at a free-standing 10-foot-tall fresnel lens, the only one displayed outside a museum setting. Other downtown attractions include Hill House, an early 19th-century dwelling with its original furnishings; the Virginia Sports Hall of Fame and Museum, which honors over 200 of the state's athletes; and the Children's Museum of Virginia, featuring kid-pleasing interactive exhibits, a climbing wall and

continued on next page

Portsmouth

⚓ **Marinas/Dockage**
  1 Tidewater Yacht Marina
  2 Public docking
    (free; no overnight)
  3 Ocean Marine Yacht Center

⊕ **Points of Interest**
  4 Courthouse Galleries
  5 Civic Center
  6 Convention & Visitors Bureau
  7 Fresnel Lens
  8 Ferry/High St. Landing
  9 Naval Shipyard Museum
  10 Lightship Museum
  11 Ferry/North Landing
  12 Hill House
  13 Children's Museum of Virginia
  14 Virginia Sports Hall of
    Fame & Museum
  17 Visual Arts Center

🍴 **Dining Area**
  18 High Street

🛍 **Shopping**

🛒 **Groceries/Carryout**
  19 Dollar General
  20 7-Eleven

☼ **Entertainment/Recreation**
  21 nTelos Pavilion at Harbor Center
  22 Commodore Theatre

✚ **Hospital**
  Naval Medical Center

🌲 **Park** ■ **Library**
? **Information**

℞ **Pharmacy**

✉ **Post Office**

  Shopping District

  Historic District

--- **Shuttle Bus Route**

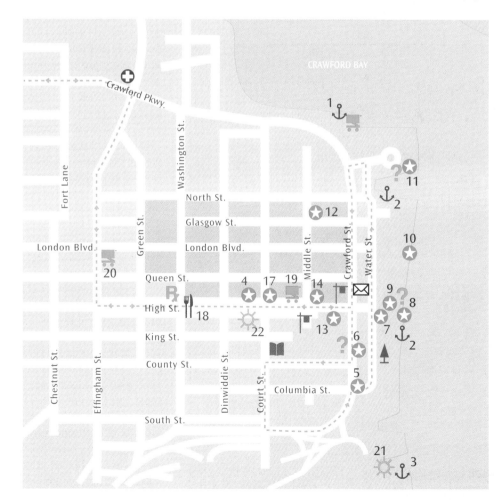

Port of Call: Portmouth *continued*

a planetarium. Tidewater Community College's Visual Arts Center and the 1846 Courthouse Galleries showcase art, lectures and performances.

Portsmouth remains lively even after the sun goes down. Movie-goers can enjoy the latest studio releases and light dinners in the handsomely restored, 1945 art deco Commodore Theatre. Concert-goers can enjoy performances by top-name musicians from the comfort of the sheltered nTelos Pavilion at Harbor Center.

Most downtown destinations, including your choice of hotels, are a stroll or shuttle bus ride from the waterfront, but taxis (757-235-5099) and rental cars are available to take visitors to city parks, Bide-A-Wee Golf Course, Hoffler Creek Wildlife Preserve, the Historic Triangle and other local attractions.

Stroll the brick sidewalks of Olde Towne and you'll find antiques stores (one specializes in nautical antiques) and specialty shops aplenty, most on High Street leading away from the river. Nearby, the Olde Towne flea market attracts nearly 100 vendors on the first Saturday of the month.

No supermarket is convenient to the waterfront, but you'll find a convenience store at Effingham Street. Tidewater Yacht Marina carries bread, milk, eggs, lunch items and other necessities, while Ocean Marine Yacht Center sells snacks, beverages and sandwiches, and offers a courtesy car for more thorough provisioning.

Seafood, Chinese, German, overstuffed sandwiches, Tex-Mex—take your pick. Going hungry in Portsmouth is a function of indecision, not lack of choice. Restaurants can be found downtown, in the historic district and in waterfront hotels and marinas; a number are concentrated on High Street.

First weekends are hopping in Portsmouth as shops and galleries host receptions and show openings on First Fridays, Olde Towne welcomes bargain hunters to the First Saturday Antiques to Flea Market and area museums offer free admission on First Sundays. Arts, culture and the water are dominant themes in annual events, including the region-wide Virginia Arts Festival and Gosport Arts Festival in May; the Cock Island Race (a sailing competition that culminates in a waterfront celebration) and River Rhythms (a music-filled counterpart to Norfolk's Harborfest) in June. in September Tidewater Marina hosts the annual Rendezvous at Mile Marker Zero for snowbirds; and in October, Great Chesapeake Bay Schooner Race participants line the docks and bulkheads.

Information: Convention & Visitors Bureau, 800-PORTS-VA or 757-393-5111; *www.visitportsva.com*.

Tidewater Yacht Marina is one of the finest marinas along the East coast located at mile marker "0" on the intracoastal waterway. With an on-site service center, fully-stocked marine store, restaurant, fuel dock and more, it's no wonder Tidewater has received so many awards and recognition. We're truly a boater's haven!

Tidewater YACHT MARINA

10 Crawford Pkwy, Portsmouth, VA 23704
tidewateryachtmarina.com • 757-393-2525

can lift ships up to 52,500 tons. Farther south on the western shore is historic Norfolk Naval Shipyard, which is entirely within Portsmouth's city limits. (The name was retained to avoid confusion with Portsmouth Naval Shipyard in Maine.) Recognized as a suitable shipbuilding site in 1620 by the earliest colonists, it was first established as Gosport Shipyard in 1767. It's the largest shipyard on the East Coast, and the U.S. Navy's oldest facility for building, remodeling and repairing its fleet.

Norfolk

4 Norfolk is a vital port to commercial shipping, a mighty naval installation, a busy yachting harbor and the beginning of the Intracoastal Waterway to Florida. It also has a very boater-friendly downtown.

The entrance to the harbor includes access to Hampton Roads (the yachting area) on the north, Newport News (the commercial and shipbuilding center) to the northwest, and Norfolk to the south and east. It is designed to be easy for a 95,000-ton aircraft carrier, so it presents no unusual problems for yachtsmen. Entering, between Fort Monroe on the north and Fort Wool on the south, is straightforward, except when hampered by the rare fog. Currents can run more than $2^{1}/_{2}$ knots, so if yours is a slow boat, use your current tables to advantage.

As you head farther up the main channel toward downtown Norfolk, you will leave a big ship anchorage to starboard and to port the largest naval base in the world: 13 enor-

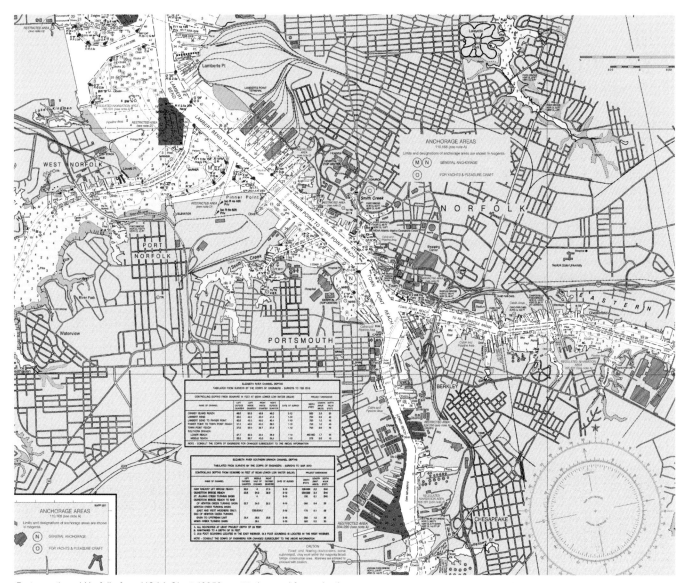

Portsmouth and Norfolk; from NOAA Chart 12253—not to be used for navigation.

mous piers that are home to aircraft carriers, an assortment of destroyers, nuclear submarines and support ships. Here, too, security has tightened; boom floats and patrol boats delineate the security perimeters around naval piers and vessels.

Just as you pass the long gray line, you're greeted by giant cranes that are likely working container ships at Norfolk International Terminal. A mile beyond, also to port, is the massive Lambert Point Coal Terminal. On a clear day, you'll begin to see the Norfolk skyline. Turn to port and leave International Terminal, as well as the Naval Medical Center Portsmouth, to starboard. On the opposite side of the river, you'll be greeted by a stunning site, the battleship *Wisconsin* and its neighbor, science center and museum NAUTICUS, and then downtown Norfolk.

Waterside Marina, at the foot of the Waterside Festival Marketplace, can accommodate up to 50 boats. (Register in the dockmaster's office, a gazebo at the southwest corner.) It's best to radio ahead on channel 16 so staff can be ready at the dock. The marina does not sell gas or diesel. Waterside

Marina is within strolling distance of the *Wisconsin*, downtown restaurants and MacArthur Center shopping mall. The GENERAL DOUGLAS MACARTHUR MEMORIAL has a fascinating collection of the general's memorabilia.

Albemarle and Dismal Swamp Canals

From Intracoastal Waterway Mile Marker Zero at the Elizabeth River's lighted buoy 36, an interesting and varied stretch of about $10^1/_2$ nautical miles leads to the community of Great Bridge in Chesapeake, Virginia, and the start of the **5 Albemarle and Chesapeake Canal.** Authorized in 1772, the canal was finally started in 1855 and finished in 1859. It is the eastern of two routes that cruisers can take southward from the Elizabeth River; the western route, the Great Dismal Swamp Canal, branches off the ICW at Deep Creek, about

continued on page 349

Port of Call
Norfolk

Energetic, sophisticated, fun—Norfolk is a port of call where there never seems to be enough time to do all you hope to do. Whether you're sightseeing, shopping, attending a cultural event or one of Norfolk's numerous celebrations, this nautically minded city will charm you. In short, Norfolk is habit forming.

The center for boating activity for cruisers has got to be Waterside, a municipal marine center that for years doubled as an unofficial city maritime gateway. In addition to all the amenities at the marina, you'll find brochures for the self-guided Cannonball Trail tour, which traces Norfolk's heritage. Along the way you'll pass window exhibits at MacArthur Center chronicling four centuries of Norfolk history and note the bronze plaques along Granby Street that honor such Hampton Roads music legends as Pearl Bailey, Ella Fitzgerald and Bruce Hornsby. You'll also pass the MacArthur Memorial (757-441-2965; *www.macarthurmemorial.org*), a museum and final resting place for another local hero, General Douglas MacArthur. At the waterfront, detour to the Pagoda Garden Tea House and Gallery (757-662-0506; *www.pagodagarden.org*) to enjoy their gardens. A Civil War trail acquaints visitors with Norfolk's role in that terrible conflict, while the Heart & Art Mermaid Story Trails offer aerobic and artistic diversion. And an abandoned railroad bed affords picturesque river views. Many attractions are accessible by NET (Norfolk Electric Transit). Route 17 includes stops at the beautifully redesigned Chrysler Museum (757-664-4200; *www.chrysler.org*), whose collection of art and Tiffany glass is world-renowned, and d'Art Center (757-620-4211; *www.d-artcenter.org*), a gallery and studio.

One must-see cluster of attractions centers on Nauticus (757-664-1000; *www.nauticus.org*), the National Maritime Center, an interactive, maritime-themed science museum. Here you'll also find Hampton Roads Naval Museum and the USS

Wisconsin. Tour boats (including the *American Rover*) ply the harbor, bound for Norfolk Naval Base, dinner cruises and excursions.

Norfolk has an active cultural life too, including the acclaimed Virginia Opera, the Virginia Symphony and Virginia Ballet Theatre. Amateur and professional theater companies and concert venues lie within walking distance of the harbor. A bit farther away is historic Attucks Theatre, a focal point of African American culture.

Baseball fans can watch the Norfolk Tides—the Baltimore Orioles' AAA team—at Harbor Park, and arena football fans can cheer the Norfolk Admirals at Norfolk Scope. MacArthur Center has 18 movie screens and a children's play area.

With dozens of upscale shops and two large department stores, MacArthur Center is a shopping mecca. It is complemented by other

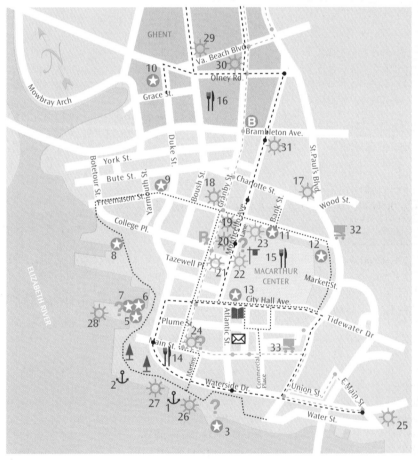

Norfolk

⚓ Marinas/Dockage
1 Waterside Marina
2 City Bulkhead*
⊙ Points of Interest
3 Ferry/Waterside Landing
5 Nauticus
6 Hampton Roads Naval Museum
7 Battleship Wisconsin
8 Pagoda Garden Tea House
  & Gallery
9 Hunter House Victorian Museum
10 Chrysler Museum of Art
11 Moses Myers House
12 Willoughby-Baylor House
13 Windows on History

🍴 Dining Areas
14 Marina/Nauticus area
15 McArthur Center
16 Gransby St./Ghent
☼ Entertainment/Recreation
17 Chrysler Hall
18 Granby Theater
19 Roper Performing Arts Center
20 NorVa Theater
21 Wells Theater/Virginia Stage
22 MacArthur Center (movies)
23 Ticketmaster
24 d'Art Center
25 Harbor Park (baseball)
26 *American Rover* (tour boat)
27 *Spirit of Norfolk* (dinner cruises)
28 *Victory Rover* (tour boat)
29 Harrison Opera House

30 Virginia Ballet Theatre
31 Norfolk SCOPE Arena
🛒 Groceries/Carryout
32 7-Eleven
33 Plume Market Deli
? Information
⚓ Park   🛍 Shopping
📖 Library   ℞ Pharmacy
✉ Post Office   ⊕ Bus Terminal
···· Cannonball Trail
    NET Route & Stops
···· (weekdays)
···· (weekends)

for major events; fees and admission apply; no overnight dockage

*Note: Dockage at Town Point Park available

Port of Call: Norfolk

downtown shops and the stores nearby. Ghent, a historic neighborhood with a mix of shops and antiques merchants, can be reached on foot (a healthy hike) or on NET. If you're low on galley supplies, you can buy basics at Waterside's City Market, and breakfast and lunch items at Plume Market Deli.

There are plenty of restaurants within walking distance of Waterside Marina, like Todd Jurich's Bistro and City Dock Restaurant. Granby Street has so many chef-owned eateries it's been dubbed Restaurant Row. Try 219 Bistro, Shula's or Granby Bistro & Deli among other Granby Street favorites. And there are perhaps an equal number of eateries along Colley Avenue in Ghent. If you prefer, Orange Peel taxi service (757-463-7500) will deliver take-out meals.

Concerts, tall ship visits, food festivals—Norfolk's calendar offers something fun almost any time you visit. But Harborfest is the city's premier event, featuring visiting tall ships, live entertainment, fireworks, a Parade of Sail and more.

Information: Convention and Visitors Bureau, 800-368-3097; www.visitnorfolktoday.com

Albemarle and Dismal Swamp canals
continued from page 347

seven miles south of Mile Marker Zero.

Whether you're headed down the A&C Canal or the Dismal Swamp, you share the road here with all manner of vessels, from skiffs to mega-yachts, as well as tug and barge traffic. Of the seven bridges between statute miles "0" and "10", the three railroad bridges are usually open, but because they're still used by rail traffic, listen closely to VHF 13 for closings. Among the highway bridges, the old Jordan Bridge (mile 2.8) has been replaced by a fixed span, with a vertical clearance of 145 feet. Also the Dominion Boulevard bridge (formerly the "Steel" and now "Veterans" bridge) now a high fixed (95 feet) span. That leaves only the Gilmerton Bridge with restricted openings. And that one is now a lift bridge with a closed clearance of 35 feet. Between the two is I-64, a bascule bridge with a closed clearance of 65 feet.

At mile "5" the ICW turns eastward at **St. Julian Creek** (entering from the west). Here, industry gives way to a more rural atmosphere. A half-mile later, the ICW curves south again at **Milldam Creek**. Don't mistake either of these creeks for the navigable waterway.

To starboard, immediately beyond the I-64 bridge, an Army Corps of Engineers sign marks the entrance to Deep Creek and the historic Dismal Swamp Canal. This scenic wilderness cruise (consisting of two locks) eventually leads to Elizabeth City, N.C., 50 statute miles from Norfolk's Mile Zero.

After the junction with the Dismal Swamp Canal, the main stem of the ICW leads to the Albemarle and

Chesapeake Canal's only lock, at **Great Bridge**, which has regular openings daily between 6 a.m. and 7 p.m. The change in elevation is only about 5 feet; two dock lines of at least 25 feet each (one for the bow and one for the stern) are sufficient. The lock operator will pass the lines around bollards at the top of the lock wall and return the bitter ends to you. The east end of the lock is opened hourly; the west end is opened about 10 minutes after the hour. For after-hours openings, hail the operator on channel 13.

South of the lock, a small bulkheaded park to starboard accommodates about 8 to 10 boats. From here, banks, restaurants, groceries, and automotive and marine supplies are within walking distance. Despite sidewalks and signals, however, the non-stop traffic on Battlefield Boulevard makes navigation by foot tricky.

For boats continuing southward along the ICW, the Great Bridge bascule bridge opens in coordination with the lock, hourly from 6 a.m. to 7 p.m., and on request after 7. Beyond the span (to starboard when heading south) is Atlantic Yacht Basin, a full-service repair facility. In addition to its convenient and protected location, AYB's fuel and transient dock is open 24 hours. On the other side of the canal is the new Great Bridge Battlefield and Waterways Historic Park and Visitors Center. Boats may dock at the small pier here free of charge and tour the park.

For those opting to take the **Dismal Swamp Canal**, be aware that there is no fuel and few services for boaters along the way. Past Deep Creek Lock, a small public dock to starboard (adjacent to a park) and a smaller bulkhead just south of the lock's associated bridge allow access to a nearby shopping center. At mile marker 28, just below the North Carolina state line, limited dock space is available at the visitor center. About 5 statute miles farther, between the other bridge and lock, temporary dockage is permitted on a long bulkhead with a nearby convenience store. However, 18 miles beyond the second (and last) lock, in Elizabeth City's revitalized waterfront, Mariners' Wharf has 48-hour free dockage along with services and area restaurants; nearby marinas offer fuel and repairs.

The Dismal Swamp Canal has two locks: **Deep Creek** in Virginia and **South Mills** in North Carolina, with openings at each at 8:30 and 11 a.m., and 1:30 and 3:30 p.m.—those these are subject to change with water conditions. Sailboats can make it all the way through by catching the 8:30 opening. Boats can raft up with other cruisers at the friendly Dismal Swamp Canal Welcome Center (877-771-8333). The Center's dock lies about 17 miles beyond the first lock and 5 statute miles before the second and offer a pleasant break, with walking trails and an exhibit hall. The canal has two lift bridges that opens in association with its lock. A pontoon foot bridge at the Welcome Center will open on signal. Call the Army Corps of Engineers' automated number (757-201-7500) for canal conditions.

Much of the Great Dismal Swamp Canal drains into the Chesapeake. With its history and canal-side hiking/biking trails, it's an enjoyable addition to the list of great cruising destinations on the Bay.

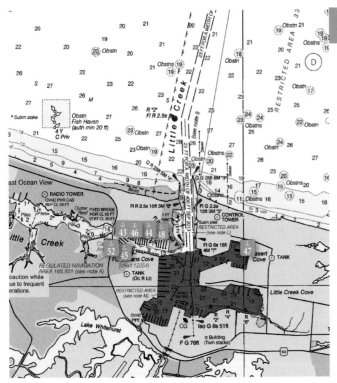

Little Creek; from NOAA Chart 12222—not to be used for navigation.

Mouth of the Bay

Little Creek

Back out on the Bay and around the corner from Hampton Roads, **Little Creek** is a popular harbor among Bay fishermen, who find it convenient to the productive areas around the Bay Bridge-Tunnel. Because it is so close to open sailing waters, it is also a favorite with sailing enthusiasts.

Little Creek is unique among Virginia harbors in that it is divided (roughly east and west) between the Naval Amphibious Base and numerous pleasure craft facilities. Thanks to the Navy, the entrance is among the deepest and best maintained on the coast. Locals are used to the large ships that come and go at the Little Creek Amphibious Base, but visitors will find the "Gator Navy" quite different from the other ships seen up and down the Bay.

The approach to Little Creek is simple. The light on the east bank of the entrance is on a tall tower, quite visible by day or night. A lighted range guides you up the channel, so it is really difficult to go astray.

Fishermans Cove, to starboard after "8", is where Little Creek's civilian boating facilities flank the narrow waterway.

● On Premises
► Nearby

Lynnhaven Inlet & Little Creek

	MLW	Overnight Slips	Gas	Diesel	Propane	Electric	Showers	Laundry	Restaurant	Lodging	Pool	Pump-out	Ice	Groceries	Marine Supplies	Bait	Boat Repair	Haul-out Services	Launch Ramp	Wi-Fi	Other
43 Bay Marine & East Beach Marina Little Cr./Fisherman's Cove 757-362-5000	6'	●	►	►		●	●	●	●	►	●	●	●	►	●	●	●	●			55-ton lift
44 Bay Point Marina Little Cr./Fisherman's Cove 757-362-8432; www.littlecreekmarina.com	6'	●	►	►		●	●	●	●	►	●	●	►	►	►	►	►	►	►	●	Wi-Fi, customer lounge
45 Cobb's Marina Little Cr./Fisherman's Cove 757-588-5401; www.cobbsmarina.com	8'	●	●	►	►	●	●	●	►		●	►	►	●	●		●	●		●	50-ton and 75-ton hoist
46 Cutty Sark Marina Little Cr./Fisherman's Cove 757-362-2942	14'	●	►	►	►	●	●	●	●	►		●	►	►	●		●	●	►	●	Restaurant; cocktails, wine, beer, boatyard
47 Little Creek Cove Marina Naval Amphibious MM Little Cr./Virgina Beach 757-462-7140; www.discovermwr.com	8'	●	●	●	►	●	●	●	►	►		●	►	●	●	►	►	●			Call during working hours, base auth. req.
48 Little Creek Marina Little Cr./Fisherman's Cove 757-362-3600; www.littlecreekmarina.com	15'	●	●		●	●	●	●	●	►	►	●	●	●	●	●	●	●		●	Wi-Fi, customer lounge
49 Long Bay Pointe Boating Resort Lynnhaven Inlet/Long Cr. 757-321-4550; www.longbaypointemarina.com	6'	●	●	●	●	●	●	►	●	►	●	►	●	►	►	●	►	►	►		Hair Salon, fitness center, 2 restaurants
50 Lynnhaven Municipal Marina Lynnhaven Inlet/Long Cr. 757-460-7590; www.vbgov.com	6'	●	►	►	►		►	►	►		●	►	►	►	►	►	►	►	►	►	Free pump-out, grill, picnic area, fish cleaning station
51 Marina Shores Lynnhaven Inlet/Long Cr. 757-496-7000; www.marinashoresmarina.com	8'	●	●	●		●	●	●	●		●	●	●	►	►	●	●	●	●		
52 Vinings Landing Marine Center Little Cr./Fisherman's Cove 757-587-8000; www.viningslanding.com	8'- 9'	●	●	●		●	●	●	●		●	●	►	►	●	►	►	►	►	●	

Marinas here generally have transient slips, and some have pools and other amenities as well as working boatyards with haul-outs and repairs. All are within a short walk of banks/ATMs and a convenience store, as well as a large shopping center with drugstore and grocery. Nearby restaurants offer everything from waterside seafood to breakfast, pizza and fast fare. And it's only a few blocks walk to the beach.

The main channel, with 8- to 10-foot depths, has no place to anchor, but you'll find a snug spot in deeper, wider water if you can get beneath the fixed bridge (20-foot vertical clearance).

Lynnhaven Inlet

Just a few miles south of Little Creek, and on the east side of the Chesapeake Bay Bridge-Tunnel, **Lynnhaven Inlet** opens into several pleasant, protected bays and offers a variety of facilities and services—but *only* if your boat requires less than 35 feet of vertical clearance. Broad Bay and Linkhorn Bay are both large but protected and easily navigated. **Lynnhaven Bay,** on the other hand, is difficult to navigate without local knowledge. You will find several marinas with

fuel and services, as well as waterfront restaurants, located just inside the inlet. Lighted navigational aids define the entrance from **Lynnhaven Roads**. This area is prone to shoaling and only the marked channel is dredged. Do not stray outside the markers. Beware of pilot boats entering and leaving the inlet; they can create an uncomfortable wake in the restricted approach. As we mentioned, Lesner Bridge (over the inlet) has a fixed vertical clearance of 35 feet.

Just inside the bridge, two channels turn east (left), flow around a small island, and then rejoin. The left (north) one is recommended because it is used by commercial traffic and is dredged regularly. The south channel is prone to shoaling.

If you take the first channel to the left, you will immediately pass the Harbor Pilot Station and two marinas. Unlike the other marinas farther in, these seldom have transient slips. The Inlet, Bubba's Crabhouse, Chick's Oyster Bar and Lynnhaven Seafood restaurants all provide dock space for customers.

About 1/2 mile after the two channels rejoin, and 1 mile from the bridge, you'll come to another fork. If you're headed directly to Broad Bay, choose the direct route to the right. If you're looking for a marina or a more scenic route, take the

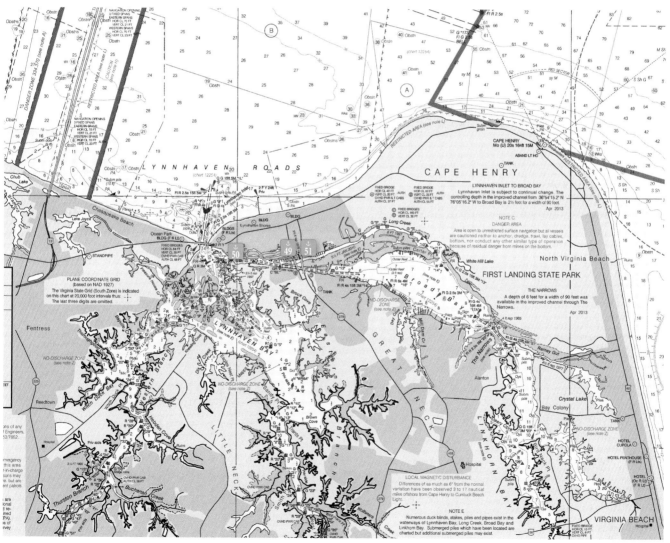

Lynnhaven Inlet; from NOAA Chart 12253—not to be used for navigation.

Lynnhaven Inlet *continued*

Long Creek route to the left; the main channel (on the right) continues eastward to **Broad Bay**. Another consideration is that the two bridges just east of the fork have a vertical clearance of 35 feet over the main channel and 20 feet over Long Creek.

At the mouth of Long Creek, you'll come to Long Bay Pointe, a resort marina with floating piers and more than 200 slips (including transient dockage). Amenities range from gas, diesel, showers and laundry to two restaurants, a hair salon, gourmet market, fitness center and fishing charters. Long Creek has been dredged to maintain 8 feet (MLW); slip depths in the marina are 6 feet. Just inside the left fork in the creek is another resort marina, Marina Shores. This friendly multi-service facility offers slips, fuel, repairs, parts, several restaurants, a pool, shops and showers.

If you continue along Long Creek another 2 miles, you'll reach Broad Bay. The area from the Inlet to Broad Bay is a no-wake zone, though it is sometimes difficult to make headway against a maximum current without moving fast enough through the water to create a wake. Most of the marinas near the mouth of the inlet have launching ramps. Most also have repair facilities.

At the eastern end of Broad Bay is **The Narrows**. A boat ramp on the north side provides public access from 64th Street in **Virginia Beach**. The area around the ramp is shoal so approach it with caution. The Narrows itself is well marked and presents no difficulty within the channel.

The Narrows leads to the northern end of **Linkhorn Bay**. Following Rainey Gut will take you eastward in depths of around 4 feet to **Crystal Lake**, a quiet, secluded anchorage surrounded by elegant residential neighborhoods. Farther south, in Linkhorn Bay, the Cavalier Golf and Yacht Club sits just east of Bird Neck Point.

Barco's Marine Railway, the largest in Virginia Beach, is located at the end of the southeast branch of Linkhorn Bay. The Virginia Beach oceanfront area is just over a mile from here.

The best anchorage in Broad Bay is southeast of flashing "14". From here you can row ashore and explore FIRST LANDING STATE PARK, where members of the Virginia Company landed before proceeding on to Jamestown. Crystal Lake is usually less crowded than Broad Bay or Linkhorn Bay. Any of the coves off Linkhorn Bay make a good anchorage.

Several natural restrictions to the tidal flow occur inside Lynnhaven Inlet—the inlet itself, the main channel just beyond the fork at Long Creek and The Narrows. These areas can have a current up to 2 knots.

Rudee Inlet

Along the Atlantic oceanfront at Virginia Beach, lies **Rudee Inlet,** six nautical miles south of the Cape Henry Light and the only way to visit Virginia Beach by water if your boat requires a clearance greater than 35 feet.

Heading east from Hampton Roads, you'll pass through the Thimble Shoal Channel opening in the Chesapeake Bay Bridge-Tunnel, between the North and South islands (also known as First and Second islands). After rounding the Cape Henry lights (the old stone light and the "newer" tower), follow the Atlantic coastline south in 20 to 30 feet of water.

Before you know it, you'll sight the Virginia Beach fishing pier, located a mile north of Rudee Inlet. A stone jetty extends out from the beach on the inlet's north side. A second jetty, on the south side, does not go all the way to the beach.

The inlet was once just a narrow cut draining water from vast inland marshes. Today, it's a busy haven for recreational boats of all sorts, ranging from PWCs to sportfishing charter

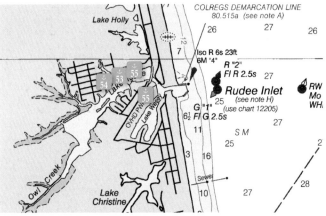

Rudee Inlet, from NOAA Chart 12208—not to be used for navigation.

● On Premises
➤ Nearby

Rudee Inlet

	MLW	Overnight Slips	Gas	Diesel	Propane	Electric	Showers	Laundry	Restaurant	Lodging	Pool	Pump-out	Ice	Groceries	Marine Supplies	Bait	Boat Repair	Haul-out Services	Launch Ramp	Wi-Fi	Other
Fisherman's Wharf Marina Rudee Inlet/Virginia Beach 757-428-2111; *www.fishermanswharfmarina.com*	8'	●	➤	➤		●	●	➤	➤		➤	●	●	➤	●	➤			➤	●	Walk to beach, inshore/offshore fishing
Rudees Inlet Station Marina Rudee Inlet/Virginia Beach 757-422-2999; *www.rudeesmarina.com*	8'	●	●	●		●	●	●	●	➤		●	●	●	●	●			➤	●	Near beach/boardwalk; 2 restaurants, outdoor bar
Virginia Beach Fishing Center Rudee Inlet/Virginia Beach 757-491-8000 or 800-725-0509; *www.virginiafishing.com*	6'	●	●	●		●	●	➤	➤	➤		●	●	●	●	●	●		➤		Closest entrance to the Atlantic Ocean

Long Creek leading from Lynnhaven Inlet to Broad Bay at Virginia Beach's back door. The bulkheaded shoreline gives the creek the look of a canal.

boats and headboats to whale-watching excursion vessels.

Enter Rudee Inlet between green "1" and red "2", just outside the jetties. If traffic permits, favor the north side of the channel when entering and leaving. The channel is subject to shoaling although dredging continues practically nonstop in an effort to ensure average depths of about 10 feet (MLW).

The Rudee Inlet Bridge (fixed, 29-foot vertical clearance), may separate you from **Lake Rudee** and its facilities. If you require greater clearance, proceed south into **Lake Wesley**, a small cove split by a peninsula at the south end, with 15 feet of water on each side. This is a quiet, protected anchorage surrounded by lovely homes. The Virginia Beach Fishing Center's Southside facility is the only marina located on the inlet side of the bridge, but provides access for high-aspect cruisers to all attractions of Rudee and Virginia Beach.

The north shore of Lake Rudee is lined with condos, marinas and restaurants. You should have no problem getting permission to tie up your dinghy while you explore on foot. There are three marinas located here—Virginia Beach Fishing Center, Fisherman's Wharf Marina and Rudee's Inlet Station Marina—each with an adjoining restaurant. In addition, Rockafellers Restaurant and Rudee's on the Inlet Restaurant & Raw Bar (with a tiki bar) offer slips for dinner tie-ups.

The marinas are within easy walking distance of Virginia Beach and all of its many diversions. A wide boardwalk extends the length of the beachfront, paralleled by a bicycle path. Within four blocks of Rudee Inlet are numerous restaurants, hotels, trolley stops, souvenir shops and a bakery. Less than 2 miles south of the inlet is the VIRGINIA AQUARIUM & MARINE SCIENCE CENTER on Owl Creek. This state-of-the-art center, Ocean Breeze Fun Park and the OLD COAST GUARD STATION MUSEUM all can be reached by trolley.

NOTE: Boaters planning to visit Rudee Inlet should check with their insurers to verify coverage outside the Bay. Limited off-shore coverage can usually be added for little extra cost.

Port of Call
Rudee Inlet

This compact inlet, just down the Atlantic coast from Cape Henry, is a mecca for all things fishing. Behind the 28-foot high fixed bridge, just down the street from Virginia Beach, lie one of the largest collections of sport-fish boats anywhere. Here you can buy a fishing boat, rent a fishing boat, charter a fishing boat or dock a fishing boat at marinas such as Rudee Inlet Station, Virginia Beach Fishing Center and Fisherman's Wharf. Here too you can eat a fresh-fish dinner at any number of popular restaurants like Rockafellar's, Rudee's on the Inlet with its swing seats and cabana bar, and Big Sam's Cafe and Raw Bar. But fishing is only part of the water-entertainment story at Rudee Inlet. Here you can go parasailing, take a pirate ship, rent paddleboards, kayaks, sailboats, jetskis or canoes and ride the Rudee Rocket. When you've done all that, you can walk a couple of blocks east and you'll be on the beach. When the time comes to exercise your mind a bit, you can climb into your boat or your dinghy and motor along Lake Rudee to visit the splendid Virginia Beach Aquarium and Marine Science Center (*virginiaaquarium.com;* 757-385-7777), where you can also watch an IMAX movie.

All of that sounds great for powerboaters, but what about sailors or tall powerboats? The best plan is to turn to port after entering Rudee Inlet, and find a spot in Lake Wesley (8 to 9 feet MLW) to drop the anchor. From there, it's a quick dinghy ride under the bridge to Rudee Inlet and all of that food, fishing and fun mentioned earlier. Alternatively, the Virginia Beach Fishing Center has a second facility just outside the bridge that can often accommodate sailboats and high-aspect powerboats.

Information: *visitrudeeinlet.com*

Rudee Inlet

⚓ **Marinas/Dockage**
  1 Virginia Beach Fishing Center
   (2 locations)
  2 Fisherman's Wharf
  3 Rudee Inlet Station Marina

🍴 **Dining Area**
  4 Big Sam's Inlet Cafe and Raw Bar
  5 Rockafellar's Restaurant
  6 Rudee's on the Inlet Restaurant
   and Cabana Bar

☼ **Entertainment/Recreation**
  7 Air America Parasail
  8 Captain Jack's Pirate Adventures
  9 Rudee Inlet Stand Up Paddle
  10 Adventure Parasail
  11 Rudee Tours
  12 Rudee Rocket
  13 Iggy Biggy Sailing
  14 Rudee Inlet Jet Ski Rentals

⊙ **Points of Interest**
  15 Virginia Beach Aquarium and
   Marine Science Center

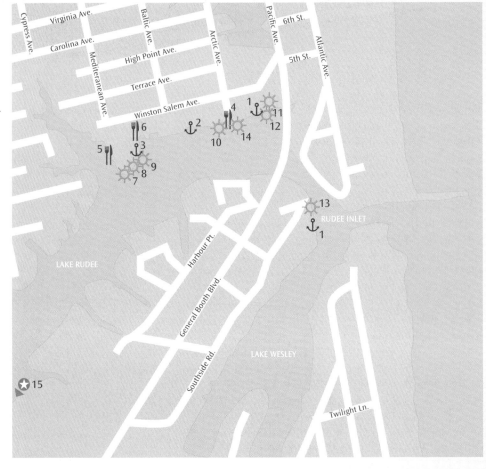

Bay Spotlight

U.S. Naval Historical Center

Clash of the Titans

On the night of March 8, 1862, while the ironclad CSS *Virginia* lay at anchor at Sewells Point at the mouth of the Elizabeth River, a pilot on board thought he saw a strange shape glide by out on Hampton Roads. It was a silhouette, really, a water-tank-on-a-raft shape, backlit by the fires of a burning federal ship, and he thought nothing of it. The crew of the *Virginia* was celebrating. That day they had dealt a devastating blow to the Union, mauling two powerful Union warships and sending shockwaves all the way to Washington. The rest of the federal blockade ships awaited them in the morning. Picking them off would be a walk in the park.

Meanwhile, the surreptitious vessel dropped anchor out on the Roads. The boat, the Union's own ironclad USS *Monitor*, had just barely made it to Hampton Roads after a nightmarish trip down the Atlantic. After two days and two sleepless nights, the ship rounded Cape Charles on the afternoon of March 8. In the distance the crew heard heavy gunfire as the *Virginia* systematically worked its way through the Union fleet.

The *Monitor* took position behind the USS *Minnesota*, the *Virginia*'s next likely victim. When the morning sun burned away the fog, sure enough the

Virginia steamed away from Sewells Point straight for the *Minnesota*. The *Monitor* slid out of the shadows to greet them.

Ignoring whatever impertinence lay before them, the *Virginia*'s gunners opened up on the *Minnesota*. Then something strange happened. The great turret on the vessel in their path slowly swiveled toward them, a port swung open and a huge cannon —11 inches wide—fired at them. The second battle of Hampton Roads had been joined.

The ironclads pummeled each other for four hours, circling like punch-drunk fighters, actually touching a couple of times. The gunners on both ships stripped down to the waist, grunting in their hellish confines as they loaded, rammed and fired, wincing as monstrous shots clanged against their armor, collapsing when the four-hour contest ended in a draw.

This titanic clash has been re-created in all its intensity for the Battle Theater of the new Monitor Center, part of the Mariners' Museum in Newport News (*www. monitorcenter.org*; 800-581-7245).

—*Paul Clancy*

SPOTLIGHT CRUISE: RUDEE INLET

An ocean "voyage," a great beach town . . . and cousins

Is Rudee Inlet part of the Chesapeake Bay? No, not strictly speaking, because you have to go out into the actual Atlantic Ocean to get there. Which is why, when I got to the end of the Bay one recent summer, I felt I just had to keep going. Well, that and my husband's cousin Jerry. You see, Cousin Jerry and his wife Cousin Helen have lived in Virginia Beach for seven years now and have been raving about it for at least five years and eleven months.

"Listen," Jerry would say, "Rudee Inlet is only six miles down the coast from the Bay, so it's an easy zip around the corner, and you're there." He and Cousin Helen would be happy to pick us up at the boat and show us around, he said.

So when Skipper the dog and I were boating in the southern Bay last June, I set up that meeting. Rick would drive down for the weekend, and we would rendezvous with the cousins.

And what a great time we had! We drove up to First Landing State Park and visited the lighthouses at Cape Henry. We took a late-night stroll along Virginia Beach's boardwalk. We lunched in Rudee Inlet Station's outdoor gliding-table restaurant, swam in the ocean, and visited the Virginia Aquarium. Jerry and Helen were right about Virginia Beach. It was a great place to visit . . . and the important thing is that we could have done and seen everything that we did—with the possible exception of First Landing State Park and the lighthouses—even without the cousins. All of it was within easy walking distance of the boat. Moreover, we could have done it in either a powerboat or a sailboat.

On the morning of the big rendezvous, Skipper and I left Lynnhaven Inlet, where we'd spent the night, and re-emerged into the Bay, just south of the Chesapeake Bay

Bridge-Tunnel. I turned the Albin 28 east to follow the shoreline. Only a few minutes later, we were off First Landing State Park, Virginia's most popular state park. It's a fan favorite for good reason: nearly 3,000 acres of trails and a mile and a quarter of beach, with overnight cabins, a launch area, swimming and fishing. We idled past the lookout tower and a couple of small boats anchored just off the beach. A few minutes after that, we reached Cape Henry at the southern limit of the Chesapeake Bay. A few more minutes and we would be in the ocean!

I dawdled off the lighthouses for a while and then followed the shoreline as it fell off south. I could keep the Albin just off the beach, since the water drops off within a 100-yards or so of the shore. As I neared Virginia Beach, however, I went out far enough to avoid the busy beach traffic but close enough to stay within easy view of the action. And action there was aplenty: banner-towing planes, ski-towing boats, small rental sailboats, swimmers, PWCs, sightseeing boats, deep-sea fishing boats. Behind all of that, the hotels, condominiums and beach businesses of Virginia Beach stretched south and west until they were lost in the haze. Now all I had to do was find the entrance to Rudee Inlet. I needn't have worried. Since Rudee Inlet is the only port between the Bay and Oregon Inlet, N.C., and because it is Virginia Beach's only access to open water and the rich fishing grounds that lie beyond, it attracts a lot of boaters. It was like watching honey bees bringing the day's pollen catch back to the hive. I simply joined the swarm.

Red and white whistling marker "RI" stands offshore, signaling boats that this is where to find the inlet. Then come flashing red "2" and flashing green "1", followed by the inlet's twin stone jetties. Since the inlet is in a perpetual state of shoaling—not surprising, given the ocean's proximity—it is also in a perpetual state of dredging, with the result that the entrance channel is usually good for 8 to 13 feet, at least until you reach the far side of the double bridges (vertical clearance 28 feet). Even there, the depth generally stays at least six feet. All bets are off after an Atlantic storm, however.

As we passed between the jetties to enter the inlet, we found ourselves fourth in line behind a trawler, two offshore fishing boats and a small bow-rider. Jockeying for space in the outgoing lane were a jet boat—well stocked with excited children and parents—a small skiff and a head boat. This was one busy place! Under the bridges, however, the waterway opened up into Lake Rudee, with large marinas cheek-by-jowl to starboard and private homes to port. Virginia Beach Fishing Center was followed by Fisherman's Wharf Marina and then Rudee's Inlet Station Marina with its the long fuel dock parallel to the channel.

I decided it was still early enough to explore the rest of Rudee Inlet before settling in and calling the cousins. I was surprised at what I found. With Skipper taking the bow watch, we idled past the inlet to Rockefeller's Restaurant and then took the long narrow island ahead of us to starboard. Suddenly we had left the buzz of the beach behind. We had also left most of the homes. Here were trees, birds and a wholly unexpected quiet—except for the periodic roar of military aircraft close overhead. On the whole, however, this was not how I had pictured Rudee Inlet at all. As we left the island behind, I could see the buildings of the Virginia Aquarium & Marine Center straight ahead. It would be easy to drop anchor here and take a dinghy to shore, I thought. To the aquarium's left, lay Owl Creek, one

Touring Rudee Inlet, Skipper and I come to the Virginia Aquarium at the end of Lake Rudee.

of the area's busiest boat ramps. There was a line of cars and boats there, too. Yet, until the next F/A-18 Hornet came subsonically zipping through, everything was utterly quiet, so quiet that Skipper curled up on the bow and went to sleep. Some lookout!

It was still early, so I decided to take a look on the other side of the bridges. Just after the entrance, the inlet splits, with Lake Rudee to the right and Lake Wesley (and no bridges) to the left. Heading back out through the bridges, I turned right and entered Lake Wesley, a charmed world of mildly idiosyncratic residences. Each seemed to have its own singular personality in a subtropical resorty kind of way. Despite its charms, however, Lake Wesley didn't seem to have much room for a boat to swing at anchor—perhaps only enough room for couple of 35 to 40 footers. However, I spotted a perfectly good alternative to the anchoring problem. Virginia Beach Fishing Center has an annex on Lake Wesley. That means that high-aspect boats have a place to tie up and still have easy access to all of the beach activities and restaurants, not to mention the Virginia Aquarium.

I was just waiting for a break in the traffic to jump in line to get back to the other side of the bridges when my cell phone rang. It was Rick. He and the cousins had gotten tired of waiting for me to call, he said, and had driven down to Rudee Inlet Station. They were currently tapping their toes on the fuel dock, waiting for me to show up so we could start having fun. I decided not to mention that Skipper and I had been having plenty of fun all morning and merely said that we would be arriving before they could say Jack Robinson. Which we did. Skipper saw them first and began to spin happily at the bow, making docking just that little bit more interesting—not what you're looking for at a strange marina full of very expensive boats. But then, we had been out on the ocean today, so we laughed at fear. Besides, we had bow-thrusters!

After a great visit with family, Skipper and I join the parade of boats leaving Rudee Inlet.

—Jody Argo Schroath

RESTAURANTS

SECTION 1

C&D Canal/Chesapeake City

Bayard House Restaurant
C&D Canal/Chesapeake City
410-885-5040; www.bayardhouse.com
Open year-round for lunch, dinner and private parties. Dinners: $21–$32. Reservations suggested. Free dockage for diners and overnight at nearby city dock. Outdoor bar. B&B on site. Specialties: Tournedos Baltimore, crabcakes, Stuffed Anaheim peppers. Enjoy a drink in the historic Hole in the Wall Bar.

Bohemia Cafe and Bakery
C&D Canal/Chesapeake City
410-885-3066; www.bohemiacafeandbakery.com
Open year-round serving breakfast and lunch. Relaxed, child-friendly atmosphere. Reasonable prices. Fresh bakery items daily. Take-out and catering services.

Chesapeake Inn Restaurant & Marina
C&D Canal/Chesapeake City
410-885-2040; www.chesapeakeinn.com
Open year-round for lunch and dinner. Dinners: $6–$15 downstairs; $15–30 upstairs. Reservations not necessary. Marina on premises; dockage for diners and overnight, 4–12'. Specialties: Seafood w/ Italian flair. Live entertainment daily, May–Sept.

Schaefer's Canal House
C&D Canal/Chesapeake City
410-885-7200; www.schaeferscanalhouse.com
Open year-round for lunch and dinner. Dinners $15–$30. Featuring seafood, steaks, pastas, sandwiches and more. Plus a great view of the C&D Canal.

Taproom
C&D Canal/Chesapeake City
410-885-2344; www.taproomcrabhouse.com
Open year-round for lunch and dinner. Dinners: $10-$25. Reservations recommended for parties of 10 or more. Marina and motel nearby. Specialty: seafood and Italian.

Northeast River

Nauti-Goose Saloon
Northeast R./North East
410-287-7880; www.nautigoose.net
Open for lunch and dinner. Dinners $14–$26. Reservations recommended. Free dockage for diners, $25 for overnight. Specialities: Seafood and prime rib buffet; Deck, bar, live entertainment on weekends.

Wellwood/Rivershack at the Wellwood
Northeast R.
410-287-6666; www.wellwoodclub.com
Open year-round (closed Mon.) for lunch, dinner and Sunday breakfast. Dinners: $8–$30. Reservations suggested. Dockage for diners and overnight at Wellwood Marina. Specialties: Oysters Rockefeller, large hardshell crabs (seasonal), fresh seafood, pasta, carryout wine/beer. Rivershack open seasonally Thurs.–Mon. for breakfast, lunch and dinner. Casual dining inside or on patio. All-you-can-eat crabs, crabcakes, sandwiches.

Woody's Crab House
Northeast R./North East
410-287-3541; www.woodyscrabhouse.com
Open year-round for lunch and dinner Mon.–Sun. Reservations not necessary. Motel nearby. Specialties: Maryland crabhouse with paper-covered tables serving crabs, crabcakes, shrimp, fresh fish, other seafood; can ship crabcakes.

Susquehanna River/Havre de Grace

Laurrapin Grille
Susquehanna R./Havre de Grace
410-939-4956; www.laurrapin.com
Open year-round for lunch and dinner, Closed Mondays. Dinners $13–$25. Reservations suggested. Fresh seafood dishes, steaks. Where Northern California meets the Chesapeake Bay. Chef-owned and operated. New bar & lounge, live music weekly.

MacGregor's Restaurant, Tavern & Banquet Room
Susquehanna R./Havre de Grace
410-939-3003; macgregorsrestaurant.com
Open year-round for lunch, dinner and Sunday brunch. Dinners: $13–$23. Reservations suggested. Specialties: Award-winning jumbo lump crabcakes, seafood, steaks, prime rib, pasta. All tables have water view, plus totally remodeled large outside deck and bar.

Tidewater Grille
Susquehanna R./Havre de Grace
410-575-7045 or 939-3313; thetidewatergrille.com
Open year-round for lunch and dinner, Sat.-Sun. breakfast. Dinners $15–$35. Reservations recommended for 5+. Dockage for diners 6'+. Specialties: fresh fish, shellfish, steaks, famous crabcakes, homemade soups, sandwiches and salads. Full-service menu, wine bar, great selection of beer and spirits.

Susquehanna River/Port Deposit

Backfin Bar & Grill
Susquehanna R./Port Deposit
410-378-2722; www.backfinblues.com
Open Wed.–Sat. for dinner, Sun. brunch 10 a.m.–4 p.m. Dinners $10–$35. Reservations suggested. Tomes Landing Marina nearby. Casual upscale dining with bar and grill and water view. Dockage available, call for details.

Lee's Landing Dock Bar
Susquehanna R./Port Deposit
443-747-4006; www.leeslandingdockbar.com
Open daily for lunch and dinner. Dinners $10–$20. Tomes Landing Marina and town dock nearby. Family friendly menu, pirate ship for kids, casual atmosphere. Free dockage for diners. Sandwiches, fish tacos, crabcakes, plus steamers, oysters.

Sassafras River/Georgetown

Kitty Knight House
Sassafras R./Georgetown
410-648-5200; www.kittyknight.com
Open daily for lunch and dinner. Inn (B&B), and restaurant in historic 1755 home. Deck dining with spectacular views; live entertainment on weekends. Dockage available for diners and overnight at Georgetown Yacht Basin. Specialties: Crab dishes, Eastern Shore cuisine, waterfront weddings. Pool, beach, kayaks.

Norm's Kitchen at Sassafras Harbor Cafe
Sassafras R./Georgetown
410-275-1300; www.normskitchen.com
Open seven days a week: Mon-Wed for breakfast and lunch; Thurs- Sun for breakfast, lunch, and dinner. Featuring 23 craft beers. Serving seafood, soups, salads, steak, daily specials. Dockage on-site at Sassafras Harbor Marina.

Sassafras Grill
Sassafras R./Georgetown
410-275-1603; granary.biz
Open seasonally for Sat.–Sun. breakfast, lunch and dinner. Dinners $7–$15. Dockage on site. Serving pizzas, soups, salads, deli sandwiches, burgers, hot dogs. Live entertainment.

Signals
Sassafras R./Skipjack Cove
410-275-2122; www.skipjackcove.com
Open seasonally Thurs.–. Sun. for lunch, dinner and Sunday breakfast. Dinners $18–$24. Reservations recommended. Skipjack Cove Marina on premises offers dockage for diners and overnight w/reservations, 13'. Motel nearby. Weekend specials, award-winning crabcakes.

the Granary
Sassafras R./Georgetown
410-275-1603; granary.biz
Open daily for lunch and dinner. Dinners $14–$30. Dockage available on site. Specialties: gourmet seafood, steaks, sandwiches, fish tacos.

Worton & Fairlee Creeks

Inn at Worton Creek
Worton Cr./Worton Cr. Marina
410-810-3466; www.theinnatwortoncreek.com
Open year-round for breakfast, lunch and dinner ($15–$25). Reservations suggested. Worton Creek Marina on premises offers dockage for diners and overnight, 6'.

Mangrove's Restaurant
Fairlee Cr./Great Oak Landing
410-778-2100; www.mearsgreatoaklanding.com
Open seasonally for lunch and dinner. Dinners $20–$30.Reservations suggested. Deli/cafe open daily. Mears Great Oak Landing Marina on premises offers dockage for diners and overnight. Motel on site. Jellyfish Joel's Beach bar on site.

Gunpowder River

Sapore Di Mare
Gunpowder R.
410-538-8066; www.saporedimare.us
Open year-round for lunch and dinner. Dinners $5.95–$18.95. Reservations not necessary. Near Marine Max Marina. Specialties: seafood and Italian.

Middle River

Carson's Creekside Restaurant
Middle R./Dark Head Cr.
410-238-0080 ; www.carsonscreekside.com
Open daily for lunch, dinner and light fare. Dinners $10–$25. Reservations recommended. Dockage (6') for diners; Stansbury Marina nearby. Seafood, steaks, sandwiches, wraps, salads. Beautiful waterfront setting, live entertainment weekends in lounge.

Island View Waterfront Cafe
Middle R./Browns Cr.
410-687-9799; www.islandviewwaterfrontcafe.com
Open seasonally for breakfast, lunch and dinner. Reservations not necessary. Dockage for diners, 3'+. Specialities: Maryland crab and cream of crab soups, crab pretzels. Wine tastings, Bay-related art shows throughout the year. Available for private parties/events. Now renting kayaks!

River Watch Restaurant And Marina
Middle R./ Hopkins Cr./River Watch Marina
410-687-1422; www.riverwatchrestaurant.com
Open year-round for lunch and dinner. Dinners: $15–$29. Reservations suggested. Marina on premises offers dockage for diners and overnight, 15'. Motel nearby. Specialties: crabcakes, seafood and steaks; live music weekends April through October.

SECTION 2

Patapsco River/Baltimore

Captain James Seafood Palace
Patapsco R./Balt. Harb./Bay View Marina
410-327-8600; www.captainjameslanding.com
Crab house and bar on the water. Open year-round for breakfast, lunch and dinner. Dinners: $12–$45. Reservations suggested. Marina on premises has dockage for diners and overnight, 15'. Specialties: steamed crabs at outdoor pavilion (May–Sept.).

Little Havana
Patapsco R./Baltimore Harbor
410-837-9903; *www.littlehavanas.com*
Open year-round for lunch and dinner, weekend brunch. Dinners: $12–$20. Reservations not necessary. Harborview Marina nearby. Specialty: Modern Cuban cuisine. Open-air deck for dining, all-day happy hour.

Phillips Harborplace Restaurants
Patapsco R./Baltimore Harbor/Harborplace
410-685-6600; *www.phillipsseafood.com*
Open year-round for lunch and dinner. Dinners: $15–$30. Reservations not necessary but accepted. Marina and motel nearby. Specialties: crabcakes, Chesapeake Bay seafood, all-you-can-eat buffet. Piano bar, carryout.

Rusty Scupper Restaurant
Patapsco R./Balt. Inner Harbor
410-727-3678; *www.selectrestaurants.com/rusty*
Open year-round for lunch, dinner and Sunday brunch. Dinners: $15–$30. Reservations suggested. Inner Harbor Marina adjacent to restaurant; motel nearby. Full-service upscale casual seafood restaurant with a great view of the Inner Harbor. Large groups welcome.

The Black Olive
Patapsco R./Fells Pt./Inner Harbor East
410-276-7141; *www.theblackolive.com*
Open year-round serving lunch and dinner fine dining $20–$50. Reservations suggested. Dockage for diners and overnight. Marinas and motel nearby. Specialties: fresh fish flown in from around the world, Greek, Mediterranean.

Patapsco River/Southern Shore Creeks

Cheshire Crab
Patapsco R./Bodkin Cr./Pleasure Cove Marina
410-360-2220; *www.cheshirecrab.com*
Open daily for lunch and dinner, Sunday brunch. Reservations recommended. Dockage for diners (7') at marina, motel nearby. Specialties: crabs, seafood, hickory-grilled steaks, ribs, chicken & fish, frozen drinks.

Mike's Crabhouse North
Patapsco R./ Cr./White Rocks Marina
410-255-7946; *www.mikesnorth.com*
Open weekends for lunch and dinner, weekday dinners. Dinners: $10.95–$26.95. Reservations not necessary. Dockage for diners. Located at White Rocks Marina. Specialties: fresh seafood, steaks, steamed hard crabs year-round, fresh fish.

Stoney Creek Inn and Crab Deck
Patapsco R./Stoney Cr.
410-439-3123; *www.stoneycreekinnrestaurant.com*
Open year-round, Tues.–Sun. for lunch and dinner. Reservations recommended. Stoney Creek Bridge Marina nearby. Serving steamed crabs, crab soup, jumbo lump crabcakes, seafood. Featured on Diners, Drive-ins and Dives.

Magothy River

Deep Creek Restaurant And Marina
Magothy R./Deep Cr.
410-757-4045 or 974-1408; *thedeepcreekrestaurant.com*
Open year-round for lunch, dinner and Sunday country buffet brunch. Dinners: $12–$26. Reservations suggested. Free dockage on premises for diners and overnight, 6 ½'. Specialties: fresh fish, steaks, seafood, sandwiches; banquets; outdoor seating.

Point Crabhouse and Grill
Magothy R./Mill Cr.
410-544-5448; *thepointcrabhouse.com*
Open year-round for lunch and dinner. Slips available at Ferry Point Marina on site. Serving fresh, local produce and seafood harvested within a 50-mile radius.

Rock Hall & Swan Creek

The Channel Restaurant
Chesapeake Bay/Buoy 21/Tolchester Marina
410-778-0751; *www.tolchestermarina.com*
Open seasonally for breakfast, lunch and dinner. Dinners: $9–$25. Reservations not accepted. Dockage for diners and overnight, 6'. B&B nearby. Specialties: crabcakes, seafood.

Harbor Shack
Rock Hall Harbor
410-639-9996; *www.harborshack.net*
Open March-October for lunch and dinner. Dinners: $12–$26. Dockage for diners. Marinas nearby. Specialties: steak, locally caught seafood dishes, Mexican fare. Live entertainment on weekends.

Osprey Point Restaurant
Swan Cr./Rock Hall
410-639-2194; *www.ospreypoint.com*
Open for dinner Wed.–Sun. starting at 5 p.m. Sun. Brunch 10:30 a.m.–2 p.m. Reservations recommended. Offering contemporary American cuisine in an upscale but low-key setting. Osprey Point also has 16 inn rooms and a floating dock marina. Dockage is free while dining. Located in the solitude of 30 beautifully wooded acres on Swan Creek.

Passages Bar & Grill
Swan Cr./Rock Hall
410-778-6697; *www.havenharbour.com*
Open year-round Fri.–Sun. serving dinner and Sat.-Sun. lunch. Shaded outdoor tables, bar, barside seating, featuring frozen tropical drinks, assorted menu.

Swan Point Inn
Swan Cr./Rock Hall
410-639-2500; *swanpointinn.net*
One block from Beach. Open Thurs.–Sun. dinner 4 p.m. (early bird specials til 7), reservations suggested. Marinas nearby; inn on premises. Specialties: Planked cooking for fresh seafood; blackened prime rib, crabcakes, freshly made pizza. Pet-friendly dining deck overlooking creek. Free shuttle from area marinas.

Waterman's Crab House
Rock Hall Harbor
410-639-2261; *www.watermanscrabhouse.com*
Open Feb.-Dec. for lunch and dinner. Dinners: $13–$30. Reservations not necessary. Dockage for diners and overnight, 6'-8' at marina nearby. 450-seat waterfront deck Live entertainment on weekends. Specialties: Authentic Eastern Shore fare-steamed crabs, crabcakes BBQ ribs.

Chestertown

the Kitchen at the Imperial
Chester R./Chestertown
410-778-5000; *www.imperialchestertown.com*
Open Thurs.–Mon. for lunch and dinner, breakfast on weekends. Bistro style dining using fresh, locally sourced ingredients.

The Fish Whistle
Chester R./Chestertown
410-778-3566; *www.fishandwhistle.com*
Open year-round for lunch and dinner. Meals range from $10–$25. Fresh seafood, all entrees made from scratch. Daily specials. Waterfront dining. Full bar w/music on weekends. Chestertown Marina nearby.

SECTION 3

Whitehall Bay

Cantler's Riverside Inn
Whitehall Bay/Mill Cr.
410-757-1467; *www.cantlers.com*
Open year-round for lunch and dinner. Dinners: $9–$25. Reservations not accepted. Dockage for diners, 10'. Marina nearby. Specialties: steamed crabs, soft crabs, rockfish, steamers and fresh fin fish; deck overlooking the waterfront.

Severn River/Annapolis

Blackwall Hitch
Severn R./Spa Cr./Eastport
410-263-3454; *theblackwallhitch.com*
Open year-round for lunch, dinner and Sunday brunch. Dinners $10–$35. Specialties: seafood, steaks, wood-fired pizza, pastas. Rooftop dining, late-night live music. Ample free parking.

Boatyard Bar & Grill
Severn R./Spa Cr./Eastport
410-216-6206; *www.boatyardbarandgrill.com*
Open year-round for breakfast, lunch and dinner. Dinners $10–$20. Annapolis City Marina nearby, short walk from City Dock. Specialties: crabcakes, local seafood specials, fish tacos, lobster rolls, burgers, steaks and salads. Kids welcome; lively atmosphere.

Carrol's Creek Cafe
Severn R./Spa Cr./Annapolis City Marina
410-263-8102; *www.carrolscreek.com*
Open year-round for lunch, dinner and Sunday brunch. Dinners: $20–$30. Reservations suggested. Dockage overnight (6') at Annapolis City Marina on premises. Motel nearby. Contemporary American cuisine specializing in seafood.

Chart House
Severn R./Spa Cr./Eastport
410-268-7166; *www.chart-house.com*
Open daily for dinner and Sunday brunch. Dinners $20–$35. Happy Hour Sun.–Thurs. in lounge overlooking Annapolis. Gourmet seafood and steaks.

Davis' Pub
Severn R./Back Cr./Eastport
410-268-7432; *www.davispub.com*
Open daily 11 a.m.–2 a.m. Dinners $8–$15. Local pub with indoor and outdoor seating. Featured on Food Network's Diners, Drive-ins and Dives. Across from 4th St. Dinghy landing. Marinas nearby.

Dock Street Bar & Grille
Severn R./Spa Creek/Annapolis
410-268-7278; *www.dockstreetbar.net*
Open year-round for lunch and dinner. Dinners $10–$25. Serving salads, burgers, crabcakes, steaks and more, all within view of City Dock and Ego Alley.

Factors Row
Severn R./Annapolis City Dock
410-280-8686; *www.factorsrowannapolis.com*
Open daily for lunch and dinner. Dinners $15–$30. City dock/marinas nearby. Specialties: Farm to table, local specialties, oysters.

Iron Rooster
Severn R./Annapolis City Dock
410-990-1600; *www.ironroosterallday.com*
Open year-round for breakfast, lunch and dinner. Breakfast served all day, starting at 7 a.m. Entrees $12–$25. Serving wide variety of fresh, scratch-made dishes.

Leeward Market
Severn R./Back Cr./Eastport
443-837-6122; *www.leewardmarketcafe.com*
Open daily for breakfast and lunch. Marinas nearby. Specialties: gourmet pizzas, sandwiches, salads, soups, fresh vegetables and market items.

Lewnes Steakhouse
Severn R./Spa Cr./Eastport
410-263-1617; *www.lewnessteakhouse.com*
Open daily for dinner. Dinners $20–$40. Serving award-winning U.S. Prime steaks, wide wine selection.

McGarvey's Saloon & Oyster Bar
Severn R./Annapolis City Dock
410-263-5700; *www.mcgarveys.net*
Open year-round for lunch and dinner (till 1 a.m.) and Sunday brunch. Dinners: $6–$20. Marina and hotel nearby. Specialties: award-winning hamburgers, steak, local oysters, crabcakes, Aviator beer on tap.

Middleton Tavern
Severn R./Annapolis
410-263-3323; www.middletontavern.com
Open year-round for lunch and dinner.
Reservations suggested for priority seating.
Specialties: Middleton oyster shooters. Outside cafe.
Marina and motel nearby.

O'Leary's Seafood Restaurant
Severn R./Spa Cr./Eastport
410-263-0884; www.olearysseafood.com
Open daily for dinner. Dinners $25–$30.
Specializing in gourmet seafood.

Purple Thread Cafe
Severn R./Annapolis City Dock
410-267-6568
Open year-round for lunch and dinner. Serving
authentic, fresh, asian fusion cuisine. Bahn Mi sandwiches, dumplings, noodle dishes, and homemade
baked goods.

Pussers Caribbean Grille
Severn R./Spa Cr./Marriott dock
410-626-0004; www.pussersusa.com
Open daily for breakfast, lunch and dinner. Dinners
$15–$25. Dockage available for diners. Caribbean
and Chesapeake seafood dishes, pasta and steak.
Lively dock bar in the heart of Ego Alley.

Ruth's Chris Steak House
Severn R./Spa Cr./Eastport
410-990-0033; www.serioussteaks.com
Open year-round for dinner. Reservations recommended. Marina and motel nearby. Specialties:
hand-cut USDA Prime beef, Maine lobster and
other fresh seafood, extensive wine list.

Sam's on the Waterfront &
Proud Mary's Dock bar
Severn R./South of Back Cr./Ches. Harbour Marina
410-263-3600; www.samsonthewaterfront.com
Open year-round for lunch and dinner and Sunday
brunch. Dinners: $14–$32. Chesapeake Harbour
Marina on premises for diners and overnight, free
for diners dining at Sam's Sunday Brunch.
Specializing in fun, regional fare with a creative
menu and the best waterfront dining inside and out.
Live music Fri.–Sat. nights and Sun. afternoon.

Severn Inn
Severn R.
410-349-4000; www.severninn.com
Open year-round for lunch, dinner and pub fare.
Reservations suggested. Dockage for diners (8'–12').
Marinas and motels nearby. At eastern end of the
Naval Academy bridge with spectacular views of the
Naval Academy and the Severn River. Specialties
include a diverse selection of fine beef and seafood.

Wild Country Seafood
Severn R./Back Cr./Eastport
410-267-6711; www.wildcountryseafood.com
Open year-round. Closed Mon. in summer, Mon.–
Wed. in winter. Working watermen serving fresh
local seafood for lunch and dinner. Crabs, rockfish,
oysters, perch; platters, sandwiches, baskets and
more. Located behind Annapolis Maritime
Museum.

South River

Coconut Joe's
South R./Rt. 2 Br.
443-837-6057; coconutjoesusa.com
Open daily for lunch and dinner. Dinners $11–$27.
Dockage for diners. Family friendly dining, play
pirate ship for kids. Three bars, dining room and
deck dining. Hawaiian-inspired menu and cocktails.
Live music.

Mike's Restaurant & Crab House
South R./Riva Br.
410-956-2784; www.mikescrabhouse.com
Open year-round for lunch and dinner. Dinners:
$10.95–$28.95. Reservations not necessary. Dockage
for diners, 18'. Marina and motel nearby. Specialties:
fresh seafood, steaks, steamed hard crabs year-
round, fresh fish. Private facilities for up to 200
guests.

Yellowfin Steak and Fish House
South R./South R. Br.
410-573-1333; www.yellowfinrest.com
Open year-round for lunch, dinner and Sun. brunch.
($18–$35) Reservations suggested. Dockage for diners
(10') by reservation. Liberty Marina and motel
nearby. Specialties: fresh center-cut black angus
steaks, seafood and fresh fish. Daily happy hour,
11:30 a.m.–7 p.m.; Sun. brunch, 11 a.m.–2 p.m.

West River/Galesville

Pirate's Cove
West R./Galesville/Pirate's Cove Marina
410-867-2300; www.piratescovemd.com
Open year-round for lunch, dinner abd Sunday
breakfasts. Dinners: $7–$22. Reservations not necessary. Dockage for diners and overnight, 12'. Motel
on premises. Specialty: fresh, broiled seafood.
Dockside dining. Dock bar, entertainment Fri.–Sun.

Thursdays Steak and Crabhouse
West R./Galesville
410-867-7200; www.thursdaysrestaurant.com
Open year-round for lunch and dinner. Dinners
$13–$20. Slips available for diners. Marinas nearby.
Specialties: Steaks, fresh seafood, steamed crabs,
sandwiches. Outdoor dining and tiki bar.

Herring Bay/Deale

Dockside Restaurant
Rockhold Cr./Deale
410-867-1138; www.docksiderestaurantmd.com
Open daily for lunch and dinner ($10–$25). Indoor
and outdoor casual dining. located at Herrington
Harbour North. Sports bar atmosphere, serving
seafood, pastas, sandwiches.

Happy Harbor
Rockhold Cr./Deale
410-867-0949; www.happyharbordeale.com
Open daily for lunch and dinner ($5–$20). Indoor
and outdoor casual dining. Dockage for diners (3'),
pubilc pier nearby. Great for groups, kid-friendly.
Reservations Recommended. Specialties: steamer
menu, sandwiches, seafood baskets, pub fare.
Breakfast Saturday and Sunday, late night menu
until midnight 7 days.

Mango's Bar & Grill
Herring Bay/Herrington Harbour S.
410-257-0095; www.mangosonthebay.com
Open daily for lunch, dinner and weekend brunch.
Dinners $17–$30. At Herrington Harbour South
Marina. Casual, but classy athosphere. Serving
inventive seafood, steak and crab dishes, plus pastas,
lite fare and sandwiches.

Skipper's Pier Waterfront Restaurant &
Dock Bar
Rockhold Cr./Deale
410-867-7110; www.skipperspier.com
Open year-round for dinner Tues.–Thurs.; lunch
and dinner Fri.–Sun. Closed Mondays. Dinners:
$9–$25. Reservations accepted for large parties.
Dockage for diners. Specialties: crabs, crabcakes,
fried green tomatoes, shrimp and grits. Plus fresh
squeezed orange crushes and house made desserts.

Kent Island/Kent Narrows

Annie's Paramount Steak & Seafood House
Kent Narrows/Mears Point Marina
410-827-7103; www.annies.biz
Open year-round for Lunch and Dinner.
Reservations highly recommended. Dinners $15-
$50. Dockage (6') on premises. Specialties: Award-
winning "Prime" Dry-Aged Certified Angus beef,
prime rib, award-winning crabcakes, fresh seafood,
pastas and veal. Voted Best Restaurant in Queen
Anne's County, Zagat Rated, Wine Spectator Award
of Excellence.

Bridges Restaurant
Kent Narrows
410-827-0282; bridgesrestaurant.net
Open year-round for lunch and dinner. Dockage
available for boats up to 70'. Overnight slilps available. Serving upscale seafood dishes, plus small plate
selection and gourmet pizzas.

Cafe Sado
Kent Island/Castle Harbor Marina
410-604-1688; www.cafesado.com
Open year-round for lunch and dinner. Closed
Mondays. Castle Harbor Marina next door.
Specialties: sushi, French southeast Asian cuisine. 27
different sushi rolls, sashimi, pan-Asian tapas.

Fisherman's Inn Restaurant and Crab Deck
Kent Narrows/South of bridge
410-827-8807; www.fishermansinn.com
Open year-round for lunch and dinner. Dinners:
$8–$23. Reservations not accepted. Free dockage for
diners, 6'. Marinas and motel on premises.
Specialties: local seafood, prime rib, surf and turf
combos. Crab Deck serving steamed crabs and local
seafood May–Oct.

Harris Crab House
Kent Narrows/North side
410-827-9500; www.harriscrabhouse.com
Open year-round for lunch and dinner. Dinners:
$12–$25. Reservations not accepted. Dockage for
diners, 6'-8'. Mears Point Marina nearby. Ice cream
shop and gift shop. Specialties: all-you-can-eat crab/
shrimp feast Mon.-Fri.; Oct.-April oyster buffet Fri.

Hemingway's Restaurant
Kent Island/E.End Bay Brdg./Bay Bridge Marina
410-604-0999; www.hemingwaysbaybridge.com
Open year-round for lunch and dinner. Dinners:
$8–$28. Reservations suggested. Dockage for diners
and overnight (5') on premises. Motel nearby.
Newly remodeled.Specialties: seafood and steaks.

Kentmorr Restaurant & Crab House
Kent Island/Kentmorr Harbour Marina
410-643-2263; www.kentmorr.com
Open year-round for lunch and dinner. Dinners
$15-$32. Reservations suggested. Dockage for diners
(4') on premises. Specialties: steamed crabs, fresh
seafood, Tiki Bar on private beach, company
picnics.

The Jetty Restaurant & Dock Bar
Kent Island/Kent Narrows
410-827-4959; www.jettydockbar.com
Open year-round for lunch and dinner. Breakfast
served on weekends. Reservations not accepted.
Dinners $8–$20. Free dockage for diners. Featuring
crabs, seafood and sandwiches. Live entertainment
on weekends; karaoke on Thursdays.

The Narrows
Kent Narrows
410-827-8113; www.thenarrowsrestaurant.com
Open year-round for lunch and dinner. Dinners:
$25–$30. Reservations suggested. Dockage for diners
and overnight, 10'. Marina and motel nearby.
Specialties: cream of crab soup, jumbo lump crabcakes, fresh fish, fine wine.

Miles River/St. Michaels

Ava's Pizzeria & Wine Bar
Miles R./St. Michaels
410-745-3081; *avaspizzeria.com*
Open daily for lunch and dinner. Reservations recommended. Dinners $10–$20. Marina nearby. Serving gourmet wood-fired pizzas, artisinal sandwiches and entrees. Wine bar.

Carpenter Street Saloon
Miles R./St. Michaels
410-745-5111
Open year-round. Restaurant open at 8 a.m. for breakfast, lunch and dinner ($9–$15). Saloon known for revelry, camaraderie and cold draft beer. Families welcome. Marina and motel nearby. Specialty: Maryland crab soup, burgers.

Crab Claw
Miles R./St. Michaels
410-745-2900; *www.thecrabclaw.com*
Open seasonally for lunch and dinner. Dinners: $12-$24. Reservations suggested. Dockage for diners, 8'-10'. Marina and motel nearby. Specialty: seafood, Maryland steamed blue crabs.

Harbourside Grill
Miles R./St. Michaels
410-745-9131; *www.harbourinn.com*
Open year round for breakfast, lunch, dinner, and Sunday Brunch. Located at St. Michaels Harbour Inn. Specialties: fine dining, mediterranean and seafood, regional Chesapeake specialties.

St. Michaels Crab & Steak House
Miles R./St. Michaels Marina
410-745-3737; *www.stmichaelscrabhouse.com*
Open seasonally (Mar.–Dec.) for lunch and dinner. (closed Wed.) Dinners: $15–$28. Reservations suggested on weekends. Newly remodeled. Dockage on premises for diners and overnight, 10'. Motel nearby. Specialty: fresh imaginatively prepared seafood, chicken and steak. Waterfront dining inside; casual tavern & outdoor seating.

Stars Restaurant
Miles R./St. Michaels/Inn at Perry Cabin
410-745-2200; 1-866-278-9601; *www.perrycabin.com*
Open year-round for breakfast, lunch, afternoon tea and dinner. Reservations suggested. Dockage for diners, 6'. Marina nearby, inn on premises. Specialties: crabcakes, European cuisine, local produce in season.

Theo's Steaks, Sides & Spirits
Miles R./St. Michaels
410-745-2106; *theossteakhouse.com*
Open daily for dinner and happy hour. Reservations recommended. Dinners $13–$40. Marina nearby. Serving gourmet steaks, steak sauces, sides, seafood and wine.

Town Dock Restaurant
Miles R./St. Michaels/St. Michaels Marina
410-745-5577 or 800-884-0103; *www.towndockrestaurant.com*
Open year-round for lunch and dinner. Dinners: $18–$32. Reservations suggested. Dockage on premises for diners and overnight, 9'. Lodging nearby. Specialty: Fine food in a casual waterfront setting featuring local seafood, prime meats.

SECTION 4

Knapps Narrows/Tilghman Island

Character's Bridge Restaurant
Knapps Narrows
410-886-1060
Open Mar.–Jan. for lunch and dinner ($13.95 and up). Marinas and motels nearby. Specialties: Fresh seafood, crabs on deck, fresh cut meats, deck bar, sports bar & occasional music on the crab deck.

Harrison's Chesapeake House
Tilghman Island/Dogwood Cove
410-886-2121; *www.chesapeakehouse.com*
Open year-round for breakfast, lunch and dinner. Dinners: $12–$30. Reservations suggested. Dockage for diners and overnight, 6'. Motel on premises. Specialties: chicken and crabcakes, steamed crabs, Friday night buffets.

Tilghman Island Inn
Knapps Narrows
410-886-2141, 800-866-2141; *www.tilghman-islandinn.com*
Open year-round for lunch and dinner. Dinners: $19–$32. Reservations suggested. Dockage at marina for diners and overnight, 3'–5'. Hotel on premises. Specialties: creative American cuisine. Deck seating.

Tred Avon River/Oxford

Latitude 38
Tred Avon R./Oxford
410-226-5303; *www.latitude38.org*
Open year-round for dinner (lunch Dec.–Apr.) and Sunday brunch. Dinners: $8–$24. Reservations suggested. Marina and motel nearby. Specialities: bar dinners $6.95, casual fine dining (local favorite), crabcakes. Dinner menu changes every 2 weeks. Complimentary transportation to/from marinas.

Pope's Tavern
Tred Avon R./Town Cr./Oxford
410-226-5220; *www.oxfordinn.net*
Open for dinner Thurs.–Mon. Lite fare and fine dining menu $12–$35. Marina nearby, complimentary shuttle in the Pope Mobile. B&B on-site. Fine dining in historic home and Inn. Seasonal menus, seafood dishes.

Robert Morris Inn
Tred Avon R./Town Cr./Oxford
410-226-5111; *www.robertmorrisinn.com*
Open for breakfast, lunch and dinner. Dinners $18–$36. Dockage for diners in, 7'. Historic setting for casual fine dining from celebrity chef Mark Salter.

Schooners on the Creek
Tred Avon R./Town Cr./Oxford
410-226-0160; *http://schoonersonthecreek.com*
Open Apr.–Oct. for lunch and dinner. Closed Wed. Reservations suggested. Dockage on premises for diners and overnight (9'). Motel nearby. Air-conditioned waterfront dining with a casual atmosphere, outdoor deck and bar. Local crabs and fresh seafood daily.

The Masthead at Pier Street
Tred Avon R./Oxford
410-226-5171; *http://themastheadatpierstreetmarina.com/*
Open seasonally for lunch and dinner. Dinners: $9–$25. Reservations recommended for large parties. Dockage on premises for diners, 7'. Outdoor bar with daily happy hour 5–7 p.m. Specialties: fresh local crabs and fresh fish, beef, BBQ ribs.

Choptank River/Cambridge

Blue Point Provision Company
Choptank R./Cambridge Hyatt
410-901-6410; *www.chesapeakebay.hyatt.com*
Open year-round for dinner. Located at the Hyatt resort marina. Serving regional seafood, rockfish, blue point oysters, crabcakes and other regional dishes. Fabulous water views.

Snapper's Waterfront Cafe
Choptank R./Cambridge Cr.
410-228-0112; *www.snapperswaterfrontcafe.com*
Open year-round for lunch, dinner and Sunday brunch (11 a.m.–4 p.m.). Dinners: $5.95–$29.95. Reservations not necessary but suggested. Dockage for diners and overnight, 6'. Marina nearby. Specialities: full service bar, waterfront deck, call for entertainment schedule.

Suicide Bridge Restaurant
Choptank R./Cabin Cr./Suicide bridge Marina
410-943-4689; *www.suicidebridge.com*
Open year-round for lunch and dinner. Dinners: $12–$25. Reservations recommended. Dockage on premises for diners and overnight-6', motel nearby. Home of the Choptank Riverboat Company—scenic river cruises. Specialties: award-winning crabcakes, fresh fish, steamed crabs and slow roasted prime rib.

Water's Edge Grill
Choptank R./Cambridge Hyatt
410-901-6400; *www.chesapeakebay.hyatt.com*
Open year-round for breakfast, lunch and dinner. Located at the Hyatt resort hotel. Serving gourmet steaks, seafood, salads, a kids' buffet.

Little Choptank/Taylors Island

Island Grille
Little Choptank R./Taylors Isl.
410-228-9094
Open Mon.–Sat. for breakfast, lunch and dinner. Dockage available at Chapel Cove Marina. Casual waterfront dining. Serving seasonal seafood specialties, steaks, hamburgers, hand-cut fries, salads, homemade soups and desserts.

Old Salty's
Honga R./Back Creek
410-397-3752; *www.oldsaltys.com*
Open for lunch and dinner. Reservatinos recommended. Phil Jones Marina nearby. Fresh local seafood, prime cuts of beef, homemade rolls and desserts.

Palm Beach Willie's
Little Choptank R./Slaughter Cr.
410-221-5111
Open Thurs.–Fri. 4 p.m., Sat.–Sun. noon. Dinners: $5–$20. Reservations suggested. Dockage (Slaughter Creek Marina) on premises for diners and overnight, 5'. Specialties: seafood, steaks and extensive menu. Live music on the deck.

Chesapeake Beach

Rod 'N Reel Restaurant
Chesapeake Beach/Fishing Cr.
410-257-2735 or 877-RODNREEL; *www.cbresorts-pa.com*
Open year-round for lunch and dinner. Dinners: $14–$27. Slips available for diners and overnight, 5'. Hotel amenities available with overnight slips. Brunch buffet Sat.–Sun.

Smokey Joe's Grill
Chesapeake Beach/Fishing Cr.
301-855-3089; *www.cbresortspa.com*
Open year-round for lunch and dinner. Dinners: $14–$20. Slips available for diners and overnight, 5'. Hotel amenities available with overnight slips. Specialties: Ribs, BBQ, chicken, steaks.

Traders Seafood Steak & Ale
Chesapeake Beach
301-855-0766; *traders-eagle.com*
Open for dinner. Specialties: seafood, steaks.

Patuxent River/Solomons

Anglers Seafood Bar & Grill
Patuxent R./Back Cr./Beacon Marina
410-326-2772; *anglers-seafood.com*
Open year-round for breakfast, lunch and dinner. Dinners: $8–$25. Dockage for diners at marina, 10'. Motel on premises. Outdoor waterfront dining. Specialty: seafood and steak.

Back Creek Bistro at Calvert Marina
Patuxent R./Back Cr.
410-326-9900; *www.backcreekbistro.com*

Fourwinds
Patuxent R./Back Cr.
410-394-6373; www.fourwindscafe.net
open for lunch and dinner Thurs.–Sun. Located at
Calvert Marina. Sandwiches, salads, soups and crabcakes.

Island Hideaway
Patuxent R./Back Cr.
410-449-6382; www.islandhideawaysolomons.com
Open year-round for lunch and dinner, weekend
breakfast. (Closed Monday) Dinners $15-$25.
Dockage available on site. Serving local seafood.
Dockside bar.

Stoney's Seafood & Crab House
Patuxent R./Island Cr./Broomes Island Marina
410-586-1888; www.stoneysbroomesisland.com
Open seasonally (Apr.–Oct.) for lunch and dinner
($10–$25). Reservations not accepted. Dockage on
premises for diners and overnight, 6'. House specialties: crabcakes, seafood, crabs.

The Dry Dock
Patuxent R./Solomons/Zahniser's Yachting Ctr.
410-326-4817; www.zahnisers.com
Open year-round serving dinner and Sunday
brunch. Dinners: $18–$32. Reservations suggested.
Dockage for diners and overnight; 15'. Specialties:
Seafood and tenderloin, menu specials changing
daily. Porch dining available.

Vera's White Sands Beach Club
Patuxent R./St. Leonard Cr./White Sands Marina
410-586-1182; www.verasbeachclub.com
Open seasonally for lunch and dinner. Prices: $14–
$30. Dockage on premises for diners and overnight,
Hotel nearby. Specialties: seafood, Maryland crabs,
steaks, exotic drinks. Live entertainment Friday and
Saturday.

SECTION 5

Lower Potomac River

Riverside Bistro
Potomac R./St. Mary's R./Carthagena Cr.
301-994-2404; dennispointmarina.net
Open seasonally for lunch and dinner Thurs.–Sat.,
and Sun. brunch. Dockage for diners and overnight
at Dennis Point Marina (on premises). Newly renovated restaurant and bar.

Shymansky's Restaurant & Marina
Potomac R./Cobb Island/Neale Sound
301-259-0300
Open year-round for breakfast (Sunday breakfast
buffet), lunch and dinner. Dinners: $12-$20.
Reservations not necessary. Dockage on premises for
diners and overnight, 6'. Specialties: seafood, weekday
specials; fresh crabs, fish and oysters in season.

Sunset Cove & Snorkel's Bar
Potomac R./Smith Cr./Pt. Lookout Marina
301-872-5020; www.pointlookoutmarina.com
Open seasonally for lunch and dinner Friday through
Monday. Sunday brunch buffet 9-12. Newly
Renovated restaurant and bar with outdoor seating.
Dockage for dinners and overnight guests at point
lookout marina (on premises).

The Reluctant Navigator
Potomac R./Herring Cr./Tall Timbers Marina
301-994-1508; talltimbersmarinasomd.com
Open seasonally (March-Dec.) for Sun. breakfast,
Fri.–Sat. lunch and dinner. Buffet Thurs.–Sun.
Dinners: $13–$28. Reservations not necessary. Year
round dockage at Tall Timbers marina for diners and
overnight, 4–6'. Specialities: buffets, holiday menus,
special occasion menus. Water views and bar.

Middle Potomac River

Captain Billy's Crabhouse
Potomac R.
301-932-4323
Open seasonally for lunch and dinner ($15–$30).
Reservations suggested for large parties. Dockage for
diners available. Goose Bay Marina (4.5-ft) nearby.
Specialties: steamed crabs, fresh seafood, steaks;
complete lunch and dinner menu. ATM.

Captain John's Crabhouse & Marina
Potomac R./Neal Sound/Captain John's Marina
301-259-2315; www.cjcrab.com
Open year-round for breakfast, lunch and dinner
($8–$20). Reservations not necessary. Dockage on
premises for diners and overnight, 5'–10' All new
slips in 2013. A true southern Md., crabhouse.
Specialties: seafood, prime rib, chicken, crabs. MD
Lottery, Keno & race trax. ATM on site. Wireless
internet. Gas for boats and cars, pump-out.

Dockside Restaurant and Blue Heron Pub
Potomac R./Monroe Cr./Colonial Beach Yacht Ct
804-224-8726; docksiderestaurantandblueheron-
pub.com
Open year-round for dinner, weekend brunch and
lunch. Closed Tuesdays. Dinners: $6–$26.
Reservations suggested. Dockage on premises for
diners and overnight, 10'. B&Bs nearby. Specialties:
local seafood, steaks, veal, pasta, chicken in British
pub atmosphere. Tiki bar in summer. Live music
Sat. night and Sun. afternoon.

Gilligan's Pier
Potomac R./Popes Cr.
301-259-4514; www.gilliganspier.com
Open daily for lunch and dinner. Dinners $14–$27.
Dockage for diners, water taxi from boats to the restaurant. Serving crabcakes, stuffed shrimp, fried
oysters, rockfish, steamer items and steaks.

Morris Point Restaurant
Potomac R./St. Clements Bay/Canoe Neck Cr.
301-769-2500; www.morris-point.com
Open year-round Fri.–Sun. for breakfast, lunch and
dinner. Dinners $11–$23. Reservations required for
large parties. Outdoor dining available. Dockage for
diners and overnight,
6'–8'. Colton's Point and Cather's marinas nearby.
Near well-protected, popular anchorage. Very close
to St. Clement's Island. Menu includes something
for every taste; all types of seafood.

Quade's Store
Potomac R./Wicomico R.
301-769-3903
Serving food Thurs.–Sun. Open daily for convenience
store items. Boat ramp, dockage for diners, 3'–10'.
Specialties: homemade crabcakes, sports bar menu.

Wilkerson's Seafood Resaurant
Potomac R./Colonial Beach
804-224-7117; www.wilkersonsseafoodrestaurant.com
Open daily at 11:30 for lunch and dinner. $8.95–
$38.95. Reservations not necessary. Dockage for
diners, 5'. Marina and motel nearby. Specialties:
rockfish, crab legs and crabcakes, steamed crabs,
fresh local oysters, weekend all you can eat buffet,
salad bar.

Upper Patuxent River

Port Tobacco Restaurant
Potomac R./Port Tobacco R.
301-392-0007; www.porttobaccorestaurant.com
Open Wed.–Thurs. for dinner; Fri.–Sun. for lunch
and dinner. Serving Po boys, steamed crabs, seafood
platters, raw bar, fresh fish. Live music on weekends.

Secret Garden Cafe
Potomac R./Occoquan R.
703-494-2848 ; www.stonehouserestaurants.com/
thesecretgarden.html
Open year-round for breakfast and lunch. Marina
and motel nearby. Specialties: informal dining and
home baking. Pre-Civil War building with terraces
and bricked patios. Prince William Marine nearby.

Tim's II at Fairview
Potomac R./Fairview Beach
540-775-7500; tims2.com
Open year-round for lunch and dinner. Dinners:
$5–$25. Dockage for diners. Steamed crabs, fried
seafood, crabcakes, oysters, sandwiches. Lots of live
music and fun events.

Tim's Rivershore Restaurant & Crabhouse
Potomac R./West shore, north of Possum Point
703-441-1375; www.timsrivershore.com
Open year-round for lunch and dinner. Dinners:
$5–$25. Reservations not accepted. Dockage for diners
and water taxi to boats anchored nearby. Specialties:
crabs, crabcakes, seafood, steaks and chicken.

Washington, D.C. Area

Cantina Marina
Potomac R./Washington Channel
202-554-8396; www.cantinamarina.com
Open Mar.–Nov. for lunch and dinner ($10–$25).
Reservations not necessary. Dockage for diners on
premises at the Gangplank Marina, 25'. Motel
nearby. Specialities: Gulf Coast and Cajun fare.

Indigo Landing Restaurant
Potomac R./Columbia Isl.
703-548-0001; www.indigolanding.com
Open year-round for lunch and dinner. Dinners:
$15–$29. Reservations suggested. Washington
Sailing Marina on premises, motel nearby.
Specialties: fresh seafood, raw bar, crabs on the deck.

Orange Anchor
Potomac R./Georgetown
202-802-9990; www.orangeanchordc.com
Open daily for lunch, dinner and weekend brunch.
Boat delivery service available. Serving oysters,
seafood, lobster rolls. Dinners $20–$40.

SECTION 6

Smith & Tangier Islands

Bayside Inn Restaurant
Smith Island/Ewell
410-425-2771; www.smithislandcruises.com
Open seasonally (May–Oct.) serving lunch daily.
Reservations suggested. Known for crabcakes and
soft crab platters and Smith Island cake for dessert.

Fisherman's Corner Restaurant
Tangier Island
757-891-2900; www.tangierisland-va.com/fisherman
Open seasonally for lunch and dinner ($15–$20).
Reservations suggested. Dockage for diners and
overnight at Parks Marina (2 blocks), 15'. Local
seafood caught daily by owners; homemade desserts.
Specialities: creamy crab bisque, crabcakes (only
Chesapeake Bay crabmeat), stuffed flounder, crab
dip and Angus NY strip steaks.

Hilda Crockett's Chesapeake House
Tangier Island
757-891-2331; www.chesapeakehousetangier.com
Open seasonally (late-April–mid-Oct.) for breakfast,
lunch and dinner. Dinners: $22 average. Parks
Marina nearby; motel on premises. Specialties: crabcakes and clam fritters. Breakfast served 7–9 a.m.
daily. lunch/dinner 11:30–5 p.m. daily.

Tangier Island Waterfront Restaurant
Tangier Island
757-891-2248; www.tangierisland-va.com/waterfront/
Open seasonally for lunch. First stop at dock on
Tangier. Watch the watermen bring in their fresh
catch. Serving fresh crabcakes, soft crabs, seafood
baskets, subs and more.

Nanticoke River

Millie's Roadhouse Grill
Nanticoke River/Vienna
410-376-3130
Open year-round for breakfast, lunch and dinner
($12–$18.95). Reservations suggested. Dockage at
nearby town wharf. Specialities: crab balls, oysters,
fresh-cut steaks. Sunday buffet noon-6 p.m.

Wicomico River

Red Roost
Wicomico R./Whitehaven/Daymarker 21
410-546-5443; *www.theredroost.com*
Open daily for dinner. Dinners $15–$25. Fresh
steamed all-you-can-eat crabs, fried chicken, fresh
seafood, seafood platters and ribs.

Little Annemessex/Crisfield

Watermen's Inn
Little Annemessex R./Crisfield
410-968-2119
Open year-round for lunch and dinner; closed
Mon.–Wed. Dinners to $23. Reservations suggested.
Somer's Cove Marina nearby.
Specialties: Menu entrees and (dinner) specials
using fresh, local (&) seasonal seafood, fruits and
vegetables. Homemade desserts. Full bar.

Onancock

Bizzotto's Gallery-Caffe
Onancock Cr./Onancock
757-787-3103; *www.esva.net/~bizzottos/caffe.htm*
Open year-round for lunch Tues.–Sat.; dinner daily.
Reservations Recommended. Town wharf and
lodging nearby. Specialty: local seafood. Oldest restaurant in town.

Blarney Stone Pub
Onancock Cr./Onancock
757-302-0300; *www.blarneystonepubonancock.com*
Open Tues.–Sun. for lunch and dinner; Irish pub
fare and more! Chef's specials, lunch specials, local
music, and family friendly. "Where friends and
neighbors gather." Short walk from the wharf.
Marina and motel nearby.

Charlotte Hotel
Onancock Cr./Onancock
757-787-7400; *www.thecharlottehotel.com*
Open to public for dinner Tues.–Sun. 4–9 p.m.
Reservations recommended. Onancock Wharf
nearby. This 1907 building has been rebuilt with a
bar, dining room and 8 guest rooms. The restaurant
features an upscale bistro menu with many local
ingredients.

Mallards at the Wharf
Onancock Cr./Onancock
757-787-8558; *www.mallardsllc.com*
Open year-round for lunch and dinner. Dinners:
$15–$25. Reservations suggested. Dockage for
diners; 8+'. Town wharf, B&Bs nearby. Local
seafood and regional fare, outdoor dockside dining
in season, live entertainment on weekends. Home of
Johnny Mo the musical chef!

Cape Charles

Kelly's Gingernut Pub
Cape Charles Harbor/Cape Charles
757-331-3222; *kellysgingernutpub.com*
Open year-round for lunch and dinner. Great selection of beers on tap.

The Oyster Farm
Kings Cr./Kings Creek Marina
757-331-8660; *www.kingscreekmarina.com*
Open year-round for lunch and dinner. Dinners:
$15–$30. Reservations suggested. Dockage on premises for diners and overnight, 6'. Featuring local
seafood & produce.

Great Wicomico River/Reedville

Crazy Crab At Reedville Marina
Great Wicomico R./Cockrell Cr.
804-453-6789; *www.reedvillemarina.com*
Open seasonally for lunch and dinner. Dinners:
$8–$22. Reservations not accepted. Dockage on
premises, 14'. Motel nearby. Specialties: seafood,
salads, beef and poultry. Waterfront deck dining.

Horn Harbor House Seafood Restaurant
Great Wicomico R./Great Wicomico Marina
804-453-3351
Open mid-March through Thanksgiving, Fri.–Sun.
5–10. Dockage on premises for diners and overnight
(8'). Fresh seafood, lobster, steaks, chops and nightly
specials. Homemade desserts.

Leadbelly's Restaurant
Great Wicomico R./Reedville/Fairport Marina
804-453-5002
Open seasonally Mon.–Sat. for lunch and dinner.
Located at Fairport Marina. Serving burgers, sand-
wiches and seafood.

Tommy's Steaks & Seafood
Great Wicomico R./Cockrell Cr.
804-453-4666; *www.tommysfinedining.com*
Open year-round for dinner. Reservations appreci-
ated. Marina and motel nearby. Casual waterfront
restaurant and bar.

Rappahannock River/Urbanna

Colonial Pizza
Rappahannock R./Urbanna Cr.
804-758-4079
Open year-round for lunch and dinner. Closed
Mondays. Dinners: $8.95–$16.95. Reservations not
accepted. Marinas and hotel nearby. Specialities:
Greek pizza, salad and subs; Greek and Italian dishes.

Something Different
Rappahannock R./Urbanna Cr.
804-758-8000; *pine3.info*
Open year-round for breakfast, lunch and dinner.
Dinners: $8.50–$19. Reservations not necessary.
Marina, motel nearby. Specialties: barbecue and
smoked meats, fine wines, cheeses, freshly roasted
peanuts, homemade ice cream, deli sandwiches,
crabcakes.

Virginia Street Cafe
Rappahannock R./Urbanna Cr.
804-758-3798
Open year-round for breakfast, lunch and dinner.
Dinners: $8.50–$19. Reservations not necessary.
Marina, motel nearby. Specialties: Fresh soft-shell
crabs, oysters, crab soup, chowders, crabcakes, hush
puppies, bread pudding and more.

Rappahannock River/White Stone

**Chesapeake Club and Commodore's
at the Tides**
Rappahannock R./Carter Cr./Tides Inn
804-438-5000 or 800-843-3746; *www.tidesinn.com*
Open breakfast, lunch and dinner. Featuring contemporary regional bistro cuisine and panoramic
water views. Patio dining available.
Commodore's open seasonally serving light fare,
informal dining. Tides Inn Marina on premises.

Willaby's Cafe
Rappahannock R./Rt. 3 Bridge
804-435-0000; *www.willabys.com*
Open Mon.–Sat. for lunch; Thurs.–Sat. for lunch
and dinner, plus Sun. brunch. Serving local
oysters, seafood, fish and chips, burgers, sandwiches and soups.

Deltaville

Cocomo's
Broad Cr./Deltaville
804-776-8822
Open year-round, Wed.–Thurs. dinner, Fri.–Sun.,
lunch and dinner .Only waterfront restaurant in
Deltaville. Seafood, sandwiches, burgers.

Taylor's Restaurant
Piankatank R./Deltaville
804-776-9611
Open year-round for lunch and dinner. Dinners:
$8–$23. Reservations recommended. Marinas and
motel nearby. Specialties: fresh seafood daily, hand-
cut steaks. Courtesy car to marinas.

Gwynn's Island

Seabreeze Restaurant
Rappahannock R./Gwynn's Island
804-725-4000
Open daily for breakfast, lunch and dinner. Dockage
on site. Great views from every seat in the house.
Fresh seafood.

Yorktown

Beach Delly
York R./Yorktown
757-886-5890; *beachdellyandpizzaria.com*
Open seasonally. Yorktown Riverwalk nearby.
Serving subs, crabcakes, pizza and local seafood.

Island Grille
York R./Yorktown
757-898-5270; *www.facebook.com/
IslandTimeCafe*
Open daily for breakfast, lunch and dinner. Dinners
$15–$30. Riverwalk Landing nearby. Serving
seafood, fresh fish, seafood platters.

Riverwalk Restaurant
York R./Yorktown
757-875-1522; *riverwalkrestaurant.net*
Open daily for lunch and dinner. Dinners $15–$30.
Riverwalk Marina nearby. Specialties: Riverwalk
clam chowder; steaks, seafood dishes, tapas menu,
pastas.

Yorktown Pub
York R./Yorktown
757-886-9964; *www.yorktownpub.com*
Open daily for lunch and dinner. Dockage nearby at
Riverwalk Landing. Serving fresh, local seafood,
steamers, oysters, crabcakes, plus pub appetizers,
sandwiches, grill specials and burgers.

Sarah Creek

York River Oyster Company
York R./Sarah Cr.
804-993-7174; *yorkriveroysterco.com*
Open daily for lunch and dinner. Dinners $15–$25.
York RIver Yacht Haven on site. Specialties: fresh,
local oysters, seafood tacos (oysters, shrimp or fish),
fish n chips, seafood platters, brick oven pizzas.

Poquoson River

Owen's Marina Restaurant
Poquoson R./Bennett Cr./Owen's Marina
757-868-8407
Open 7 days a week for breakfast, lunch and
dinner. gas and diesel. top quality seafood, burgers.
Deep water at fuel dock. Dockage at adjacent York
Haven Marina.

Surf Rider, Poquoson
Poquoson R./Bennett's Ck/Whitehouse Cove Marina
757-868-0080; www.surfriderrestaurant.com
Open year-round for lunch and dinner.
Reservations not accepted. Dockage for diners.
Specialties: seafood, steak and homemade desserts.

Hampton

Marker 20
Hampton R./Hampton
757-726-9410; www.marker20.com
Open year-round for lunch and dinner, plus Sat.–
Sun. breakfast. Dinners: $7–$15.Reservations not
accepted. Marinas and motel nearby. Specialties:
seafood, microbrews. Open late, live music.

Regatta Grille and Oyster Alley
Hampton R./Hampton Marina Hotel
757-727-9700; www.hamptonmarinahotel.com
Both restaurants at the Hampton Marina Hotel.
Regatta Grille open daily for breakfast, lunch and
dinner, serving seafood, steaks and extensive wine
list. Oyster Alley open seasonally for lunch and
dinner, live music on the outdoor patio at the
marina.

Surf Rider, Hampton
Hampton R./Sunset Creek/Bluewater Yachting Ctr
757-723-9366; www.surfriderrestaurant.com
Open year-round for lunch and dinner.
Reservations not accepted. Dockage for diners and
overnight at Bluewater Yachts (on premises).
Specialties: Seafood, steak and homemade desserts.

James River

Captain Chuck-A-Mucks
Ship's Store and Grill
James R./Pagan R./Jones Cr.
757-356-1005; www.captainchuck-a-mucks.com
Open for lunch and dinner Tues.–Sun. in summer.
Call for spring/fall/winter hours. Dockage for diners.
Specializing in fresh seafood, including soft crabs (in
season), shrimp, oysters, fresh fish, salads, hand-cut
steaks and 1/2 lb. burgers, plus homemade crabcakes, she-crab soup, key lime pie and much more.

Colonial Harbor Restaurant
James R./Chickahominy R./Colonial Harbor Marina
804-966-5523; www.colonialharbor.com
Open seasonally for breakfast, lunch and dinner
Fri.–Sun. Dinners: $3–$14. Reservations not necessary. Dockage on premises for diners and overnight,
8'. Specialty: seafood.

Crab Shack on the James
James R./James River Bridge
757-245-CRAB; www.crabshackonthejames.com
Open for lunch and dinner. Reservations not
accepted. Marina facilities and motel nearby. Enjoy
dining homemade meals cooked to order while
having a panoramic view of the James River and
spectacular sunsets.

Smithfield Inn
James R./Pagan R./Smithfield
757-357-1752; www.smithfieldinn.com
Open year-round for lunch and dinner. Dinners:
$15–$31. Reservations suggested. Smithfield Station
marina nearby; B&B on premises. Specialties: jumbo
lump crabcakes, Smithfield pork, Smithfield ham
rolls and ham biscuits.

Smithfield Station
James R./Pagan R./Smithfield Station
757-357-7700; www.smithfieldstation.com
Open year-round for breakfast, lunch and dinner.
Dinners: $19–$38. Reservations suggested. Dockage
for diners and overnight, 8'. Marina and lodge on
premises. Specialty: seafood, steaks, frozen drinks,
full service bar.

Elizabeth River/Norfolk

456 Fish on Granby
Elizabeth R./Norfolk
757-625-4444; www.456fish.com
Open daily for dinner; Sun. brunch. Reservations
suggested. Dinners $18–30. Waterside Marina
nearby. Serving seafood, steaks, sides to share.

Bodega
Elizabeth R./Norfolk
757-622-8527; www.bodegaongranby.com
Open daily for dinner. Dinners $18–$30. Waterside
Marina nearby. Serving small plates, big drinks—
Spanish/Mediterranean tapas, seafood, housemade
bread, fresh ingredients.

D'egg Diner
Elizabeth R./Norfolk
757-626-3447; www.deggnorfolk.com
Open daily for breakfast and lunch. Waterside
Marina nearby. Serving omelettes, breakfast sandwiches and dishes; wraps, sandwiches, soups and
salads.

Freemason Abbey Restaurant
Elizabeth R./Norfolk
757-622-3966; www.freemasonabbey.com
Open year-round for lunch, dinner and Sun.
brunch. Dinners: $9.95–$20.95. Reservations suggested. Marina and lodging nearby. Specialties
include crab soup, seafood, prime rib and pasta
dishes served in casual atmosphere of a renovated
19th-century church.

Granby Bistro & Deli
Elizabeth R./Norfolk
757-622-7003; granbybistroanddeli.com
Open Mon.–Sat. for breakfast and lunch. Waterside
Marina nearby. Breakfast specials, deli and specialty
sandwiches.

Norfolk Seafood Company/
Big Easy Oyster Bar
Elizabeth R./Norfolk
757-227-6222; www.norfolkseafoodco.com
Open Tues.–Sat. for dinner. Reservations suggested.
Dinners $19–$30. Seafood, oyster bar, upscale
dining.

Todd Jurich's Bistro
Elizabeth R./Norfolk
757-622-3210; www.toddjurichsbistro.com
Open year-round for lunch and dinner. Dinners:
$19–$36. Reservations suggested. Dockage for diners
and overnight (20') at nearby Waterside Marina.
AAA 4 Diamond Award and Wine Spectator Best of
Award of Excellence.

Elizabeth River/Portsmouth/Chesapeake

757 Crave on the Harbor
Elizabeth R./Portsmouth
757-966-7919; www.757cravers.com
Open year-round for breakfast, lunch and dinner.
Dinners: $12–$25. Panoramic view of the harbor
from Tidewater Marina. Free dockage for diners.
Serving seafood, fish tacos, pastas, breakfast special-
ties.

Amber Lantern
Elizabeth R./Chesapeake
757-227-3057; www.toprackmarina.com
Open uear-round for dinner. (Closed Mondays).
Located at Top Rack Marina. Serving crabcakes,
seafood, fine dining with outdoor dining.

Baron's Pub
Elizabeth R./Portsmouth
757-399-4840
Open year-round for lunch and dinner. Dinners:
$5.95–$18.95. Friendly, local pub atmosphere with
live music. Marinas (Ocean Marine, Tidewater
Yacht, Scott's Creek) and motel nearby.

Lobscouser Restaurant
Elizabeth R./Portsmouth
757-397-2728; www.lobscouser.com
Open year-round for lunch and dinner. Dinners:
$8–$25. Reservations suggested. Marinas and
lodging nearby. Fine seafood dining in casual,
elegant surroundings in heart of Olde Towne
Portsmouth.

Little Creek/Lynnhaven Inlet

Chick's Oyster Bar
Lynnhaven Inlet/Virginia Beach
757-481-5757; www.chicksoysterbar.com
Open year-round for lunch, dinner and Sun.
brunch. Dinners: $7–$17. Two-day advance reservations accepted. Dockage for diners; marinas nearby.
Specialties: fresh seafood, shellfish, platters. Delivery
to boats.

Cutty Sark Marina & Restaurant
Little Creek/Cutty Sark Marina
757-362-2942
Open year-round for breakfast, lunch and dinner.
Reservations not necessary. Dockage on premises
for diners and overnight. Lodging nearby.

Lynnhaven Fish House
Lynnhaven Pier/Virginia Beach
757-481-0003; www.lynnhavenfishhouse.net
Open year-round for lunch and dinner. Dinners:
$18–$39. Lynnhaven Marina nearby.Specialty: fresh
seafood, daily catch, at least 12 varieties per day.

One Fish Two Fish
Lynnhaven Inlet/Long Creek/Long Bay Pointe
Marina
757-496-4350; www.onefish-twofish.com
Open for dinner ($18–$35). Reservations suggested.
Dockage for diners at resort marina on premises.

Surf Rider, Marina Shores
Lynnhaven Inlet/Marina Shores Marina
757-481-5646; www.surfriderrestaurant.com
Open year-round for lunch and dinner.
Reservations not accepted. Dockage on premises for
diners and overnight. Specialties: seafood, steak and
homemade desserts.

Surf Rider, Vinings Landing
Little Cr./Norfolk/Vinings Landing Marina
757-480-5000; www.surfriderrestaurant.com
Open year-round for lunch and dinner.
Reservations not accepted. Dockage for diners.
Specialties: Seafood, steak and homemade desserts.

Rudee Inlet

Big Sam's Inlet Cafe & Raw Bar
Rudee Inlet/Virginia Beach
757-428-4858; www.bigsamsrawbar.com
Open for breakfast, lunch and dinner. Marina
nearby. Specialties: award-winning pancakes, jumbo
lump crabcakes, 7-11 a.m. Happy Hour on Bloody
Mary's and Screwdrivers 3-7 p.m. Tiki Time on
wings, clams, oysters and shrimp as well as drinks
and beers. Casual atmosphere.

Rockafeller's Restaurant
Rudee Inlet/Virginia Beach
757-422-5654; www.rockafellers.com
Open daily for lunch and dinner. Dinners: $14–$25.
Dockage for diners. Reservations suggested for 6 or
more. Indoor & outdoor dining available. Specialties
include fresh fish and other seafood.

Rudee's on the Inlet Restaurant and
Cabana Bar
Rudee Inlet/Virginia Beach/Rudee's Inlet Station
Marina
757-425-1777; www.rudees.com
Open year-round for lunch, dinner and Sun.
brunch. Dinners: $9–$13. Reservations not necessary. Dockage for diners and overnight at Rudee's
Marina on premises. Lodging nearby. Specialties:
locally caught fish, hand-cut steaks, raw bar, overstuffed sandwiches. Cabana/tiki bar.

BIG Improvements For Boaters

The town of Urbanna used BIG (Boating Infrastructure Grant) funds to install transient boat slips, bulkheads, a pedestrian walkway, new power pedestals and ADA compliant restroom facilities with showers and laundry.

Today more than 12 million boats cruise and fish in the waters of the United States. Recreational boating is a growing economic activity, and in many ways exceeds that of waterborne commerce. Boating Infrastructure Grant (BIG) funding is available to help marinas meet the increasing demand for transient boater tie-ups and sanitary facilities. The BIG program protects the integrity of our waterways by ensuring that these boaters have places to seek refuge, dispose of waste properly and use onshore facilities instead of discharging into the Virginia waters. For more information on Boating Infrastructure Grant funding, contact Preston Smith at 804-864-7468 or at Preston.Smith@vdh.virginia.gov.

KEEP OUR WATER CLEAN – USE PUMPOUTS

SPORT FISH RESTORATION

VDH VIRGINIA DEPARTMENT OF HEALTH
Protecting You and Your Environment
www.vdh.virginia.gov

VIRGINIA CLEAN MARINA

Cruise Guide Index

INDEX

Advertiser's Index